SO-BMG-910

MASTER
VISUALLY™
Windows® Me
Millennium Edition

Visual™

From
maranGraphics™

&

IDG Books Worldwide, Inc.
An International Data Group Company
Foster City, CA • Indianapolis • Chicago • New York

Master VISUALLY™ Windows® Me Millennium Edition

Published by
IDG Books Worldwide, Inc.
An International Data Group Company
919 E. Hillsdale Blvd., Suite 400
Foster City, CA 94404

Copyright© 2000 by maranGraphics Inc.
5755 Coopers Avenue
Mississauga, Ontario, Canada
L4Z 1R9

All rights reserved. No part of this book, including interior design, cover design, and icons, may be reproduced or transmitted in any form, by any means (electronic, photocopying, recording, or otherwise) without prior written permission from maranGraphics.

Library of Congress Catalog Card No.: 00-107997

ISBN: 0-7645-3496-3

Printed in the United States of America

10 9 8 7 6 5 4 3 2 1

10/QW/RR/QQ/MG

Distributed in the United States by IDG Books Worldwide, Inc.
Distributed by CDG Books Canada Inc. for Canada; by Transworld Publishers Limited in the United Kingdom; by IDG Norge Books for Norway; by IDG Sweden Books for Sweden; by IDG Books Australia Publishing Corporation Pty. Ltd. for Australia and New Zealand; by TransQuest Publishers Pte Ltd. for Singapore, Malaysia, Thailand, Indonesia, and Hong Kong; by Gotop Information Inc. for Taiwan; by ICG Muse, Inc. for Japan; by Intersoft for South Africa; by Eyrolles for France; by International Thomson Publishing for Germany, Austria and Switzerland; by Distribuidora Cuspide for Argentina; by LR International for Brazil; by Galileo Libros for Chile; by Ediciones ZETA S.C.R. Ltda. for Peru; by WS Computer Publishing Corporation, Inc. for the Philippines; by Contemporanea de Ediciones for Venezuela; by Express Computer Distributors for the Caribbean and West Indies; by Micronesia Media Distributor, Inc. for Micronesia; by Chips Computadoras S.A. de C.V. for Mexico; by Editorial Norma de Panama S.A. for Panama; by American Bookshops for Finland.
For corporate orders, please call maranGraphics at 800-469-6616.
For general information on IDG Books Worldwide's books in the U.S., please call our Consumer Customer Service department at 800-762-2974.
For reseller information, including discounts and premium sales, please call our Reseller Customer Service department at 800-434-3422.
For information on where to purchase IDG Books Worldwide's books outside the U.S., please contact our International Sales department at 317-572-3993 or fax 317-572-4002.
For consumer information on foreign language translations, please contact our Customer Service department at 800-434-3422, fax 800-550-2747, or e-mail rights@idgbooks.com.
For information on licensing foreign or domestic rights, please phone 650-653-7000 or fax 650-653-7500.
For sales inquiries and special prices for bulk quantities, please contact our Sales department at 650-655-3200.
For information on using IDG Books Worldwide's books in the classroom or for ordering examination copies, please contact our Educational Sales department at 800-434-2086 or fax 317-572-4005.
For press review copies, author interviews, or other publicity information, please contact our Public Relations department at 650-653-7000 or fax 650-653-7500.
For authorization to photocopy items for corporate, personal, or educational use, please contact maranGraphics at 800-469-6616.
Screen shots displayed in this book are based on pre-release software and are subject to change.

LIMIT OF LIABILITY/DISCLAIMER OF WARRANTY: THE PUBLISHER AND AUTHOR HAVE USED THEIR BEST EFFORTS IN PREPARING THIS BOOK. THE PUBLISHER AND AUTHOR MAKE NO REPRESENTATIONS OR WARRANTIES WITH RESPECT TO THE ACCURACY OR COMPLETENESS OF THE CONTENTS OF THIS BOOK AND SPECIFICALLY DISCLAIM ANY IMPLIED WARRANTIES OF MERCHANTABILITY OR FITNESS FOR A PARTICULAR PURPOSE. THERE ARE NO WARRANTIES WHICH EXTEND BEYOND THE DESCRIPTIONS CONTAINED IN THIS PARAGRAPH. NO WARRANTY MAY BE CREATED OR EXTENDED BY SALES REPRESENTATIVES OR WRITTEN SALES MATERIALS. THE ACCURACY AND COMPLETENESS OF THE INFORMATION PROVIDED HEREIN AND THE OPINIONS STATED HEREIN ARE NOT GUARANTEED OR WARRANTED TO PRODUCE ANY PARTICULAR RESULTS, AND THE ADVICE AND STRATEGIES CONTAINED HEREIN MAY NOT BE SUITABLE FOR EVERY INDIVIDUAL. NEITHER THE PUBLISHER, NOR AUTHOR SHALL BE LIABLE FOR ANY LOSS OF PROFIT OR ANY OTHER COMMERCIAL DAMAGES, INCLUDING BUT NOT LIMITED TO SPECIAL, INCIDENTAL, CONSEQUENTIAL, OR OTHER DAMAGES. FULFILLMENT OF EACH COUPON OFFER IS THE RESPONSIBILITY OF THE OFFEROR.

Trademark Acknowledgments

maranGraphics Inc. has attempted to include trademark information for products, services and companies referred to in this guide. Although maranGraphics Inc. has made reasonable efforts in gathering this information, it cannot guarantee its accuracy.

All brand names and product names used in this book are trade names, service marks, trademarks, or registered trademarks of their respective owners. IDG Books Worldwide and maranGraphics Inc. are not associated with any product or vendor mentioned in this book.

FOR PURPOSES OF ILLUSTRATING THE CONCEPTS AND TECHNIQUES DESCRIBED IN THIS BOOK, THE AUTHOR HAS CREATED VARIOUS NAMES, COMPANY NAMES, MAILING ADDRESSES, E-MAIL ADDRESSES AND PHONE NUMBERS, ALL OF WHICH ARE FICTITIOUS. ANY RESEMBLANCE OF THESE FICTITIOUS NAMES, COMPANY NAMES, MAILING ADDRESSES, E-MAIL ADDRESSES AND PHONE NUMBERS TO ANY ACTUAL PERSON, COMPANY AND/OR ORGANIZATION IS UNINTENTIONAL AND PURELY COINCIDENTAL.

maranGraphics has used their best efforts in preparing this book. As Web sites are constantly changing, some of the Web site addresses in this book may have moved or no longer exist. maranGraphics does not accept responsibility nor liability for losses or damages resulting from the information contained in this book. maranGraphics also does not support the views expressed in the Web sites contained in this book.

Permissions

Hilgraeve Inc.

www.hilgraeve.com, copyright Hilgraeve, Inc., 2000

Microsoft

© 2000 Microsoft Corporation. All rights reserved.

Wal-Mart

Copyright © 2000 Wal-Mart Stores, Inc.

Yahoo

Reproduced with permission of Yahoo! Inc. 2000 by Yahoo! Inc. YAHOO! and the YAHOO! logo are trademarks of Yahoo! Inc.

Permission Also Granted

America's Top 40

CBS Sportsline

CDNow

Discovery

Sunkist

© 2000 maranGraphics, Inc.
The 3-D illustrations are the copyright of maranGraphics, Inc.

U.S. Corporate Sales	U.S. Trade Sales
Contact maranGraphics at (800) 469-6616 or fax (905) 890-9434.	Contact IDG Books at (800) 434-3422 or (650) 653-7000.

ABOUT IDG BOOKS WORLDWIDE

Welcome to the world of IDG Books Worldwide.

IDG Books Worldwide, Inc., is a subsidiary of International Data Group, the world's largest publisher of computer-related information and the leading global provider of information services on information technology. IDG was founded more than 30 years ago by Patrick J. McGovern and now employs more than 9,000 people worldwide. IDG publishes more than 290 computer publications in over 75 countries. More than 90 million people read one or more IDG publications each month.

Launched in 1990, IDG Books Worldwide is today the #1 publisher of best-selling computer books in the United States. We are proud to have received eight awards from the Computer Press Association in recognition of editorial excellence and three from Computer Currents' First Annual Readers' Choice Awards. Our best-selling ...For Dummies® series has more than 50 million copies in print with translations in 31 languages. IDG Books Worldwide, through a joint venture with IDG's Hi-Tech Beijing, became the first U.S. publisher to publish a computer book in the People's Republic of China. In record time, IDG Books Worldwide has become the first choice for millions of readers around the world who want to learn how to better manage their businesses.

Our mission is simple: Every one of our books is designed to bring extra value and skill-building instructions to the reader. Our books are written by experts who understand and care about our readers. The knowledge base of our editorial staff comes from years of experience in publishing, education, and journalism — experience we use to produce books to carry us into the new millennium. In short, we care about books, so we attract the best people. We devote special attention to details such as audience, interior design, use of icons, and illustrations. And because we use an efficient process of authoring, editing, and desktop publishing our books electronically, we can spend more time ensuring superior content and less time on the technicalities of making books.

You can count on our commitment to deliver high-quality books at competitive prices on topics you want to read about. At IDG Books Worldwide, we continue in the IDG tradition of delivering quality for more than 30 years. You'll find no better book on a subject than one from IDG Books Worldwide.

John Kilcullen
Chairman and CEO
IDG Books Worldwide, Inc.

Steven Berkowitz
President and Publisher
IDG Books Worldwide, Inc.

Eighth Annual
Computer Press
Awards ≥1992

Ninth Annual
Computer Press
Awards ≥1993

Tenth Annual
Computer Press
Awards ≥1994

Eleventh Annual
Computer Press
Awards ≥1995

IDG is the world's leading IT media, research and exposition company. Founded in 1964, IDG had 1997 revenues of $2.05 billion and has more than 9,000 employees worldwide. IDG offers the widest range of media options that reach IT buyers in 75 countries representing 95% of worldwide IT spending. IDG's diverse product and services portfolio spans six key areas including print publishing, online publishing, expositions and conferences, market research, education and training, and global marketing services. More than 90 million people read one or more of IDG's 290 magazines and newspapers, including IDG's leading global brands — Computerworld, PC World, Network World, Macworld and the Channel World family of publications. IDG Books Worldwide is one of the fastest-growing computer book publishers in the world, with more than 700 titles in 36 languages. The "...For Dummies®" series alone has more than 50 million copies in print. IDG offers online users the largest network of technology-specific Web sites around the world through IDG.net (http://www.idg.net), which comprises more than 225 targeted Web sites in 55 countries worldwide. International Data Corporation (IDC) is the world's largest provider of information technology data, analysis and consulting, with research centers in over 41 countries and more than 400 research analysts worldwide. IDG World Expo is a leading producer of more than 168 globally branded conferences and expositions in 35 countries including E3 (Electronic Entertainment Expo), Macworld Expo, ComNet, Windows World Expo, ICE (Internet Commerce Expo), Agenda, DEMO, and Spotlight. IDG's training subsidiary, ExecuTrain, is the world's largest computer training company, with more than 230 locations worldwide and 785 training courses. IDG Marketing Services helps industry-leading IT companies build international brand recognition by developing global integrated marketing programs via IDG's print, online and exposition products worldwide. Further information about the company can be found at www.idg.com.   1/24/99

maranGraphics is a family-run business
located near Toronto, Canada.

At maranGraphics, we believe in producing great computer books–one book at a time.

Each maranGraphics book uses the award-winning communication process that we have been developing over the last 25 years. Using this process, we organize screen shots, text and illustrations in a way that makes it easy for you to learn new concepts and tasks.

We spend hours deciding the best way to perform each task, so you don't have to! Our clear, easy-to-follow screen shots and instructions walk you through each task from beginning to end.

Our detailed illustrations go hand-in-hand with the text to help reinforce the information. Each illustration is a labor of love–some take up to a week to draw!

We want to thank you for purchasing what we feel are the best computer books money can buy. We hope you enjoy using this book as much as we enjoyed creating it!

Sincerely,

The Maran Family

Please visit us on the Web at:
www.maran.com

CREDITS

Authors:
Ruth Maran & Paul Whitehead

Directors of Copy Development:
Kelleigh Johnson
Wanda Lawrie

Copy Developers:
Roxanne Van Damme
Raquel Scott
Cathy Benn
Stacey Morrison
Luis Lee

Technical Consultant:
Gerald Vidas

Project Manager:
Judy Maran

Editors:
Teri Lynn Pinsent
Roderick Anatalio

Screen Captures and Editing:
James Menzies

Layout Designer:
Treena Lees

Screen Artists:
Dave Thornhill
Jimmy Tam

Screen Shot Permissions:
Jennifer Amaral

Indexer:
Kelleigh Johnson

*Senior Vice President and
Publisher, IDG Books Technology
Publishing Group:*
Richard Swadley

*Publishing Director, IDG Books
Technology Publishing Group:*
Barry Pruett

*Editorial Support, IDG Books
Technology Publishing Group:*
Martine Edwards
Lindsay Sandman
Sandy Rodrigues

Post Production:
Robert Maran

ACKNOWLEDGMENTS

Thanks to the dedicated staff of maranGraphics, including
Jennifer Amaral, Roderick Anatalio, Cathy Benn, Sean Johannesen,
Kelleigh Johnson, Wanda Lawrie, Luis Lee, Treena Lees, Jill Maran,
Judy Maran, Robert Maran, Ruth Maran, Russ Marini, James Menzies,
Suzana Miokovic, Stacey Morrison, Teri Lynn Pinsent, Steven Schaerer,
Norm Schumacher, Raquel Scott, Manish Thadani, Dave Thornhill,
Natalie Tweedie, Roxanne Van Damme and Paul Whitehead.

Finally, to Richard Maran who originated the easy-to-use
graphic format of this guide. Thank you for your
inspiration and guidance.

1

GETTING STARTED

1) WINDOWS ME BASICS

2) VIEWING FILES

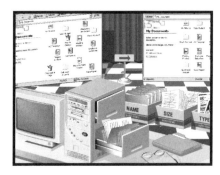

TABLE OF CONTENTS

3) WORK WITH FILES

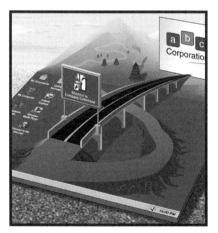

WINDOWS ME ACCESSORIES

TABLE OF CONTENTS

3 CUSTOMIZE WINDOWS ME

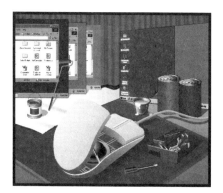

TABLE OF CONTENTS

4 — *WINDOWS ME AND MULTIMEDIA*

5 CONNECT TO OTHER COMPUTERS

TABLE OF CONTENTS

NETWORKING

17) WORK ON A NETWORK

18) SET UP AND MONITOR A NETWORK

7 COMMUNICATE WITH OTHERS

8 WINDOWS ME AND THE INTERNET

TABLE OF CONTENTS

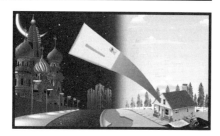

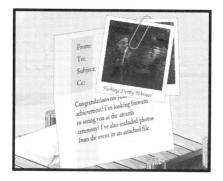

9 MANAGE HARDWARE AND SOFTWARE

TABLE OF CONTENTS

INTRODUCTION TO WINDOWS ME

Windows Me (Millennium Edition) is an operating system which ensures that all parts of your computer work together smoothly and efficiently. Windows Me controls the hardware on your computer and starts and operates your programs. Windows Me allows you to easily use your computer for work or play.

Working With Files

When you create and save a document, Windows stores the document as a file. You can open, sort, move, copy, rename, print, search for and delete your files. If you accidentally delete a file, you can usually restore the file from the Recycle Bin. You can create folders to organize your files and you can place shortcuts on your desktop to help you easily access your favorite files and folders.

Entertaining Features

When you need a break from your work, you can play games such as Solitaire and Pinball. You can also play video and sound files, listen to music CDs and listen to radio station broadcasts on the Internet. You can make Windows more entertaining by assigning sounds to program events. You can watch television programs on your computer using WebTV or use Windows Movie Maker to transfer, organize and edit home movies on your computer before sharing them with friends and family.

Accessory Programs

Windows includes several programs you can use to perform tasks. You can use WordPad to compose simple documents or use Paint to create graphic images. You can perform calculations using the on-screen Calculator

and make telephone calls from your computer using Phone Dialer. The Imaging program lets you view and work with images stored on your computer.

Customization and Personalization

You can change the appearance and behavior of Windows to suit your needs. You can place the taskbar in a more convenient location on the screen. You can display a picture on your desktop or change the colors used to display screen elements. Changing the resolution allows you to display more or less information on the screen. You can also have a screen saver appear when you are not using your computer. You can also add programs you frequently use to the Start menu and have programs start automatically each time you start Windows. The Accessibility options can help make the computer easier to use for people with special needs.

Disk Management

Windows Me allows you to optimize the performance of your computer. You can view the amount of used and free space on your hard drive. You can also use ScanDisk to locate and repair any errors that are found on your hard drive. Disk Cleanup allows you to remove unneeded files from your computer to free up disk space and Disk Defragmenter better organizes the files on your hard drive.

Working With Hardware and Software

You can use the wizards included with Windows to easily install a new hardware device or program. The wizards guide you step by step through the installation process. Many hardware devices will install automatically when you connect the device to your computer. Windows provides many ways for you to view information about your hardware devices and modify the settings for your devices. Windows also provides Troubleshooters to assist you when your hardware devices and programs do not work properly.

Connecting to Other Computers

There are many ways you can connect to other computers. You can use a dial-up connection to connect to your computer at work when you are traveling. You can use HyperTerminal as a telnet program to connect to a computer on the Internet. A direct cable connection allows you to use a cable to connect two computers to share information. The Briefcase feature allows you to work on your files when you are away from the office. When you return to the office, Briefcase can automatically update the files on your office computer.

Networking

You can share your files and printer with people on your network. You can also determine the type of access that others will have to your shared resources. My Network Places allows you to view the shared resources on your network. WinPopup allows you to exchange short messages with other people on your network. Windows also provides a wizard that helps you quickly set up a home network.

Access the Internet

Windows includes Internet Explorer, which allows you to browse through information on the Web. You can display, search for and print Web pages of interest and create a list of your favorite Web pages. Outlook Express allows you to exchange e-mail messages with people around the world. You can read, send, reply to, forward, print and delete e-mail messages. You can also use the address book to store the e-mail addresses of people you frequently send messages to. Outlook Express also allows you to read and send newsgroup messages.

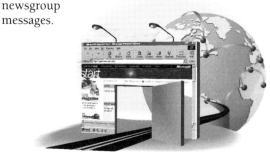

WHAT'S NEW IN WINDOWS ME

Ease of Use

Windows Me is easier to use than previous versions of Windows. Windows Me automatically personalizes your Start menu by temporarily hiding programs you do not use on a regular basis. This allows you to quickly access the programs you regularly use.

Windows Me also offers a Help feature that includes articles, instructions and information about all the features in Windows Me. The Help feature allows you to easily search for information about a specific topic. The Help feature also includes Assisted support, which you can use to quickly access help information and technical support on the Internet. You can even submit a question about Windows Me directly to a Microsoft support professional.

Windows Me also allows you to compress folders on your computer and extract files from compressed folders. Creating compressed folders is useful if you want to save storage space on your computer or if you want to speed up the transfer of files over the Internet.

Work With Pictures

Windows Me includes many improved features that allow you to create and edit pictures. Pictures you create can be inserted into other programs or displayed as a screen saver or wallpaper on your desktop.

Windows Me provides the My Pictures folder, which is a convenient place to store and view pictures. The My Pictures folder provides a thumbnail view of pictures you select so you can preview them without opening each one. The Image Preview feature also allows you to easily view, magnify, print and rotate pictures.

Windows Image Acquisition (WIA) allows you to manage images you create using devices such as scanners, digital cameras and image manipulation software. This allows you to efficiently retrieve, store and organize saved images on your computer.

Work With Multimedia

Windows Me includes an enhanced version of Windows Media Player, which allows you to play music CDs, listen to radio station broadcasts over the Internet and view video or animation files on your computer. You can customize how Windows Media Player looks and functions. You can also use the Media Guide to access the latest music, movies and videos on the Internet.

Windows Movie Maker allows you to transfer your home movies to your computer. You can then organize and edit the movies before sharing them with friends and family.

The Media Library allows you to organize all the media files on your computer.

Communicate With Others

MSN Messenger Service is an instant messaging program that allows you to communicate with other people who use the service. You can see who is online and send instant messages or files to other people. You can also talk to another person using a microphone and easily access your e-mail messages.

If you have more than one computer at home, you can set up a home network so you can exchange information between the computers. Computers on a home network may be able to use one Internet connection to access the Internet at the same time.

Windows Me also includes several games that you can play on your own, on a network with other Windows users or with people on the Internet. When playing a game on the Internet, Windows Me matches you with other players. You can chat with the other players by sending messages such as "It's your turn" or "Play again?".

Computer Optimization

Windows Me includes many improved features to help you optimize your computer's performance. If you are experiencing problems with your computer, you can use the System Restore feature to return your computer to a time before the problems occurred.

Windows Me can automatically notify you if a new Windows feature becomes available on the Internet. You can then install the feature to update and improve the performance of your computer.

The System File Protection (SFP) feature in Windows Me ensures that critical system files are not accidentally replaced on your computer. This helps to avoid system errors and keeps your computer running efficiently.

Hardware Enhancements

Windows Me supports more hardware types than previous versions of Windows. The enhanced Plug and Play system allows you to connect many devices to a computer running Windows Me without having to perform any manual software installation or hardware configuration. Computers running the Windows Me operating system can also be connected to devices such as home appliances, which are now being created with communication capabilities.

You can place your computer on standby, which turns off items that use power when you do not use the computer for a period of time. Some computers also support the hibernate option, which saves everything on your computer and then automatically turns off the computer. When you restart your computer after hibernation, any open programs and documents will appear as you left them on your computer.

PARTS OF THE WINDOWS ME SCREEN

The Windows Me screen displays various items that give you quick access to Windows features.

My Documents

Provides a convenient place to store your documents.

My Computer

Lets you view all the folders and files stored on your computer.

My Network Places

Lets you view all the folders and files available on your network.

Recycle Bin

Stores deleted files and allows you to recover them later.

Online Services

Allows you to sign on to popular online services, such as America Online.

Title Bar

Displays the name of an open window. The title bar of the window you are currently using is blue in color.

Menu Bar

Provides access to lists of commands available in a window.

Toolbar

Contains buttons that provide quick access to frequently used menu commands.

Window

A rectangle on your screen that displays information. A window can be moved and sized.

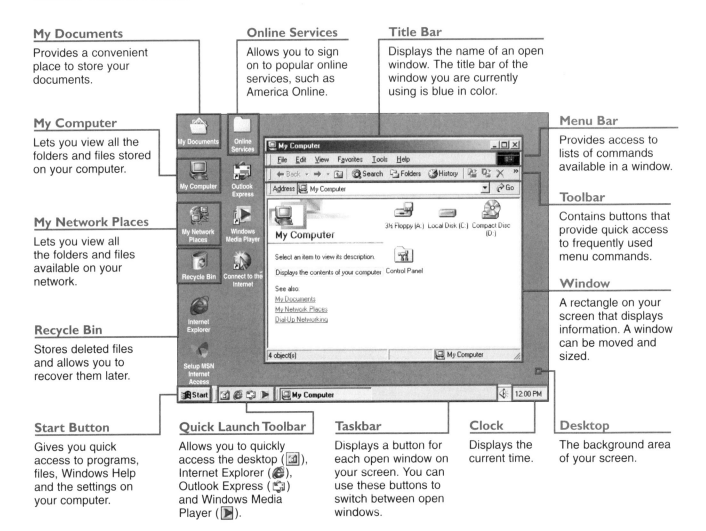

Start Button

Gives you quick access to programs, files, Windows Help and the settings on your computer.

Quick Launch Toolbar

Allows you to quickly access the desktop (), Internet Explorer (), Outlook Express () and Windows Media Player ().

Taskbar

Displays a button for each open window on your screen. You can use these buttons to switch between open windows.

Clock

Displays the current time.

Desktop

The background area of your screen.

USING THE MOUSE

A mouse is a handheld device that allows you to select and move items on your screen. When you move the mouse on your desk, the mouse pointer on your screen moves in the same direction.

The mouse pointer assumes different shapes, such as ▷ or Ⅰ, depending on its location on the screen and the task you are performing.

Click

Press and release the left mouse button. A click is used to select an item on the screen.

Double-click

Quickly press and release the left mouse button twice. A double-click is used to open a document or start a program.

Right-click

Press and release the right mouse button. A right-click is used to display a list of frequently used commands for an item.

Drag and Drop

Position the mouse pointer over an item on the screen and then press and hold down the left mouse button as you move the mouse to where you want to place the item. Then release the button. Dragging and dropping allows you to easily move an item to a new location.

Cleaning the Mouse

You should occasionally remove the small cover on the bottom of the mouse and clean the ball inside the mouse. Make sure you also remove dust and dirt from the inside of the mouse to help ensure smooth motion of the mouse.

Mouse Pads

A mouse pad provides a smooth surface for moving the mouse on your desk. A mouse pad also reduces the amount of dirt that enters the mouse and protects your desk from scratches. Hard plastic mouse pads attract less dirt and provide a smoother surface than fabric mouse pads.

START WINDOWS ME

Windows automatically starts when you turn on your computer. You may need to enter a user name and password.

If your computer is connected to a network, your user name and password identify you to the network and verify that you have permission to access the network resources. If you share your computer with other people, your user name and password enable you to have a personalized working environment.

The first time you start Windows, the Windows Millennium Edition Preview may appear. The preview displays a short video and then gives you quick access to information about new Windows features.

If your computer was not shut down properly the last time you used the computer, Windows automatically runs ScanDisk to check your hard drive for errors. For information about ScanDisk, see page 512.

How can I display the Windows Millennium Edition Preview again?

✔ From the Start menu, click Programs and select Accessories. Then click Entertainment and select Windows Millennium Edition Preview. To display the preview, your screen resolution must be set at 800x600 or higher. To change the screen resolution, see page 172.

START WINDOWS ME

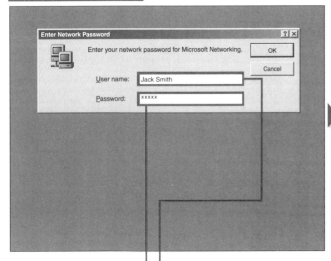

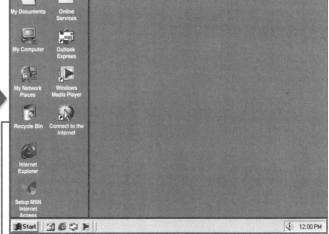

■ **1** Turn on your computer and monitor.

■ A dialog box may appear, asking you to enter your password.

■ This area displays your user name. To enter a different name, drag the mouse I over this area to highlight the name and then type the new name.

2 Type your password and then press the Enter key.

Note: You can click Cancel to start Windows without logging on to your network.

■ Windows starts.

■ This area displays your desktop icons.

■ This area displays the taskbar.

Note: The screen resolution in this book was changed to make the information on the screen larger and easier to view. To change the screen resolution, see page 172.

SHOW THE DESKTOP

You can use the Show Desktop button to minimize all the open windows on your screen so you can clearly view the desktop. This allows you to quickly access the items on your desktop, such as My Computer, the Recycle Bin and shortcuts to programs and documents you frequently use.

Windows allows you to perform many tasks at once, so you may often have several windows open on your screen at the same time. When you want to perform another task, such as starting a program or opening a My Computer window, you can minimize all the open windows, rather than closing or moving the windows, to view the desktop.

The Show Desktop button does not close any of the open windows. The windows are minimized to buttons on the taskbar. You can return all the windows to your screen at once by using the Show Desktop button or one at a time by using the taskbar buttons.

SHOW THE DESKTOP

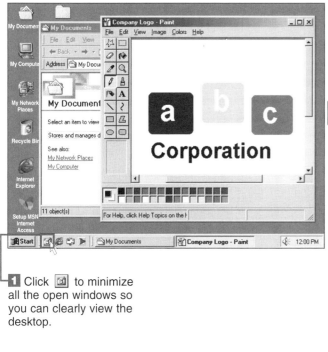

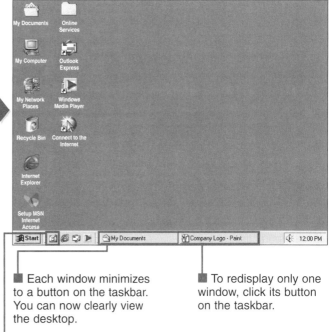

■1 Click 🗗 to minimize all the open windows so you can clearly view the desktop.

■ Each window minimizes to a button on the taskbar. You can now clearly view the desktop.

■ You can click 🗗 again to redisplay all the windows.

■ To redisplay only one window, click its button on the taskbar.

USING THE START MENU

You can use the Start menu to start programs, access recently used documents, search for files, access computer settings, get help with Windows and more.

When you click the Start button on the taskbar, the Start menu appears, providing quick access to Windows features. You can also use the keyboard to display the Start menu.

The Start menu contains a Programs menu. When you display the Programs menu, a short version of the menu may appear, displaying the items you have recently used. You can expand the menu to display all the items on the menu. When you select an item from the expanded menu, the item is automatically added to the short version of the menu.

You can access the Start menu while you are working in any program. This is useful if you want to quickly start a new program without having to close or minimize the current program. For example, you may want to open a spreadsheet program while working with WordPad to compare data in the two programs.

USING THE START MENU

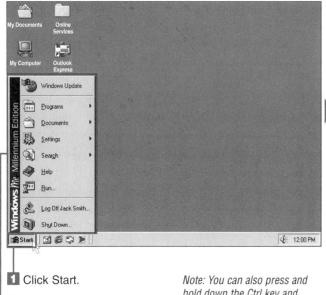

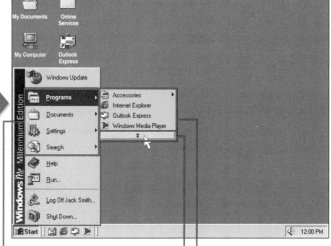

1 Click Start.

■ The Start menu appears.

Note: You can also press and hold down the Ctrl key and then press the Esc key to display the Start menu. If you have the Windows key (⊞) on your keyboard, you can also press this key to display the Start menu.

2 To display another menu, position the mouse ⍟ over a menu item with an arrow (▶).

■ Another menu appears.

■ Windows may display a short version of the menu, which displays only the items you have recently used.

3 To display all the items on the menu, position the mouse ⍟ over ⩔.

How can I find a program that does not appear on the Start menu?

✔ Try to locate the program using either My Computer, Windows Explorer or the Search feature. For information about the Search feature, see page 78.

Can I add an item to the Start menu?

✔ You can add any program or file to the Start menu. Find the item you want to add and then drag the item to the Start button. Do not release the mouse button and the Start menu will appear. Continue dragging the item to the location on the Start menu or Programs menu where you want the item to appear.

Can I rearrange the items on the Programs menu?

✔ You can move an item on the Programs menu by dragging the item to a new location.

How do I make the Programs menu always display all of its items?

✔ Right-click an empty area of the taskbar. From the menu that appears, click Properties. In the Taskbar and Start Menu Properties dialog box, select the Use personalized menus option (☑ changes to ☐).

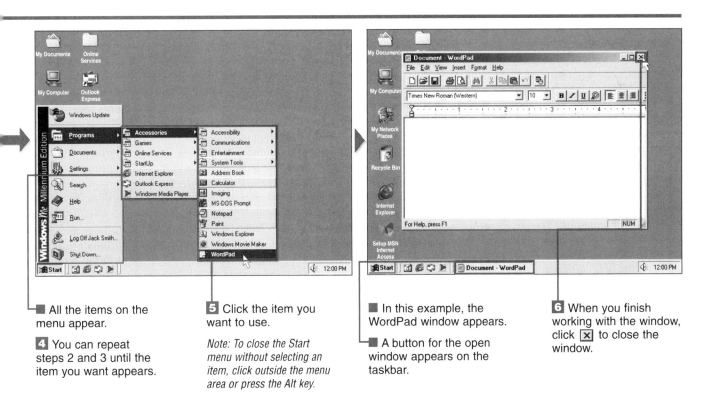

■ All the items on the menu appear.

4 You can repeat steps 2 and 3 until the item you want appears.

5 Click the item you want to use.

Note: To close the Start menu without selecting an item, click outside the menu area or press the Alt key.

■ In this example, the WordPad window appears.

■ A button for the open window appears on the taskbar.

6 When you finish working with the window, click ☒ to close the window.

USING RUN TO START A PROGRAM

You can use the Run command to quickly start a program. The Run command is especially useful for programs that do not appear on the Start menu.

There are many programs that Windows does not display on the Start menu, such as programs that can be used to change the settings on your computer. This helps to avoid the accidental

misuse of these programs. For example, if you type regedit in the Run dialog box, the Registry Editor starts. The Registry Editor allows you to change your system registry settings. Incorrect use of this program may cause serious damage to your computer.

You may also have MS-DOS and older Windows programs, such as games, that are not displayed on the Start menu. You can use

the Run command to start these types of programs.

When you begin typing the name of a program you want to start using the Run command, Windows may display a list of matching programs that you can choose from. You can also display a list of programs you have recently started using the Run command and then choose a program from the list.

USING RUN TO START A PROGRAM

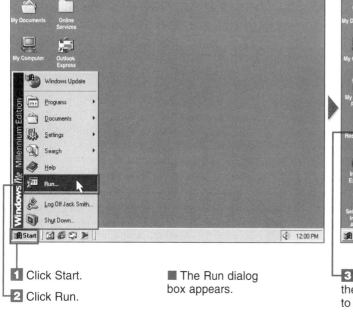

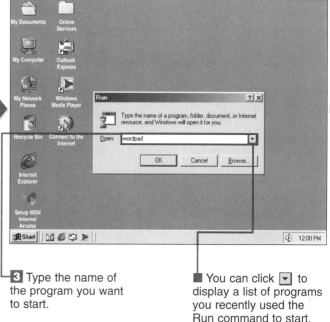

1 Click Start.

2 Click Run.

■ The Run dialog box appears.

3 Type the name of the program you want to start.

■ You can click ▼ to display a list of programs you recently used the Run command to start. You can then select the program you want to start from the list.

What if I do not know the name of the program I want to start?

✓ You can click the Browse button in the Run dialog box to find a program you want to start.

Can I use the Run command to open items other than programs?

✓ The Run command can open many types of items. For example, if you type the address of a page on the Web, such as www.maran.com, Windows will connect to the Internet, open your Web browser and display the Web page. You can also type the path and name of a file or folder, such as c:\My Documents\notes.txt, to open the file or folder.

Is there another way to quickly start a program?

✓ You can add the program to the Start menu. Drag the program from your desktop or an open window to the Start button. When you want to start the program, click the Start button and then select the program.

Windows cannot find the program I want to start. What should I do?

✓ Some programs do not register the program path in the Windows Registry. You should type the path and program name, such as c:\Windows\Freecell.exe, to start these programs.

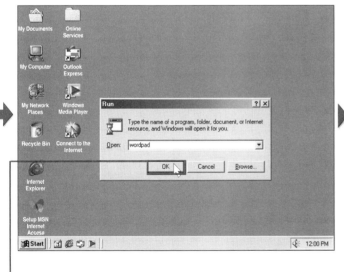

4 Click OK to start the program.

■ The program starts.

■ When you finish working with the program, click ☒ to close the program.

MAXIMIZE OR MINIMIZE A WINDOW

You may want to maximize a window to fill your screen so you can see more of the information in the window. You can also minimize a window to put the window aside so you can concentrate on other tasks.

Maximizing a window enlarges the window to fill your screen.

This allows you to view more of the contents of the window.

When you are not using a window, you can minimize the window to remove it from your screen. Minimizing a window reduces the window to a button on your taskbar that displays all or part of the name of the window.

When you are ready to once again use a minimized window, you can restore the window. Restoring a minimized window displays the window in its original size and location.

If you have many open windows on your screen, you can save time by minimizing all of the windows at once.

MAXIMIZE A WINDOW

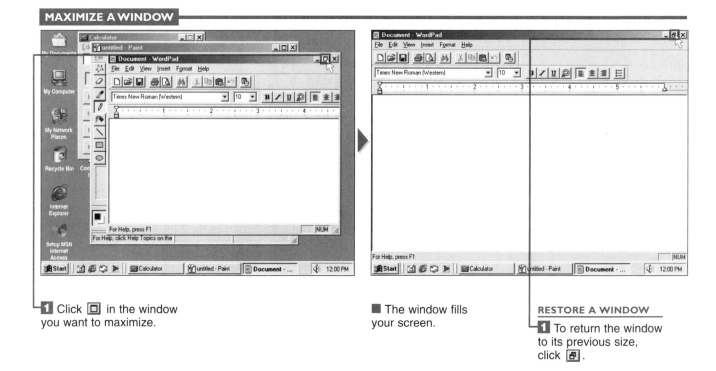

1 Click ▣ in the window you want to maximize.

■ The window fills your screen.

RESTORE A WINDOW

1 To return the window to its previous size, click ▣.

I keep clicking the wrong button when I try to maximize a window. Is there an easier way to maximize a window?

✔ You can double-click the title bar of a window to maximize the window. Double-clicking the title bar again will return the window to its original size. You can also increase the size of the buttons at the top right corner of a window to make the buttons more visible. Right-click a blank area on the desktop and then click Properties. In the Display Properties dialog box, click the Appearance tab. In the Item area, select Caption Buttons and then type a larger number in the Size area.

How do I close a minimized window?

✔ If you no longer need a window that is minimized on your screen, right-click the button for the window on the taskbar and then select Close.

Can I make the taskbar disappear to provide more room to work with a maximized window?

✔ You can use the Auto hide feature to temporarily hide the taskbar. For more information, see page 48.

MINIMIZE A WINDOW

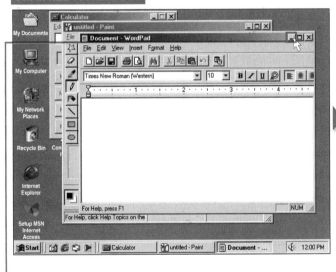

■1 Click ▣ in the window you want to minimize.

■ The window reduces to a button on the taskbar. To redisplay the window, click the button.

MINIMIZE ALL WINDOWS

■1 To minimize all windows displayed on your screen, right-click an empty area on the taskbar. A menu appears.

■2 Click Minimize All Windows.

MOVE OR SIZE A WINDOW

You can have many windows open on your desktop at one time. Adjusting the location and size of windows can help you work with their contents more easily.

You can move a window to a new location if it covers important items on your screen. If you have more than one window open, you can adjust the position of the windows to ensure that you can view the contents of each window. You can click on any open window to bring it to the front so you can clearly view its contents.

You can increase the size of a window to see more of its contents. You can reduce the size of a window to view items covered by the window.

Just as you can move and size windows on your desktop, you can also move and size windows in open programs.

MOVE A WINDOW

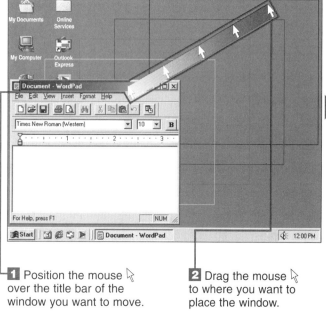

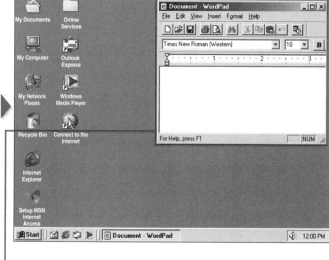

1 Position the mouse ↕ over the title bar of the window you want to move.

2 Drag the mouse ↕ to where you want to place the window.

■ An outline of the window indicates the new location.

■ The window moves to the new location.

How can I see the contents of a window as I move or size the window?

✔ Right-click a blank area on your desktop. On the menu that appears, select Properties. Click the Effects tab and then select the Show window contents while dragging option (☐ changes to ☑).

Can I move or size a maximized window?

✔ You will not be able to move or size a window that has been maximized. You must restore the window before you can move or size it. To restore a window, see page 14.

Can I move a window entirely off the screen?

✔ You can move most of a window off the screen but some of the window will still be visible. This allows you to put a document aside, as you might on a real desk.

Can all program windows be sized?

✔ Some programs, like Calculator, have windows that cannot be sized.

SIZE A WINDOW

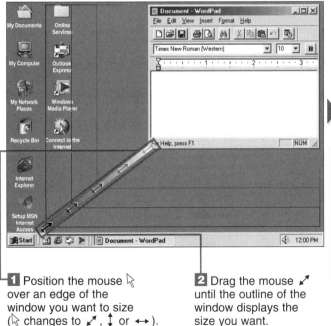

1 Position the mouse ⓚ over an edge of the window you want to size (ⓚ changes to ↗, ↕ or ↔).

2 Drag the mouse ↗ until the outline of the window displays the size you want.

■ The window changes to the new size.

SWITCH BETWEEN WINDOWS

When you have more than one window open on your screen, you can switch between the windows.

Although you are able to have several windows open, you can work in only one window at a time. This window is called the active window and appears in front of all the other windows. The title

bar of the active window is a different color than the title bar of the other open windows.

The taskbar displays a button for each open window on your screen. Each taskbar button displays all or part of the name of the window it represents.

You can make a window active by clicking its button on the taskbar.

You can also use your keyboard to switch between open windows.

The ability to have multiple windows open and switch between them is very useful. Switching between windows allows you to perform several tasks at once, such as consulting a report while you answer your e-mail and prepare a presentation.

SWITCH BETWEEN WINDOWS

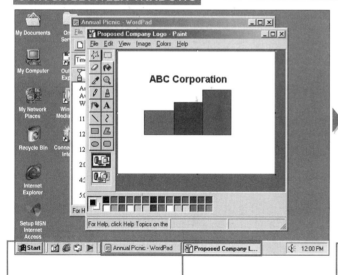

■ The taskbar displays a button for each open window on your screen.

■ Each button for an open program displays the name of the file and program.

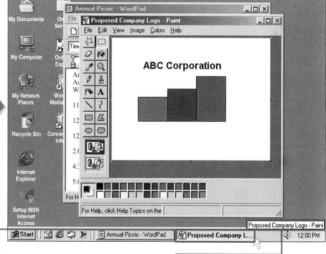

■ A button that displays periods (...) does not have enough room to display all of its information. To display all the information for a button, position the mouse ⍔ over the button.

■ After a moment, a yellow box appears, displaying all the information for the button.

The taskbar is not displayed on my screen. How do I get the taskbar to appear?

✔ If you have turned on the Auto hide feature, you can display the taskbar by moving the mouse pointer to where the taskbar was last seen. You can also press and hold down the Ctrl key and then press the Esc key to display the taskbar and the Start menu.

What can I do if my taskbar will not reappear?

✔ Your taskbar may have been resized. Move the mouse pointer to the edge of the screen where the taskbar was last seen. When the mouse pointer changes to a double-headed arrow ($\updownarrow$ or $\leftrightarrow$), drag the taskbar back onto the screen.

Are there other ways to make an open window active?

✔ You can click any part of an open window to make it the active window. You can also use your keyboard to change the active window. Press and hold down the Alt key and then press the Esc key until the window you want to work with appears in front of all other windows.

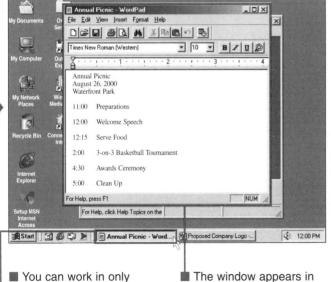

■ You can work in only one window at a time.

1 Click the button on the taskbar for the window you want to work with.

■ The window appears in front of all other windows. You can now clearly view the contents of the window.

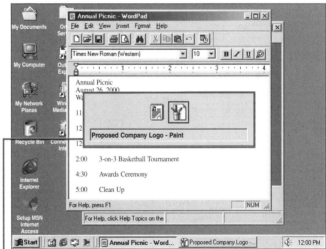

USING THE KEYBOARD

1 Press and hold down the Alt key and then press the Tab key.

■ A box appears, displaying an icon for each open window.

2 Still holding down the Alt key, press the Tab key until the box displays the name of the window you want to work with. Then release the Alt key.

ARRANGE WINDOWS

Y ou can arrange the open windows on your desktop to make them easier to work with or to display more of their contents.

You can have several windows open at the same time. Similar to a real desk, you can have many items, such as an agenda, a letter and a budget, all open on your desktop at once. Windows allows you to arrange and

organize these items so they are easier to use.

You can choose to cascade your open windows. The Cascade Windows command displays windows one on top of the other so that you can see the title bar of each window. You can move between the open windows by clicking the title bar of the window you want to view.

You can use the Tile Windows Horizontally or Tile Windows Vertically command to arrange multiple open windows one above the other or side by side. Tiling windows allows you to easily compare the contents of your windows and drag information from one window to another.

ARRANGE WINDOWS

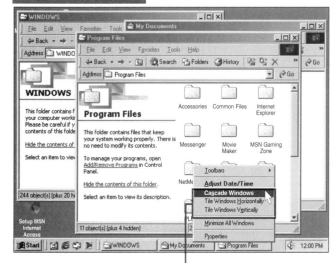

1 Right-click an empty area on the taskbar. A menu appears.

2 Click the way you want to arrange the open windows on your screen.

CASCADE

■ The windows neatly overlap each other. You can clearly see the title bar of each window.

■ You can click the title bar of the window you want to work with to make that window active. The window will appear in front of all other windows.

How do I make a window appear in front of all other windows?

✔ Click any part of the window. You can also click the window's button on the taskbar.

How do I change back to the previous window arrangement?

✔ To immediately change back to the previous window arrangement, right-click an empty area on the taskbar and then select Undo.

Why are some of my program windows not tiling correctly?

✔ Some programs with a fixed window size, such as Calculator, cannot be tiled.

Why can't I see a difference between the Tile Windows Horizontally command and the Tile Windows Vertically command?

✔ Tiled windows are displayed the same way on your screen when there are four or more windows open.

How do I cascade or tile only some of the windows I have open?

✔ Minimize the windows you do not want to cascade or tile before you use the Cascade Windows or Tile commands.

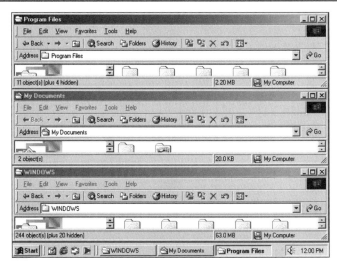

TILE HORIZONTALLY

■ The windows appear one above the other. You can view the contents of each window.

■ You can easily compare the contents of the windows and exchange information between the windows.

■ You can click anywhere in the window you want to work with to make that window active.

TILE VERTICALLY

■ The windows appear side by side. You can view the contents of each window.

■ You can easily compare the contents of the windows and exchange information between the windows.

■ You can click anywhere in the window you want to work with to make that window active.

SELECT COMMANDS

Windows provides menus and dialog boxes that allow you to access commands and features. You can use your mouse or keyboard to select commands.

Each menu contains a group of related commands. Some menu commands, such as Undo and Copy, immediately perform an action when they are selected.

Some menu commands, such as Open With and Add to Favorites, open a dialog box. These commands are usually followed by three dots (...). A dialog box appears when Windows needs more information to perform an action. Dialog boxes have areas where you can enter text or select options from a list.

You can use some menu commands to turn an option on or off. If an option is on, a check mark (✔) or a bullet (●) appears to the left of the command.

If a small arrow (▶) appears to the right of a menu command, the command will open another menu that contains more commands.

SELECT COMMANDS

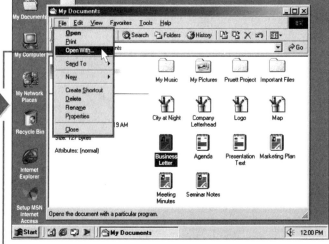

1 Click the name of the menu you want to display.

■ To select a menu with the keyboard, press the Alt key and then press the key for the underlined letter in the menu name (example: F for File).

2 Click the name of the command you want to select.

■ To select a command with the keyboard, press the key for the underlined letter in the command name (example: H for Open With).

■ To close a menu without selecting a command, click outside the menu or press the Alt key.

Why do some menu commands appear dimmed?

✔ Commands that appear dimmed are currently not available. You must perform a specific task before you can access the commands. For example, you must select a file to make the Cut and Copy commands in the Edit menu available.

Are there shortcut keys for menu commands?

✔ Many menu commands offer keyboard shortcuts you can use to quickly select the commands. For example, Ctrl+C copies a selected file. If a command has a keyboard shortcut, the shortcut appears beside the command in the menu.

What is the difference between option buttons (○) and check boxes (☐)?

✔ When a list of choices displays option buttons (○), you can select only one option. The selected option displays a dark center (◉). When a list of choices displays check boxes (☐), you can select as many options as you want. Selected options display a check mark (☑).

Is there another way to select commands?

✔ Yes. Most items in Windows, including the desktop and the taskbar, have a shortcut menu that appears when you right-click the item. The shortcut menu includes the most frequently used commands for the item.

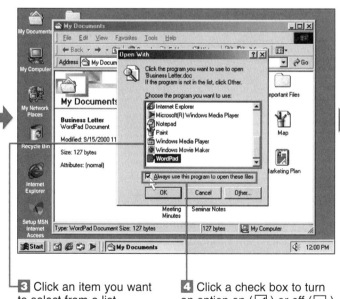

3 Click an item you want to select from a list.

■ To move through the options in a dialog box with the keyboard, press the Tab key. Press the up or down arrow keys to select an item from a list.

4 Click a check box to turn an option on (☑) or off (☐).

■ To turn an option on (☑) or off (☐) with the keyboard, press the Spacebar.

5 Click OK or press the Enter key to confirm your selections.

■ You can click Cancel or press the Esc key to leave the dialog box without making any changes.

GETTING HELP

Y ou can use the Home page to browse through lists of commonly used help topics, recently viewed help topics and other resources. The Home page appears automatically each time you open the Windows Help and Support window and is a good starting point for finding help information.

When you select a commonly used help topic, a list of related help topics appears. You can continue selecting topics of interest to find the help information you need. For example, the Using Windows Millennium Edition topic contains help topics you may find useful if you are using Windows for the first time or if you are upgrading from a previous version of Windows. The Personalizing Your Computer topic contains help topics that teach you how to customize Windows.

The Home page includes topics that can help you fix a problem you are experiencing with your computer. For example, you can select the Use System Restore topic to return your computer to a time before a problem occurred.

The Home page also provides access to resources, such as online support and help topics you have recently viewed.

USING THE HOME PAGE

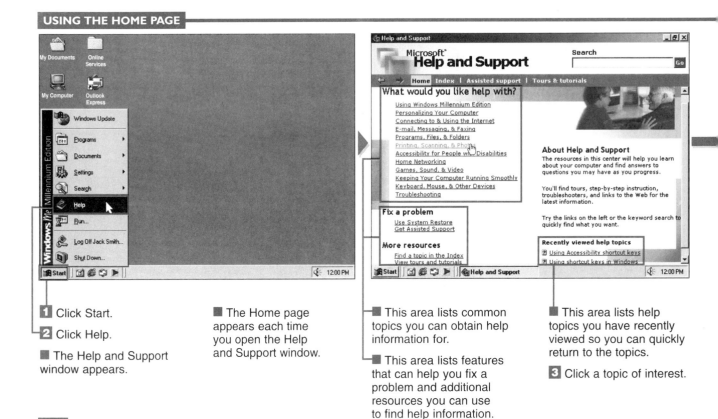

■1 Click Start.

■2 Click Help.

■ The Help and Support window appears.

■ The Home page appears each time you open the Help and Support window.

■ This area lists common topics you can obtain help information for.

■ This area lists features that can help you fix a problem and additional resources you can use to find help information.

■ This area lists help topics you have recently viewed so you can quickly return to the topics.

■3 Click a topic of interest.

MASTER IT

How do I return to the Home page?

✔ You can click Home in the Help and Support window to return to the Home page at any time.

How can I find more information about a help topic?

✔ Position the mouse pointer over the help topic (↖ changes to 👆). After a few seconds, a yellow box appears, displaying a description of the help topic.

How can I quickly display help information?

✔ When working in a folder window, press the F1 key to quickly open the Help and Support window. When you are working in a program, pressing the F1 key will usually open the help feature provided by the program.

Why do some help topics display blue text?

✔ You can click a word or phrase that appears in blue to have Windows open the window or dialog box needed to perform the task.

Why do some help topics display green text?

✔ You can click a word or phrase that appears in green to have Windows display a definition of the word or phrase. To hide the definition, click anywhere on the screen.

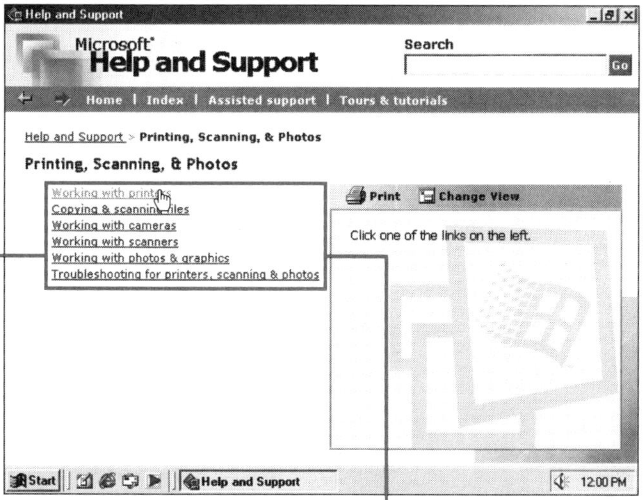

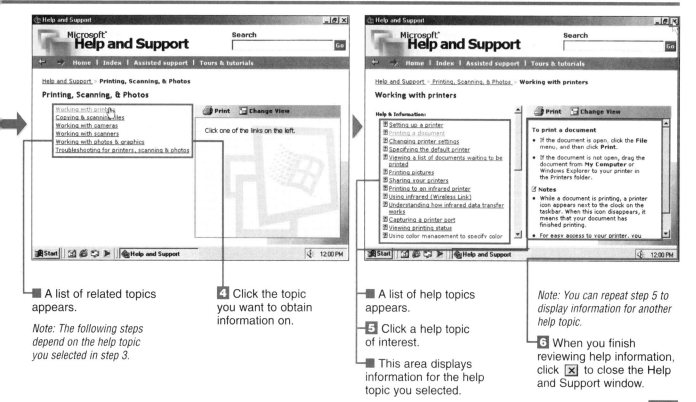

■ A list of related topics appears.

Note: The following steps depend on the help topic you selected in step 3.

4 Click the topic you want to obtain information on.

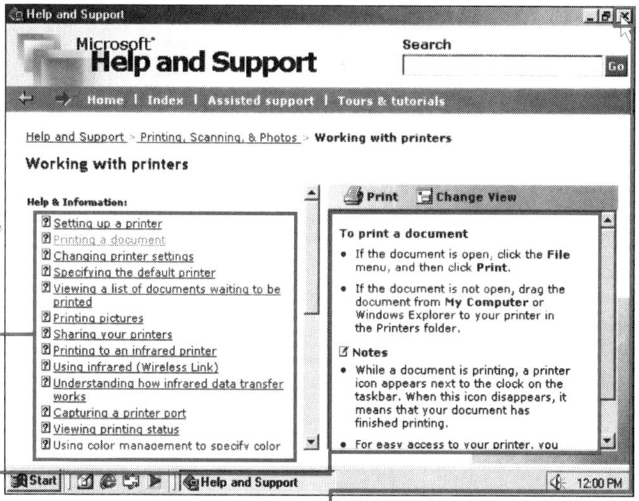

■ A list of help topics appears.

5 Click a help topic of interest.

■ This area displays information for the help topic you selected.

Note: You can repeat step 5 to display information for another help topic.

6 When you finish reviewing help information, click ☒ to close the Help and Support window.

GETTING HELP (CONTINUED)

The search tool provided by Windows Help allows you to find information for specific help topics. You can type one or more words and have Windows display help topics that contain the words.

To help ensure your search produces the results you want, you should enter only the words you are looking for. For example,

if you want information on saving files, type "save files" instead of "I need information on saving files."

When the search is complete, Windows displays a list of the matching help topics. Windows organizes the topics into one or more categories to help you quickly find the help topic of interest. These categories can

include Help & Information, Troubleshooting, Technical Resources and Tours & Tutorials.

If Windows displays many help topics, you can narrow your search by adding another word or searching for a more specific word.

After you find the help topic you want, you can display the help information for the topic.

SEARCH FOR HELP INFORMATION

1 Click Start.

2 Click Help.

■ The Help and Support window appears.

3 To search for help information, click this area and then type a word or short phrase that describes the topic of interest.

4 Press the Enter key to start the search.

Is there another way to narrow my search?

✔ You can use the AND, OR or NOT operator to narrow your search. For example, if you want to find help topics on sharing resources but you do not want information on sharing printers, you can type **share NOT printers**.

How can I find a help topic related to the currently displayed information?

✔ Many help topics display a Related Topics link at the end of the help information. You can click the link to view a list of related help topics and then select the topic you want to display. If a help topic has only one related topic, the information for the related topic will immediately appear when you click the Related Topics link.

Can I find definitions for the terms used in Windows?

✔ You can type **glossary** in the search area and then press the Enter key to find the Glossary of Windows terms help topic. After you select the topic, you can click a term to display a definition for the term.

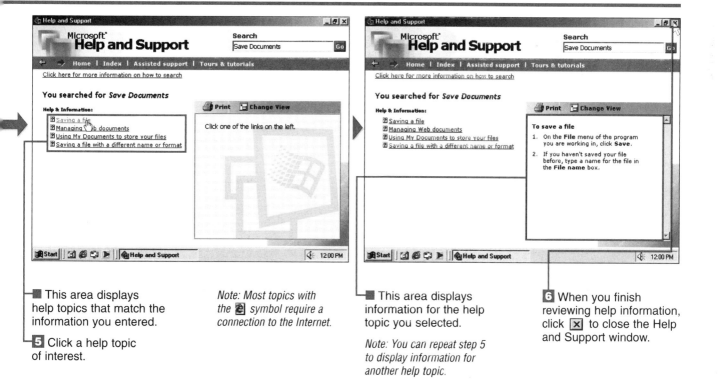

■ This area displays help topics that match the information you entered.

5 Click a help topic of interest.

Note: Most topics with the [icon] symbol require a connection to the Internet.

■ This area displays information for the help topic you selected.

Note: You can repeat step 5 to display information for another help topic.

6 When you finish reviewing help information, click [X] to close the Help and Support window.

GETTING HELP (CONTINUED)

The Windows help feature includes an index that displays an alphabetical list of all the Windows help topics. You can use the index to find information the same way you would use the index in a book.

You can use the scroll bar to browse through the index to locate a help topic of interest.

If you want to quickly find a specific help topic, you can type the first few characters of the help topic you want to find. Windows will instantly take you to the topic's location in the index.

Windows categorizes topics so you can quickly find the information you need. For example, if you want to add

an item to your computer, you can type the word "adding." Listed under "adding," you will find help topics for adding fonts, new users, printers and programs to your computer.

After you find the help topic you want, you can display the help information for the topic.

USING THE INDEX

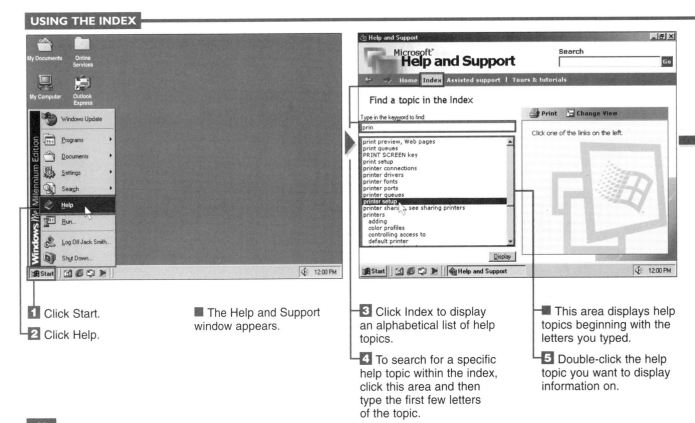

1 Click Start.

2 Click Help.

■ The Help and Support window appears.

3 Click Index to display an alphabetical list of help topics.

4 To search for a specific help topic within the index, click this area and then type the first few letters of the topic.

■ This area displays help topics beginning with the letters you typed.

5 Double-click the help topic you want to display information on.

Can I reduce the size of the Help and Support window?

✔ You can hide the left side of the Help and Support window to reduce the size of the window. This is useful if you need access to your desktop while viewing help information. Click Change View to hide the left side of the Help and Support window. Click ▣ to once again display the entire window.

How can I display help information in a larger area of the Help and Support window?

✔ Position the mouse pointer over the left edge of the area displaying the help information (↖ changes to ✛). Then drag the mouse until the outline of the area displays the size you want.

How do I return to a help topic I have already viewed?

✔ You can click the Back (⇐) or Forward (⇒) button in the Help and Support window to return to a help topic you have viewed.

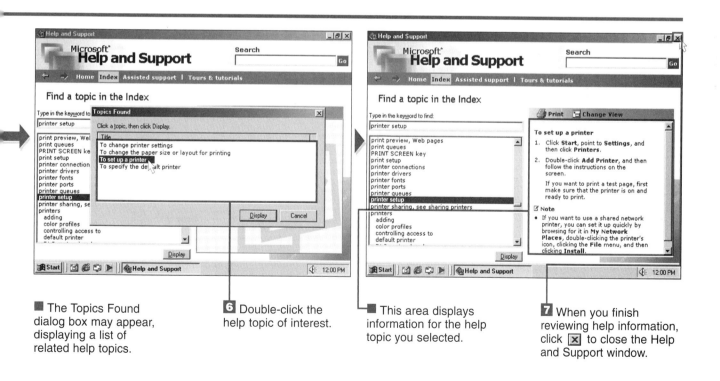

■ The Topics Found dialog box may appear, displaying a list of related help topics.

6 Double-click the help topic of interest.

■ This area displays information for the help topic you selected.

7 When you finish reviewing help information, click ⊠ to close the Help and Support window.

GETTING HELP (CONTINUED)

You can use assisted support to find help information and technical support on the Internet. You must be connected to the Internet to use most of the features in assisted support.

You can select the Microsoft Corporation option to submit a question about Windows Me to a Microsoft support professional. Once you submit a question, you can check the status of the question. You can also review responses to questions you previously submitted.

Assisted support allows you to view information about your computer. This information could help you troubleshoot a problem you are experiencing with your computer.

Support communities can also be used to access help information. You can select the MSN Computing Central Forums option to discuss computer topics, such as hardware, software and multimedia, with other Windows Me users. The MSN Computing Central Message Boards option allows you to use various message boards to share information, get advice and obtain technical support.

If you select a support community, you can specify which forum or message board you want to access.

USING ASSISTED SUPPORT

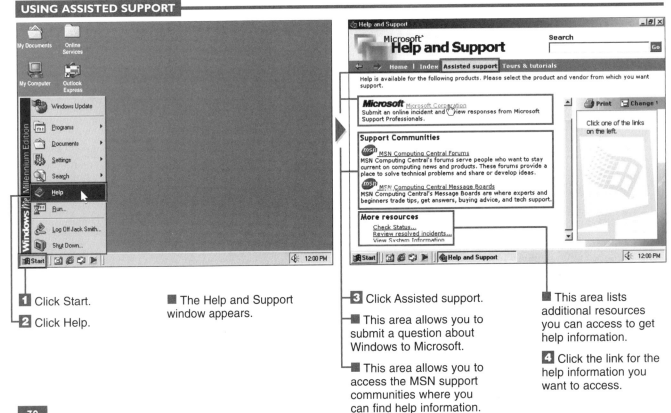

1 Click Start.

2 Click Help.

■ The Help and Support window appears.

3 Click Assisted support.

■ This area allows you to submit a question about Windows to Microsoft.

■ This area allows you to access the MSN support communities where you can find help information.

■ This area lists additional resources you can access to get help information.

4 Click the link for the help information you want to access.

Y ou can take a tour or tutorial to learn more about Windows Me.

The Windows Millennium Edition Preview tour introduces some of the features offered by Windows Me, including improved functionality, home networking and Internet access. To run the Windows Millennium Edition Preview tour, your screen resolution must be 800 by 600 or higher. To change your screen resolution, see page 172.

A tour can provide you with information about a specific Windows feature. For example, you can take the Desktop tour to learn about items on the desktop, such as the Start button and the taskbar.

Most tours contain headings that you can select to display additional information or start a new tour. Some tours, such as the Internet Explorer 5.5 tour, display a Web page on the World Wide Web. You must be connected to

the Internet to take a tour that displays a Web page.

You can take a tutorial to find out how to perform a task in Windows. For example, the Learning to use the mouse tutorial teaches you how to select items on your screen using the mouse.

USING TOURS AND TUTORIALS

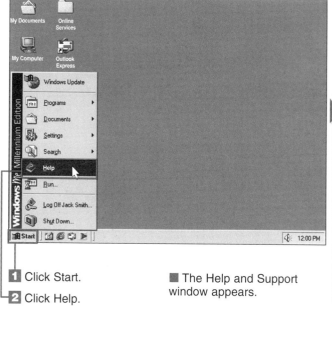

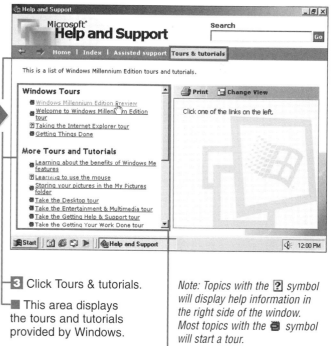

1 Click Start.

2 Click Help.

■ The Help and Support window appears.

3 Click Tours & tutorials.

■ This area displays the tours and tutorials provided by Windows.

Note: Topics with the ? symbol will display help information in the right side of the window. Most topics with the symbol will start a tour.

4 Click a topic of interest.

GETTING HELP (CONTINUED)

You can produce a paper copy of the help topic displayed on your screen. Printing a help topic can be useful because it is often difficult to remember all of the information in a Help and Support window.

A printed copy of a help topic allows you to review a task from beginning to end before you start the task.

In some circumstances, you may not be able to view the information in a Help and Support window while performing a task. For example, if you are completing a task that requires you to restart your computer, you will not be able to refer to the help information while the computer is restarting. A printed copy of the topic will help you complete the task.

A printed reference of a help topic can also help you learn about Windows features. For example, becoming familiar with all of the Windows shortcut keys can take a long time, but a printed reference can help you memorize them.

PRINT A HELP TOPIC

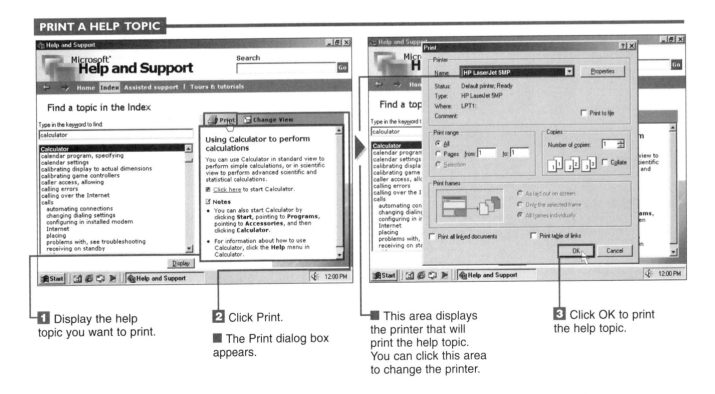

1 Display the help topic you want to print.

2 Click Print.

■ The Print dialog box appears.

■ This area displays the printer that will print the help topic. You can click this area to change the printer.

3 Click OK to print the help topic.

You can find help information about the items in a dialog box you are using.

If you are unfamiliar with a dialog box, you can use the Help button (?) to display help information. When you click the Help button and then click an item in the dialog box, a box containing help information

appears. The help information explains what the item you selected does and how you can use the item. The help information stays on the screen while you learn about the item.

You must click the Help button each time you want to display help information for an item in a dialog box.

If the Help button is not available in the dialog box, you can press the F1 key to display help information. You can also right-click an item in a dialog box and then click What's This? to display help information.

GETTING HELP IN A DIALOG BOX

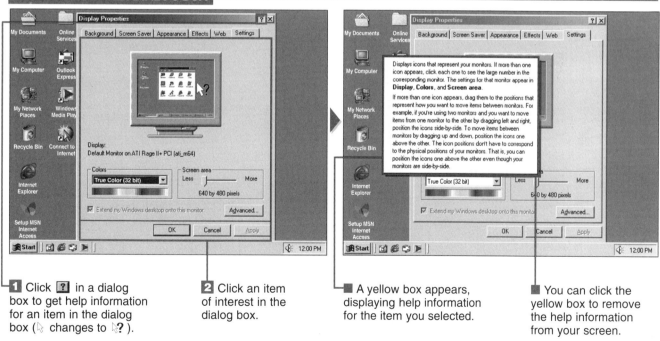

1 Click ? in a dialog box to get help information for an item in the dialog box (⬄ changes to ⬄?).

2 Click an item of interest in the dialog box.

■ A yellow box appears, displaying help information for the item you selected.

■ You can click the yellow box to remove the help information from your screen.

SHUT DOWN OR LOG OFF WINDOWS ME

You should always shut down Windows before turning off your computer. Shutting down properly allows Windows to save settings you have changed, disconnect from the network and warn you about users on the network who may be accessing your files. Turning off your computer without shutting down properly may cause you to lose data.

There are several shut down options you can choose from. The Shut down option shuts down your computer so you can turn off the power. Before shutting down Windows, make sure you close all programs you have open.

If your computer is not operating properly, you can use the Restart option to restart your computer to try to fix the problem.

The Stand by option places the computer in a low-power mode. Stand by mode is useful if you do not need to use your computer for a short period of time. You should save all your open documents before choosing Stand by mode.

If you share your computer with other people, you can log off Windows so another person can log on to Windows or the network.

SHUT DOWN WINDOWS ME

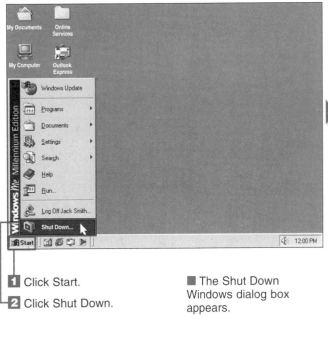

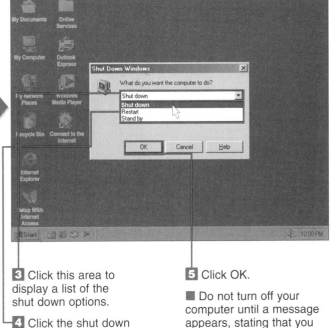

1 Click Start.

2 Click Shut Down.

■ The Shut Down Windows dialog box appears.

3 Click this area to display a list of the shut down options.

4 Click the shut down option you want to use.

5 Click OK.

■ Do not turn off your computer until a message appears, stating that you can safely turn off the computer. Some computers will turn off automatically.

Why isn't the Stand by option available on my computer?

✔ Your computer may not have power management capabilities or the power management feature may be turned off. You can consult the documentation that came with your computer to determine if your computer supports power management features.

How can I resume using my computer when it is in Stand by mode?

✔ When you are ready to use your computer, move the mouse or press a key on your keyboard.

What is the Hibernate option in the Shut Down Windows dialog box for?

✔ The Hibernate option is only available if the computer supports the hibernation feature. This feature is useful when you need to quickly turn off the computer, but wish to continue your work from where you stopped. When you select the Hibernate option, all the current settings are saved, including which windows are open and which programs are running. The computer and monitor are then turned off. When you turn on your computer again, your desktop will look exactly as it did when the computer was turned off.

LOG OFF WINDOWS ME

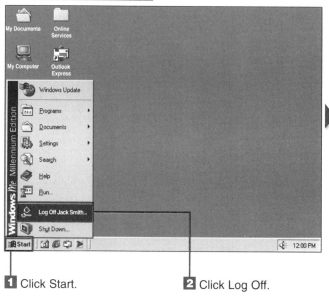

1 Click Start.

2 Click Log Off.

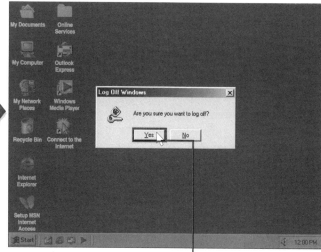

■ The Log Off Windows dialog box appears.

3 Click Yes to log off Windows.

■ A dialog box will appear, asking for your user name and password.

COMPUTER HARDWARE
Devices You Attach to a Computer

Keyboard

A keyboard is used to enter information and instructions into a computer. Many keyboards have buttons that you can press to perform tasks on your computer, such as adjusting the sound volume or accessing the Internet.

Speakers and Headphones

Speakers and headphones are used to listen to sounds created by a sound card. Headphones allow you to listen to sounds privately. Many computer speakers include an amplifier and can be plugged into a power outlet or run on batteries.

Video Camera

A video camera is used to create video files or for videoconferencing. Videoconferencing allows you to have face-to-face conversations with other people on a network.

Mouse

A mouse is a handheld device that allows you to select and move items on your screen. There are many alternatives to the mouse, including trackballs, touch-sensitive pads and tablets that use pens. Some mice have a wheel between the buttons that you can use to scroll through information in a window.

Monitor

A monitor displays text and images generated by a computer. The size of a monitor is measured diagonally across the screen. Common monitor sizes range from 14 to 21 inches.

Microphone

A microphone plugs into a sound card to allow you to record speech and other sounds onto your computer. Not all microphones are compatible with all types of sound cards.

Printer

A printer produces a paper copy of documents created on a computer. Laser printers produce high-quality printouts. Ink-jet printers produce medium-quality printouts and make color printing affordable. Dot matrix printers produce low-quality printouts and are often used to print multi-part forms.

Removable Drive

A removable drive stores and retrieves large amounts of data on removable disks. The disks you use with a removable drive can contain from 100 MB to 2 GB of information. You can use a removable drive to store information, back up information on your computer or transfer large amounts of information between computers.

Modem

A modem allows computers to exchange information through telephone lines. You can use a modem to connect to the Internet. There are two types of modems. Internal modems are expansion cards that fit inside your computer. External modems plug into the back of your computer. The speed of a modem determines how fast it can send and receive information through telephone lines. The most common modem speed is 56 Kbps.

High-Speed Internet Connection Devices

You can use a cable modem, Integrated Services Digital Network (ISDN) line or Digital Subscriber Line (DSL) to obtain a high-speed connection to the Internet. A cable modem uses the same type of cable as your television. An ISDN line connects to a dedicated telephone line, while a DSL line uses a regular telephone line. To connect to the Internet using an ISDN or DSL connection, your computer must have an ISDN or DSL connection device installed.

Scanner

A scanner converts paper documents into a format your computer can use. The resolution used by a scanner determines the amount of detail the scanner can detect. Scanner resolution is measured in dots per inch (dpi).

Tape Drive

A tape drive stores and retrieves information on tape cartridges. You can use a tape drive to back up files, archive old or rarely used files or transfer large amounts of information. There are many types of tape drives available, including the Travan drive, the QIC (Quarter-Inch Cartridge) drive and the DAT (Digital Audio Tape) drive.

Port

A port is a connector at the back of a computer where you plug in an external device, such as a printer or modem. This allows instructions and data to flow between the computer and the device. A parallel port has 25 pins and connects a printer, removable drive or tape drive. The computer uses the letters LPT, followed by a number, to identify a parallel port. A serial port has either 9 or 25 pins and is used to connect many types of devices, such as a mouse or modem. The computer uses the letters COM, followed by a number, to identify a serial port. Your computer also has additional ports to connect devices such as your monitor, keyboard or joystick. Universal Serial Bus (USB) and FireWire ports provide a way to connect several devices using only one port. Infrared ports let a computer communicate with devices by using infrared light instead of cables.

COMPUTER HARDWARE

Inside a Computer

Floppy Drive

A floppy drive stores and retrieves information on floppy disks. A double-density (DD) floppy disk can store 720 KB of information. This type of disk has one hole at the top of the disk. A high-density (HD) floppy disk can store 1.44 MB of information. This type of disk has two holes at the top of the disk.

CD-ROM Drive

A CD-ROM drive reads information stored on compact discs. You can use a CD-ROM drive to install programs, play games directly from CD-ROM discs and listen to music CDs. CD-ROM discs can store up to 650 MB of information. You cannot record information using a CD-ROM drive. To record information on a disc, you can use a CD-Recordable (CD-R) drive with a CD-R disc. You can record information on a CD-R disc only once. To be able to record information on a disc more than once, you can use a CD-ReWritable (CD-RW) drive with a CD-RW disc.

DVD-ROM Drive

A Digital Versatile Disc-ROM (DVD-ROM) drive reads information stored on DVD-ROM or CD-ROM discs. A DVD-ROM disc is similar in size and shape to a CD-ROM disc but can store a lot more information. DVD-ROM discs can store up to 17 GB of information and are often used for storing movies.

Expansion Slot

An expansion slot is a socket where you plug in an expansion card to add a new feature to your computer. The number of expansion slots on your computer determines how many different expansion cards you can add to the computer.

Hard Drive

A hard drive is the primary device that a computer uses to store information. Most computers have one hard drive, named drive C. Most new hard drives have 4 GB or more of storage space.

Bytes

Bytes are used to measure the amount of information a device can store.

One byte represents one character.

One kilobyte (KB) is 1,024 characters. This is approximately equal to one page of text.

One megabyte (MB) is 1,048,576 characters. This is approximately equal to one novel.

One gigabyte (GB) is 1,073,741,824 characters. This is approximately equal to 1,000 novels.

Motherboard

A motherboard is the main circuit board of a computer. All of the computer's electronic components plug into the motherboard.

TV Tuner Card

TV tuner cards are used to watch television on your computer. The television broadcast appears in a window on the desktop. TV tuner cards often provide features such as closed captioning and TV listings.

Central Processing Unit (CPU)

The Central Processing Unit (CPU) is the main chip in a computer. The CPU processes instructions, performs calculations and manages the flow of information through a computer system. The most popular CPU chips available in new computers are the Pentium III and Celeron processors made by Intel and the Athlon and Duron processors made by AMD. Each type of processor is available in several speeds. The faster the speed, the faster the computer operates. Processor speed is measured in megahertz (MHz).

Bus

The bus is the electronic pathway in a computer that carries information between devices. Common bus types include ISA (Industry Standard Architecture), SCSI (Small Computer Systems Interface) and PCI (Peripheral Component Interconnect). AGP (Accelerated Graphics Port) is a bus type used to provide faster video speeds.

Network Interface Card

A Network Interface Card (NIC) physically connects each computer to a network. This card controls the flow of information between the network and the computer. A network is a group of connected computers that allows people to share information and devices.

Video Card

A video card translates instructions from a computer into information a monitor can display. Some computers have video capabilities built into the motherboard.

Memory

Memory, also known as Random Access Memory (RAM), temporarily stores information inside a computer. The information stored in RAM is lost when you turn off your computer. The amount of memory a computer has determines the number of programs a computer can run at once and how fast programs will operate. Most new computers have at least 64 MB of RAM.

Video Capture Card

A video capture card is used for videoconferencing or transforming video from a video camera or a VCR into files that can be used by a computer. Most video capture cards also have TV capabilities that allow you to watch television on a computer.

Sound Card

A sound card allows a computer to play and record sounds. A sound card is used to play music CDs as well as narration, music and sound

effects during games. Sound cards also allow you to record from a microphone, stereo or other audio device. Some computers have sound capabilities built into the motherboard.

USING MY COMPUTER

My Computer provides access to all of the drives, folders and files on your computer. My Computer also gives you quick access to the Control Panel folder, which contains items you can use to change your computer's settings. Each item in a My Computer window displays an icon to help you distinguish between the different types of items, such as a folder or text file.

You can use My Computer to browse through the files and folders on your computer and open files or folders of interest to display their contents. A folder can contain items such as documents, programs and other folders. Folders keep items organized and easy to find and use.

When you select an item in the My Computer window, Windows displays information about the item in the left side of the window.

My Computer can help you manage and organize your files and folders. You can create, rename, copy, move or delete files and folders in a My Computer window.

USING MY COMPUTER

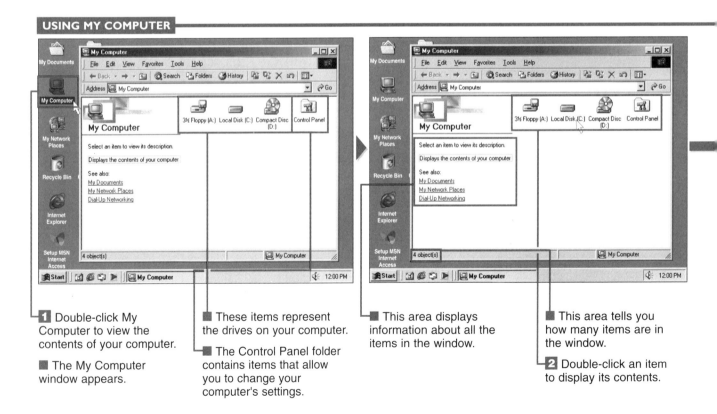

1 Double-click My Computer to view the contents of your computer.

■ The My Computer window appears.

■ These items represent the drives on your computer.

■ The Control Panel folder contains items that allow you to change your computer's settings.

■ This area displays information about all the items in the window.

■ This area tells you how many items are in the window.

2 Double-click an item to display its contents.

Why don't the contents of some folders appear when I double-click the folder?

✔ Some folders contain important files that help keep your computer working properly. Windows does not automatically display the contents of these folders to prevent you from accidentally changing or deleting the files. To view the contents of the folder, click the View the entire contents of this folder link.

Can Windows display the contents of each folder I open in its own window?

✔ Yes. To have each folder open in its own window, click the Start button, click Settings and then click Control Panel. Double-click Folder Options and then click the Open each folder in its own window option.

How can I open an item if I have trouble double-clicking?

✔ Right-click the item and then select Open from the menu that appears.

Is there another way to display the contents of a drive or folder on my computer?

✔ Click ▼ beside the Address area in the My Computer window to display a list of the drives and folders on your computer. Then click the drive or folder you want to view. The contents of the drive or folder you selected appear in the window.

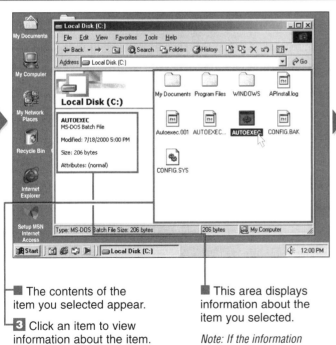

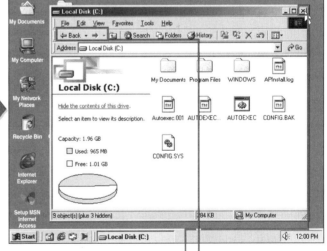

■ The contents of the item you selected appear.

-3 Click an item to view information about the item. The item is highlighted.

■ This area displays information about the item you selected.

Note: If the information does not appear, increase the size of the window. To size a window, see page 16.

■ You can once again display information about all the items by clicking a blank area in the list of items.

4 To continue browsing through the information on your computer, double-click each item of interest.

■ You can click ⬅ Back or ➡ to move through the drives and folders you have previously viewed.

5 When you finish browsing, click ✕ to close the window.

41

CHANGE VIEW OF ITEMS

You can change the view of items in a window. The view you select determines the information you will see in the window.

Windows displays a picture, or icon, to represent each type of item in a window. For example, the 🗀 icon indicates the item is a folder.

When you first use Windows, items are displayed as large icons.

The Large Icons view makes it easy to see the types of items available in a window.

You can choose the Small Icons view or List view to see more items in a window.

The Details view displays item information in columns. You can change the width of the columns in the Details view to make the information easier to view.

The Thumbnails view displays a miniature version, called a thumbnail, of each image file in a window. Non-image files display an icon to indicate the type of file.

Changing the view of items affects only the open window. Each window remembers the view you selected and displays the items in that view the next time you open the window.

CHANGE VIEW OF ITEMS

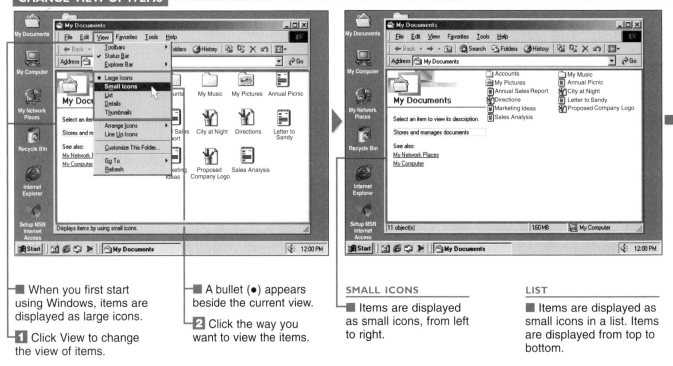

■ When you first start using Windows, items are displayed as large icons.

1 Click View to change the view of items.

■ A bullet (●) appears beside the current view.

2 Click the way you want to view the items.

SMALL ICONS

■ Items are displayed as small icons, from left to right.

LIST

■ Items are displayed as small icons in a list. Items are displayed from top to bottom.

Can I refresh the items displayed in a window?

✔ You can press the F5 key to update the items displayed in a window. This is useful if you are viewing the contents of floppy disks. When you switch disks, you can press the F5 key to display the contents of the second floppy disk in the window.

Is there a shortcut for changing the view?

✔ To quickly change the view of items, click ▦▾ in the window and then select the way you want to view the items. If you cannot see ▦▾, you may have to increase the size of the window. To size a window, see page 16.

How can I add additional column headings to the Details view?

✔ Right-click a column heading and then select the name of the column you want to add. You can click the More option to view additional column headings you can add.

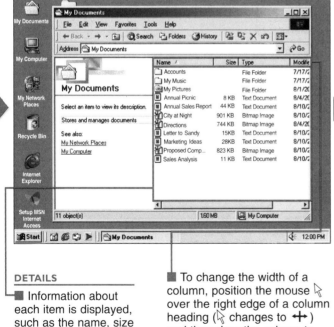

DETAILS

■ Information about each item is displayed, such as the name, size and type of item.

■ To change the width of a column, position the mouse over the right edge of a column heading (changes to ↔) and then drag the column to a new width.

Note: To resize a column to fit the longest item, double-click the right edge of the column heading.

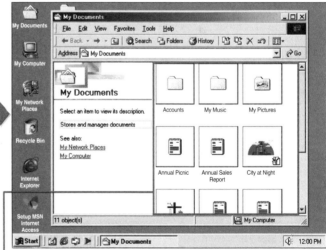

THUMBNNAILS

■ A miniature version of each image file is displayed. Non-image files display an icon to indicate the type of file.

Note: The Thumbnails view is not available in some windows.

SORT ITEMS

You can sort the items displayed in a window. This can help you find files and folders more easily.

Windows allows you to sort items by name, type, size or date.

Sorting by name displays items alphabetically, from A to Z. If you know the name of the item you want to find, try sorting by name.

Sorting by type displays items alphabetically according to the file type. If you are looking for a file of a specific type, try sorting by type.

Sorting by size displays items by their size, from smallest to largest. To find a large file, try sorting by size.

Sorting by date displays items according to the date they were last saved, from oldest to newest.

If you know when the file you want to find was last saved, try sorting by date.

If a window displays column headings, you can use the headings to sort items.

Regardless of how you sort items, Windows sorts files and folders separately.

SORT ITEMS

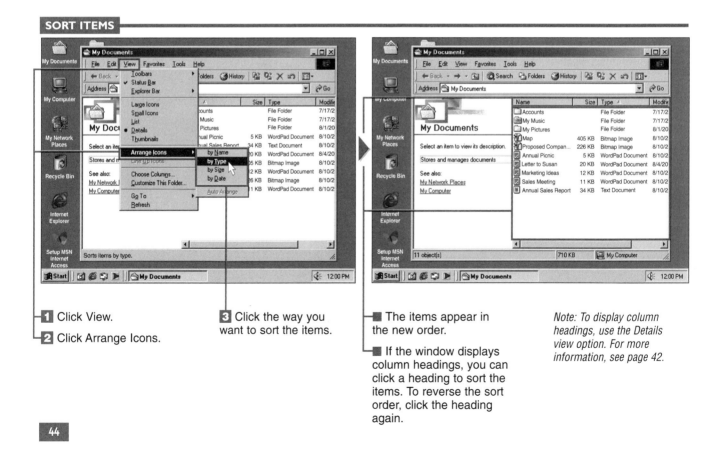

1 Click View.

2 Click Arrange Icons.

3 Click the way you want to sort the items.

■ The items appear in the new order.

■ If the window displays column headings, you can click a heading to sort the items. To reverse the sort order, click the heading again.

Note: To display column headings, use the Details view option. For more information, see page 42.

SCROLL THROUGH A WINDOW

A scroll bar allows you to browse through information in a window. This is useful when a window is not large enough to display all the information it contains. Some dialog boxes also display scroll bars that you can use to view all of the items in a list.

The location of the scroll box on the scroll bar indicates which part of the window you are viewing.

For example, when the scroll box is halfway down the scroll bar, you are viewing information in the middle of the window. The size of the scroll box varies, depending on the amount of

information the window contains and the size of the window.

You can purchase a mouse that has a wheel between the left and right mouse buttons. Moving this wheel also allows you to scroll through information in a window.

SCROLL UP OR DOWN

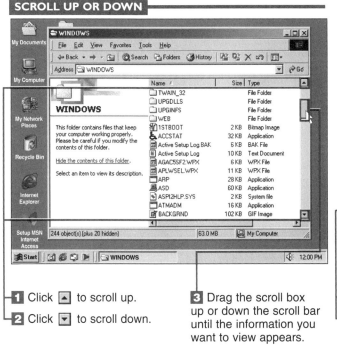

-1 Click ▲ to scroll up.

-2 Click ▼ to scroll down.

3 Drag the scroll box up or down the scroll bar until the information you want to view appears.

SCROLL LEFT OR RIGHT

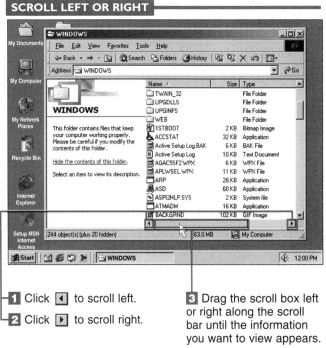

-1 Click ◄ to scroll left.

-2 Click ► to scroll right.

3 Drag the scroll box left or right along the scroll bar until the information you want to view appears.

ARRANGE ICONS AUTOMATICALLY

You can have Windows automatically arrange icons to fit neatly in a window or on the desktop. If your icons are scattered or piled one on top of another, arranging the icons will make the contents of your window or desktop easier to view.

You can use the Auto Arrange feature in a window to place

icons at a fixed distance from one another in rows and columns. The icons will remain neatly arranged even if you size the window or add and remove icons.

When you arrange icons on your desktop, Windows arranges the icons in columns, starting at the left edge of your screen.

When the Auto Arrange feature is turned on, you cannot move an icon to a blank area away from the other icons, but you can move an icon to a new location within the rows or columns. The other icons will shift to make space for the icon and will remain neatly arranged.

ARRANGE ICONS IN A WINDOW

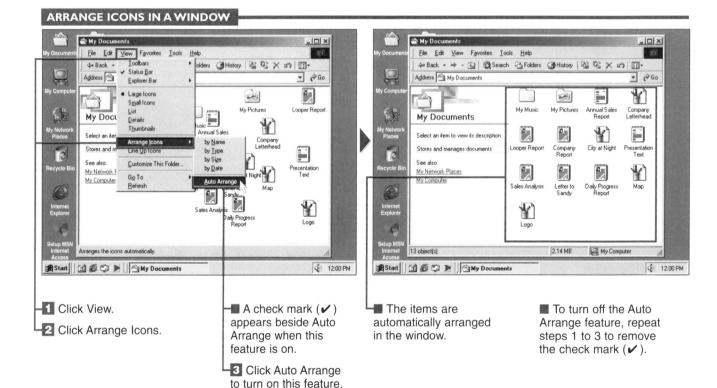

■1 Click View.

■2 Click Arrange Icons.

■ A check mark (✔) appears beside Auto Arrange when this feature is on.

■3 Click Auto Arrange to turn on this feature.

■ The items are automatically arranged in the window.

■ To turn off the Auto Arrange feature, repeat steps 1 to 3 to remove the check mark (✔).

Why is the Auto Arrange feature not available?

✔ The Auto Arrange feature is not available when items in a window are displayed in the List or Details view. To change the view of items in a window, see page 42.

Is there another way to line up icons?

✔ To have Windows move the icons to the nearest row or column in a window, click the View menu and select Line Up Icons. Unlike the Auto Arrange feature, the icons will not automatically rearrange if you add, remove or move items in the window. To line up the icons on the desktop, right-click a blank area of the desktop and then select Line Up Icons.

How can I move icons closer together or farther apart?

✔ You can change the horizontal and vertical spacing of icons. Right-click a blank area on the desktop and then select Properties. Choose the Appearance tab and in the Item area, select Icon Spacing (Horizontal) or Icon Spacing (Vertical). To change the spacing between icons, double-click the Size area and then type a new number.

ARRANGE ICONS ON THE DESKTOP

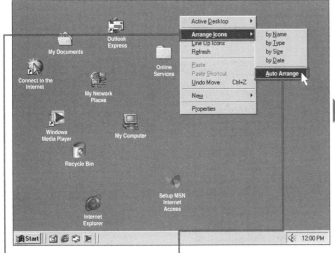

1 Right-click a blank area on your desktop. A menu appears.

2 Click Arrange Icons.

■ A check mark (✔) appears beside Auto Arrange when this feature is on.

3 Click Auto Arrange to turn on this feature.

■ The items are automatically arranged on the desktop.

■ To turn off the Auto Arrange feature, repeat steps 1 to 3 to remove the check mark (✔).

DISPLAY OR HIDE A TOOLBAR OR THE STATUS BAR

Toolbars allow you to quickly access commonly used commands and features. The status bar provides information about the items displayed in a window. You can display or hide these bars to suit your needs.

Toolbars appear at the top of a window. The Standard Buttons toolbar contains buttons that

allow you to quickly select commonly used commands, such as Search, Delete and Undo. You can use the Address Bar toolbar to quickly access another drive or folder on your computer. You can also type a Web page address in the Address Bar toolbar to access the Web without first starting your Web browser. The Links toolbar contains links you can select to quickly access useful Web pages.

The Radio toolbar allows you to select a radio station you want to listen to over the Internet.

The status bar appears at the bottom of a window and displays information about all the items in the window or the selected item. For example, when you select a file, the status bar displays the type and size of the file.

DISPLAY OR HIDE A TOOLBAR

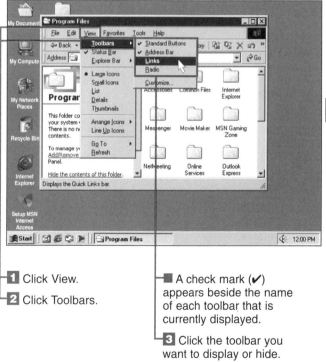

1 Click View.

2 Click Toolbars.

■ A check mark (✔) appears beside the name of each toolbar that is currently displayed.

3 Click the toolbar you want to display or hide.

■ The Standard Buttons toolbar displays buttons for commonly used commands.

■ The Address Bar toolbar displays the location of the open folder and allows you to quickly access another drive or folder.

■ The Links toolbar allows you to quickly access useful Web pages. To view more of the Links toolbar, double-click the toolbar.

■ The Radio toolbar allows you to listen to radio broadcasts over the Internet.

Can I customize the Standard Buttons toolbar?

✔ Yes. Select the View menu, choose Toolbars and then click Customize. To add a button to the toolbar, double-click the button in the Available toolbar buttons area. To remove the text from the toolbar buttons or change where the text appears, click the Text options area and then select the text option you want to use.

How can I move a toolbar?

✔ Position the mouse over the raised line at the left edge of the toolbar you want to move (⇖ changes to ↔). Drag the toolbar to a new location. You can place more than one toolbar on the same line.

Can I change the size of toolbars when more than one toolbar appears on the same line?

✔ Position the mouse over the raised line at the left edge of a toolbar (⇖ changes to ↔). Then drag the raised line until the toolbars display the size you want.

How can I view all the items on a toolbar?

✔ When all the items on a toolbar are not displayed, ʺ appears at the right edge of the toolbar. Click ʺ to display a list of additional items.

DISPLAY OR HIDE THE STATUS BAR

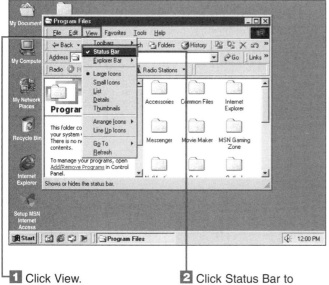

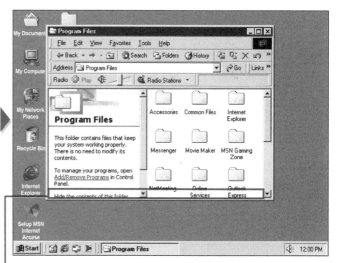

1 Click View.

■ A check mark (✔) appears beside Status Bar if the bar is currently displayed.

2 Click Status Bar to display or hide the bar.

■ In this example, the status bar disappears.

CHANGE FOLDER VIEW OPTIONS

You can customize the way Windows displays the contents of folders.

You can have Windows regularly search the network for shared folders and printers. The shared resources Windows finds appear in My Network Places.

When you first display the Control Panel window, all the items do not appear in the window. You can choose to display all the items in the Control Panel window and all other windows.

You can have Windows display the location of folders in the Address bar or title bar of a window.

You can also hide the three-letter file extension for file types that Windows recognizes.

To improve the stability of Windows, you can have each folder open in a separate part of your computer's memory.

Windows can remember the way you display items in each folder and redisplay the items the same

way the next time you open the folder.

You can choose to display the My Documents folder on the desktop so you can quickly access the folder.

When you position the mouse pointer over a folder or desktop item, Windows can display a description of the item in a small box.

CHANGE FOLDER VIEW OPTIONS

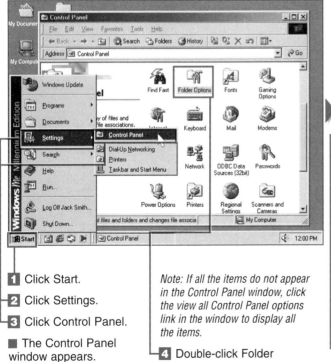

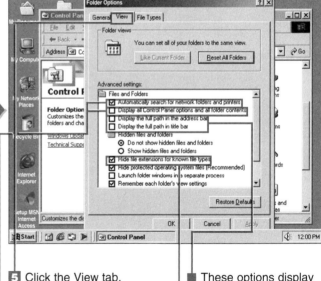

1 Click Start.

2 Click Settings.

3 Click Control Panel.

■ The Control Panel window appears.

Note: If all the items do not appear in the Control Panel window, click the view all Control Panel options link in the window to display all the items.

4 Double-click Folder Options.

■ The Folder Options dialog box appears.

5 Click the View tab.

■ This option regularly searches the network for shared folders and printers.

■ This option displays all items in the Control Panel folder and all other folders.

■ These options display the location of the open folder in the Address bar and in the title bar of a window.

■ This option hides the three-letter file extension for file types that Windows recognizes.

50

Can I return to Windows default folder view options?

✔ Yes. In the Folder Options dialog box, click the View tab and then click the Restore Defaults button.

I customized the view of items in a folder. Can I make all the other folders use the same settings?

✔ Yes. Open the folder that displays the settings you customized. On the Tools menu, click Folder Options. Select the View tab and click the Like Current Folder button. To return all folders on your computer to the default settings, click the Reset All Folders button. For information about changing the view of items, see page 42.

Should I display extensions for my files?

✔ File extensions can help you identify the types of files you are viewing. For example, viewing the file extensions would help you realize that the Notepad file you thought was named "read.me" is actually saved as "read.me.txt".

Why would I want to hide the hidden and system files?

✔ Hidden and system files are files that Windows and your programs need to run. If you change or delete hidden or system files, your computer may no longer operate properly.

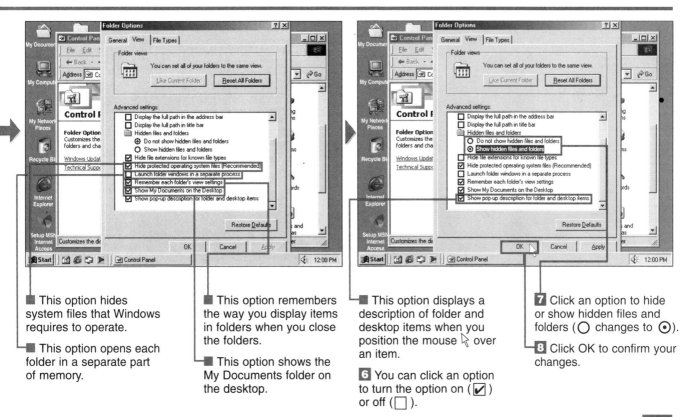

■ This option hides system files that Windows requires to operate.

■ This option opens each folder in a separate part of memory.

■ This option remembers the way you display items in folders when you close the folders.

■ This option shows the My Documents folder on the desktop.

■ This option displays a description of folder and desktop items when you position the mouse over an item.

6 You can click an option to turn the option on (☑) or off (☐).

7 Click an option to hide or show hidden files and folders (○ changes to ⊙).

8 Click OK to confirm your changes.

51

USING WINDOWS EXPLORER

Like a map, Windows Explorer shows you the location of every file and folder on your computer. Windows Explorer helps you understand how your files and folders are organized.

Windows Explorer has two panes. The left pane shows the structure of the drives and folders on your computer. You can expand the information

available in the left pane to show drives and folders that are hidden from view. You can also reduce the information in the left pane to provide an overview of the items available on your computer.

When you select a drive or folder in the left pane, Windows Explorer displays the contents of the drive or folder in the right pane.

To change the size of the left and right panes, you move the vertical bar that separates the two panes. You may want to make the right pane larger to clearly view the contents of a folder.

You can use Windows Explorer to manage and organize files. For example, you can move, rename, delete and open files in Windows Explorer.

USING WINDOWS EXPLORER

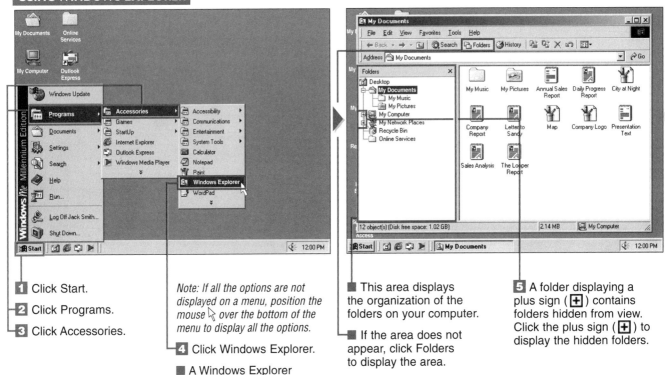

1 Click Start.

2 Click Programs.

3 Click Accessories.

Note: If all the options are not displayed on a menu, position the mouse ⦈ over the bottom of the menu to display all the options.

4 Click Windows Explorer.

■ A Windows Explorer window appears.

■ This area displays the organization of the folders on your computer.

■ If the area does not appear, click Folders to display the area.

5 A folder displaying a plus sign (⊞) contains folders hidden from view. Click the plus sign (⊞) to display the hidden folders.

Why don't the contents of some folders appear when I click the name of the folder?

✔ Some folders contain important files that help keep your computer working properly. Windows does not automatically display these files to prevent you from accidentally deleting or modifying them. For example, the first time you display the contents of the WINDOWS folder, no files or folders are displayed. To view the contents of the folder, click the View the entire contents of this folder link.

Can I start Windows Explorer without using the Start menu?

✔ Yes. Right-click My Computer and then select Explore.

How do I open a file or folder using Windows Explorer?

✔ You can double-click a file or folder in the right pane.

How can I quickly display all the hidden folders within a folder?

✔ You can display all the hidden folders within a folder by selecting the folder and then pressing the asterisk (*) key on the numeric keypad. To once again hide all the folders, click the minus sign (☐) beside the top folder and then press the F5 key.

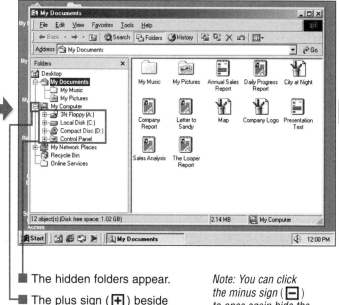

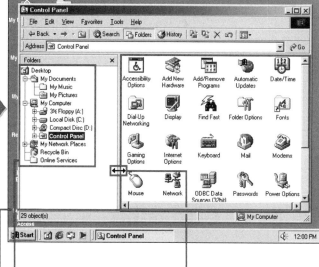

■ The hidden folders appear.

■ The plus sign (⊞) beside the folder changes to a minus sign (☐). This indicates that the hidden folders within the folder are displayed.

Note: You can click the minus sign (☐) to once again hide the folders within the folder.

6 To display the contents of a folder, click the name of the folder.

■ This area displays the contents of the folder.

7 To change the size of the left and right panes in the window, position the mouse ↖ over the vertical bar that separates the two panes (↖ changes to ↔). Then drag the bar to a new location.

SELECT FILES

Before you can work with a file or folder, you often need to select the item. For example, you must first select a file or folder you want to copy, move, delete or open.

When you select a file or folder, Windows highlights the item and displays information about the item in the left side of the window. Information you can

view for a file includes the file's type, the date the file was last modified, the size of the file and the file's attributes. If you select an image or Web page, a small preview of the image or Web page appears in the left side of the window.

You can select and work with multiple files and folders. This lets you perform the same

procedure on several items at the same time.

When you select multiple files in a window, you can view the number of selected files and the total size of the selected files in the left side of the window.

SELECT FILES

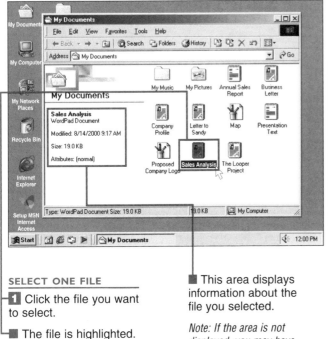

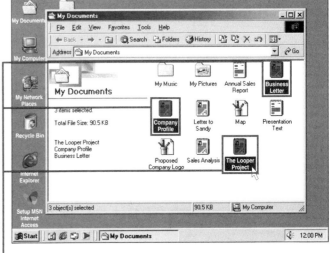

SELECT ONE FILE

■1 Click the file you want to select.

■ The file is highlighted.

■ This area displays information about the file you selected.

Note: If the area is not displayed, you may have to increase the size of the window. To size a window, see page 16.

SELECT RANDOM FILES

■1 Press and hold down the Ctrl key as you click each file you want to select.

How do I deselect all the files and folders in a window?

✔ Click a blank area in the window.

Is there an easy way to select all but a few files in a window?

✔ Select all the files in the window and then hold down the Ctrl key as you click the files you do not want to select. You can also select the files you do not want and then choose the Edit menu and select Invert Selection.

How do I deselect one file or folder from a group of selected items?

✔ Hold down the Ctrl key while you click the file or folder you want to deselect.

Is there another way to select a group of files?

✔ To select a group of files, position the mouse pointer to the left of the first file you want to select and then drag the mouse pointer to form a rectangle around the files.

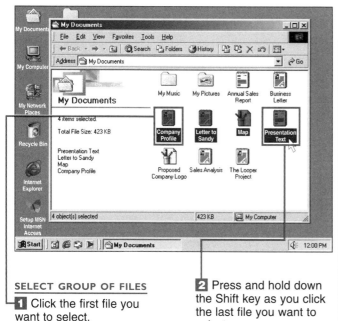

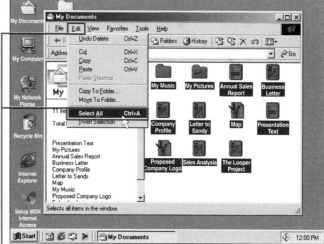

SELECT GROUP OF FILES

1 Click the first file you want to select.

2 Press and hold down the Shift key as you click the last file you want to select.

SELECT ALL FILES

1 Click Edit to select all the items in a window.

2 Click Select All.

Note: The Select All dialog box appears if the window contains hidden items. Click OK to select only the displayed items.

OPEN FILES

You can open a file directly from a My Computer window or a Windows Explorer window to display its contents on the screen. Opening a file allows you to review and make changes to the file.

Each file on your computer is associated with a specific program. When you open a file, the associated program starts automatically. For example,

text files are associated with the Notepad program. When you open a text file, the Notepad program starts and the file is opened.

You can select a different program to open a file. For example, Windows automatically opens an image file in the Image Preview utility. To edit an image, you need to open the image in an image editing program. You

can use the Open With dialog box to specify which program you want to open a file. You can also specify if the new program should always open the file and every file of that type.

The Open With dialog box automatically appears when Windows does not know which program to use to open a file.

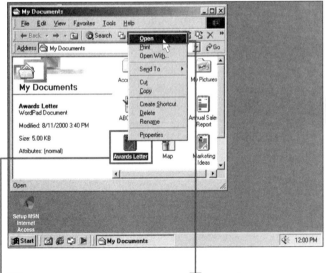

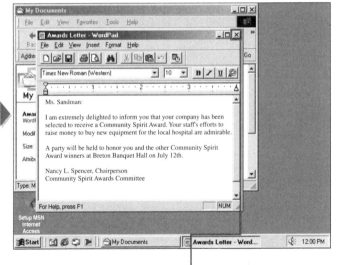

1 Right-click the file you want to open. A menu appears.

2 Click Open.

Note: You can double-click the file instead of performing steps 1 and 2.

■ Windows starts the appropriate program and displays the contents of the file. You can now review and make changes to the file.

■ When you finish working with the file, click ☒ to close the file and exit the program.

How do I find a file I want to open?

✔ You can use My Computer or Windows Explorer to browse through the contents of your computer. For information on My Computer, see page 40. For information on Windows Explorer, see page 52.

How can I find files of a specific type?

✔ From the Start menu, click Search and then select For Files or Folders. Click Search Options and then select the Type option (☐ changes to ☑). In the area that appears, select the type of file you want to find and then click Search Now. For more information on the Search feature, see page 78.

Why does a menu appear when I click Open With?

✔ After you open a file in a different program, a menu may appear when you click the Open With command. The menu displays programs that can be used to open the file and the Choose Program option, which allows you to display the Open With dialog box.

OPEN FILES IN A DIFFERENT PROGRAM

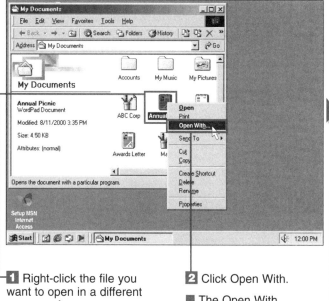

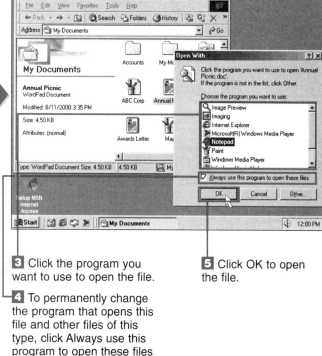

1 Right-click the file you want to open in a different program. A menu appears.

2 Click Open With.

■ The Open With dialog box appears.

3 Click the program you want to use to open the file.

4 To permanently change the program that opens this file and other files of this type, click Always use this program to open these files (☐ changes to ☑).

5 Click OK to open the file.

OPEN RECENTLY USED FILES

Windows remembers the last files you opened and displays the names of the files in a list on the Start menu. You can quickly open any of these files to review or make changes to the files.

Windows displays the list of recently used files in alphabetical order to make it easier to find the file you want to open. An icon

appears beside each file to indicate the program associated with the file. When you select a file, the associated program starts and the file opens. Selecting a file from the list saves you from searching through folders on your computer to find a file you want to open.

The Start menu also includes shortcuts to the My Documents

and My Pictures folders to help you quickly access the files and images stored in these folders.

You can clear the list of recently used files at any time. Clearing the list is useful when the list becomes cluttered or contains files you no longer need. Clearing the list of recently used files will not remove the files from your computer.

OPEN RECENTLY USED FILES

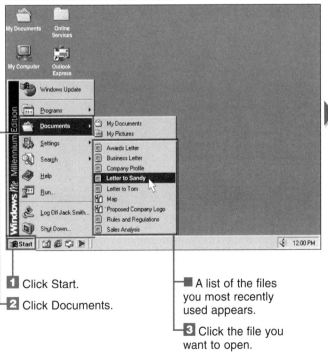

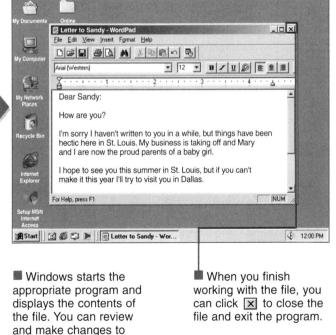

1 Click Start.

2 Click Documents.

■ A list of the files you most recently used appears.

3 Click the file you want to open.

■ Windows starts the appropriate program and displays the contents of the file. You can review and make changes to the file.

■ When you finish working with the file, you can click ☒ to close the file and exit the program.

How do I find a file that is not on the list of recently used files?

✔ If the file you want to open is not on the list of recently used files, you can have Windows search for the file. To find files, see page 78.

Why is a file I recently used not listed in the Start menu?

✔ A file will not appear in the list of recently used files if you use a program that cannot add files to the list. For example, if you open a file in an e-mail program, the file will not appear in the list.

How can I add files to the list of recently used files?

✔ You can add a file to the list by opening the file. To open a file, double-click the file.

I cannot make changes to the image files I open. What is wrong?

✔ Windows automatically opens images in the Image Preview window, which allows you to preview images. To edit an image, you must open the image in an image editing program.

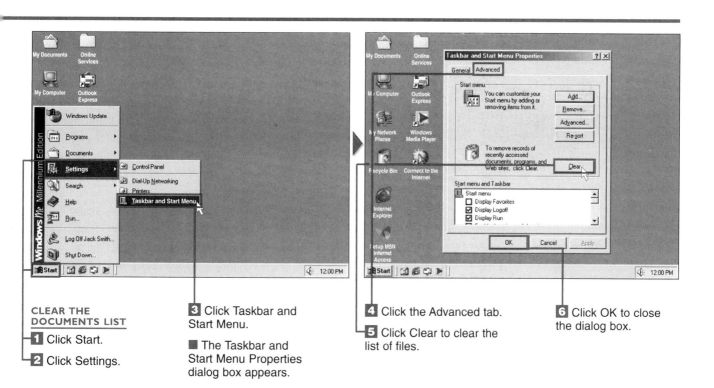

CLEAR THE DOCUMENTS LIST

1 Click Start.

2 Click Settings.

3 Click Taskbar and Start Menu.

■ The Taskbar and Start Menu Properties dialog box appears.

4 Click the Advanced tab.

5 Click Clear to clear the list of files.

6 Click OK to close the dialog box.

PREVIEW IMAGES

You can use the Image Preview window to view your image files without opening an image editing program.

When you select an image in a window, the left side of the window displays a miniature version of the image. Displaying an image in the Image Preview window allows you to preview the image in more detail.

Image Preview allows you to zoom into a part of an image you want to view in more detail or zoom out of the image to see more of the image.

If you want to preview how the image will look when printed, you can choose to display the image at its actual size. You can also view the image in the size that fits best in the Image Preview window. This is useful

if you want to view the entire image at once.

You can rotate the image clockwise or counter clockwise in the window. This is useful if you want to turn the image on its side or view the image upside down.

By default, most images on your computer are stored in the My Pictures folder located in the My Documents folder.

PREVIEW IMAGES

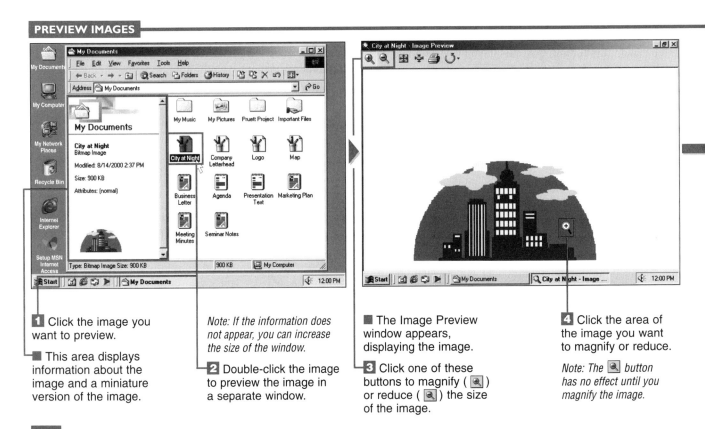

■ Click the image you want to preview.

■ This area displays information about the image and a miniature version of the image.

Note: If the information does not appear, you can increase the size of the window.

■ Double-click the image to preview the image in a separate window.

■ The Image Preview window appears, displaying the image.

■ Click one of these buttons to magnify (🔍) or reduce (🔍) the size of the image.

■ Click the area of the image you want to magnify or reduce.

Note: The 🔍 button has no effect until you magnify the image.

Can I print an image displayed in the Image Preview window?

✔ Yes. Click 🖨 in the Image Preview window to print the image. The Printing better pictures dialog box appears, asking if you want tips on printing pictures. Click Yes or No to specify if you want tips. If you click Yes, a window displaying printing tips appears. Click OK in the Print dialog box to print the picture. If you do not want the Printing better pictures dialog box to appear the next time you print a picture, click the In the future, do not ask this question option (☐ changes to ☑).

How can I open an image in an image editing program?

✔ Right-click the image file you want to open and select Open With. If the Open With dialog box appears, select the program you want to use to open the image and then click OK. If a menu appears when you select the Open With command, select the program you want to use to open the file from the menu. If the program you want to use does not appear on the menu, click Choose Program to display additional options.

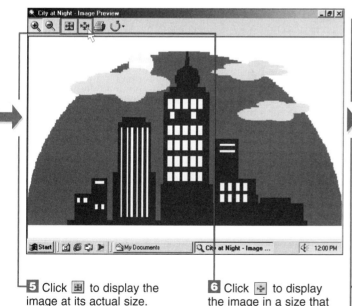

5 Click ▦ to display the image at its actual size.

6 Click ✥ to display the image in a size that fits best in the window.

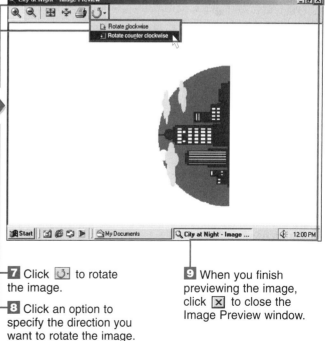

7 Click ↻ to rotate the image.

8 Click an option to specify the direction you want to rotate the image.

9 When you finish previewing the image, click ✕ to close the Image Preview window.

MOVE OR COPY DATA

You can move or copy data to a different place in a document or from one document to another.

You can select text, numbers or images in a document and share the data with other documents, without having to retype or recreate the data. You can also share data between programs. For example, you can move an image created in Paint to a WordPad document.

The Clipboard is a temporary storage area for data you are moving or copying.

When you move data, Windows removes the data from the original document and places the data in the Clipboard. The data disappears from the original document.

When you copy data, Windows makes a copy of the data and places the copy in the Clipboard.

The data remains in its place in the original document.

When you paste data into a document, Windows places the data from the Clipboard into the document. The data appears in the document where you positioned the insertion point.

MOVE OR COPY DATA

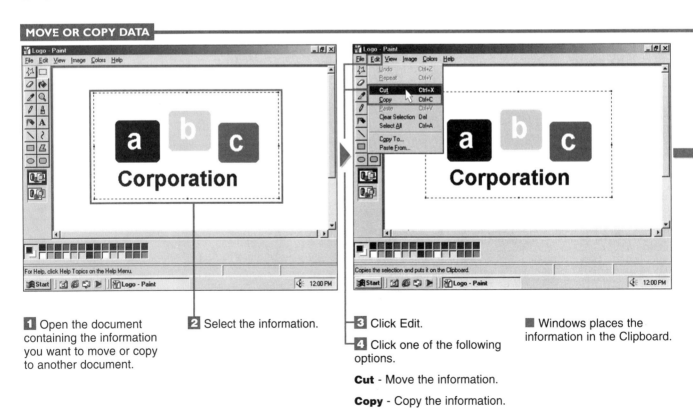

1 Open the document containing the information you want to move or copy to another document.

2 Select the information.

3 Click Edit.

4 Click one of the following options.

Cut - Move the information.

Copy - Copy the information.

■ Windows places the information in the Clipboard.

How do I select the data I want to move or copy?

✔ In most programs, you can drag the mouse over the data you want to select. Selected data usually appears highlighted on your screen. To select an image in Paint, click ▭ and then drag the mouse ╋ over the image you want to select until a dotted line surrounds the image you want to move or copy.

Can I put several items in the Clipboard and then paste them all at the same time?

✔ The Clipboard can hold only one item at a time. When you place a new item in the Clipboard, the previous item is replaced.

Can I move or copy data in a dialog box?

✔ Most Windows programs allow you to use the keyboard to move or copy data whenever you do not have access to menus or toolbars. To move data, select the data and then press Ctrl+X on your keyboard. To copy data, select the data and then press Ctrl+C. To paste data, position the insertion point where you want the data to appear and then press Ctrl+V.

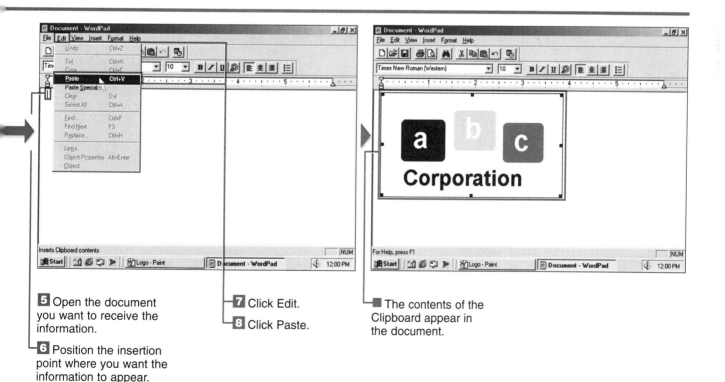

5 Open the document you want to receive the information.

6 Position the insertion point where you want the information to appear.

7 Click Edit.

8 Click Paste.

■ The contents of the Clipboard appear in the document.

USING DRAG AND DROP TO EXCHANGE DATA

You can use the mouse to drag information from its current location to a new location.

You can drag and drop information within a document or between two documents. You may also be able to drag and drop information between programs.

If both documents are displayed on the screen, you can select the information you want and drag it to the new location.

If you want to move or copy information to a program that is minimized on the taskbar, you can select the information and drag it to the program's button on the taskbar. Continue holding down the mouse button until the program window opens and then drag the information to where you want it to appear.

If you see a black circle with a slash through it ($\bigcirc$) when you

try to drag and drop information, you cannot place the information where the mouse pointer is. For example, you cannot drag text from a document into a Paint window.

Drag and drop will not work for all programs. If you are having trouble dragging and dropping, you can check your program's manual or help information to see if the program supports the feature.

USING DRAG AND DROP TO EXCHANGE DATA

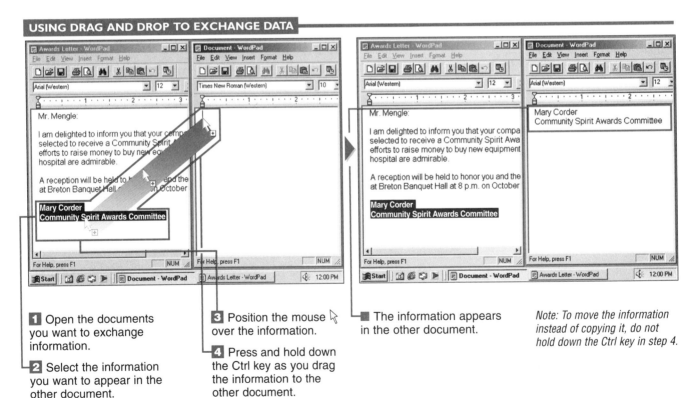

1 Open the documents you want to exchange information.

2 Select the information you want to appear in the other document.

3 Position the mouse over the information.

4 Press and hold down the Ctrl key as you drag the information to the other document.

■ The information appears in the other document.

Note: To move the information instead of copying it, do not hold down the Ctrl key in step 4.

COPY SCREEN OR WINDOW CONTENTS

You can take a picture of the entire desktop or just the active window or dialog box. This is useful if you are trying to explain a computer problem or procedure and you want a visual example to illustrate what you are explaining.

When you copy the desktop, active window or active dialog

box, the image is stored in the Clipboard. You can place the image in a program such as Paint or WordPad and then print the image or e-mail the image to another person.

You can buy programs that provide options the Print Scrn key does not offer. For example, Screen Thief by Villa Software

lets you copy a program menu or a selected area on the screen. There are also programs, such as Lotus ScreenCam, that can record a series of movements on your screen and save them as a movie.

COPY SCREEN OR WINDOW CONTENTS

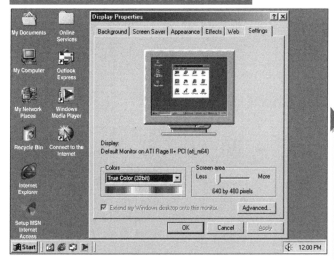

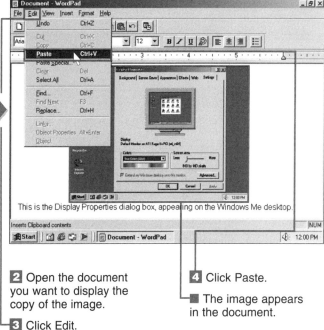

This is the Display Properties dialog box, appearing on the Windows Me desktop.

■ **1** Press the Print Scrn key to copy the entire screen.

■ To copy just the active window or dialog box, press and hold down the Alt key as you press the Print Scrn key.

■ Windows places a copy of the image in the Clipboard.

2 Open the document you want to display the copy of the image.

3 Click Edit.

4 Click Paste.

■ The image appears in the document.

PUT PART OF DOCUMENT ON THE DESKTOP

You can place frequently used information on your desktop. Information you place on the desktop is called a scrap. Scraps give you quick access to information and are useful if you frequently add standard information to new documents.

Document scraps save you time since you do not have to retype the information over and over.

For example, you can create a scrap containing your name, address and phone number. You can then drag the scrap into a document whenever you need the information. You can also create a scrap for images, such as your company logo.

When creating a scrap, make sure the document from which you are dragging information is not maximized. If the document

is maximized, you will not be able to drag the information to the desktop.

Scraps are available only for programs that allow you to drag and drop information to other programs. For example, you cannot create scraps using a Microsoft Notepad document.

PUT PART OF DOCUMENT ON THE DESKTOP

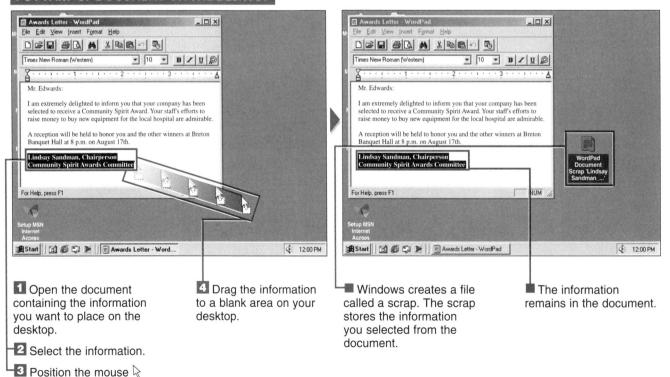

1 Open the document containing the information you want to place on the desktop.

2 Select the information.

3 Position the mouse over the information.

4 Drag the information to a blank area on your desktop.

■ Windows creates a file called a scrap. The scrap stores the information you selected from the document.

■ The information remains in the document.

How do I select the information in a document that I want to drag to the desktop?

✔ The way you select information depends on the program you are working with. To select text in WordPad, position the mouse I over the first word you want to select and then drag the mouse over the text. To select an image in WordPad, click the image.

How do I rename a scrap?

✔ Right-click the scrap on the desktop. From the menu that appears, select Rename. Type the new name for the scrap and press the Enter key.

How can I view or edit the contents of a scrap?

✔ When you double-click a scrap, the program you used to create the scrap opens and displays the scrap. You can edit the scrap as you would edit any document.

How can I remove a scrap I no longer need?

✔ You can work with a scrap as you would work with any file on your desktop. To remove a scrap you no longer need, drag the scrap to the Recycle Bin.

USING SCRAPS

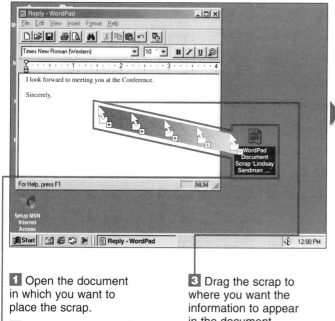

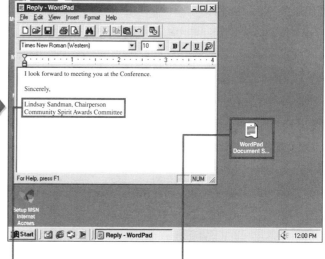

1 Open the document in which you want to place the scrap.

2 Position the mouse ↕ over the scrap.

3 Drag the scrap to where you want the information to appear in the document.

■ The information appears in the document.

■ The scrap remains on your desktop. You can place the information in as many documents as you wish.

MOVE OR COPY FILES

You can move or copy files when you want to reorganize files on your hard drive, share documents with a colleague or take work home on a floppy disk. Copying files is also useful for making backup copies.

When you move a file, you delete the file from its original location.

When you copy a file, you create a second file that is exactly the

same as the first. You can place the copy in another location on your computer, on a network, floppy disk or removable media. If you create a copy of a file in the same folder, Windows will add "Copy of" to the file name.

When you drag and drop a file, the result depends on the file's destination. When you drag a file to a new location on the same drive, Windows moves the file.

When you drag a file to a different drive, Windows copies the file.

You can use the Send To menu to quickly send copies of files to a floppy disk.

You can also move and copy folders. When you move or copy a folder, all files in the folder are also moved or copied.

MOVE FILES

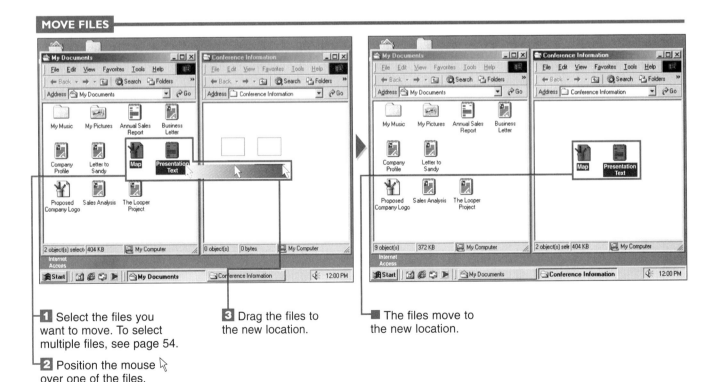

■1 Select the files you want to move. To select multiple files, see page 54.

■2 Position the mouse ⍒ over one of the files.

■3 Drag the files to the new location.

■ The files move to the new location.

How do I move a file to a different drive?

✔ When you drag a file to a different drive, a plus sign (✚) appears under the mouse pointer, indicating that Windows will make a copy of the file. To move the file, hold down the Shift key.

I frequently move files to the same folder. How can I simplify this task?

✔ You can add the folder to the Send To menu. For information about adding destinations to the Send To menu, see page 96. You can also place a shortcut to the folder on your desktop. For information about creating shortcuts, see page 90.

Is there another way to move or copy files?

✔ Using the right mouse button, drag the files you want to move or copy to the new location. From the menu that appears, select Move Here or Copy Here. You can also select the files and then right-click one of the files. On the menu that appears, click Cut or Copy to move or copy the files. Open the folder where you want to place the files. Right-click a blank area in the folder and then click Paste.

COPY FILES

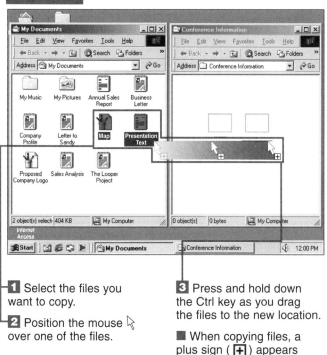

1 Select the files you want to copy.

2 Position the mouse over one of the files.

3 Press and hold down the Ctrl key as you drag the files to the new location.

■ When copying files, a plus sign (✚) appears under the mouse pointer.

COPY FILES TO A FLOPPY DISK

1 Select the files you want to copy to a floppy disk.

2 Right-click one of the files. A menu appears.

3 Click Send To.

4 Click the drive that contains the floppy disk.

RENAME FILES

You can change the name of a file to better describe the contents of the file. You should only rename files that you have created.

When renaming your files, choose a name that will identify the file, such as the name of a client, a project or an event. Renaming a file can help make the file easier to find.

In Windows, you can use up to 215 characters to name a file. You can include spaces and periods in a file name. The only characters you cannot use to name a file are the symbols \ / : * ? | " < or >.

You should try to keep your file names relatively short since some programs cannot work with extremely long file names. For example, MS-DOS and

Windows 3.1 programs do not support long file names. If you use these programs, you should use file names made up of no more than eight characters followed by a three-character extension, such as report.txt.

RENAME FILES

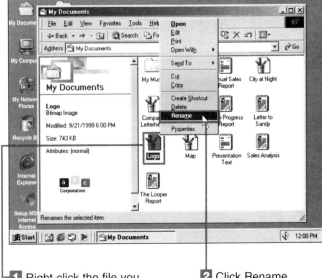

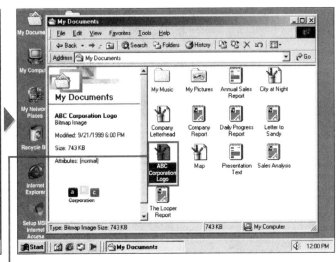

■1 Right-click the file you want to rename. A menu appears.

■2 Click Rename.

■ A box appears around the file name.

■3 Type a new name for the file and then press the Enter key.

Note: You can edit the file name instead of replacing the entire name. Click the file name where you want to edit the name and make the change.

■ If you change your mind while typing a new name, press the Esc key to cancel your changes.

Is there another way to rename a file?

✔ Click the name of the file you want to rename. Wait a moment and click the name again. Then type a new name for the file.

Can I use both upper and lower case letters to name a file?

✔ You can type upper and lower case letters to make file names easier to read, but Windows does not recognize the difference between upper and lower case letters. For example, Windows sees readme, ReadMe and README as identical file names.

Can I use the same file name for two different files?

✔ You can use the same file name for two different files if the files are located in different folders or the files are different file types, such as a document and image file.

Can I rename folders?

✔ You can rename folders the same way you rename files. You should only rename folders that you have created so you do not change the names of folders that Windows or your programs require to operate. Windows does not allow you to change the name of some system folders, such as the System and System32 folders.

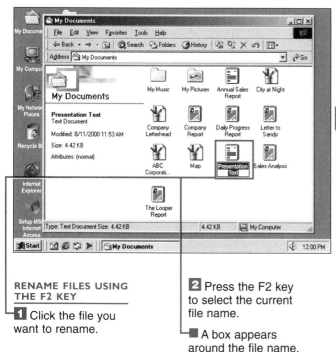

RENAME FILES USING THE F2 KEY

■1 Click the file you want to rename.

■2 Press the F2 key to select the current file name.

■ A box appears around the file name.

■3 Type a new name for the file and then press the Enter key.

DELETE FILES

You can remove files, folders and programs you no longer need to free up space on your computer. If you delete a folder, Windows will erase all the files and folders within the folder. To protect you from accidentally erasing important files, Windows stores deleted files in the Recycle Bin.

As a precaution, Windows asks you to confirm the files you are deleting. Make sure you do not delete system files required to run Windows or files required by programs you still use. Do not delete any file unless you are certain you no longer need the file.

Before you delete files, consider the value of the files. You may want to save copies on a removable disk or a backup tape in case you need the files later. The cost of disks and tapes is small compared to the time and effort of recreating a file.

DELETE FILES

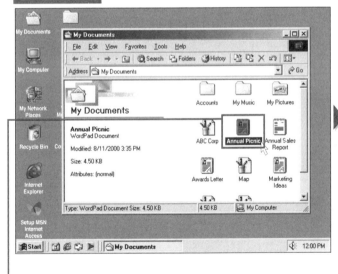

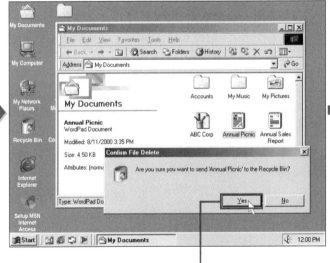

1 Select the files you want to delete. To select multiple files, see page 54.

2 Press the Delete key.

■ A dialog box appears, confirming the deletion.

3 Click Yes to delete the files.

How do I delete a confidential file so it cannot be recovered?

✔ Select the file and then press the Shift and Delete keys. The file will be deleted from your computer and will not appear in the Recycle Bin.

Is there another way to delete a file?

✔ You can drag and drop a file onto the Recycle Bin to delete the file.

Are all deleted files placed in the Recycle Bin?

✔ Files deleted from floppy disks, removable disks, locations on your network or at the MS-DOS command prompt are not placed in the Recycle Bin and cannot be recovered.

Can I delete any file on my computer?

✔ You should delete only files that you have created. If you want to delete other files to free up space on your hard drive, you can use the Disk Cleanup tool. For more information, see page 510.

Can I prevent the Confirm File Delete dialog box from appearing each time I delete a file?

✔ Right-click the Recycle Bin and then select Properties. On the Global tab, click the Display delete confirmation dialog option (☑ changes to ☐).

DELETE A FOLDER

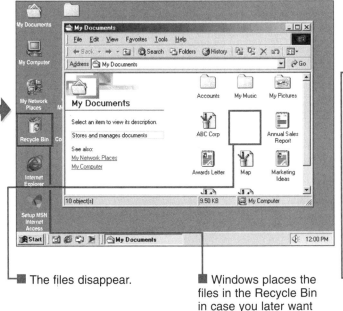

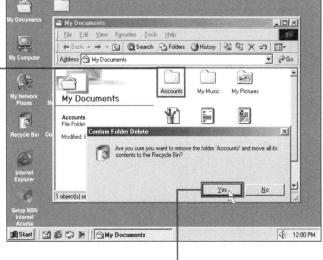

■ The files disappear.

■ Windows places the files in the Recycle Bin in case you later want to restore the files. To restore a deleted file, see page 74.

1 Click the folder you want to delete.

2 Press the Delete key.

■ A dialog box appears, confirming the deletion.

3 Click Yes to delete the folder and all the files and folders it contains.

RESTORE DELETED FILES

The Recycle Bin is a special folder that stores the files you have deleted. If you have accidentally deleted a file, you will probably find the file in the Recycle Bin. You can then restore the file to its original location on your computer. If you restore a file that was originally located in a folder that has also been deleted, Windows will recreate the folder and restore the file in the folder.

You cannot restore files deleted from floppy disks, removable media, locations on your network or the MS-DOS command prompt. Files deleted from these sources are permanently deleted.

When you are certain that you no longer need the files in the Recycle Bin, you can use the Empty Recycle Bin command to remove all the deleted files and increase the available disk space

on your computer. When you empty the Recycle Bin, all the files are permanently removed from your computer.

When the Recycle Bin fills up with deleted files, Windows will permanently remove older files to make room for recently deleted files.

RESTORE DELETED FILES

1 Double-click Recycle Bin to display all the files you have deleted.

■ The Recycle Bin window appears.

2 Click the file you want to restore.

Note: To restore multiple files, select all the files you want to restore. To select multiple files, see page 54.

■ This area displays information about the file you selected.

3 Click File.

4 Click Restore.

■ The file disappears from the Recycle Bin window. Windows restores the file to its original location.

Note: You can restore a deleted folder the same way you restore a deleted file. When you restore a folder, Windows also restores all the files in the folder.

Why doesn't the Recycle Bin window display information about a file I selected?

✔ To display information about a selected file in the left side of the Recycle Bin window, you may have to increase the size of the window. To size a window, see page 16.

Can I view the contents of a file located in the Recycle Bin?

✔ To view the contents of a deleted file, drag the file from the Recycle Bin window to the desktop and then double-click the file to display its contents.

Can I restore all the files in the Recycle Bin at once?

✔ Yes. Click a blank area in the Recycle Bin window and then click the Restore All button in the left side of the window.

How can I quickly empty the Recycle Bin?

✔ Right-click the Recycle Bin icon on the desktop. From the menu that appears, select Empty Recycle Bin.

Can I permanently delete only some of the files in the Recycle Bin?

✔ Yes. Select each file you want to delete in the Recycle Bin window and then press the Delete key.

EMPTY THE RECYCLE BIN

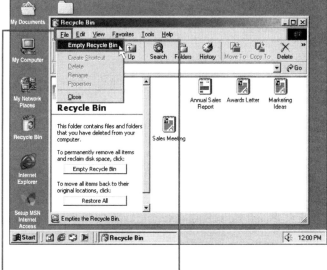

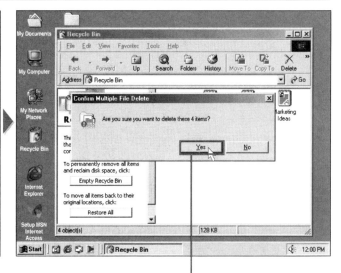

■1 Click File in the Recycle Bin window.

■2 Click Empty Recycle Bin.

■ A dialog box appears, confirming the deletion.

■3 Click Yes to permanently remove all the files from the Recycle Bin.

■ The files disappear and are permanently removed from your computer.

CHANGE RECYCLE BIN PROPERTIES

The Recycle Bin protects your files by temporarily storing the files you delete. You can change the properties of the Recycle Bin to specify the kind of protection you want.

If you have more than one drive on your computer, you can specify the Recycle Bin settings for each drive.

The Recycle Bin normally uses up to 10% of a hard drive's space to store deleted files. For example, on a 4 GB drive, the Recycle Bin may use up as much as 400 MB. By checking the status of files in the Recycle Bin for a week or two, you can estimate how much space is needed to safeguard a day's, week's or month's worth of work. You can then adjust the size of the Recycle Bin accordingly.

You can choose to permanently delete files from your computer rather than send them to the Recycle Bin. Permanently deleted files cannot be restored.

Windows normally displays a confirmation dialog box when you delete a file. To delete files more quickly, you can change the Recycle Bin properties so the dialog box will no longer appear.

CHANGE RECYCLE BIN PROPERTIES

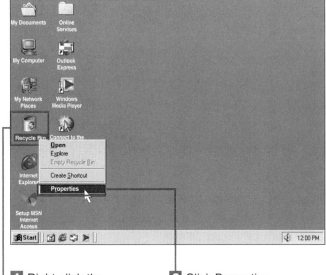

1 Right-click the Recycle Bin. A menu appears.

2 Click Properties.

■ The Recycle Bin Properties dialog box appears.

3 You can click an option to use different Recycle Bin settings for each drive or the same settings for all of your drives (○ changes to ⊙).

■ If you chose to use different settings for each drive, you can use these tabs to change the settings for each drive.

How can I view the maximum amount of space reserved for the Recycle Bin on a drive?

✔ In the Recycle Bin Properties dialog box, click the tab for the drive whose Recycle Bin properties you want to view. Windows displays the maximum space reserved on the drive for the Recycle Bin.

Can I adjust the size of the Recycle Bin for my removable hard drive?

✔ No. The Recycle Bin does not store files you delete from removable media, such as floppy disks and removable hard drives.

Can I bypass the Recycle Bin and permanently delete a file without changing the settings for all files?

✔ To delete a file or group of files permanently, select the file(s) and then hold down the Shift key while you press the Delete key. In the dialog box that appears, click Yes to confirm your deletion. If the file is already in the Recycle Bin, just delete the file as you would delete any file. To delete a file, see page 72.

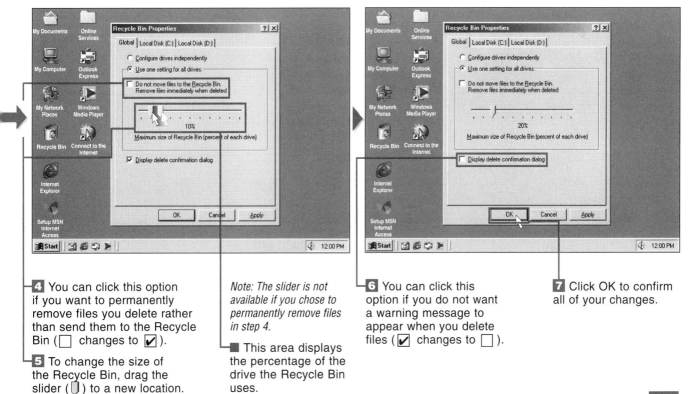

■4 You can click this option if you want to permanently remove files you delete rather than send them to the Recycle Bin (☐ changes to ☑).

■5 To change the size of the Recycle Bin, drag the slider (⬍) to a new location.

Note: The slider is not available if you chose to permanently remove files in step 4.

■ This area displays the percentage of the drive the Recycle Bin uses.

■6 You can click this option if you do not want a warning message to appear when you delete files (☑ changes to ☐).

■7 Click OK to confirm all of your changes.

77

SEARCH FOR FILES

If you cannot remember the name or location of a file you want to work with, you can have Windows search for the file.

You can have Windows search for a file by name. This is useful if you know all or part of the file name. For example, searching for a file named "report" will find every file or folder with a name that contains the word "report."

If you know a word or phrase that a file contains, you can have Windows search for the file using this information. Searching by file content will slow down your search.

You can specify which area of your computer you want Windows to search for a file. If you select My Computer, Windows will search all the drives and folders on your

computer. This is useful if you cannot remember where a file is located.

You can also search for a file based on the date the file was last modified. This is useful if you know the file was last worked on during a specific time period.

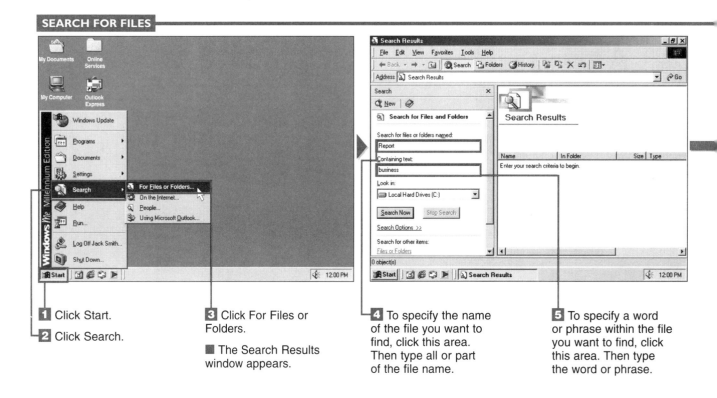

■1 Click Start.

■2 Click Search.

■3 Click For Files or Folders.

■ The Search Results window appears.

■4 To specify the name of the file you want to find, click this area. Then type all or part of the file name.

■5 To specify a word or phrase within the file you want to find, click this area. Then type the word or phrase.

How do I start a new search?

✔ Click the New button at the top of the search area to clear the search information you have entered and start a new search.

Can I change the way Windows searches for files by date?

✔ Yes. Windows automatically searches for files based on the date they were last modified. You can also have Windows search for files based on the date the files were created or last accessed. Click the area below the Date option and then select the way you want to search for files by date.

Can I use wildcard characters to find files?

✔ You can use an asterisk (*) or a question mark (?) to find files. The asterisk (*) represents one or more characters. The question mark (?) represents a single character. For example, type **d*** to find all files with names beginning with the letter d.

How can I search for a file on my network?

✔ Click ▼ beside the Look in area and then select Browse. You can use the My Network Places option in the dialog box that appears to specify the network location that you want to search.

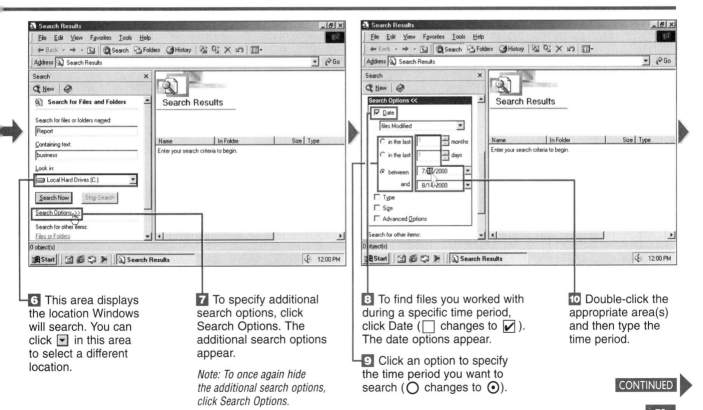

6 This area displays the location Windows will search. You can click ▼ in this area to select a different location.

7 To specify additional search options, click Search Options. The additional search options appear.

Note: To once again hide the additional search options, click Search Options.

8 To find files you worked with during a specific time period, click Date (☐ changes to ✔). The date options appear.

9 Click an option to specify the time period you want to search (◯ changes to ◉).

10 Double-click the appropriate area(s) and then type the time period.

CONTINUED ▶

79

SEARCH FOR FILES (CONTINUED)

The search options provided by Windows allow you to narrow your search for a file. You can use all, some or just one of the options.

You can specify the type of file you want to find. This is useful if you want to locate a specific type of file, such as an application or a bitmap image.

Windows can also search for a file based on size. You can search for files that are larger or smaller than the size you specify.

Windows includes advanced options that allow you to specify additional information for a search. You can choose not to search all the folders in the location you specified or to search for files that exactly match the upper and

lower case letters of the text you specified.

When the search is complete, Windows displays all the matching files and information about each file, such as location and size. You can open and work with a file Windows finds as you would open and work with a file in any window.

SEARCH FOR FILES (CONTINUED)

◼11 To find files of a specific type, click Type (☐ changes to ☑). The file type options appear.

◼12 This area displays the file type Windows will search for. You can click this area to select a different file type.

◼13 To find files of a specific size, click Size (☐ changes to ☑). The file size options appear.

◼14 This area specifies that Windows will search for files that are at least the size you specify. You can click this area to select a different option.

◼15 Double-click this area and then type a file size in kilobytes (KB).

How can I stop a search once Windows has found the file I am looking for?

✔ Click the Stop Search button at any time to end a search.

Can I search for other types of information?

✔ Besides files, Windows allows you to search the Internet for Web pages of interest. You can also search for a person using an address book on your computer or a directory service on the Internet. To search for a Web page or a person, perform steps 1 to 3 on page 78, selecting the On the Internet option or the People option in step 3.

Can I save a search so I can use the same settings again?

✔ From the File menu, select Save Search. Type a name for the search and then click the Save button. By default, Windows saves the search settings as a file in the My Documents folder.

Is there a faster way to find a file I recently used?

✔ To view a list of recently used files, click Start and then select Documents. You can then click the file you want to open.

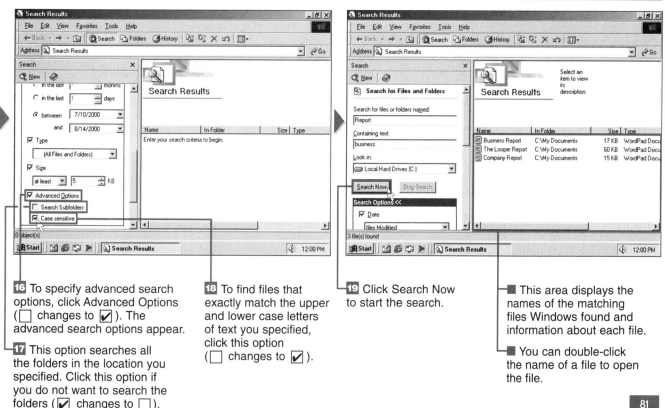

16 To specify advanced search options, click Advanced Options (☐ changes to ☑). The advanced search options appear.

17 This option searches all the folders in the location you specified. Click this option if you do not want to search the folders (☑ changes to ☐).

18 To find files that exactly match the upper and lower case letters of text you specified, click this option (☐ changes to ☑).

19 Click Search Now to start the search.

■ This area displays the names of the matching files Windows found and information about each file.

■ You can double-click the name of a file to open the file.

81

UNDO YOUR LAST ACTION

When you change your mind or make a mistake, Windows can help you undo your last action.

Windows can undo actions such as renaming, deleting, copying or moving a file. The word that appears beside the Undo command indicates which action is available to undo. You may be able to undo up to the last 10 actions.

If the Undo command is not available, you cannot undo your last action. For example, you cannot undo a delete command after you empty the Recycle Bin. You also cannot undo a save or an undo command. If you move a file to a folder that already has a file with the same name, Windows asks if you want to replace the file located in the folder. If you replace the file, you will not be able to undo the action to restore the original file.

Many applications, such as Microsoft Word and Excel, also offer the Undo command.

UNDO YOUR LAST ACTION

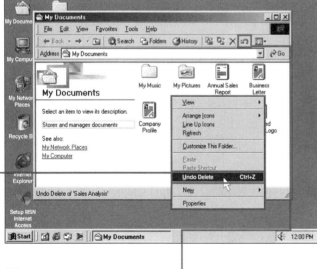

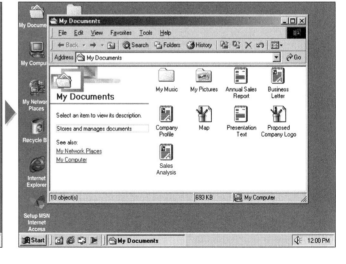

1 Right-click a blank area on your desktop or in a window. A menu appears.

2 Click Undo.

■ You can also click 🔄 in a window to undo your last action.

Note: If you cannot see 🔄, you may have to increase the size of the window. To size a window, see page 16.

■ Windows reverses your last action.

Note: In this example, the Sales Analysis file reappears.

CLOSE MISBEHAVING PROGRAMS

You can view the status of the programs running on your computer and close a program that is no longer working properly without shutting down Windows or other programs. You can close a misbehaving program even when you do not have access to the program's menus or commands.

When a program fails to respond to mouse or keyboard commands, Windows identifies the program as not responding. Windows may detect that a program is not responding before you do and display a warning message. You may also discover, while using a program, that it is not behaving as it should.

When you close a program that is not responding, you lose all the unsaved information in the program. Closing a misbehaving program should not affect the operation of your other open programs or Windows.

CLOSE MISBEHAVING PROGRAMS

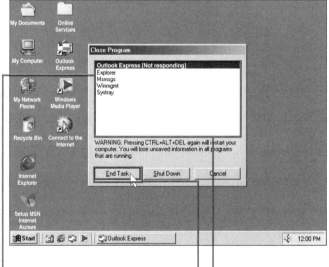

1 When a program stops responding, press and hold down the Ctrl and Alt keys and then press the Delete key.

■ The Close Program dialog box appears.

■ This area lists the programs that are currently running.

2 Click the program that is misbehaving.

Note: [Not responding] appears beside the name of a misbehaving program.

3 Click End Task.

■ A dialog box appears, stating that the program is not responding.

4 Click End Task to close the program.

CREATE A NEW FOLDER

You can create a new folder to better organize the information stored on your computer.

When you begin using your computer, you can create new folders to store your work. Storing files in personalized folders will help you quickly locate your files.

You can create folders within other folders to help further organize information. For example, you can create a folder named "letters." This folder can store other folders named "clients," "colleagues" and "personal." You can also create folders on your desktop to organize any shortcuts you have created.

You can create as many folders as you need to organize your files by date, project or type. Use a system that makes sense to you and will help you find your files.

A folder name can contain up to 215 characters and can include spaces. Folder names cannot contain the \ / : * ? " < > or | characters.

CREATE A NEW FOLDER

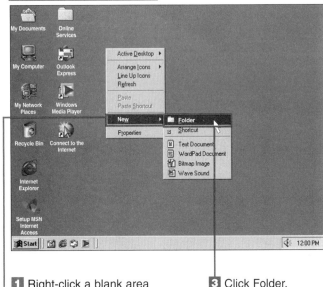

1 Right-click a blank area on the desktop or in the window where you want to place the new folder.

2 Click New.

3 Click Folder.

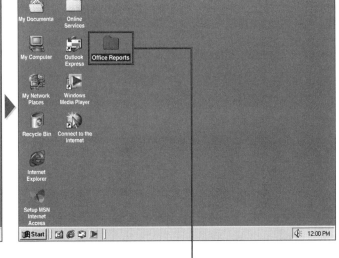

■ The new folder appears with a temporary name.

4 Type a name for the new folder and then press the Enter key.

CREATE A NEW FILE

You can create, name and store a new file in the location you want without having to start any programs. This allows you to focus on the organization of your work, rather than the programs you need to accomplish your tasks.

Before writing a letter or creating a new picture, you can first determine where you want to

store the new file. By selecting the location of the file first, you can organize your work and later find the file more easily.

Once you decide on the location of a new file, you can create and name the file. A file name can contain up to 215 characters and can include spaces. File names cannot contain the \ / : * ?"< > or | characters.

The types of new files you can create depend on the programs installed on your computer. By default, you can create a text document, WordPad document, bitmap image and wave sound.

CREATE A NEW FILE

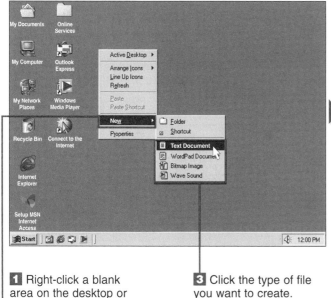

1 Right-click a blank area on the desktop or in the window where you want to place the new file.

2 Click New.

3 Click the type of file you want to create.

■ The new file appears with a temporary name.

4 Type a name for the new file and then press the Enter key.

DISPLAY AND CHANGE FILE PROPERTIES

You can find information about a file or folder by reviewing its properties. When viewing the properties of a file, you can change the name of the file. You can also see the file's type and the program Windows will use to open the file.

You can view where the file is stored on your computer, the size of the file and the amount of disk space required to store the file. You can also find the date and time the file was created, last changed and last opened.

Each file has attributes that you can verify or change. The Read-only attribute prevents you from saving changes you make to the file. The Hidden attribute is used to hide and protect files Windows needs to operate. The Archive attribute is used to determine if the file has changed since the last backup.

When the Properties dialog box displays additional tabs, you can find even more information about a file. For example, when you view the properties for a sound file, you can use the additional tabs to view the copyright information or play the sound.

DISPLAY AND CHANGE FILE PROPERTIES

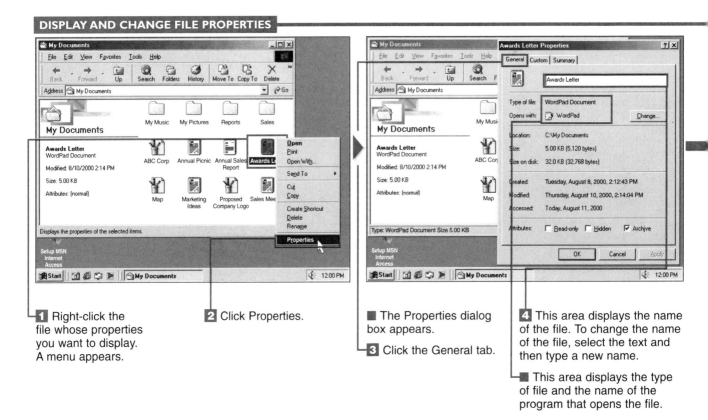

1 Right-click the file whose properties you want to display. A menu appears.

2 Click Properties.

■ The Properties dialog box appears.

3 Click the General tab.

4 This area displays the name of the file. To change the name of the file, select the text and then type a new name.

■ This area displays the type of file and the name of the program that opens the file.

Why are the size of the file and the amount of disk space required to store the file different in the Properties dialog box?

✔ The size of the file indicates the actual number of bytes required to store the file. However, when a file is stored on a disk, Windows stores the file in blocks of space, called clusters, which are made up of many bytes. The amount of disk space required to store the file is based on the number of clusters in which the file is stored.

I turned the Hidden attribute on. Why is the file still visible?

✔ You need to press the F5 key to refresh the contents of the current window.

How do I display hidden files?

✔ To display hidden files, click the Start button, choose Settings, and then select Control Panel. Double-click Folder Options, click the View tab and then select the Show hidden files and folders option.

What does the Read-only attribute do?

✔ The Read-only attribute prevents a file from being changed. You can open a Read-only file, but if you make changes to the file, you must save the file with a new name. This is useful for files such as letterhead or blank forms that you do not want altered.

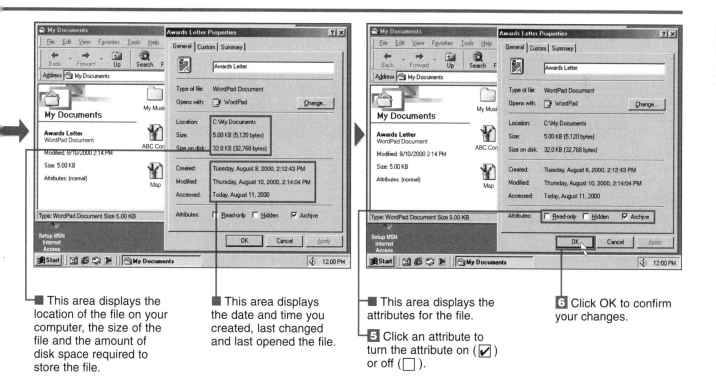

■ This area displays the location of the file on your computer, the size of the file and the amount of disk space required to store the file.

■ This area displays the date and time you created, last changed and last opened the file.

■ This area displays the attributes for the file.

5 Click an attribute to turn the attribute on (☑) or off (☐).

6 Click OK to confirm your changes.

CHANGE THE PROGRAM THAT OPENS A FILE

You can change the program Windows uses to open a file. For example, if Notepad currently opens a file, you can choose another program, such as WordPad, to open the file.

Changing the program that opens a file affects all the files with the same extension. For example, if you change the program that opens a file with the .bmp extension, all files with the .bmp extension will open in the new program.

You can display the properties of a file to view the name of the program that currently opens the file and select a new program from a list.

A specific icon represents each type of file on your computer. When you choose a new program to open a file, the icons for all files of that type change to match the program you selected.

After you add a new program to your computer, Windows' settings may automatically be changed to open some types of files in the new program. You can change the program that opens these types of files to reverse the changes. Changing the program that opens a file type also lets you use your favorite program to open files of certain type.

CHANGE THE PROGRAM THAT OPENS A FILE

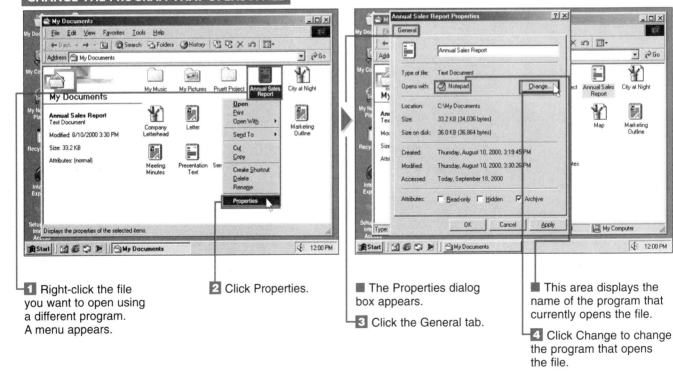

1 Right-click the file you want to open using a different program. A menu appears.

2 Click Properties.

■ The Properties dialog box appears.

3 Click the General tab.

■ This area displays the name of the program that currently opens the file.

4 Click Change to change the program that opens the file.

The program I want to use is not listed in the Open With dialog box. What can I do?

✔ In the Open With dialog box, click the Other button to locate the program on your computer.

Can I change the icon for a file type without changing the program that opens the file?

✔ Yes. You may want to change the icon for a file type to one that better represents the file type. See page 210 for information about changing the icon for a file type.

Can I change the program that opens a file one time only?

✔ Yes. Right-click the file and then select Open With. In the Open With dialog box, click the program you want to use to open the file. Make sure the Always use this program to open these files option does not display a check mark and then click OK. The next time you right-click the same type of file and choose Open With, a menu will appear, displaying programs you have used to open the file. To display the Open With dialog box and choose a different program, click Choose Program.

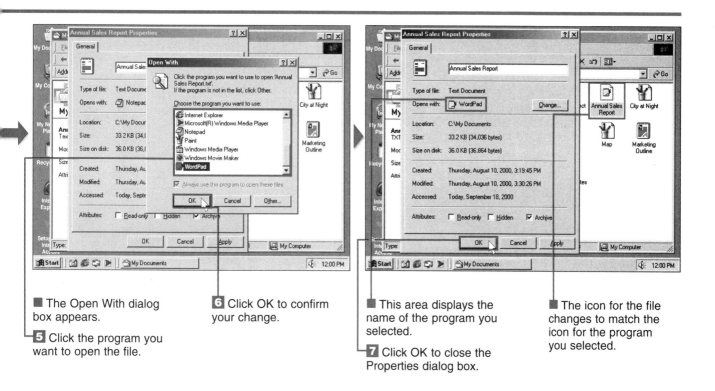

■ The Open With dialog box appears.

5 Click the program you want to open the file.

6 Click OK to confirm your change.

■ This area displays the name of the program you selected.

7 Click OK to close the Properties dialog box.

■ The icon for the file changes to match the icon for the program you selected.

CREATE A SHORTCUT

You can create a shortcut to provide a quick way of opening an item you use regularly.

A shortcut icon resembles the original item, but displays an arrow (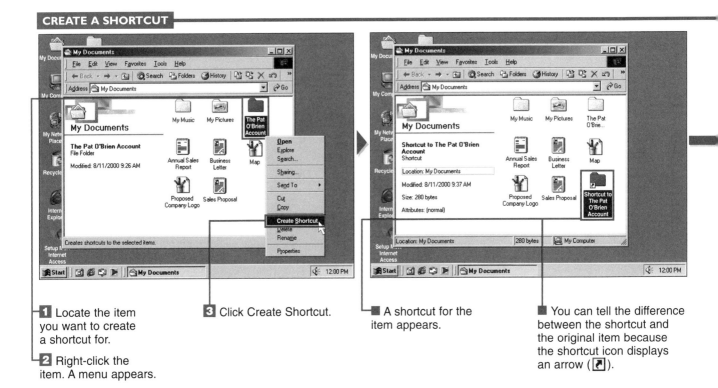) in the bottom left corner. A shortcut is a link that contains the information needed to locate the original item, but does not contain the item itself.

You can place a shortcut on the desktop, inside a folder or on the Start menu. Shortcuts allow you to access items on your computer, such as programs, files, folders, drives, printers and Control Panel items, without having to search for the item's actual location.

Shortcuts make working with files easier. For example, you

can use shortcuts to access all of the files for a project from one folder, without having to move the original files. This is particularly useful if some of the files are stored on other computers on a network.

CREATE A SHORTCUT

■1 Locate the item you want to create a shortcut for.

■2 Right-click the item. A menu appears.

■3 Click Create Shortcut.

■ A shortcut for the item appears.

■ You can tell the difference between the shortcut and the original item because the shortcut icon displays an arrow ().

Are there other ways to create a shortcut?

✔ To place a shortcut for an item on the desktop, right-click the item. On the menu that appears, click Send To and then select Desktop (create shortcut). You can also use the right mouse button to drag an item to the location where you want to place a shortcut for the item. From the menu that appears, select Create Shortcut(s) Here.

Can I rename a shortcut?

✔ Yes. Click the shortcut and then press the F2 key. Type a new name for the shortcut and then press the Enter key.

How do I delete a shortcut?

✔ Click the shortcut and then press the Delete key. Deleting a shortcut for an item will not remove the original item from your computer.

What happens if I try to use a shortcut to a file that has been deleted?

✔ Windows displays a dialog box that indicates there is a problem with the shortcut. Windows may also display the name of a file that best matches the missing file. You can change the shortcut to refer to this file or delete the shortcut.

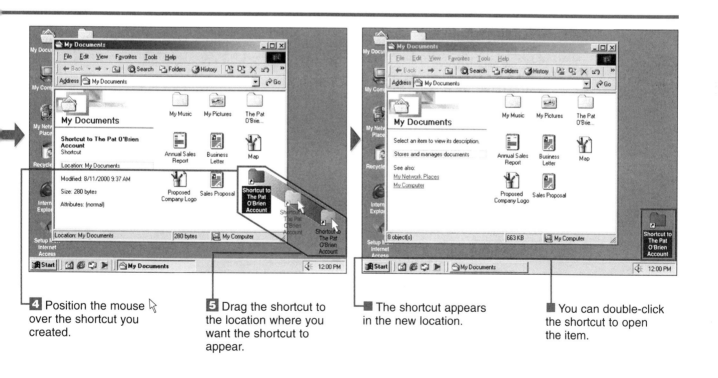

■4 Position the mouse ▷ over the shortcut you created.

■5 Drag the shortcut to the location where you want the shortcut to appear.

■ The shortcut appears in the new location.

■ You can double-click the shortcut to open the item.

CHANGE SHORTCUT PROPERTIES

Windows allows you to view and change the properties of a shortcut.

You can change the name of the shortcut. Changing the name of a shortcut will not change the name of the original item.

When viewing the properties of a shortcut, you can view the size of the shortcut and the amount of disk space used to store the

shortcut. You can also see the date and time the shortcut was created, last changed and last accessed. The item the shortcut refers to is also displayed in the Properties dialog box.

If you are changing the properties of a shortcut for a program or file, you may want to specify a new default folder. A default folder usually contains the files required to start the program associated

with the shortcut. Specifying a different default folder is useful when the files needed to start the program are not saved in the current default folder.

You can specify a keyboard shortcut that allows you to press a single key or a combination of keys to open the item the shortcut refers to.

CHANGE SHORTCUT PROPERTIES

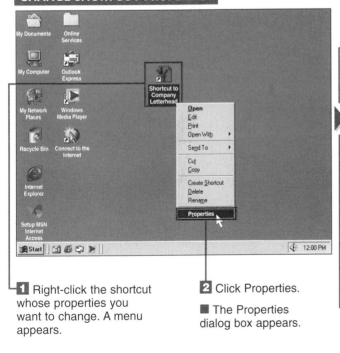

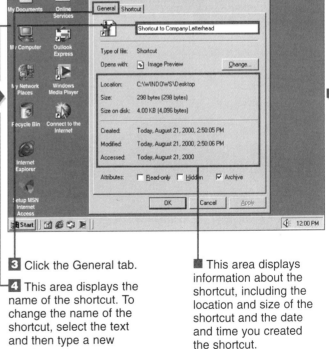

1 Right-click the shortcut whose properties you want to change. A menu appears.

2 Click Properties.

■ The Properties dialog box appears.

3 Click the General tab.

4 This area displays the name of the shortcut. To change the name of the shortcut, select the text and then type a new name.

■ This area displays information about the shortcut, including the location and size of the shortcut and the date and time you created the shortcut.

How can I quickly find the original item a shortcut refers to?

✔ In the Properties dialog box for the shortcut, select the Shortcut tab and then click the Find Target button.

What keyboard keys can I assign to a shortcut?

✔ You can assign a combination of the Ctrl and Alt keys and a letter or number, such as Ctrl+Alt+Y. You can also assign a function key, such as F9. When you assign a function key to a shortcut, the shortcut cancels whatever function the key had. For example, if you assign the F2 key to a shortcut, you will no longer be able to use the F2 key to rename files.

Can I use a keyboard shortcut to open a program or file?

✔ If the shortcut for the program or file is located on the Start menu or the desktop, you can create a keyboard shortcut that will open the program or file. For example, you can create a shortcut on your desktop to a screen saver file and then create a keyboard shortcut that will instantly activate the screen saver.

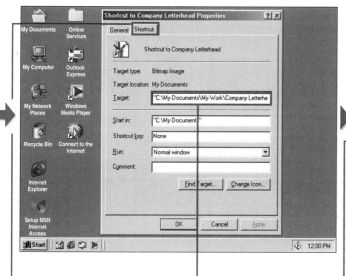

5 Click the Shortcut tab.

6 This area displays the location and name of the item the shortcut refers to. To change this information, select the text and then type a new location and name.

7 This area displays the location and name of the default folder used by the item. To change this information, select the text and then type a new folder location and name.

8 Click this area to create a keyboard shortcut that will instantly activate the shortcut. Then press the keyboard key(s) you want to assign to the shortcut.

CONTINUED

CHANGE SHORTCUT PROPERTIES
(CONTINUED)

W hen changing the properties of a shortcut, you can choose how you want the item to appear when you use the shortcut to open the item. You can have the item open in a normal window, minimized as a button on the taskbar or maximized to fill your screen.

If an item, such as a program, requires the full screen area, you

may want to display the item as a maximized window. If you have an item that opens automatically every time you start Windows, you may want the item to open minimized as a button on the taskbar so you can display the item only when needed.

You can create a comment that describes the shortcut. The comment will appear when

you position the mouse pointer over the icon for the shortcut.

You can change the icon for a shortcut to better represent the shortcut. Windows provides a selection of icons you can choose from. When you change the icon for a shortcut, the appearance of the original item does not change.

CHANGE SHORTCUT PROPERTIES (CONTINUED)

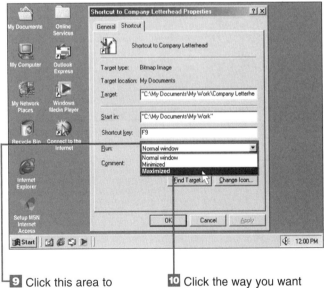

9 Click this area to specify how you want the item to appear when you use the shortcut to open the item.

10 Click the way you want the item to appear. The item can appear in a normal window, minimized as a button on the taskbar or maximized to fill the screen.

11 Click this area if you want to add a comment that describes the shortcut. Then type the comment.

■ This area displays the icon currently used for the shortcut.

12 Click Change Icon to change the icon for the shortcut.

Can I change the icon Windows uses for a specific type of file?

✔ Each type of file on your computer is represented by an icon. You can change the icon used for a specific type of file by modifying the file type. Windows will change the icon for all files of that type on your computer. To change the icon for a file type, see page 210.

Where can I find more icons for my shortcuts?

✔ In the Change Icon dialog box, double-click the File name area. Type **c:\windows\moricons.dll** and then press the Enter key to display more icons. You can also use the Browse button to search for more icons on your computer.

I selected to have a program open maximized, but it is not working. What is wrong?

✔ Some programs cannot open in a different window size. For example, the Calculator program cannot open minimized as a button on the taskbar or maximized to fill your screen.

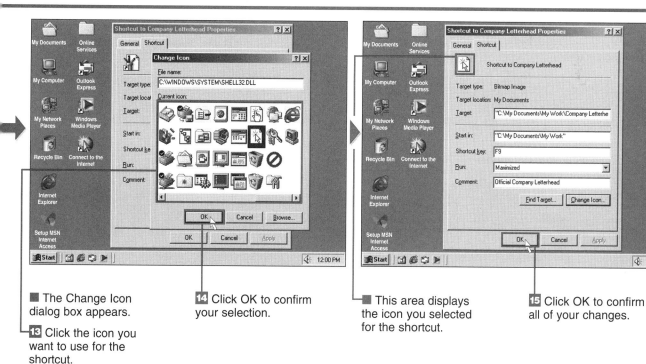

■ The Change Icon dialog box appears.

13 Click the icon you want to use for the shortcut.

14 Click OK to confirm your selection.

■ This area displays the icon you selected for the shortcut.

15 Click OK to confirm all of your changes.

ADD DESTINATIONS TO SEND TO MENU

The Send To menu allows you to send copies of files to another location. You can customize the Send To menu to include the programs, folders and devices to which you most often send files.

Windows automatically displays your floppy drive, the desktop and the My Documents folder on the Send To menu. The menu also

displays the Mail Recipient item, which allows you to quickly send a file in an e-mail message.

You can place a shortcut for a folder or a device, such as a printer, on the Send To menu. This allows you to send a file directly to a specific folder or device.

You may also want to add a program to the Send To menu

so you can quickly open files in the program. For example, if you frequently use WordPad to open files created in other programs, you can place a shortcut for the WordPad program on the Send To menu. You can then use the menu to quickly open files in WordPad.

You must add a shortcut for an item to the SendTo folder in order to have the item appear on the Send To menu.

ADD DESTINATIONS TO SEND TO MENU

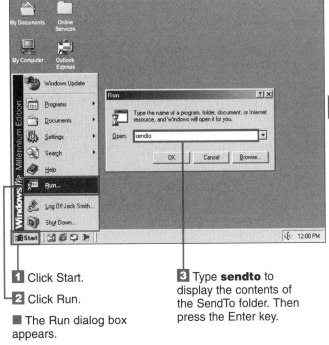

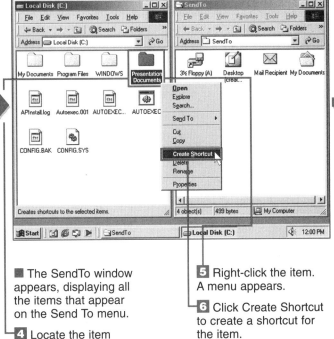

■1 Click Start.

■2 Click Run.

■ The Run dialog box appears.

■3 Type **sendto** to display the contents of the SendTo folder. Then press the Enter key.

■ The SendTo window appears, displaying all the items that appear on the Send To menu.

■4 Locate the item you want to add to the Send To menu.

■5 Right-click the item. A menu appears.

■6 Click Create Shortcut to create a shortcut for the item.

Where is the SendTo folder located on my computer?

✔ The SendTo folder is located on your hard drive (C:), within the WINDOWS folder. The SendTo folder is a hidden folder. You may need to show hidden folders before you can see the SendTo folder. To show hidden folders, see page 192.

Can I use folders to organize the information on the Send To menu?

✔ You can create a folder in the SendTo folder and then move items to the new folder. To create a folder, see page 84. The folder will appear at the top of the Send To menu with an arrow (▶) indicating there are more choices. You can click the folder to display the choices.

Can I add shared folders on the network to the Send To menu?

✔ Adding shared folders to the Send To menu is useful if you frequently store files on the network. Double-click the My Network Places icon on the desktop and then locate the folder you want to add to the Send To menu. Create a shortcut for the folder and then place the shortcut in the SendTo folder on your computer.

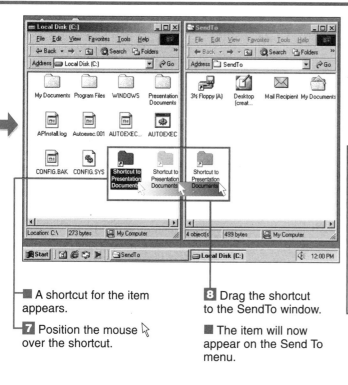

■ A shortcut for the item appears.

7 Position the mouse ▷ over the shortcut.

8 Drag the shortcut to the SendTo window.

■ The item will now appear on the Send To menu.

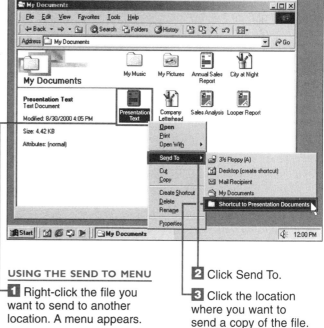

USING THE SEND TO MENU

1 Right-click the file you want to send to another location. A menu appears.

2 Click Send To.

3 Click the location where you want to send a copy of the file.

CREATE A COMPRESSED FOLDER

Compressed folders work the same way as regular folders, except that the files and folders stored in the folder are compressed, or squeezed, into a smaller file. Creating compressed folders is useful if you want to save storage space on your computer or if you want to transfer files over the Internet more quickly.

You can store folders and files, such as word processing documents, in a compressed folder. You can also store program files in a compressed folder, but you should never run a program from a compressed folder. You should also never store system files in a compressed folder.

Windows allows you to assign a password to a compressed folder to make the folder more secure. This is referred to as encrypting. Encrypting a compressed folder ensures that only those who know the password will be able to open files in the folder.

Before encrypting a compressed folder, you should make sure the folder contains all the files you want the folder to store. Files you add to the compressed folder after the folder has been encrypted will not be password protected.

CREATE A COMPRESSED FOLDER

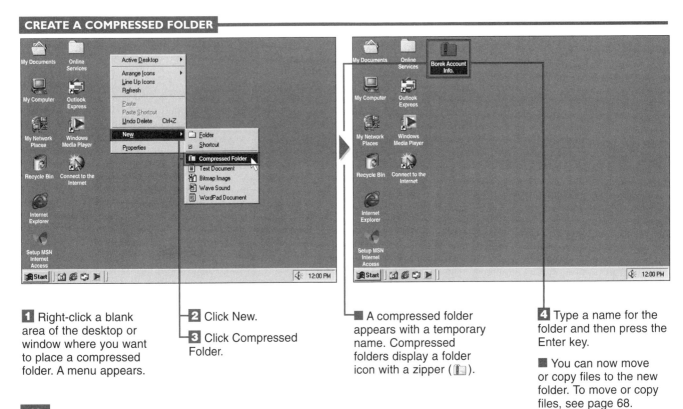

1 Right-click a blank area of the desktop or window where you want to place a compressed folder. A menu appears.

2 Click New.

3 Click Compressed Folder.

■ A compressed folder appears with a temporary name. Compressed folders display a folder icon with a zipper (🗜).

4 Type a name for the folder and then press the Enter key.

■ You can now move or copy files to the new folder. To move or copy files, see page 68.

Why isn't the Compressed Folder command available?

✔ You need to add the Compressed Folders component to your computer. Compressed Folders is located in the System Tools category. To add Windows components, see page 538.

Can I work with compressed drives on my computer?

✔ You cannot compress drives in Windows Me, but you can use DriveSpace to work with compressed drives and removable disks on your computer. To start DriveSpace, click the Start button, click Programs, select Accessories, click System Tools and choose DriveSpace. If the DriveSpace command is not available, you may need to add the Disk compression tools component to your computer. The component is found in the System Tools category. To add Windows components, see page 538.

How can I change the password for an encrypted compressed folder?

✔ To change the password, you must first decrypt the folder. Right-click the compressed folder and select Decrypt. Then perform steps 1 to 5 below to encrypt the folder again with a new password.

Can a computer running another operating system access the files in a compressed folder?

✔ You can use a Zip compression program, such as WinZip, to access the files in a compressed folder from a computer running another operating system. For information about WinZip, visit the www.winzip.com Web site.

ENCRYPT A COMPRESSED FOLDER

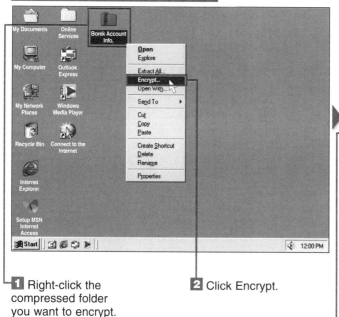

1 Right-click the compressed folder you want to encrypt. A menu appears.

2 Click Encrypt.

■ The Encrypt dialog box appears.

3 Type the password you want to use to prevent unauthorized people from opening the files in the compressed folder.

4 Click this area and type the password again.

5 Click OK.

EXTRACT FILES FROM A COMPRESSED FOLDER

You can use the Extract Wizard to extract all the files and folders from a compressed folder at once. You need to extract files from a compressed folder before you can save changes you make to the files.

You can also use the Extract Wizard to extract compressed files you have downloaded from the Internet. Files offered on the

Internet are often compressed to allow them to transfer over the Internet more quickly.

Windows will create a new folder to store the files you extract from a compressed folder. The wizard indicates where the new folder will be stored.

If the compressed folder was encrypted, Windows will ask you to enter the password required

to access the folder. The extracted files in the new folder will no longer be encrypted, but the original compressed folder will remain encrypted.

Before you can work with compressed folders, you need to add the Compressed Folders component to your computer. The component is located in the System Tools category. To add Windows components, see page 538.

EXTRACT FILES FROM A COMPRESSED FOLDER

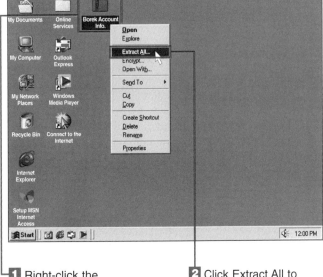

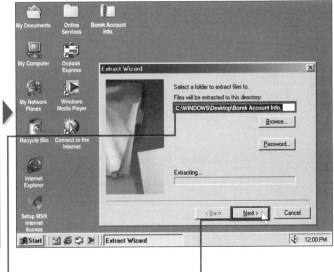

1 Right-click the compressed folder that contains the files you want to extract.

2 Click Extract All to extract all the files in the folder.

■ The Extract Wizard appears.

■ This area displays the location and name of the folder where Windows will place the extracted files.

3 Click Next to continue.

How do I extract a single file or folder from a compressed folder?

✔ Drag the file or folder from the compressed folder to a new location. A compressed version of the file or folder remains in the compressed folder. To delete a file or folder in the compressed folder, click the file or folder and press the Delete key.

Can I specify a different location to store extracted files?

✔ Yes. In the Extract Wizard, click the Browse button. A dialog box appears, allowing you to select another location to store the extracted files.

How do I delete a compressed folder?

✔ Click the compressed folder you want to delete and then press the Delete key. All the files and folders within the compressed folder will also be deleted.

After I extract files from a compressed folder, can I have the contents of the new folder automatically display on my screen?

✔ Yes. In the Extract Wizard, click the Show extracted files option (☐ changes to ☑). This allows you to quickly view the extracted files after the wizard is closed.

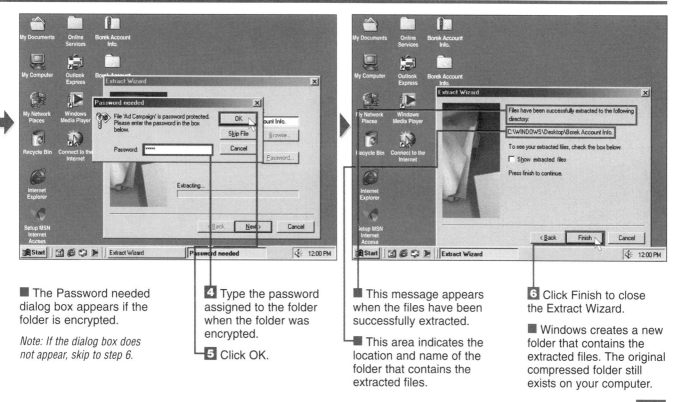

■ The Password needed dialog box appears if the folder is encrypted.

Note: If the dialog box does not appear, skip to step 6.

4 Type the password assigned to the folder when the folder was encrypted.

5 Click OK.

■ This message appears when the files have been successfully extracted.

━ This area indicates the location and name of the folder that contains the extracted files.

6 Click Finish to close the Extract Wizard.

■ Windows creates a new folder that contains the extracted files. The original compressed folder still exists on your computer.

PRINT FILES

You can produce a paper copy of a file without having to open the program that created the file. This allows you to quickly print a file from a window or the desktop.

You can select many different types of files and print them all at the same time. For example, you can print a document, a

spreadsheet and a picture at once.

When you print a file, Windows starts the program associated with the file and briefly opens the file on your screen. Windows closes the program when the file has been sent to the printer. When you print files, Windows sends the files to your default printer. You can

print files to a different printer by changing the default printer. To change the default printer, see page 110.

You can also create a shortcut for a printer on your desktop. When you want to print files, you can drag the files onto the shortcut for the printer. For more information about shortcuts, see page 90.

PRINT FILES

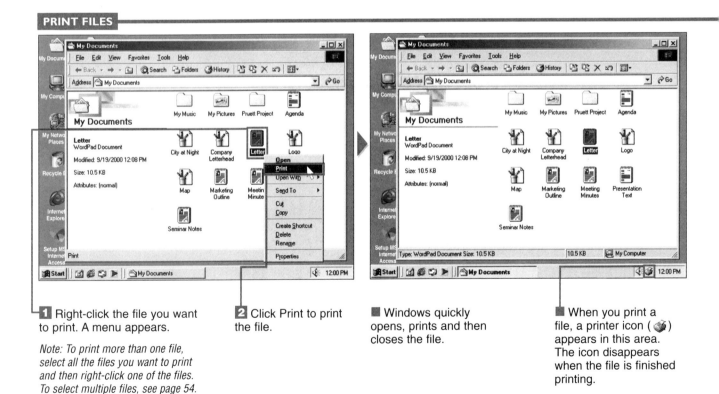

1 Right-click the file you want to print. A menu appears.

Note: To print more than one file, select all the files you want to print and then right-click one of the files. To select multiple files, see page 54.

2 Click Print to print the file.

■ Windows quickly opens, prints and then closes the file.

■ When you print a file, a printer icon (🖨) appears in this area. The icon disappears when the file is finished printing.

Why is the Print command not available when I right-click a file?

✔ Windows does not recognize the type of file and does not know which program to use to open and print the file. To specify which program Windows should use, right-click the file, click Properties and then click the Change button. In the Open With dialog box, click the program you want to open and print the file. You must also use this method if you try to print a file of a type Windows does not recognize by dragging the file to a printer shortcut.

Why does a dialog box appear when I print a picture?

✔ The Printing better pictures dialog box appears, asking if you want tips on printing pictures. Click Yes or No to specify if you want tips. If you click Yes, a window displaying printing tips appears. Click OK in the Print dialog box to print the picture. If you do not want the Printing better pictures dialog box to appear the next time you print a picture, click the In the future, do not ask this question option (☐ changes to ☑).

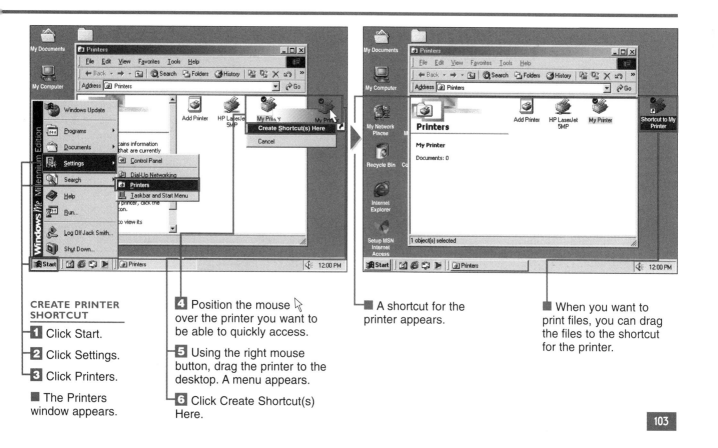

CREATE PRINTER SHORTCUT

1 Click Start.

2 Click Settings.

3 Click Printers.

■ The Printers window appears.

4 Position the mouse ↖ over the printer you want to be able to quickly access.

5 Using the right mouse button, drag the printer to the desktop. A menu appears.

6 Click Create Shortcut(s) Here.

■ A shortcut for the printer appears.

■ When you want to print files, you can drag the files to the shortcut for the printer.

VIEW PRINTING STATUS

Y ou can view information about the files you have sent to the printer.

You can display a print queue window for each printer installed on your computer. A print queue window displays information about the current status of the printer and the files waiting to print. The title bar for a print queue window displays the name of the printer.

Each file that is printing or waiting to print is listed in the print queue window. The columns in the window list information about each print job, including the file name, the status of the file and the name of the person who is printing the file. The Progress column indicates the size of each file. While a file is printing, the Progress column keeps track of how much of the document has

been sent to the printer. You can also view the time and date each file was sent to the printer.

While a file is printing, a printer icon appears next to the clock on the taskbar. This icon disappears when the file has finished printing.

VIEW PRINTING STATUS

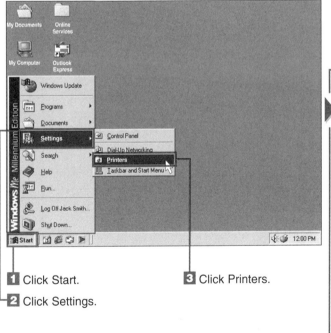

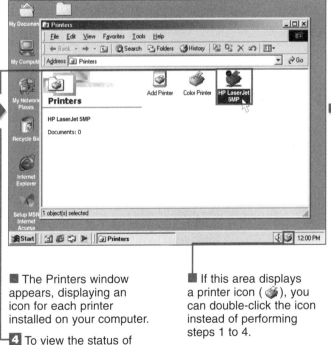

1 Click Start.

2 Click Settings.

3 Click Printers.

■ The Printers window appears, displaying an icon for each printer installed on your computer.

4 To view the status of the print jobs for a printer, double-click the printer icon.

■ If this area displays a printer icon ( ), you can double-click the icon instead of performing steps 1 to 4.

How can I change the order of print jobs?

✔ Open the print queue window and then drag a file to a new location in the list of print jobs. A file that is currently being printed will not be affected if you change its order in the print queue. You cannot change the order of print jobs sent to a network printer.

What happens when I close the print queue window?

✔ Closing the print queue window does not affect the files waiting to print. The printer icon (🖨) remains on the taskbar until the files are finished printing.

How can I view information about all available printers at once?

✔ In the Printers window, choose the View menu and then select Details. Windows displays information about the number of files waiting to print and the printer status for each printer. Viewing information about all the printers at once can help you decide which printer you should use to print files.

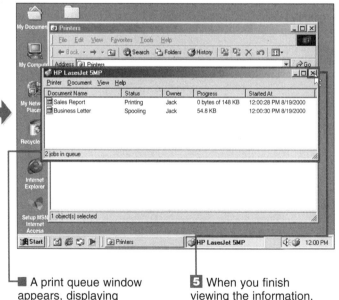

■ A print queue window appears, displaying information about each file waiting to print. The file at the top of the list will print first.

5 When you finish viewing the information, click ✕ to close the window.

INSTANTLY VIEW PRINTING STATUS

■ When you print files, the printer icon (🖨) appears in this area. The printer icon disappears when the files are finished printing.

1 To see how many files are waiting to print, position the mouse ⬎ over the printer icon (🖨).

■ A box appears, displaying the number of files.

PAUSE PRINTING

You can pause the printer connected to your computer to temporarily stop all print jobs. Pausing the printer is useful when you want to change the toner or add more paper to the printer.

You can also pause the printing of a specific document. Pausing the printing of a document is useful when you want to allow more

important documents to print first. When you print a document, Windows creates a file and sends the file to the printer. Pausing a document intercepts the file. The length of time allowed for you to pause a document depends on the number and size of files waiting to print and the speed of the printer and your computer.

When you pause a document, the document keeps its place in the print queue. The print queue is the list of files waiting to be printed. When you resume printing the document, the document prints according to its location in the print queue.

PAUSE PRINTING

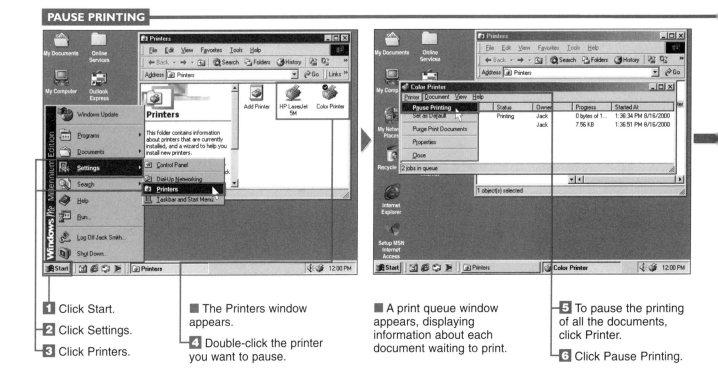

1 Click Start.

2 Click Settings.

3 Click Printers.

■ The Printers window appears.

4 Double-click the printer you want to pause.

■ A print queue window appears, displaying information about each document waiting to print.

5 To pause the printing of all the documents, click Printer.

6 Click Pause Printing.

What happens if I pause a document that is currently printing?

✔ If you pause a document while it is printing, there may be problems with the next print job. The printer may not print other documents until you resume or cancel the printing of the paused document.

Can I pause printing on a network printer?

✔ When using a network printer, you can only pause your own print jobs. You cannot pause the printer or the print jobs of other people on your network unless you are the network administrator.

Why is the Pause Printing command not available for my printer?

✔ Spooling may be turned off for the printer. To turn spooling on, right-click the printer icon in the Printers window and select Properties. In the Properties dialog box, select the Details tab and click the Spool Settings button. In the Spool Settings dialog box, select Spool print jobs so program finishes printing faster and click OK. For more information about spooling, see page 120.

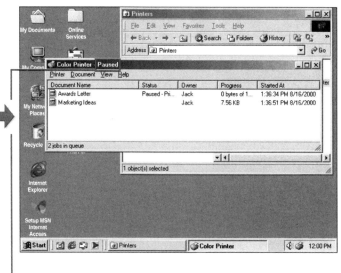

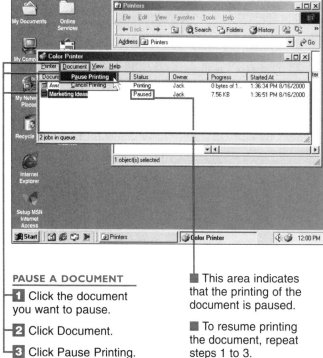

■ This area displays the word "Paused" to indicate that all the print jobs are paused.

■ To resume printing, repeat steps 5 and 6.

PAUSE A DOCUMENT

1 Click the document you want to pause.

2 Click Document.

3 Click Pause Printing.

■ This area indicates that the printing of the document is paused.

■ To resume printing the document, repeat steps 1 to 3.

CANCEL PRINTING

You can stop a document from printing if you have made a mistake and need to make a correction. The Cancel Printing command is available even if a document has already started printing.

Windows allows you to cancel a single print job or cancel the entire print queue. A print queue is a list of documents waiting to

be printed. When using a network printer, you can only cancel your own print jobs. You cannot cancel the print jobs of other people on your network unless you are the network administrator.

When you cancel the printing of a single document or all the print jobs, Windows will not give you a warning or an undo option. Do not cancel any print jobs unless

you are sure you do not want to print the documents. You may want to pause the printer first, before deciding if you want to cancel the print jobs. For information on pausing a printer, see page 106.

CANCEL PRINTING A DOCUMENT

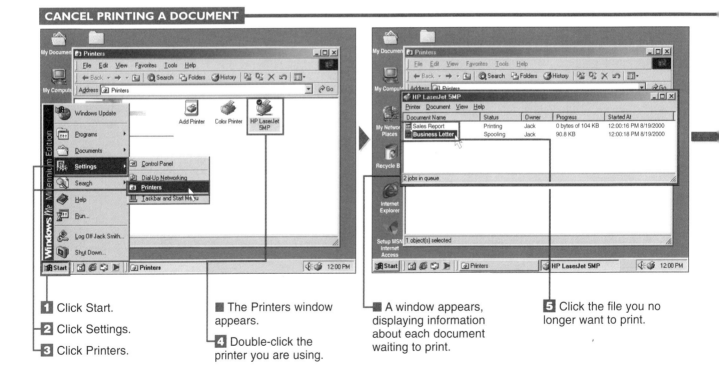

■ **1** Click Start.

■ **2** Click Settings.

■ **3** Click Printers.

■ The Printers window appears.

■ **4** Double-click the printer you are using.

■ A window appears, displaying information about each document waiting to print.

■ **5** Click the file you no longer want to print.

Can I cancel a document while it is printing?

✔ You can cancel a document if the document has already started printing, but this may cause problems with the next document waiting to print. If you are using an older printer, the printer may have to be reset.

How can I quickly cancel all print jobs?

✔ To cancel all print jobs sent to a printer, right-click the printer icon in the Printers window and select Purge Print Documents from the menu that appears.

How can I get quick access to the list of files waiting to print?

✔ You can create a shortcut icon to the printer on your desktop. Using the right mouse button, drag the icon for the printer from the Printers window to your desktop. Select Create Shortcut(s) Here from the menu that appears. You can now double-click the shortcut icon to quickly access the list of files waiting to print at any time.

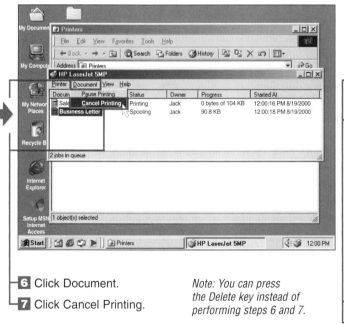

6 Click Document.

7 Click Cancel Printing.

Note: You can press the Delete key instead of performing steps 6 and 7.

■ The file disappears from the list and will not be printed.

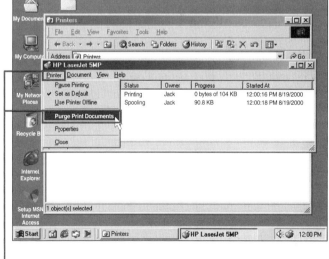

CANCEL ALL FILES

1 Click Printer.

2 Click Purge Print Documents.

■ All the files disappear from the list and will not be printed.

SET THE DEFAULT PRINTER

If you have access to more than one printer, you can select which printer you want to automatically print your documents. The printer you select is referred to as the default printer.

When selecting a default printer, you should select the printer that you use most often and that offers the capabilities you need.

Windows will automatically use the default printer to print your files unless you specify another printer. You may occasionally want to print a document on another printer. When you print a document, most programs will display a Print dialog box that allows you to select the printer you want to use.

In some situations, a Print dialog box will not be available and your document will be sent directly to the default printer. For example, a Print dialog box is not available when you right-click a file and select the Print command. In such cases, changing the default printer is the only way to choose a different printer.

SET THE DEFAULT PRINTER

1 Click Start.

2 Click Settings.

3 Click Printers.

■ The Printers window appears, displaying the printers installed on your computer.

■ The default printer displays a check mark (✓).

4 Right-click the printer you want to set as your default printer. A menu appears.

5 Click Set as Default.

6 Click ✕ to close the Printers window.

USE A PRINTER OFFLINE

You can tell Windows that a printer is not currently available and you want to use the printer offline. This allows you to save your print jobs and print them later.

You may want to use a printer offline when you are working with a portable computer and you do not have access to a printer or when a network printer is unavailable because it needs

paper, toner or maintenance. In both cases, Windows will save your print jobs until you can access the printer again. Your documents will be sent to the printer as soon as you tell Windows you are no longer using your printer offline.

By using your printer offline, you save the time of having to reopen documents and print them later. You also eliminate

the chance that you will forget which documents you wanted to print.

The Use Printer Offline command is only available for portable computers or for computers using a network printer. To temporarily use a local printer offline, you can use the Pause Printing command. See page 106 for information about pausing a printer.

USE A PRINTER OFFLINE

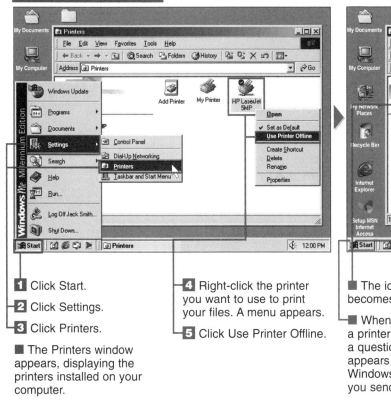

1 Click Start.

2 Click Settings.

3 Click Printers.

■ The Printers window appears, displaying the printers installed on your computer.

4 Right-click the printer you want to use to print your files. A menu appears.

5 Click Use Printer Offline.

■ The icon for the printer becomes dim.

■ When you print files, a printer icon displaying a question mark ( ) appears on the taskbar. Windows will store the files you send to the printer.

■ To once again use the printer online and print the stored files, repeat steps 1 to 5.

RENAME A PRINTER

You can change the name of a printer to help you identify the printer. This is useful when you have access to more than one printer.

The Printers window displays an icon for each printer installed on your computer. The name of each printer appears below each icon in the window.

Printer names can be up to 31 characters long, including letters, numbers, spaces and special characters. Long, descriptive printer names make it easier to identify a printer. For example, a printer named "Kim's color printer in room 204" is much easier to identify than a printer named "Printer 2."

When you rename your printer, the new name will appear in the Print dialog boxes in all of your programs. This helps you select the printer when printing a document.

Renaming a printer will not have any effect on documents currently waiting to print.

RENAME A PRINTER

1 Click Start.

2 Click Settings.

3 Click Printers.

■ The Printers window appears.

4 Click the name of the printer you want to rename.

5 Wait a moment and then click the name of the printer again or press the F2 key on your keyboard.

■ The name of the printer appears in a box.

6 Type a new name for the printer and then press the Enter key.

DELETE A PRINTER

If you no longer use a printer, you should delete the printer from your computer.

When you delete a printer, you remove the software that runs the printer from your computer. The icon for the printer will disappear from the Printers window and Windows will no longer display the printer in the Print dialog boxes of your programs.

If Windows detects that it no longer needs the files used to communicate with the printer, Windows offers to remove the files for you. If you are removing the printer permanently, you should delete the printer files. If you intend to reconnect the printer later, you should keep the files, especially if they were provided on a floppy disk or CD-ROM disc with the printer or were downloaded from the Internet.

Windows will display a warning message if you delete your default printer. The default printer is the printer that automatically prints your documents. If you have another printer installed on your computer, Windows will make this printer the new default printer. If you do not have another printer installed on your computer, Windows indicates this in the warning message.

DELETE A PRINTER

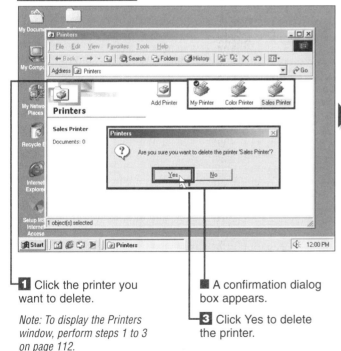

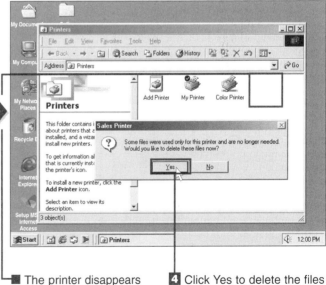

■1 Click the printer you want to delete.

Note: To display the Printers window, perform steps 1 to 3 on page 112.

■2 Press the Delete key.

■ A confirmation dialog box appears.

■3 Click Yes to delete the printer.

■ The printer disappears from the Printers window.

■ A second confirmation dialog box may appear.

■4 Click Yes to delete the files that operate the printer.

Note: Windows displays a warning message if you have deleted your default printer. If you have another printer installed on your computer, Windows sets this printer as your new default printer.

INSTALL A PRINTER

Before you can use a printer attached to your computer, you need to install the printer on your computer. A printer connected directly to your computer is called a local printer. You only need to install a printer once.

The Add Printer Wizard asks you a series of questions and then sets up the printer according to the information you provide. The wizard helps ensure that your new printer is installed correctly and works properly.

When installing a printer, you must specify the manufacturer and model of the printer. Windows supports hundreds of printer models from over 60 different manufacturers, including Hewlett-Packard, Epson and Panasonic.

Windows includes a printer driver for most printer models. A printer driver is software that enables Windows to communicate with your printer. When you install a printer, Windows selects the correct printer driver for your printer.

INSTALL A PRINTER

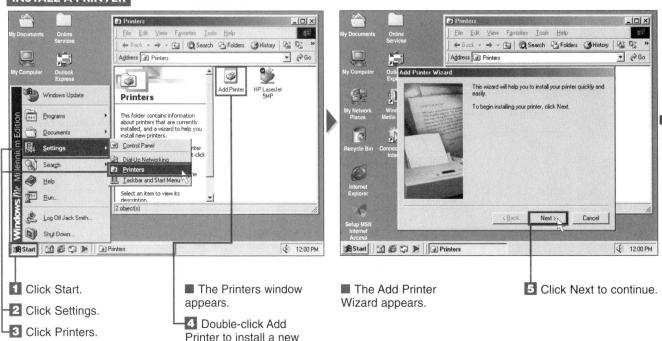

1 Click Start.

2 Click Settings.

3 Click Printers.

■ The Printers window appears.

4 Double-click Add Printer to install a new printer.

■ The Add Printer Wizard appears.

5 Click Next to continue.

The printer I want to install does not appear in the list. What should I do?

✔ You can use the installation disk that came with the printer to install the printer. Insert the installation disk into the drive. Click the Have Disk button in the Add Printer Wizard and then press the Enter key.

Which printer should I choose if no documentation or disk was supplied with my printer?

✔ If your printer does not appear in the list, you can select a printer that closely resembles your printer. For example, select a similar model made by the same manufacturer. You can also select the Generic printer, but this option provides only basic features for a printer.

Do I need to use the installation disk that came with my printer if my printer appears in the list?

✔ If you purchased a printer after the release of Windows Me, the installation disk may contain a more up-to-date printer driver. Insert the installation disk into the drive. Click the Have Disk button in the Add Printer Wizard and then press the Enter key.

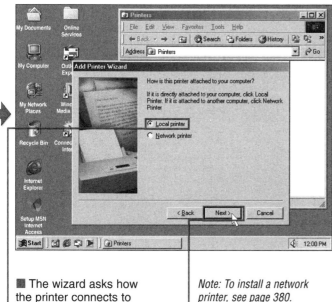

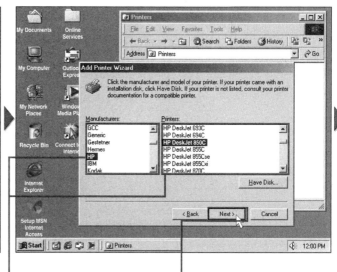

■ The wizard asks how the printer connects to your computer.

6 Click Local printer to install a printer that connects directly to your computer (○ changes to ⊙).

Note: To install a network printer, see page 380.

7 Click Next to continue.

8 Click the manufacturer of your printer.

9 Click the model of your printer.

Note: If the printer you want to use does not appear in the list, see the top of this page.

10 Click Next to continue.

CONTINUED

INSTALL A PRINTER (CONTINUED)

When installing a printer, you must specify which port the printer is connected to. A port is a socket at the back of a computer where you plug in a device. In most cases, printers are attached to a computer's parallel port, called LPT1.

The wizard allows you to name your printer to help identify the printer. A printer name can be up to 31 characters long. Giving a printer a descriptive name can help other people using the printer easily identify the printer.

If you have more than one printer installed on your computer, you can specify whether you want the printer to be your default printer. Files you print automatically print to the default printer. If you have only one printer installed on your computer, it is automatically set as the default printer.

Windows allows you to print a test page to confirm that your printer is working properly. The test page contains information about the printer. You may want to keep the page for future reference.

INSTALL A PRINTER (CONTINUED)

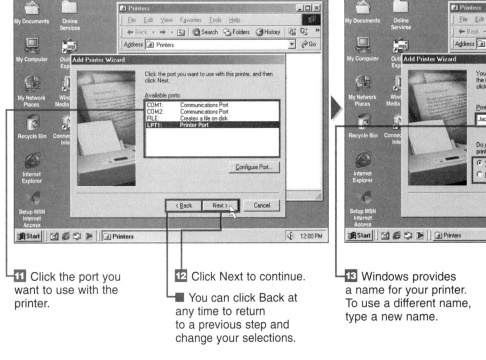

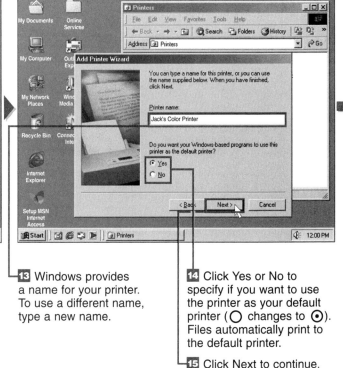

■11 Click the port you want to use with the printer.

■12 Click Next to continue.

■ You can click Back at any time to return to a previous step and change your selections.

■13 Windows provides a name for your printer. To use a different name, type a new name.

■14 Click Yes or No to specify if you want to use the printer as your default printer (○ changes to ⊙). Files automatically print to the default printer.

■15 Click Next to continue.

How can I later print another test page?

✔ You can print another test page at any time. In the Printers window, right-click the printer and click Properties on the menu that appears. Then click the Print Test Page button.

What happens when I install a printer with Plug and Play capabilities?

✔ A Plug and Play printer is a printer that Windows can automatically detect after you plug in the printer and turn on the computer. Windows displays the Add New Hardware Wizard to help you install the new printer. Follow the instructions on your screen to install the printer.

I am having printer problems. Where can I get help?

✔ Windows includes a Printing Troubleshooter that can help you with many common printer problems. To use the Printing Troubleshooter, click Start and select Help. In the Search text box, type "printing troubleshooter" and press Enter. A link appears for the Printing Troubleshooter. Click the link and then follow the instructions that appear in the right pane.

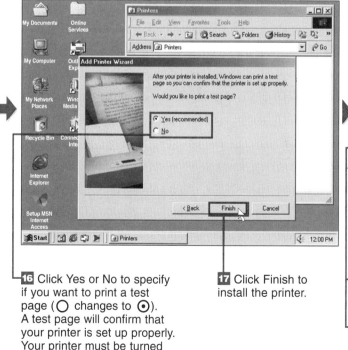

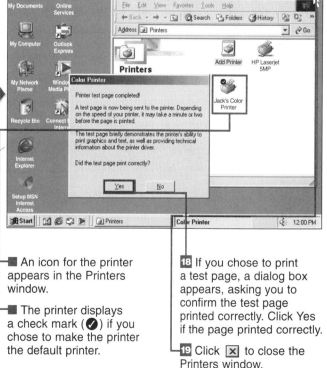

16 Click Yes or No to specify if you want to print a test page (○ changes to ⊙). A test page will confirm that your printer is set up properly. Your printer must be turned on to print a test page.

17 Click Finish to install the printer.

■ An icon for the printer appears in the Printers window.

■ The printer displays a check mark (✔) if you chose to make the printer the default printer.

18 If you chose to print a test page, a dialog box appears, asking you to confirm the test page printed correctly. Click Yes if the page printed correctly.

19 Click ⊠ to close the Printers window.

CHANGE PRINTER SETTINGS

You can change a printer's settings to suit your needs. Changing a printer's settings will affect all the documents it prints. The settings you can change depend on the printer you are using.

Changing a printer's general settings can be useful when the printer is shared with other people on a network. You can add a comment about your printer that

can be seen by other people on the network when they install the printer and view its properties.

If many people on the network use your printer or you often print several documents at once, you can have the printer insert a separator page between each printed document. The separator page prints before each document and helps identify who printed the document. The Full separator page

uses a large font. The Simple separator page uses the printer's default font. You can only change the separator page setting if the printer is attached directly to your computer. If you are using a printer connected to a network, you cannot change this setting.

Windows allows you to print a test page to confirm the printer is working properly.

CHANGE PRINTER SETTINGS

1 Click Start.

2 Click Settings.

3 Click Printers.

■ The Printers window appears.

4 Click the printer whose settings you want to change.

5 Click File.

6 Click Properties.

■ The Properties dialog box appears.

Should I print a test page?

✔ A test page confirms that the printer is working properly and provides information about the printer's driver. You can compare the driver information on the test page to the driver information on the printer manufacturer's Web site to determine if a more up-to-date printer driver is available.

My test page did not print correctly. What can I do?

✔ In the dialog box that appears when you print a test page, click the No button. Windows will open the Help and Support window and display the Printing Troubleshooter. Follow the instructions on your screen to try to resolve the problem.

Can I create my own separator page?

✔ Yes. You can use files in the Windows metafile (.wmf) format as a separator page. Advanced graphics programs, such as CorelDRAW, can save files in the .wmf format. When you use your own separator page, Windows does not print the name of the user on the page. In the Properties dialog box, click the General tab and then select the Browse button to find the .wmf file you want to use.

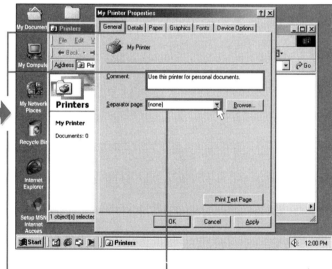

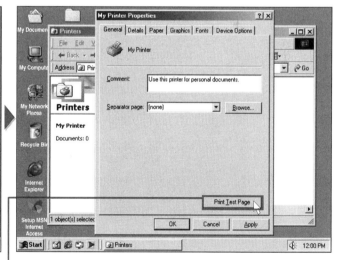

GENERAL SETTINGS

1 Click the General tab.

2 You can click this area and type a comment about the printer.

3 This area specifies if a separator page will print between each printed document. You can click ▼ in this area to select the type of separator page you want to use.

Note: You can only select a separator page if the printer is directly attached to your computer.

4 You can click Print Test Page to print a test page to make sure the printer is set up correctly.

Note: A dialog box will appear, stating that the test page is being sent to the printer. If the test page prints correctly, click Yes.

CONTINUED

CHANGE PRINTER SETTINGS
(CONTINUED)

You can change settings that specify how your computer works with a printer.

You can view which port the printer uses to connect to your computer. You can also view the driver the printer uses. A driver is a program that allows your computer to communicate with the printer. The driver determines which settings are available for the printer.

The spool settings control how information is sent to the printer. When you print a document, Windows creates a file on your hard drive to store the document until the printer is ready. When the printer is ready, Windows sends the file from your hard drive to the printer. Once the file is sent, you can resume using your computer. This process is called spooling and means that you do not have to wait for the printer

to print your document before performing another task on your computer.

If your printer is capable of sending information back to the computer, you should leave the bi-directional support option enabled. This feature allows Windows to provide additional information about your print jobs, such as displaying a message when a document finishes printing.

CHANGE PRINTER SETTINGS (CONTINUED)

DETAILS SETTINGS

1 Click the Details tab.

■ This area displays the port used by the printer or the location of the printer on the network.

■ This area displays the name of the driver that enables the printer to communicate with your computer.

2 These areas display how long Windows will wait for the printer to be online and ready to print before reporting an error. To change the number of seconds, double-click an area and type a new number of seconds.

3 Click Spool Settings to change how Windows sends your documents to the printer.

What are the Timeout settings used for?

✔ The Not selected setting indicates how long Windows will attempt to contact the printer when the printer is offline. The Transmission retry setting indicates how long Windows will wait for the printer to successfully print a document. If you have problems printing large documents, you may want to increase the number of seconds for the Transmission retry setting.

What are spool data formats?

✔ Spool data formats control the way information waiting to be printed is saved on your hard drive. EMF is the most efficient format for spooling data, but some printers cannot use this format. If you are having problems printing, try using the RAW format.

Which spool settings should I choose?

✔ If you want your documents printed quickly, select the Print directly to the printer setting. If you want to be able to use your computer soon after sending a document to the printer, select the Spool print jobs so program finishes printing faster setting. This setting offers two options. The Start printing after first page is spooled option will free up the program faster.

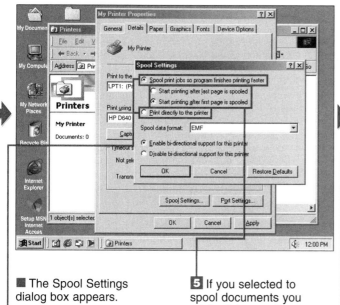

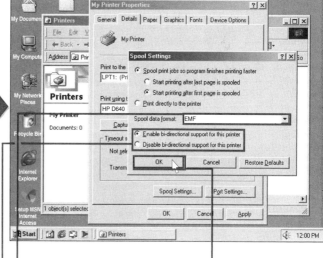

■ The Spool Settings dialog box appears.

4 Click an option to specify if you want to spool documents you print or print directly to the printer (○ changes to ⊙).

5 If you selected to spool documents you print, click an option to specify when you want Windows to send information to the printer (○ changes to ⊙).

6 This area displays the format Windows uses to store information waiting to be printed. You can click this area to select another format.

7 Click an option to specify if you want Windows to be able to receive information sent by the printer (○ changes to ⊙).

8 Click OK to close the Spool Settings dialog box.

CONTINUED ▶

CHANGE PRINTER SETTINGS
(CONTINUED)

Y ou can specify the size of paper you want to use to print your documents. For example, you may want to set up a printer to always print on legal-size paper or envelopes. The available paper sizes depend on the paper sizes supported by the printer. Some printers can be set up to print on non-standard paper sizes.

You can also change the orientation of the pages you print. Portrait is the standard orientation. The Landscape orientation is often used to print certificates and wide tables.

Windows also allows you to specify where the paper you want to use is located in the printer, such as the upper or lower tray. You can set some printers to

automatically select the appropriate paper source for the documents you print.

You may also be able to change the settings that control how graphics are printed. You can change the resolution and the type of dithering used to produce graphics. You can also have graphics print darker or lighter on a page.

CHANGE PRINTER SETTINGS (CONTINUED)

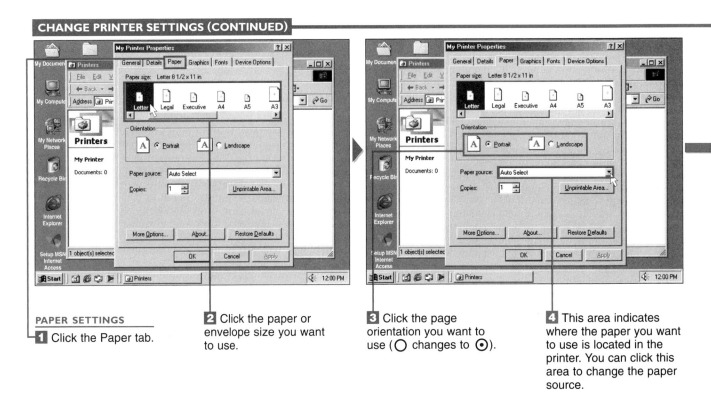

PAPER SETTINGS

■1 Click the Paper tab.

■2 Click the paper or envelope size you want to use.

■3 Click the page orientation you want to use (○ changes to ⊙).

■4 This area indicates where the paper you want to use is located in the printer. You can click this area to change the paper source.

What is resolution?
✔ Resolution is the number of dots printed per inch. Generally, higher resolution settings produce better quality images, but documents take longer to print.

What is dithering?
✔ Dithering is the technique of using dots of different colors to create the illusion of a wide range of gray tones or colors. This technique is used by most kinds of printers to enhance the appearance of images.

Can I change the printer settings for only one document?
✔ Yes. Open the document you want to print. From the File menu, select Page Setup or Print Setup to change the printer settings for the document.

How can I save time if I use different printer settings each time I print?
✔ You can install more than one copy of the printer, called a virtual printer, and then specify different settings for each printer. For example, you can create one virtual printer to print envelopes and another virtual printer to print using the letterhead tray. When printing, you can select the virtual printer you want to use. To install a printer, see page 114.

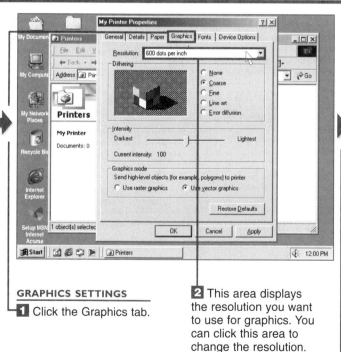

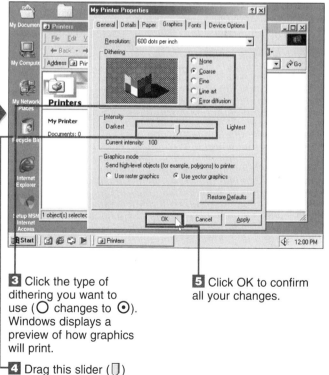

GRAPHICS SETTINGS

■1 Click the Graphics tab.

■2 This area displays the resolution you want to use for graphics. You can click this area to change the resolution.

■3 Click the type of dithering you want to use (○ changes to ◉). Windows displays a preview of how graphics will print.

■4 Drag this slider (⬚) to specify how dark you want to print graphics in your documents.

■5 Click OK to confirm all your changes.

START AN MS-DOS PROMPT WINDOW

You can use the MS-DOS Prompt window to work with MS-DOS commands and programs in Windows.

Windows can run many MS-DOS games and programs without any problem. If Windows cannot run an MS-DOS program, a message may appear in the MS-DOS Prompt window indicating that the program is not suitable for use with Windows.

To make the MS-DOS Prompt window easier to use, you can enlarge the window to fill your entire screen. Some MS-DOS programs, especially games, can only run in full screen mode. You can also change the size of text displayed in the MS-DOS Prompt window. When you change the size of text, the size of the MS-DOS Prompt window changes to accommodate the new text size.

Although you can have several MS-DOS Prompt windows open at the same time, they require some of your computer's resources. Running programs in several MS-DOS Prompt windows at once may slow down your computer's performance.

START AN MS-DOS PROMPT WINDOW

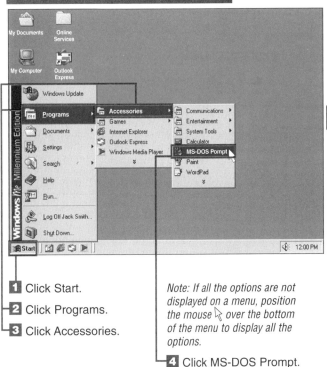

1 Click Start.

2 Click Programs.

3 Click Accessories.

Note: If all the options are not displayed on a menu, position the mouse ⟍ over the bottom of the menu to display all the options.

4 Click MS-DOS Prompt.

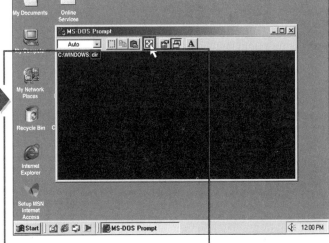

■ The MS-DOS Prompt window appears.

■ You can enter MS-DOS commands and start MS-DOS programs in the window. In this example, we enter the **dir** command to list the contents of the current directory.

5 Click 🔳 to have the MS-DOS Prompt window fill the entire screen.

Note: You can also hold down the Alt key and then press the Enter key.

Is there another way to close the MS-DOS Prompt window?

✔ You can click ☒ to close the window. If you have a program open, a message may appear warning that you will lose any unsaved information. You should use a program's quit or exit command to exit the program before closing the MS-DOS Prompt window.

How can I find out what commands I can use in the MS-DOS Prompt window?

✔ In the MS-DOS Prompt window, type **cd c:\windows\command** and then press the Enter key to open the folder that contains many of the MS-DOS commands included with Windows. Then type **dir** to list the commands.

How can I find out what each MS-DOS command does?

✔ In the MS-DOS Prompt window, type the name of a command followed by **/?**. For example, you can type **move /?** to find out what the move command does.

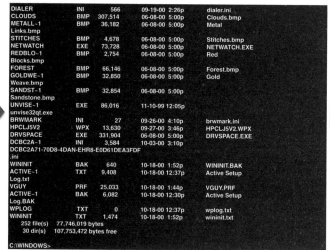

■ The MS-DOS Prompt window fills the entire screen.

6 To return the MS-DOS screen to a window, hold down the Alt key and then press the Enter key.

7 Click this area to change the size of the text.

8 Click the font size you want to use.

■ The text in the window appears in the new size.

9 When you finish using the MS-DOS Prompt window, type **exit** and then press the Enter key to close the window.

125

INSTALL AND RUN MS-DOS PROGRAMS

Programs designed to work with MS-DOS can be installed and used in Windows.

Before you can use an MS-DOS program, you usually need to locate and run an installation program that sets up the program on your computer. The installation program file usually starts with the word "install," "setup" or "go."

Many MS-DOS programs provide a file with documentation to help you install the program. These files are often named "readme." You should read the file before installing a program.

When you install an MS-DOS game, the program will often ask questions about the devices on your computer, such as a joystick or sound card. The program will then set itself up to work with your computer.

Some MS-DOS programs do not need to be installed. You can copy all of the program's files into a folder on your computer and then use the program file in the folder to start the program.

MS-DOS programs you install do not appear on the Start menu. See page 230 for information about adding programs to the Start menu.

INSTALL AN MS-DOS PROGRAM

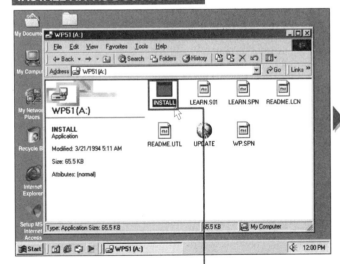

1 Locate the installation file for the MS-DOS program you want to install.

Note: The installation file may be on your computer, a floppy disk or CD-ROM.

2 Double-click the installation file.

■ The installation program starts.

3 Follow the instructions on your screen. Every program will install differently. In this example, we install WordPerfect 5.1.

How can I delete an MS-DOS program?

✔ To delete a program, follow the instructions provided in the program's documentation. If no documentation is provided, you can drag the folder that contains the program files to the Recycle Bin to delete the program. Make sure the folder does not contain any documents you still need. You should also remove any shortcuts to the program on the desktop and the Start menu.

Why does my MS-DOS program indicate that there is no room left on my hard drive?

✔ Some MS-DOS programs may be incompatible with the FAT32 file system used by Windows. Contact the manufacturer of your program to see if an updated version of the program is available.

My MS-DOS program is not working properly. What should I do?

✔ You can control the way an MS-DOS program works with Windows. If a program is not working properly, it may help to change some of the program settings. Right-click the program icon and click Properties. The Properties dialog box lets you modify settings such as the amount of memory the program requires or how the program is displayed on the screen.

RUN AN MS-DOS PROGRAM

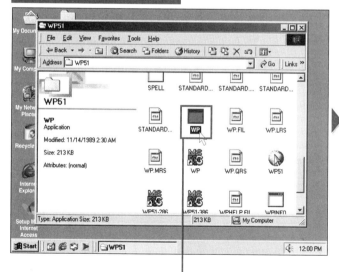 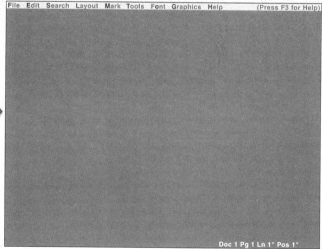

1 Locate the file that runs the program.

Note: The file name often contains the name of the program.

2 Double-click the file.

■ The program starts.

COPY TEXT FROM AN MS-DOS PROGRAM

Y ou can copy information from an MS-DOS program and place the information in a Windows program.

When using Windows, you can still use your old MS-DOS programs and files. If your Windows programs cannot open your old MS-DOS files, you can use your older files by opening them in an MS-DOS program. You can then copy

the information you need from the old documents and paste the information into a document in a Windows program. Copying and pasting information from MS-DOS programs saves you from having to print a copy of the document and then retype the information in a Windows program.

You can also copy and paste the results of commands displayed

in the MS-DOS Prompt window. For example, you can copy the directory listing created using the dir command and paste the listing into a document.

When you copy information from an MS-DOS program, you lose the format of the text. The program you copy the text to will display the pasted text in the default font of the program.

COPY TEXT FROM AN MS-DOS PROGRAM

1 Start the MS-DOS program that contains the information you want to copy.

Note: To display the MS-DOS Prompt window, see page 124. To run an MS-DOS program, see page 126.

2 Click 🔲 to turn on the marking mode.

■ A flashing cursor appears at the top of the window.

3 Position the mouse ⌀ over the top left corner of the area you want to copy.

4 Drag the mouse ⌀ until you highlight the area you want to copy.

5 Click 🔳 to copy the information to the Clipboard.

Can I take a picture of an MS-DOS window?

✔ Yes. Click anywhere in the window and then press Alt+Print Scrn. Open the document you want to display the picture of the MS-DOS window, choose the Edit menu and then select Paste.

Can I copy text from an MS-DOS program displayed in full screen mode?

✔ You can copy all the text from the screen at once by pressing the Print Scrn key. You cannot copy specific text when an MS-DOS program is displayed in full screen mode.

Is there an easier way to select the text I want to copy?

✔ You can use the QuickEdit mode instead of having to turn on the marking mode each time you want to select text in an MS-DOS program. To turn on the QuickEdit mode, click 🖼 to open the Properties dialog box. Select the Misc tab and click QuickEdit (☐ changes to ✔). In the QuickEdit mode, you can use the mouse to highlight text at all times. You cannot use the mouse as a pointing device in an MS-DOS program when the QuickEdit mode is on.

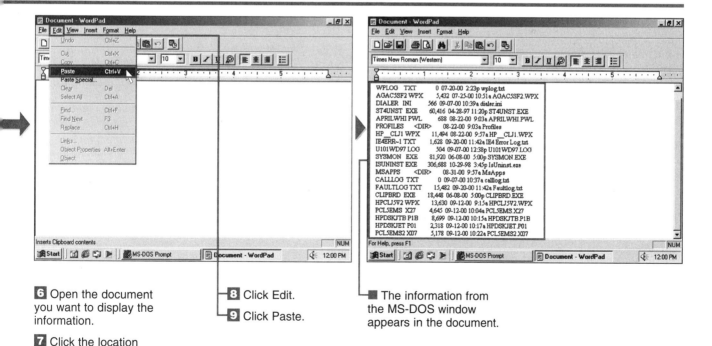

■6 Open the document you want to display the information.

■7 Click the location where you want to place the information.

■8 Click Edit.

■9 Click Paste.

■ The information from the MS-DOS window appears in the document.

START WORDPAD

WordPad is a word processing program included with Windows. You can use WordPad to create simple documents, such as letters and memos. You can also use WordPad to review and edit files created in other word processing programs, such as Microsoft Word.

Word processing is similar to using a typewriter. You use some special keyboard keys, such as the Tab key, just as you do when using a typewriter. One of the advantages of using a word processor is that you do not need to press the Enter key at the end of each line when typing text in a document. The text automatically moves to the next line.

Entering text in a document is only the beginning of word processing. When you finish typing the text, you can make changes to the content and appearance of your document.

If you need more advanced features than those offered in WordPad, you can purchase a more powerful word processor, such as Microsoft Word or Corel WordPerfect. These programs include features such as tables, graphics, a spell checker and a thesaurus.

START WORDPAD

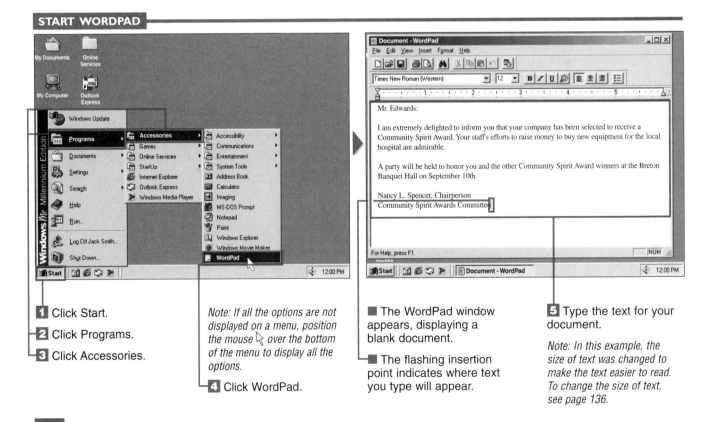

1 Click Start.

2 Click Programs.

3 Click Accessories.

Note: If all the options are not displayed on a menu, position the mouse ⌖ over the bottom of the menu to display all the options.

4 Click WordPad.

■ The WordPad window appears, displaying a blank document.

■ The flashing insertion point indicates where text you type will appear.

5 Type the text for your document.

Note: In this example, the size of text was changed to make the text easier to read. To change the size of text, see page 136.

SAVE A DOCUMENT

You can save your document to store it for future use. This allows you to later review and edit the document. When you save a document, you should use a descriptive name that will help you find the document later.

You may want to save a document as soon as you create the document and then regularly save your changes. If there is an equipment failure or power loss, you will lose the work you have completed since the last time you saved the document.

By default, Windows stores WordPad documents you save in the My Documents folder. You can choose to save your document in another location. For example, you may want to save a document you frequently work with on the desktop for easier access.

Can I save my document in a different format?

✔ WordPad automatically saves your document in the Word for Windows 6.0 format. To save your document in a different format, click the Save as type area in the Save As dialog box and then select the way you want to save the document.

SAVE A DOCUMENT

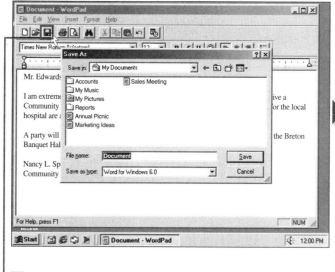

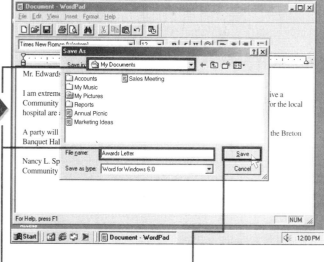

1 Click ▣ to save the document.

■ The Save As dialog box appears.

Note: If you previously saved the document, the Save As dialog box does not appear since you have already named the document.

2 Type a name for the document.

■ This area shows the location where WordPad will save the document. You can click this area to change the location.

3 Click Save to save the document.

OPEN A DOCUMENT

You can open a saved document to review and make changes to the document.

You can also open a new document to start writing a letter, memo or report. When you open a new document, you must choose the type of document you want to create.

The Word 6 Document type is the default document type for WordPad

documents and is useful if you plan to later work with the document in Microsoft Word version 6 or later. The Rich Text Document type can be used by many word processors, including some word processors for Macintosh computers. Rich text can contain formatting, such as bold or underlined text. The Text Document type can be used by all word processors but contains no formatting. The Unicode Text Document type allows you to create

documents using characters from different languages, such as Greek.

WordPad allows you to work with only one document at a time, so make sure you save the document you are working with before opening another. You can work with several documents at once by starting WordPad several times and opening a document in each program window.

OPEN A SAVED DOCUMENT

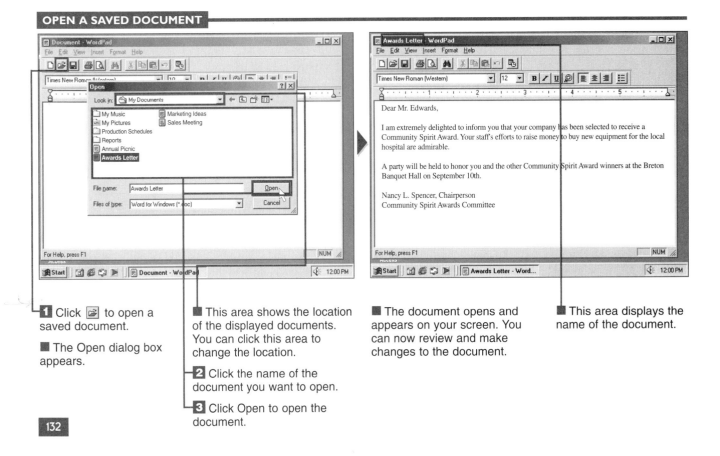

■ Click 📂 to open a saved document.

■ The Open dialog box appears.

■ This area shows the location of the displayed documents. You can click this area to change the location.

2 Click the name of the document you want to open.

3 Click Open to open the document.

■ The document opens and appears on your screen. You can now review and make changes to the document.

■ This area displays the name of the document.

Why can't I see the saved document I want to open?

✔ If the document you want to open is not listed in the Open dialog box, the document may have been saved as a different file type. To view all the documents in the current location, click the Files of type area and then select All Documents.

How do I print a document I have opened?

✔ Select the File menu and then click Print. In the Print dialog box, select the option for the pages you want to print and then click OK. You can also click the Print button ( ) to quickly print an entire document. To preview a document before printing, click the Print Preview button ( ).

Is there a faster way to open a saved document?

✔ The names of the last four documents you worked with in WordPad appear on the File menu. To open one of these documents, click the name of the document. The Start menu also displays the last 15 documents you worked with in Windows. To open one of these documents, click the Start button, select Documents and then click the name of the document you want to open.

OPEN A NEW DOCUMENT

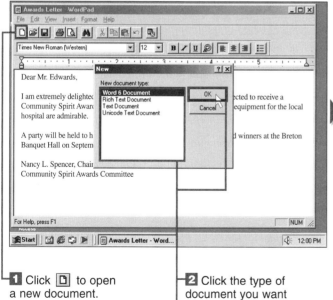

1 Click to open a new document.

■ The New dialog box appears.

2 Click the type of document you want to open.

3 Click OK.

■ A new document appears.

EDIT AND MOVE TEXT

The ability to edit a document makes a word processor a more powerful tool than a typewriter. You can insert, delete and reorganize the text in your document without having to retype the entire document.

You can add new text to a document. The existing text will shift to make room for the text you add.

You can delete text you no longer need from a document. The remaining text will shift to fill any empty spaces.

Moving text allows you to try out different ways of organizing the text in a document. You can find the most effective structure for a document by experimenting with different placements of sentences and paragraphs.

You can also place a copy of text in a different location in your document. This will save you time since you can repeat information without having to retype the text. If you plan to make major changes to a paragraph, you may want to copy the paragraph before you begin. This gives you two copies of the paragraph-the original paragraph and a paragraph with the changes.

EDIT TEXT

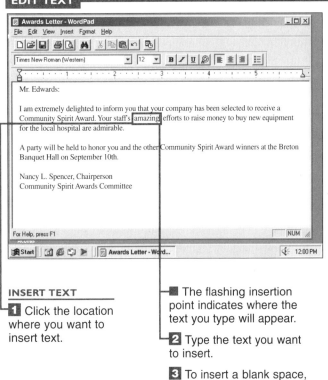

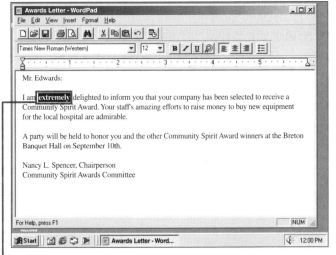

INSERT TEXT

1 Click the location where you want to insert text.

■ The flashing insertion point indicates where the text you type will appear.

2 Type the text you want to insert.

3 To insert a blank space, press the Spacebar.

DELETE TEXT

1 Select the text you want to delete.

2 Press the Delete key to remove the text.

■ To delete one character at a time, click to the left of the first character you want to delete. Press the Delete key for each character you want to remove.

How do I select text?

✔ To select a word, double-click the word. To select one line of text, click in the left margin beside the line you want to select. To select a paragraph, double-click in the left margin beside the paragraph you want to select. To select all the text in a document, choose the Edit menu and then click Select All. To select any amount of text, drag the mouse pointer until you highlight all the text you want to select.

Can I cancel a change I made?

✔ WordPad remembers the last change you made. Click the Undo button ( ) to cancel the last change you made. You can click the Undo button again to cancel previous changes.

How can I find or change every occurrence of a word or phrase in a document?

✔ To find every occurrence of a word or phrase in your document, click the Find button ( ). To change every occurrence of a word or phrase in your document, click the Edit menu and then choose Replace.

MOVE TEXT

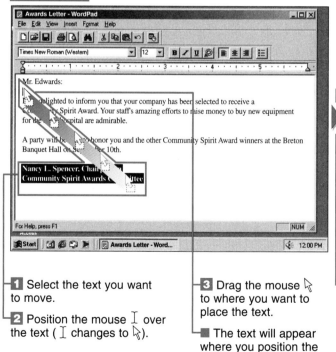

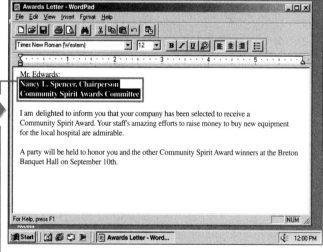

1 Select the text you want to move.

2 Position the mouse I over the text (I changes to).

3 Drag the mouse to where you want to place the text.

■ The text will appear where you position the insertion point on your screen.

■ The text moves to the new location.

■ To copy text, perform steps 1 to 3, except press and hold down the Ctrl key as you perform step 3.

FORMAT CHARACTERS

You can make text in your document look more attractive by using various fonts, sizes, styles and colors.

When you first enter text in WordPad, the text appears in the Times New Roman font. The default size for text is 10 points and the default color is black.

Several other fonts are also installed with Windows, including Arial and Courier New. The fonts available in WordPad depend on your printer and the setup of your computer.

WordPad measures the size of text in points. There are 72 points in one inch. Due to differences in design, two fonts may appear to be different sizes even though they are displayed using the same point size.

You can change the style of text using the Bold, Italic and Underline features. These features are often used to emphasize different types of text, such as titles.

You can change the color of text to draw attention to headings or important information in your document.

FORMAT CHARACTERS

CHANGE THE FONT

1 Select the text you want to change.

2 Click ▼ in this area to display a list of the available fonts.

3 Click the font you want to use.

■ The text changes to the new font.

CHANGE THE FONT SIZE

1 Select the text you want to change.

2 Click ▼ in this area to display a list of the available font sizes.

3 Click the font size you want to use.

■ The text changes to the new size.

How can I change the format of all the new text that I type in a document?

✔ Before you begin typing the text you want to format differently, select the format you want to use. Any new text you type will display the new format.

Is there another way that I can format selected text?

✔ Choose the Format menu and select Font. The Font dialog box appears allowing you to change the formatting of selected text. The dialog box also displays an area where you can preview the font settings you choose.

Can I add fonts to my computer?

✔ You can purchase fonts at most computer stores and obtain fonts on the Internet. To install fonts on your computer, see page 196. If you have installed other programs on your computer, WordPad can use the fonts provided with these programs.

Can I use colored text if I do not have a color printer?

✔ You can add color to your text, but any colors you add will appear as shades of gray when printed on a black-and-white printer. You can use color effectively in documents that you will only view on-screen.

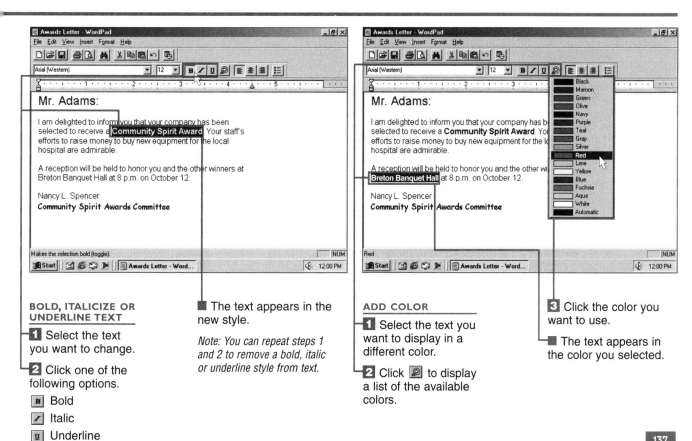

BOLD, ITALICIZE OR UNDERLINE TEXT

1 Select the text you want to change.

2 Click one of the following options.

B Bold

/ Italic

U Underline

■ The text appears in the new style.

Note: You can repeat steps 1 and 2 to remove a bold, italic or underline style from text.

ADD COLOR

1 Select the text you want to display in a different color.

2 Click 🖉 to display a list of the available colors.

3 Click the color you want to use.

■ The text appears in the color you selected.

FORMAT PARAGRAPHS

You can format the paragraphs in a WordPad document to help organize the document and make the document easier to read.

Aligning text allows you to line up the edge of a paragraph along a margin. Most documents are left aligned so the edge of each paragraph lines up along the left margin. Right alignment is often used to line up dates or addresses along the right margin. You can also center paragraphs between the left and right margins. Centering paragraphs is most effective for headings and titles. WordPad does not allow you to line up text along both the left and right margins at the same time.

You can change the tabs in your document. This is useful for lining up columns of information.

By default, WordPad sets a tab every 0.5 inches.

You can indent a paragraph from the left, right or both margins. Indenting paragraphs is often used to set apart quotations. You can indent just the first line of a paragraph so you do not need to press the Tab key at the beginning of every new paragraph.

FORMAT PARAGRAPHS

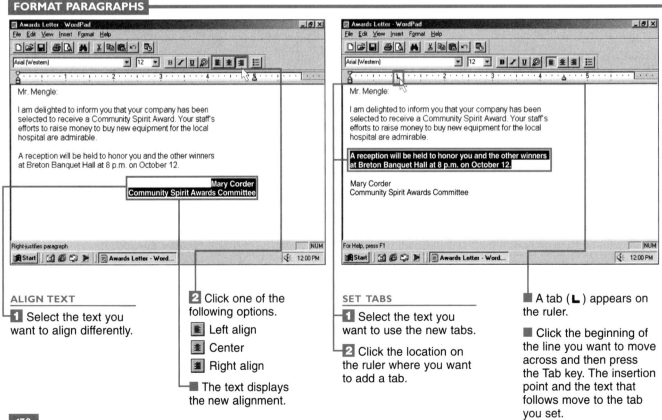

ALIGN TEXT

1 Select the text you want to align differently.

2 Click one of the following options.

- ▤ Left align
- ▤ Center
- ▤ Right align

■ The text displays the new alignment.

SET TABS

1 Select the text you want to use the new tabs.

2 Click the location on the ruler where you want to add a tab.

■ A tab (**L**) appears on the ruler.

■ Click the beginning of the line you want to move across and then press the Tab key. The insertion point and the text that follows move to the tab you set.

How do I display the ruler on my screen?

✔ From the View menu, select Ruler to display or hide the ruler. When the ruler is displayed, a check mark appears beside Ruler in the View menu.

Can I format more than one paragraph at a time?

✔ You can format as many paragraphs as you want. WordPad applies your changes to all the paragraphs that are currently selected.

How can I move or delete a tab?

✔ Select the text containing the tab you want to move or delete. To move a tab, drag the tab (**L**) to a new location on the ruler. To delete a tab, drag the tab off the ruler. Only tabs in the currently selected paragraphs are affected.

How can I clear all the tabs from a section of text?

✔ Select the text containing the tabs you want to remove. From the Format menu, select Tabs to display the Tabs dialog box. Then click the Clear All button. You can also use this dialog box to set tabs.

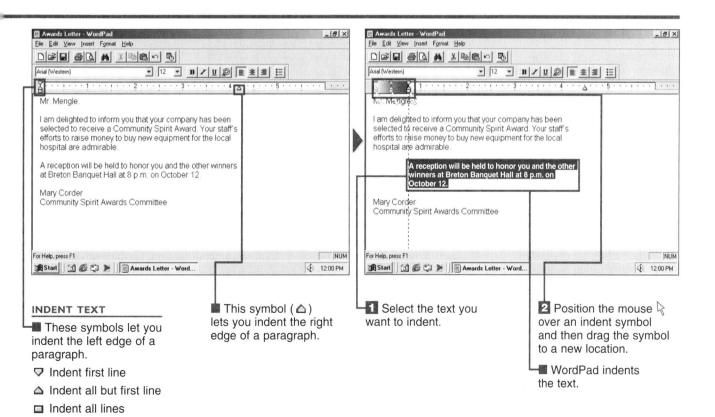

INDENT TEXT

■ These symbols let you indent the left edge of a paragraph.

▽ Indent first line

△ Indent all but first line

▢ Indent all lines

■ This symbol (△) lets you indent the right edge of a paragraph.

■1 Select the text you want to indent.

■2 Position the mouse ▷ over an indent symbol and then drag the symbol to a new location.

■ WordPad indents the text.

FORMAT PAGES

You can adjust the appearance of the pages in your document to suit your needs.

WordPad sets each page in your document to print on letter-sized paper. If you want to use a different paper size, you can change this setting. The available paper sizes depend on the printer you are using.

You can change the orientation of pages in your document. The Portrait orientation prints across the short side of a page and is used for most documents. The Landscape orientation prints across the long side of a page and is often used for certificates and tables.

You can change the margins to suit your document. A margin is the amount of space between text and

the edge of your paper. Changing margins lets you accommodate letterhead and other specialty paper.

The Page Setup dialog box displays a sample of how your document will appear when printed.

The changes you make affect the entire document.

FORMAT PAGES

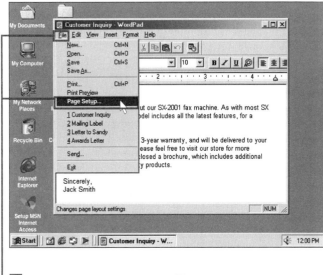

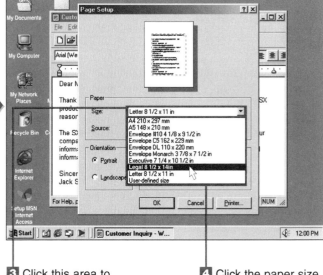

-1 Click File.

-2 Click Page Setup.

■ The Page Setup dialog box appears.

3 Click this area to display a list of the available paper sizes.

4 Click the paper size you want to use.

Can I change how WordPad measures the margins?

✔ From the View menu, select Options. Click the Options tab and select the preferred unit of measure. You can choose from inches, centimeters, points and picas. There are 72 points in one inch and 6 picas in one inch. The unit of measure you select will be used throughout WordPad.

How do I change the margins for only part of my document?

✔ If you want to change the left and right margins for only part of your document, you must change the indentation of the paragraphs. See page 138. You cannot change the top and bottom margins for only part of your document.

My printer stores letterhead in one location and plain paper in another. How can I tell WordPad which paper to use?

✔ In the Page Setup dialog box, click the area beside Source and then select the location of the paper you want to use to print the document.

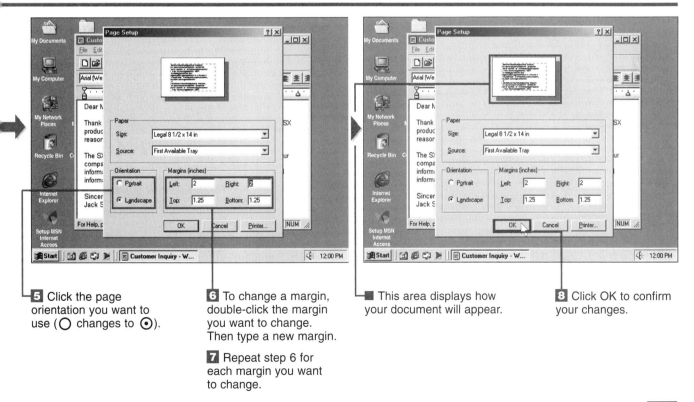

5 Click the page orientation you want to use (○ changes to ◉).

6 To change a margin, double-click the margin you want to change. Then type a new margin.

7 Repeat step 6 for each margin you want to change.

■ This area displays how your document will appear.

8 Click OK to confirm your changes.

START PAINT

Paint is a simple drawing program included with Windows that you can use to create and edit pictures. Pictures you create in Paint can be printed, inserted into other programs or displayed as wallpaper on your desktop.

A Paint picture is made up of a grid of tiny colored dots, called pixels. Paint uses the number of pixels from the left and top of the picture to indicate the position of the mouse pointer on your screen. You can view the

position of the mouse pointer at the bottom of the Paint window. Using the position can help you line up objects in your picture.

Although Paint offers many features to help you create pictures, you may want to obtain a more sophisticated image editing program, such as Jasc Paint Shop Pro or Adobe Photoshop. You can obtain Paint Shop Pro at the www.jasc.com Web site and Photoshop at the www.adobe.com Web site.

How do I close Paint?

✔ Before closing Paint, make sure you save any changes you made to the picture. To save a picture, see page 148. Click ☒ in the top right corner of the Paint window to close the program.

START PAINT

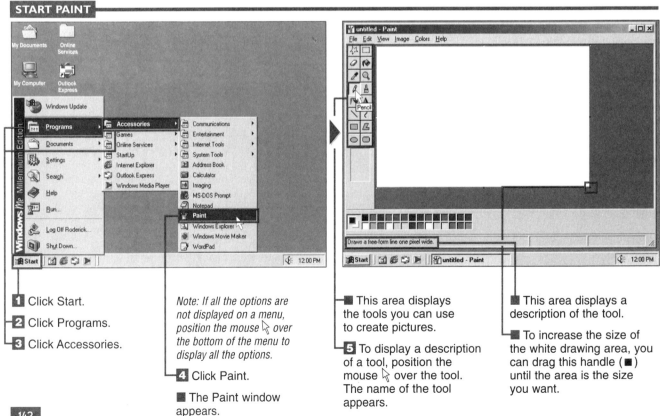

1 Click Start.

2 Click Programs.

3 Click Accessories.

Note: If all the options are not displayed on a menu, position the mouse over the bottom of the menu to display all the options.

4 Click Paint.

■ The Paint window appears.

■ This area displays the tools you can use to create pictures.

5 To display a description of a tool, position the mouse over the tool. The name of the tool appears.

■ This area displays a description of the tool.

■ To increase the size of the white drawing area, you can drag this handle (■) until the area is the size you want.

DRAW SHAPES

Y ou can use Paint's tools to draw shapes such as rectangles, rounded rectangles, circles, ellipses and polygons. You can use the Polygon tool to draw many different kinds of multi-sided shapes, ranging from simple triangles to complex objects.

Before you draw a shape, you can specify whether you want to outline the shape, fill the shape with a color or both. You can also specify the colors you want to use for the outline and the inside of the shape.

How do I draw a circle or a square?

✔ To draw a circle, select the Ellipse tool (⬭). To draw a square, select the Rectangle tool (⬜). Then press and hold down the Shift key as you draw the shape.

Can I change the border thickness of a shape?

✔ When you draw a shape, the border thickness is the same as the thickness currently selected for the Line or Curve tool. To change the border thickness, click the Line or Curve tool and then select the thickness you want in the area below the toolbox.

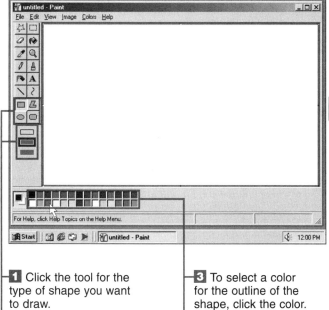

■1 Click the tool for the type of shape you want to draw.

■2 Click an option to specify if you want the shape to display an outline, an inside color or both.

■3 To select a color for the outline of the shape, click the color.

■4 To select a color for the inside of the shape, right-click the color.

■5 Position the mouse + where you want to begin drawing the shape.

■6 Drag the mouse + until the shape is the size you want.

■7 If you selected ◿ in step 1, repeat steps 5 and 6 until you finish drawing all the lines for the shape. Then immediately double-click the mouse to complete the shape.

DRAW LINES AND USE BRUSHES

You can draw three different types of lines in your pictures. You can draw pencil lines, straight lines and curved lines. You can also use brushes to paint brush strokes or spray areas of a picture.

The Pencil tool draws a thin line and allows you to draw lines and curves more freely than the Line or Curve tool.

The Line tool allows you to draw a perfectly straight line when you drag the mouse from one point to another.

When you use the Curve tool, the line begins as a perfectly straight line. You can then bend or twist the line to create the curve you want.

The Brush tool is similar to the Pencil tool, but it has many

different brush styles that you can choose from, including some that work like a calligraphy pen.

You can use the Airbrush tool to spray areas of color onto a picture and create shading effects. When using the Airbrush tool, the slower you drag the mouse, the darker the color appears in your picture.

DRAW LINES

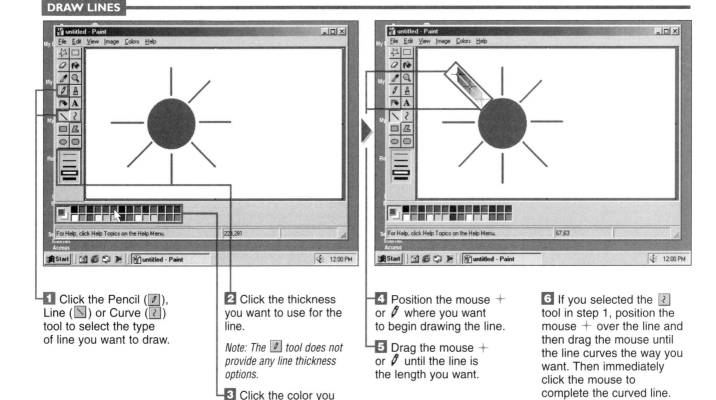

1 Click the Pencil (🖉), Line (◥) or Curve (◝) tool to select the type of line you want to draw.

2 Click the thickness you want to use for the line.

Note: The 🖉 tool does not provide any line thickness options.

3 Click the color you want to use for the line.

4 Position the mouse ✛ or 🖉 where you want to begin drawing the line.

5 Drag the mouse ✛ or 🖉 until the line is the length you want.

6 If you selected the ◝ tool in step 1, position the mouse ✛ over the line and then drag the mouse until the line curves the way you want. Then immediately click the mouse to complete the curved line.

How do I draw a perfectly horizontal line?

✔ You can draw perfectly horizontal, vertical or 45-degree diagonal lines by holding down the Shift key while you draw the line. This method works for the Pencil, Line and Curve tools only.

How can I zoom in to draw precise lines?

✔ Click the View menu, choose Zoom and then select Large Size. To access more zoom levels, click the View menu, choose Zoom and then select Custom. When you are finished, you can return to the normal zoom level. Click the View menu, choose Zoom and then select Normal Size.

How do I move an item in a picture?

✔ To move an item in a picture, click 🔲. Choose an option in the area below the toolbox to move the item with 🔳 or without 🔳 the background. To select the item, drag the mouse over the item until a line surrounds the item. Right-click the color you want to use to fill the space left after you move the item. Then position the mouse over the item and drag it to a new location.

USE BRUSHES

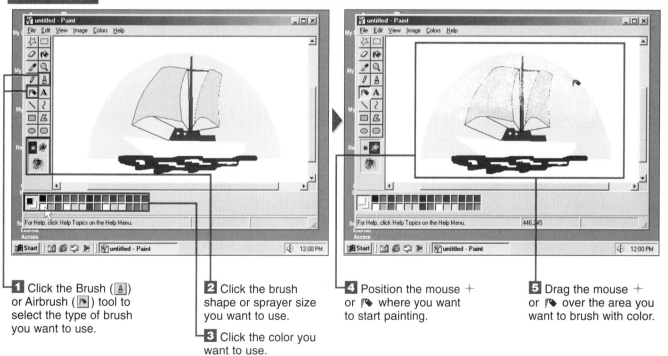

1 Click the Brush (🖌) or Airbrush (🖍) tool to select the type of brush you want to use.

2 Click the brush shape or sprayer size you want to use.

3 Click the color you want to use.

4 Position the mouse + or 🖍 where you want to start painting.

5 Drag the mouse + or 🖍 over the area you want to brush with color.

ADD TEXT

Y ou can add text to your picture to provide written information or explanations.

When adding text to a picture, you first need to create a text box that will hold the text. Text you type will automatically wrap to fit within the text box.

Paint does not have a spell-checker, so you should check the spelling of your text as you type the text. You will not be able to make changes to the text after you select another tool or click outside the text box.

Can I use text from another document?

✔ Yes. Open the program that contains the text and then select and copy the text. Display the Paint window and create a text box large enough to fit the text. Click the Edit menu and select Paste to place the text in the text box.

How can I format text?

✔ The Fonts toolbar appears when you add text to a picture. You can use the options on the toolbar to change the font, size and style of the text. If the Fonts toolbar does not appear, click the View menu and then select Text Toolbar.

ADD TEXT

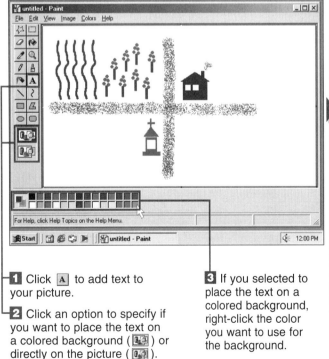

1 Click A to add text to your picture.

2 Click an option to specify if you want to place the text on a colored background (⬚) or directly on the picture (⬚).

3 If you selected to place the text on a colored background, right-click the color you want to use for the background.

4 Click the color you want to use for the text.

5 Position the mouse + where you want the top left corner of the text box to appear and then drag the mouse until the text box is the size you want.

6 Type the text.

7 Click outside the text box when you finish typing the text.

FILL AREA WITH COLOR

You can change the color of any solid object in a picture or any area that has a solid border.

If there are gaps in the border of the object you are filling with color, the color will leak out into the surrounding area. Make sure you fix the gaps in the object's border before you begin to fill the object with color.

Filling an area with color is useful if you want to color an entire object or create a pattern of colors between lines drawn inside an object.

You can also change the color of the entire background of your picture by clicking a blank area of your picture.

Can I copy a color from one area of my picture to another area?

✔ Yes. If you want several areas of your picture to display the same color, click 🖉 and then click the area displaying the color you want to copy. Then select 🖎 and click the area you want to display the color.

How do I cancel the last change I made?

✔ Click the Edit menu and then select Undo.

FILL AREA WITH COLOR

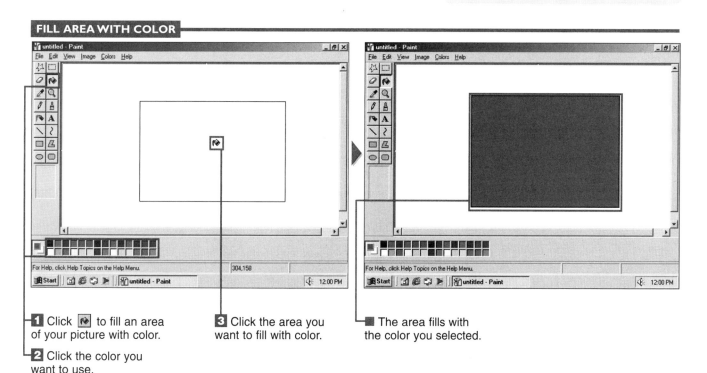

■1 Click 🖎 to fill an area of your picture with color.

■2 Click the color you want to use.

■3 Click the area you want to fill with color.

■ The area fills with the color you selected.

SAVE AND OPEN A PICTURE

You can save your picture to store it for future use. This allows you to later review and make changes to the picture. You should regularly save changes you make to a picture to avoid losing your work due to a computer problem or power failure.

Paint saves pictures you create in the bitmap format. Pictures stored in the bitmap format usually have the .bmp extension.

You should store your pictures in a location on your computer that will be easy to find. By default, Paint stores pictures you create in the My Pictures folder.

You can open a saved picture to display the picture on your screen. This allows you to review and make changes to the picture. In the Open dialog box, Windows displays a miniature version of each picture stored in the My Pictures folder.

Paint allows you to work with only one picture at a time. Make sure you save the picture you are currently working with before opening another picture. You can work with many pictures at the same time by starting the Paint program several times and opening a picture in each program window.

SAVE A PICTURE

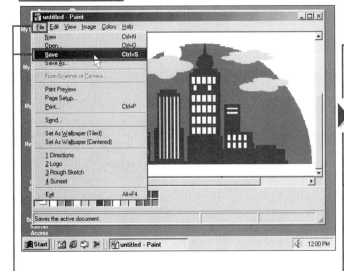

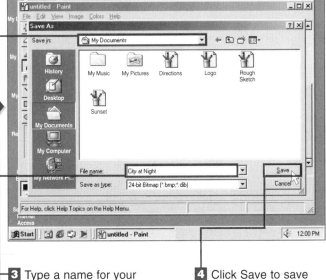

1 Click File.

2 Click Save.

■ The Save As dialog box appears.

Note: If you previously saved the picture, the Save As dialog box will not appear since you have already named the picture.

3 Type a name for your picture.

■ This area shows the location where Paint will store the picture. You can click this area to change the location.

4 Click Save to save your picture.

Is there a faster way to open a picture?

✔ The names of the last four pictures you opened in Paint appear on the File menu. Click the name of the picture you want to open.

Can I open a picture from a window or the desktop?

✔ You can open a picture from a window or the desktop by double-clicking the icon for the picture. Windows will display the picture in the Image Preview window, which allows you to preview the picture. To make changes to the picture, you must open the picture in Paint.

Can I change the number of colors used to save a picture?

✔ You can select the number of colors used to save a picture from the Save as type area in the Save As dialog box. Saving a picture with fewer colors results in a smaller file size.

How do I print a picture displayed on my screen?

✔ Select the File menu and then click Print. In the Print dialog box, click the OK button to print the picture. To preview the picture before printing, select the File menu and then click Print Preview.

OPEN A PICTURE

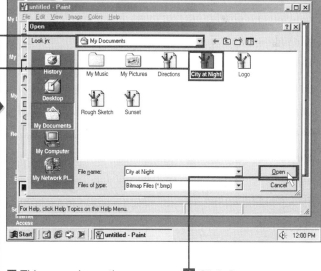

1 Click File.

2 Click Open.

■ The Open dialog box appears.

■ This area shows the location of the displayed pictures. You can click this area to change the location.

3 Click the picture you want to open.

4 Click Open to open the picture.

■ The picture opens and appears on your screen.

ERASE PART OF A PICTURE

Y ou can remove an area from your picture. Paint offers four different eraser sizes that you can use. Choose the small eraser size when you want to be precise in your erasing. The large eraser size is useful when you want to erase a large area of your picture.

You can use any color to erase an area of your picture. The

color you select should match the background color of your picture. For example, use a white eraser when the area you want to erase has a white background and a colored eraser when the area you want to erase has a colored background.

Is there another way to erase a large area of my picture?

✔ To select the area you want to erase, click the Select tool (▢) and then drag the mouse over the area you want to erase until a line surrounds the area. Right-click the color you want to use to erase the area and then press the Delete key.

ERASE PART OF A PICTURE

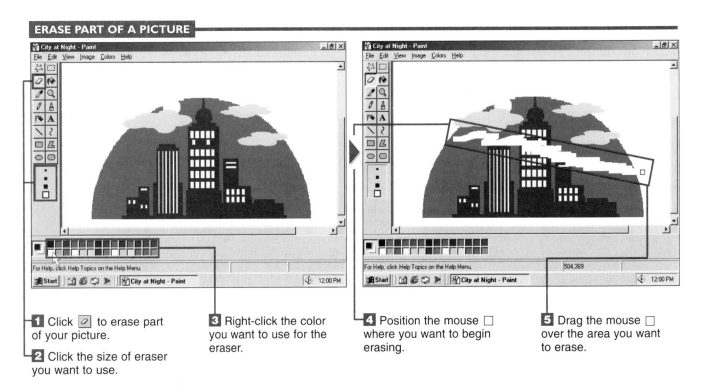

1 Click ⬚ to erase part of your picture.

2 Click the size of eraser you want to use.

3 Right-click the color you want to use for the eraser.

4 Position the mouse ⬚ where you want to begin erasing.

5 Drag the mouse ⬚ over the area you want to erase.

USE A PICTURE AS DESKTOP BACKGROUND

You can use any picture created in Paint as a background for your desktop. This is an easy way to customize your desktop.

Your picture will be the same size on the desktop as it appears in the Paint window.

Paint allows you to choose how the picture is displayed on your desktop. A picture can be tiled to cover the entire screen or centered on your desktop.

How can I remove a picture from my desktop background?

✔ You can use the Display Properties dialog box to remove a picture from your desktop background. Right-click a blank area of the desktop and then select Properties. On the Background tab, choose None from the list of wallpaper and then click OK.

Can I change the size of a picture I have created?

✔ Yes. Click the Image menu and select Stretch/Skew. In the Stretch area, change the horizontal and vertical percentages to increase or decrease the size of the picture.

USE A PICTURE AS DESKTOP BACKGROUND

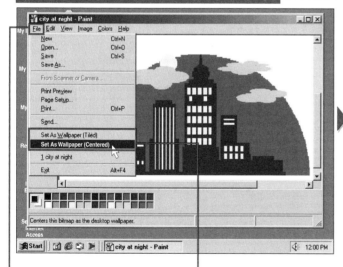

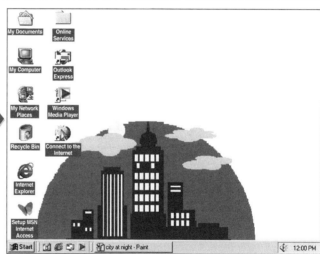

■ You must save a picture before you can use the picture as your desktop background. To save a picture, see page 148.

1 Click File.

2 Click the wallpaper option you want to use.

Tiled - Repeats picture to cover the desktop.

Centered - Displays picture centered on the desktop.

■ The picture appears on your desktop.

USING CALCULATOR

Windows provides a calculator to help you perform calculations. You can work with the Calculator in either the Standard or Scientific view.

The Calculator's Standard view allows you to perform basic mathematical calculations. In this view, the Calculator resembles a small handheld calculator.

You can use the Scientific view to perform more complex mathematical calculations. This view lets you calculate factorial numbers, numbers raised to an exponent, sines, cosines or tangents of numbers and much more.

You can enter information into the Calculator by using your mouse to click the Calculator buttons or by using the keys on your keyboard,

including the keys on the numeric keypad. To be able to enter numbers using the numeric keypad, the Num Lock setting must be on. A status light on the keyboard indicates this setting is on. You may need to press the Num Lock key on your keyboard to turn on the setting.

The result of each calculation you perform appears at the top of the Calculator window.

USING CALCULATOR

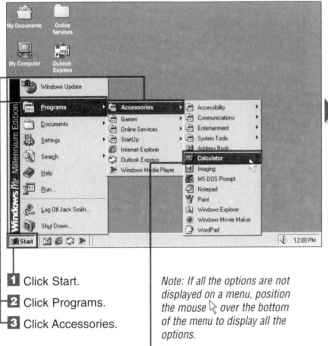

1 Click Start.

2 Click Programs.

3 Click Accessories.

Note: If all the options are not displayed on a menu, position the mouse ⌕ over the bottom of the menu to display all the options.

4 Click Calculator.

■ The Calculator window appears.

5 To enter information into the Calculator, click each button as you would press the buttons on a handheld calculator.

Note: You can also use the keys on your keyboard to enter information.

■ This area displays the numbers you enter and the result of each calculation.

■ You can click [C] to start a new calculation at any time.

How can I determine what a button on the Calculator does?

✔ Right-click a button of interest. A box containing the text "What's This?" appears. Click this box to display information about the button. You can click a blank area on your screen to remove the information.

Can I have the Calculator display commas in large numbers?

✔ Yes. Using commas can help make the numbers displayed in the Calculator window easier to read. To display commas, choose the View menu and select Digit grouping.

How can I copy the result of a calculation into another program?

✔ To copy the result of a calculation, press Ctrl+C on the keyboard. In the other program, position the insertion point where you want to paste the result and then press Ctrl+V on the keyboard. You can also use this technique to copy a number you have selected from another program into the Calculator.

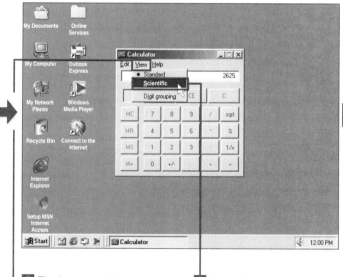

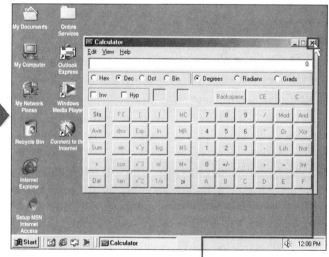

6 To change to the Scientific view of the Calculator, click View.

7 Click Scientific.

■ The Scientific view of the Calculator appears. This view offers additional features that allow you to perform advanced scientific and statistical calculations.

Note: To return to the Standard view, perform steps 6 and 7, selecting Standard in step 7.

8 When you finish using the Calculator, click ☒ to close the Calculator window.

USING NOTEPAD

Notepad is a fast and easy-to-use text editor that can help you accomplish many tasks. Notepad does not require a lot of your computer's resources to run.

You can use Notepad to create text documents that do not require formatting and are smaller than 64 K. Most word processors and desktop publishing programs can

open documents created in Notepad. Notepad can also be used to create and edit Web pages and to view .log and .ini files.

By default, Notepad displays each paragraph in a document on one line. To read an entire line, you have to scroll from left to right in the window. You can use Notepad's Word Wrap feature to wrap the text to fit in the window.

Wrapping text can make the document easier to read.

You can have Notepad enter the current time and date set in your computer into a document. This is useful if you use Notepad to create Web pages and want to quickly record when the page was created.

USING NOTEPAD

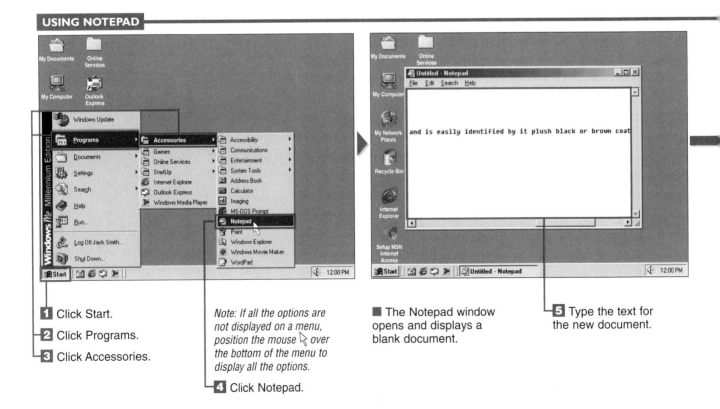

1 Click Start.

2 Click Programs.

3 Click Accessories.

Note: If all the options are not displayed on a menu, position the mouse ⟍ over the bottom of the menu to display all the options.

4 Click Notepad.

■ The Notepad window opens and displays a blank document.

5 Type the text for the new document.

How do I save a document in Notepad?

✔ Choose the File menu and then select Save. The first time you save a document, the Save As dialog box appears, allowing you to name the document.

How do I open a document I previously saved?

✔ Choose the File menu, select Open and then double-click the document you want to open. Notepad lets you work with only one document at a time. If you are currently working with a document, save the document before opening another.

Is there a way to have Notepad automatically enter the time and date into my document?

✔ If you type .LOG on the first line of a document, Notepad will add the current time and date to the end of the document each time you open the document.

How can I find a word in a Notepad document?

✔ Click at the beginning of the document. Then choose the Search menu and select Find to search for a specific word.

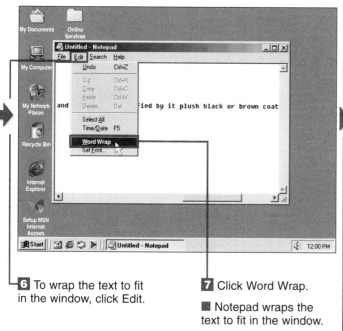

6 To wrap the text to fit in the window, click Edit.

7 Click Word Wrap.

■ Notepad wraps the text to fit in the window.

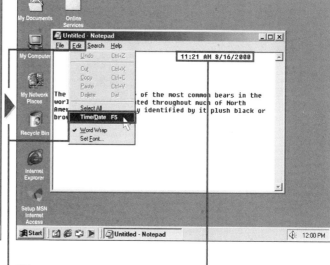

8 To insert the current time and date at the location of the flashing insertion point, click Edit.

9 Click Time/Date.

■ Notepad inserts the current time and date into your document.

Note: You can also press the F5 key to insert the current time and date.

USING CHARACTER MAP

You can use Character Map to include special characters in your documents that are not available on your keyboard. Special characters can include upper and lower case accented letters such as é, graphical characters such as ✍, one character fractions such as ¼ and symbols such as ©.

There are many sets of characters, or fonts, that you can choose from.

The Character Map window displays all of the characters for each font. Many fonts contain regular numbers and letters in addition to the special characters, while some fonts contain only special characters. For example, the Wingdings font contains a variety of bullet characters and arrows.

You can view an enlarged version of each character a font offers.

This can help you select the characters you want to add to your documents.

Once you have selected the special characters you want to use, you can copy the special characters from Character Map and paste them into your documents. Keep in mind that you can only paste characters into documents created in Windows-based programs.

USING CHARACTER MAP

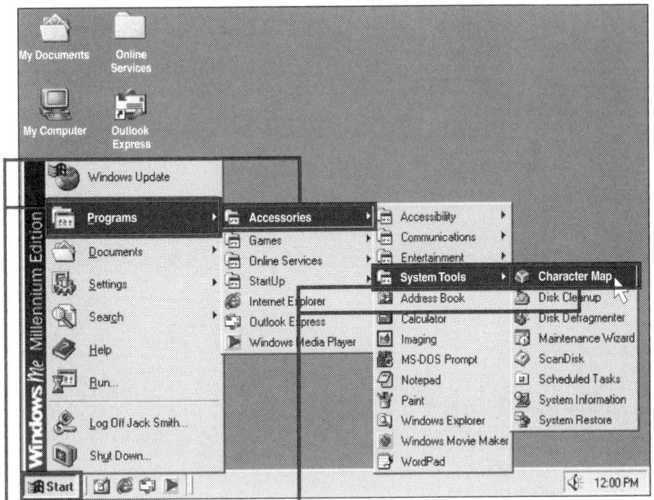

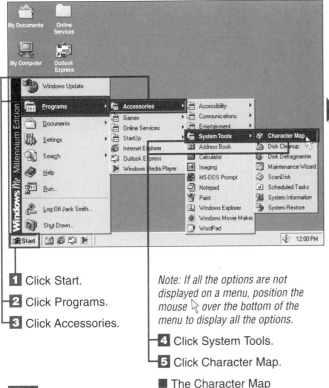

1 Click Start.

2 Click Programs.

3 Click Accessories.

Note: If all the options are not displayed on a menu, position the mouse over the bottom of the menu to display all the options.

4 Click System Tools.

5 Click Character Map.

■ The Character Map window appears.

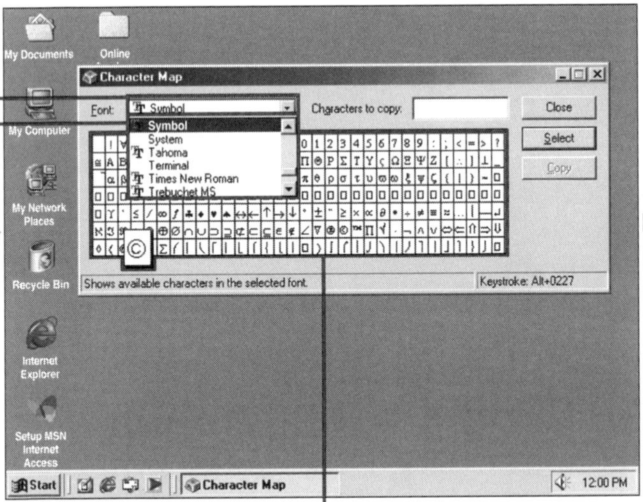

6 Click this area to display a list of the available fonts.

7 Click the font that contains the set of characters you want to display.

■ This area displays the characters for the font you selected.

8 To display an enlarged version of a character, position the mouse over the character and then hold down the left mouse button.

MASTER VISUALLY WINDOWS ME

Why isn't Character Map displayed on the Start menu?

✔ You need to add the Character Map component to your computer. Character Map is found in the System Tools category. To add Windows components, see page 538.

How can I make Character Map easier to access?

✔ If you use Character Map regularly, you can leave it open on the desktop or minimize it to a button on the taskbar. You can also have the Character Map start automatically each time you start Windows. See page 238 to start a program automatically.

Can I add special characters to a document without opening Character Map?

✔ Many special characters have a keystroke combination you can use to quickly add the character to a document. For example, to enter the copyright sign ©, hold down the Alt key as you enter 0169. When you click a character in the Character Map window, the combination for the character appears in the bottom right corner of the window. When using a keystroke combination, make sure you use the numeric keypad on your keyboard to enter numbers. Also, make sure the fonts selected in Character Map and in the document you are entering the character into are the same.

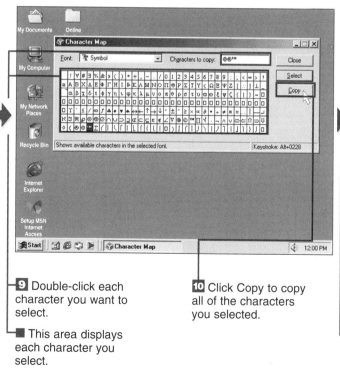

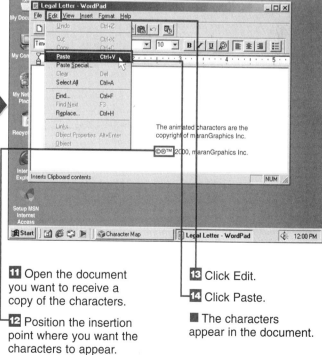

-9 Double-click each character you want to select.

■ This area displays each character you select.

10 Click Copy to copy all of the characters you selected.

11 Open the document you want to receive a copy of the characters.

-12 Position the insertion point where you want the characters to appear.

13 Click Edit.

-14 Click Paste.

■ The characters appear in the document.

USING CLIPBOARD VIEWER

You can use Clipboard Viewer to view and save the information currently stored in the Clipboard.

The Clipboard temporarily stores the last item you selected to copy or move. Most programs can access and use the information stored in the Clipboard.

The information that appears in the Clipboard Viewer window

depends on the type of item you placed in the Clipboard. When you place an item such as an image or text in the Clipboard, you can view the entire item. When you place an item such as a file or folder in the Clipboard, you can view only the path of the item, which indicates the location and name of the file or folder.

When you place part of a sound file in the Clipboard, you can

view only the icon that represents the item. When you place part of a video file in the Clipboard, you may be able to view a frame from the video.

You can save information stored in the Clipboard and reuse the information later. The information will be saved in a file with the .clp extension.

USING CLIPBOARD VIEWER

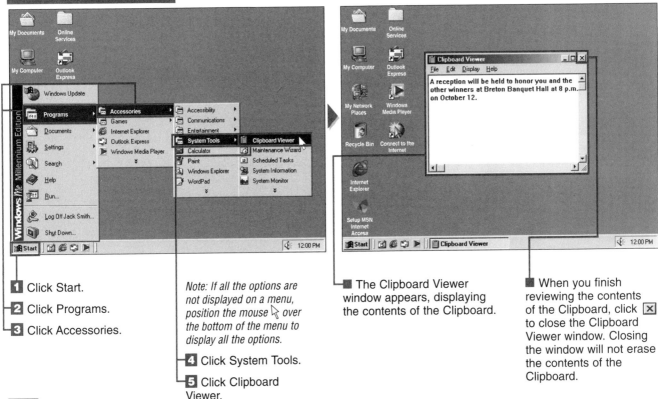

1 Click Start.

2 Click Programs.

3 Click Accessories.

Note: If all the options are not displayed on a menu, position the mouse ⃕ over the bottom of the menu to display all the options.

4 Click System Tools.

5 Click Clipboard Viewer.

■ The Clipboard Viewer window appears, displaying the contents of the Clipboard.

■ When you finish reviewing the contents of the Clipboard, click ☒ to close the Clipboard Viewer window. Closing the window will not erase the contents of the Clipboard.

Why isn't Clipboard Viewer on the Start menu?

✔ You may need to install the Clipboard Viewer component on your computer. The Clipboard Viewer component is located in the System Tools category on your computer. To add a Windows component, see page 538.

How long does information stay in the Clipboard?

✔ The Clipboard stores one item at a time. When you move or copy a new item, the new item replaces the item currently stored in the Clipboard. When you shut down Windows, the item stored in the Clipboard is deleted.

How do I open a Clipboard file I saved?

✔ In the Clipboard Viewer window, select the File menu and then click Open. In the Open dialog box, double-click the Clipboard file you want to open.

Why does the image appear distorted in the Clipboard Viewer window?

✔ Clipboard Viewer automatically sizes images to fit the window. In some cases, you can choose the Display menu and then select the DIB Bitmap or Bitmap command to display the image at the original size. You can also resize the window to change the size of the image.

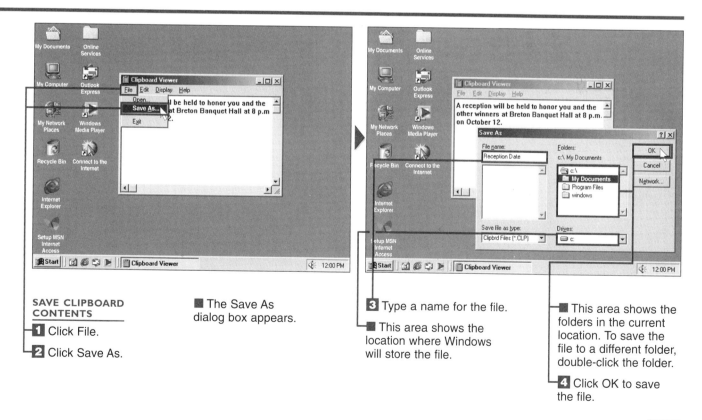

SAVE CLIPBOARD CONTENTS

1 Click File.

2 Click Save As.

■ The Save As dialog box appears.

3 Type a name for the file.

■ This area shows the location where Windows will store the file.

■ This area shows the folders in the current location. To save the file to a different folder, double-click the folder.

4 Click OK to save the file.

USING IMAGING

You can use Imaging to view and work with images stored on your computer, such as pictures you have copied from a digital camera or documents you have scanned using a scanner.

You can open most image formats in Imaging, including the JPEG, GIF, BMP and TIFF formats. You can change the

way an image appears on your screen in Imaging. For example, you can magnify or reduce the size of the image and rotate the image to the left or right.

Imaging also allows you to add text to an image. Information you add to an image is called an annotation. Adding annotations is useful when you want an image to contain your remarks

and comments. For example, you can add notes to a scanned document. You can save or print an annotation with an image. You can only add annotations to images saved in the BMP or TIFF format.

USING IMAGING

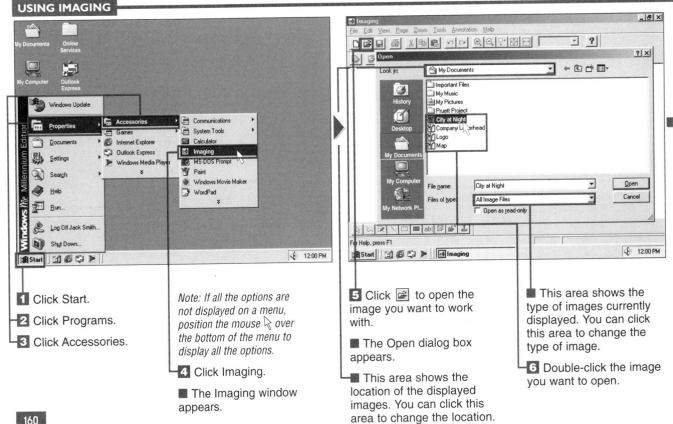

1 Click Start.

2 Click Programs.

3 Click Accessories.

Note: If all the options are not displayed on a menu, position the mouse ⟍ over the bottom of the menu to display all the options.

4 Click Imaging.

■ The Imaging window appears.

5 Click 📂 to open the image you want to work with.

■ The Open dialog box appears.

■ This area shows the location of the displayed images. You can click this area to change the location.

■ This area shows the type of images currently displayed. You can click this area to change the type of image.

6 Double-click the image you want to open.

How do I size an image to fit on my screen?

✔ You can click 🔲 to view the entire image on your screen or you can click 🔲 to make the image fit the width of your screen.

What other annotations can I add to an image?

✔ You can add a note or a rubber stamp to your image. To add a note, click 🗗 and then click where you want the note to appear. Type the text for the note and then click 🔲. To add a rubber stamp, click 🔲 and select the stamp you want to use. Click where you want the stamp to appear and then click 🔲.

Can I move or delete an annotation?

✔ Yes. Click the Annotation Selection tool (🔲). To move an annotation, drag the annotation to a new position. To delete an annotation, click the annotation and then press the Delete key. You cannot move or delete annotations that have been saved with a BMP image.

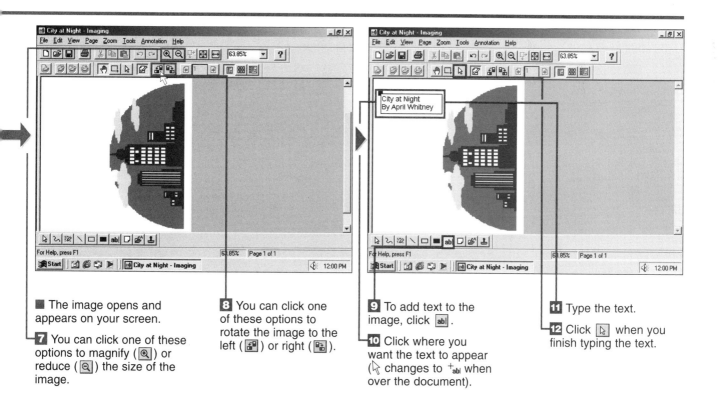

■ The image opens and appears on your screen.

7 You can click one of these options to magnify (🔍) or reduce (🔍) the size of the image.

8 You can click one of these options to rotate the image to the left (🔲) or right (🔲).

9 To add text to the image, click 🔲.

10 Click where you want the text to appear (🔲 changes to ⁺ₐᵦₗ when over the document).

11 Type the text.

12 Click 🔲 when you finish typing the text.

USING PHONE DIALER

You can use Phone Dialer to make telephone calls. To use Phone Dialer, you must have a modem installed on your computer and you need to connect your telephone to the modem. When you use Phone Dialer to make a call, you can pick up the telephone receiver to talk.

Phone Dialer allows you to enter a phone number in

several ways. You can enter the phone number using the number keys in the numeric keypad on your keyboard. You can also use the mouse to click the numbers on the dial pad in the Phone Dialer window.

You can create speed-dial buttons to store phone numbers you dial frequently. When you store a number in a speed-dial button, you can click the button

to quickly dial the phone number.

You can have other programs that use the telephone line open at the same time you use Phone Dialer, but only one program can use the telephone line at a time.

USING PHONE DIALER

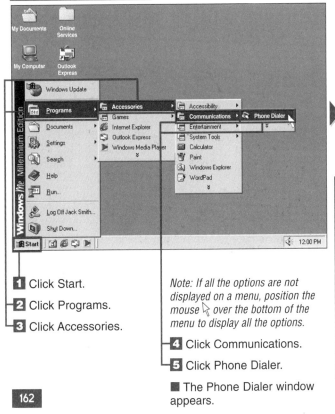

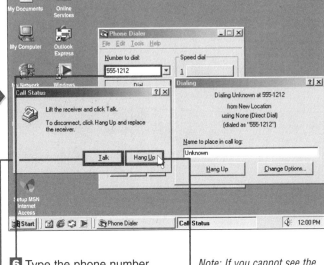

■ Click Start.

■ Click Programs.

■ Click Accessories.

Note: If all the options are not displayed on a menu, position the mouse over the bottom of the menu to display all the options.

■ Click Communications.

■ Click Phone Dialer.

■ The Phone Dialer window appears.

■ Type the phone number you want to dial and then press the Enter key.

■ The Dialing and Call Status dialog boxes appear.

■ Lift the receiver of your telephone and click Talk.

Note: If you cannot see the Talk button, click the Call Status button on the taskbar to display the Call Status dialog box.

■ When you finish with the call, click Hang Up and replace the receiver.

How can I view a list of my phone calls?

✔ In the Phone Dialer window, choose the Tools menu and then select Show Log to display a list of all your phone calls.

Is there a quick way to dial a phone number I recently called?

✔ Phone Dialer stores the phone numbers you recently called. In the Phone Dialer window, click ▼ in the Number to dial area. Select the number you want to dial and press the Enter key.

How can I change the information stored in my speed-dial buttons?

✔ In the Phone Dialer window, click Edit. In the Edit Speed Dial dialog box, click the speed-dial button you want to change and enter the new information. Then click Save.

How can I stop Phone Dialer from treating a local call as a long-distance call?

✔ Phone Dialer will automatically dial a 1 before any area codes that differ from yours. In the Phone Dialer window, click the Tools menu and then select Dialing Properties. Click the Area Code Rules button and then click the New button beside Do not dial 1 for numbers with the following area codes. Then enter the area code you want to treat as a local call.

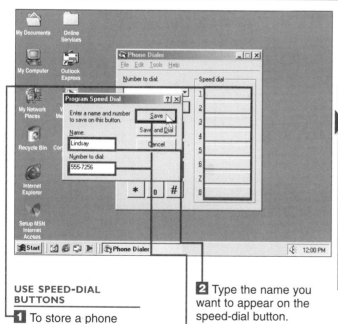

USE SPEED-DIAL BUTTONS

■1 To store a phone number you frequently dial, click an empty speed-dial button.

■ The Program Speed Dial dialog box appears.

■2 Type the name you want to appear on the speed-dial button.

■3 Click this area and then type the phone number.

■4 Click Save to save the information.

■ The name you entered appears on the button.

■ To dial a stored phone number, click the speed-dial button for the number.

163

SET THE DATE AND TIME

Y ou can set the correct date and time in your computer. Setting the correct date and time is important because Windows uses this information to identify when you create and update files. If your computer's calendar and clock are accurate, you will be able to find your files more easily.

Your computer maintains the date and time even when you turn off your computer. Windows also

adjusts the time automatically to compensate for daylight savings time. When you turn on your computer after daylight savings time occurs, Windows will display a message indicating that the clock settings were updated.

Windows uses four digits to display the year. This allows Windows to work properly with dates before and after the year 2000.

If complete accuracy of your computer's clock is important to you, there are programs available that will synchronize your computer's clock with one of the very precise clocks on the Internet.

SET THE DATE AND TIME

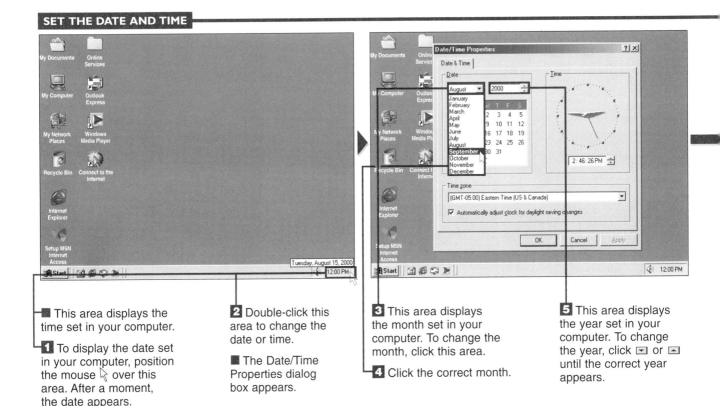

■ This area displays the time set in your computer.

1 To display the date set in your computer, position the mouse ⌖ over this area. After a moment, the date appears.

2 Double-click this area to change the date or time.

■ The Date/Time Properties dialog box appears.

3 This area displays the month set in your computer. To change the month, click this area.

4 Click the correct month.

5 This area displays the year set in your computer. To change the year, click ▾ or ▴ until the correct year appears.

How can I remove the clock from my taskbar?

✔ Right-click an empty area of the taskbar. From the menu that appears, click Properties. In the Taskbar and Start Menu Properties dialog box, click the Show clock option (☑ changes to ☐).

How can Windows help me get to my appointments on time?

✔ There are many time management programs, such as Microsoft Outlook and Lotus Organizer, that use the date and time set in your computer to keep track of your appointments. These programs usually provide audio and visual warnings in advance of your scheduled appointments.

Can I change the format Windows uses to display the date and time?

✔ You can have Windows display a shorter version of the date or use a 24-hour clock format to display the time. Click Start, choose Settings and then select Control Panel. In the Control Panel window, double-click the Regional Settings icon. In the Regional Settings Properties dialog box, use the options on the Date and Time tabs to change the format of the date and time. For more information, see page 166.

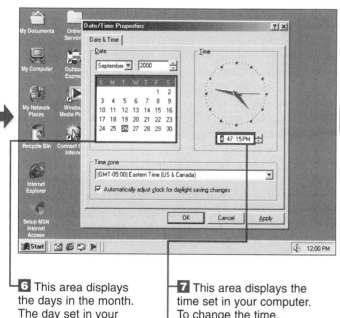

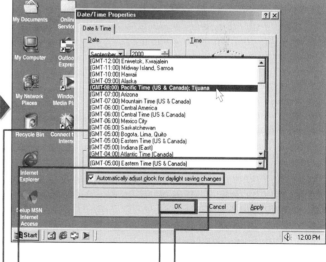

6 This area displays the days in the month. The day set in your computer is highlighted. To change the day, click the correct day.

7 This area displays the time set in your computer. To change the time, double-click the part of the time you want to change.

8 Type the correct information.

9 This area displays the time zone set in your computer. To change the time zone, click this area.

10 Click the correct time zone.

11 Windows will automatically adjust the computer's clock for daylight savings time. You can click this option to turn off the option (☑ changes to ☐).

12 Click OK to confirm all your changes.

CHANGE REGIONAL SETTINGS

You can change the way numbers, currency, times and dates are displayed on your computer. This allows you to use the settings common to your language and region of the world.

When you select a new language and geographic region for your computer, Windows displays a preview of how the new settings will affect numbers, currency, times and dates. The new settings

may also affect how these items are sorted in some programs.

Most North Americans use a period (.) to indicate the decimal point and a comma (,) to separate large numbers. These settings are not universal. In fact, in many regions, these settings are reversed.

When you receive a document from a computer set to a different language, Windows may adjust some of the numbers, currency,

times and dates in the document to the language and region you have selected.

Changing regional settings only affects the way programs display numbers, currency, times and dates. To change the language displayed in items such as menus and the Help feature, you must install Windows and your favorite programs in the language you want to use.

CHANGE REGIONAL SETTINGS

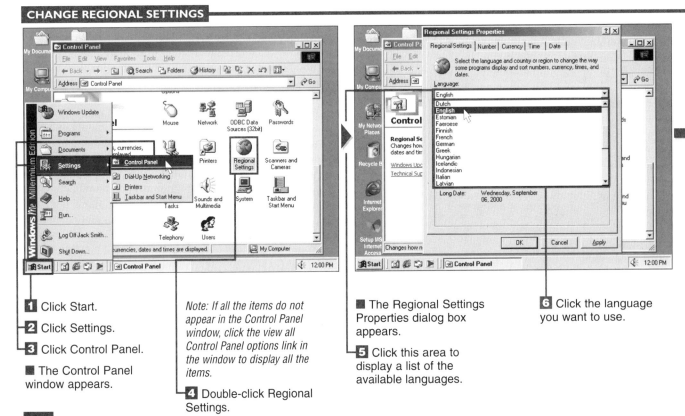

■ Click Start.

■ Click Settings.

■ Click Control Panel.

■ The Control Panel window appears.

Note: If all the items do not appear in the Control Panel window, click the view all Control Panel options link in the window to display all the items.

■ Double-click Regional Settings.

■ The Regional Settings Properties dialog box appears.

■ Click this area to display a list of the available languages.

■ Click the language you want to use.

Can I use my keyboard to enter text in another language?

✔ Yes. You can change your keyboard language settings to work with the language you selected. This allows you to use the keyboard layout and any special characters for the language. In the Control Panel window, double-click Keyboard. In the Keyboard Properties dialog box, select the Language tab. Click the Add button and then select the language you want to work with. An icon appears on the taskbar that allows you to easily switch between keyboard language settings. You will need to install the Multilanguage Support component to enter text in non-Latin alphabets. To install Windows components, see page 538.

Can I customize the regional settings?

✔ Yes. You can use the Regional Settings Properties dialog box to customize some number, currency, time and date settings to your own personal preference. For example, to change the clock to a 24-hour clock, click the Time tab and then select a time style where the hours are represented by the capital letter H.

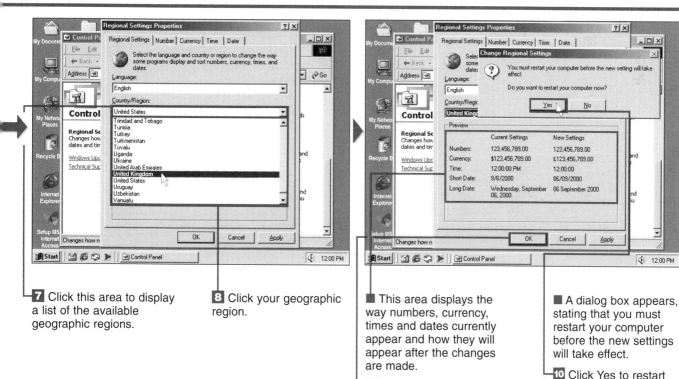

■7 Click this area to display a list of the available geographic regions.

■8 Click your geographic region.

■ This area displays the way numbers, currency, times and dates currently appear and how they will appear after the changes are made.

■9 Click OK to confirm your changes.

■ A dialog box appears, stating that you must restart your computer before the new settings will take effect.

■10 Click Yes to restart your computer now.

CHANGE YOUR DESKTOP BACKGROUND

Like hanging posters on your walls or placing pictures on your desk, you can customize the Windows desktop to create a friendly and personalized working environment.

Wallpaper is an image or Web page you display on your desktop. You can center a large image on the desktop or tile a small image so it repeats over the entire desktop. You can also stretch an image to cover your desktop.

You can search the Internet for sites providing images you can use as wallpaper. Collections of clip art and photographs found in computer stores can also be used as wallpaper.

You can create personal wallpaper from photographs or your own artwork by using a scanner. You can also create wallpaper images using the Paint program included with Windows. Windows automatically adds any image

you save in Paint to the list of available wallpaper.

When you select a wallpaper image, Windows may ask you to turn on the Active Desktop feature. This feature allows you to display Web page content that updates automatically on your desktop.

CHANGE YOUR DESKTOP BACKGROUND

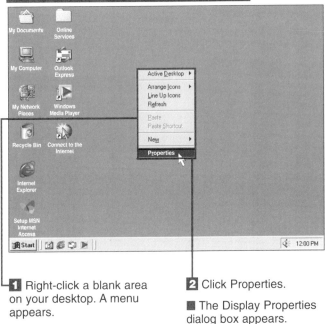

1 Right-click a blank area on your desktop. A menu appears.

2 Click Properties.

■ The Display Properties dialog box appears.

3 Click the wallpaper you want to use.

4 Click this area to select how you want to display the wallpaper on your desktop.

5 Click the way you want to display the wallpaper.

Center - Places wallpaper in the middle of your desktop.

Tile - Repeats wallpaper until it covers your entire desktop.

Stretch - Stretches wallpaper to cover your entire desktop.

How do I use clip art, scanned photographs or images stored on my computer as wallpaper?

✔ In the Display Properties dialog box, click the Browse button to locate the image you want to use. You can use many different types of images, including images with the .bmp, .gif, .jpg, .dib, .png or .htm extension.

Does Windows provide additional wallpaper that I can use?

✔ You can add more wallpaper to the Display Properties dialog box by installing the Desktop Wallpaper component, which is located in the Accessories category. To add a Windows component, see page 538.

Can I display patterns on my desktop?

✔ You can select a pattern to add a design to your desktop. A pattern alternates between black and the color of the background. In the Display Properties dialog box, click the Pattern button and then select the pattern you want to use.

How can I use an image displayed on a Web page as my wallpaper?

✔ When viewing a page on the Web, right-click the image you want to use as your wallpaper. On the menu that appears, click Set as Wallpaper.

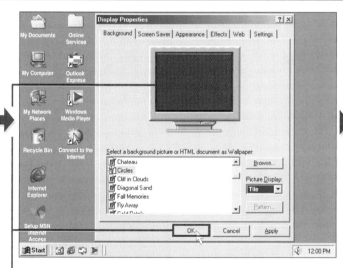

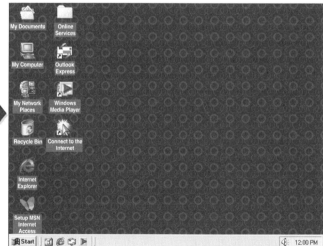

■ This area displays how the wallpaper you selected will look on your desktop.

6 Click OK to confirm your changes.

■ A dialog box appears if the wallpaper you selected requires you to enable the Active Desktop feature.

7 Click Yes to enable the Active Desktop feature.

■ Your desktop displays the wallpaper you selected.

■ To remove wallpaper from your desktop, perform steps 1 to 3, selecting (None) in step 3. Then perform step 6.

CHANGE SCREEN COLORS

You can change the colors displayed on your screen to personalize and enhance Windows.

Windows offers several schemes that you can choose from. A scheme is a pre-defined screen appearance that includes colors, text sizes and styles. Choosing a scheme allows you to make adjustments to many screen elements in one step.

High Contrast schemes are designed for people with vision impairments. High color schemes are designed for computers displaying more than 256 colors. VGA schemes are designed for computers limited to 16 colors. For information on changing the number of colors your computer displays, see page 174.

You can change the font, size, color and style of individual items

to create your own unique scheme. For example, if you find the text on menus and under icons too small to read or have trouble clicking small buttons, you can change the size of these items to suit your needs and preferences.

CHANGE SCREEN COLORS

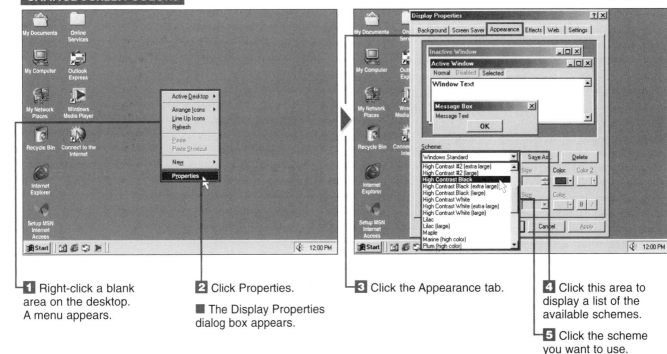

1 Right-click a blank area on the desktop. A menu appears.

2 Click Properties.

■ The Display Properties dialog box appears.

3 Click the Appearance tab.

4 Click this area to display a list of the available schemes.

5 Click the scheme you want to use.

How do I change my screen back to the original scheme?

✔ In the Display Properties dialog box, select the Windows Standard scheme to return to the original scheme.

How can I save the changes I have made to a scheme?

✔ In the Display Properties dialog box, click Save As to save the changes you made to a scheme. Windows will not display a warning if this procedure will replace a scheme that already exists. If you do not want to replace an existing scheme, make sure you use a different name when saving the scheme.

Why are some options in the Display Properties dialog box unavailable?

✔ Some options do not apply to certain items. For example, if an item does not display text, such as the scrollbar, then you cannot change the font, size, color or style of the text for the item. The number of colors your screen displays may also affect which options are available.

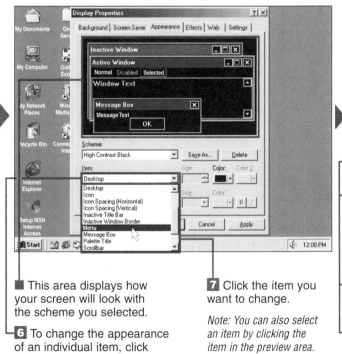

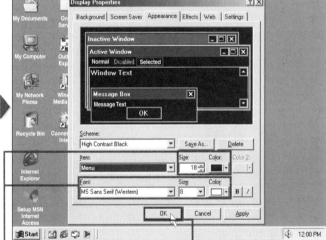

■ This area displays how your screen will look with the scheme you selected.

6 To change the appearance of an individual item, click this area.

7 Click the item you want to change.

Note: You can also select an item by clicking the item in the preview area.

8 Use these options to change the size and color of the item you selected.

9 Use these options to change the font, size, color and style of text in the item you selected.

Note: The available options depend on the item you selected.

10 Repeat steps 6 to 9 for each item you want to change.

11 Click OK to confirm your changes.

CHANGE THE SCREEN RESOLUTION

You can change the screen resolution to adjust the size of the image displayed on your screen. Your monitor and video card determine which screen resolutions you can use.

Screen resolution is measured by the number of horizontal and vertical pixels. A pixel is the smallest point on a screen. The most common screen resolutions

are 640 by 480 pixels and 800 by 600 pixels.

Lower screen resolutions display larger images so you can see the information on your screen more clearly. Some games are designed to run at a specific screen resolution. You may need to use a lower resolution to have a game fill your entire screen.

Higher screen resolutions display smaller images so you can display more information on your screen at once. A higher resolution allows you to see more of a word processing document or more cells in a spreadsheet without scrolling. In a graphics program, a higher resolution allows you to see more detail without zooming in or out.

CHANGE THE SCREEN RESOLUTION

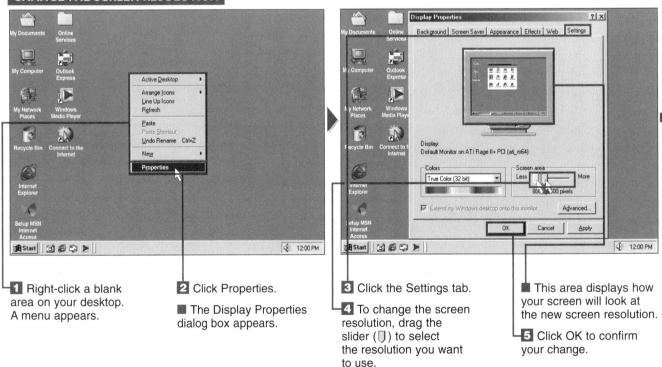

1 Right-click a blank area on your desktop. A menu appears.

2 Click Properties.

■ The Display Properties dialog box appears.

3 Click the Settings tab.

4 To change the screen resolution, drag the slider (🔲) to select the resolution you want to use.

■ This area displays how your screen will look at the new screen resolution.

5 Click OK to confirm your change.

Why do I have wide black borders around the edge of my screen or lose part of the desktop when I change the screen resolution?

✔ You may need to make adjustments to your monitor after changing the screen resolution. Consult the manual included with your monitor for information about the monitor controls that you can use to make the necessary adjustments.

Is there an easier way to change the screen resolution?

✔ In the Display Properties dialog box, click the Settings tab and then click the Advanced button. You can then select the Show settings icon on task bar option to display the monitor icon on the taskbar. You can then click the monitor icon to select a new screen resolution.

I find it difficult to read screen items when I change to a higher resolution. What can I do?

✔ You can increase the size of text in menus and other screen items to make the text easier to read. In the Display Properties dialog box, click the Settings tab and then click the Advanced button. Click the General tab and in the Font Size area, select Large Fonts.

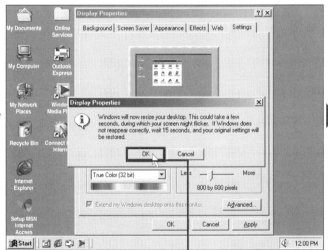

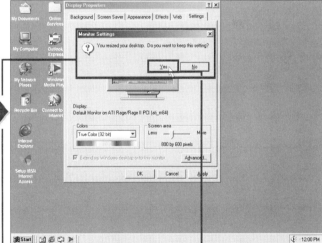

■ A dialog box appears, stating that Windows will take a few seconds to change the screen resolution. Your screen may flicker during this time.

6 Click OK to change the screen resolution.

■ Windows resizes the information on your screen.

■ The Monitor Settings dialog box appears, asking if you want to keep the new screen resolution.

7 Click Yes to keep the screen resolution.

Note: If your screen does not reappear correctly, wait fifteen seconds and Windows will restore your original screen resolution.

CHANGE THE COLOR DEPTH

olor depth refers to the number of colors your screen displays. You can increase the number of colors your screen displays to improve the quality of images and the general appearance of your screen.

Windows offers several different color depth settings. You can choose between the 16 Colors, 256 Colors, High Color (16 bit) and True Color (24 and 32 bit)

color depths. The 16 Colors setting is often used to display low-resolution images. The 256 Colors setting is suitable for most home and business applications. The High Color setting displays over 65 thousand colors while the True Color settings display over 16 million colors.

You may want to display more colors on your screen when viewing photographs, playing

videos or playing games on your computer. Some programs, particularly games, require you to use a specific color depth.

The number of colors your screen can display depends on the capabilities of your computer's video card and monitor.

CHANGE THE COLOR DEPTH

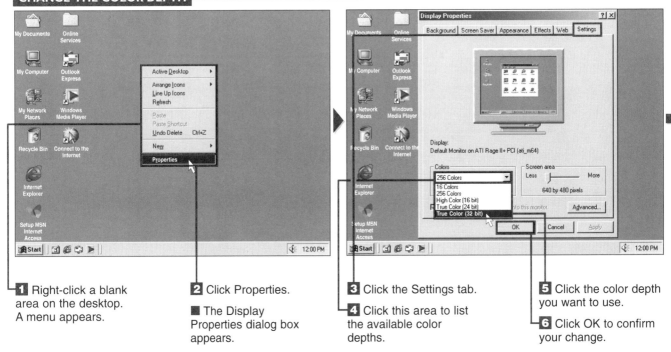

1 Right-click a blank area on the desktop. A menu appears.

2 Click Properties.

■ The Display Properties dialog box appears.

3 Click the Settings tab.

4 Click this area to list the available color depths.

5 Click the color depth you want to use.

6 Click OK to confirm your change.

How can I stop Windows from asking me to restart the computer each time I change the color depth setting?

✔ On the Settings tab, click the Advanced button. In the dialog box that appears, select the General tab and choose an option to automatically restart the computer every time you change the color depth setting or always apply the new setting without restarting the computer.

Can all monitors use the True Color depth settings?

✔ All modern monitors are capable of using the True Color depth settings to display millions of colors.

Will a higher color depth setting affect my computer's performance?

✔ Although your computer may work slightly faster at lower color depth settings compared to higher color depth settings, the speed difference is minor.

Will certain Windows features work only with higher color depth settings?

✔ Some Windows features will work only when you use a higher color depth setting. For example, you need to display 256 or more colors to use the animated hourglasses set of mouse pointers or to smooth the edges of fonts to make the fonts more readable. To change the mouse pointer set, see page 200. To smooth the edges of fonts, see page 180.

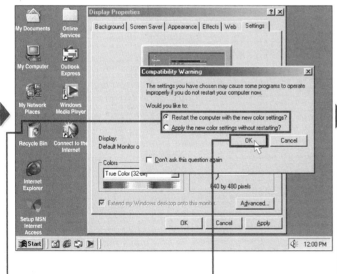

■ The Compatibility Warning dialog box appears, stating that some programs may not operate properly if you do not restart your computer.

7 Click an option to specify if you want to restart your computer (○ changes to ⊙).

8 Click OK to confirm your selection.

■ The System Settings Change dialog box appears if you selected to restart your computer.

9 Click Yes to restart your computer.

■ When your computer restarts, Windows will use the new color depth you specified.

SET UP A SCREEN SAVER

A screen saver is a moving picture or pattern that appears on your screen when you do not use your computer for a period of time. You can use a screen saver to hide your work while you are away from your desk. Windows provides several interesting screen savers that you can use.

When you do not use your computer for a certain period

of time, Windows starts the screen saver. You can select the number of minutes the computer must be inactive before the screen saver appears. Adjusting the time period before a screen saver starts is useful to prevent the screen saver from disrupting your work while you are reviewing information on your screen.

Screen savers were originally designed to prevent screen burn,

which occurs when an image appears in a fixed position on the screen for a period of time. Today's monitors are less susceptible to screen burn, but people still use screen savers for their entertainment value.

SET UP A SCREEN SAVER

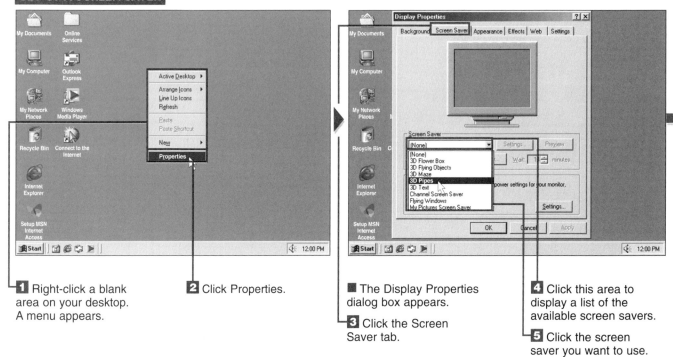

■1 Right-click a blank area on your desktop. A menu appears.

■2 Click Properties.

■ The Display Properties dialog box appears.

■3 Click the Screen Saver tab.

■4 Click this area to display a list of the available screen savers.

■5 Click the screen saver you want to use.

Where can I find more screen savers?

✔ When you install Windows, only a limited number of screen savers are installed. You can add more screen savers by installing all of the Screen Savers component, which is located in the Accessories category on your computer. To add a Windows component, see page 538. You can also buy screen savers at computer stores or download screen savers from the Internet.

What does the My Pictures Screen Saver do?

✔ The My Pictures Screen Saver option displays the images stored in your My Pictures folder on your screen in random order. The My Pictures folder is located within the My Documents folder on your desktop.

Can I customize my screen savers?

✔ After you select a screen saver, you can click the Settings button to customize the screen saver. Each screen saver offers options that you can change.

How can I preview a screen saver?

✔ When choosing a screen saver, you can click the Preview button to see how the screen saver will appear on your screen. To end the preview, move the mouse or press a key on your keyboard.

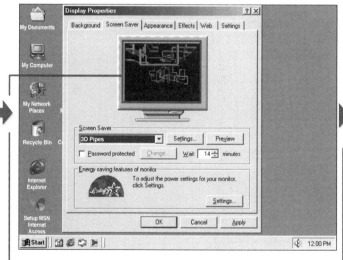

■ This area displays how the screen saver will appear on your screen.

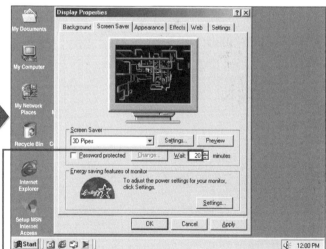

6 To specify the number of minutes your computer must be inactive before the screen saver will appear, double-click this area. Then type the number of minutes.

CONTINUED ▶

SET UP A SCREEN SAVER (CONTINUED)

S creen savers can add a level of security and privacy to your work.

You can use the screen saver password feature to prevent other people from using your computer when you are away from your desk. A screen saver password helps to keep your documents private and protects your work from unauthorized changes.

If you assign a password to your screen saver, you must enter the password correctly to remove the screen saver and use your computer. This makes it difficult for people to use your computer without your permission.

When you choose a password, you should not use words that people can easily associate with you, such as your name or

favorite hobby. An effective password contains a mixture of letters and numbers. To keep your password secure, do not write it down in an area where it can be easily found. You may also want to change your password every few weeks.

SET UP A SCREEN SAVER (CONTINUED)

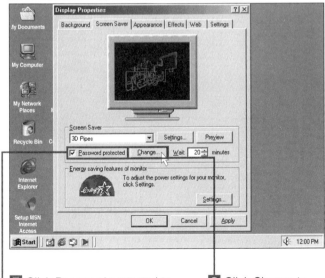

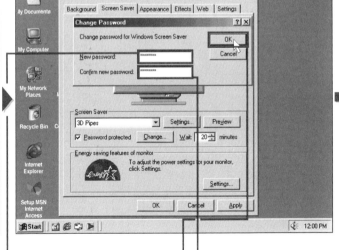

7 Click Password protected to assign a password that must be entered to remove the screen saver (☐ changes to ☑).

Note: If you do not want to assign a password to the screen saver, skip to step 13.

8 Click Change to specify the password you want to use.

■ The Change Password dialog box appears.

9 Type a password for the screen saver. A symbol (ˣ) appears for each character you type to prevent others from seeing your password.

10 Click this area and then type the password again to confirm the password.

11 Click OK.

How do I stop a screen saver from appearing?

✔ You can turn off the screen saver. In the Display Properties dialog box, select the Screen Saver tab. Click the area below Screen Saver and then select (None).

What impact does a screen saver have on my computer?

✔ A screen saver can use a lot of your computer's resources when displayed on your screen, especially if the screen saver contains detailed graphics. You should turn off the screen saver if your computer will be performing unattended tasks that require a lot of processing power, such as updating information in a database.

How secure is my computer when I use a screen saver password?

✔ A screen saver password does not fully protect your computer. Other people can access your computer by simply restarting the computer.

Can I change my screen saver password later?

✔ Yes. You can change the password at any time. Open the Display Properties dialog box and click the Screen Saver tab. Then perform steps 8 to 13 below to change the password.

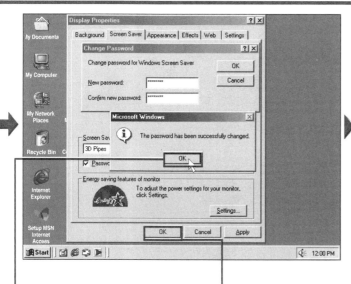

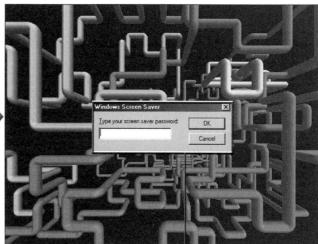

■ A dialog box appears, stating that the password was successfully changed.

12 Click OK to close the dialog box.

13 Click OK to close the Display Properties dialog box.

■ The screen saver appears when you do not use your computer for the number of minutes you specified.

■ You can move the mouse or press a key on your keyboard to remove the screen saver.

■ If you assigned a password to the screen saver, the Windows Screen Saver dialog box appears, asking for your password. Type your password and then press the Enter key.

CHANGE DESKTOP ICONS AND VISUAL EFFECTS

You can customize Windows by changing the appearance of desktop icons and the visual effects that Windows uses.

Windows allows you to choose a new icon for the My Computer, My Documents, My Network Places and the full and empty Recycle Bin items on your desktop. Windows includes many different icons for you to choose from.

You can use animation effects to enhance the way menus appear on the screen.

Windows also allows you to smooth the edges of fonts to make text on your screen easier to read.

You can display large icons for items on your desktop. Displaying large icons is useful if you are using a high screen resolution,

such as 1024x768 or higher. To change the screen resolution, see page 172.

You can display icons using all the colors your computer can display to improve the appearance of icons.

You can also choose to see the contents of a window you are moving or resizing.

CHANGE DESKTOP ICONS AND VISUAL EFFECTS

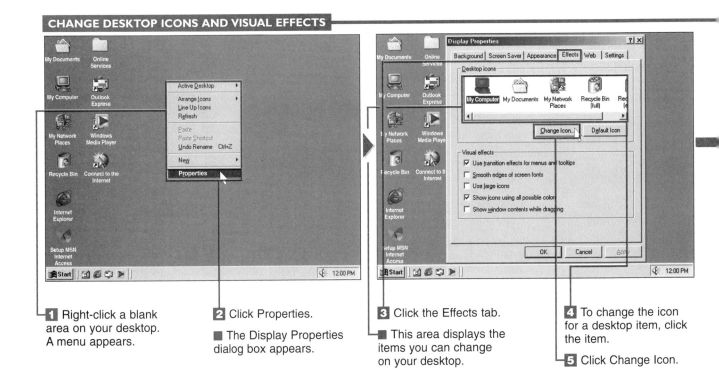

1 Right-click a blank area on your desktop. A menu appears.

2 Click Properties.

■ The Display Properties dialog box appears.

3 Click the Effects tab.

■ This area displays the items you can change on your desktop.

4 To change the icon for a desktop item, click the item.

5 Click Change Icon.

Are there other icons I can use?

✔ Yes. There are many icons available for you to download on the Internet. After downloading an icon you want to use, you can click the Browse button in the Change Icon dialog box to locate the file for the icon on your computer.

Can I change the appearance of all the icons on my desktop at once?

✔ You can apply a theme to your desktop to change the appearance of all desktop icons. Each desktop theme includes a set of coordinated items such as icons, wallpaper, sounds and mouse pointers. See page 182 to apply a theme.

How can I change an icon on my desktop back to its original icon?

✔ In the Display Properties dialog box, click the Effects tab. Select the icon you want to change back to the original icon and then click the Default Icon button.

Will using visual effects make my computer operate slower?

✔ Some of the visual effects may affect your computer's performance if the computer only meets or just exceeds the minimum system requirements for Windows. You may be able to improve the computer's performance by turning off these effects.

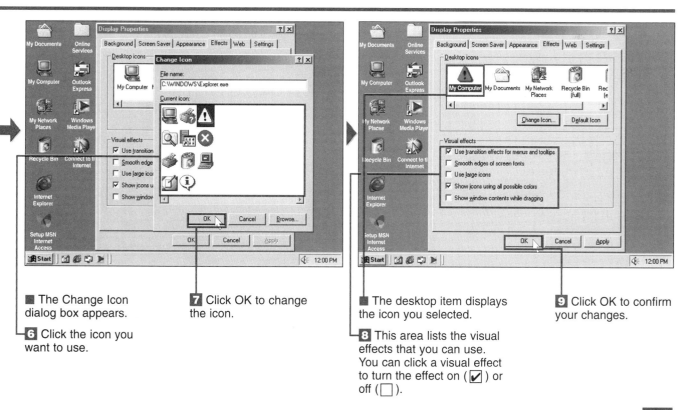

■ The Change Icon dialog box appears.

6 Click the icon you want to use.

7 Click OK to change the icon.

■ The desktop item displays the icon you selected.

8 This area lists the visual effects that you can use. You can click a visual effect to turn the effect on (✔) or off (☐).

9 Click OK to confirm your changes.

USING A DESKTOP THEME

Y ou can use a desktop theme to change the appearance of your desktop. Windows offers several themes, including a baseball, jungle and mystery theme. Each desktop theme contains several coordinated items including wallpaper, a screen saver, a color scheme, sounds, mouse pointers, icons and fonts.

The themes you should use depend on the number of colors your screen displays. If your screen displays 256 colors, you should only use the 256 color themes. If your screen displays more than 256 colors, you can use both the 256 and high color themes. Although you can select a high color theme when your screen displays 256 colors, you may experience odd color effects.

You can customize a desktop theme by selecting only the theme settings you want to use. For example, you could turn on the Screen saver setting to display a moving picture on your screen when you do not use your computer for a period of time. You could also turn off the Desktop wallpaper setting if you do not want to display a colorful design on your desktop.

USING A DESKTOP THEME

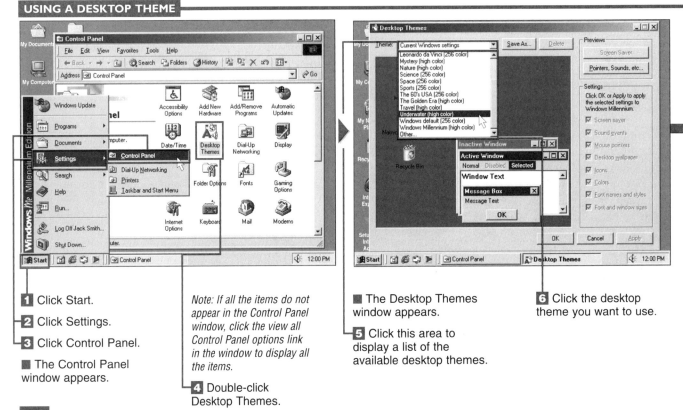

1 Click Start.

2 Click Settings.

3 Click Control Panel.

■ The Control Panel window appears.

Note: If all the items do not appear in the Control Panel window, click the view all Control Panel options link in the window to display all the items.

4 Double-click Desktop Themes.

■ The Desktop Themes window appears.

5 Click this area to display a list of the available desktop themes.

6 Click the desktop theme you want to use.

Why doesn't the Desktop Themes item appear in the Control Panel window?

✔ You need to add the Desktop Themes category of components to your computer. To add Windows components, see page 538.

The fonts in the theme I want to use are hard to read. Can I use the fonts from the Windows default theme instead?

✔ Yes. Select the Windows default theme in the Desktop Themes window and make sure all of the settings are selected. Click Apply to apply the theme. Select the desktop theme you want to use and click the Font names and styles setting as well as the Font and window sizes setting (☑ changes to ☐). When you apply the new desktop theme, the Windows default font settings will be displayed.

Can I save my customized desktop theme?

✔ Yes. After you select the settings you want to use and confirm your changes, you can use the Save As button in the Desktop Themes window to name and save the customized theme.

How can I change back to my original desktop theme?

✔ Select Windows default from the list of available themes in the Desktop Themes window.

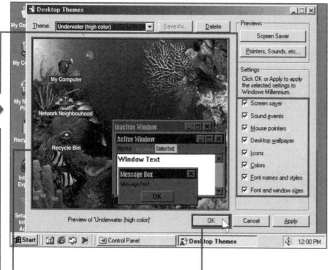

■ This area displays a preview of the theme you selected.

7 Windows will apply the theme you selected to each setting that displays a check mark. You can click a setting to add (☑) or remove (☐) a check mark.

8 Click OK to confirm your changes.

■ Windows applies the desktop theme you selected.

ADD AN ACTIVE DESKTOP ITEM

Adding Active Desktop items to your desktop allows you to display active content from the Web on your screen. Active content is information that constantly changes, such as a stock ticker or a weather map. Adding active content to your desktop gives you easy access to items you refer to on a regular basis.

Microsoft's Desktop Gallery provides a variety of Active

Desktop items that you can add to your desktop. The Active Desktop items are organized into categories, such as news, sports and entertainment. Each category contains related Active Desktop items. For example, the entertainment category contains items such as movie and entertainment news.

There are many interesting Active Desktop items. For example, you

can personalize your desktop with a comic strip or a map feature that allows you to quickly find street addresses. Some Active Desktop items contain sounds or videos.

You can also add a Web page to your desktop. For example, you could add a search tool such as Yahoo! or AltaVista to your desktop so you can quickly search for topics of interest on the Web.

ADD AN ACTIVE DESKTOP ITEM

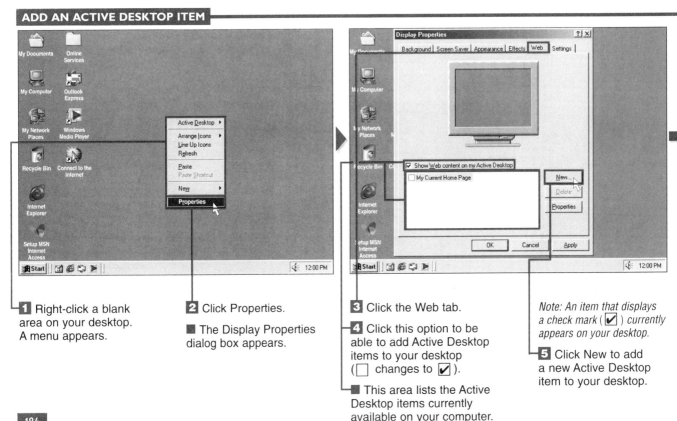

1 Right-click a blank area on your desktop. A menu appears.

2 Click Properties.

■ The Display Properties dialog box appears.

3 Click the Web tab.

4 Click this option to be able to add Active Desktop items to your desktop (☐ changes to ☑).

■ This area lists the Active Desktop items currently available on your computer.

Note: An item that displays a check mark (☑) currently appears on your desktop.

5 Click New to add a new Active Desktop item to your desktop.

Why does a Security Warning dialog box appear when I display the Desktop Gallery?

✔ If the Security Warning dialog box appears when you display the Desktop Gallery, Microsoft needs to transfer information to your computer. Click Yes to transfer the information to your computer.

What is the My Current Home Page item in the list of Active Desktop items?

✔ The My Current Home Page item displays your home page on your desktop. Your home page is the Web page that appears each time you start your Web browser. To display your home page on the desktop, click the box beside the My Current Home Page item (☐ changes to ✔).

Is there another way that I can add a Web page to my desktop?

✔ When viewing a Web page in Internet Explorer, use the right mouse button to drag the icon that appears beside the address of the page in the Address bar to your desktop. Then select the Create Active Desktop item(s) Here option.

Can I add an image or Web page stored on my computer to my desktop?

✔ Yes. In the New Active Desktop Item dialog box, click the Browse button to locate the image or Web page on your computer.

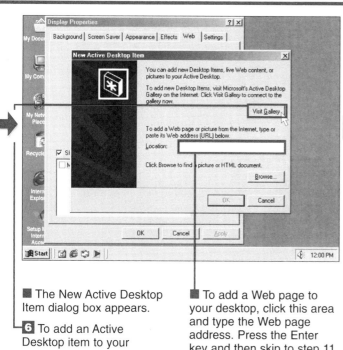

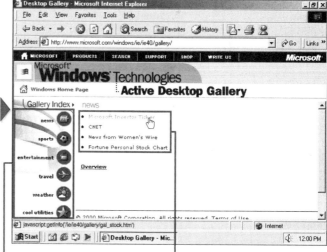

■ The New Active Desktop Item dialog box appears.

6 To add an Active Desktop item to your desktop, click Visit Gallery to display the Desktop Gallery on the Internet.

■ To add a Web page to your desktop, click this area and type the Web page address. Press the Enter key and then skip to step 11.

Note: If you are not connected to the Internet, a dialog box appears that allows you to connect.

■ The Microsoft Internet Explorer window opens and displays the Desktop Gallery Web page.

7 Click a category to display Active Desktop items of interest.

■ This area displays the Active Desktop items in the category you selected.

8 Click an Active Desktop item of interest.

CONTINUED ▶

ADD AN ACTIVE DESKTOP ITEM
(CONTINUED)

After selecting a category of interest in the Desktop Gallery, you can view information about an Active Desktop item in the category. This helps you decide which items you want to add to your desktop.

When you add an Active Desktop item to your desktop, the item is copied to your computer and

automatically appears on your desktop. You can move an Active Desktop item to any position on your desktop. The Active Desktop item will be displayed even when you are not connected to the Internet.

An item you add to your desktop will be automatically updated on a regular basis. Most Active Desktop

items contain information that must be updated to continue being useful, such as a weather map. Active Desktop items automatically update at times that have been preset by the item's designer. Keep in mind that Active Desktop items will update only when you are connected to the Internet.

ADD AN ACTIVE DESKTOP ITEM (CONTINUED)

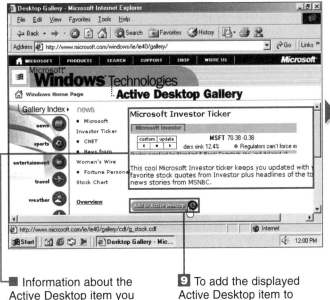

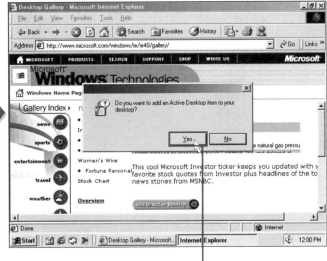

■ Information about the Active Desktop item you selected appears.

Note: You can repeat steps 7 and 8 on page 185 to view information about other Active Desktop items.

9 To add the displayed Active Desktop item to your desktop, click Add to Active Desktop.

■ A dialog box appears, asking if you want to add the Active Desktop item to your desktop.

10 Click Yes to add the Active Desktop item to your desktop.

Can I change the size of an Active Desktop item?

✔ Yes. Position the mouse pointer over an edge of the item (⬉ changes to ↔ or ⬈) and then drag the item to a new size. Some Active Desktop items cannot be sized.

How do I remove an Active Desktop item?

✔ In the Display Properties dialog box, select the Web tab. Click the box beside the item you want to remove from your desktop (☑ changes to ☐). You can repeat this procedure to redisplay the item at any time (☐ changes to ☑). To permanently remove an item from your computer, select the item and then click the Delete button. You cannot delete the My Current Home Page item.

How can I quickly remove all the Active Desktop items from my desktop?

✔ Right-click a blank area on the desktop. Click Active Desktop and then select Show Web Content. You can repeat this procedure to redisplay all the items.

Can an Active Desktop item fill the screen?

✔ Yes. Position the mouse pointer over the top of the Active Desktop item. On the gray bar that appears, click ▣.

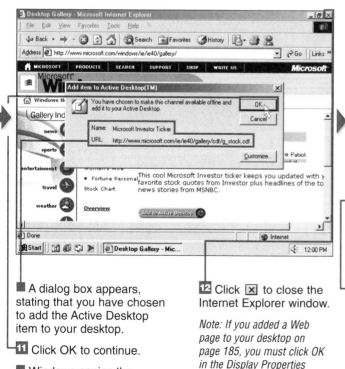

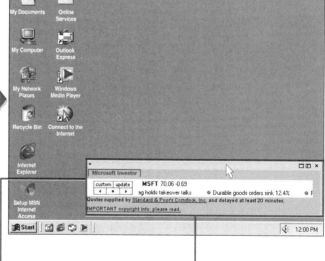

■ A dialog box appears, stating that you have chosen to add the Active Desktop item to your desktop.

11 Click OK to continue.

■ Windows copies the necessary information to your computer.

12 Click ✖ to close the Internet Explorer window.

Note: If you added a Web page to your desktop on page 185, you must click OK in the Display Properties dialog box.

■ The Active Desktop item appears on your desktop.

■ The Active Desktop item will update automatically only when you are connected to the Internet.

■ To move an Active Desktop item, position the mouse ⬉ over the top edge of the item. When a gray bar appears, drag the bar to a new location.

CUSTOMIZE FOLDER APPEARANCE

Y ou can customize the appearance of a folder on your computer. The changes you make are saved with the folder and will appear every time you work with the folder. You must have Web content enabled to customize a folder. For information about enabling Web content in folders, see page 192.

You can customize a folder by changing the way information appears in the folder, adding a background image and adding a comment about the folder.

You can select a template to specify how you want information to appear when you display the contents of a folder. The Standard template displays information about a

selected item in the left side of the window. The Classic template displays only icons in a window. The Simple template provides a good starting point if you plan to design your own folder template. The Image Preview template shows a preview of a selected image in the left side of the window. This template is useful for a folder that contains many image files.

CUSTOMIZE FOLDER APPEARANCE

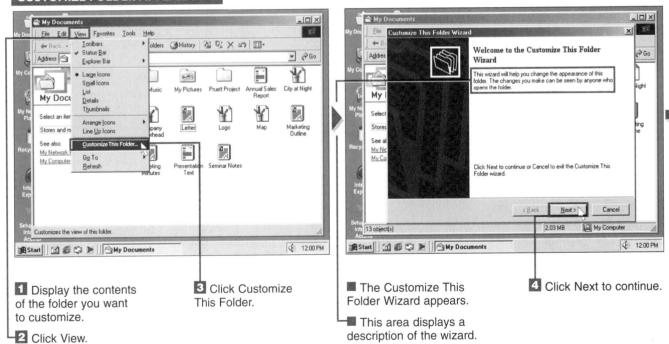

1 Display the contents of the folder you want to customize.

2 Click View.

3 Click Customize This Folder.

■ The Customize This Folder Wizard appears.

■ This area displays a description of the wizard.

4 Click Next to continue.

Why isn't the Customize This Folder command available for a folder?

✔ You cannot customize the appearance of some folders, including the My Computer folder, the Control Panel folder, the Printers folder, the Dial-Up Networking folder and the Scheduled Tasks folder.

How do I remove the customizations from a folder?

✔ Display the contents of the folder you want to change. Click the View menu and select Customize This Folder. Click Next and then select the Remove customizations option (○ changes to ⊙). Click Next and then follow the instructions on your screen to remove some or all of the customizations.

How do I design my own folder template?

✔ After you select the template you want to use as a starting point for your own template in the Customize This Folder wizard, select the I want to edit this template option (☐ changes to ☑) and then click Next. The wizard displays the HTML (HyperText Markup Language) code for the template in a Notepad document. You can edit the HTML code to specify exactly how you want the folder to look.

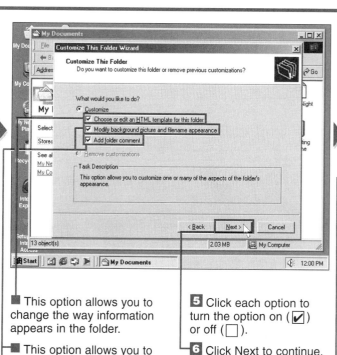

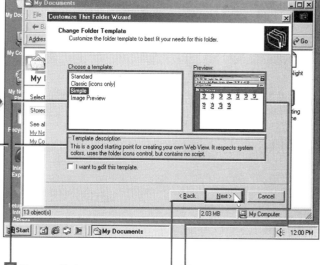

■ This option allows you to change the way information appears in the folder.

■ This option allows you to add a background image to the folder.

■ This option allows you to add a comment to the folder.

5 Click each option to turn the option on (☑) or off (☐).

6 Click Next to continue.

Note: The options available in the next screens depend on the options you selected in step 5.

7 To specify how you want information to appear in the folder, click the template you want to use.

■ This area displays a description of the selected template.

■ This area displays a preview of how information will appear in the folder.

8 Click Next to continue.

CONTINUED

CUSTOMIZE FOLDER APPEARANCE (CONTINUED)

You can give a folder on your computer a distinctive look by adding a background image to the folder. Windows includes many background images that you can choose from.

When you select the background image you want to use, Windows displays a preview of how the image will appear in the folder window. If the background image

you select does not fill the entire window, Windows repeats the image to fill the window.

You can also add a comment to a folder to provide information about the folder. When you browse through the folders on your computer, you may be able to view the comment in the left side of a window when you select the icon for the folder. You can

use HTML (HyperText Markup Language) code to format the text in the comment.

If you share a customized folder on your network, everyone on the network will be able to see the template and background image you selected, but they will not see the comment you added. To share a folder on a network, see page 374.

CUSTOMIZE FOLDER APPEARANCE (CONTINUED)

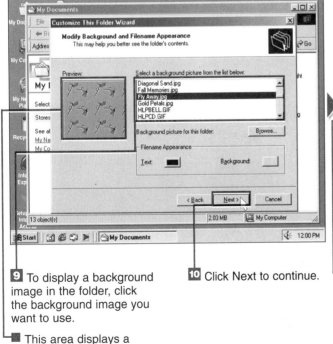

■9 To display a background image in the folder, click the background image you want to use.

■ This area displays a preview of the background image you selected.

■10 Click Next to continue.

■11 To enter a comment about the folder, type a comment.

■12 Click Next to continue.

■ You can click Back at any time to return to a previous step and change your selections.

What if the wizard does not display the name of the background image I want to use?

✔ Click the Browse button to locate the image you want to use. You can use images you created or images you obtained on the Internet or at computer stores. The image must be in the BMP, GIF, JPG or DIB format.

What is HTML code?

✔ HTML code is a set of tags used to format text. For example, you can use HTML tags to bold text in a comment. Place <B> in front of the comment and </B> after the comment. Similarly, you can use the <I> and </I> tags to italicize text.

After I add a background image to a folder, the names of icons are hard to read. How can I fix this?

✔ You can change the color of the text, the color of the text background, or both. Perform steps 1 to 6 starting on page 188, selecting only the Modify background picture and filename appearance option in step 5. In the Filename Appearance area, use the Text and Background buttons to select new colors for the text and the background of the text.

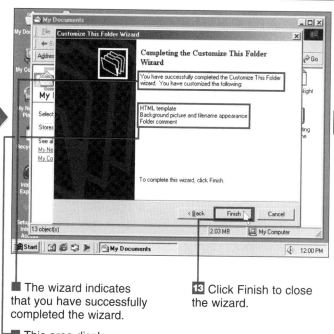

■ The wizard indicates that you have successfully completed the wizard.

■ This area displays the options you have customized.

13 Click Finish to close the wizard.

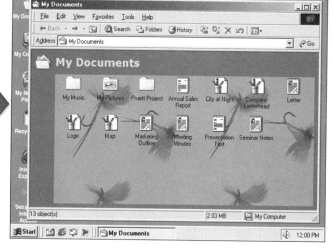

■ The folder displays the changes you made.

CHANGE FOLDER OPTIONS

You can change the way your desktop and folders look and act.

You can have your desktop act like a Web page or like a classic Windows desktop. Windows allows you to enable the Active Desktop feature so you can view and monitor items from the Web, such as your home page or a stock ticker, on your desktop.

You can choose whether you want to view Web content in your folders or display your folders in the classic style. When you view Web content in folders, Windows displays descriptive text and hyperlinks in the left side of open windows.

When opening folders, you can have each folder you open appear in the same window or in a different window. Opening folders in the same window reduces clutter on your desktop. Opening folders in different windows allows you to view the contents of several folders at once.

Windows also allows you to change the way you open items on your computer. You can choose to open items using a single-click or a double-click. If you choose the Single-click option, you can specify when you want items to display an underline.

CHANGE FOLDER OPTIONS

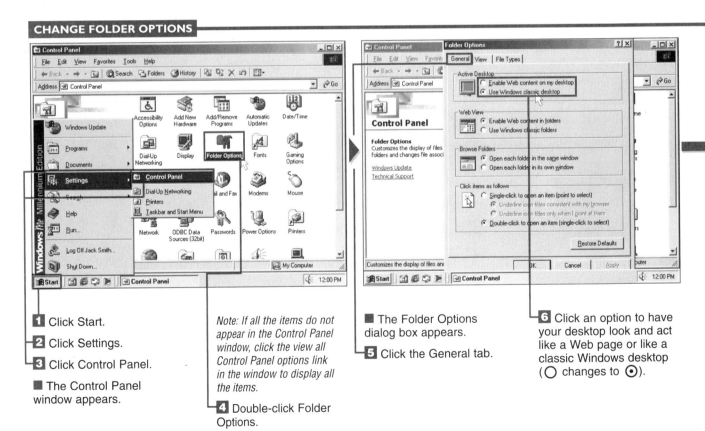

1 Click Start.

2 Click Settings.

3 Click Control Panel.

■ The Control Panel window appears.

Note: If all the items do not appear in the Control Panel window, click the view all Control Panel options link in the window to display all the items.

4 Double-click Folder Options.

■ The Folder Options dialog box appears.

5 Click the General tab.

6 Click an option to have your desktop look and act like a Web page or like a classic Windows desktop (○ changes to ⊙).

How do I select items when using the Single-click option?

✔ To select an item, position the mouse pointer over the item. To select a group of items, position the mouse pointer over the first item. Hold down the Shift key and then position the mouse pointer over the last item. To select random items, hold down the Ctrl key and position the mouse pointer over each item you want to select.

How can I quickly return to the original folder settings?

✔ If you do not like the changes you made, you can click the Restore Defaults button in the Folder Options dialog box to quickly return to the original folder settings.

How do I add Web content to my desktop?

✔ When you enable the Active Desktop feature, you can display Web content on your desktop by adding Active Desktop items. You can add items such as a three-dimensional clock or a weather map. To add Active Desktop items, see page 184.

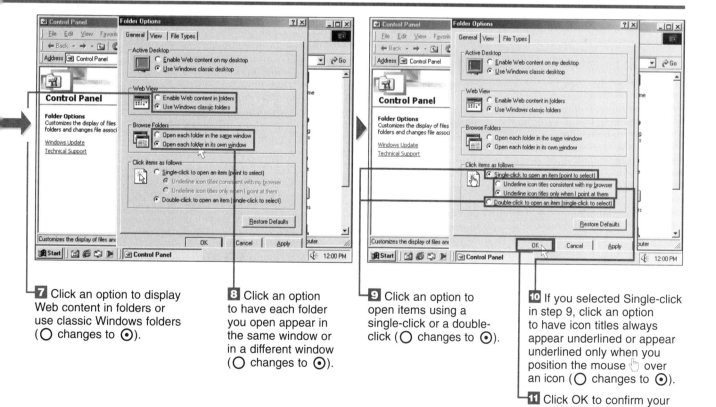

7 Click an option to display Web content in folders or use classic Windows folders (○ changes to ⊙).

8 Click an option to have each folder you open appear in the same window or in a different window (○ changes to ⊙).

9 Click an option to open items using a single-click or a double-click (○ changes to ⊙).

10 If you selected Single-click in step 9, click an option to have icon titles always appear underlined or appear underlined only when you position the mouse ⌐ over an icon (○ changes to ⊙).

11 Click OK to confirm your changes.

VIEW FONTS ON YOUR COMPUTER

You can view the fonts on your computer to see what they look like before using the fonts in your documents.

A font is a set of characters with a particular design. There are a wide variety of fonts you can use. Fonts can be serious and corporate or fancy and funny.

Most of the fonts included with Windows are TrueType fonts. In the FONTS window, the icon for a TrueType font displays two letter Ts. A TrueType font generates characters using mathematical formulas so you can change the size of a TrueType font without distorting the font. A TrueType font will print exactly as it appears on the screen.

Windows uses system fonts to display text in menus and dialog boxes. In the FONTS window, the icon for a system font displays a red A. These fonts are only available in specific sizes. Although system fonts may appear in a program's font list, they may not be suitable for some printing tasks.

Windows displays information about each font on your computer as well as samples of each font in various sizes.

VIEW FONTS ON YOUR COMPUTER

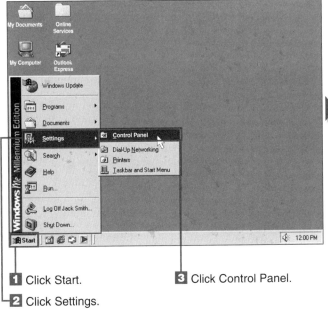

1 Click Start.

2 Click Settings.

3 Click Control Panel.

■ The Control Panel window appears.

Note: If all the items do not appear in the Control Panel window, click the view all Control Panel options link in the window to display all the items.

4 Double-click Fonts to view the fonts available on your computer.

Why do many font names appear more than once in the FONTS window?

✔ Windows displays variations of many fonts, such as bold and italic versions. In the View menu, click Hide Variations to remove the variations and display only the basic style for each font.

How can I change the way Windows displays items in the FONTS window?

✔ Click (🔲) to display items as large icons. Click (▦) to display items as small icons in a list. Click (AB) to have Windows display how similar each font is to a font you select. Then click the area beside List fonts by similarity to and select a font. Click (🏢) to view file information for each item in the FONTS window.

What are printer fonts?

✔ Printer fonts are fonts that are stored in a printer's memory. Nearly all printers include printer fonts. Printer fonts do not appear in the FONTS window and may not be accurately represented on your screen. This type of font may appear in a program's font list and is indicated by a printer icon (🖨).

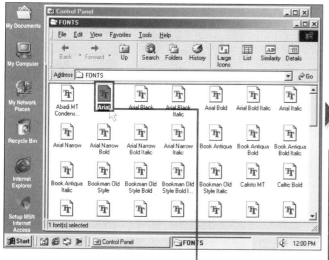

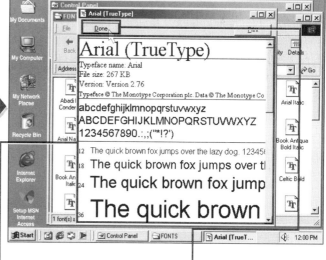

■ The FONTS window appears.

■ Each icon in the FONTS window represents a font installed on your computer. The icon for a TrueType font displays two letter Ts. The icon for a system font displays a red A.

5 Double-click a font of interest to view information about the font.

■ A window appears, displaying information about the font you selected and samples of the font in various sizes.

6 When you finish reviewing the information, click Done to close the window.

ADD AND DELETE FONTS

Y ou can add fonts to your computer to give you more choices when creating documents.

Windows includes several standard fonts. The fonts included with Windows and any other fonts you add are available in all Windows-based programs on your computer.

There are thousands of fonts available that you can add to

your computer. When obtaining fonts, look for TrueType fonts since they are the most commonly used font in Windows. A TrueType font generates characters using mathematical formulas. This type of font will print exactly as it appears on your screen.

You can buy fonts wherever software is sold. You can also obtain free fonts on the Internet.

To find fonts on the Internet, simply search for "TrueType fonts." To search the Web, see page 444.

There are fonts available for many different types of operating systems. When you buy fonts or obtain fonts on the Internet, make sure you choose the Windows version of the fonts.

ADD FONTS

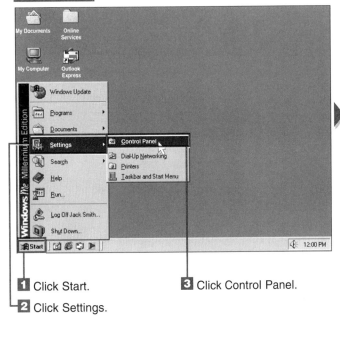

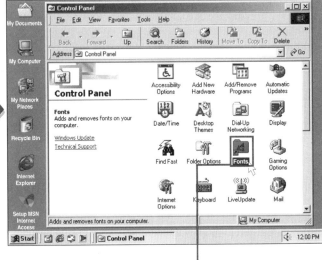

1 Click Start.

2 Click Settings.

3 Click Control Panel.

■ The Control Panel window appears.

Note: If all the items do not appear in the Control Panel window, click the view all Control Panel options link in the window to display all the items.

4 Double-click Fonts to add new fonts to your computer.

How many fonts can I install?

✔ There is no limit to the number of fonts you can install, but keep in mind that fonts take up storage space on your computer. You may also find a long list of fonts becomes cluttered and difficult to use.

Is there an easy way to manage fonts?

✔ There are several programs, such as Adobe Type Manager, that can arrange fonts into groups. You can then select the group of fonts you want to work with. You may want to group fonts that you use for a specific task, such as word processing or desktop publishing.

Is there a faster way to install a font?

✔ When the FONTS window is open on your screen, you can drag and drop the icon for a new font into the FONTS window. An icon for the font will appear in the window, but the original font file will remain in its original location on your computer. You can only place font files in the FONTS window. If you try to place another type of file in the FONTS window, Windows will display an error message.

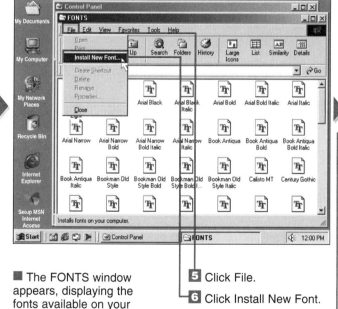

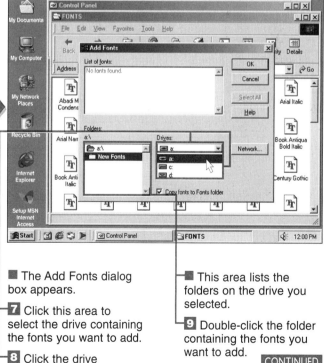

■ The FONTS window appears, displaying the fonts available on your computer.

5 Click File.

6 Click Install New Font.

■ The Add Fonts dialog box appears.

7 Click this area to select the drive containing the fonts you want to add.

8 Click the drive containing the fonts.

■ This area lists the folders on the drive you selected.

9 Double-click the folder containing the fonts you want to add.

CONTINUED ▶

ADD AND DELETE FONTS
(CONTINUED)

When adding fonts, you can select one font or all of the available fonts in the folder. Windows copies the new fonts to the FONTS folder so you can use the fonts in your documents.

You can also remove fonts you no longer use from your computer. You can select several fonts and delete them at the same time.

Fonts that display a red A in the FONTS window are required by Windows. Many other programs also install their own special fonts. Before you delete a font you did not add, make sure the font is not required by a program.

If you delete a font that is used by Windows or a Windows program, a different font will be used to replace the one you deleted. You

may not like the substitution Windows makes.

Deleted fonts are sent to your Recycle Bin. To be safe, you may want to make a backup copy of a font before you delete the font.

ADD FONTS (CONTINUED)

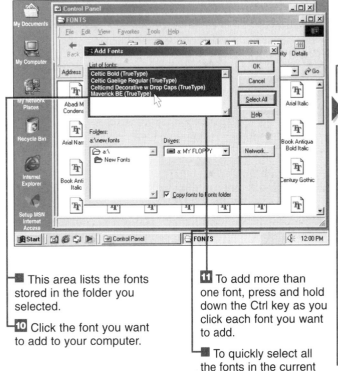

■ This area lists the fonts stored in the folder you selected.

10 Click the font you want to add to your computer.

11 To add more than one font, press and hold down the Ctrl key as you click each font you want to add.

■ To quickly select all the fonts in the current folder, click Select All.

12 Windows will place a copy of the fonts you selected in the Fonts folder. You can click this option if you do not want to copy the fonts to the Fonts folder (✔ changes to ☐).

13 Click OK to add the fonts you selected to your computer.

■ The fonts appear in the FONTS window.

Can I prevent Windows from copying fonts I add to the FONTS folder?

✔ Yes. You can use the fonts directly from their current location. This allows you to add fonts from a network drive without using disk space on your computer. If the fonts are changed on the network, you can easily access the updated font. In the Add Fonts window, select the Copy fonts to Font folder option (☑ changes to ☐).

Is there another way to delete fonts?

✔ In the Fonts window, position the mouse pointer over the font you want to delete. Then drag the font onto the Recycle Bin. The icon for the font will not disappear from the window until the next time you open the FONTS window.

How can I restore a font that I accidentally deleted?

✔ You can open your Recycle Bin to retrieve a font you deleted by mistake. In the Recycle Bin window, right-click the font you want to retrieve and then click Restore from the menu that appears.

DELETE FONTS

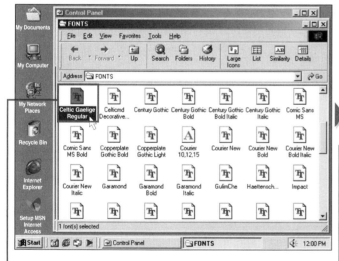

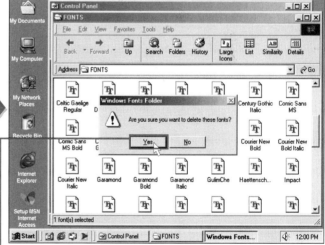

■1 Click the font you want to delete.

■ To delete more than one font, press and hold down the Ctrl key as you click each font you want to delete.

■2 Press the Delete key.

■ A confirmation dialog box appears.

■3 Click Yes to delete the font.

■ The font disappears from the FONTS window. Windows places the font in the Recycle Bin.

CHANGE MOUSE SETTINGS

You can change the way your mouse works to make it easier to use. The Mouse Properties dialog box offers many options you can adjust to suit your needs.

The left mouse button is used to select and drag items. The right mouse button is used to display a list of commands for a selected item. If you are left-handed, you

can switch the functions of the left and right mouse buttons to make the mouse easier to use.

You can change the amount of time that can pass between two clicks of the mouse button for Windows to recognize a double-click. Double-clicking is most often used to open an item. If you are a new mouse user or you have difficulty double-clicking,

you may find a slower speed easier to use. You can try out the double-click speed to find the setting you prefer.

You can also turn on the ClickLock option to allow you to drag items or select text without having to continuously hold down the mouse button.

CHANGE MOUSE SETTINGS

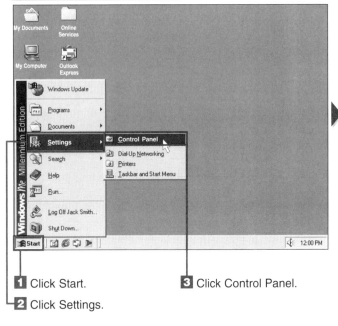

■ Click Start.

■ Click Settings.

■ Click Control Panel.

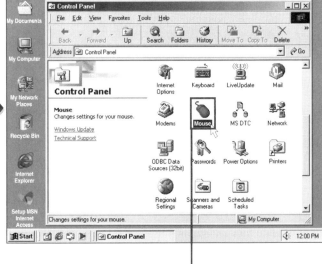

■ The Control Panel window appears.

Note: If all the items do not appear in the Control Panel window, click the view all Control Panel options link in the window to display all the items.

■ Double-click Mouse to change the settings for your mouse.

My mouse pointer jumps around or gets stuck on the screen. What can I do?

✔ Your may need to clean your mouse. Turn the mouse over and remove and clean the roller ball. Then use a cotton swab to remove the dirt from the rollers inside the mouse.

Should I use a mouse pad?

✔ A mouse pad provides a smooth surface for moving the mouse on your desk. You should use a mouse pad to reduce the amount of dirt that enters the mouse and protect your desk from scratches. Hard plastic mouse pads attract less dirt and provide a smoother surface than fabric mouse pads.

How can I use the ClickLock mouse setting to work with text and items on my screen?

✔ To select text, position the mouse pointer to the left of the text you want to select and briefly hold down the mouse button. Then click at the end of the text. To drag items, position the mouse pointer over the item you want to move and briefly hold down the mouse button. Then click where you want to place the item.

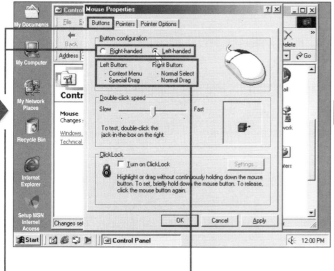

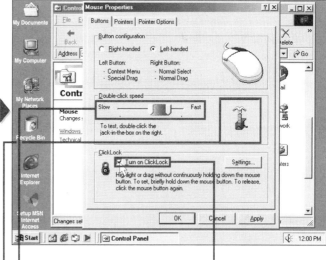

■ The Mouse Properties dialog box appears.

5 Click the Buttons tab.

6 To switch the functions of the left and right mouse buttons, click an option to specify if you are right-handed or left-handed (○ changes to ⊙).

■ This area describes the functions of the left and right mouse buttons. The functions depend on the option you selected.

7 To change the double-click speed, drag the slider (⬚) to a new position.

8 Double-click this area to test the double-click speed. A jack-in-the-box appears when you double-click at the correct speed.

9 To select or drag items without having to continuously hold down the mouse button, click this option (☐ changes to ✔).

CONTINUED ▶

CHANGE MOUSE SETTINGS (CONTINUED)

You can personalize your mouse by changing the look of the mouse pointers and the way the pointer moves on your screen.

Windows includes several sets of mouse pointers including animated and large pointers. You can choose to display a different set of mouse pointers.

You can change how fast the mouse pointer moves on your screen. You can also have the mouse pointer automatically appear over the default button in many dialog boxes. The default button in many dialog boxes is the OK button.

You can leave a trail of mouse pointers as you move the mouse around your screen to help you follow the movement of the pointer. You can also specify the length of the mouse pointer trails.

You can hide the mouse pointer when you type. The mouse pointer will reappear when you move the mouse pointer on your screen.

If you need help locating the mouse pointer on your screen, you can have Windows display moving circles around the mouse pointer when you press the Ctrl key.

CHANGE MOUSE SETTINGS (CONTINUED)

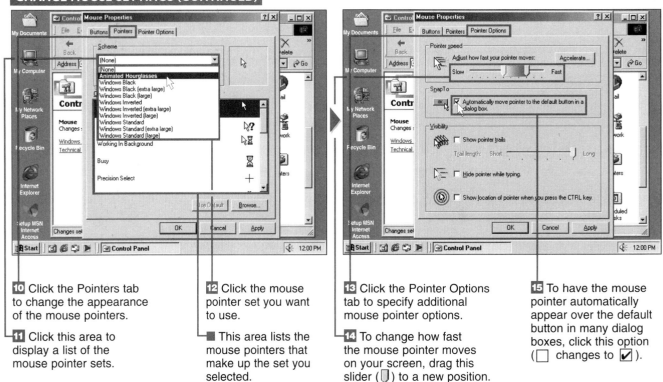

10 Click the Pointers tab to change the appearance of the mouse pointers.

11 Click this area to display a list of the mouse pointer sets.

12 Click the mouse pointer set you want to use.

■ This area lists the mouse pointers that make up the set you selected.

13 Click the Pointer Options tab to specify additional mouse pointer options.

14 To change how fast the mouse pointer moves on your screen, drag this slider (🔘) to a new position.

15 To have the mouse pointer automatically appear over the default button in many dialog boxes, click this option (☐ changes to ☑).

202

Why does my Mouse Properties dialog box have additional options?

✔ If you installed software that came with your mouse, you may find additional options in the Mouse Properties dialog box.

Why does each set of mouse pointers contain so many shapes?

✔ The mouse pointer assumes different shapes depending on its location on your screen and the task you are performing. For example, the standard mouse pointer turns into an hourglass when your computer is busy, or changes to a double-headed arrow when you are adjusting the size of a window.

How can I change the appearance of individual pointers in a set of mouse pointers?

✔ In the Mouse Properties dialog box, display the Pointers tab and then double-click the mouse pointer you want to change. In the Browse dialog box that appears, double-click the mouse pointer you want to use. After you have customized a set of mouse pointers, you can click the Save As button to name and save the set.

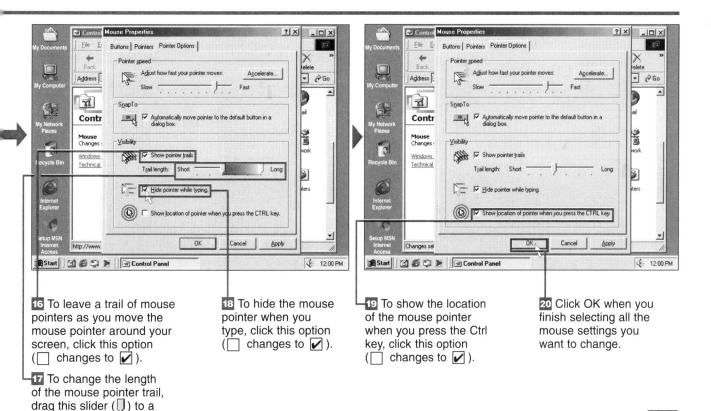

16 To leave a trail of mouse pointers as you move the mouse pointer around your screen, click this option (☐ changes to ✔).

17 To change the length of the mouse pointer trail, drag this slider (⬜) to a new position.

18 To hide the mouse pointer when you type, click this option (☐ changes to ✔).

19 To show the location of the mouse pointer when you press the Ctrl key, click this option (☐ changes to ✔).

20 Click OK when you finish selecting all the mouse settings you want to change.

CHANGE KEYBOARD SETTINGS

Y ou can change the way your keyboard responds to your commands. For example, you can change the way a character repeats when you hold down a key on your keyboard. This is useful if you often use repeated characters to underline, separate or emphasize text.

The Repeat delay setting adjusts the length of time a key must be

held down before the character starts to repeat. The Repeat rate setting determines how quickly characters appear on your screen when you hold down a key. You can test the settings while making adjustments.

You can also change the speed at which the cursor blinks. The cursor, or insertion point, indicates where the text you

type will appear in a document. The cursor should blink fast enough so it is easy to find, but slow enough so it is not distracting. You can preview your cursor blink rate to find a setting you prefer.

CHANGE KEYBOARD SETTINGS

1 Click Start.

2 Click Settings.

3 Click Control Panel.

4 Double-click Keyboard.

■ The Control Panel window appears.

Note: If all the items do not appear in the Control Panel window, click the view all Control Panel options link in the window to display all the items.

■ The Keyboard Properties dialog box appears.

Can I make my keyboard easier to use?

✔ Windows offers various accessibility options that you can select to make your keyboard easier to use. For example, you can have Windows ignore repeated keystrokes or play tones when you press the Caps Lock, Num Lock or Scroll Lock keys. For more information, see page 244.

I have trouble using my keyboard to type my documents. What can I do?

✔ You can use the On-Screen Keyboard. The On-Screen Keyboard allows you to use your mouse to select characters you want to enter in a document. For more information, see page 242.

What is the correct typing position to help avoid wrist strain?

✔ You should keep your elbows level with the keyboard. Always keep your wrists straight and higher than your fingers while working on the keyboard. You can use a wrist rest to elevate your wrists and ensure they remain straight at all times. If you start to experience any pain, tingling or numbness while working, take a break. If the sensation continues, you should see a doctor.

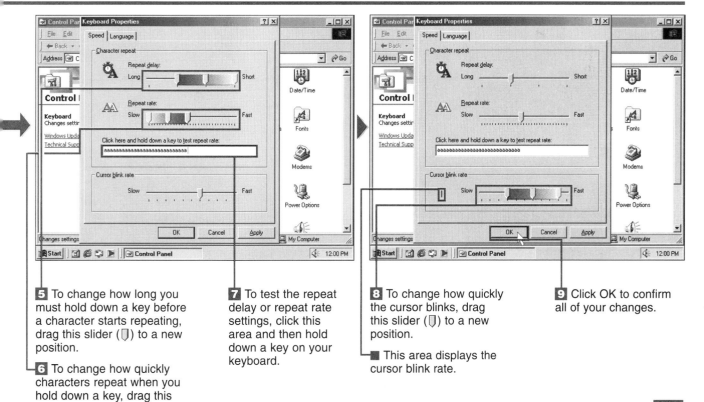

5 To change how long you must hold down a key before a character starts repeating, drag this slider (🔲) to a new position.

6 To change how quickly characters repeat when you hold down a key, drag this slider (🔲) to a new position.

7 To test the repeat delay or repeat rate settings, click this area and then hold down a key on your keyboard.

8 To change how quickly the cursor blinks, drag this slider (🔲) to a new position.

■ This area displays the cursor blink rate.

9 Click OK to confirm all of your changes.

CREATE A NEW FILE TYPE

Many files on your computer are associated with a certain program. Windows uses extensions to associate file types with programs. For example, a file called report.txt is a Text Document type of file and is associated with the Notepad program. Windows automatically recognizes many common types of files, such as text, sound, picture and video files.

You can create a new file type to tell Windows how you want to work with a certain type of file. For example, you can create a file type for letters you create that have the .let extension and associate the WordPad program with the file type. Before creating a new file type, you can view a list of all the extensions and associated file types that are currently registered with Windows. Any new file types

you create will be added to this list.

After creating a new file type, you can assign a unique icon to make the file type easier to identify in your folders. To change the icon for a file type, see page 210.

CREATE A NEW FILE TYPE

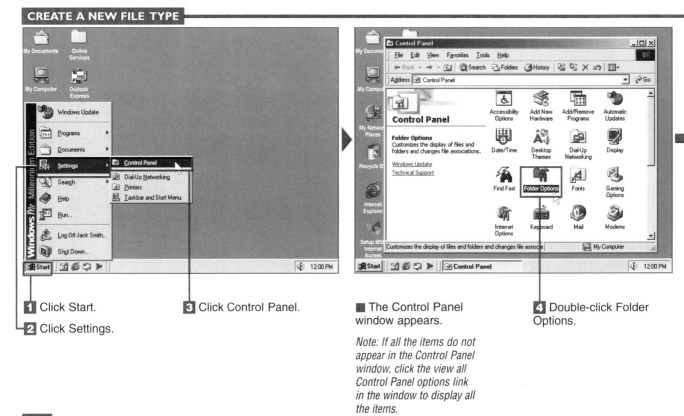

1 Click Start.

2 Click Settings.

3 Click Control Panel.

■ The Control Panel window appears.

Note: If all the items do not appear in the Control Panel window, click the view all Control Panel options link in the window to display all the items.

4 Double-click Folder Options.

Is there a faster way to create a new file type?

✔ When you double-click a file of a type that is not registered with Windows, the Open With dialog box appears. You can use the dialog box to create a new file type. Click the program you want to use to open and work with files of this type. Then make sure the Always use this program to open these files option displays a check mark (☑). Windows will create a new file type using the extension of the file. The next time you double-click a file of this type, the file will open in the program you selected.

After creating a file type with the .let extension, I named a document report.let. Why did Windows rename the document report.let.doc?

✔ Some Windows programs add default extensions to files saved without an extension or with a non-standard extension such as .let. To use a non-standard extension when saving a document, type the name of the file inside quotation marks (""). For example, type "report.let" as the file name.

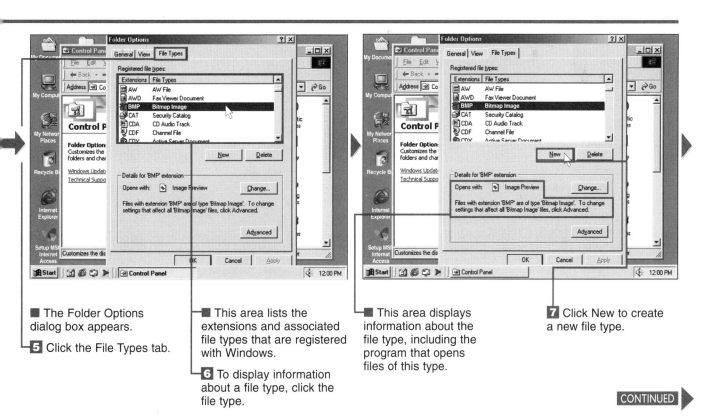

■ The Folder Options dialog box appears.

5 Click the File Types tab.

■ This area lists the extensions and associated file types that are registered with Windows.

6 To display information about a file type, click the file type.

■ This area displays information about the file type, including the program that opens files of this type.

7 Click New to create a new file type.

CONTINUED ▶

CREATE A NEW FILE TYPE
(CONTINUED)

When creating a new file type, you must provide an extension for the file type. File extensions are usually three letters that appear after the period at the end of a file name, such as .doc or .txt.

When creating a new file type, you can associate the new file type with an existing file type or create

a brand-new file type. If you associate the new file type with an existing file type, Windows will copy the characteristics of the existing file type to the new file type. For example, if you associate the .let extension with the WordPad Document file type, Windows will handle the new file type the same way it handles WordPad Document files. If you

create a brand-new file type, you will have to select the program that will open files of that type.

After you create a file type, you can edit the file type. For example, you can change which program you want to open files of that type when you double-click the files. To edit a file type, see page 212.

CREATE A NEW FILE TYPE (CONTINUED)

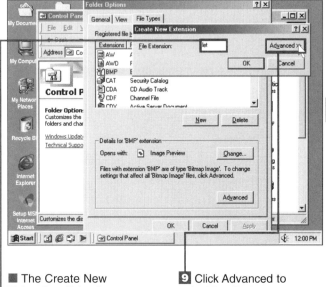

■ The Create New Extension dialog box appears.

8 Click this area and then type an extension for the new file type.

9 Click Advanced to select the file type you want to associate with the new extension.

10 Click this area to display a list of file types that you can associate with the extension.

11 Click the file type you want to associate with the extension.

Note: To create a brand-new file type, select <New>.

How can I delete a file type I created?

✔ In the Folder Options dialog box, select the File Types tab. Click the file type you want to delete and then click the Delete button. When you delete a file type, the files will not be associated with any program and Windows will display the Open With dialog box when you double-click the files.

Can I use more than three letters in a file name extension?

✔ You can create longer file extensions, such as .budget, but make sure your extensions do not contain any spaces or periods. If you share files with people who use older programs, these programs may not be able to work with files with long file name extensions.

Why can't I see the file extensions?

✔ Windows, by default, does not display the file extensions for registered file types. In the Folder Options dialog box, select the View tab and click Hide file extensions for known file types to display the file extensions (☑ changes to ☐).

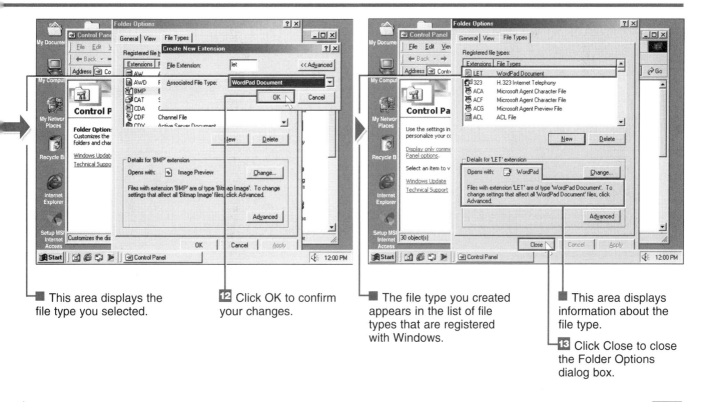

■ This area displays the file type you selected.

12 Click OK to confirm your changes.

■ The file type you created appears in the list of file types that are registered with Windows.

■ This area displays information about the file type.

13 Click Close to close the Folder Options dialog box.

CHANGE ICON FOR A FILE TYPE

Windows uses a specific icon to represent each type of file on your computer. Icons help you identify each type of file and the kind of information each file contains. You can change the icon Windows displays for a file type. Windows provides many icons you can choose from.

In addition to identifying the contents of a file, the icon normally indicates the program that is used to open a file. For example, if WordPad is used to open a file, Windows will display the WordPad icon with the name of the file.

If you create your own file type, you may want to change the icon to one that better represents the file type.

All files with the same extension will display the icon you select.

For example, if you change the icon for the file type that uses the .let extension, Windows will change the icon of all files with the .let extension.

Changing icons is a good way to give your computer a fresh look, but it may cause confusion if you share your computer with other people.

CHANGE ICON FOR A FILE TYPE

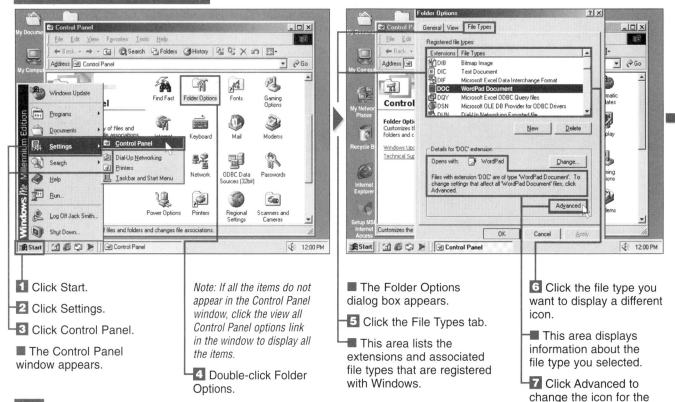

1 Click Start.

2 Click Settings.

3 Click Control Panel.

■ The Control Panel window appears.

Note: If all the items do not appear in the Control Panel window, click the view all Control Panel options link in the window to display all the items.

4 Double-click Folder Options.

■ The Folder Options dialog box appears.

5 Click the File Types tab.

■ This area lists the extensions and associated file types that are registered with Windows.

6 Click the file type you want to display a different icon.

■ This area displays information about the file type you selected.

7 Click Advanced to change the icon for the file type.

Are there more icons available on my computer?

✔ Yes. In the Change Icon dialog box, you can click the Browse button to find files containing icons on your computer. Files that contain icons often have the .dll or .exe extension. A file that contains a single icon often has the .ico extension. You can find additional icons in the C:\Windows\moricons.dll file.

How do I change the appearance of the icons displayed on my desktop?

✔ To change the icon for a shortcut on your desktop, right-click the shortcut and select Properties. Click Change Icon and then click the icon you want to use. To change the appearance of the My Computer, My Documents, My Network Places and Recycle Bin icons on your desktop, see page 180.

Can I create my own icons?

✔ There are several programs available that allow you to create your own icons. Microangelo from Impact Software (www.impactsoft.com) and Icon Forge from NeoSoft (www.testware.co.uk/utils.htm) are both available as shareware programs and can be downloaded from the Internet. A shareware program is a program that you can use for free for a limited time.

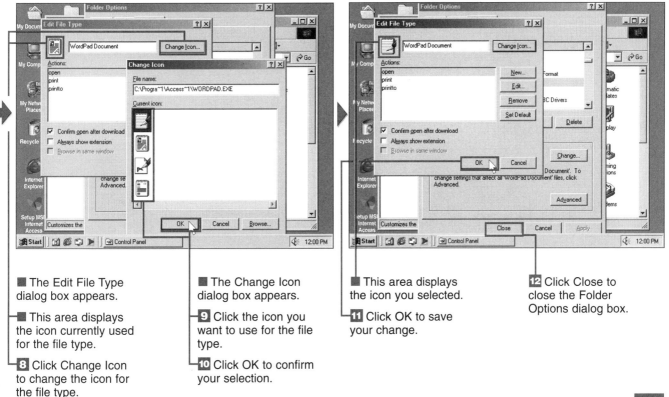

■ The Edit File Type dialog box appears.

■ This area displays the icon currently used for the file type.

8 Click Change Icon to change the icon for the file type.

■ The Change Icon dialog box appears.

9 Click the icon you want to use for the file type.

10 Click OK to confirm your selection.

■ This area displays the icon you selected.

11 Click OK to save your change.

12 Click Close to close the Folder Options dialog box.

EDIT A FILE TYPE

You can make changes to a file type. You should be careful when making changes to file types, since this can affect the way the files work.

You can change the description of a file type to one that better suits the file type. For example, you may want to change the description of a file type from

WordPad Document to Business Letter to make files of that type easier to identify. When you view items in a window using the Details view, Windows displays a description of the file type. To change the view of items in a window, see page 42.

Most file types have one or more actions. An action is a command that allows you to work with the

file type. Common actions include Open and Print. When you right-click a file, the actions available for the file type appear on the shortcut menu. You can change the name that appears on the shortcut menu for an action. You can also change which program performs an action.

see page 42

EDIT A FILE TYPE

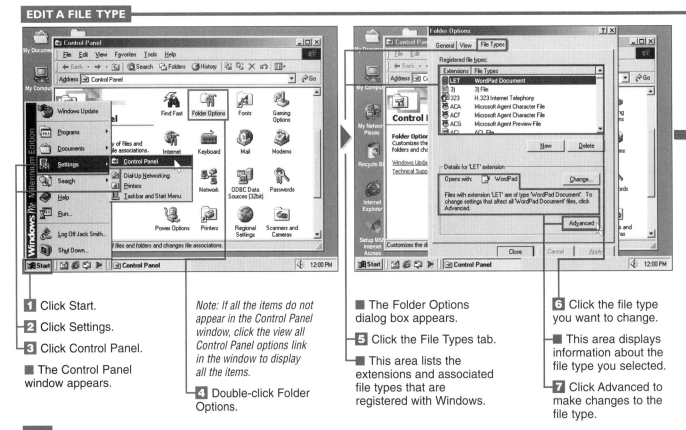

1 Click Start.

2 Click Settings.

3 Click Control Panel.

■ The Control Panel window appears.

Note: If all the items do not appear in the Control Panel window, click the view all Control Panel options link in the window to display all the items.

4 Double-click Folder Options.

■ The Folder Options dialog box appears.

5 Click the File Types tab.

■ This area lists the extensions and associated file types that are registered with Windows.

6 Click the file type you want to change.

■ This area displays information about the file type you selected.

7 Click Advanced to make changes to the file type.

212

Can I create a new action?

✔ You can create as many actions as you need. Display the Edit File Type dialog box for the file type you want to change and then click the New button. Type a name for the action and then click the Browse button. Select the program you want to perform the action and then click the Open button.

How do I remove an action I no longer want a file type to use?

✔ Display the Edit File Type dialog box for the file type and select the action you want to remove. Then click the Remove button.

How can I tell Windows which action I want to make the default action?

✔ The default action for most file types is Open. To change the default action, display the Edit File Type dialog box for the file type and select the action you want to make the default action. Then click the Set Default button. The default action is performed when you double-click a file. When you right-click a file, the default action for the file type appears in bold on the shortcut menu.

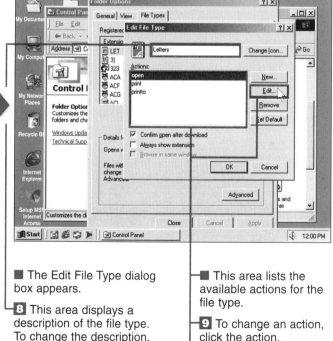

■ The Edit File Type dialog box appears.

8 This area displays a description of the file type. To change the description, type a new description.

■ This area lists the available actions for the file type.

9 To change an action, click the action.

10 Click Edit to change the action.

■ The Editing action for type dialog box appears.

11 This area displays the name of the action that appears on the shortcut menu for files of this type. To change the name, type a new name.

■ This area shows the location and the name of the program used to perform the action.

12 To change the program used to perform the action, click Browse.

CONTINUED

EDIT A FILE TYPE (CONTINUED)

When editing a file type, you can change the program you want to perform an action. For example, if Notepad currently opens the file type, you can change the Open action to use another program, such as WordPad, to open files of that type. If a file type has several actions, you can change the program that performs each action.

You can have Windows always open files of a certain type as soon as they finish downloading. This allows you to work with the downloaded files right away. Before you open a file you downloaded, you should check the file for viruses. If you open a file that contains a virus, the information on your computer could be damaged.

You can choose to display the three-letter extension for files of a certain type. Displaying file extensions can help you identify the types of files you are viewing.

Changes you make to a file type will affect all files of that type.

EDIT A FILE TYPE (CONTINUED)

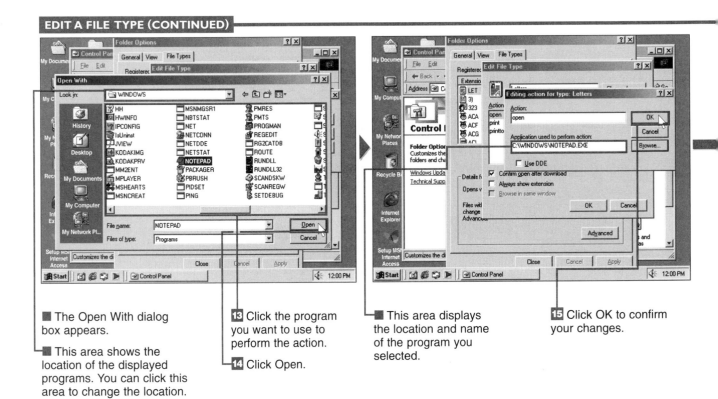

■ The Open With dialog box appears.

■ This area shows the location of the displayed programs. You can click this area to change the location.

13 Click the program you want to use to perform the action.

14 Click Open.

■ This area displays the location and name of the program you selected.

15 Click OK to confirm your changes.

I used Browse to select a program I want to perform an action, but Windows states it cannot find the program. Why?

✔ You may have selected the program's shortcut. Shortcuts display an arrow (🔗) in their icon and only contain the information needed to find a program. When you want to change the program that performs an action, you must select the original program file.

Can I show the extensions for all my files?

✔ Yes. Display the Folder Options dialog box, select the View tab and then click the Hide file extensions for known file types option (☑ changes to ☐).

Can I specify which character on the keyboard performs an action when I right-click a file?

✔ Yes. Display the Editing action for type dialog box for the action you want to specify a character for and type a name for the action. To specify which character in the action is used to perform the action, precede the character with an ampersand (&), such as **Open with &WordPad**. When the shortcut menu is displayed for a file of that type, you can press the key for the character you specified to perform the action.

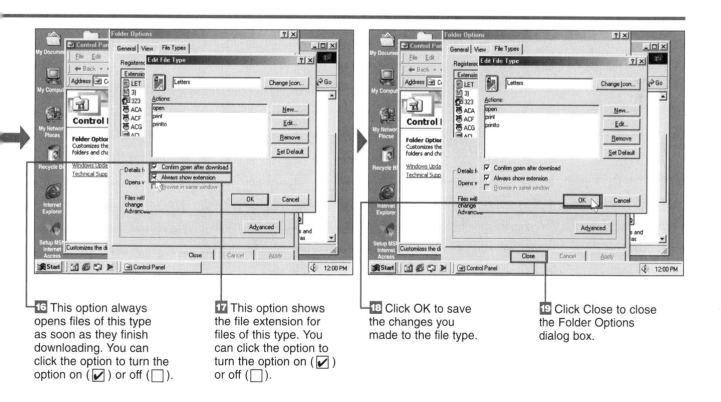

16 This option always opens files of this type as soon as they finish downloading. You can click the option to turn the option on (☑) or off (☐).

17 This option shows the file extension for files of this type. You can click the option to turn the option on (☑) or off (☐).

18 Click OK to save the changes you made to the file type.

19 Click Close to close the Folder Options dialog box.

USING MULTIPLE MONITORS

Windows allows you to use more than one monitor to expand your desktop area. For example, graphic artists often use multiple monitors to display the image they are working with on one monitor and their tools on another monitor. You can also use multiple monitors to display several documents at once or stretch a document across more than one monitor to view more of the document without scrolling.

Each monitor you use must have its own video adapter. Each video adapter must support the ability to work with multiple monitors.

When using multiple monitors, one monitor will be the primary monitor. The primary monitor displays the taskbar and desktop items. You must use the primary monitor to work with certain programs.

Although all the monitors display the same background and screen saver, you can specify a different color depth and screen resolution for each monitor.

You can change the arrangement of the monitor icons in the Display Properties dialog box. This determines how you move items from one monitor to the other.

USING MULTIPLE MONITORS

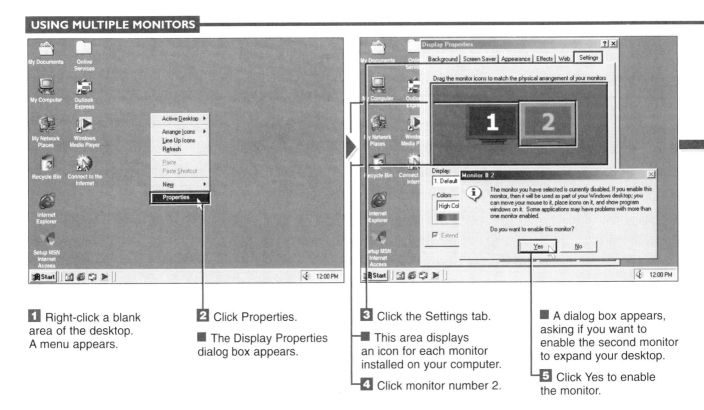

1 Right-click a blank area of the desktop. A menu appears.

2 Click Properties.

■ The Display Properties dialog box appears.

3 Click the Settings tab.

■ This area displays an icon for each monitor installed on your computer.

4 Click monitor number 2.

■ A dialog box appears, asking if you want to enable the second monitor to expand your desktop.

5 Click Yes to enable the monitor.

MASTER IT

How do I install a second monitor?

✔ Follow the manufacturer's instructions to add the video adapter for the second monitor to your computer. When you turn on your computer, Windows will detect the new video adapter and automatically install the appropriate software. If Windows does not detect the video adapter, see page 546 for information about installing hardware.

Can I change which monitor is the primary monitor?

✔ Yes. To change the primary monitor, shut down Windows and turn off your computer and monitors. Plug the monitor you want to use as the primary monitor into the primary video adapter and plug the other monitor into the secondary video adapter. Then restart your computer.

How do I determine which monitor an icon in the Display Properties dialog box represents?

✔ Right-click the monitor icon and select Identify. The monitor will display the number of the icon it corresponds to.

How do I stop using a secondary monitor?

✔ In the Display Properties dialog box, click the Settings tab and then click the monitor you want to stop using. Click the Extend my Windows desktop onto this monitor option (☑ changes to ☐).

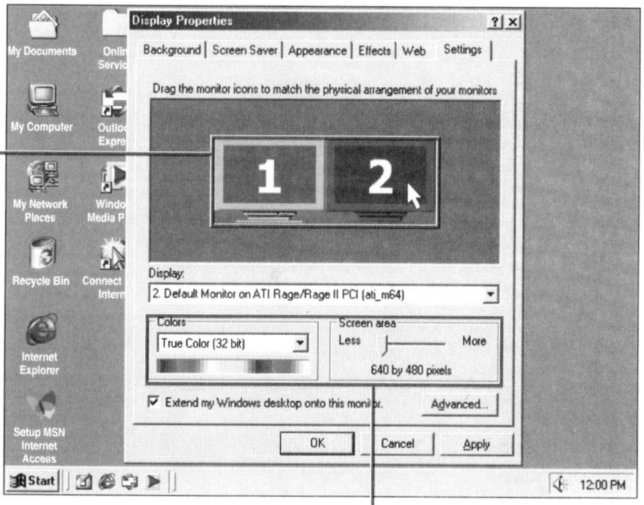

6 To display the settings for a monitor, click the icon for the monitor of interest.

■ This area displays the number of colors and the screen resolution for the monitor you selected.

Note: To change the number of colors for a monitor, see page 174. To change the screen resolution for a monitor, see page 172.

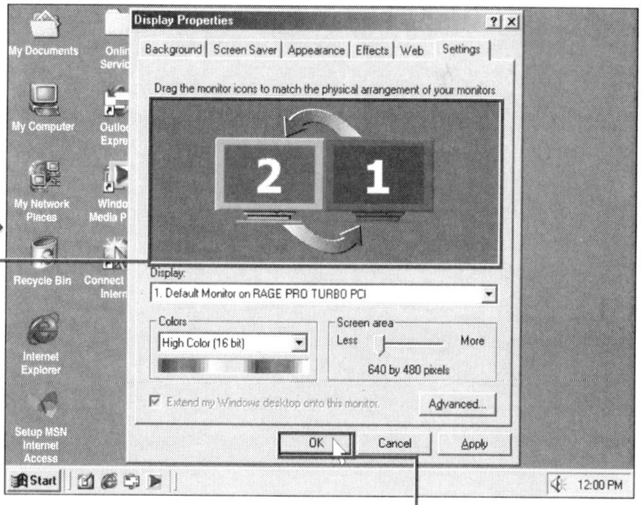

7 To change the arrangement of the monitors, position the mouse ↖ over a monitor icon and then drag the monitor icon to a new location.

Note: The position of the monitor icons determines how you will move items between the monitors.

8 Click OK to confirm your changes.

SET UP MULTIPLE USERS

I f you share your computer with family members or colleagues, you can set up the computer so each person can have their own personalized settings.

Setting up your computer for more than one person allows you to meet the needs of each person. For example, if children use your computer, you can personalize the settings so that shortcuts to their favorite games and programs are available on the desktop.

Setting up a computer for multiple users is also useful when a person requires two or more custom settings. For example, if you use your computer to perform demonstrations, you can display the Windows default settings during demonstrations and then return to your personalized settings later.

Windows asks you to specify a user name and password for each person you set up on the

computer. If you are currently using a user name and password to start Windows, you can use your current user name to set yourself up as the first user.

Windows stores each person's settings with their user name. When a person enters their user name and password to log on to Windows, their personalized settings are displayed.

SET UP MULTIPLE USERS

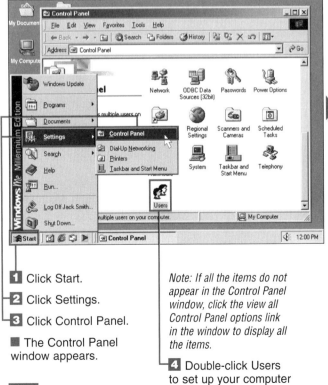

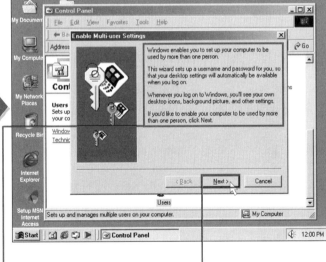

1 Click Start.

2 Click Settings.

3 Click Control Panel.

■ The Control Panel window appears.

Note: If all the items do not appear in the Control Panel window, click the view all Control Panel options link in the window to display all the items.

4 Double-click Users to set up your computer for multiple users.

■ The Enable Multi-user Settings wizard appears the first time you set up your computer for multiple users.

■ This area describes the wizard.

5 Click Next to continue.

Will other users be able to view my files and use the programs I install?

✔ Yes. Each user set up on the computer will be able to access all the programs and files on the computer, but they may not be able to access all the resources on the network. Users may need to place their own shortcuts to new programs on the desktop and Start menu.

Once new users are set up, how do we switch from one user to another?

✔ The current user must log off so another person can log on and use the computer with their personalized settings. Click the Start button and then select Log Off. Click Yes in the Log Off Windows dialog box. Windows displays a dialog box that enables another person to log on using their user name and password.

How do I return my computer to a single-user system?

✔ From the Start menu, click Settings and select Control Panel. Double-click Passwords. Click the User Profiles tab and then select the All users of this computer use the same preferences and desktop settings option (◯ changes to ◉).

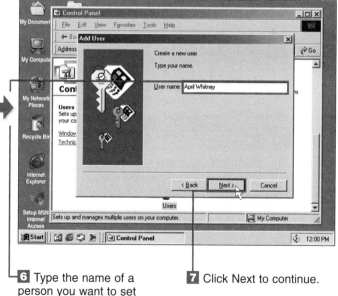

-6 Type the name of a person you want to set up to use this computer.

-7 Click Next to continue.

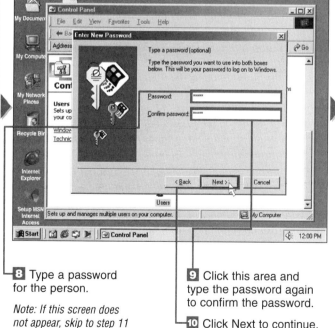

-8 Type a password for the person.

Note: If this screen does not appear, skip to step 11 on page 220.

-9 Click this area and type the password again to confirm the password.

-10 Click Next to continue.

CONTINUED ▶

SET UP MULTIPLE USERS (CONTINUED)

When setting up your computer for multiple users, Windows lets you specify which items each person can customize. For example, users can have their own settings for the My Documents folder, but share a common Start menu. When a common item is modified, every user that shares the item will see the modifications the next time they log on.

You can allow each person to customize the appearance of the desktop and have the Documents menu list only the most recently opened documents for each user.

Each person can also change and organize the items that appear on the Start menu.

You may want each person to have their own Favorites folder. This allows each user to have a customized list of their favorite folders and Web pages.

Each user can also have personalized Downloaded Web pages information. This ensures that Web-related folders, such as Temporary Internet Files, contain information specific to each user.

You can also let each person customize the contents and appearance of the My Documents folder on the desktop.

Windows lets you specify how you want to customize the settings. You can have Windows use the current set up of the computer to create items or create new items using Windows' default settings.

SET UP MULTIPLE USERS (CONTINUED)

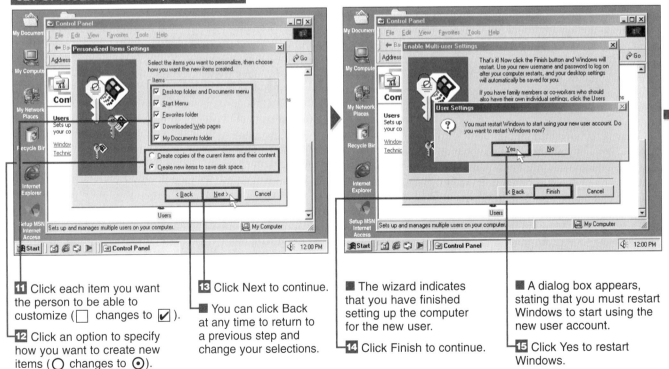

■11 Click each item you want the person to be able to customize (☐ changes to ✔).

■12 Click an option to specify how you want to create new items (○ changes to ⊙).

■13 Click Next to continue.

■ You can click Back at any time to return to a previous step and change your selections.

■ The wizard indicates that you have finished setting up the computer for the new user.

■14 Click Finish to continue.

■ A dialog box appears, stating that you must restart Windows to start using the new user account.

■15 Click Yes to restart Windows.

How do I add another user?

✔ In the User Settings dialog box, click the New User button and then enter the information for the new user. You can also create a new user each time Windows starts. In the dialog box that appears each time Windows starts, drag the mouse I over the name that appears in the User name area to highlight the name and then type a name for the new user. Press the Tab key and enter a password for the new user.

How do I change the password for a user?

✔ In the User Settings dialog box, click the name of the user whose password you want to change. Click the Set Password button and then specify a new password. You must know the user's original password.

How do I remove a user from my computer?

✔ In the User Settings dialog box, click the name of the user you want to remove and then click the Delete button.

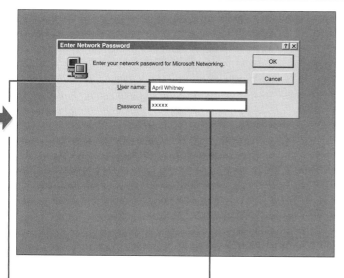

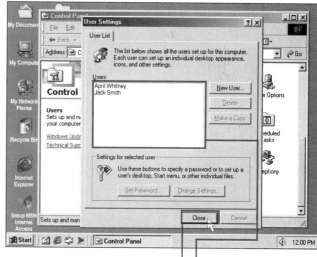

■ Each time Windows starts, a dialog box appears, asking you to enter a user name and password.

16 Drag the mouse I over the name that appears in this area to highlight the name. Then type the name of the user you want to log on as.

17 Click this area and type the password for the user. Then press the Enter key.

■ Windows starts the computer with the user's customized settings.

DISPLAY LIST OF USERS

1 To display a list of users set up on your computer, perform steps 1 to 4 on page 218.

■ The User Settings dialog box appears.

■ This area displays the name of each person set up to use this computer.

2 Click Close to close the dialog box.

MOVE AND SIZE THE TASKBAR

You can move and size the taskbar to accommodate your preferences. The taskbar is the starting point for most of the tasks you perform in Windows. The taskbar contains the Start button and displays the name of each open window on your screen as well as the current time. The Quick Launch toolbar appears beside the Start button

on the taskbar and contains shortcut icons to the desktop, Internet Explorer, Outlook Express and Windows Media Player.

Windows initially displays the taskbar at the bottom of your screen. You may want to move the taskbar to a different side of your screen. Since other

software programs display their menus at the top of the screen, you may prefer to have the taskbar also appear at the top of your screen.

You can adjust the size of the taskbar. Increasing the size of the taskbar provides more space to display information about open windows.

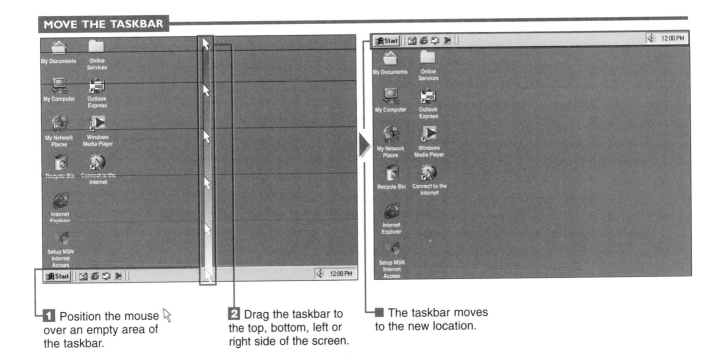

MOVE THE TASKBAR

1 Position the mouse ℞ over an empty area of the taskbar.

2 Drag the taskbar to the top, bottom, left or right side of the screen.

■ The taskbar moves to the new location.

Why has my taskbar disappeared?

✔ You may have accidentally sized the taskbar to a thin line at the edge of your screen. Position the mouse pointer over the edge of the screen where you last saw the taskbar. When ⌖ changes to ↕ or ↔, you can drag the mouse to increase the size of the taskbar.

How can I see more information about a small button on the taskbar?

✔ Position the mouse pointer over the button. After a few seconds, a box appears displaying the full name of the window the button represents.

How can I use the taskbar to display the current date?

✔ Position the mouse pointer over the time displayed on the taskbar. After a few seconds, Windows displays the current date.

How do I correct the time displayed on the taskbar?

✔ Double-click the time displayed on the taskbar to open the Date/Time Properties dialog box. This dialog box allows you to change the date and time set in your computer. For more information, see page 164.

SIZE THE TASKBAR

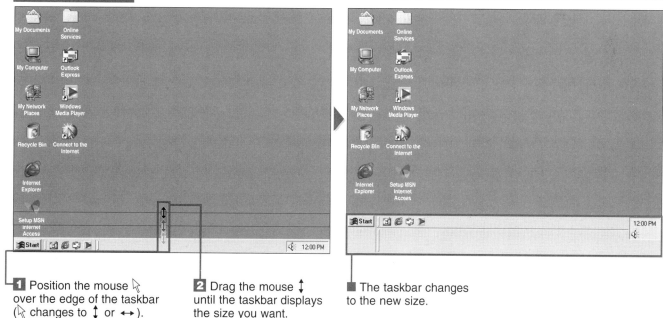

1 Position the mouse ⌖ over the edge of the taskbar (⌖ changes to ↕ or ↔).

2 Drag the mouse ↕ until the taskbar displays the size you want.

■ The taskbar changes to the new size.

ADD A TOOLBAR TO THE TASKBAR

Windows includes several ready-made toolbars that you can add to the taskbar. Toolbars contain buttons to provide easy access to files, programs and Windows features.

The Links and Address toolbars allow you to access the Web without first starting your Web browser. You can click a link in the Links toolbar to access a useful Web site. You can type

a Web page address in the Address toolbar to access the Web page from your desktop. The Desktop toolbar contains all the items on your desktop. The Quick Launch toolbar allows you to quickly access the desktop, Internet Explorer, Outlook Express and Windows Media Player.

You can create a new toolbar from any folder on your computer and place the toolbar on your desktop

or on the taskbar. For example, you can create toolbars from the Control Panel, Printers and My Documents folders to quickly access the items in the folders. If all the documents you frequently use are stored in one folder, you can create a toolbar from the folder to be able to quickly open the documents.

ADD A TOOLBAR TO THE TASKBAR

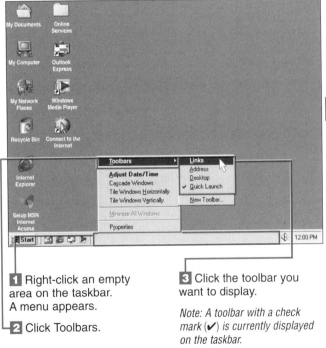

1 Right-click an empty area on the taskbar. A menu appears.

2 Click Toolbars.

3 Click the toolbar you want to display.

Note: A toolbar with a check mark (✔) is currently displayed on the taskbar.

■ The toolbar you selected appears on the taskbar.

■ You can repeat steps 1 to 3 to remove a toolbar from the taskbar.

How do I change the size of a toolbar on the taskbar?

✔ Position the mouse over the raised line on the toolbar you want to size (⤢ changes to ↔). Drag the raised line to the left or right until the toolbar displays the size you want.

Can I add an item to the Quick Launch toolbar?

✔ You can place a shortcut to an item such as a program, document or folder on the Quick Launch toolbar. To do so, drag the item to the Quick Launch toolbar.

Why doesn't the toolbar display all the items in the folder?

✔ If all the items in a folder cannot fit on the toolbar, » appears at the end of the toolbar. You can click » to view the items that are not displayed.

Can I move a toolbar?

✔ Yes. Position the mouse over the top or left edge of the toolbar you want to move and then drag the toolbar to any edge of your screen.

How do I remove a toolbar?

✔ Right-click a blank area of the toolbar you want to remove and then select Close.

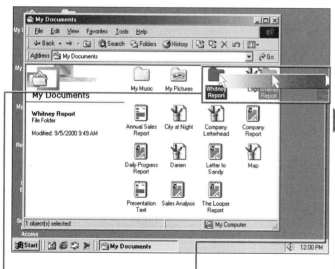

CREATE A NEW TOOLBAR

1 Locate the folder that contains the items you want to appear in a toolbar.

2 Position the mouse ⤢ over the folder.

3 Drag the folder to an edge of your screen.

Note: To create a new toolbar on the taskbar, drag the folder to an empty area on the taskbar.

■ The contents of the folder appear in a toolbar.

CHANGE THE TASKBAR AND START MENU SETTINGS

Y ou can change the taskbar and Start menu settings to suit your needs.

You can use the Always on top option to ensure that the taskbar is always visible, even when a window fills the entire screen. You can turn off this option to provide more working space in a window.

You can use the Auto hide option to hide the taskbar when you are not using it. Hiding the taskbar provides more working space on your desktop.

The Show small icons in Start menu option reduces the amount of space the Start menu takes up when displayed.

The Show clock option displays or hides the clock on the taskbar.

The Use personalized menus option hides items on the Start menu that you rarely use. This can help you quickly locate the items you use often. If you want Windows to always display all the items on the Start menu, you can turn the option off.

CHANGE GENERAL SETTINGS

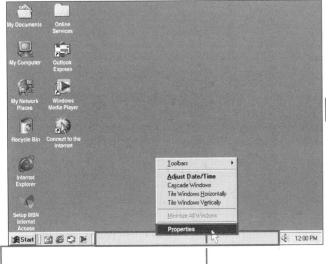

1 Right-click an empty area of the taskbar. A menu appears.

2 Click Properties.

■ The Taskbar and Start Menu Properties dialog box appears.

3 Click the General tab.

4 This option ensures that the taskbar is always visible, even when a window fills the entire screen. You can click this option if you do not want the taskbar to always be visible (☑ changes to ☐).

MASTER IT

How can I make the taskbar appear when the Auto hide option is on?

✔ Position the mouse over the area where you last saw the taskbar. You can also press Ctrl+Esc to display the taskbar and Start menu.

How do I display hidden programs on the Start menu when I use the personalized menus option?

✔ You can display hidden programs on the Start menu by clicking ⹁ at the bottom of a menu.

What happens when the number of buttons on the taskbar exceeds the available space?

✔ Two small arrows (⬆ and ⬇) appear to the right of the taskbar buttons. You can click these arrows to scroll through buttons not currently displayed on the taskbar.

How can I change the time displayed on the taskbar?

✔ The taskbar displays the time set in your computer. To change the time, double-click the time to display the Date/Time Properties dialog box. You can use this dialog box to change the time and date set in your computer. For more information, see page 164.

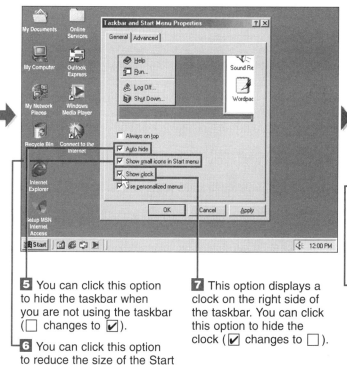

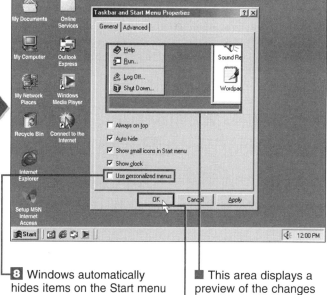

5 You can click this option to hide the taskbar when you are not using the taskbar (☐ changes to ☑).

6 You can click this option to reduce the size of the Start menu (☐ changes to ☑).

7 This option displays a clock on the right side of the taskbar. You can click this option to hide the clock (☑ changes to ☐).

8 Windows automatically hides items on the Start menu you rarely use. You can click this option to have Windows always display all the items on the menu (☑ changes to ☐).

■ This area displays a preview of the changes you made.

9 Click OK to confirm your changes.

CONTINUED

CHANGE THE TASKBAR AND START MENU SETTINGS (CONTINUED)

The advanced Start menu and taskbar settings allow you to specify how you want the Start menu to look and act.

You can specify if you want the Favorites menu, the Log Off command and the Run command to appear on the Start menu. The Favorites menu contains Web pages and folders you frequently access. The Log Off command allows you to log off your computer or network. The Run command lets you start a new program.

If you no longer want to be able to reorganize the items on the Start menu by dragging and dropping items, you can turn off this feature.

Windows allows you to display the contents of the Control Panel, Dial-Up Networking, My Documents, My Pictures and Printers folders on the Start menu. This is useful if you frequently access items in these folders.

If the Programs menu contains too many items to fit in one

column, Windows adds another column to display the additional items. You can make the Programs menu a scrolling menu to display all the items in one column.

By default, a shortcut menu appears when you right-click the taskbar. You can stop this menu from appearing. You can also make it impossible to move and resize the taskbar.

CHANGE ADVANCED SETTINGS

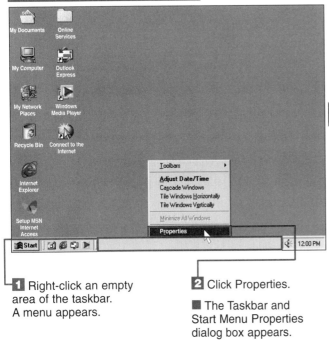

1 Right-click an empty area of the taskbar. A menu appears.

2 Click Properties.

■ The Taskbar and Start Menu Properties dialog box appears.

3 Click the Advanced tab.

■ This area lists the available options for the Start menu and taskbar.

■ These options display the Favorites menu, Log Off command and Run command on the Start menu.

■ This option allows you to drag items from one location to another on the Start menu.

228

Is there another way to display the Taskbar and Start Menu Properties dialog box?

✔ Yes. Click the Start button, select Settings and then click Taskbar and Start Menu.

How do I scroll through the items on the Programs menu?

✔ If you have changed the Programs menu to a scrolling menu, Windows will display small arrows (▲ and ▼) at the top and bottom of the menu. To scroll through the Programs menu and view the hidden items, position the mouse pointer over an arrow.

How do I add items to the Favorites menu?

✔ Internet Explorer allows you to add Web pages you frequently visit to the Favorites menu. You can also add folders to the Favorites menu. For more information, see pages 446 to 449.

How can I organize the items on the Start menu after I turn off the drag and drop feature?

✔ You can use the Start Menu window to organize the Start menu. For more information, see page 236.

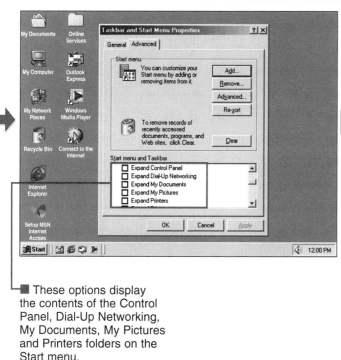

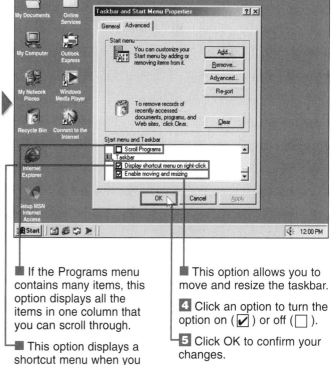

■ These options display the contents of the Control Panel, Dial-Up Networking, My Documents, My Pictures and Printers folders on the Start menu.

■ If the Programs menu contains many items, this option displays all the items in one column that you can scroll through.

■ This option displays a shortcut menu when you right-click the taskbar.

■ This option allows you to move and resize the taskbar.

4 Click an option to turn the option on (✔) or off (☐).

5 Click OK to confirm your changes.

ADD A PROGRAM TO THE START MENU

You can add programs to the Start menu so you can quickly open them. You can also add files you frequently use to the Start menu for quick access. Having programs and files you frequently use on the Start menu saves you time, since you do not have to search for the items on your computer.

Most programs designed for Windows will place a shortcut

on the Start menu when you install the program. If a program does not appear on the Start menu, you can add the program yourself.

When you add a program or file to the Start menu, Windows creates a shortcut to the program or file and adds the shortcut to the Start menu. The original program or file remains in the same location on your computer.

When searching for the program or file you want to add to the Start menu, you can have Windows show just programs or all the items in the current location. When adding a file to the Start menu, you should display all the items in the location.

ADD A PROGRAM TO THE START MENU

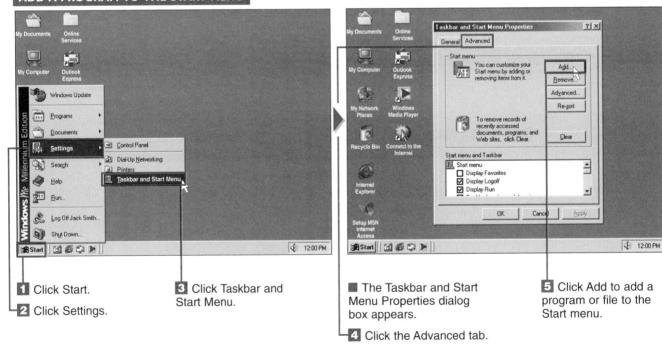

1 Click Start.

2 Click Settings.

3 Click Taskbar and Start Menu.

■ The Taskbar and Start Menu Properties dialog box appears.

4 Click the Advanced tab.

5 Click Add to add a program or file to the Start menu.

Is there another way to open the Taskbar and Start Menu Properties dialog box?

✔ You can right-click an empty area of the taskbar and then select Properties.

How can I quickly add a program or file to the Start menu?

✔ Locate the program or file on your computer that you want to add to the Start menu and then drag the item to the Start button. The program or file will appear at the top of the Start menu. If you want the program or file to appear in a different location on the Start menu, drag the item to the location where you want it to appear.

Can I add items on the network to the Start menu?

✔ Yes. In the Browse dialog box, click the My Network Places icon to access the information available on your network. You can then locate the shared item on your network that you want to add to the Start menu.

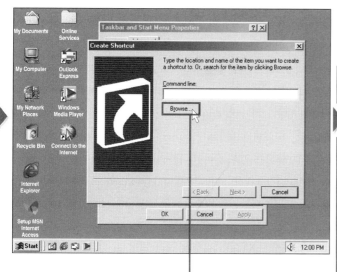

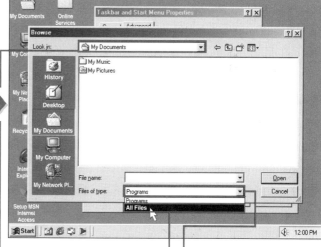

■ The Create Shortcut dialog box appears.

6 Click Browse to search for the program or file that you want to add to the Start menu.

■ The Browse dialog box appears.

■ This area shows the location of the displayed folders and programs. You can click this area to change the location.

7 Click this area to specify that you want to display all the items in the current location.

8 Click All Files to display all the items.

CONTINUED ▶

ADD A PROGRAM
TO THE START MENU (CONTINUED)

After you select the program or file you want to add to the Start menu, you can place the item on the main Start menu or inside one of the folders the Start menu contains. For example, you can select the Programs folder if you want an item to appear on the Programs menu.

If you want a program to open automatically each time you start Windows, you can place the program in the StartUp folder. This is useful for programs and files you frequently use.

You can give the program or file a descriptive name. Windows will suggest a name for the item based on the name of the original

program or file. The name you choose will appear only on the Start menu and will not affect the name of the original program or file. When naming a program or file, use a short name so the Start menu will not take up too much space when displayed on your screen.

ADD A PROGRAM TO THE START MENU (CONTINUED)

■9 Click the program or file you want to add to the Start menu.

■10 Click Open.

■ This area displays the location and name of the program or file you selected.

■11 Click Next to continue.

Can I create a new folder to contain the program or file I add to the Start menu?

✔ If you cannot find an appropriate folder on the Start menu for a program or file, you can create a new folder. In the Select Program Folder dialog box, click the folder you want to contain the new folder and select the New Folder button. Then type a name for the new folder.

Why does Windows ask me to choose an icon for the program I am adding to the Start menu?

✔ If you are adding a program that Windows does not recognize, such as an MS-DOS program, Windows asks you to select the icon you want to represent the program.

Can I rename a program or file I added to the Start menu?

✔ Yes. Display the Start menu and right-click the program or file you want to rename. Select Rename from the menu that appears and then type a new name.

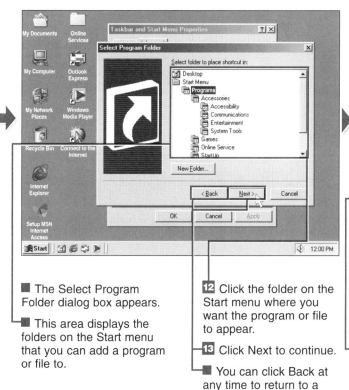

■ The Select Program Folder dialog box appears.

■ This area displays the folders on the Start menu that you can add a program or file to.

12 Click the folder on the Start menu where you want the program or file to appear.

13 Click Next to continue.

■ You can click Back at any time to return to a previous step and change your selections.

14 Type a name for the program or file that you want to appear on the Start menu.

15 Click Finish to add the program or file to the Start menu.

16 Click OK to close the Taskbar and Start Menu Properties dialog box.

■ The program or file will now appear on the Start menu.

REMOVE A PROGRAM FROM THE START MENU

You can remove a program you no longer want to appear on the Start menu. Removing programs you do not need reduces clutter on the Start menu.

Most programs designed for Windows will place a shortcut on the Start menu while they are being installed. Even after you delete a program from your computer, the Start menu may still display the shortcut to the program. You can make the Start menu appear less cluttered by removing programs that are no longer available on your computer or programs you rarely use.

You can also remove files or folders you added to the Start menu. When you remove a folder from the Start menu, all of the items in the folder are also removed. Before removing a folder from the Start menu, you should view the contents of the folder to make sure you will not remove items you frequently work with.

REMOVE A PROGRAM FROM THE START MENU

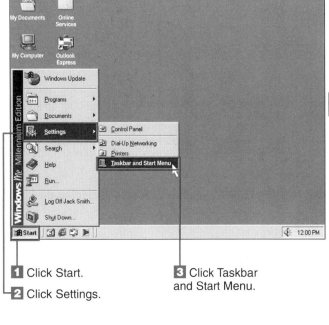

■ **1** Click Start.

■ **2** Click Settings.

■ **3** Click Taskbar and Start Menu.

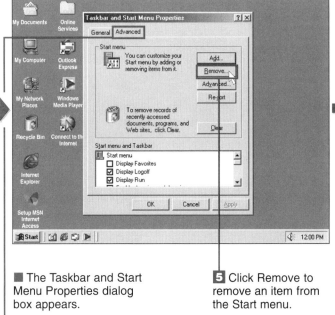

■ The Taskbar and Start Menu Properties dialog box appears.

■ **4** Click the Advanced tab.

■ **5** Click Remove to remove an item from the Start menu.

■ The Remove Shortcuts/Folders dialog box appears.

234

Is there a faster way to delete an item from the Start menu?

✔ On the Start menu, right-click the item you want to delete and then select Delete from the menu that appears.

Does removing a program from the Start menu delete the program from my computer?

✔ Removing a program from the Start menu does not delete the program from your computer. The Start menu displays only shortcuts to programs, not the actual programs. To delete a program from your computer, see page 544.

How can I restore an item I accidentally removed from the Start menu?

✔ You can use the Recycle Bin to restore any items you accidentally removed from the Start menu. To restore a deleted item from the Recycle Bin, see page 74. If the item is not in the Recycle Bin, you can add the item to the Start menu again. To add an item to the Start menu, see page 230.

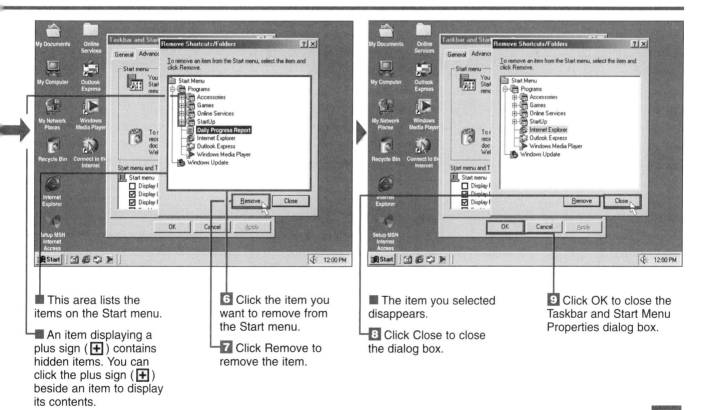

■ This area lists the items on the Start menu.

■ An item displaying a plus sign (⊞) contains hidden items. You can click the plus sign (⊞) beside an item to display its contents.

⬛6 Click the item you want to remove from the Start menu.

⬛7 Click Remove to remove the item.

■ The item you selected disappears.

⬛8 Click Close to close the dialog box.

⬛9 Click OK to close the Taskbar and Start Menu Properties dialog box.

ORGANIZE THE START MENU

You can create folders to organize the items on the Start menu. Each new folder you create will appear as a submenu on the Start menu.

When you install a new program, a shortcut for the program usually appears on the Start menu to give you quick access to the program. Eventually, the Start menu may become cluttered. You can

create folders to organize the programs into logical groups. Items organized into folders are easier to find. For example, you can create a new folder named Utilities that will list the utility programs you frequently use.

When creating a new folder on the Start menu, you should use a descriptive name for the folder that clearly indicates what items the folder contains. The Start

menu will expand to display the entire name of the folder you add. Try to use a short folder name so the Start menu will not take up too much space when displayed on your screen.

You can drag items from other Start menu locations to the new folder or you can place new items in the folder. To add items to the Start menu, see page 230.

ORGANIZE THE START MENU

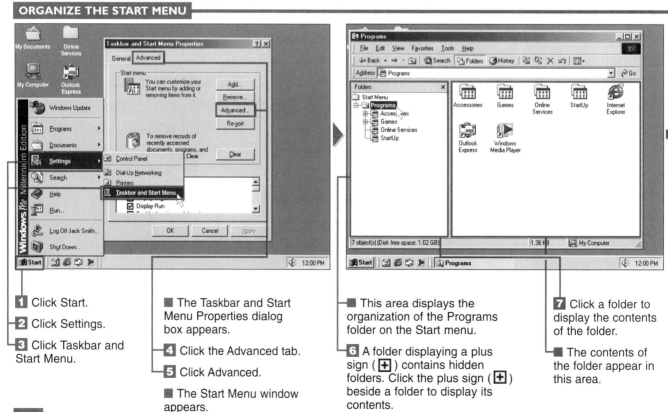

1 Click Start.

2 Click Settings.

3 Click Taskbar and Start Menu.

■ The Taskbar and Start Menu Properties dialog box appears.

4 Click the Advanced tab.

5 Click Advanced.

■ The Start Menu window appears.

■ This area displays the organization of the Programs folder on the Start menu.

6 A folder displaying a plus sign (⊞) contains hidden folders. Click the plus sign (⊞) beside a folder to display its contents.

7 Click a folder to display the contents of the folder.

■ The contents of the folder appear in this area.

How do I move an item to a different folder on the Start menu?

✔ In the Start Menu window, drag the item from the right pane of the window to the folder you want to contain the item in the left pane of the window. You can also move items directly on the Start menu. Click the Start button and position the mouse pointer over the item. Drag the item to the location on the menu where you want the item to appear.

How do I delete items from the Start menu?

✔ In the Start Menu window, click the item you want to remove and then press the Delete key. Windows will not remove the item from your computer, but you will no longer be able to access the item using the Start menu.

Is there an easy way to reorganize items I moved around on the Start menu?

✔ You can sort some sections of the Start menu. Click the Start button and display the section of the menu you want to sort. Right-click the section and then click Sort by Name to arrange the items on the menu alphabetically.

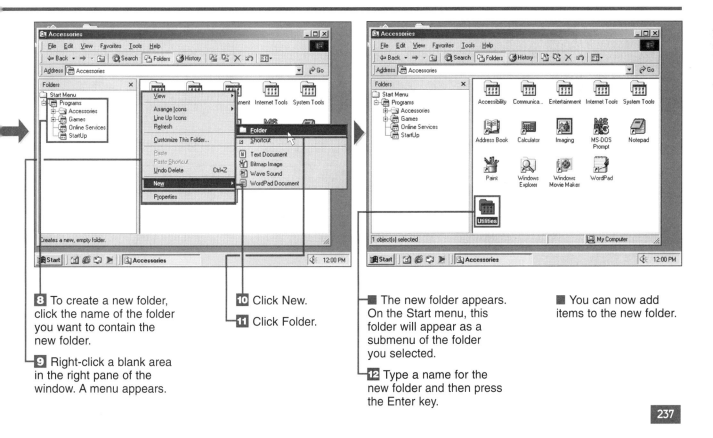

8 To create a new folder, click the name of the folder you want to contain the new folder.

9 Right-click a blank area in the right pane of the window. A menu appears.

10 Click New.

11 Click Folder.

■ The new folder appears. On the Start menu, this folder will appear as a submenu of the folder you selected.

12 Type a name for the new folder and then press the Enter key.

■ You can now add items to the new folder.

237

START A PROGRAM AUTOMATICALLY

You can have a program start automatically each time you turn on your computer.

Having a program start automatically is useful for programs you use every day and for programs you want to be able to access immediately.

Before you can start a program automatically, you need to locate the program on the Start menu

and create a shortcut to the program. You then add the shortcut for the program to the StartUp folder. Each program in the StartUp folder will start automatically each time you turn on your computer.

Your StartUp folder may already contain several programs. Some programs, such as virus checkers, are automatically added to the StartUp folder when you install them.

You can also have a file open automatically by placing a shortcut for the file in the StartUp folder. This is useful for files you frequently use, such as an order form. To create a shortcut for a file, see page 90.

Make sure you do not place too many programs in your StartUp folder, as this will increase the time it takes Windows to start.

START A PROGRAM AUTOMATICALLY

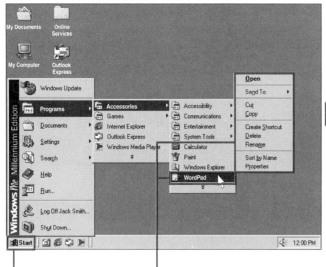

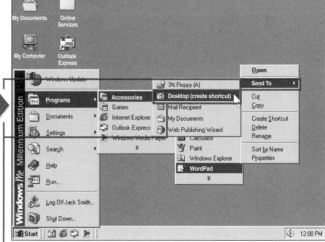

1 Click Start to display the Start menu.

2 Position the mouse over the program you want to start automatically each time you turn on your computer.

3 Right-click the program. A menu appears.

4 Click Send To.

5 Click Desktop (create shortcut).

6 To close the Start menu, click outside the menu.

■ A shortcut for the program appears on your desktop.

How do I stop a program from starting automatically?

✔ You can delete the shortcut for the program from the StartUp folder. Display the contents of the StartUp window, click the shortcut you want to delete and then press the Delete key.

How do I quickly display a list of all the programs that will start automatically?

✔ Click the Start button to display the Start menu. Click Programs and then select StartUp. A list of all the programs that will start automatically appears.

Can I stop a program from opening on the desktop and have it appear as a button on the taskbar?

✔ Yes. Display the contents of the StartUp window, right-click the shortcut for the program and then click Properties. Select the Shortcut tab in the dialog box that appears and then choose the Minimized option in the Run area.

How can I have a program start automatically if it does not appear on the Start menu?

✔ Locate the program that you want to start automatically. Then create a shortcut for the program and drag the shortcut to the StartUp folder. To create a shortcut, see page 90.

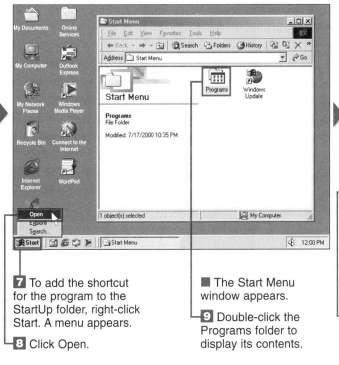

7 To add the shortcut for the program to the StartUp folder, right-click Start. A menu appears.

8 Click Open.

■ The Start Menu window appears.

9 Double-click the Programs folder to display its contents.

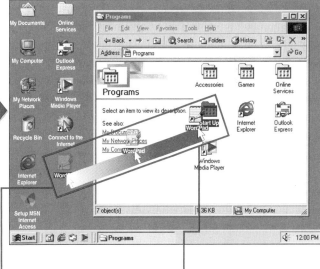

■ The contents of the Programs folder appear.

10 Position the mouse over the shortcut for the program you want to start automatically.

11 Drag the shortcut to the StartUp folder.

■ Windows places the shortcut for the program in the StartUp folder. Each program in the StartUp folder will start automatically each time you turn on your computer.

239

USING MAGNIFIER

If you have difficulty reading the information displayed on your screen, you can use Magnifier to enlarge an area of the screen. The enlarged area appears in a window at the top of your screen.

You can customize Magnifier's settings to suit your needs. Magnifier is initially set to double the size of the area displayed in the magnifier window. You can

increase or decrease the amount of magnification.

By default, Magnifier displays an enlarged view of the area surrounding the mouse pointer. Magnifier also follows keyboard commands and the insertion point.

You can change the colors displayed in the magnifier window to their complementary colors. For example, white changes to black.

Magnifier allows you to use a high contrast color scheme, which is useful for people with vision impairments. Windows will change the screen colors and increase the size of text and other items to make the screen easier to see.

You can have the Magnifier Settings window automatically minimize when you start Magnifier and you can hide the magnifier window at any time.

USING MAGNIFIER

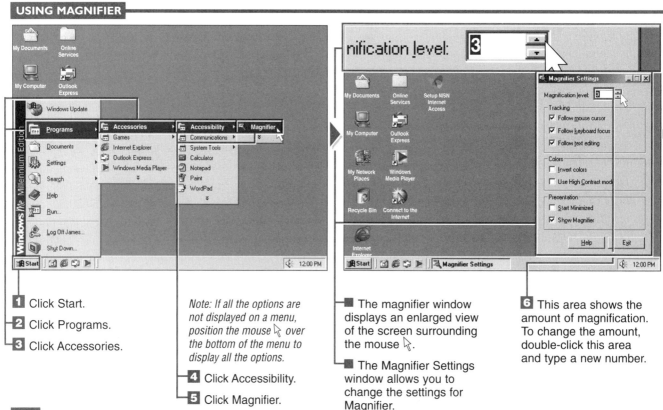

1 Click Start.

2 Click Programs.

3 Click Accessories.

Note: If all the options are not displayed on a menu, position the mouse ⇗ over the bottom of the menu to display all the options.

4 Click Accessibility.

5 Click Magnifier.

■ The magnifier window displays an enlarged view of the screen surrounding the mouse ⇗.

■ The Magnifier Settings window allows you to change the settings for Magnifier.

6 This area shows the amount of magnification. To change the amount, double-click this area and type a new number.

How can I change the size of the magnifier window?

✔ Position the mouse pointer over the bottom edge of the window (↘ changes to ↕). Drag the edge of the window until the window is the size you want.

How can I move the magnifier window?

✔ Position the mouse pointer inside the window (↘ changes to 🖑). Drag the window to any edge of your screen. You can also create a floating window by dragging the window into the middle of your screen.

Can I use the keyboard to change Magnifier's settings?

✔ If your keyboard has a Windows key (🎴), you can use the keyboard to change Magnifier's settings. To change the amount of magnification, hold down the Windows key as you press the up or down arrow keys to increase or decrease the magnification amount. To turn the Follow mouse cursor setting on or off, hold down the Windows key as you press the Page Down key. To turn the Invert colors setting on or off, hold down the Windows key as you press the Page Up key.

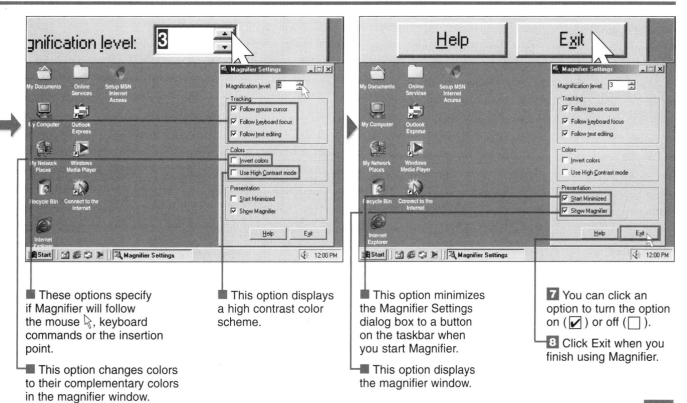

■ These options specify if Magnifier will follow the mouse ↘, keyboard commands or the insertion point.

■ This option changes colors to their complementary colors in the magnifier window.

■ This option displays a high contrast color scheme.

■ This option minimizes the Magnifier Settings dialog box to a button on the taskbar when you start Magnifier.

■ This option displays the magnifier window.

7 You can click an option to turn the option on (☑) or off (☐).

8 Click Exit when you finish using Magnifier.

241

USING ON-SCREEN KEYBOARD

I f you have limited mobility, you can display a keyboard on your screen. This keyboard allows you to type when you are unable to use a conventional keyboard.

You can specify the way you want to type. You can use a mouse to click the keyboard characters you want to type. You can also position the mouse pointer over a key until Windows types the character for

you. You can specify the length of time you must position the mouse pointer over a key.

You can also use the Joystick or key to select option to have Windows scan the on-screen keyboard and highlight each row of keys. When Windows highlights the row containing the key you want, you can use a special hardware device to select the row. Windows then scans the

row and highlights individual keys so you can select the character you want to type. You can specify the amount of time keys are highlighted during a scan.

You can visit the Microsoft Accessibility Web page at www.microsoft.com/enable to find more information about programs for people with special needs.

USING ON-SCREEN KEYBOARD

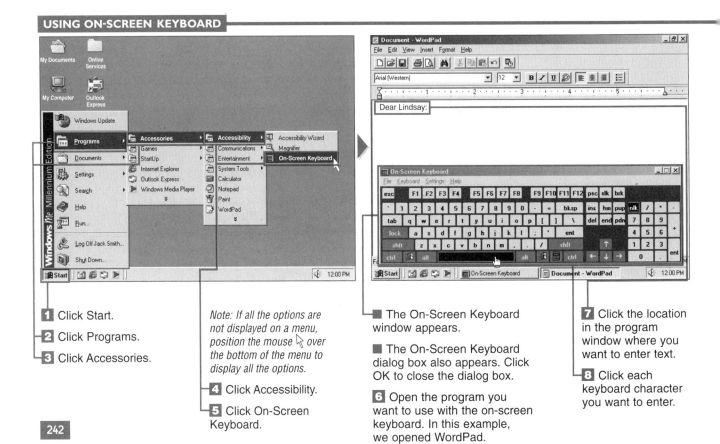

1 Click Start.

2 Click Programs.

3 Click Accessories.

Note: If all the options are not displayed on a menu, position the mouse over the bottom of the menu to display all the options.

4 Click Accessibility.

5 Click On-Screen Keyboard.

■ The On-Screen Keyboard window appears.

■ The On-Screen Keyboard dialog box also appears. Click OK to close the dialog box.

6 Open the program you want to use with the on-screen keyboard. In this example, we opened WordPad.

7 Click the location in the program window where you want to enter text.

8 Click each keyboard character you want to enter.

Why isn't the Joystick or key to select option available on my computer?

✓ You need to connect a special hardware device to your computer to make this option available. There are different types of devices available, such as devices that allow you to use the computer with your mouth.

Can I change the font of the on-screen keyboard characters?

✓ Yes. This is useful if you find the on-screen keyboard characters difficult to see. Choose the Settings menu and click Font. Then select the font, font style and size you want to use. Changing the font of the on-screen keyboard characters does not change the font of the characters you type.

Can I change the appearance of the keyboard?

✓ Yes. Select the Keyboard menu and then click the way you want to display the keyboard. A dot (●) appears beside the currently selected options. If you do not want to display a numeric keypad, you can choose the Standard Keyboard. To group the keys together in the window, choose the Block Layout. Most keyboards have 101 keys, but you can display a 102-key universal keyboard or a 106-key keyboard that has additional Japanese characters.

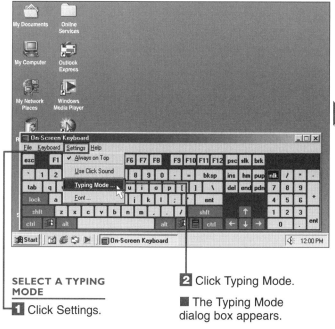

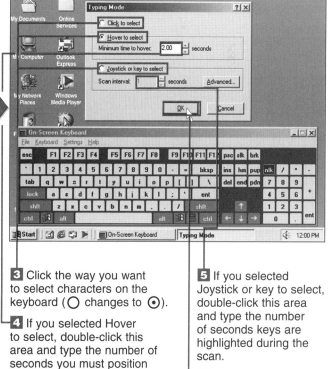

SELECT A TYPING MODE

1 Click Settings.

2 Click Typing Mode.

■ The Typing Mode dialog box appears.

3 Click the way you want to select characters on the keyboard (○ changes to ⊙).

4 If you selected Hover to select, double-click this area and type the number of seconds you must position the mouse ⬚ over a key to select the character.

5 If you selected Joystick or key to select, double-click this area and type the number of seconds keys are highlighted during the scan.

6 Click OK.

243

USING THE ACCESSIBILITY OPTIONS

You can customize the way your computer operates to accommodate special needs and situations. The Windows accessibility options allow you to make a computer easier to use if you have physical restrictions or when using a mouse is not practical.

Windows offers several options designed to make your keyboard easier to use. StickyKeys helps users who have difficulty pressing two keys at the same time. When you press the Shift, Ctrl or Alt key on your keyboard, the key will remain active while you press another key.

FilterKeys reduces the keyboard's sensitivity to repeated keystrokes and plays a tone every time you press a key.

ToggleKeys allows you to hear tones when you press the Caps Lock, Num Lock or Scroll Lock keys.

Some programs provide additional help information about the keyboard. You can have your programs display the extra help information when the information is available.

Windows also allows you to replace sound cues with visual ones. SoundSentry flashes parts of your screen when your computer makes a sound. ShowSounds provides captions for speech and sound events in some programs.

USING THE ACCESSIBILITY OPTIONS

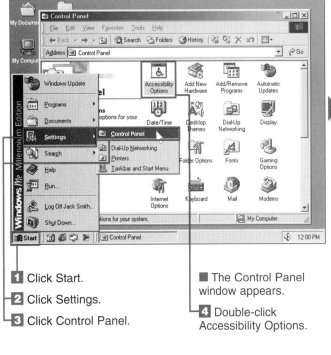

1 Click Start.

2 Click Settings.

3 Click Control Panel.

■ The Control Panel window appears.

4 Double-click Accessibility Options.

■ The Accessibility Properties dialog box appears.

5 Click the Keyboard tab to view the keyboard options.

6 Click this option if you want to press the Shift, Ctrl or Alt key and have the key remain active while you press another key (☐ changes to ☑).

Why did StickyKeys stop working?

✔ Windows automatically turns off StickyKeys when you press two keys at once. To have StickyKeys remain on even when you accidentally press two keys at once, display the Accessibility Properties dialog box and click the Keyboard tab. Select the Settings button in the StickyKeys area and then click the Turn StickyKeys off if two keys are pressed at once option (☑ changes to ☐).

My keyboard is still sensitive, even with FilterKeys turned on. What should I do?

✔ You may need to adjust the settings for FilterKeys. In the Accessibility Properties dialog box, click the Keyboard tab and then select the Settings button in the FilterKeys area to adjust the settings.

Can I use keyboard shortcuts to enable accessibility features?

✔ Yes. You can use keyboard shortcuts to enable most accessibility features. In the Accessibility Properties dialog box, select the Settings button for the feature you want to use a keyboard shortcut. In the Settings dialog box, click the Use shortcut option in the Keyboard shortcut area (☐ changes to ☑). The area indicates which keys to use for the shortcut.

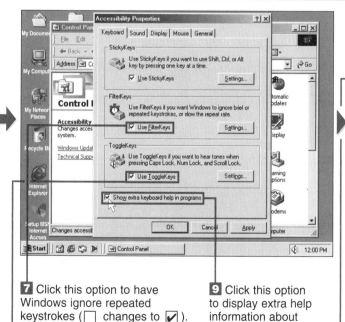

7 Click this option to have Windows ignore repeated keystrokes (☐ changes to ☑).

8 Click this option to hear sounds when you press the Caps Lock, Num Lock or Scroll Lock key (☐ changes to ☑).

9 Click this option to display extra help information about the keyboard in your programs when the information is available (☐ changes to ☑).

10 Click the Sound tab to view the sound options.

11 Click this option to display visual warnings when your computer makes sounds (☐ changes to ☑).

12 Click this option to display captions for sounds your programs make (☐ changes to ☑).

CONTINUED

USING THE ACCESSIBILITY OPTIONS (CONTINUED)

The accessibility options can make your screen easier to read and allow you to perform mouse actions using your keyboard.

If you find the screen difficult to read, you can change to the High Contrast screen display. Windows will change the color and size of text and other items to make the screen easier to read.

You can change the speed at which the cursor blinks and the width of the cursor. The cursor, also called the insertion point, indicates where the text you type will appear in a document.

MouseKeys allows you to control the mouse pointer using the numeric keypad on your keyboard instead of the mouse. This can be useful in situations where a mouse

is difficult to use, such as when using a portable computer.

If you share a computer with other users who do not want to use the accessibility options, you can have Windows automatically turn off these features when your computer is not in use. You can also use visual and sound cues to indicate when an accessibility option is turned on or off using a keyboard shortcut.

USING THE ACCESSIBILITY OPTIONS (CONTINUED)

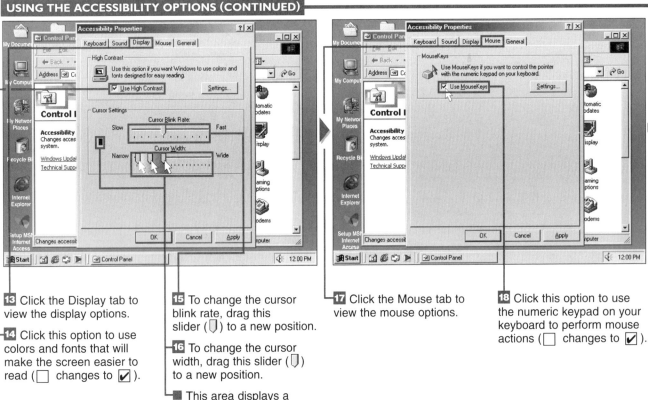

■13 Click the Display tab to view the display options.

■14 Click this option to use colors and fonts that will make the screen easier to read (☐ changes to ☑).

■15 To change the cursor blink rate, drag this slider (🖰) to a new position.

■16 To change the cursor width, drag this slider (🖰) to a new position.

■ This area displays a preview of the cursor settings you selected.

■17 Click the Mouse tab to view the mouse options.

■18 Click this option to use the numeric keypad on your keyboard to perform mouse actions (☐ changes to ☑).

After I turn on the MouseKeys feature, what keys can I use to control the mouse pointer?

✔ The Num Lock key must be on to use the MouseKeys feature. A light on your keyboard indicates the status of the Num Lock key.

How do I know if an accessibility feature is turned on?

✔ Some accessibility features display an icon on the right side of your taskbar to indicate that they are turned on. For example, StickyKeys display the 🖭 icon and Filterkeys displays the 🕑 icon.

What is the SerialKey devices option?

✔ This option allows you to connect an alternative input device, such as a speech recognition device, to your computer's serial port. This enables people to communicate with their computers when they cannot use the mouse or keyboard. In the Accessibility Properties dialog box, click the General tab and then select the Support SerialKey devices option (☐ changes to ✔).

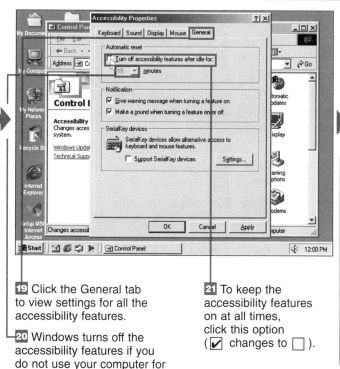

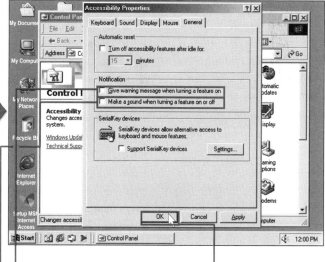

19 Click the General tab to view settings for all the accessibility features.

20 Windows turns off the accessibility features if you do not use your computer for the amount of time displayed in this area. To change the amount of time, click this area to select a new time.

21 To keep the accessibility features on at all times, click this option (✔ changes to ☐).

22 This option displays a message when you use a keyboard shortcut to turn an accessibility feature on. To turn this option off, click the option (✔ changes to ☐).

23 This option makes a sound when you use a keyboard shortcut to turn an accessibility feature on or off. To turn this option off, click the option (✔ changes to ☐).

24 Click OK to confirm all of your changes.

USING THE ACCESSIBILITY WIZARD

The Accessibility Wizard can help you set up Windows to meet your vision, hearing and mobility needs. Although the accessibility options were designed to help people with special needs operate a computer, there are some options that may be of interest to all users.

The wizard asks you to select the smallest text you can read. The text size option you select effects your screen immediately.

If you select the largest text size, Windows automatically starts Microsoft Magnifier. Magnifier appears at the top of your screen and displays an enlarged view of the area surrounding the mouse pointer.

The wizard allows you to choose the way you want text and items to appear on your screen. You can increase the font size used in title bars, menus and other features. If Magnifier is not already displayed, you can choose to display Magnifier. You can also disable the Personalized Menus feature to ensure Windows displays all the items on the Programs menu at all times.

USING THE ACCESSIBILITY WIZARD

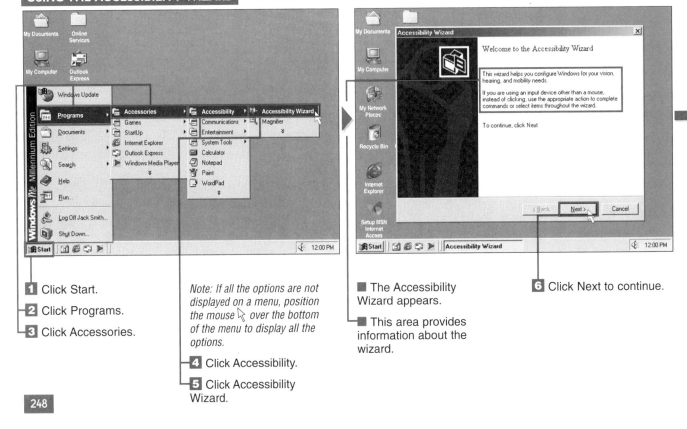

1 Click Start.

2 Click Programs.

3 Click Accessories.

Note: If all the options are not displayed on a menu, position the mouse ⟨ over the bottom of the menu to display all the options.

4 Click Accessibility.

5 Click Accessibility Wizard.

■ The Accessibility Wizard appears.

■ This area provides information about the wizard.

6 Click Next to continue.

Why did the Magnifier Settings window appear on my screen when Magnifier started?

✔ The Magnifier Settings window allows you to change the settings for Magnifier. If you do not want to use Magnifier, click the Exit button in the Magnifier Settings window. To keep Magnifier open but minimize the Magnifier Settings window, click ⬜ in the window.

Can I turn on Magnifier without starting the wizard?

✔ Yes. Click the Start button, select Programs, choose Accessories, click Accessibility and then select Magnifier. For more information about Magnifier, see page 240.

Is there another way to make the text on my screen easier to read?

✔ If you are currently using a high screen resolution, you can select the Switch to a lower screen resolution option in step 9 below. A lower screen resolution increases the size of text and items so you can see the information on your screen more clearly. This option is only available if your screen displays a resolution of 1024x768 or higher. For more information about changing the screen resolution, see page 172.

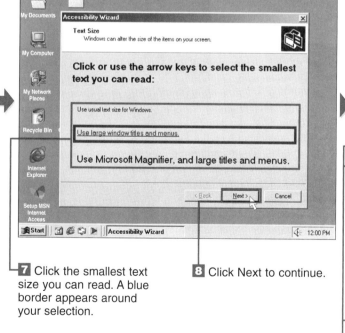

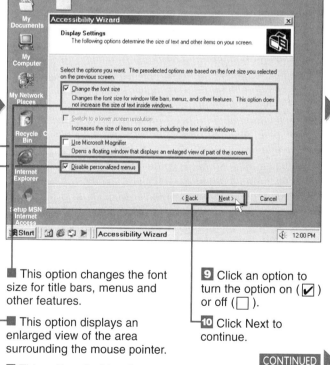

7 Click the smallest text size you can read. A blue border appears around your selection.

8 Click Next to continue.

■ This option changes the font size for title bars, menus and other features.

■ This option displays an enlarged view of the area surrounding the mouse pointer.

■ This option disables the Personalized Menus feature.

9 Click an option to turn the option on (✔) or off (⬜).

10 Click Next to continue.

CONTINUED

USING THE ACCESSIBILITY WIZARD (CONTINUED)

The Accessibility Wizard displays a list of statements and asks you to select each statement that applies to you. The statements you select helps the wizard decide which accessibility options will benefit you the most when using Windows.

If you have difficulty seeing, you can select options that will make viewing information on your screen easier. You can increase the size of

scroll bars, window borders and icons. You can also select a high contrast color scheme.

If you have difficulty hearing, you can have Windows display visual warnings when sound events occur on your computer. Windows can also display captions for sounds in some programs.

There are many options you can select to make the keyboard and mouse easier to use. For example,

you can have Windows ignore repeated keystrokes or you can use the numeric keypad instead of the mouse to move the pointer on your screen.

The administrative options are useful if more than one person uses your computer. For example, you can have Windows automatically turn off accessibility options after the computer is idle for a certain number of minutes.

USING THE ACCESSIBILITY WIZARD (CONTINUED)

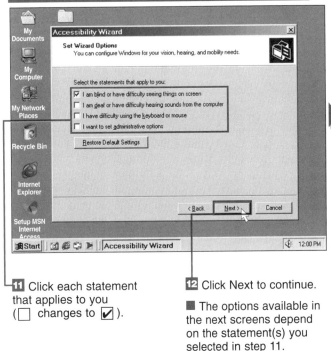

■11 Click each statement that applies to you
(☐ changes to ☑).

■12 Click Next to continue.

■ The options available in the next screens depend on the statement(s) you selected in step 11.

■13 Click the scroll bar and window border size you want to use. A blue border appears around your selection.

■14 Click Next to continue.

Is there another way to turn on accessibility options?

✔ Yes. Click the Start button, choose Settings and then select Control Panel. In the Control Panel window, there are several icons that you can use to turn on accessibility options. The Accessibility Options icon includes many of the same options available in the Accessibility Wizard. The Mouse and Keyboard icons allow you to specify how you want to use the mouse and keyboard. The Display icon allows you to adjust your screen resolution, color settings and the size of items such as scroll bars.

How do I return to the default color scheme after I complete the Accessibility Wizard?

✔ Right-click a blank area on the desktop and select Properties. In the Display Properties dialog box, select the Appearance tab. In the Scheme area, click ▾ and then select Windows Standard to return to the default color scheme.

Are there more advanced accessibility features available?

✔ The accessibility features that come with Windows provide a minimum level of functionality for people with special needs. There are programs available that offer more support. For information about these programs, visit the Microsoft Accessibility Web site at www.microsoft.com/enable.

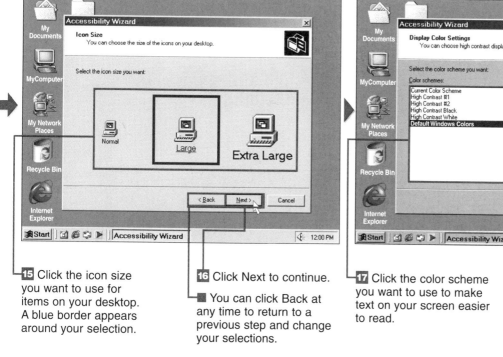

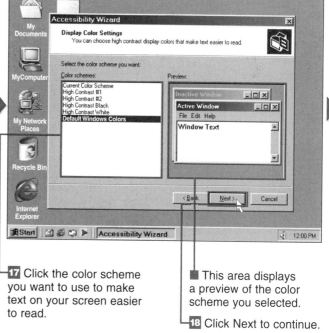

15 Click the icon size you want to use for items on your desktop. A blue border appears around your selection.

16 Click Next to continue.

■ You can click Back at any time to return to a previous step and change your selections.

17 Click the color scheme you want to use to make text on your screen easier to read.

■ This area displays a preview of the color scheme you selected.

18 Click Next to continue.

CONTINUED ▶

USING THE ACCESSIBILITY WIZARD (CONTINUED)

If you selected the statement that specifies you have difficulty seeing, you can select a size and color for the mouse pointer. This can help make the mouse pointer easier to see.

After you select all the accessibility options you want to use, you can save the options as a file on your computer, a floppy disk or the

network. Saving the accessibility options on your computer allows you to quickly set up and use the same accessibility options again. This is useful if someone removes the accessibility options from your computer. Saving the options on a floppy disk or the network is useful if you want to set up another computer to use the same accessibility options.

When you open a file containing accessibility options, the Accessibility Wizard opens and automatically selects all the options for you. An Accessibility Wizard file displays the 🗐 icon.

When you complete the Accessibility Wizard, the wizard displays a list of the accessibility options you changed.

USING THE ACCESSIBILITY WIZARD (CONTINUED)

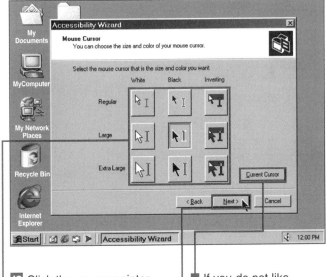

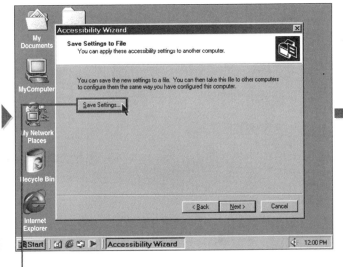

19 Click the mouse pointer that displays the size and color you want to use.

■ The mouse pointer changes immediately.

■ If you do not like the mouse pointer you selected, you can click Current Cursor to return to the previous mouse pointer.

20 Click Next to continue.

21 Click Save Settings to save the accessibility options you selected. Saving the accessibility options allows you to set up and use the same options on another computer.

■ The Save As dialog box appears.

How do I change back to the default pointer set once the Accessibility Wizard is complete?

✔ Click the Start button, choose Settings and then select Control Panel. In the Control Panel window, double-click the Mouse icon. In the Mouse Properties dialog box, select the Pointers tab. In the Scheme area, click ▼ and then select (None) to return to the default pointer set.

How can I return to my original screen settings?

✔ To return to your original screen settings, perform steps 1 to 10 starting on page 248 to start the Accessibility Wizard. When the wizard asks you to select the statements that apply to you, click the Restore Default Settings button and then follow the instructions on your screen.

Where can I find more information about the accessibility options Windows offers?

✔ The Windows help feature provides more information about the accessibility options that Windows offers. Click the Start button and then select Help. In the Help and Support window, click the Accessibility for People with Disabilities link. For more information about using the Windows help feature, see page 24.

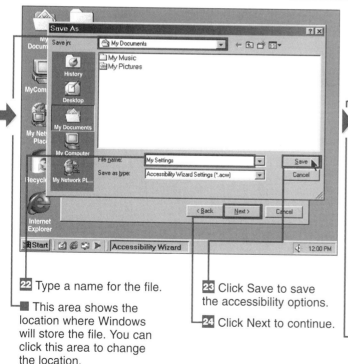

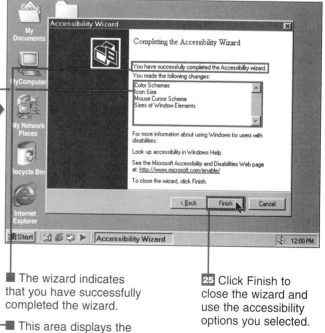

■22 Type a name for the file.

■ This area shows the location where Windows will store the file. You can click this area to change the location.

■23 Click Save to save the accessibility options.

■24 Click Next to continue.

■ The wizard indicates that you have successfully completed the wizard.

■ This area displays the changes you have made.

■25 Click Finish to close the wizard and use the accessibility options you selected.

ASSIGN SOUNDS TO PROGRAM EVENTS

You can have Windows play sounds when you perform certain tasks on your computer. Assigning sounds to tasks can make working with Windows more fun and interesting.

You need a sound card and speakers to hear sounds on your computer. If your sound card and speakers are set up properly, you will hear a short musical

introduction each time Windows starts.

The sounds on your computer can help provide information about which tasks Windows is performing, let you know that new e-mail has arrived or alert you to a program error.

You can add or change the sounds for many events on your computer

at once by choosing a sound scheme. A sound scheme is a set of related sounds that usually have a theme, such as jungle sounds or musical instruments.

When assigning sounds to events, you can preview the sound that will play for each event.

ASSIGN SOUNDS TO MANY EVENTS AT ONCE

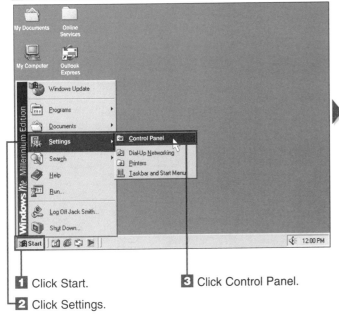

1 Click Start.

2 Click Settings.

3 Click Control Panel.

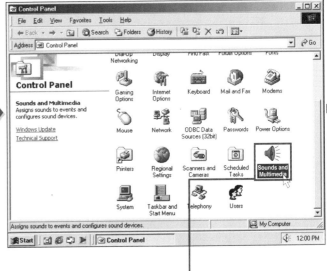

■ The Control Panel window appears.

Note: If all the items do not appear in the Control Panel window, click the view all Control Panel options link in the window to display all the items.

4 Double-click Sounds and Multimedia.

Where can I get more sound schemes?

✔ When you install Windows, only the Windows Default sound scheme is installed. You can install additional sound schemes by adding the Multimedia Sound Schemes component located in the Multimedia category. To add a Windows component, see page 538. You can also download sound schemes from the Internet.

How do I stop Windows from playing sounds for events?

✔ To stop Windows from playing sounds for events, display the Sounds and Multimedia Properties dialog box. In the Scheme area, select No Sounds.

How do I adjust the volume of the sounds?

✔ In the Sounds and Multimedia Properties dialog box, drag the sound volume slider (🔊) left or right to decrease or increase the volume. Changing the volume in this dialog box will adjust the volume for all sounds on your computer, such as sound from a music CD or video. You can also change the volume by clicking the speaker icon (🔊) on the taskbar. In the volume control box that appears, drag the slider (▭) up or down to increase or decrease the volume.

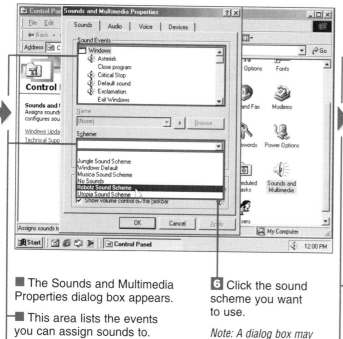

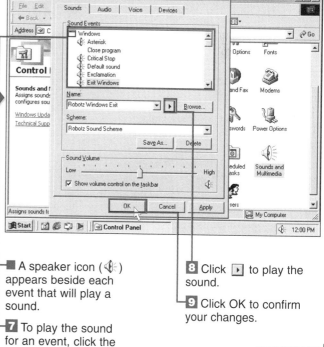

■ The Sounds and Multimedia Properties dialog box appears.

■ This area lists the events you can assign sounds to.

5 Click this area to display a list of sound schemes. Each sound scheme will change the sounds for many events at once.

6 Click the sound scheme you want to use.

Note: A dialog box may appear, asking if you want to save the previous sound scheme. To continue without saving, click No.

■ A speaker icon (🔊) appears beside each event that will play a sound.

7 To play the sound for an event, click the event.

8 Click ▶ to play the sound.

9 Click OK to confirm your changes.

CONTINUED ▶

ASSIGN SOUNDS TO
PROGRAM EVENTS (CONTINUED)

You can assign a sound to a specific event. There are over 30 events to which you can assign sounds on your computer. You may want to play familiar music from a cartoon when Windows closes or hear a sigh of relief when you restore a window. You can mix and match sound files to create a

personalized sound scheme for your computer.

You can use sound files included with Windows or sound files you downloaded from the Internet. You can also use sound files you have created. The sound files you use must be saved in the Wave format. Wave files have the .wav extension, such as chimes.wav.

Windows does not include a tool that allows you to convert other types of sound files to the Wave format.

When assigning a sound to an event, you can listen to a preview of the sound.

ASSIGN SOUND TO ONE EVENT

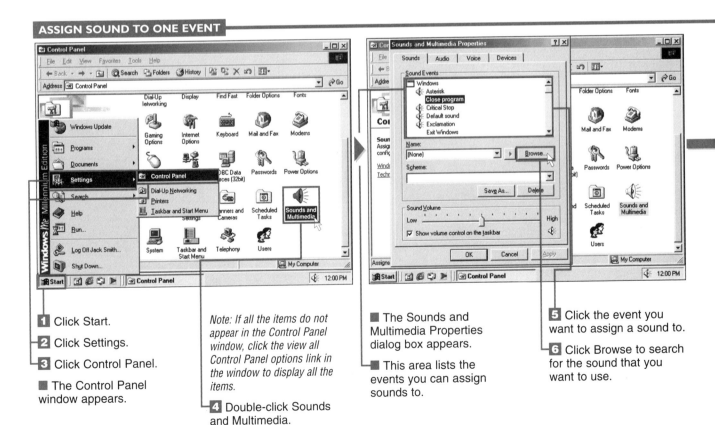

1 Click Start.

2 Click Settings.

3 Click Control Panel.

■ The Control Panel window appears.

Note: If all the items do not appear in the Control Panel window, click the view all Control Panel options link in the window to display all the items.

4 Double-click Sounds and Multimedia.

■ The Sounds and Multimedia Properties dialog box appears.

■ This area lists the events you can assign sounds to.

5 Click the event you want to assign a sound to.

6 Click Browse to search for the sound that you want to use.

Can I save the sound scheme I created?

✔ Yes. Saving a sound scheme enables you to use other sound schemes and return to your personalized scheme later. In the Sounds and Multimedia Properties dialog box, click the Save As button. Type a name for the sound scheme and then click OK.

How do I delete a sound scheme I created?

✔ In the Sounds and Multimedia Properties dialog box, click the Scheme area to display the list of available sound schemes. Select the sound scheme you want to delete and then click the Delete button.

How do I create my own sound files?

✔ You can use the Sound Recorder program to record sounds from a microphone, CD player or stereo onto your computer. For information about using Sound Recorder, see page 260.

Is there another way to assign a sound to an event?

✔ To assign a sound to an event, locate the sound file that you want to play when the event occurs. Then drag the sound file onto the event in the Sounds and Multimedia Properties dialog box.

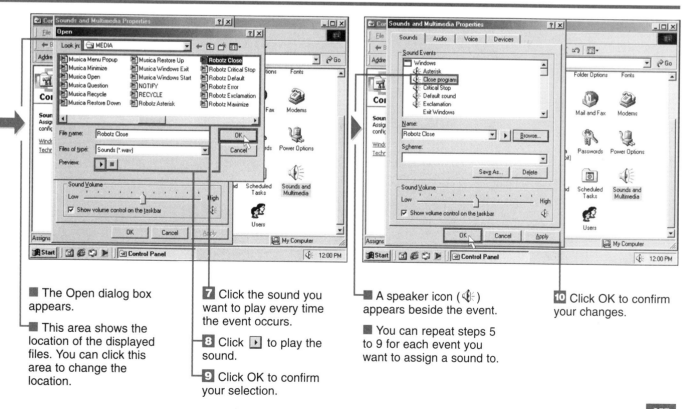

■ The Open dialog box appears.

■ This area shows the location of the displayed files. You can click this area to change the location.

7 Click the sound you want to play every time the event occurs.

8 Click ▶ to play the sound.

9 Click OK to confirm your selection.

■ A speaker icon (🔊) appears beside the event.

■ You can repeat steps 5 to 9 for each event you want to assign a sound to.

10 Click OK to confirm your changes.

USING VOLUME CONTROL

When playing sounds, such as music CDs or videos, on your computer, you can adjust the volume of sound coming from your speakers.

You can use the volume control box to raise or lower the overall volume on your computer or mute all the sound.

The Volume Control window allows you to change the volume of specific devices on your computer. For example, if your CD plays too loud, you can lower the volume of the CD player without affecting the volume of other devices.

You can also change the balance between the left and right speakers for each device on your computer. For example, if one speaker is

further away than the other, you can make that speaker louder.

You can have the Volume Control window display devices that are used for playing back or recording sounds and then specify which devices you want to display. For example, you can choose to display the microphone or CD Audio device in the window. The available devices depend on your sound card.

CHANGE VOLUME OF ALL SOUND

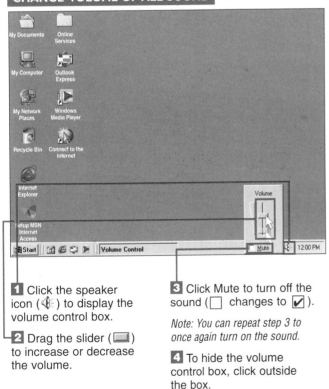

1 Click the speaker icon (◀) to display the volume control box.

2 Drag the slider (▭) to increase or decrease the volume.

3 Click Mute to turn off the sound (☐ changes to ☑).

Note: You can repeat step 3 to once again turn on the sound.

4 To hide the volume control box, click outside the box.

CHANGE VOLUME OF SPECIFIC DEVICES

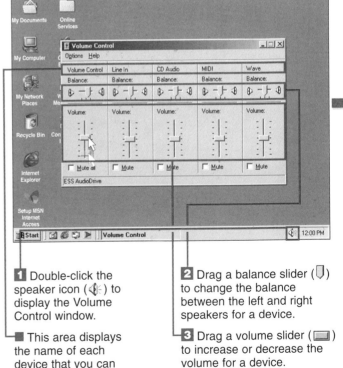

1 Double-click the speaker icon (◀) to display the Volume Control window.

■ This area displays the name of each device that you can control the volume for.

2 Drag a balance slider (▯) to change the balance between the left and right speakers for a device.

3 Drag a volume slider (▭) to increase or decrease the volume for a device.

The speaker icon does not appear on my taskbar. How can I display the icon?

✔ The speaker icon will not appear on your taskbar if your sound card is not properly installed. If your sound card is properly installed, click the Start button, choose Settings and select Control Panel. Double-click Sounds and Multimedia and select the Sounds tab. Then click the Show volume control on the taskbar option (☐ changes to ☑).

Why does my computer make beeping sounds even after I have muted the sound?

✔ The beeping sounds are coming from the computer's internal speaker. Windows usually cannot control this speaker. You may have to physically disconnect the internal speaker to mute the beeping sounds.

Why does adjusting the CD Audio volume not change the volume of my CDs?

✔ You may need to change how Windows Media Player plays CDs on your computer. Click ▶ on the taskbar to display the Windows Media Player window. Click the Tools menu and choose Options. Then select the CD Audio tab and click the Digital playback option in the Playback Setting area (☑ changes to ☐).

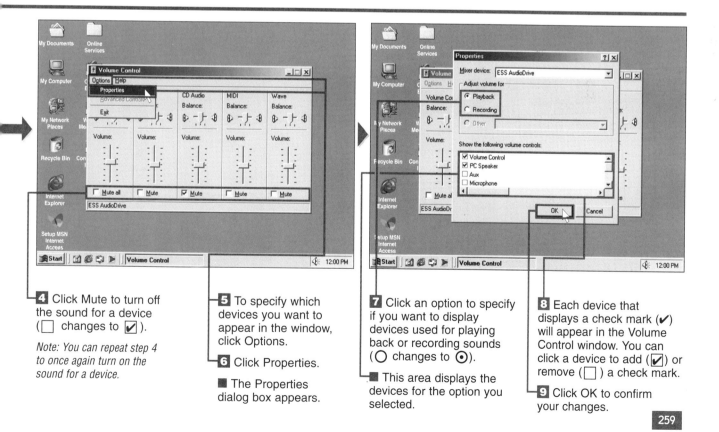

■4 Click Mute to turn off the sound for a device (☐ changes to ☑).

Note: You can repeat step 4 to once again turn on the sound for a device.

■5 To specify which devices you want to appear in the window, click Options.

■6 Click Properties.

■ The Properties dialog box appears.

■7 Click an option to specify if you want to display devices used for playing back or recording sounds (○ changes to ◉).

■ This area displays the devices for the option you selected.

■8 Each device that displays a check mark (✔) will appear in the Volume Control window. You can click a device to add (☑) or remove (☐) a check mark.

■9 Click OK to confirm your changes.

USING SOUND RECORDER

Y ou can use Sound Recorder to record, play and edit sounds on your computer. You can record sounds from a microphone, CD player, stereo, VCR or any other sound device you connect to your computer. You need a sound card and speakers to record and play sounds.

You can add recorded sounds to a document to provide additional information or to provide

entertainment. For example, a sales report could include a voice recording of a speech given by the company president.

You can also record sounds, effects or comments and have them play when specific events occur on your computer, such as when you close a program. This can help personalize your computer. To assign sounds to program events, see page 254.

When playing a recording, you can move to the beginning or end of the recording. You can also move to a specific location in a recording.

Sound Recorder allows you to perform basic sound recording and editing tasks. There are many other more sophisticated sound recording and editing programs that you can obtain on the Internet and at computer stores.

USING SOUND RECORDER

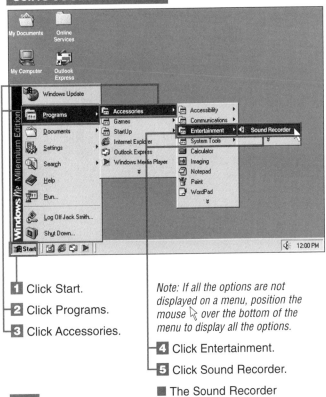

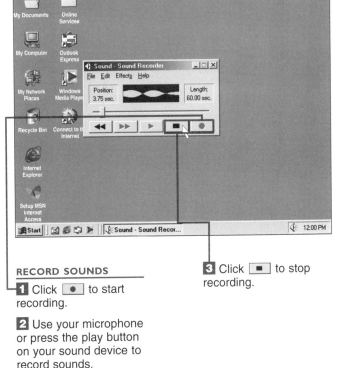

1 Click Start.

2 Click Programs.

3 Click Accessories.

Note: If all the options are not displayed on a menu, position the mouse over the bottom of the menu to display all the options.

4 Click Entertainment.

5 Click Sound Recorder.

■ The Sound Recorder window appears.

RECORD SOUNDS

1 Click ● to start recording.

2 Use your microphone or press the play button on your sound device to record sounds.

3 Click ■ to stop recording.

How do I save my recording?

✔ In the Sound Recorder window, click the File menu and select Save As to save your recording as a file on your computer. To open a saved recording, select the File menu and click Open. Then select the recording you want to open and click the Open button.

How can I begin a new recording?

✔ In the Sound Recorder window, choose the File menu and then select New.

How can I change the volume of the playback?

✔ Click the speaker icon (🔊) on the taskbar to change the volume of the playback. In the volume control box that appears, drag the slider (▭) to increase or decrease the volume.

The recording is too quiet or too loud. Can I change the recording volume?

✔ In the Sound Recorder window, the green line shows the volume level of your recording. If the green line barely moves, you should increase the recording volume. If the green line reaches the top and bottom of the box, you should decrease the recording volume. To adjust the recording volume, click Edit and then select Audio Properties. In the Sound Recording area, click the Volume button. Then adjust the volume slider for the sound device you are recording from.

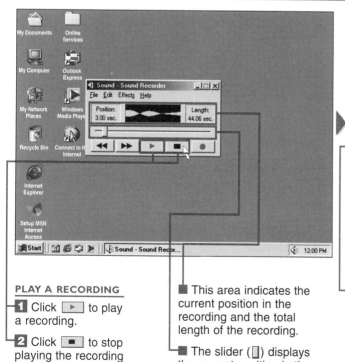

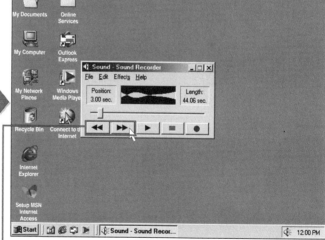

PLAY A RECORDING

1 Click ▶ to play a recording.

2 Click ■ to stop playing the recording at any time.

■ This area indicates the current position in the recording and the total length of the recording.

■ The slider (▯) displays the current position in the recording.

3 Click one of these buttons to move to the beginning or end of the recording.

◄◄ Move to beginning

►► Move to end

Note: You can drag the slider (▯) to move to a specific position in the recording.

CONTINUED

USING SOUND RECORDER
(CONTINUED)

Sound Recorder has several sound effects you can use to change your recording. You can adjust the volume of your recording to make it louder or softer. You can also speed up your recording to create a chipmunk effect or slow down the recording to create a spooky and mysterious effect. You may also want to add an echo to your recording or play the recording backwards.

Sound Recorder allows you to insert another sound file into an existing recording. You can choose the exact position in a recording where you want to insert the other sound file. The sound file you insert will replace the original recording from the point of insertion to the end of the inserted file.

Inserting a sound file into an existing recording lets you create

one sound file containing your favorite sounds. For example, you can create a Halloween sound file by inserting howls and screams into a recording of spooky music.

There are many sound files available on the Internet that you can insert into another recording. Sound Recorder can only work with files in the Wave format. Wave files have the .wav file extension.

USING SOUND RECORDER (CONTINUED)

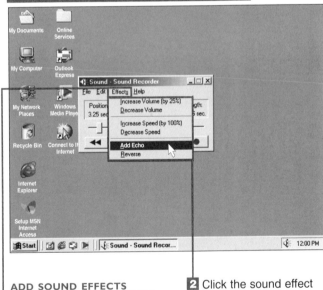

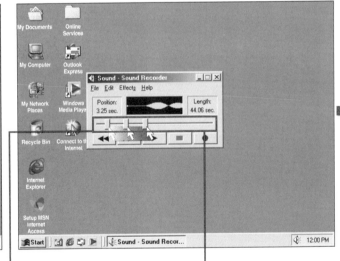

ADD SOUND EFFECTS

■1 Click Effects to add a sound effect to a recording.

■2 Click the sound effect you want to use.

■ You can repeat steps 1 and 2 for each sound effect you want to use.

INSERT A SOUND FILE

■1 To specify where you want to insert a sound file into the current recording, position the mouse over the slider ( ).

■2 Drag the slider ( ) to where you want to insert a sound file.

Note: The sound file you insert will replace the original recording from the position of the slider ( ) to the end of the inserted file.

How do I undo a mistake?

✔ In the Sound Recorder window, click the File menu and then select Revert. This command will undo all the changes you made since you last saved the recording. You should save your recording every time you make a successful change.

How can I mix two sound files together so both sounds play at the same time?

✔ Mixing two sound files together is useful if you are adding a music background to a voice recording. Position the slider (▯) in one sound file where you want the second sound file to start playing. On the Edit menu, click Mix with File. Select the sound file you want to mix with your current recording and then click the Open button.

Can I change the quality of a recording?

✔ Sound Recorder normally records sounds in Radio Quality. You may want to record sounds in CD Quality to improve the recording quality or in Telephone Quality to create a smaller file size. To record sounds using a different quality, click the File menu and then select Properties. Then click the Convert Now button. Click the Name area and then select the quality you want to use.

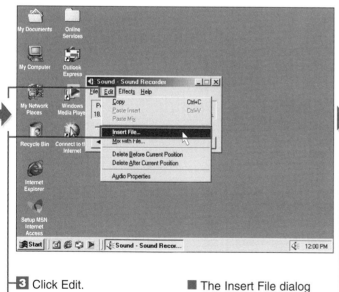

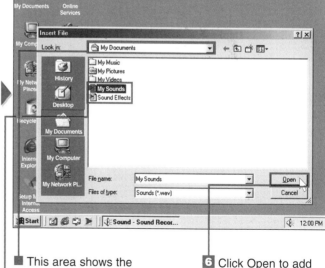

-3 Click Edit.

-4 Click Insert File.

■ The Insert File dialog box appears.

■ This area shows the location of the displayed files. You can click this area to change the location.

-5 Click the sound file you want to insert.

6 Click Open to add the sound file to the current recording.

PLAY GAMES

Windows includes several games that you can play on your own or with people on the Internet. Games are a fun way to improve your mouse skills and hand-eye coordination.

You can play single-player card games, including Classic Solitaire, Spider Solitaire and FreeCell. Minesweeper and Pinball are other games you can play on your own.

If you are on a network with other Windows users, up to four people can join in a game of Classic Hearts.

Windows also offers games, such as Backgammon, Checkers, Hearts, Reversi and Spades, which you can play on the Internet. When you select an Internet game, the MSN Zone.com dialog box appears. Windows may automatically send your computer ID and information about your system to the Zone.com Web site to help administer the game.

When playing a game on the Internet, Windows matches you with other players. You can chat with the other players by sending messages such as "It's your turn" or "Play again?".

The games included with Windows are an introduction to the types of games you can play in Windows. You can obtain additional games at computer stores or on the Internet.

PLAY GAMES

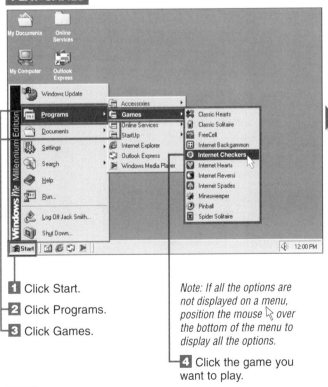

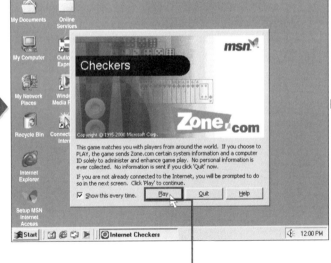

1 Click Start.

2 Click Programs.

3 Click Games.

Note: If all the options are not displayed on a menu, position the mouse ⬚ over the bottom of the menu to display all the options.

4 Click the game you want to play.

■ If you selected an Internet game, the MSN Zone.com dialog box appears.

Note: If you selected a non-Internet game, the game appears. Skip to step 8.

5 Click Play to have Windows match you with other players from around the world and start the game.

Note: If you are not currently connected to the Internet, a dialog box appears that allows you to connect.

MASTER VISUALLY WINDOWS ME

Windows Me and Multimedia

IV

How can I learn how to play a game?

✔ You can press the F1 key to display help information in most games.

How do I start a new game?

✔ To start a new session of a game you play on your own, press the F2 key. When playing an Internet game, select the Game menu and then click Find New Opponent(s).

Where can I find other games to play on the Internet?

✔ The MSN Gaming Zone Web site at www.zone.com provides many games you can play on the Internet.

How do I play a game of Classic Hearts on a network?

✔ When you start the Classic Hearts game, a dialog box appears. Type the name of your computer and then select the I want to be dealer option and click OK. Then wait for other users on the network to join the game. To join the game, users on the network can select the I want to connect to another game option and click OK. When asked for the dealer's name, users will enter the name of your computer.

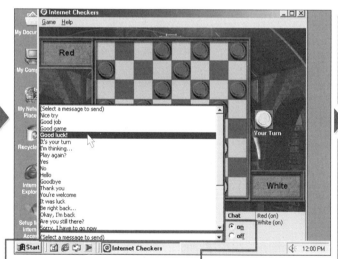

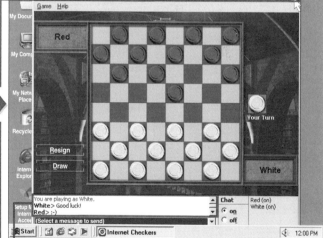

■ A window appears, displaying the game. In this example, the Internet Checkers window appears.

6 To send a message to your opponent, click this area to display a list of messages that you can send.

7 Click the message you want to send.

■ This area displays the message you sent, the ongoing conversation and information about the current game.

8 When you finish playing the game, click ⊠ to close the window.

■ If you are playing an Internet game, a message will appear to confirm that you want to leave the game. Click Yes to leave the game.

INSTALL A GAME CONTROLLER

Y ou can install a game
controller on your computer.
A game controller is a device,
such as a joystick or gamepad, that
allows you to interact with a game.

A game controller allows you to
easily control the direction of
movement in a game, such as
forward, backward or at an angle.
You can use a mouse instead of a
game controller in many games,
but the greater control that a game

controller offers can enhance
games such as flight simulators.

Before installing a game
controller, you should connect
the controller to your computer.
A game controller can connect
to a game port, serial port or
a USB port on your computer.

Windows provides a list of popular
types of game controllers. You can
select your game controller from
this list. Windows then chooses the

appropriate driver for the controller
you select. A driver is software that
allows Windows to communicate
with your game controller.

When installing a game controller,
you can specify whether the
controller has a rudder. A rudder
is a device that adds more features
to the controller. Specifying that a
controller has a rudder allows you
to use the rudder when playing
games.

INSTALL A GAME CONTROLLER

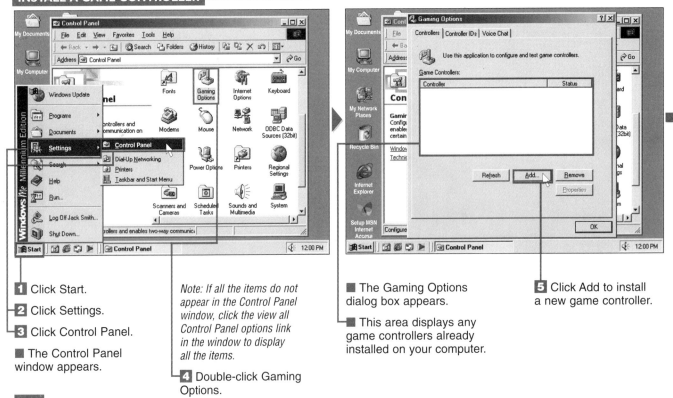

1 Click Start.

2 Click Settings.

3 Click Control Panel.

■ The Control Panel
window appears.

*Note: If all the items do not
appear in the Control Panel
window, click the view all
Control Panel options link
in the window to display
all the items.*

4 Double-click Gaming
Options.

■ The Gaming Options
dialog box appears.

■ This area displays any
game controllers already
installed on your computer.

5 Click Add to install
a new game controller.

My game controller does not appear in the list. What should I do?

✔ You can use the installation disk that came with the game controller to install the controller. Insert the installation disk into the drive. In the Add Game Controller dialog box, click the Add Other button. In the dialog box that appears, click the Have Disk button.

Can I install a controller that doesn't appear in the list if I do not have an installation disk?

✔ You can click the Custom button in the Add Game Controller dialog box to specify the features of your controller. The name you specify for the controller will appear in the list of available game controllers. You can also try choosing a game controller in the list that closely resembles your controller.

Do I have to install a Plug and Play game controller?

✔ No. After you physically connect a Plug and Play game controller to your computer and turn on the computer, Windows will usually automatically detect and install the game controller for you. If Windows requires information to install the game controller, Windows will ask you for the information.

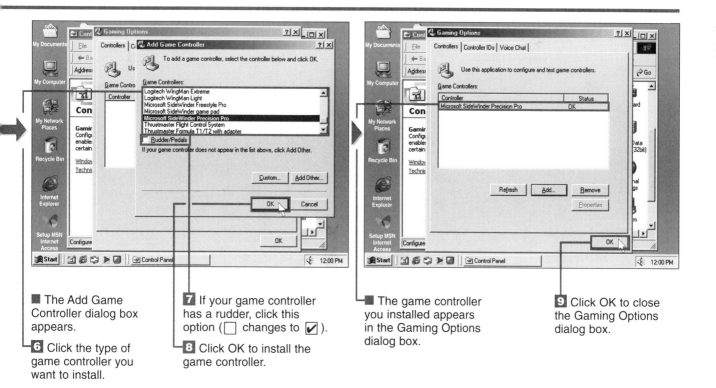

■ The Add Game Controller dialog box appears.

6 Click the type of game controller you want to install.

7 If your game controller has a rudder, click this option (☐ changes to ☑).

8 Click OK to install the game controller.

■ The game controller you installed appears in the Gaming Options dialog box.

9 Click OK to close the Gaming Options dialog box.

ADJUST GAME CONTROLLER SETTINGS

After you have installed a game controller on your computer, you can adjust and fine-tune the settings for the controller. Fine-tuning a game controller's settings is often referred to as calibrating a game controller.

Adjusting the settings of a game controller can help improve the performance of the controller

and ensure you will be able to properly control the direction of movement in a game, such as forward, backward or at an angle.

Many games are designed to operate with specific types of game controllers. Each game controller is different and may require you to adjust different settings before it works properly

with the game you are playing. For example, if you are using a joystick, you may need to adjust the range of motion for the joystick and any specialized buttons on the joystick, such as a Point of View (POV) button.

ADJUST GAME CONTROLLER SETTINGS

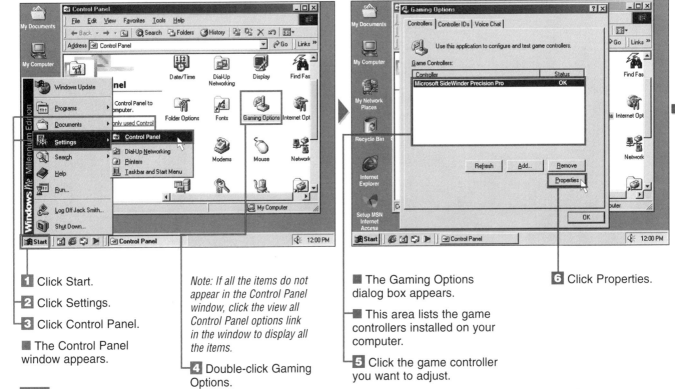

1 Click Start.

2 Click Settings.

3 Click Control Panel.

■ The Control Panel window appears.

Note: If all the items do not appear in the Control Panel window, click the view all Control Panel options link in the window to display all the items.

4 Double-click Gaming Options.

■ The Gaming Options dialog box appears.

■ This area lists the game controllers installed on your computer.

5 Click the game controller you want to adjust.

6 Click Properties.

How can I test my game controller?

✔ After you finish setting up your game controller, display the Game Controller Properties dialog box and then click the Test tab. Windows lets you test certain features of the game controller to make sure the controller is working the way you want.

Why do some features of my game controller not work?

✔ Some game controllers offer advanced features and are more complicated to set up. You may have to use the software that came with the controller to set it up. Check the game controller's documentation to find out how to properly set up the controller.

I notice a delay in the response of my game controller when playing games on the Internet. What could be wrong?

✔ Hardware devices, such as your modem, may be conflicting with your game controller. To turn off the feature that may be causing the problem, display the Gaming Options dialog box and click the Controller IDs tab. Then select the Poll with interrupts enabled option (☑ changes to ☐).

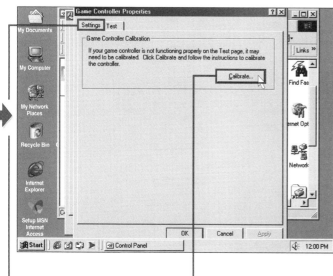

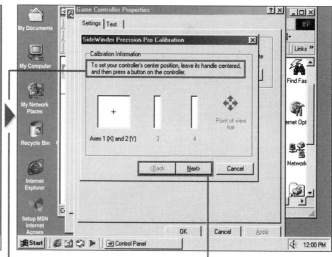

■ The Game Controller Properties dialog box appears.

7 Click the Settings tab.

8 Click Calibrate to adjust the settings for the game controller.

■ The Calibration dialog box appears.

9 Follow the instructions on your screen. Each game controller may have different settings you can adjust.

■ You can click Next or Back to move to the next or previous step.

Note: The Next button changes to Finish when the calibration is complete.

CHANGE PROPERTIES OF A CD-ROM OR DVD-ROM DRIVE

Y ou can change the way Windows works with your CD-ROM or DVD-ROM drive.

You can change the level of volume produced by your CD-ROM or DVD-ROM drive.

If you have digital speakers, you may want to enable the digital audio playback feature. This allows the drive to send the sound directly to your digital speakers, which can improve sound quality.

Some CD-ROM and DVD-ROM drives do not support this feature.

You can specify whether you want Windows to automatically detect a CD or DVD you place in your computer's CD-ROM or DVD-ROM drive. If the CD or DVD is a program disc with autorun capabilities, the initial window will automatically appear. If you insert a music CD, the Windows Media Player program will open and play the CD.

Windows also allows you to reserve a drive letter for your CD-ROM or DVD-ROM drive. Reserving a drive letter prevents Windows from changing the drive letter for the CD-ROM or DVD-ROM drive when you add other devices to your computer. This helps ensure that programs that use the drive will always be able to find the files they need.

CHANGE PROPERTIES OF A CD-ROM OR DVD-ROM DRIVE

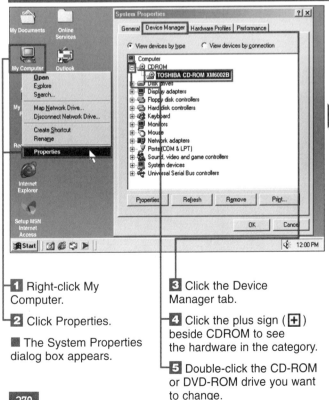

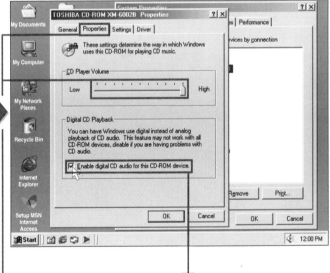

1 Right-click My Computer.

2 Click Properties.

■ The System Properties dialog box appears.

3 Click the Device Manager tab.

4 Click the plus sign (⊞) beside CDROM to see the hardware in the category.

5 Double-click the CD-ROM or DVD-ROM drive you want to change.

■ A Properties dialog box appears.

6 Click the Properties tab.

7 To increase or decrease the volume for the CD-ROM or DVD-ROM drive, drag the slider (⬒) to the right or left.

8 To enable digital audio for the CD-ROM or DVD-ROM drive, click this option (☐ changes to ☑).

Note: Some CD-ROM and DVD-ROM drives do not support digital audio.

Can I stop a CD or DVD from automatically starting when I put it in a drive?

✔ Yes. Hold down the Shift key while you insert the CD or DVD into the drive.

What is the DMA option on the Settings tab in the Properties dialog box for?

✔ Some CD-ROM and DVD-ROM drives support the DMA (Direct Memory Access) option, which allows information on a disc to transfer between main memory and the CD-ROM or DVD-ROM drive without having to be processed by the computer's CPU. This can help your CD-ROM or DVD-ROM drive operate more efficiently. To turn this option on, click the option (☐ changes to ✔).

How can I improve the performance of my CD-ROM or DVD-ROM drive?

✔ Make sure that the CD-ROM or DVD-ROM drive's cache is set to the largest setting. The cache stores information from a CD-ROM or DVD-ROM disc in memory where it can be accessed more quickly than from the disc. In the System Properties dialog box, select the Performance tab and then click the File System button. Click the CD-ROM tab and drag the slider (⬇) to the right to increase the cache setting.

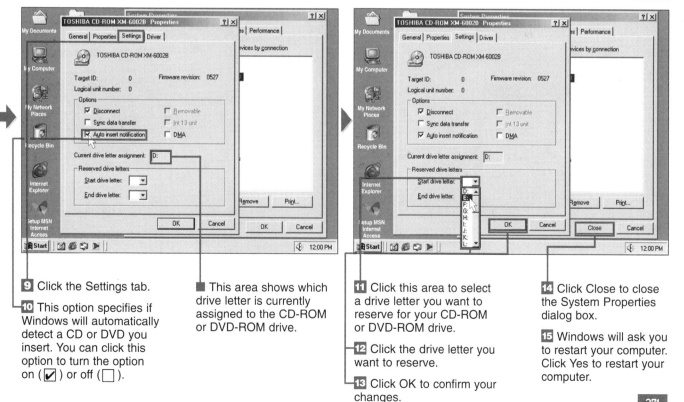

9 Click the Settings tab.

10 This option specifies if Windows will automatically detect a CD or DVD you insert. You can click this option to turn the option on (✔) or off (☐).

■ This area shows which drive letter is currently assigned to the CD-ROM or DVD-ROM drive.

11 Click this area to select a drive letter you want to reserve for your CD-ROM or DVD-ROM drive.

12 Click the drive letter you want to reserve.

13 Click OK to confirm your changes.

14 Click Close to close the System Properties dialog box.

15 Windows will ask you to restart your computer. Click Yes to restart your computer.

SCAN A DOCUMENT

The Scanner and Camera Wizard allows you to use a scanner to turn paper documents, such as forms and newspaper clippings, into pictures you can use on your computer.

You need a Windows Image Acquisition (WIA) compatible scanner to scan a document using the Scanner and Camera Wizard. You can check the documentation that came with your scanner to determine if it is WIA compatible.

To scan documents with a scanner that is not WIA compatible, use the software that came with the scanner.

Before scanning a document, the Scanner and Camera Wizard asks you to specify whether you are scanning a color, grayscale or black and white picture. Specifying the type of picture helps the wizard efficiently scan the document.

The Scanner and Camera Wizard also displays a preview of the scanned picture. You can use the preview to adjust the area the wizard will scan.

You can save a scanned picture in the JPEG, Bitmap or TIFF file format. The file format you should choose depends on how you plan to use the picture. For example, the JPEG file format is useful for pictures you intend to place on a Web page.

SCAN A DOCUMENT

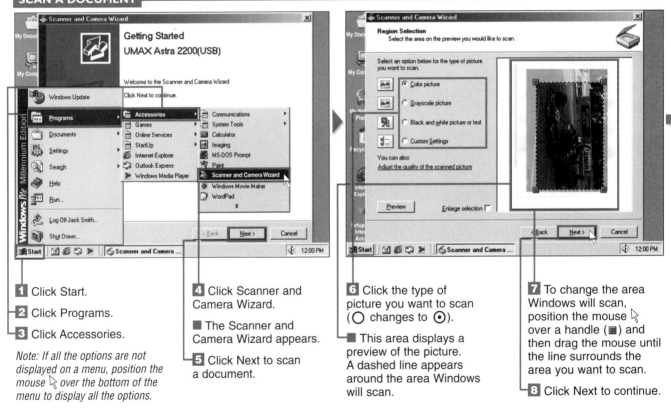

1 Click Start.

2 Click Programs.

3 Click Accessories.

Note: If all the options are not displayed on a menu, position the mouse ⟍ over the bottom of the menu to display all the options.

4 Click Scanner and Camera Wizard.

■ The Scanner and Camera Wizard appears.

5 Click Next to scan a document.

6 Click the type of picture you want to scan (○ changes to ⊙).

■ This area displays a preview of the picture. A dashed line appears around the area Windows will scan.

7 To change the area Windows will scan, position the mouse ⟍ over a handle (■) and then drag the mouse until the line surrounds the area you want to scan.

8 Click Next to continue.

How do I specify custom settings for a picture I want to scan?

✔ Perform steps 1 to 5 below and then click the Adjust the quality of the scanned picture link. The Advanced Properties dialog box appears, displaying the settings you can customize, such as brightness and contrast. When you are finished adjusting the settings, click OK to return to the Scanner and Camera Wizard.

Can I store a scanned picture in a location other than the My Pictures folder?

✔ Yes. In the Scanner and Camera Wizard, click the Browse button beside the Save picture in this folder area. In the Browse For Folder dialog box, select the location where you want to save the picture.

How do I install a scanner on my computer?

✔ Attach the scanner to your computer. If the scanner is a Plug and Play scanner, Windows can automatically detect and install the scanner for you when you turn on the computer. If Windows does not automatically install your scanner, display the Control Panel window and double-click Scanners and Cameras. In the Scanners and Cameras window, double-click Add Device and then follow the instructions on your screen.

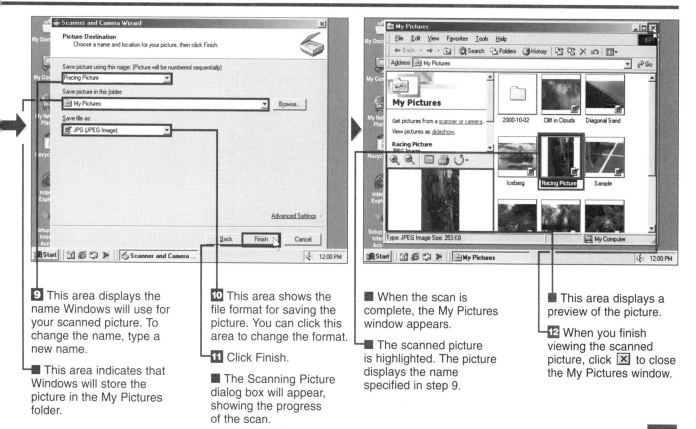

9 This area displays the name Windows will use for your scanned picture. To change the name, type a new name.

■ This area indicates that Windows will store the picture in the My Pictures folder.

10 This area shows the file format for saving the picture. You can click this area to change the format.

11 Click Finish.

■ The Scanning Picture dialog box will appear, showing the progress of the scan.

■ When the scan is complete, the My Pictures window appears.

■ The scanned picture is highlighted. The picture displays the name specified in step 9.

■ This area displays a preview of the picture.

12 When you finish viewing the scanned picture, click ☒ to close the My Pictures window.

COPY PICTURES FROM A DIGITAL CAMERA

You can take pictures using a digital camera and then use the Scanner and Camera Wizard to copy the pictures from the camera to your computer. This allows you to edit and print the pictures, as well as add the pictures to documents or e-mail messages.

You need a Windows Image Acquisition (WIA) compatible digital camera to use the Scanner

and Camera Wizard. Check the documentation that came with your camera to determine if it is WIA compatible. If your digital camera is not WIA compatible, you can use the software that came with the camera to copy pictures to your computer.

You may need to set your digital camera to a specific mode, such as the Connect mode, before you can copy pictures to your computer.

By default, the Scanner and Camera Wizard will copy all the pictures on your digital camera to your computer. If you want to copy only specific pictures, you can select the pictures.

You can specify the name you want to use to save your pictures on your computer. You can also specify if you want to delete the pictures from the camera once they have been copied to your computer.

COPY PICTURES FROM A DIGITAL CAMERA

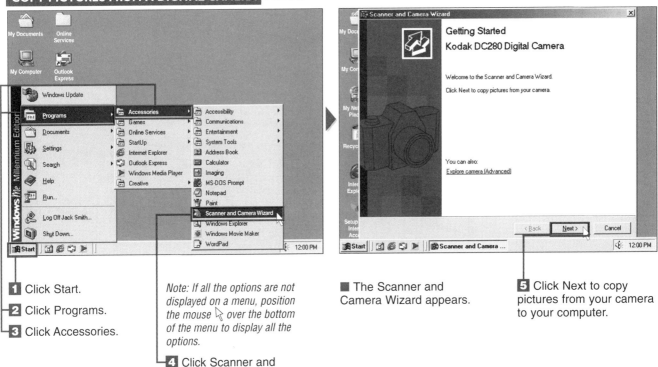

1 Click Start.

2 Click Programs.

3 Click Accessories.

Note: If all the options are not displayed on a menu, position the mouse ▷ over the bottom of the menu to display all the options.

4 Click Scanner and Camera Wizard.

■ The Scanner and Camera Wizard appears.

5 Click Next to copy pictures from your camera to your computer.

Why did the Select Device dialog box appear when I started the Scanner and Camera Wizard?

✔ The Select Device dialog box appears if you have more than one imaging device installed on your computer, such as a scanner and digital camera. Select your digital camera in the dialog box and click OK.

Can I work with the pictures before I copy them to my computer?

✔ Yes. In the Scanner and Camera Wizard, click the Explore camera (Advanced) link to browse through the pictures stored on the camera. You can click a picture to display a list of links you can use to work with the picture. For example, you can preview the picture, save the picture on your computer or delete the picture from the camera.

How do I install a digital camera on my computer?

✔ Attach the digital camera to your computer. If the digital camera is a Plug and Play camera, Windows can automatically detect and install the camera for you when you turn on the computer. If Windows does not automatically install your camera, display the Control Panel window and double-click Scanners and Cameras. In the Scanners and Cameras window, double-click Add Device and then follow the instructions on your screen.

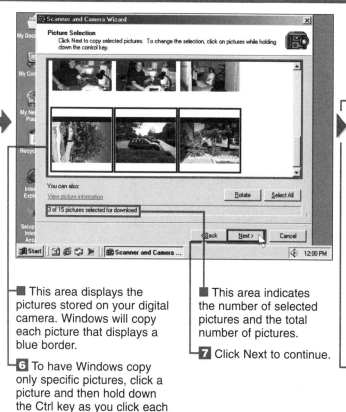

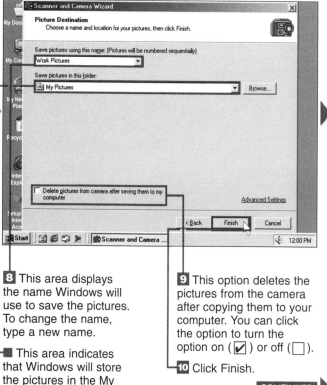

■ This area displays the pictures stored on your digital camera. Windows will copy each picture that displays a blue border.

6 To have Windows copy only specific pictures, click a picture and then hold down the Ctrl key as you click each picture you want to copy.

■ This area indicates the number of selected pictures and the total number of pictures.

7 Click Next to continue.

8 This area displays the name Windows will use to save the pictures. To change the name, type a new name.

■ This area indicates that Windows will store the pictures in the My Pictures folder.

9 This option deletes the pictures from the camera after copying them to your computer. You can click the option to turn the option on (✔) or off (☐).

10 Click Finish.

CONTINUED

COPY PICTURES FROM A DIGITAL CAMERA (CONTINUED)

When you copy pictures from a digital camera, Windows creates a subfolder in the My Pictures folder to store the pictures. The My Pictures folder is located in the My Documents folder on your desktop. By default, Windows names the subfolder with the current date, such as 2000-09-25.

Once the pictures have been copied to your computer, Windows automatically displays the contents of the subfolder on your screen. Each picture in the subfolder displays the name specified for the pictures. Windows also sequentially numbers the pictures so that each picture is saved in a separate file with a unique name.

You can view a slideshow of the pictures you copied to your computer. Windows displays the slideshow using the full screen and automatically advances through the pictures.

Windows displays the slideshow toolbar, which you can use to move through the pictures in the slideshow. The toolbar also allows you to stop, restart and exit the slideshow. Windows will temporarily hide the toolbar if you do not use it for a period of time. You can move the mouse on your screen to redisplay the toolbar at any time.

COPY PICTURES FROM A DIGITAL CAMERA (CONTINUED)

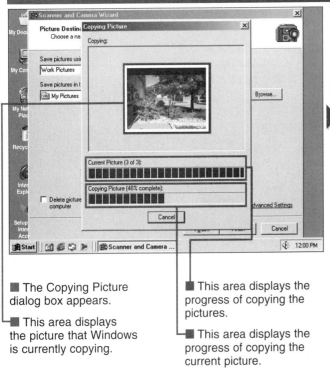

■ The Copying Picture dialog box appears.

■ This area displays the picture that Windows is currently copying.

■ This area displays the progress of copying the pictures.

■ This area displays the progress of copying the current picture.

■ The subfolder that stores the pictures appears, displaying the pictures copied from the camera.

■ Windows uses the current date to name the subfolder.

■ Each picture is sequentially numbered and displays the name specified in step 8.

Can I work with the preview of a picture in the subfolder?

✔ Click a picture you want to work with. A preview appears in the left pane of the window. You can use the toolbar in the left pane to work with the preview. For example, click 🔍 or 🔍 and then click the preview of the picture to zoom in or out. The 🖼 button allows you to preview the picture in the Image Preview window. You can click 🖨 to print the picture. To rotate the picture, click 🔄 and then select the way you want to rotate the picture.

Can I use the pictures I copied from my digital camera as a screen saver?

✔ Windows provides a screen saver that displays a slideshow of all the pictures stored in the My Pictures folder and its subfolders. To set up the screen saver, right-click a blank area of the desktop and select Properties. In the Display Properties dialog box, select the Screen Saver tab. Click 🔽 in the Screen Saver area and then select My Pictures Screen Saver. For more information about screen savers, see page 176.

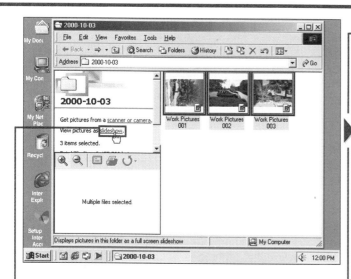

VIEW A SLIDESHOW

1 Click the slideshow link to start a full-screen slideshow of all the pictures stored in the subfolder.

■ Windows displays a picture in the subfolder using the full screen.

2 To start or stop the slideshow at any time, click the Start (▷) or Stop (⏸) button.

Note: To display the slideshow toolbar, move the mouse ⇖ on your screen.

3 To move through the pictures in the slideshow, click the Previous Picture (◁◁) or Next Picture (▷▷) button.

4 When you finish viewing the slideshow, click ✕.

USING WEBTV FOR WINDOWS

You can use WebTV for Windows to watch television programs on your computer. You need a TV tuner card to watch programs on your computer. You also need a sound card and speakers to hear sounds in television programs you watch.

When you first start WebTV for Windows, you can have the program scan for local TV

channels and place them into your Program Guide. The scan can take a few minutes. While the scan is in progress, you can see which channels are accepted and which channels are rejected. You can also enter your ZIP code so Windows will be able to find TV listings for your area.

If you have access to the Internet, you can visit the

Microsoft TV Listings Web site and get free TV listings for your area. Even if you do not have a TV tuner card, you can still use WebTV for Windows to view TV listings on your computer. WebTV for Windows will display the TV listings in the Program Guide so you can see when your favorite television programs will start.

START WEBTV FOR WINDOWS

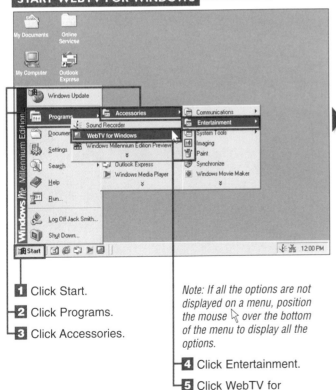

Scan For Channels

Scanning identifies local TV channels and puts them into your Program Guide. It takes a few minutes to scan all the channels.

To scan now, click **Start Scan**.

To postpone scanning, click **Next**.

Start Scan

Next

1 Click Start.

2 Click Programs.

3 Click Accessories.

Note: If all the options are not displayed on a menu, position the mouse ⬚ over the bottom of the menu to display all the options.

4 Click Entertainment.

5 Click WebTV for Windows.

■ The Scan For Channels screen appears the first time you start WebTV for Windows.

■ WebTV for Windows can scan for local TV channels and place them in your Program Guide. The scan may take a few minutes.

6 Click Start Scan to start the scan.

How can I verify that my computer has the hardware required to use WebTV for Windows?

✔ You can consult your computer hardware retailer or visit the www.microsoft.com/windowsme/upgrade/compat Web site to search for hardware that has been tested for use with Windows Me. In the Product category area, you can search by Video Capture/TV Tuner to find hardware devices for use with WebTV for Windows.

Why isn't WebTV for Windows on my Start menu?

✔ You need to install the WebTV for Windows component on your computer. To install Windows components, see page 538.

Is there a faster way to start WebTV for Windows?

✔ Yes. Click the Launch WebTV for Windows icon (🔲) on the Quick Launch toolbar. If you do not see the Launch WebTV for Windows icon, click » on the toolbar and then select the Launch WebTV for Windows option.

Will I be able to watch all the programs offered by my cable provider?

✔ You should be able to watch all the programs offered by your cable provider, except for programs that require an external tuning device. Programs that require an external tuning device include pay-per-view programs and digital broadcasts.

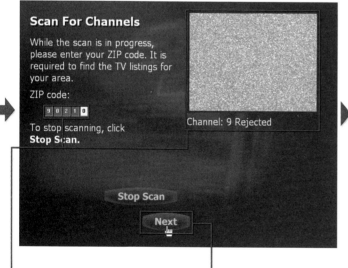

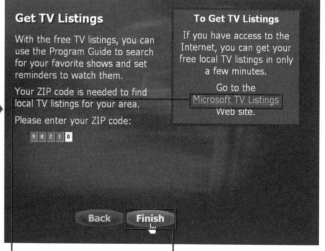

■ During the scan, this area displays the channels and whether the channels are accepted or rejected.

⑦ Click this area and type your ZIP code. Windows will use your ZIP code to find TV listings for your area.

⑧ When the scan is complete, click Next to continue.

⑨ If you have access to the Internet, you can click the Microsoft TV Listings link to visit the Microsoft TV Listings Web site and get free TV listings for your area.

Note: If you select the link, follow the instructions at the Web site to get the TV listings.

⑩ Click Finish to complete the setup of WebTV for Windows.

CONTINUED ►

USING WEBTV FOR WINDOWS (CONTINUED)

The Program Guide allows you to view information about television programs.

The Program Guide displays the channels offered by your cable provider and the names of the programs available on each channel. Windows displays programs that are currently playing in a different color than programs that are not currently playing.

You can select a program to see a brief description of the program. The description may include parental rating information. Symbols may also appear, providing you with additional information about the program. The ♻ symbol indicates the program is a rerun. When the ⌨ symbol is displayed, closed captioning is available. When the 🎧 symbol is displayed, stereo sound is available. The

yellow 🖉 symbol indicates enhancements are available. Enhancements can include background facts about a program or the ability to chat with other viewers.

If you select a program that is currently playing, WebTV for Windows will display the program in a small area above the description.

USING THE PROGRAM GUIDE

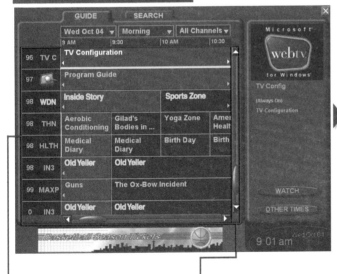

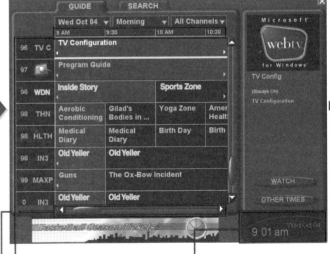

■ This area displays the channels and the programs playing on each channel.

■ You can use this scroll bar to browse through the channels.

■ This area displays the times for the displayed programs.

■ You can use this scroll bar to see the programs playing at other times.

■ This area displays the current time and date. To quickly return to the current time and date in the Program Guide, click the time.

Why doesn't my Program Guide display any program information?

✔ If you did not get your local TV listings when you first started WebTV for Windows, the Program Guide will not display any program information. To get the TV listings, double-click channel 96 to display your TV Configuration channel. Click Go To and then select Get TV Listings. Enter your ZIP code and click the Microsoft TV Listings link to connect to a Web site. Follow the instructions on your screen to get the TV listings. When the TV listings are downloaded to your computer, close your Web browser and click Close in the TV Configuration channel. You can use this procedure to update the TV listings at any time.

Can I have the Program Guide display only the channels I want to watch?

✔ Yes. Press the F10 key to display the TV toolbar and then click the Settings button. Each channel that displays a check mark (✔) will appear in the Program Guide. You can click the check box beside a channel to add or remove a check mark.

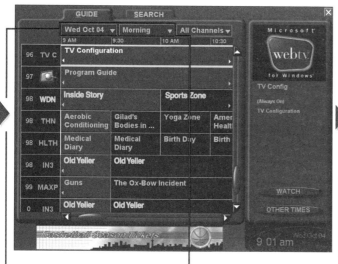

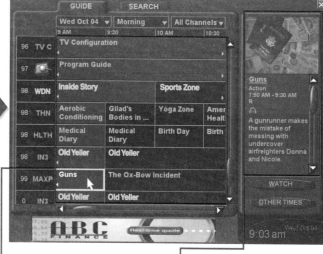

■ This area shows the date for the displayed programs. You can click this area to view the programs playing on another day.

■ This area shows the time of day for the displayed programs. You can click this area to view the programs playing at another time.

1 Click a program of interest.

■ This area displays the program and a description of the program.

CONTINUED

USING WEBTV FOR WINDOWS (CONTINUED)

Once you find a television program in the Program Guide you want to watch, you can use the entire screen to display the program.

You need a TV tuner card and sound card to see and hear a program you want to watch. Depending on the TV tuner card and sound card you are using, you may have to use an audio cable to connect the cards to hear sound.

If you are using multiple monitors, you will only be able to display the program on the primary monitor. For information about using multiple monitors, see page 216.

When you are watching a program, WebTV for Windows allows you to display the TV banner and the TV toolbar at the top of your screen. The TV banner displays the number of

the channel you are viewing and a brief description of the program you are watching. You can use the TV banner to change channels. The TV toolbar appears below the TV banner and includes buttons that allow you to quickly display the Program Guide, change settings and get help with WebTV for Windows.

WATCH PROGRAMS

1 Click a program of interest.

■ This area displays the program and a description of the program.

2 To use the entire screen to display the program, click Watch.

■ The program fills the screen.

3 To view the TV banner and TV toolbar, move the mouse ⬁ over the top of the screen or press the F10 key.

Can I watch a program in a window?

✔ When you are watching a program, you can press the F6 key to switch between full-screen viewing and window viewing. Window viewing allows you to perform other tasks on your computer while you watch the program.

How do I quickly change channels using my keyboard?

✔ You can type the number of the channel you want to view and then press the Enter key.

How can I close WebTV for Windows?

✔ You can press the Alt+F4 keys to close WebTV for Windows at any time.

Can I increase or decrease the volume using my keyboard?

✔ To increase the volume, press the Windows logo (🪟)+Ctrl+V keys. To decrease the volume, press the Windows logo (🪟)+Shift+V keys. To mute the sound, press the Windows logo (🪟)+V keys.

Can I have WebTV for Windows display closed captioning?

✔ Yes. Press the F10 key and then click the Settings button. Click the Show closed captioning option (☐ changes to ☑).

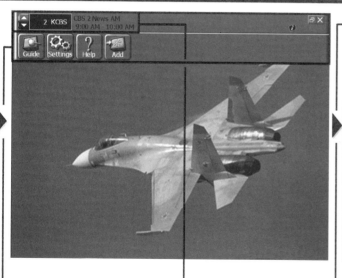

■ The TV banner and TV toolbar appear.

Note: To remove the TV banner and TV toolbar, press the F10 key.

■ This area displays the channel number and information about the displayed program.

■ You can click the Channel up (🔼) or Channel down (🔽) arrow to move through the channels.

Note: You can also press the Page Up and Page Down keys to move through the channels.

4 To return to the Program Guide, click Guide.

CONTINUED ▶

USING WEBTV FOR WINDOWS (CONTINUED)

You can use the Program Guide to search for programs of interest. The Search tab allows you to quickly locate the programs you want to watch.

You can search for a program by category. The categories offered in the Program Guide include Action, Comedy, Drama, Sports and many more.

You can also find a program by searching for the name of the program or the name of the station that broadcasts the program. If you want to find a program starring a certain actor or actress, you can search for the name of the actor or actress.

The Program Guide displays the names of the matching programs it finds and information about

the programs, such as the channels that offers the programs and when the programs will play.

You can choose to narrow your search to display only programs that play on a certain day. You can also sort the programs the Program Guide finds by the time the programs will play or by the titles of the programs.

SEARCH FOR PROGRAMS

1 Click the Search tab.

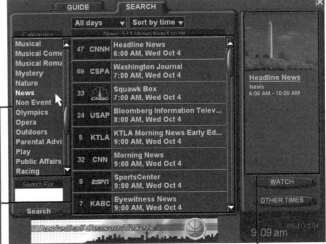

SEARCH BY CATEGORY

1 To view channels that offer programs in a specific category, click the category of interest.

■ This area lists the programs in the category you selected.

■ This area displays a description of the selected program.

Note: To view the description of another program, click the program.

Do I need to know the exact name of a program, actor or actress?

✔ No. You can type as much of the name as you know and WebTV for Windows will attempt to find a match. For example, you can type **Trav** to find movies starring the actor John Travolta.

How can I get more information about a program?

✔ You can click the name of the program in the description area. Windows opens Internet Explorer and searches the Web for Web pages that match the words in the program name. You can select a Web page you want to view from the list of Web pages Internet Explorer finds.

How can I find the other times a program will play?

✔ If you click the Search tab while you are previewing a program in the Program Guide, the Search tab will display the other times the program will play. You can also select a program in the Program Guide and then click the Other Times button.

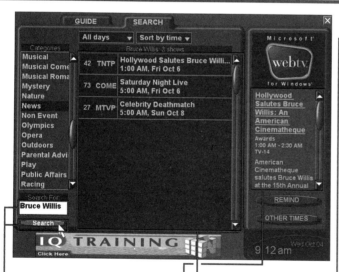

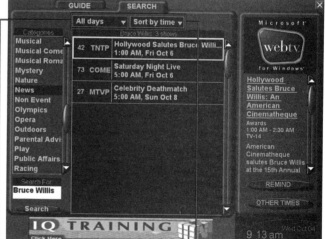

SEARCH BY WORD

1 To search for programs using specific information, click this area and then type the name of the program, station, actor or actress you want to search for.

2 Click Search.

■ This area lists the programs that match the information you entered.

■ This area displays a description of the selected program.

CUSTOMIZE SEARCH RESULTS

■ This area shows the days the displayed programs will play. You can click this area to display programs playing on a specific day.

■ This area shows how the programs are sorted. You can click this area to sort the programs by time or title.

PLAY A MUSIC CD

You can use your computer to play music CDs while you work. You need a CD-ROM drive, a sound card and speakers to play music CDs.

When you insert a music CD into your CD-ROM drive, the Windows Media Player window opens automatically and the CD starts playing.

If you are connected to the Internet when you play a music CD, Windows Media Player

attempts to download information from the Internet, such as the name of the artist and the name of each song. If this information is unavailable, Windows Media Player displays the track number of each song instead. After the information is downloaded, Windows will recognize the CD each time it is inserted and display the information for the CD.

Windows Media Player has many of the same controls as a standard

CD player. You can use controls to play, pause and stop a CD. You can also use controls to play the previous or next song or play the songs in random order.

Once a CD starts playing, you can continue to work with other programs on your computer. Playing a CD should have very little effect on the speed of your other programs.

PLAY A MUSIC CD

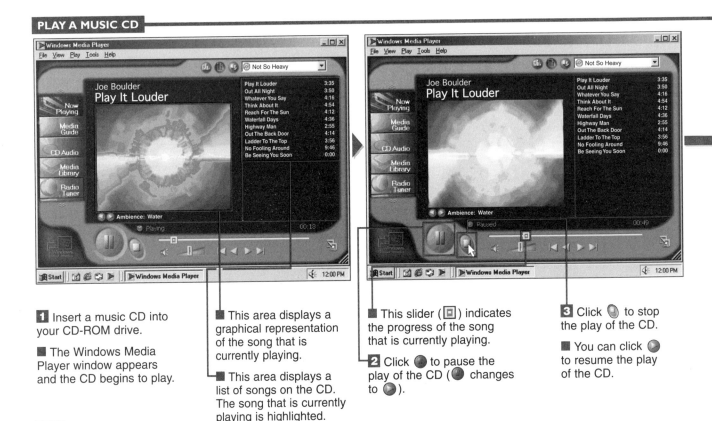

■1 Insert a music CD into your CD-ROM drive.

■ The Windows Media Player window appears and the CD begins to play.

■ This area displays a graphical representation of the song that is currently playing.

■ This area displays a list of songs on the CD. The song that is currently playing is highlighted.

■ This slider (▣) indicates the progress of the song that is currently playing.

■2 Click ◉ to pause the play of the CD (◉ changes to ◉).

■3 Click ◉ to stop the play of the CD.

■ You can click ◉ to resume the play of the CD.

Can I change the graphical representation of the song?

✔ Yes. Click the View menu, select Visualizations, select a type of graphical representation and then click the name of the graphical representation you want to display.

Is there another way to start Windows Media Player?

✔ Click the Windows Media Player button (▶) on the taskbar.

How do I hide the playlist displayed on the Now Playing tab?

✔ Click 🔘 to hide the playlist. To redisplay the playlist, click 🔘 again.

Can I listen to a music CD privately?

✔ You can listen to a music CD privately by plugging headphones into the jack at the front of your CD-ROM drive. If your CD-ROM drive does not have a headphone jack, you can plug the headphones into the back of your computer where the speakers plug in.

I am not connected to the Internet. How can I have the playlist display song titles?

✔ Right-click the track number of a song in the playlist and select Edit from the menu that appears. Then type the title of the song and press the Enter key.

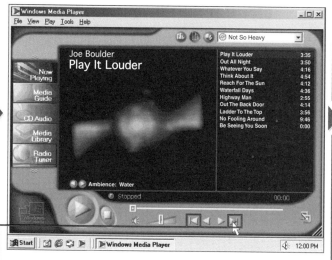

■ **4** Click one of the following options to move through the songs on the CD.

◄ Play the previous song

► Play the next song

■ **5** To play a specific song in the list, double-click the song. The song is highlighted.

■ **6** Click 🔘 to play the songs on the CD in random order.

■ You can click 🔘 to once again play the songs on the CD in order.

CONTINUED ▶

PLAY A MUSIC CD (CONTINUED)

When playing a music CD, you can temporarily mute the sound. You can also adjust the volume of the sound to suit your needs. If you are using headphones that are plugged into your CD-ROM drive, you can adjust the volume using the volume control on the front of the CD-ROM drive. The volume also depends on the computer's master volume setting. For more information, see page 258.

You can view additional information about the CD you are playing by viewing the contents of the CD Audio tab in the Windows Media Player window.

Windows Media Player allows you to copy songs to your computer. This is useful if you want to create a customized playlist of songs from various CDs. You can then play the songs at any time without having to insert the CDs into your computer.

Depending on the configuration of your hardware, you may be able to listen to the CD while you are copying songs.

The songs you copy from a music CD are stored in the Media Library in Windows Media Player.

PLAY A MUSIC CD (CONTINUED)

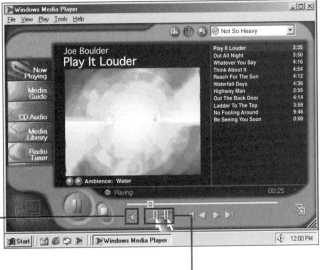

7 Click <img> to turn off the sound (<img> changes to <img>).

■ You can click <img> to once again turn on the sound.

8 To adjust the volume of the sound, drag this slider (<img>) left or right to decrease or increase the volume.

9 Click the CD Audio tab to view more information about the songs on the CD.

■ This area displays information about the songs on the CD, including the name of each song and the name of the artist.

■ To once again display the graphical representation of the current song, click the Now Playing tab.

How do I play a song I copied to my computer?

✔ The songs you copy to your computer appear on the Media Library tab. To play a song on the Media Library tab, perform steps 1 to 3 on page 298.

Can I adjust the quality of the songs I copy?

✔ Yes. From the Tools menu, click Options. In the Options dialog box, click the CD Audio tab. In the Copy Settings area, drag the slider (⬚) to the right or left to increase or decrease the quality of the copy. Songs copied using lower quality take up less storage space on your computer.

How can I find more information about the current CD?

✔ If you are connected to the Internet, select the CD Audio tab and then click the Album Details button to display information such as a review of the CD and a biography of the artist.

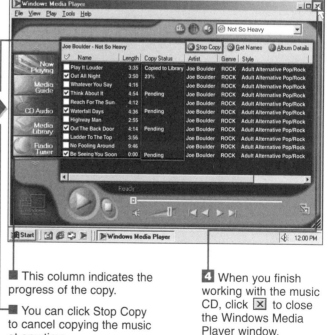

COPY A MUSIC CD

1 Click the CD Audio tab.

2 Windows Media Player will copy each song that displays a check mark (☑) to your computer. Click the box beside each song you do not want to copy to remove the check mark (☐).

3 Click Copy Music to copy the music to your computer.

■ This column indicates the progress of the copy.

■ You can click Stop Copy to cancel copying the music at any time.

4 When you finish working with the music CD, click ☒ to close the Windows Media Player window.

LISTEN TO RADIO STATIONS ON THE INTERNET

Y ou can use Windows Media Player to listen to radio stations from around the world that broadcast on the Internet. You need a sound card, speakers and an Internet connection to use your computer to listen to radio stations.

Windows Media Player provides several methods you can use to search for radio stations that

broadcast on the Internet. To find a radio station that plays a specific type of music, you can search by a format, such as new age or oldies. You can search by band to find radio stations that broadcast on AM, FM or that broadcast only on the Internet. If you are interested in listening to a radio station that broadcasts in another language or from another country, search by language or location.

You can also specify a call sign, frequency or keyword to find a radio station of interest. For example, you can enter a call sign, such as CNN, or a frequency, such as 102.3. Searching by a keyword, such as "rock" or "news," is useful when you are not sure which station you want to listen to.

LISTEN TO RADIO STATIONS ON THE INTERNET

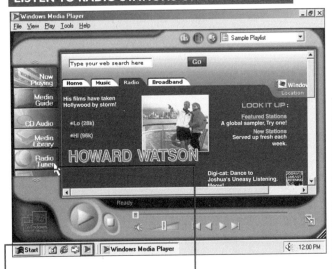

DISPLAY THE RADIO TUNER

1 Click ▶ to start Windows Media Player.

■ The Windows Media Player window appears.

2 Click the Radio Tuner tab to listen to radio stations on the Internet.

Note: If you are not connected to the Internet, a dialog box appears that allows you to connect.

SEARCH FOR RADIO STATIONS

1 Click this area to display the ways you can search for radio stations.

2 Click the way you want to search for radio stations.

■ An area appears that allows you to specify which radio stations you want to search for.

How do I find more information about a radio station displayed on the Radio Tuner tab?

✔ Position the mouse pointer over the name of the radio station (↖ changes to 🖑). After a few seconds, a yellow box appears, displaying a description of the station.

Can I sort the radio stations in the results of a search?

✔ You can click a heading displayed in the results of a search to sort the radio stations. For example, sorting by the Station Name column displays names alphabetically from A to Z. To reverse the sort order, click the heading again.

Is there a way to narrow my search for a radio station?

✔ On the Radio Tuner tab, click the Search button. In the Advanced Station Search dialog box, select the search options you want to use. Click the Find button to start the search.

Can I browse the Web while listening to a radio station?

✔ Yes. You can use your Web browser to view Web pages and use Windows Media Player to play a radio station at the same time.

3 Click this area to display the options for the search method you chose in step 2.

4 Click the option you want to use.

Note: If you selected Callsign, Frequency or Keyword in step 2, an area appears where you can specify the information you want to search for. Click the area and type the information. Then press the Enter key.

■ This area lists the radio stations that match the information you specified.

■ This area indicates the number of the current page and the total number of pages in the results.

■ If the results contain more than one page, you can click Next or Previous to display the next or previous page.

CONTINUED ▶

LISTEN TO RADIO STATIONS ON THE INTERNET (CONTINUED)

You can play a radio station you find in a search or a radio station featured on the Radio Tuner tab.

Before Windows plays a radio station on the Internet, information is partially transferred and temporarily stored in a section of memory on your computer called a buffer. While the radio station plays, information will continuously transfer from the Internet and be temporarily stored in the buffer. This ensures that any interruptions to the information transferring from the Internet will not cause interruptions to the radio station playing on your computer.

The Web page for the currently playing radio station appears as a button on your taskbar. You can display the Web page on your screen to view the contents of the page.

You can add your favorite radio stations to the My Presets list on the Radio Tuner tab. Initially, this list is empty. Adding radio stations to the My Presets list allows you to create a personalized list of radio stations that can be quickly accessed at any time.

LISTEN TO RADIO STATIONS ON THE INTERNET (CONTINUED)

PLAY A RADIO STATION

■ This area displays a list of featured radio stations.

■ If you searched for radio stations, this area displays the results of the search.

1 Double-click the name of the radio station you want to play.

■ After a moment, the radio station begins to play.

■ This area displays information about the radio station.

■ The Web page for the radio station appears as a button on the taskbar. To display the Web page, click the button.

2 To adjust the volume of the radio station broadcast, drag the slider (▯) left or right to decrease or increase the volume.

3 To stop playing the radio station, click ◉.

How can I change the size of the Presets and Station Finder areas displayed on the Radio Tuner tab?

✔ To change the size of the Presets and Station Finder areas, position the mouse pointer over the bar between the areas (⇘ changes to ↔). Drag the mouse ↔ until the areas display the size you want.

Can I create another preset list besides the Featured and My Presets lists?

✔ Yes. In the Presets area, click the Edit button. In the Edit Preset Lists dialog box, select the text in the Add new list area and type a name for the list you want to create. Then click the Add button. You can add radio stations to the new list as you would add stations to the My Presets list.

Is there another way to adjust the volume of a radio station?

✔ Click the speaker icon (🔊) on the taskbar to adjust your computer's master volume setting. This setting affects how loud you can play the radio station using the volume slider on the Radio Tuner tab. For more information on your computer's master volume setting, see page 258.

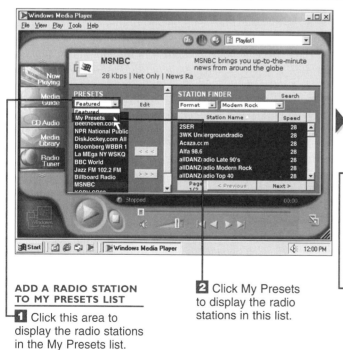

ADD A RADIO STATION TO MY PRESETS LIST

1 Click this area to display the radio stations in the My Presets list.

2 Click My Presets to display the radio stations in this list.

■ This area displays the radio stations in the My Presets list.

Note: The My Presets list initially appears empty. You can add radio stations to the list to create a personalized list of radio stations.

3 Click a radio station you want to add to the My Presets list.

4 Click ⟨⟨⟨ to add the radio station to the My Presets list.

USING THE MEDIA GUIDE

The Media Guide is a Web page that is updated daily to provide you with access to the latest music, movies and videos on the Internet. You must have a connection to the Internet to use the Media Guide.

The Media Guide displays tabs that contain information about different types of media. The tabs help you quickly find information of interest.

Each tab contains several links that you can select to display information on various topics. Selecting a link may display additional information in the Media Guide, open a Web page in your Web browser or play media files such as movie clips or music videos. You can play all media files accessed through the Media Guide in Windows Media Player.

Keep in mind that the information found in the Media Guide is hosted by the WindowsMedia.com Web site and changes daily. This means that the Media Guide shown below may look different than the Media Guide displayed on your screen.

USING THE MEDIA GUIDE

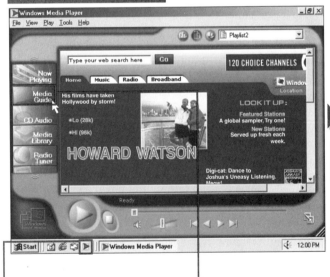

■1 Click ▶ to start Windows Media Player.

■ The Windows Media Player window appears.

■2 Click the Media Guide tab.

Note: If you are not connected to the Internet, a dialog box appears that allows you to connect.

■ This area displays the Media Guide. The Media Guide is a Web page that provides access to the latest media on the Internet.

■3 Click a tab to display information for a particular type of media.

Why does the Media Guide appear each time I start Windows Media Player?

✔ If you are connected to the Internet when you start Windows Media Player, the Media Guide automatically appears. To avoid having to wait for the Media Guide to load each time you start Windows Media Player, select the Tools menu and click Options. In the Options dialog box, click the Player tab and then select the Start player in Media Guide option (☑ changes to ☐).

Can I search for media files by a specific artist in the Media Guide?

✔ Yes. Click the Home tab and then select the Artist search option (◯ changes to ◉). Click the box below the option, type the name of the artist you want to search for and then press the Enter key.

Why are there speeds listed next to a media file in the Media Guide?

✔ These are the Internet connection speeds the Media Guide recommends that you use to download and play the media file. If you have a high-speed Internet connection, such as a cable modem, you can select the higher speed. If you have a slower Internet connection or if you are not concerned about the quality of playback, you can select a slower speed.

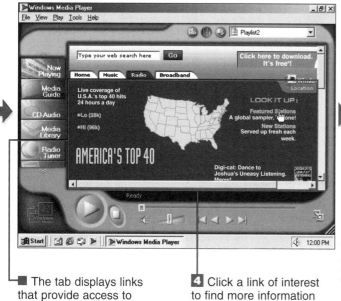

■ The tab displays links that provide access to information on various topics.

4 Click a link of interest to find more information on the topic.

■ Information on the topic appears.

5 You can repeat step 4 until you find information of interest.

6 When you finish using the Media Guide, click ☒ to close the Windows Media Player window.

USING THE MEDIA LIBRARY

You can use the Media Library to organize and work with media files, including sound and video files. The Media Library displays the names of media files on your computer and may also display links to radio stations you have listened to on the Internet. For information about listening to a radio station on the Internet, see page 290.

The Media Library allows you to search for all the media files stored on your computer, including media files that your programs use. You can also specify whether you want to search system folders for media files in the WAV and MIDI formats. Windows uses these media files to play sounds when events occur on your computer.

You can obtain media files from many sources. The Media Guide provides access to the latest music, movies and videos on the Internet. For more information about the Media Guide, see page 294. There are also Web sites that offer sound and video files, such as soundamerica.com, earthstation1.com and www.jurassicpunk.com. Many computer stores offer collections of media files that you can purchase.

SEARCH COMPUTER FOR MEDIA FILES

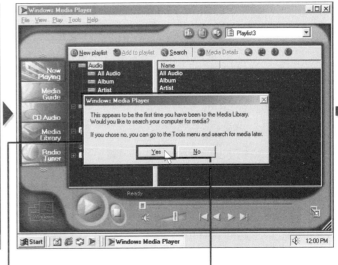

1 Click ▶ to start Windows Media Player.

■ The Windows Media Player window appears.

2 Click the Media Library tab.

■ The first time you visit the Media Library, a dialog box appears, asking if you want to search your computer for media files.

Note: If the dialog box does not appear and you want to search your computer for media files, press the F3 key and then skip to step 4.

3 Click Yes to search your computer for media files.

How can I add one sound or video file to the Media Library?

✔ In the Windows Media Player window, select the File menu and click Open. In the Open dialog box, locate the file you want to add and then click the Open button. You can also double-click a media file on the desktop or in a window to open and automatically add the file to the Media Library.

Can I add a song from a music CD to the Media Library?

✔ To add a song from a music CD to the Media Library, you must copy the song from the CD to your computer. For more information, see page 288.

How do I add a radio station to the Media Library?

✔ Radio stations displayed in the Presets area of the Radio Tuner tab may automatically appear in the Radio Tuner Presets category. For information on the Presets area of the Radio Tuner tab, see page 292. To add a radio station that is currently playing to the All Audio category, choose the File menu, select Add to Library and then click Add Currently Playing Track.

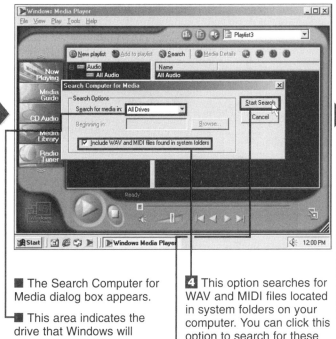

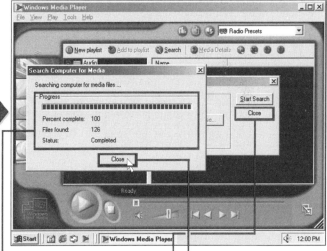

■ The Search Computer for Media dialog box appears.

■ This area indicates the drive that Windows will search for media files. You can click this area to change the drive.

4 This option searches for WAV and MIDI files located in system folders on your computer. You can click this option to search for these files (☐ changes to ☑).

5 Click Start Search to start the search.

■ Windows searches your computer for media files.

■ This area shows the progress of the search.

6 When the search is complete, click Close to close the dialog box.

7 Click Close to close the Search Computer for Media dialog box.

CONTINUED ▶

USING THE MEDIA LIBRARY
(CONTINUED)

The Media Library organizes your media files into several categories. For example, sound files can be found in the All Audio, Album, Artist and Genre categories. Some categories contain hidden items. For example, the Artist category contains the names of artists. You can browse through categories and items to find the media file you want to play.

You can play a media file directly from the Media Library. You only need to connect to the Internet to listen to a radio station that broadcasts over the Internet.

The Media Library includes a category called My Playlists. You can add a new playlist to the My Playlists category. This is useful if you want to create a personalized playlist that contains the media files you frequently access or if

you want to group together sound and video files.

There is no limit to the number of media files you can add to a playlist, but you can only add files that are listed in the Media Library.

You can play all the media files in a playlist. The media files play in the order they appear in the playlist.

VIEW MEDIA FILES

■ The Media Library organizes your media files into categories.

1 A category displaying a plus sign (⊞) contains hidden items. You can click the plus sign (⊞) beside a category to display its hidden items (⊞ changes to ⊟).

Note: To once again hide the items in a category, click the minus sign (⊟) beside the category.

2 Click a category or item that contains media files of interest.

■ This area displays the media files in the category or item you selected.

3 To play a media file, double-click the file.

Note: For more information about playing media files, see page 300.

How can I search for a specific media file in the Media Library?

✓ On the Media Library tab, click the Search button. In the Search Library for Media dialog box, type a word you want to search for and then click the Search Now button. When the search is complete, click the View Results button to close the dialog box and view a playlist that contains the results of the search.

Can I change the order in which media files play in a playlist?

✓ Yes. Click the playlist you want to change. Select a media file in the playlist and then click the ⊙ or ⊙ button to move the file up or down in the list.

How do I delete a playlist from the Media Library?

✓ Select a media file in the playlist you want to delete and then click the ⊗ button. From the menu that appears, select Delete Playlist. Deleting a playlist will not remove the media files from the Media Library. Deleted playlists are stored in the Deleted Items category.

CREATE A PLAYLIST

1 Click New playlist.

■ The New Playlist dialog box appears.

2 Type a name for the playlist and then press the Enter key.

■ The new playlist appears in the My Playlists category.

3 To add a media file to a playlist, locate the file in Media Library and then click the file in this area.

4 Click Add to playlist.

5 Click the playlist you want to add the media file to.

■ Windows adds the media file to the playlist.

Note: To play all the media files in a playlist, double-click the playlist.

PLAY MEDIA FILES

Windows Media Player allows you to play sound and video files on your computer. You need a sound card and speakers to play sound on your computer.

The Media Library organizes your sound and video files into categories. You can browse through the categories in the Media Library to locate the media file you want to play.

If you play a video file, the video automatically appears on the Now Playing tab in the Windows Media Player window. If you play a sound file, you can listen to the sound while you view a graphical representation of the sound on the Now Playing tab.

While a media file is playing, a slider (▣) indicates how much of the file is left to play. Once a file is finished playing, you can select

another file you want to play or let Windows Media Player play the next file in the list.

Windows Media Player lets you control how a file plays. You can play, pause and stop a file. You can also turn off the sound or adjust the volume of a file.

PLAY MEDIA FILES

1 Click ▶ to start Windows Media Player.

■ The Windows Media Player window appears.

2 Click the Media Library tab.

3 Locate the sound or video file you want to play. To locate a file in Media Library, see page 296.

4 Double-click the file you want to play.

■ If you selected a video file, the video appears on the Now Playing tab.

Note: If you selected a sound file, the sound plays. You can click the Now Playing tab to display a graphical representation for the sound.

■ This area displays a list of your sound or video files. The file that is currently playing appears highlighted.

Note: To play another file in the list, double-click the file.

Is there another way to play a media file?

✔ Yes. You can use a My Computer or Windows Explorer window to locate media files on your computer. You can then double-click the media file you want to play.

Can I change the audio and video settings Windows Media Player uses to play media files?

✔ Yes. Select the Now Playing tab and then click 📷. An area appears in the bottom left corner of the Now Playing tab. Click ◀ or ▶ in the area to view the audio and video settings you can change. To hide the area, click 📷 again.

How can I move through the media files in the list?

✔ At the bottom of the Windows Media Player window, click ◀ to play the previous file or ▶ to play the next file.

I changed the volume using the volume slider (▯).Why didn't I get the result I expected?

✔ The volume used in Windows Media Player also depends on the computer's master volume setting. For information about changing the computer's master volume setting, see page 258.

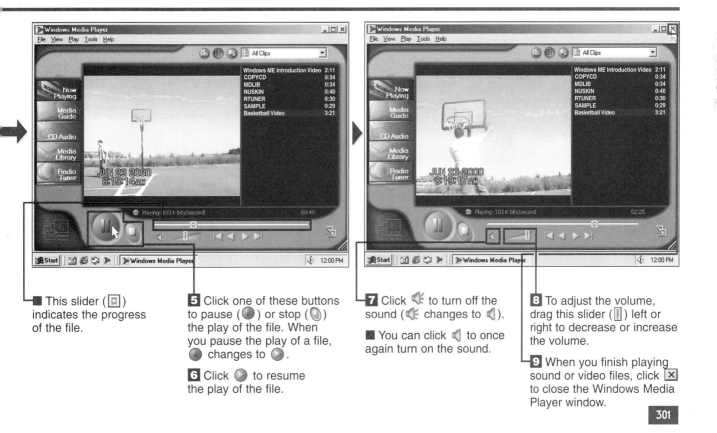

■ This slider (▯) indicates the progress of the file.

5 Click one of these buttons to pause (⏸) or stop (⏹) the play of the file. When you pause the play of a file, ⏸ changes to ▶.

6 Click ▶ to resume the play of the file.

7 Click 🔇 to turn off the sound (🔇 changes to 🔈).

■ You can click 🔈 to once again turn on the sound.

8 To adjust the volume, drag this slider (▯) left or right to decrease or increase the volume.

9 When you finish playing sound or video files, click ✕ to close the Windows Media Player window.

CHANGE SKIN OF WINDOWS MEDIA PLAYER

You can change the skin of Windows Media Player to customize how the player looks and functions. Windows Media Player allows you to play media files, such as sounds and videos, and listen to radio stations that broadcast over the Internet.

Windows Media Player includes several skins for you to choose

from, including Headspace, Rusty and Toothy. When you apply a skin, Windows Media Player automatically switches to compact mode to display the new skin.

Compact mode displays a smaller player window, which provides more room on your screen for using other programs. However, in compact mode, you do not have access to all the features available

in Windows Media Player. For example, you cannot change the skin of Windows Media Player. The number of features available in compact mode depends on the skin you select. You can switch to full mode at any time to access all the Windows Media Player features.

CHANGE SKIN OF WINDOWS MEDIA PLAYER

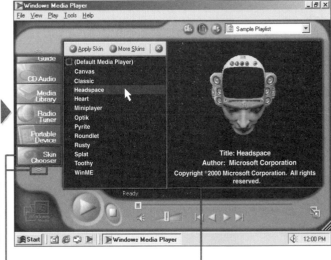

1 Click ▶ to start Windows Media Player.

■ The Windows Media Player window appears.

2 Click the Skin Chooser tab to change the skin of Windows Media Player.

■ If the Skin Chooser tab is not displayed, click this arrow until the tab appears.

■ This area lists the available skins that you can use with Windows Media Player.

3 Click the skin you want to use.

Where can I obtain more skins for Windows Media Player?

✔ You can obtain more skins for Windows Media Player on the Internet. On the Skin Chooser tab, click the More Skins button to display a Web page that offers skins you can use. When you select the skin you want to use, the skin transfers to your computer and appears in your list of available skins.

How do I delete a skin?

✔ On the Skin Chooser tab, select the skin you want to delete and then click the Delete button (⊘).

Can I change back to the original Windows Media Player skin?

✔ Yes. On the Skin Chooser tab, select the Default Media Player skin and then click the Apply Skin button.

How can I quickly switch from full mode to compact mode?

✔ Click 🔳 in the bottom right corner of the Windows Media Player window. The last skin you selected will be displayed.

Can I access some full mode features when in compact mode?

✔ You can press Shift+F10 to display a shortcut menu, which provides access to some of the features that are available in full mode.

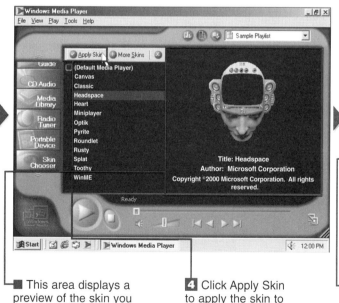

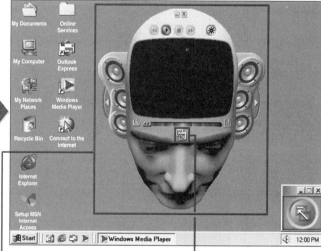

■ This area displays a preview of the skin you selected.

4 Click Apply Skin to apply the skin to Windows Media Player.

■ Windows Media Player appears in compact mode and displays the skin you selected.

■ To once again display Windows Media Player in full mode, click 🔳.

Note: The location of 🔳 depends on the skin you selected.

COPY FILES TO A PORTABLE DEVICE

Windows Media Player allows you to copy audio files from the Media Library to a portable device such as an MP3 player. This allows you to copy music files that you want to take with you from your computer to a portable music player.

Before copying files to your portable device, you must first add the files to the Media Library.

For information about using the Media Library, see page 296. You can transfer any audio files stored in the Media Library to your portable device, including files you downloaded from the Internet or copied from a music CD. To copy files to the Media Library from a music CD, see page 289.

Windows allows you to choose the sound category or playlist

that contains the files you want to copy.

You can also view the total amount of space on the device, the amount of used and free space and the amount of space required to store the files you selected to copy. When you copy files to your portable device, Windows Media Player compresses the files to reduce the amount of space the files will use.

COPY FILES TO A PORTABLE DEVICE

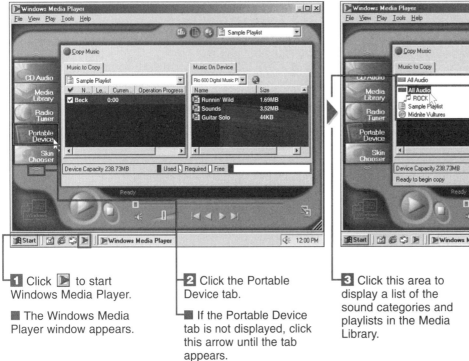

■1 Click ▶ to start Windows Media Player.

■ The Windows Media Player window appears.

■2 Click the Portable Device tab.

■ If the Portable Device tab is not displayed, click this arrow until the tab appears.

■3 Click this area to display a list of the sound categories and playlists in the Media Library.

■4 Click the sound category or playlist that contains the files you want to copy.

Can I copy a media file with the .wma extension to my portable device?

✔ You can copy media files with the .wma, .asf, .wav and .mp3 extensions.

Can I specify a quality setting for the files I copy?

✔ Yes. Click the Tools menu and select Options. On the Portable Device tab, click the Select quality level option and then drag the slider ([ ]) to specify the quality setting you want to use. Dragging the slider to the right increases the size and quality of files you copy. Dragging the slider to the left reduces the size and quality of the files.

How do I delete a file from my portable device?

✔ Select the file that you want to delete in the Music On Device area, click ⊗ and then click Delete. You can click Delete All to remove all the files on the portable device.

Can I quickly select only a few files to copy?

✔ Click the check mark icon ✔ at the top of the Music to Copy list to remove the check marks from all the items. Then click the box beside each item you want to copy (☐ changes to ☑).

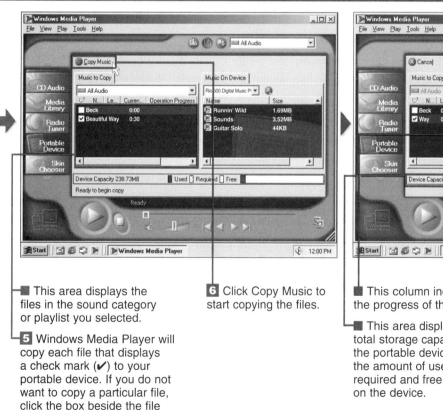

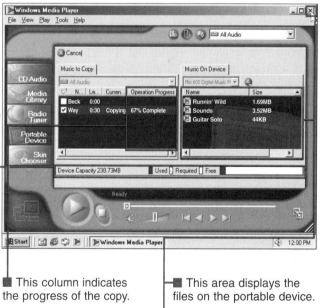

■ This area displays the files in the sound category or playlist you selected.

5 Windows Media Player will copy each file that displays a check mark (✔) to your portable device. If you do not want to copy a particular file, click the box beside the file (☐ changes to ☑).

6 Click Copy Music to start copying the files.

■ This column indicates the progress of the copy.

■ This area displays the total storage capacity of the portable device and the amount of used, required and free space on the device.

■ This area displays the files on the portable device.

7 When you finish copying files to the portable device, click ☒ to close the Windows Media Player window.

RECORD A VIDEO

You can use Windows Movie Maker to transfer audio and video files to your computer. You can then organize and edit the files to create movies.

For Windows Movie Maker to work properly, you must have the equivalent of a 300 MHz Pentium II computer, at least 64 MB of memory and 2 GB of free hard disk space.

Before using Windows Movie Maker, you need to install and set up the equipment needed to transfer video or audio content to your computer. You will need to install a video capture card to record video from a video camera, television broadcast, VCR or DVD player. You may not need a video capture card if you are using a Web camera. You can record audio from a stereo component, radio, audio tape, video tape or compact disc.

You can choose the type of material you want to record and the period of time Windows Movie Maker will record material.

Windows Movie Maker automatically breaks a video you record into smaller segments, called clips. If you choose not to create clips, Windows creates one clip for the video.

You can also choose a quality setting for your recording.

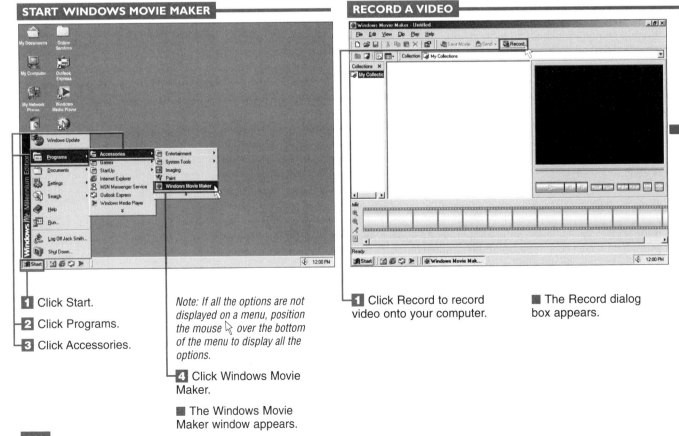

START WINDOWS MOVIE MAKER

1 Click Start.

2 Click Programs.

3 Click Accessories.

Note: If all the options are not displayed on a menu, position the mouse ⓡ over the bottom of the menu to display all the options.

4 Click Windows Movie Maker.

■ The Windows Movie Maker window appears.

RECORD A VIDEO

1 Click Record to record video onto your computer.

■ The Record dialog box appears.

Why does a Welcome screen appear when I start Windows Movie Maker?

✔ The Microsoft Windows Movie Maker Tour appears the first time you start Windows Movie Maker. You can click a topic of interest to display information about the topic. Click Exit to close the tour.

Can I import a video saved on my computer to Windows Movie Maker?

✔ In the Windows Movie Maker window, click File and select Import. Locate the file you want, select the file and then click Open. Windows Movie Maker will create a new collection to store clips for the video file you import.

What quality setting should I use to record my video?

✔ When selecting a quality setting for your video, you should consider how people will view your movie. For example, if people will view your movie on the Internet or in an e-mail message, consider the time the movie will take to transfer to a person's computer. The higher the quality setting, the longer a movie will take to transfer.

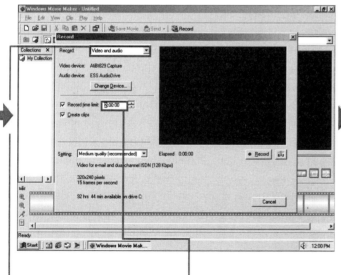

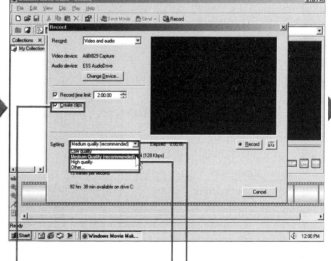

■ This area displays the type of material you will record. You can click this area to change the type of material.

2 This area displays the total amount of time that you can record video. To change the amount of time, click the part of the time you want to change and type a new number.

Note: If you do not want to have a time limit, click Record time limit (✔ changes to ☐).

3 This option automatically breaks up video you record into smaller segments, called clips. If you do not want to create clips, click this option to turn off the option (✔ changes to ☐).

4 Click this area to display a list of the available quality settings that you can use to record the video.

5 Click the quality setting you want to use.

CONTINUED ▶

RECORD A VIDEO (CONTINUED)

Windows automatically stores each video you record in the My Videos folder, which is located within the My Documents folder on your computer. Windows creates the My Videos folder the first time you start Windows Movie Maker. You can choose to save your video in a different location.

When you save your video, Windows Movie Maker stores all the clips for the video in one folder, called a collection. The collection appears in the left pane of the window, displaying the name you specified when saving the video.

The clips in the collection appear in the right pane of the window. Each video clip consists of a

number of still images, called frames. To help you identify the clips, Windows displays the first frame of each video clip.

After recording a video, you can organize and edit your collection of clips to create a movie. After creating a movie, you can view the movie on your computer, send it to people in e-mail or display it on your Web page.

RECORD A VIDEO (CONTINUED)

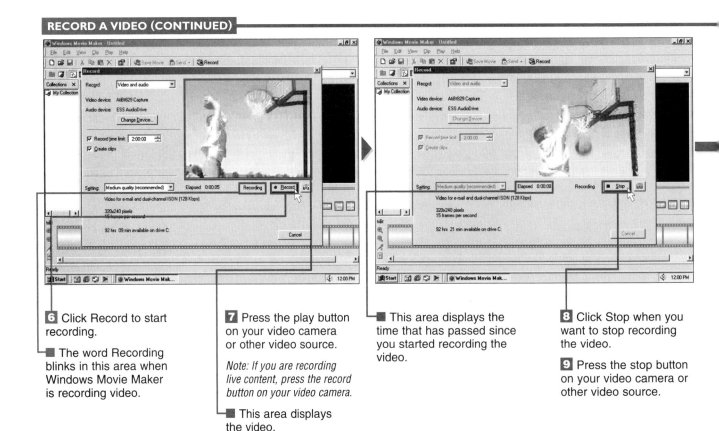

6 Click Record to start recording.

■ The word Recording blinks in this area when Windows Movie Maker is recording video.

7 Press the play button on your video camera or other video source.

Note: If you are recording live content, press the record button on your video camera.

■ This area displays the video.

■ This area displays the time that has passed since you started recording the video.

8 Click Stop when you want to stop recording the video.

9 Press the stop button on your video camera or other video source.

Can I change the way clips are displayed?

✔ When viewing clips, click 🎞️ and select the way you want to view the clips. The List view displays the clips in a list. The Details view displays additional information about the clips, including the date the clips were recorded and the length of each clip.

How do I rename or delete a collection?

✔ Select the collection you want to change. To rename the collection, click the Edit menu and choose Rename. Type a new name for the collection and then press the Enter key. To delete the collection, click 🗙.

How do I delete a clip from a collection?

✔ Click the collection that contains the clip you want to delete. Select the clip and then click 🗙.

How do I organize a collection of clips?

✔ You can create folders within a collection to help you organize the clips. Click the collection you want to organize and select 📁. Type a name for the new folder and press the Enter key. To move clips to the new folder, drag the clips from the left pane to the new folder in the right pane.

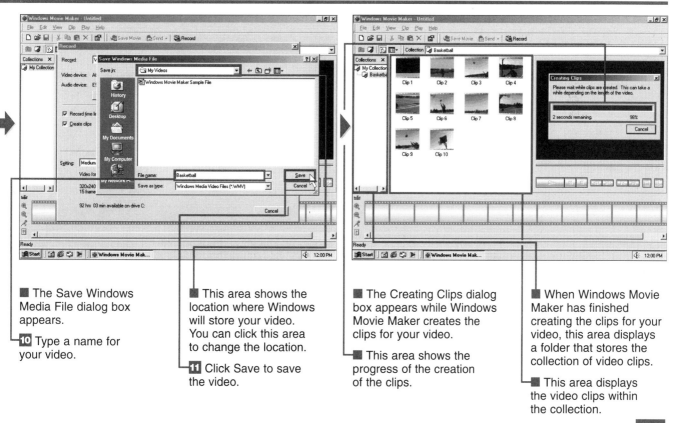

■ The Save Windows Media File dialog box appears.

🔟 Type a name for your video.

■ This area shows the location where Windows will store your video. You can click this area to change the location.

1️⃣1️⃣ Click Save to save the video.

■ The Creating Clips dialog box appears while Windows Movie Maker creates the clips for your video.

■ This area shows the progress of the creation of the clips.

■ When Windows Movie Maker has finished creating the clips for your video, this area displays a folder that stores the collection of video clips.

■ This area displays the video clips within the collection.

PLAY A VIDEO CLIP

You can play each video clip you have recorded on your computer. Playing video clips can help you determine which clips you want to include in your movie.

Each time you record a video, Windows Movie Maker creates a collection to store all the clips for the video. To locate the video clip

you want to play, you can browse through collections.

The area in the Windows Movie Maker window where the video clip plays is called the monitor. While a video clip is playing, a slider (⬇) on the monitor indicates how much of the video clip is left to play. The monitor also displays buttons that let you

control the play of the video clip. You can play, pause and stop a video clip.

The monitor also has buttons you can use to move to a still image, called a frame, in a video clip. You can move backward or forward through the video clip, frame by frame.

PLAY A VIDEO CLIP

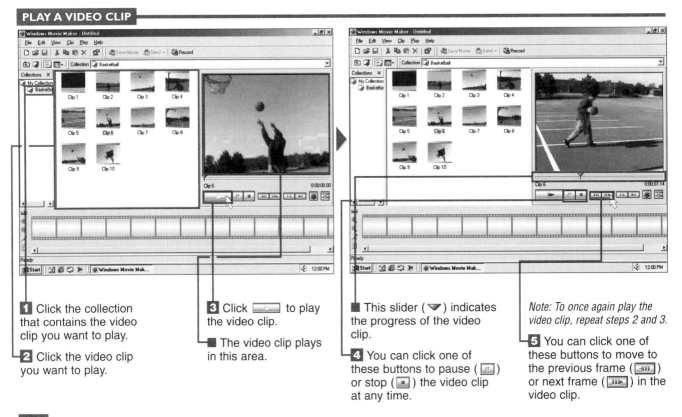

■ 1 Click the collection that contains the video clip you want to play.

■ 2 Click the video clip you want to play.

■ 3 Click [⬜] to play the video clip.

■ The video clip plays in this area.

■ This slider (⬇) indicates the progress of the video clip.

■ 4 You can click one of these buttons to pause ([⏸]) or stop ([⏹]) the video clip at any time.

Note: To once again play the video clip, repeat steps 2 and 3.

■ 5 You can click one of these buttons to move to the previous frame ([◄ǁ]) or next frame ([ǁ►]) in the video clip.

ADD A VIDEO CLIP
TO THE STORYBOARD

Y ou can add each video
clip that you want to
include in your movie to
the storyboard. The storyboard
displays the order in which
video clips will appear in your
movie.

Depending on the resolution
of your screen, the storyboard
may not be displayed on your
screen. You can use the scrollbar

to view the storyboard or you
can change the resolution of
your screen to show more
information on the screen at
once. For information about
changing the screen resolution,
see page 172.

In addition to the method
shown below, you can drag the
video clip to the location on the
storyboard where you want to

add the video clip. A vertical bar
on the storyboard indicates the
location where the video clip
will appear. You cannot leave
empty spaces between clips on
the storyboard.

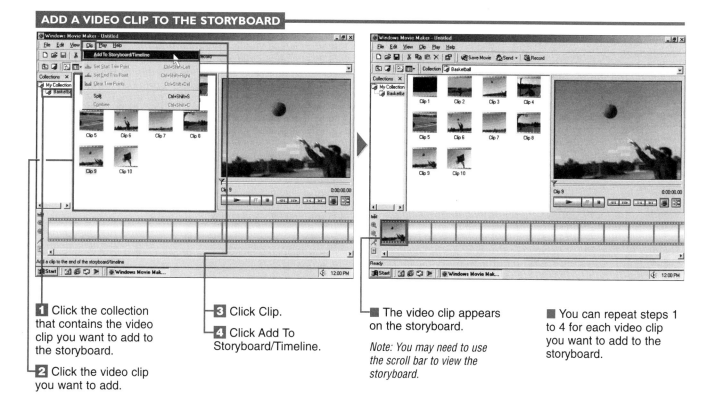

ADD A VIDEO CLIP TO THE STORYBOARD

1 Click the collection
that contains the video
clip you want to add to
the storyboard.

2 Click the video clip
you want to add.

3 Click Clip.

4 Click Add To
Storyboard/Timeline.

■ The video clip appears
on the storyboard.

*Note: You may need to use
the scroll bar to view the
storyboard.*

■ You can repeat steps 1
to 4 for each video clip
you want to add to the
storyboard.

PREVIEW A MOVIE

You can preview all the video clips you added to the storyboard as a movie. Previewing a movie is useful if you want to see what the video clips look like together before you save the movie on your computer.

The entire movie will play on the monitor in the Windows Movie Maker window. You can pause or stop the preview of a movie at any time. You can also move to a specific video clip in the movie at any time.

Can I have the movie I am previewing fill the screen?

✔ Yes. This is useful when you want to see the overall effect of the movie when played on a full screen. When you are previewing a movie, click the Full Screen button ( ) on the monitor to have the movie fill the entire screen. When you are finished viewing the movie on the full screen, click the screen to return to the Windows Movie Maker window.

PREVIEW A MOVIE

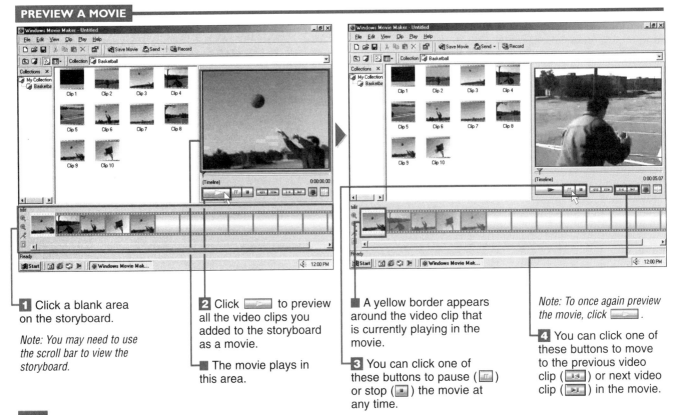

1 Click a blank area on the storyboard.

Note: You may need to use the scroll bar to view the storyboard.

2 Click ☐ to preview all the video clips you added to the storyboard as a movie.

■ The movie plays in this area.

■ A yellow border appears around the video clip that is currently playing in the movie.

3 You can click one of these buttons to pause ( ) or stop ( ) the movie at any time.

Note: To once again preview the movie, click ☐ .

4 You can click one of these buttons to move to the previous video clip ( ) or next video clip ( ) in the movie.

CHANGE THE WORKSPACE VIEW

The workspace is the area at the bottom of the Windows Movie Maker window that allows you to edit your movie. There are two views you can switch between in the workspace–the storyboard view and the timeline view.

The storyboard view is displayed by default. This view displays the order that video clips will appear in your movie.

The storyboard view is useful if you want to review or change the order of the video clips in your movie.

The timeline view shows the video clips in your movie on a timeline. This view is useful when you want to review or change the amount of time video clips will play in your movie. You can also view sound clips in this view.

How can I use the 🔍 and 🔍 buttons that appear to the left of the timeline?

✔ These buttons allow you to zoom in and out of the timeline. You can click the Zoom In button (🔍) to view a more detailed timeline. If you want to see less detail, you can click the Zoom Out button (🔍).

CHANGE THE WORKSPACE VIEW

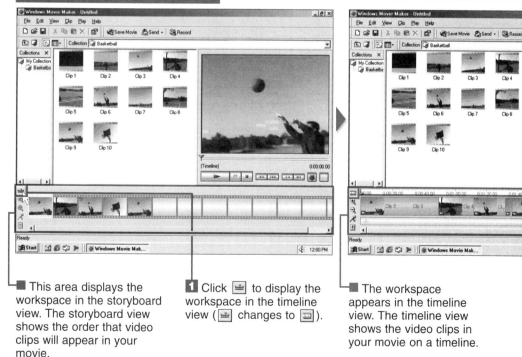

■ This area displays the workspace in the storyboard view. The storyboard view shows the order that video clips will appear in your movie.

Note: You may need to use the scroll bar to view the storyboard.

1 Click 🔲 to display the workspace in the timeline view (🔲 changes to 🔲).

■ The workspace appears in the timeline view. The timeline view shows the video clips in your movie on a timeline.

■ You can click 🔲 to once again display the workspace in the storyboard view.

WORK WITH VIDEO CLIPS

Windows Movie Maker allows you to work with video clips to edit a movie on your computer.

After adding the video clips you want to use to the storyboard, you can change the order of the clips to change the order they will play in your movie. When you move a video clip, any surrounding video clips shift to make room for the clip.

You can trim a video clip on the storyboard to remove parts of the clip that you do not want to play in your movie.

To trim a video clip, you can set a start trim point, an end trim point or both. A start trim point specifies where a video clip will start playing, while an end trim point specifies where a video clip will stop playing.

Trimming a video clip will reduce the file size of your movie. A movie with a smaller file size will take up less storage space on your computer and transfer more quickly over the Internet.

Any changes you make to a video clip in the workspace will not affect the video clip stored in Windows Movie Maker.

REARRANGE VIDEO CLIPS

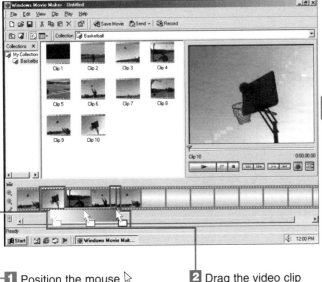

1 Position the mouse ▷ over the video clip that you want to move to a different location on the storyboard.

Note: You may need to use the scroll bar to view the storyboard.

2 Drag the video clip to a new location. A vertical bar indicates the new location.

■ The video clip appears in the new location.

■ The surrounding video clips automatically move to make room for the video clip.

How do I trim a video clip in the timeline view?

✔ Click the video clip you want to trim on the timeline. Handles (▲ or ◢) appear on the video clip. Position the mouse pointer over a handle and then drag the mouse ↔ to a new position to set the trim point. To display the timeline view, see page 313.

Is there a way to create a smooth transition from one video clip to another?

✔ Yes. You can create a smooth transition between video clips by overlapping the clips. In the timeline view, click the video clip to the right of a video clip you want to display a transition. Then drag the video clip to the left to overlap the clip.

How do I remove a video clip from the storyboard?

✔ Click the video clip you no longer want to include on the storyboard and then press the Delete key.

How do I remove the trim points I set?

✔ Click the video clip you trimmed. Choose the Clip menu and then select Clear Trim Points. Clearing trim points may cause clips to overlap in the movie.

TRIM A VIDEO CLIP

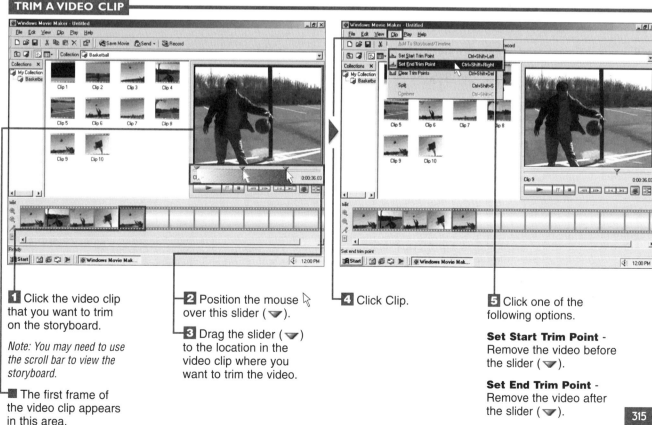

1 Click the video clip that you want to trim on the storyboard.

Note: You may need to use the scroll bar to view the storyboard.

■ The first frame of the video clip appears in this area.

2 Position the mouse over this slider (▼).

3 Drag the slider (▼) to the location in the video clip where you want to trim the video.

4 Click Clip.

5 Click one of the following options.

Set Start Trim Point - Remove the video before the slider (▼).

Set End Trim Point - Remove the video after the slider (▼).

SAVE AND OPEN A PROJECT

A project is a rough draft of your movie that contains all the video clips you added to the storyboard. You can save your project to store it for future use.

Saving a project allows you to later review and make changes to the project. You should regularly save changes you make to a project to avoid losing your work due to a computer problem or power failure. Windows Movie Maker usually

saves project files with the .mswmm extension.

You should store your projects in a location on your computer that will be easy to find. By default, Windows Movie Maker stores projects you create in the My Videos folder, which is located in the My Documents folder on your desktop.

You can open a saved project to display the video clips on the

storyboard. This allows you to review and make changes to the project, such as adding, removing or rearranging the video clips. For information about working with video clips, see page 314.

Windows Movie Maker allows you to work with only one project at a time. Make sure you save the project you are currently working with before opening another project.

SAVE A PROJECT

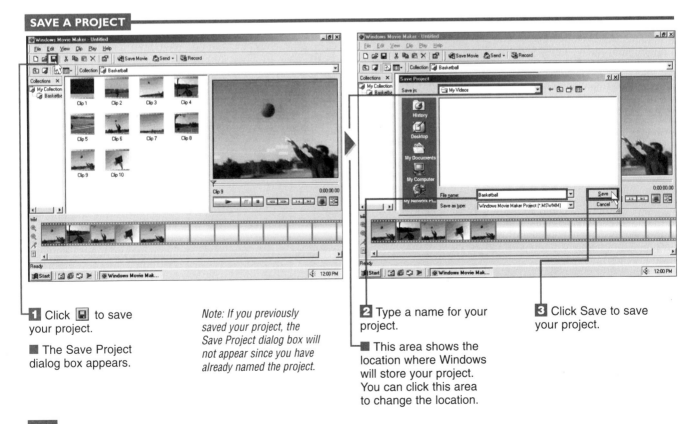

◢1 Click 🔳 to save your project.

■ The Save Project dialog box appears.

Note: If you previously saved your project, the Save Project dialog box will not appear since you have already named the project.

◢2 Type a name for your project.

■ This area shows the location where Windows will store your project. You can click this area to change the location.

◢3 Click Save to save your project.

Is there another way to open a project?

✔ The Start menu displays the last 15 items you worked with in Windows. To open one of these items, click the Start button, select Documents and then click the name of the project you want to open.

How do I create a new project in Windows Movie Maker?

✔ You can click 🗅 to create a new project. You should make sure you save your current project before creating a new one.

Can I save a project with a new name?

✔ Yes. If you plan to make major changes to a project, you may want to save the project with a new name. This gives you two copies of the project–the original project and a project with all the changes. To save a project with a new name, click the File menu and select Save Project As. In the Save As dialog box that appears, type a new name for the project and then click Save.

OPEN A PROJECT

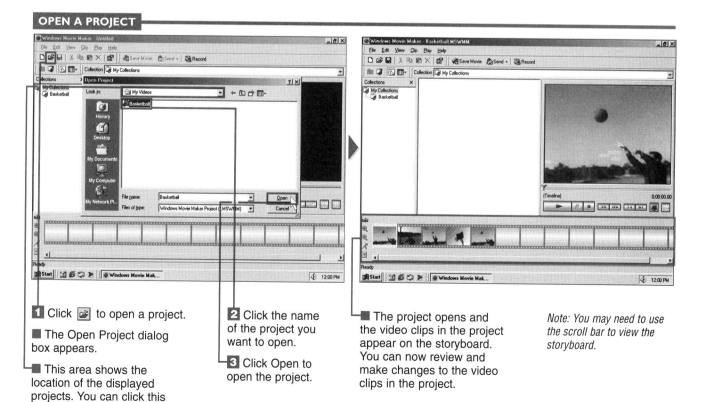

1 Click 🗁 to open a project.

■ The Open Project dialog box appears.

■ This area shows the location of the displayed projects. You can click this area to change the location.

2 Click the name of the project you want to open.

3 Click Open to open the project.

■ The project opens and the video clips in the project appear on the storyboard. You can now review and make changes to the video clips in the project.

Note: You may need to use the scroll bar to view the storyboard.

RECORD NARRATION

Windows Movie Maker allows you to record voice narration for a movie. This is ideal for narrating a presentation or home video. You need a full-duplex sound card, microphone and speakers to record narration.

You can record narration in the timeline view. If the movie you want to record narration for

already contains sound, you can turn off this sound while you record your narration. You may also be able to change the volume of your narration depending on the microphone and sound card on your computer.

When recording narration, you can watch the movie and view the amount of time that has passed since you started recording.

Once the narration is complete, Windows Movie Maker allows you to save the narration as a sound file with the .wav extension on your computer. The sound file will appear as a sound clip below the video clips on the timeline and will also appear as a sound clip for the current collection in the Windows Movie Maker window.

RECORD NARRATION

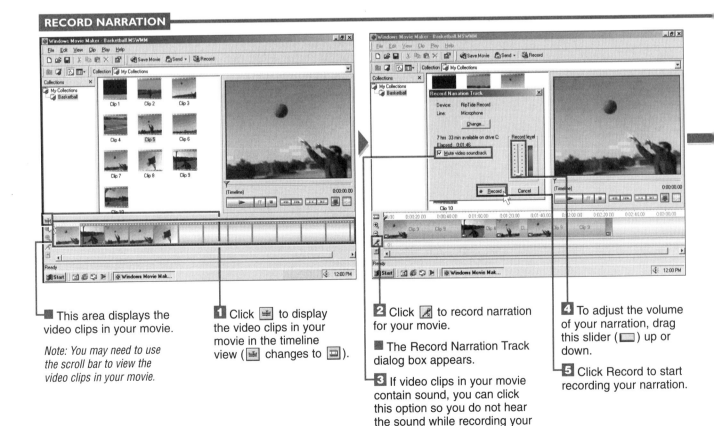

■ This area displays the video clips in your movie.

Note: You may need to use the scroll bar to view the video clips in your movie.

1 Click 🔲 to display the video clips in your movie in the timeline view (🔲 changes to 🔲).

2 Click 🔲 to record narration for your movie.

■ The Record Narration Track dialog box appears.

3 If video clips in your movie contain sound, you can click this option so you do not hear the sound while recording your narration (☐ changes to ☑).

4 To adjust the volume of your narration, drag this slider (🔲) up or down.

5 Click Record to start recording your narration.

MASTER IT

How do I remove narration from a movie?

✔ Click the sound clip on the timeline and then press the Delete key. The sound clip will not be removed from the collection in the Windows Movie Maker window.

How can I make the narration I recorded louder than the sound the movie already has?

✔ Click the Set audio levels button (🔳) to the left of the timeline. In the Audio Levels dialog box, drag the slider (🔲) to the right to increase the volume of the narration you recorded.

Can I specify when the sound clip will start playing?

✔ Yes. You can drag the sound clip to a new position on the timeline to change when the clip will start playing.

Can I record narration for a movie using a device other than a microphone?

✔ Yes. In the Record Narration Track dialog box, click the Change button. The Configure Audio dialog box appears. In the Input line area, click 🔽 and then select the device you want to use.

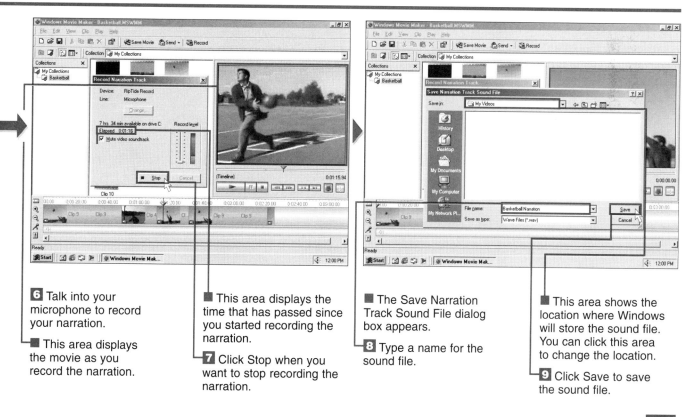

6 Talk into your microphone to record your narration.

■ This area displays the movie as you record the narration.

■ This area displays the time that has passed since you started recording the narration.

7 Click Stop when you want to stop recording the narration.

■ The Save Narration Track Sound File dialog box appears.

8 Type a name for the sound file.

■ This area shows the location where Windows will store the sound file. You can click this area to change the location.

9 Click Save to save the sound file.

SAVE A MOVIE

A fter you add all the video clips that you want to include in your movie to the storyboard, you can save the movie on your computer. Saving a movie allows you to play the movie at any time.

Once you save a movie, you can send the movie in an e-mail to friends and family. You should try to keep your movies under 1 MB, or 1000 KB. The computer

receiving the message must have the necessary software to play the movie. You can also add the movie to a Web page and then transfer the page to your Web server to make the movie available to everyone on the Web. A Web server is a computer that stores Web pages.

If you plan to add a movie to a Web page, you can specify the quality setting you want to use

for the movie. Higher quality settings result in larger movie file sizes. Make sure you do not select a higher quality setting than you used to record your video.

You can include information about the movie, such as the title and description of the movie. People who view your movie in Windows Media Player will see the information you enter.

SAVE A MOVIE

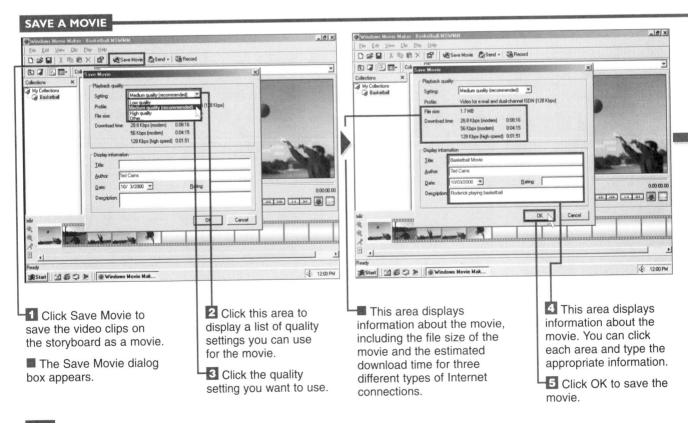

■1 Click Save Movie to save the video clips on the storyboard as a movie.

■ The Save Movie dialog box appears.

■2 Click this area to display a list of quality settings you can use for the movie.

■3 Click the quality setting you want to use.

■ This area displays information about the movie, including the file size of the movie and the estimated download time for three different types of Internet connections.

■4 This area displays information about the movie. You can click each area and type the appropriate information.

■5 Click OK to save the movie.

How do I send a movie to the Web server?

✔ In the Windows Movie Maker window, click Send and then select Web Server. In the Send Movie to a Web Server dialog box, enter the quality setting and information you want to use for the movie and click OK. Enter the name of the movie you want to send to the Web server and click OK. In the Send To Web dialog box, select the Web server you want to send the movie to and enter your user name and password. To view the movie on the Web, click Visit Site Now. To view the movie later, click Close.

What if my Web server is not displayed in the Send To Web dialog box?

✔ You may have to set up your Web server in Windows Movie Maker. In the Send To Web dialog box, click New. You must then enter the name of the Web server and the File Transfer Protocol (FTP) address of the server. You must also specify the address of your Web site.

How do I e-mail a movie?

✔ You can send a saved movie as an attachment in an e-mail message. See page 470.

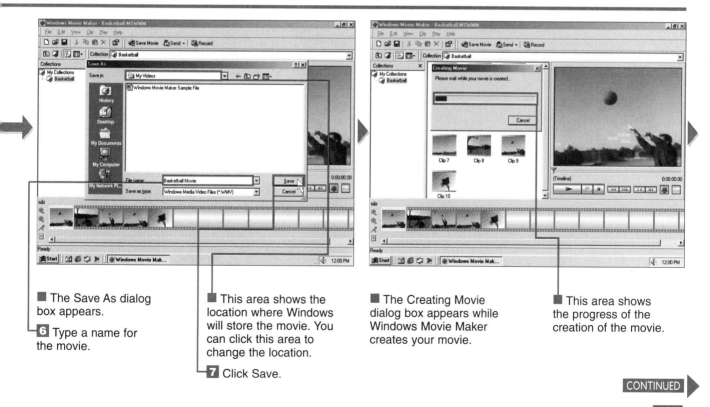

■ The Save As dialog box appears.

6 Type a name for the movie.

■ This area shows the location where Windows will store the movie. You can click this area to change the location.

7 Click Save.

■ The Creating Movie dialog box appears while Windows Movie Maker creates your movie.

■ This area shows the progress of the creation of the movie.

CONTINUED

SAVE A MOVIE (CONTINUED)

After you save a movie on your computer, you can view the movie in Windows Media Player.

If you do not want to view the movie immediately after you create the movie, you can play the movie at a later time. To play a movie you have saved, double-click the movie in the My Videos folder, which is located within the My Documents folder on your desktop.

While a movie is playing in Windows Media Player, a slider (🔲) indicates how much of the file is left to play. Windows Media Player lets you control how a file plays. You can play, pause and stop a file. You can also turn off the sound or adjust the volume of a file.

Windows Media Player allows you to play only one movie at a time. Once a movie is finished playing, you can select another movie you want to play.

SAVE A MOVIE (CONTINUED)

■ A dialog box appears when Windows Movie Maker has finished creating and saving your movie.

8 Click Yes to watch the movie now.

Note: If you do not want to watch the movie now, click No.

■ The Windows Media Player window appears.

■ The movie plays in this area.

9 You can click a button to pause (🔘) or stop (🔘) the movie at any time.

Note: The pause button changes to 🔘 after you pause or stop the movie. To play the movie again, click 🔘.

10 When you finish viewing the movie, click ⊠ to close the Windows Media Player window.

EXIT WINDOWS MOVIE MAKER

When you finish using Windows Movie Maker, you can exit the program. You should always exit Windows Movie Maker and all other programs before turning off your computer.

Before exiting the program, Windows Movie Maker may ask if you want to make a backup of your collections file. The collections file

stores information about your video clips. If your collections files becomes damaged or you accidentally delete a collection or video clip, you can use the backup copy to restore the collections file.

You can specify a name for the backup copy. When you save a backup copy, you should use a descriptive name that will help you find the copy later. Windows

Movie Maker usually saves the backup copy of your collections file with the .bak extension.

You should store your backup files in a location on your computer that will be easy to find. By default, Windows Movie Maker stores backup copies of the collections file in the My Videos folder, which is located in the My Documents folder on your desktop.

EXIT WINDOWS MOVIE MAKER

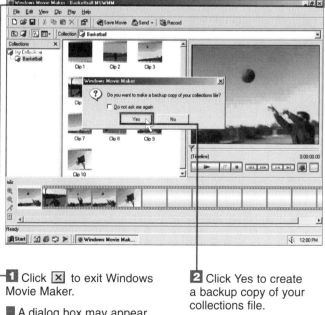

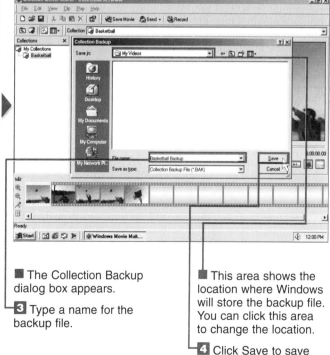

1 Click ☒ to exit Windows Movie Maker.

■ A dialog box may appear, asking if you want to make a backup copy of your collections file. Your collections file stores information about your video clips.

2 Click Yes to create a backup copy of your collections file.

■ The Collection Backup dialog box appears.

3 Type a name for the backup file.

■ This area shows the location where Windows will store the backup file. You can click this area to change the location.

4 Click Save to save the backup file.

INSTALL A MODEM

You can install a modem on your computer. The Install New Modem wizard guides you step by step through the installation process.

A modem is a device that allows computers to exchange information using telephone lines. A modem allows you to connect to the Internet or to another computer, such as a computer at work.

There are two types of modems. An external modem attaches to a computer using a cable. External modems are portable and easy to fix if a problem arises. An internal modem is located inside a computer and is less expensive than an external modem. Both types of modems provide the same features.

Windows will try to detect a new modem on your computer.

If Windows cannot detect a new modem, you will need to select the modem from a list.

When you install a modem, Windows also installs the necessary software, called a driver. A driver allows your computer to communicate with the modem.

INSTALL A MODEM

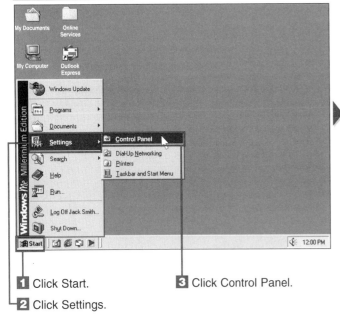

1 Click Start.

2 Click Settings.

3 Click Control Panel.

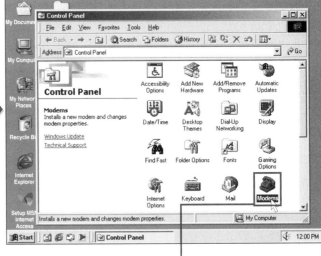

■ The Control Panel window appears.

Note: If all the items do not appear in the Control Panel window, click the view all Control Panel options link in the window to display all the items.

4 Double-click Modems.

Do I have to use the Install New Modem wizard to install a new modem?

✔ No. When you physically connect a Plug and Play modem to your computer and turn on the computer, Windows will usually automatically detect and install the modem for you.

Can I install more than one modem?

✔ Yes. To install another modem, perform steps 1 to 4 on page 324 to display the Modems Properties dialog box. Click Add to start the Install New Modem wizard and then follow the instructions on your screen.

Why would I install more than one modem?

✔ You can use more than one modem to increase the speed of the connection to your Internet Service Provider (ISP). To use multiple modems, click the Start button, choose Settings and select Dial-Up Networking. Right-click the icon for the connection to your ISP and select Properties. Select the Multilink tab and click the Use additional devices option. Click the Add button and then use the drop-down list to select an additional modem. You should make sure your ISP supports multiple modem connections.

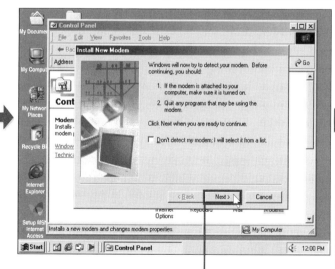

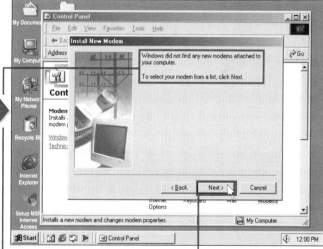

■ The Install New Modem wizard appears.

■ If your modem is attached to your computer, make sure the modem is turned on. You should also close any open programs before installing your modem.

5 Click Next to continue.

■ Windows searches for the modem on your computer. Your screen may temporarily go blank during the search.

■ This message appears if Windows did not find any modems attached to your computer.

Note: If the message "Your modem has been set up successfully" appears, skip to step 12.

6 Click Next to continue.

CONTINUED

INSTALL A MODEM (CONTINUED)

I f Windows did not detect a new modem, you need to select the manufacturer and model of the modem from a list. Windows supports over 100 modem models from 13 different manufacturers.

When installing a modem, you may need to specify which port the modem should use. A port is a connector that allows instructions and data to flow between the

computer and a device. Most modems use a serial, or COM, port. If Windows detected your modem, you do not need to specify a port.

You must also ensure that the settings Windows uses for the modem match the settings on the modem. You can use the Device Manager to view the settings Windows uses for the modem. For information about Device Manager, see page 570.

You may have to adjust the settings on the modem to correspond with the settings used by Windows. You can adjust the settings on the modem by using the software that came with the modem or by manually adjusting the jumpers or switches on the modem. Consult the modem's documentation before making any adjustments.

INSTALL A MODEM (CONTINUED)

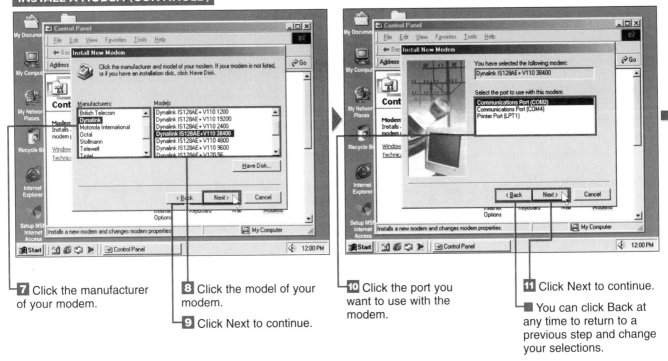

◢7 Click the manufacturer of your modem.

◢8 Click the model of your modem.

◢9 Click Next to continue.

◢10 Click the port you want to use with the modem.

◢11 Click Next to continue.

■ You can click Back at any time to return to a previous step and change your selections.

The modem I want to install does not appear in the list. What should I do?

✔ You can use the installation disk that came with the modem to install the modem. Insert the installation disk into the drive. Click the Have Disk button in the Install New Modem wizard and then press the Enter key. If you do not have a disk for the modem, try selecting a modem that closely resembles your modem. The documentation that came with your modem should indicate a model that your modem is compatible with. You can also select a Standard modem type, but this option provides only basic options for a modem.

What can I do if the modem does not work after I install the modem?

✔ You can use the Modem Troubleshooter to help you solve common modem problems. Click the Start button and select Help. In the Search area, type **modem troubleshooter** and then press the Enter key.

How do I remove a modem I no longer use?

✔ Perform steps 1 to 4 on page 324 to display the Modem Properties dialog box. Select the modem you want to remove and click Remove.

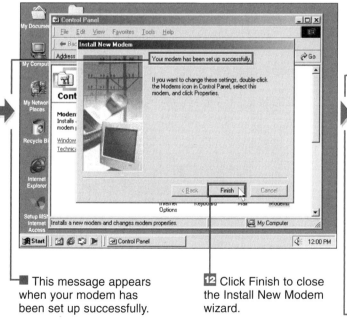

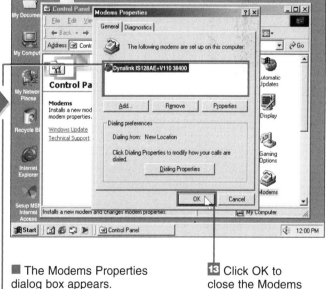

■ This message appears when your modem has been set up successfully.

12 Click Finish to close the Install New Modem wizard.

■ The Modems Properties dialog box appears.

■ This area displays the modem you installed on your computer.

13 Click OK to close the Modems Properties dialog box.

■ You can now use the new modem.

CHANGE THE MODEM DIALING PROPERTIES

You can change the dialing properties for your modem. Dialing properties are settings that determine how your modem will dial phone numbers. Changing the dialing properties may be helpful when you are having problems connecting to another computer. You may also need to change the dialing properties depending on the location where

you are using your computer. For example, using your computer at the office requires different dialing properties than using your computer in a hotel room.

When you installed your modem, Windows set up a dialing location called "New Location" and specified the dialing properties for the location. You can use a more

descriptive name to better identify where you are dialing from, such as "Office."

When changing the modem dialing properties, you can tell Windows which country and area code you are calling from. Your modem will use this information to determine if a call will be local or long distance.

CHANGE THE MODEM DIALING PROPERTIES

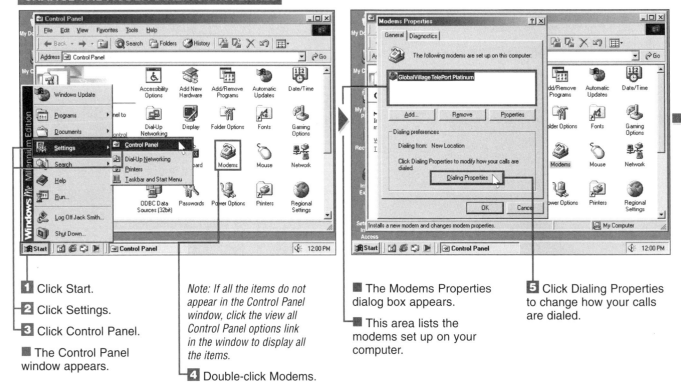

1 Click Start.

2 Click Settings.

3 Click Control Panel.

■ The Control Panel window appears.

Note: If all the items do not appear in the Control Panel window, click the view all Control Panel options link in the window to display all the items.

4 Double-click Modems.

■ The Modems Properties dialog box appears.

■ This area lists the modems set up on your computer.

5 Click Dialing Properties to change how your calls are dialed.

How can I set different dialing properties for each location where I plan to use my computer?

✔ In the Dialing Properties dialog box, click the New button. Click OK and then type a name for the new location. You can now enter the dialing properties for the new location. To later review or change the properties you set for a location, display the Dialing Properties dialog box and click ▼ in the I am dialing from area. Then select the location you want from the list that appears.

How can I dial a long distance phone number within my area code?

✔ In the Dialing Properties dialog box, click the Area Code Rules button. Click the New button in the When calling within my area code section and then enter the first three digits of the phone number.

Can I make Windows use 10-digit calling?

✔ Yes. In the Dialing Properties dialog box, click the Area Code Rules button. In the When calling within my area code section, click Always dial the area code (10-digit dialing). To enable 10-digit dialing for other area codes, click the New button in the When calling to other area codes section and then enter the area code.

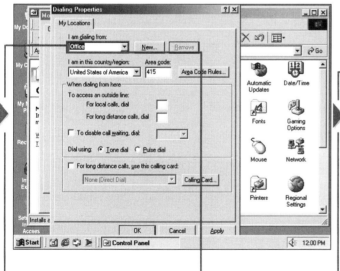

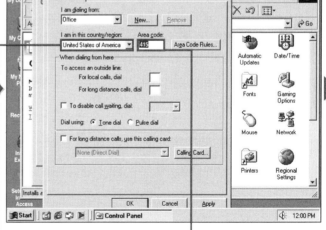

■ The Dialing Properties dialog box appears.

■ This area displays the name of the current location. The dialog box displays the properties for this location.

6 To change the name of the current location, type a new name.

■ This area displays the country or region you are dialing from. Click this area to select a different country or region.

■ This area displays your area code. To change the area code, double-click this area and then type a new area code.

CONTINUED ▶

CHANGE THE MODEM DIALING PROPERTIES (CONTINUED)

W hen changing the modem dialing properties, you can specify any special numbers you need to enter. For example, some companies and hotels require you to dial a special number to access an outside line for local or long distance calls.

You can also specify whether you want to use tone or pulse dialing. Tone dialing is the most common type of dialing used by phone companies.

If you have the call waiting feature, you can have Windows automatically disable the feature when you use your modem. You should turn off the call waiting feature when using your modem, since this feature could disrupt the modem connection. The call waiting feature is automatically restored when you end the modem connection. You should check with your local phone company to find out which code you must use to

disable call waiting. The most common code is *70.

You can also set up your modem to use a calling card. A calling card allows you to make long distance calls and have the charges billed to the owner of the calling card. Calling cards can be used where long distance calls are not permitted.

CHANGE THE MODEM DIALING PROPERTIES (CONTINUED)

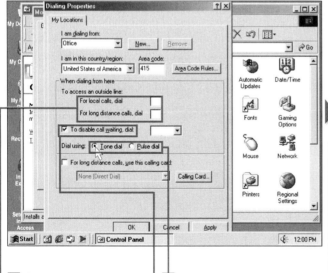

7 If you need to dial numbers to access an outside line for local calls or long distance calls, click an area and then type the numbers.

8 Click Tone dial or Pulse dial to specify which type of dialing to use (○ changes to ⊙).

9 To disable call waiting when using the modem, click this option (☐ changes to ✔).

10 Click ▼ in this area to display a list of codes that can disable call waiting.

11 Click the code that disables call waiting.

Note: If the code you want to use does not appear in the list, type the code in the area provided.

12 To use a calling card for long distance calls, click this option (☐ changes to ✔).

Where can I get a calling card?

✔ Most phone companies offer calling cards to their customers. There are many types of calling cards available. Some cards offer incentives, such as discount rates, to attract new customers. Many businesses and organizations use calling cards to track long distance calls.

What should I do if my calling card is not listed?

✔ In the Calling Card dialog box, click New. Enter the name of the Calling Card, press Enter and then click OK. Enter your PIN number and the access numbers for the calling card. Click the Long Distance Calls and International Calls buttons to enter the sequence required to make long distance and international calls. The sequence is provided by the phone company and may be printed on the card.

I have set up different dialing properties for different locations. How do I select a different location when using my modem?

✔ When you use your modem to connect to another computer, a dialog box usually appears, allowing you to select the location you want to use.

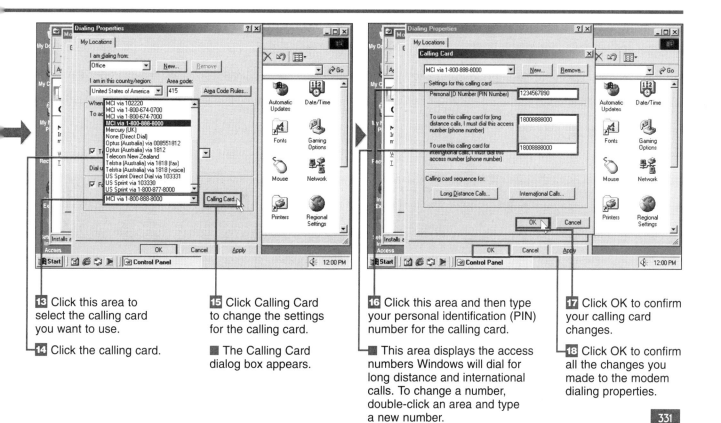

13 Click this area to select the calling card you want to use.

14 Click the calling card.

15 Click Calling Card to change the settings for the calling card.

■ The Calling Card dialog box appears.

16 Click this area and then type your personal identification (PIN) number for the calling card.

■ This area displays the access numbers Windows will dial for long distance and international calls. To change a number, double-click an area and type a new number.

17 Click OK to confirm your calling card changes.

18 Click OK to confirm all the changes you made to the modem dialing properties.

CHANGE THE MODEM SETTINGS

Y ou can change the settings for a modem installed on your computer to help the modem operate more effectively.

The settings you can change depend on the type of modem you are using. Also, some settings may not be available if the correct driver for your modem is not installed on your computer. A driver is software that allows your computer to communicate with the modem.

You can view and change the port your modem uses. A port is a connector that allows instructions and data to flow between the computer and the modem. Most modems connect to a COM, or serial, port.

A modem has a speaker that lets you hear the modem as it dials and connects to another modem. You may be able to adjust the speaker volume.

You can specify the maximum speed setting for your modem. This allows you to change the maximum speed that your modem can send and receive information. The speed of a modem is measured in bits per second (bps). The maximum speed setting should match the fastest speed setting of your modem. Check your modem's documentation to determine the modem's maximum speed.

CHANGE THE MODEM SETTINGS

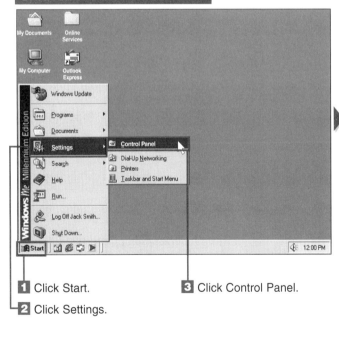

1 Click Start.

2 Click Settings.

3 Click Control Panel.

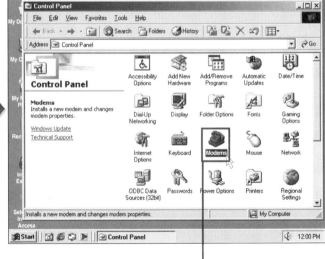

■ The Control Panel window appears.

Note: If all the items do not appear in the Control Panel window, click the view all Control Panel options link in the window to display all the items.

4 Double-click Modems.

MASTER IT

How can I find out if I have the correct modem driver installed on my computer?

✔ In the Modems Properties dialog box, select the Diagnostics tab. Select the modem you want to check the driver for and then click Driver. You can also check the modem's documentation to determine which driver you should have installed.

Why is my modem slow even though I specified a high maximum speed?

✔ Modems must use the same speed when exchanging information. When a fast modem connects to a slower modem, the modems will exchange information at the slower speed.

How do I prevent my modem from using a slow speed?

✔ Many phone lines are affected by interference that may result in slow transmission speeds. If you tell Windows to only connect at a specific speed, a connection will not be made with another modem unless Windows can connect at the maximum speed you specified. To lock the modem speed, click the Only connect at this speed option in the Properties dialog box. This option is not available for some modems.

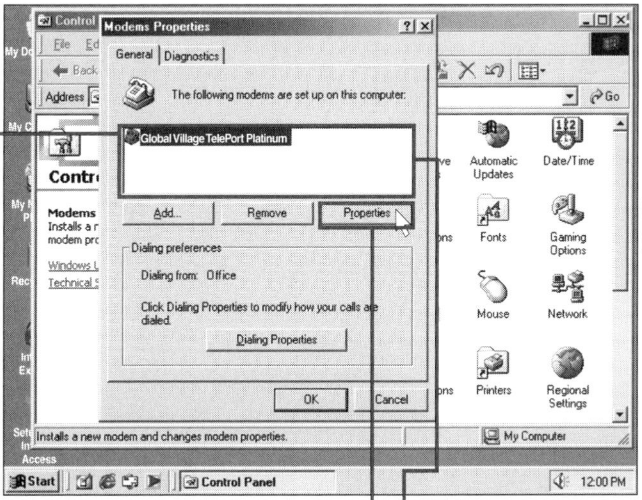

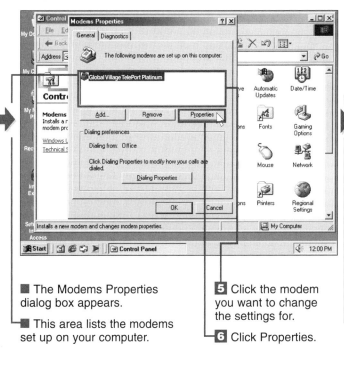

■ The Modems Properties dialog box appears.

■ This area lists the modems set up on your computer.

5 Click the modem you want to change the settings for.

6 Click Properties.

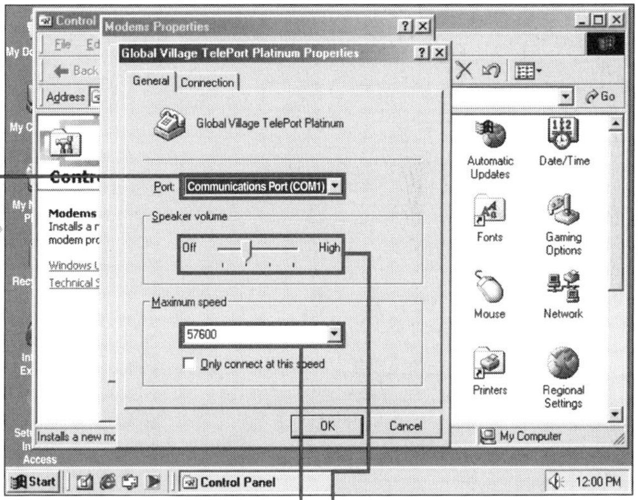

■ The Properties dialog box appears.

7 This area displays the port your modem uses. You can click this area to change the port.

8 You can drag this slider (⎕) to lower or raise the speaker volume for your modem.

9 This area displays the maximum speed your modem can use. You can click this area to change the maximum speed.

CONTINUED

CHANGE THE MODEM SETTINGS
(CONTINUED)

You can change the connection settings for a modem. Changing a modem's connection settings helps the modem better communicate with other modems.

Before two modems can exchange information, the modems must use the same data, parity and stop bit settings. You will see unreadable text on your screen if the other modem uses different bit settings.

The data bits contain the actual information exchanged between computers. The parity bits are used to determine whether errors occur during the transfer of information. The stop bits indicate when each data bit begins and ends. The most common bit settings are 8 data bits, no parity bits and 1 stop bit.

You can specify whether you want to wait for a dial tone before the modem starts dialing. You can also

tell Windows how long you want to wait before canceling or disconnecting a call. Having Windows disconnect a call when your modem is idle for a period of time can help prevent the accumulation of online charges.

Most modems are already set up to use the most common options, so you will likely not need to change the connection settings for your modem.

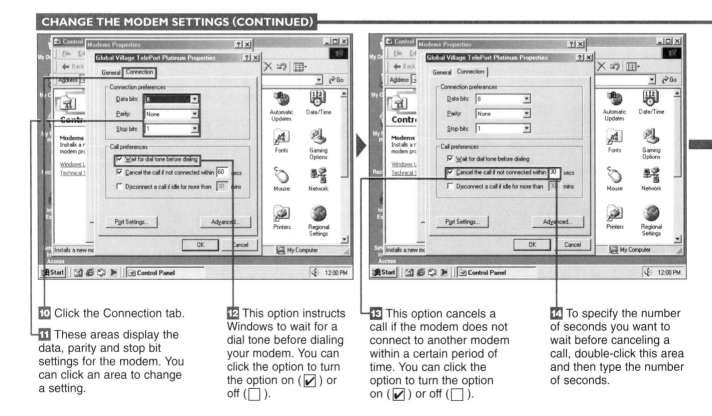

10 Click the Connection tab.

11 These areas display the data, parity and stop bit settings for the modem. You can click an area to change a setting.

12 This option instructs Windows to wait for a dial tone before dialing your modem. You can click the option to turn the option on (☑) or off (☐).

13 This option cancels a call if the modem does not connect to another modem within a certain period of time. You can click the option to turn the option on (☑) or off (☐).

14 To specify the number of seconds you want to wait before canceling a call, double-click this area and then type the number of seconds.

Why should I have my modem wait for a dial tone before dialing?

✔ With some phone systems, a modem may not receive a dial tone as soon as it connects to the phone system. You can help ensure your modem will be able to dial the number by having the modem wait for a dial tone before dialing.

Why is my call not connecting?

✔ There are many reasons that a call may not connect. Problems sometimes occur with the phone system or the other modem may not be set to answer calls. The computer receiving the call may also be turned off. Usually, 60 seconds is an adequate length of time to wait before canceling a call.

Are there any other connection settings I can change?

✔ You can change the way your computer communicates with your modem. For example, you can specify the type of error control, flow control and modulation you want the modem to use. To change these settings, display the Connections tab in the Properties dialog box and click the Advanced button.

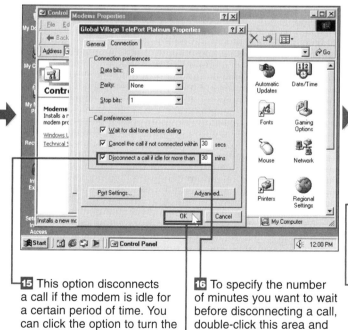

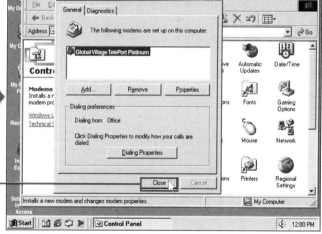

15 This option disconnects a call if the modem is idle for a certain period of time. You can click the option to turn the option on (✔) or off (☐).

16 To specify the number of minutes you want to wait before disconnecting a call, double-click this area and then type the number of minutes.

17 Click OK to confirm all your changes.

18 Click Close to close the Modems Properties dialog box.

SET UP A DIAL-UP CONNECTION TO ANOTHER COMPUTER

Y ou can set up a dial-up connection that will allow you to connect to another computer using a modem. When you are connected to the other computer, you can work with files on the computer as if the files were stored on your own computer. You can also print files and access information on a network.

Connecting to another computer is useful when you are at home or traveling and you need information stored on your computer at work.

When you set up a connection to another computer, you must provide information about the computer you want to contact, such as the area code and phone number of the computer.

You only need to set up a connection to another computer once. After the connection is set

up, Windows displays an icon for the connection in the Dial-Up Networking window.

Before you can use the dial-up connection to contact the other computer, the computer you want to connect to must be turned on and set up as a dial-up server. To set up a dial-up server, see page 346.

SET UP A CONNECTION TO ANOTHER COMPUTER

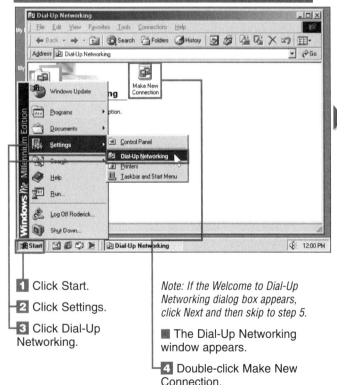

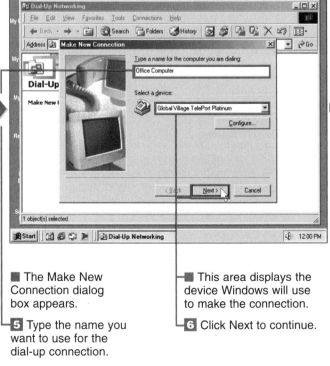

1 Click Start.

2 Click Settings.

3 Click Dial-Up Networking.

Note: If the Welcome to Dial-Up Networking dialog box appears, click Next and then skip to step 5.

■ The Dial-Up Networking window appears.

4 Double-click Make New Connection.

■ The Make New Connection dialog box appears.

5 Type the name you want to use for the dial-up connection.

■ This area displays the device Windows will use to make the connection.

6 Click Next to continue.

Can I set up a dial-up connection to the Internet?

✔ To set up a dial-up connection to your Internet service provider's computer system, you can use the Internet Connection Wizard. Once you connect to your Internet service provider's computer system, you can access the resources available on the Internet. See page 432 to use the Internet Connection Wizard.

How do I securely connect to a private network over the Internet?

✔ You must first add the Virtual Private Networking component found in the Communications category to your computer. See page 538 to add a Windows component. The private network you will connect to must support PPTP (Point-to-Point Tunneling Protocol).

To connect to a private network over the Internet, you should first set up a connection to an Internet Service Provider (ISP). Then perform steps 1 to 5 below. Click the Select a Device area, select Microsoft VPN Adapter and then click Next. In the Host name or IP Address box, type the name or IP address of the virtual private networking server you want to connect to. Then follow the instructions on your screen to complete the connection. When you want to connect to the private network, you must connect to your ISP before connecting to the private network.

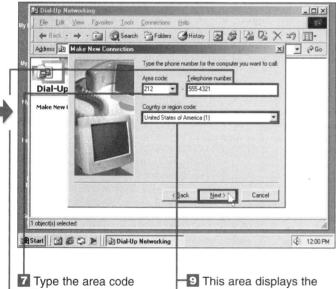

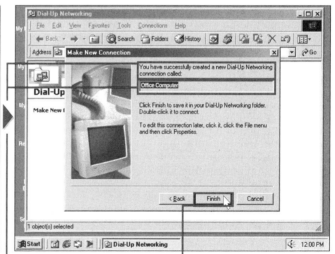

7 Type the area code of the computer you want to contact.

8 Click this area and type the telephone number of the computer.

9 This area displays the country or region where the computer is located. You can click this area to change the country or region.

10 Click Next to continue.

■ A message appears, stating that you have successfully created a new dial-up connection.

■ This area displays the name you assigned to the connection.

11 Click Finish to save the connection.

■ An icon for the connection appears in the Dial-Up Networking window. To use this icon to dial in to the other computer, see page 338.

DIAL IN TO ANOTHER COMPUTER

After you set up a connection to another computer, you can dial in to the computer to access information on the computer. For example, you can dial in to a computer at work to access files you need while you are away from the office. If the computer is connected to a network, you may be able to access information on the network. If the computer is running Windows, you can use My Network Places

to gain access to shared folders and printers on the computer. For information about My Network Places, see page 362.

Windows displays an icon in the Dial-Up Networking window for each connection to another computer you have set up. To set up a dial-up connection to another computer, see page 336.

When connecting to another computer, Windows displays

information about the connection, such as the telephone number Windows will dial and the location you are dialing from.

If the computer you are connecting to requires you to enter a password, you will need to enter the password to connect to the computer. You can have Windows save your password so you do not have to enter it each time you want to connect to the computer.

DIAL IN TO ANOTHER COMPUTER

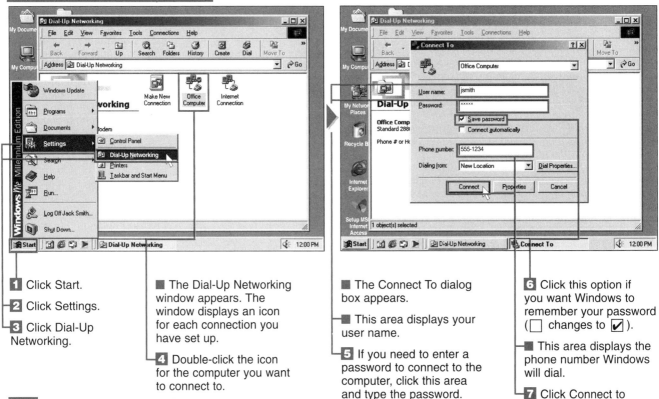

■ **1** Click Start.

■ **2** Click Settings.

■ **3** Click Dial-Up Networking.

■ The Dial-Up Networking window appears. The window displays an icon for each connection you have set up.

■ **4** Double-click the icon for the computer you want to connect to.

■ The Connect To dialog box appears.

■ This area displays your user name.

■ **5** If you need to enter a password to connect to the computer, click this area and type the password.

■ **6** Click this option if you want Windows to remember your password (☐ changes to ☑).

■ This area displays the phone number Windows will dial.

■ **7** Click Connect to connect to the computer.

Is there a faster way to dial in to another computer?

✔ Yes. If you saved your password in step 6 below, you can click the Connect automatically option in the Connect To dialog box. The next time you double-click the icon for the computer in the Dial-up Networking window, Windows will automatically dial in to the computer.

How can I monitor a connection I have made?

✔ When you are connected to another computer, double-click 🖳 on the taskbar to display the Connected to dialog box. This dialog box displays information about the connection, such as the speed of the connection and the amount of time you have been connected.

Why did my modem disconnect from the other computer?

✔ There may be interference on the phone line. Try connecting again to get a better phone line connection. Your local phone company may be able to help you reduce phone line interference. Your modem may also disconnect from another computer if you do not use your computer for a period of time or if the computer you are connected to is turned off.

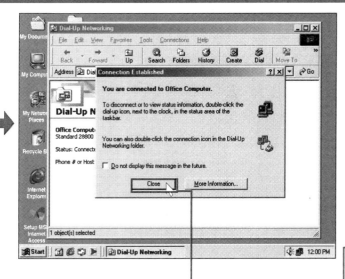

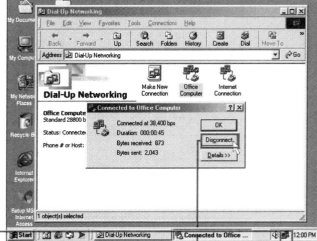

■ The Connection Established dialog box appears when you are successfully connected to the other computer.

8 Click Close to close the dialog box.

■ You can now access information on the other computer.

END THE CONNECTION

■ An icon (🖳) appears in this area when you are connected to the other computer.

1 When you want to end the connection, double-click the icon (🖳).

■ The Connected to dialog box appears.

2 Click Disconnect to end the connection.

CHANGE SETTINGS FOR A DIAL-UP CONNECTION

Y ou can change the settings for a dial-up connection to specify how your computer dials in to another computer.

You can change the area code and phone number Windows uses to contact another computer.

You can also specify the country or region where the computer you want to contact is located. This allows Windows to determine the country code it will use to dial the connection.

By default, Windows will use the area code and country code when dialing the other computer. If you choose not to use this information, you will not be able to change the location you are dialing from when you try to connect to the other computer.

If your computer has more than one device installed that can be used to connect to another computer, such as a modem, ISDN or Virtual Private

Networking (VPN) adapter, you can select the device you want to use to make the connection.

When you change the settings for a dial-up connection, the new settings will affect only that connection. Your other dial-up connections remain unchanged.

CHANGE SETTINGS FOR A DIAL-UP CONNECTION

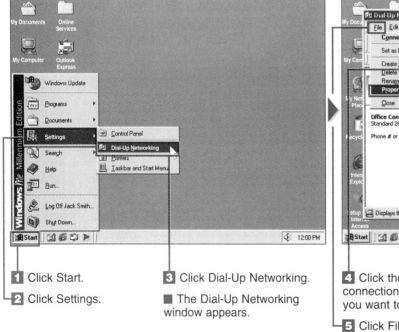

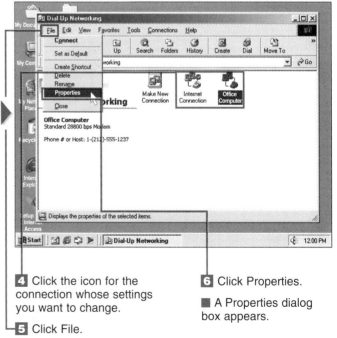

1 Click Start.

2 Click Settings.

3 Click Dial-Up Networking.

■ The Dial-Up Networking window appears.

4 Click the icon for the connection whose settings you want to change.

5 Click File.

6 Click Properties.

■ A Properties dialog box appears.

Can I display the terminal window when dialing a connection?

✔ You may want to display the terminal window to send additional commands to your modem before dialing or display the window after dialing to help troubleshoot a faulty connection. On the General tab of the Properties dialog box, click the Configure button to display the Modem Properties dialog box. Select the Options tab and in the Connection control area, click an option to specify when you want to display the terminal window.

Can I stop Windows from automatically dialing the phone number for a connection?

✔ Yes. On the General tab of the Properties dialog box, click the Configure button to display the Modem Properties dialog box. Select the Options tab and then click the Operator assisted or manual dial option.

What settings can I change for all dial-up connections?

✔ You can specify if you want Windows to display a confirmation dialog box or an icon on the taskbar after a connection is established. You can also specify security settings for all your dial-up connections. In the Dial-Up Networking window, click the Connections menu and select Settings. Then choose the options you want to use on the General and Security tabs.

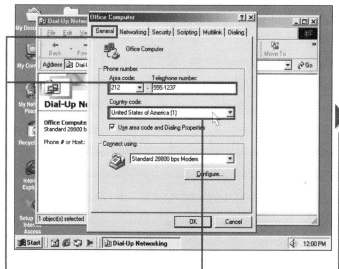

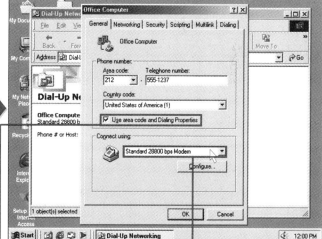

GENERAL SETTINGS

■1 Click the General tab.

■2 This area displays the area code and telephone number Windows will use to contact the other computer. To change a number, double-click an area and type a new number.

■3 This area displays the country where the other computer is located. You can click this area to change the country.

■4 This option uses the area code and country code when dialing the connection. You can click this option to turn the option on (✔) or off (☐).

■5 This area displays the device Windows will use to make the connection. You can click this area to change the device.

CONTINUED ▶

CHANGE SETTINGS FOR A DIAL-UP CONNECTION (CONTINUED)

You can specify the type of dial-up server that matches the operating system on the computer you want to connect to.

To speed up the transfer of information, Windows allows you to compress information you receive or send. The compression software used by the computers must be compatible.

Windows can create a log file in your Windows folder, called ppplog, which records information each time you use the connection. Log files can be useful in

determining the source of connection problems.

You can specify the network protocol the computers should use to exchange information. You can also specify the user name, password and domain name you use to log on to the other computer or network. If you leave the password area empty, you will be asked to type the password each time you use the connection.

If you have saved your password, you can have Windows log on to another computer automatically

when you double-click the icon for the connection.

You can also have your computer log on to the network using the user name and password you used to log on to Windows.

For greater security, you can have your computer send or receive only encrypted passwords and data. Encrypting converts information into code during transfer to prevent unauthorized people from viewing the information.

CHANGE SETTINGS FOR A DIAL-UP CONNECTION (CONTINUED)

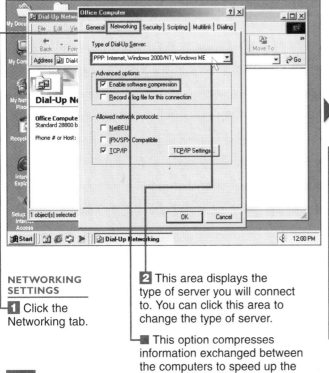

NETWORKING SETTINGS

1 Click the Networking tab.

2 This area displays the type of server you will connect to. You can click this area to change the type of server.

■ This option compresses information exchanged between the computers to speed up the transfer of information.

■ This option records information about the connection in a file each time you use the connection.

■ These options determine which network protocols your computer uses to communicate with the other computer.

3 Windows will use each option that displays a check mark (✔). You can click an option to turn the option on (✔) or off (☐).

Why would I need to enter a domain name?

✔ A domain is a set of computers on a network that are administered together. When you log on to a network, your logon information is verified with the domain or server listed. You usually do not need to enter a domain name when connecting to your Internet service provider.

How do I encrypt information I send?

✔ When you choose to send or receive only encrypted passwords or data, Windows will automatically encode the information for you. Windows will also automatically decode the information you receive. In order to use this feature, the computer you are contacting must also support encrypted passwords or data.

Which network protocols should I choose?

✔ The TCP/IP protocol is the most common protocol and is usually used when connecting to the Internet and Wide Area Networks (WANs). You can click the TCP/IP Settings button on the Networking tab to change the TCP/IP protocol settings. To determine which protocols you need to use, contact your network administrator or the owner of the computer you are connecting to.

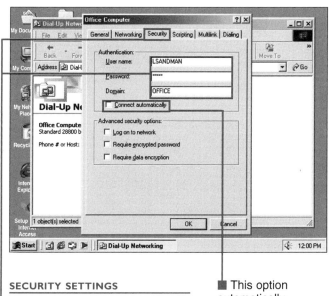

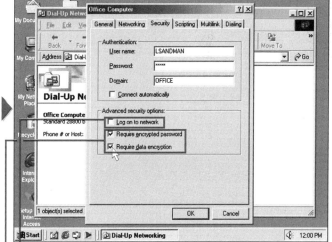

SECURITY SETTINGS

1 Click the Security tab.

2 These areas display the user name, password and domain name used to log on to the other computer or network. To change the information, double-click an area and type the new information.

■ This option automatically connects you to the other computer without requesting any information.

■ This option logs you on to the network using the user name and password you typed when you logged on to Windows.

■ These options specify that only encrypted passwords and encrypted data can be sent or received by your computer.

3 Windows will use each option that displays a check mark (✔). You can click an option to turn the option on (☑) or off (☐).

CONTINUED

CHANGE SETTINGS FOR A DIAL-UP CONNECTION (CONTINUED)

Y ou can create a script file that provides information, such as your user name and password, to a dial-up connection. You can specify the location and name of the script file you want to use and have the script run one command at a time, making it easier to check the script for errors.

Windows will start the terminal window minimized as a button on your taskbar. If you want to view information in the terminal window, you can turn off this option.

You can choose to make the connection the default Internet connection and then specify whether you want to dial the connection yourself or have Windows automatically dial it for you. Windows can automatically dial the connection only when a network connection is not available or always use the dial-up connection.

When a connection is not made on the first attempt, you can specify how many times Windows should

redial the number and the amount of time that should pass between each redial attempt.

You can also specify when Windows will disconnect an idle connection and turn off the confirmation dialog box Windows displays before automatically disconnecting.

When the program that initiated the connection closes, you can have Windows automatically close the connection or keep the connection open.

CHANGE SETTINGS FOR A DIAL-UP CONNECTION (CONTINUED)

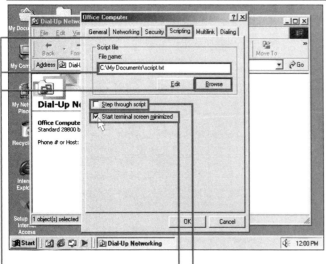

SCRIPTING SETTINGS

1 Click the Scripting tab.

2 Click this area and type the location and name of the script file you want to use.

■ To search for the file on your computer, click Browse.

■ This option runs one command of the script at a time.

■ This option minimizes the window that displays the script information.

3 You can click an option to turn the option on (✔) or off (☐).

DIALING SETTINGS

1 Click the Dialing tab.

2 Click this option to make this connection the default Internet connection (☐ changes to ✔).

3 If you selected the option in step 2, click an option to specify when you want to dial the Internet connection (○ changes to ⊙).

4 Double-click this area and type the number of times you want Windows to redial a connection after failing to connect.

How do I create a script file?

✔ A script file contains commands, parameters and expressions that send and retrieve information from the computer you are connecting to. To create a Dial-Up Networking script, you can use a text editor, such as WordPad or Notepad. You can find information about the scripting commands you need to create a script file in a document called SCRIPT located in the Windows folder on your hard drive.

Can I edit a script before assigning it to a connection?

✔ To edit a script before assigning it to a connection, click the Edit button on the Scripting tab. The script file appears in the Notepad window, allowing you to make changes to the script.

Can I install more than one connection device?

✔ You can use more than one connection device to increase the speed of the connection. To use multiple connection devices, display the Properties dialog box for the connection, select the Multilink tab and then click the Use additional devices option (○ changes to ◉). Click the Add button and then use the drop-down list to select an additional device. You should make sure the computer you dial supports multiple connection devices.

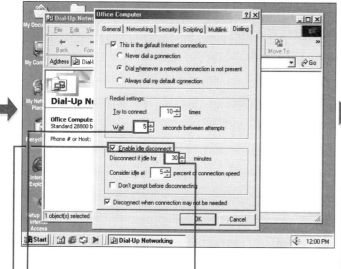

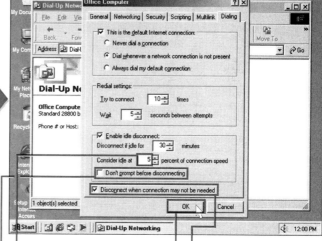

5 Double-click this area and type the number of seconds you want Windows to wait between each redial attempt.

6 This option will disconnect the connection when the connection is idle for a period of time. You can click the option to turn the option on (☑) or off (☐).

Note: If you turned the option off in step 6, skip to step 10.

7 Double-click this area and type the number of minutes you want to wait before disconnecting the connection.

8 Double-click this area and type the percentage of the connection speed you want to consider as idle.

9 Click this option to automatically disconnect without displaying a confirmation message first (☐ changes to ☑).

10 This option disconnects the connection when you close the program that made the connection. You can click the option to turn the option on (☑) or off (☐).

11 Click OK to confirm all your changes.

SET UP A DIAL-UP SERVER

You can set up a computer so you can dial in to the computer from another location. Setting up a dial-up server is ideal for someone who wants to access information stored on a computer while away from the office. A modem must be installed on the dial-up server and the server must be turned on before you can dial in to the computer.

You can dial in to the dial-up server to access information stored on the computer and the network attached to the computer. Connecting to the dial-up server also allows you to print documents on printers located at the office.

You can assign a password so only people who know the password can access the dial-up server.

Many networks have a dedicated dial-up server that accepts calls from computers that require access to the network. These dedicated dial-up servers are often called remote access servers.

After you set up a dial-up server, you need to set up a dial-up connection to the server on your portable or home computer. See page 336 to set up a connection.

SET UP A DIAL-UP SERVER

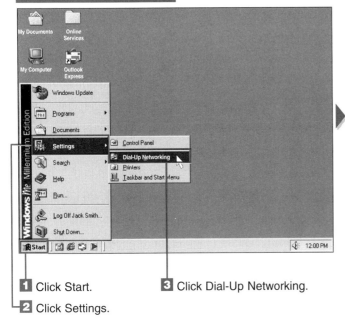

1 Click Start.

2 Click Settings.

3 Click Dial-Up Networking.

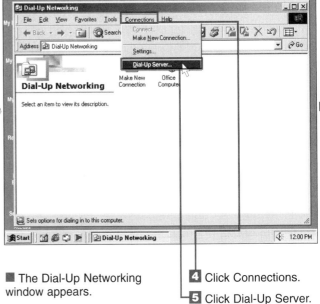

■ The Dial-Up Networking window appears.

Note: If the Welcome to Dial-Up Networking dialog box appears, click Cancel to close the dialog box.

4 Click Connections.

5 Click Dial-Up Server.

Why is the Dial-Up Server option not available?

✔ You may need to install the Dial-Up Server component on your computer. You will find this component in the Communications category. To add Windows components, see page 538.

What resources will be available on the computer I set up as a dial-up server?

✔ Any shared information and printers on the dial-up server will be available when you access the dial-up server. To share information, see page 374. To share a printer, see page 378.

Do I need to change the settings on the dial-up server?

✔ If you have trouble connecting to a dial-up server, you may need to change the server type on the dial-up server. To change the server type, display the Dial-Up Server dialog box and click the Server Type button. Then select the type of dial-up server that matches the operating system on the computer you will use to connect to the server.

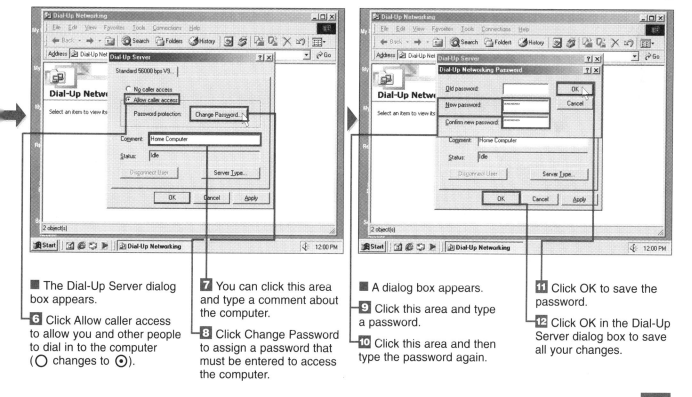

■ The Dial-Up Server dialog box appears.

6 Click Allow caller access to allow you and other people to dial in to the computer (○ changes to ⊙).

7 You can click this area and type a comment about the computer.

8 Click Change Password to assign a password that must be entered to access the computer.

■ A dialog box appears.

9 Click this area and type a password.

10 Click this area and then type the password again.

11 Click OK to save the password.

12 Click OK in the Dial-Up Server dialog box to save all your changes.

USING DIRECT CABLE CONNECTION

You can use a cable to connect two computers to share information and other resources. This is useful if you want to connect a portable computer to a desktop computer at work. Unlike a regular network, neither computer needs a network interface card.

When setting up a direct cable connection, you must set up one computer as the host and the other computer as the guest.

The host is the computer that provides the resources, such as files and printers. The guest is the computer that can access resources on the host and on the network attached to the host.

Make sure you plug the cable into both computers before you begin. You can choose from two types of cable. A serial cable allows you to connect the computers over a long distance but transfers information slowly. A parallel cable transfers

information faster than a serial cable and is the best choice for most direct cable connections.

Before setting up a direct cable connection, you must share resources on the host computer. To turn on sharing, see page 372. To share information, see page 374. To share a printer, see page 378. You should also make sure both computers have the NetBEUI protocol installed. To install a network protocol, see page 390.

SET UP DIRECT CABLE CONNECTION

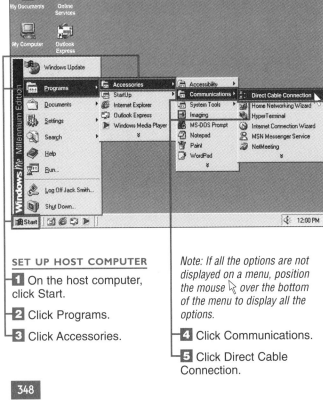

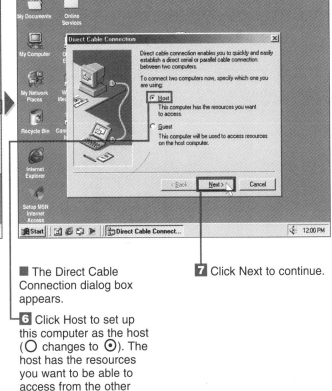

SET UP HOST COMPUTER

1 On the host computer, click Start.

2 Click Programs.

3 Click Accessories.

Note: If all the options are not displayed on a menu, position the mouse ⓛ over the bottom of the menu to display all the options.

4 Click Communications.

5 Click Direct Cable Connection.

■ The Direct Cable Connection dialog box appears.

6 Click Host to set up this computer as the host (O changes to ⊙). The host has the resources you want to be able to access from the other computer.

7 Click Next to continue.

348

Why isn't Direct Cable Connection available on the Start menu?

✔ You need to install the Direct Cable Connection component on your computer. The Direct Cable Connection component is located in the Communications category. To add Windows components, see page 538.

How can I prevent unauthorized people from accessing the host?

✔ You can set a password to prevent unauthorized people from accessing the host. Before selecting Finish in step 10 below, click the Use password protection option and then select the Set Password button. In the Direct Cable Connection Password dialog box, specify the password that a guest must enter to connect to the host.

Is there another way to connect computers?

✔ You can use the Home Networking Wizard to connect computers and set up a home network. For more information about setting up a home network, see page 406.

Will I have to set up the direct cable connection every time I want to connect the host and guest computers?

✔ After you set up a connection, you can reconnect the host and guest computers at any time. To re-establish a direct cable connection, see page 352.

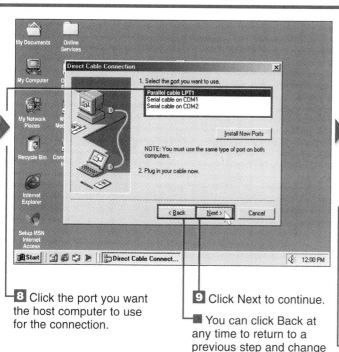

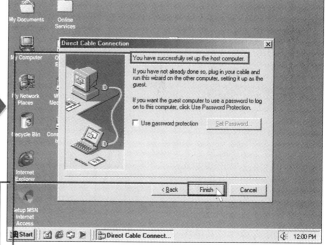

8 Click the port you want the host computer to use for the connection.

9 Click Next to continue.

■ You can click Back at any time to return to a previous step and change your selections.

■ This message appears when you have successfully set up the host computer.

10 Click Finish.

■ A window appears, stating that the computer is waiting for the guest computer to connect.

■ You are now ready to set up the guest computer.

CONTINUED ▶

USING DIRECT CABLE CONNECTION (CONTINUED)

Y ou must set up the guest computer before you can use the computer to access resources on the host. Make sure you set up the host computer before setting up the guest computer. To set up the host computer, see page 348.

You must specify the port you want the guest computer to use for the connection. You must

select the same type of port you chose for the host computer.

When you finish setting up the guest computer, Windows connects the guest computer to the host. While the computers are connected, the guest computer can access the shared resources on the host computer. If the host computer is attached to a network, the guest will also

be able to access the network and all shared resources on the network.

If any of the shared resources on the host computer are password-protected, you will need to enter a password to access the resources.

You cannot use a direct cable connection to share an Internet connection.

SET UP DIRECT CABLE CONNECTION (CONTINUED)

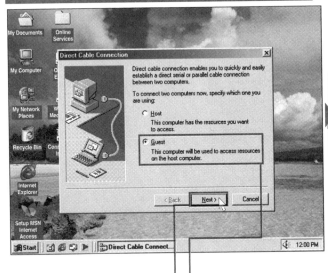

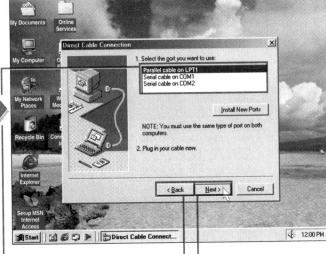

SET UP GUEST COMPUTER

1 On the guest computer, perform steps 1 to 5 on page 348 to display the Direct Cable Connection dialog box.

2 Click Guest to set up this computer as the guest (○ changes to ⊙).

3 Click Next to continue.

4 Click the port you want the guest computer to use for the connection.

5 Click Next to continue.

■ You can click Back at any time to return to a previous step and change your selections.

Can I use the host computer to access information on the guest computer?

✔ Yes. On the guest computer, share the information you want to access. On the host computer, double-click the My Network Places icon and then click the Search button. In the Computer Name area, type the name of the guest and then press the Enter key. Double-click the guest computer icon to display the shared items on the computer.

How do I print using the host computer's printer?

✔ Right-click the shared printer in the window that displays the host's shared items. From the menu that appears, select Connect to install the printer's software on the guest computer. Follow the instructions on your screen to install the printer. When you want to print, choose the printer in the program's Print dialog box.

I had to disconnect the printer from the host to plug in the cable for the direct cable connection. How can I print using the host?

✔ From the Control Panel on the host, select the Printers folder and then click the printer you want to use. Choose the File menu and select Pause Printing. Windows will store any files you send to the printer. When you reconnect the host to the printer, select the Pause Printing command again to print the files.

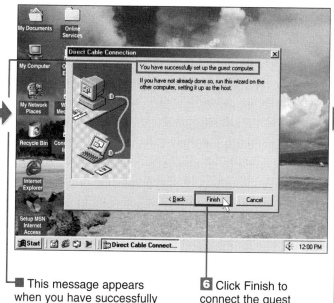

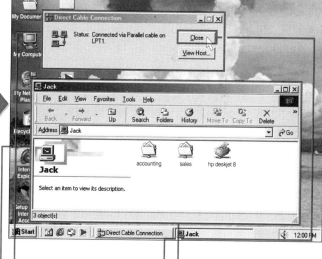

■ This message appears when you have successfully set up the guest computer.

6 Click Finish to connect the guest and host computers.

■ A window appears, telling you the status of the connection.

■ When the computers are connected, a window appears that displays the items shared by the host computer.

■ You can open and work with the folders and files as if the information were stored on the guest computer.

7 When you finish working with the files, click Close to end the connection.

CONTINUED ▶

USING DIRECT CABLE CONNECTION (CONTINUED)

Y ou only need to set up a direct cable connection once. After you set up a connection, you can reconnect the host and guest computers at any time. Windows uses the settings you specified when you set up the connection to re-establish the connection.

You can leave the cable connected to the host computer all the time.

You can re-attach the cable to the guest computer whenever you need to reconnect the computers.

Before re-establishing a direct cable connection, you must make sure that the resources you want to access on the host computer are still shared.

You can open and work with all the shared resources on the host

computer as if the resources were stored on the guest computer. Besides opening files and folders, you may be able to run shared programs that are located on the host computer. You can run programs that do not require special files to be stored on the guest computer.

RE-ESTABLISH DIRECT CABLE CONNECTION

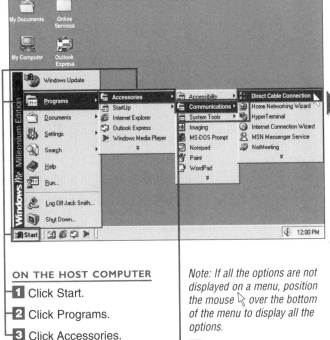

ON THE HOST COMPUTER

1 Click Start.

2 Click Programs.

3 Click Accessories.

Note: If all the options are not displayed on a menu, position the mouse over the bottom of the menu to display all the options.

4 Click Communications.

5 Click Direct Cable Connection.

■ The Direct Cable Connection window appears.

6 Click Listen.

■ A window appears, stating that the computer is waiting for the guest computer to connect.

How can I quickly display the Direct Cable Connection window?

✔ You can create a desktop shortcut that will allow you to quickly display the window. On the Start menu, right-click Direct Cable Connection. From the menu that appears, click Send To and then select Desktop (create shortcut). You can double-click the icon that appears on the desktop to quickly display the Direct Cable Connection window.

How can I change the settings for a direct cable connection?

✔ In the Direct Cable Connection window, click the Change button. You can change settings such as the port used by a computer for the connection or the password you set for the host computer.

Can I work with the host's files on the guest computer when the computers are not connected?

✔ Yes. When the computers are connected, create a Briefcase on the guest computer and add the host's files to the Briefcase. You can now work with the host's files on the guest computer when the computers are not connected. When you reconnect the computers, you can update the files on the host computer. For more information about the Briefcase feature, see page 354.

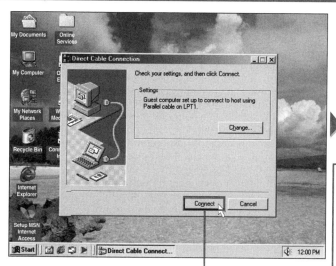

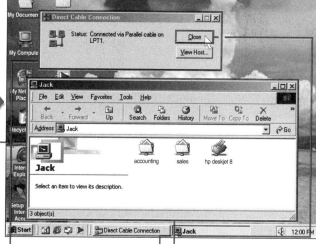

ON THE GUEST COMPUTER

1 Perform steps 1 to 5 on page 352 to display the Direct Cable Connection window.

2 Click Connect to connect the guest and host computers.

■ A window appears, telling you the status of the connection.

■ When the computers are connected, a window appears that displays the items shared by the host computer.

■ You can open and work with the folders and files as if the information were stored on the guest computer.

3 When you finish working with the files, click Close to end the connection.

USING BRIEFCASE

The computer in your office may be the computer you use most often to work with files, but you may also use a home or portable computer. When you place a file in a Briefcase, you can easily transport the file between computers. Briefcase ensures that you are always working with the most up-to-date version of a file, regardless of the computer you use to edit the file.

When you place a folder in a Briefcase, all of the files in the folder are added to the Briefcase. The Briefcase contains a copy of your files. The original files remain on your main computer.

You can move a Briefcase to a floppy disk or other type of removable disk so you can work with the files on another computer.

When at home or traveling, you can work with Briefcase files as you would work with any files. When you are ready to return to your main computer, make sure you save and close all Briefcase files you edited and close the Briefcase window before removing the disk containing the Briefcase from the computer's drive.

USING BRIEFCASE

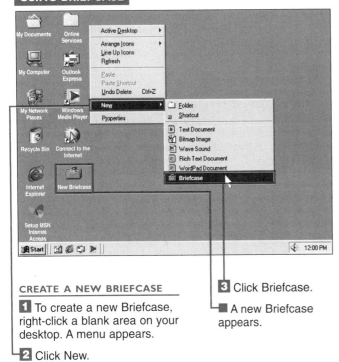

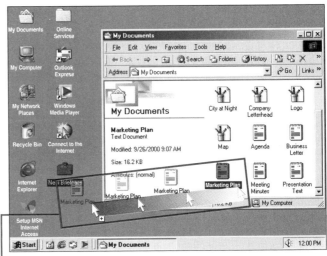

CREATE A NEW BRIEFCASE

1 To create a new Briefcase, right-click a blank area on your desktop. A menu appears.

2 Click New.

3 Click Briefcase.

■ A new Briefcase appears.

WORK WITH BRIEFCASE FILES

1 Drag each file or folder to the Briefcase that you want to work with while away from your main computer.

Note: The first time you copy a file to a Briefcase, Windows displays a welcome message. Click Finish to close the message.

I want to create a Briefcase. Why isn't the Briefcase command displayed on the menu?

✔ You need to install the Briefcase component before you can create a Briefcase. The Briefcase component is found in the Accessories category. To add Windows components, see page 538. Briefcase is automatically installed on portable computers.

Can I create more than one Briefcase?

✔ Yes. You can create as many Briefcases as you need. If you create more than one Briefcase, you may want to rename each Briefcase so you can easily tell them apart. You can rename a Briefcase the same way you rename a file. To rename a file, see page 70.

Is there another way to place files in a Briefcase?

✔ Right-click the file or folder you want to place in the Briefcase. Click Send To and then select My Briefcase. This procedure only works if your Briefcase is named "My Briefcase."

Why can't I use a Briefcase on my home computer?

✔ You must install the Briefcase component on every computer you want to use to work with Briefcase files.

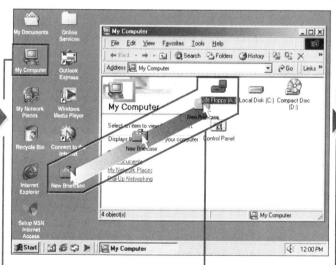

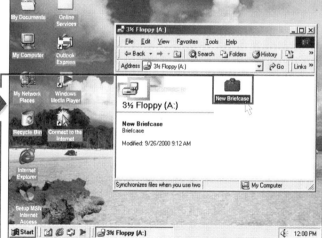

2 Insert a floppy disk or other removable disk into a drive on your computer.

3 Double-click My Computer to display the My Computer window.

4 Drag the Briefcase to the drive that contains the disk.

■ Windows moves the Briefcase to the disk. You can now transfer the Briefcase to your other computer.

5 Insert the disk into a drive on your other computer.

6 Display the contents of the drive containing the disk.

7 Double-click the Briefcase to display its contents. You can open and edit the files in the Briefcase as you would open and edit any files.

8 When you finish working with the files, remove the disk and return the disk to your main computer.

CONTINUED

USING BRIEFCASE (CONTINUED)

Briefcase lets you work with files while you are away from your main computer. When you change a file in the Briefcase, the original file on your main computer becomes out-of-date. Briefcase can update the files you changed. You can update all files or only specific files.

The update process ensures that the original files and the

Briefcase copies are the same. Briefcase compares the files it contains with the files on your main computer and shows you which files need to be updated. You can replace the original file with the Briefcase file, replace the Briefcase file with the original file or skip replacing the file completely.

By default, Briefcase replaces the older version of the file

with the newer version of the file. If both the original and Briefcase copies have been changed, Briefcase will indicate this and will not update the file.

Do not rename or move the original files on your main computer and do not rename the files in the Briefcase. If you do, Briefcase will not be able to properly update the files.

USING BRIEFCASE (CONTINUED)

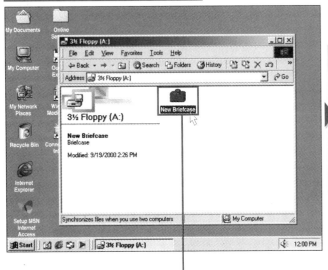

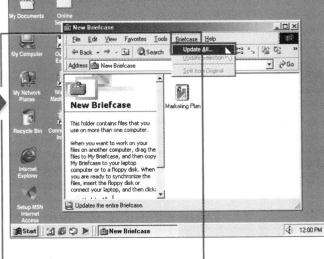

UPDATE BRIEFCASE FILES

1 Insert the floppy disk or other removable disk that contains the Briefcase into a drive on your main computer.

2 Display the contents of the drive containing the disk.

3 Double-click the Briefcase.

■ A window appears, displaying the contents of the Briefcase.

4 Click Briefcase to update the files.

5 Click Update All.

Note: You can also click the Update All button (Update All) to update the files.

How can I quickly update only some of the files in a Briefcase?

✔ In the Briefcase window, select the files you want to update. Click the Briefcase menu and select Update Selection.

Can I permanently prevent a Briefcase file from updating?

✔ In the Briefcase window, select the file you do not want to update. Click the Briefcase menu and select Split from Original. This lets you keep the changed version of the file in the Briefcase and the original file on the main computer.

I created a new file in a Briefcase while working at home. Will the file be updated to my main computer?

✔ The file will be updated to your main computer if you created the file in an existing folder in the Briefcase. If you did not create the file in an existing folder, the file will not be updated because Windows will not know where to store the file on your main computer.

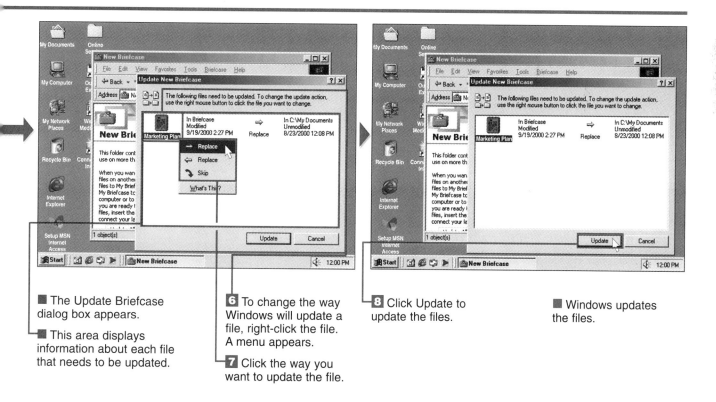

■ The Update Briefcase dialog box appears.

■ This area displays information about each file that needs to be updated.

6 To change the way Windows will update a file, right-click the file. A menu appears.

7 Click the way you want to update the file.

8 Click Update to update the files.

■ Windows updates the files.

USING HYPERTERMINAL

yperTerminal allows your computer to communicate with another computer.

Some computers on the Internet only offer information by telnet. HyperTerminal is commonly used as a telnet program to connect to a computer on the Internet and access this information. You must connect to the Internet before you can use HyperTerminal as a telnet program.

Before you can access telnet information using HyperTerminal, you need to set up a connection to the computer on the Internet that offers the information. You need to specify the host address of the computer you want to connect to and the port number that indicates the port HyperTerminal will use to connect to the other computer.

The host address and port number you enter depend on the computer you connect to. HyperTerminal allows you to enter the host address as a domain name, such as telnet.abccorp.com, or as an IP (Internet Protocol) number, such as 172.20.135.71. The port number for telnet sites is 23.

SET UP A NEW CONNECTION

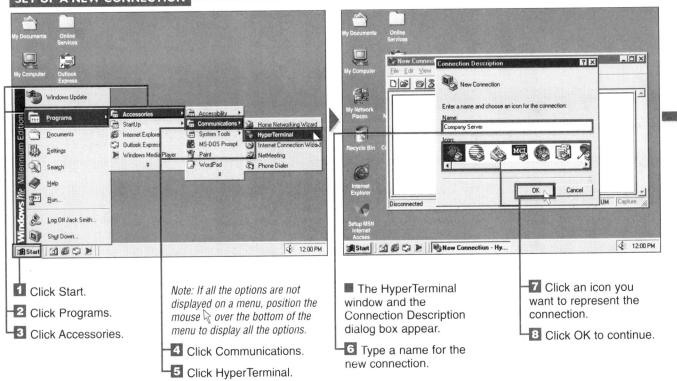

■1 Click Start.

■2 Click Programs.

■3 Click Accessories.

Note: If all the options are not displayed on a menu, position the mouse ⍾ over the bottom of the menu to display all the options.

■4 Click Communications.

■5 Click HyperTerminal.

■ The HyperTerminal window and the Connection Description dialog box appear.

■6 Type a name for the new connection.

■7 Click an icon you want to represent the connection.

■8 Click OK to continue.

Why doesn't HyperTerminal appear on the Start menu?

✔ You may need to add the HyperTerminal component to your computer. HyperTerminal is found in the Communications category. To add Windows components, see page 538.

Where can I get the latest version of HyperTerminal?

✔ HyperTerminal is continuously updated to add more features. You can get an updated or more powerful version of HyperTerminal on the Web at www.hilgraeve.com.

Can I use HyperTerminal to connect to another computer using my modem?

✔ Yes. Connecting to another computer using your modem is useful if the other computer uses a modem and HyperTerminal to transfer information, such as when connecting to a Bulletin Board Service (BBS) or a friend's computer. Perform steps 1 to 8 below to display the Connect To dialog box. In the Country/region area, click ▼ and select your country. In the Area code and Phone number areas, type the area code and phone number of the computer you want to connect to. In the Connect using area, click ▼ and then select the modem you will use to connect to the other computer. In the Connect dialog box, click the Dial button.

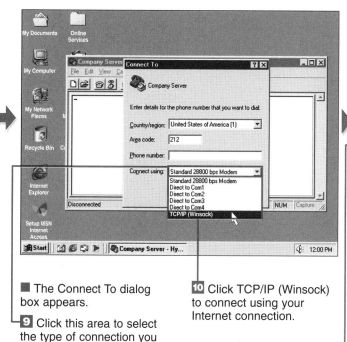

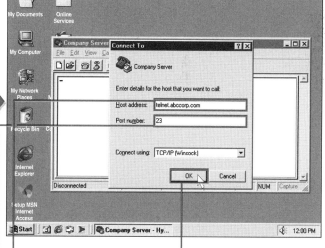

■ The Connect To dialog box appears.

9 Click this area to select the type of connection you will use.

10 Click TCP/IP (Winsock) to connect using your Internet connection.

11 Click this area and type the host address of the computer you want to connect to.

■ This area displays the port number HyperTerminal will use to connect to the other computer.

12 Click OK to connect to the other computer.

Note: If you are not currently connected to the Internet, a dialog box appears that allows you to connect.

CONTINUED ►

359

USING HYPERTERMINAL (CONTINUED)

When you connect to another computer that offers telnet information, you usually need to log on to the computer to access and work with the information on the computer. To log on, you need to enter your user name and password.

Once you are connected to the other computer, you can enter commands to work with the information on the computer. For example, entering the dir command usually allows you to list the contents of the current directory. When you are finished working with the other computer, you usually disconnect from the computer by typing the exit command.

HyperTerminal allows you to save a connection you set up. Saving the connection prevents you from having to enter the same information each time you use the connection. Windows saves the connection in the C:/Program Files/Accessories/HyperTerminal folder on your computer. You can use the saved connection at any time to quickly reconnect to the computer.

SET UP A NEW CONNECTION (CONTINUED)

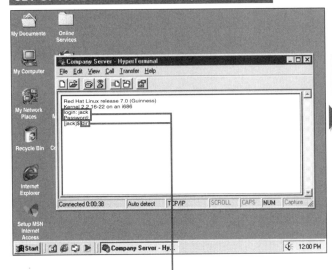

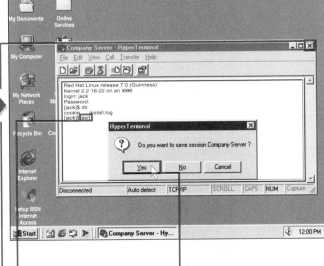

■ You are now connected to the other computer.

■ Before you can access information on the other computer, you may need to log on to the computer.

13 To log on to the computer, type your user name and press Enter.

14 Type your password and press Enter.

■ You can now enter commands to work with information on the computer.

15 When you want to end the connection to the other computer, type the command that logs you off the computer and then press Enter.

16 Click ☒ to close the HyperTerminal window.

■ A message appears, asking if you want to save the information you entered for the connection.

17 Click Yes to save the connection.

Can I save the text from a HyperTerminal session in a text file?

✓ Yes. Capturing text is useful if you want to work with the information in a HyperTerminal session later. From the Transfer menu, click Capture Text. In the Capture text dialog box, type the location and name of the file where you want to save the text. The file name should have the .txt extension so you can later work with the text in a text editor such as Notepad. Click Start to start capturing text. When you want to stop capturing text, choose the Transfer menu, click Capture Text and then click Stop.

Can I view images using HyperTerminal?

✓ No. HyperTerminal is only capable of displaying text. You will not be able to view images using HyperTerminal.

How do I change the font of text displayed in the HyperTerminal window?

✓ You can change the font of text to make the text easier to read. From the View menu, select Font. In the Font dialog box, choose the font, style and size settings you want the text to display.

USE A SAVED CONNECTION

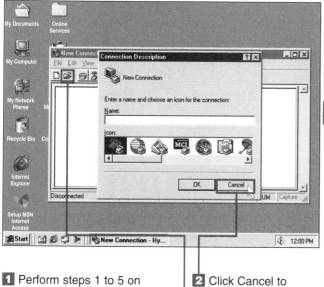

1 Perform steps 1 to 5 on page 358.

■ The HyperTerminal window and the Connection Description dialog box appear.

2 Click Cancel to close the Connection Description dialog box.

3 Click 📂.

■ The Open dialog box appears, displaying your saved connections.

4 Click the connection you want to use to connect to another computer.

5 Click Open to use the connection.

BROWSE THROUGH A NETWORK

Y ou can use My Network Places to browse through the shared resources available on your network, such as files and printers.

Using My Network Places to locate resources on a network is similar to using My Computer to locate information on your own computer.

Each item in the My Network Places window displays an icon to help

you distinguish between the types of items on the network, such as computers (🖳) and folders (📁).

When browsing through a network, you select the workgroup that contains the resources you want to access. A workgroup is a group of computers that frequently share resources. You can then select the computer that contains the resources you want to work with.

You can work with the information shared on a network as you would work with information stored on your own computer. You may need to enter a password before you can access some shared resources. If you do not know what password to type, ask your network administrator or the person who shares the folder.

BROWSE THROUGH A NETWORK

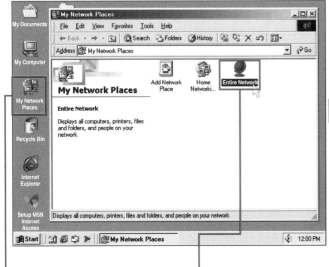

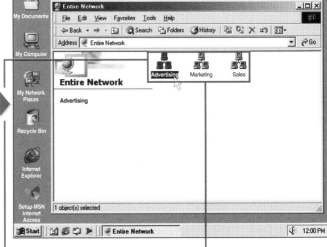

1 Double-click My Network Places to browse through the resources on your network.

■ The My Network Places window appears.

2 Double-click Entire Network to view all the workgroups on your network.

■ The workgroups on your network appear.

Note: If the workgroups on your network do not appear, click the View the entire contents of this folder link in the window to display the workgroups.

3 Double-click the workgroup that contains the computer you want to access.

Can I use Windows Explorer to browse through a network?

✓ Yes. Open Windows Explorer and double-click My Network Places in the window. Then double-click Entire Network to display a list of all the workgroups on your network. For information about using Windows Explorer, see page 52.

Why do some folders appear in the My Network Places window?

✓ Windows automatically places shortcuts to shared folders that you have previously accessed in the My Network Places window. You can double-click one of these folders to display its contents. To delete a shortcut to a folder from the My Network Places window, click the folder you want to delete and then press the Delete key.

Why can't I access information on the network?

✓ You may need to install the network protocol used by your network to exchange information. A network protocol is a set of rules that determines how computers on a network communicate. To install a network protocol, see page 390.

Why can I no longer access a shared folder on the network?

✓ The computer that stores the folder may be turned off or the folder may no longer be shared.

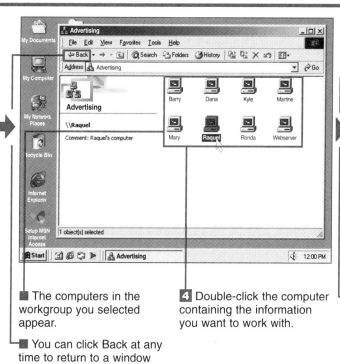

■ The computers in the workgroup you selected appear.

■ You can click Back at any time to return to a window you have previously viewed.

4 Double-click the computer containing the information you want to work with.

■ The folders and printers shared by the computer appear.

■ You can work with the information shared by the computer as you would work with information stored on your own computer.

Note: You may be asked to type a password to access some shared folders.

5 When you finish working with information on your network, click ✕ to close the window.

363

SEARCH FOR A COMPUTER

You can quickly locate a computer on your network. Searching for a computer is especially useful if your network contains hundreds of computers.

If you are searching for a computer on a large network, Windows may take a while to display the names of any computers it finds. You can cancel the search at any time.

After the search is complete, Windows displays a list of all the computers that match the name you specified. Windows also indicates the location of each computer that was found and displays a comment for each computer.

Once you find a computer, you can browse through the information

and equipment shared by the computer. You can access the information stored on the computer as if the information were stored on your own computer. Windows may ask you to enter a password to access some shared items.

SEARCH FOR A COMPUTER

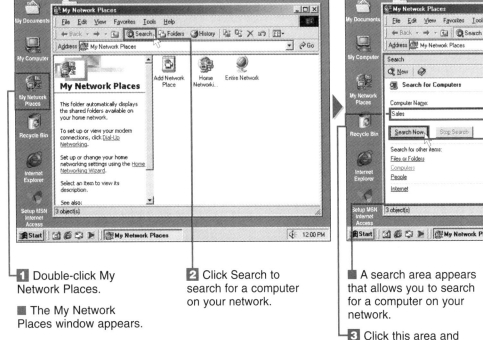

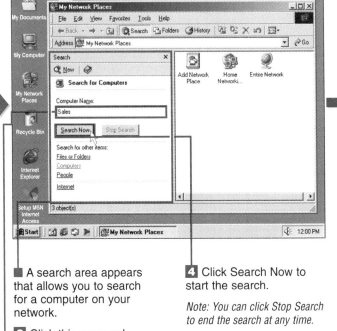

1 Double-click My Network Places.

■ The My Network Places window appears.

2 Click Search to search for a computer on your network.

■ A search area appears that allows you to search for a computer on your network.

3 Click this area and then type the name of the computer you want to find.

4 Click Search Now to start the search.

Note: You can click Stop Search to end the search at any time.

Can I use wildcard characters to help me search for a computer?

✔ You can use an asterisk (*) or a question mark (?) to help you find a computer in your workgroup when you know only part of the computer's name. A workgroup is a group of computers on a network that frequently share information. The asterisk (*) represents one or more characters. The question mark (?) represents a single character. For example, type Jon* to find a computer named Jonathon.

How do I start a new search?

✔ Click the New button at the top of the search area to clear the computer name you entered and start a new search.

How can I change the order of the computers that Windows finds?

✔ You can sort the list of computers by name, location or comment. Click the heading of the column you want to use to sort the computers. Windows will sort the items alphabetically.

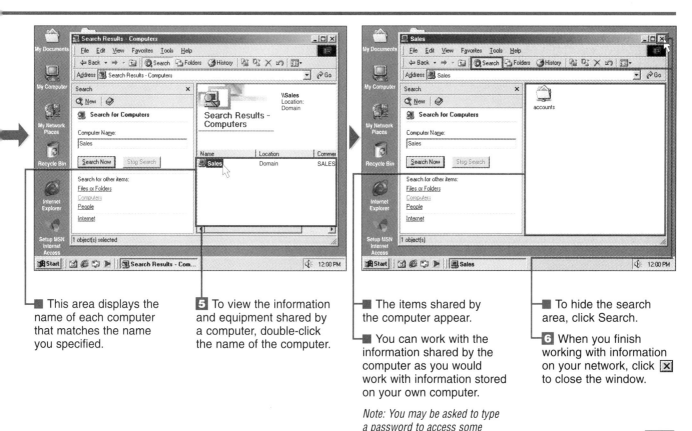

■ This area displays the name of each computer that matches the name you specified.

5 To view the information and equipment shared by a computer, double-click the name of the computer.

■ The items shared by the computer appear.

■ You can work with the information shared by the computer as you would work with information stored on your own computer.

Note: You may be asked to type a password to access some shared items.

■ To hide the search area, click Search.

6 When you finish working with information on your network, click ☒ to close the window.

MAP A NETWORK DRIVE

You can assign, or map, a drive letter to a drive or folder on the network. Mapping a network drive provides a quick way to access information on another computer on the network. You can access a drive or folder on the other computer as if the drive or folder were on your own computer.

If you frequently use information stored on another computer, mapping a network drive can

save you time. Accessing a drive or folder on the network that has not been mapped may require you to spend time searching for the drive or folder. Instead, you can have Windows connect to a mapped network drive and display an icon for the drive in the My Computer window each time you start Windows.

Mapping a network drive is also useful if you are working with MS-DOS or older Windows-based

programs. Although Windows allows you to use up to 215 characters to name a folder, older programs may not be able to read folder names that contain more than 8 characters. Mapping a network drive uses a single letter to represent a folder on the network, such as F:, allowing older programs to access the folder.

MAP A NETWORK DRIVE

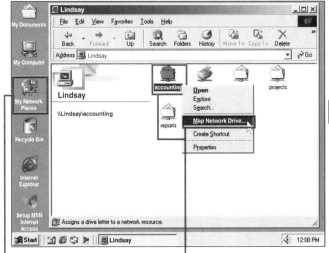

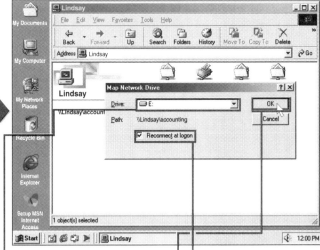

1 Double-click My Network Places to browse through the information on your network.

■ The My Network Places window appears.

2 Locate the drive or folder on your network that you want to be able to quickly access.

Note: To use My Network Places to find information on your network, see page 362.

3 Right-click the drive or folder. A menu appears.

4 Click Map Network Drive.

■ The Map Network Drive dialog box appears.

■ This area displays the drive letter that Windows will assign to the drive or folder. You can click this area to select a different letter.

5 This option indicates whether Windows will connect to the drive or folder every time you start Windows. You can click this option to turn the option on (✔) or off (☐).

6 Click OK.

How do I disconnect a mapped network drive?

✔ In the My Computer window, right-click the mapped network drive you want to disconnect from and then click Disconnect.

Why does an X appear through a mapped network drive?

✔ In the My Computer window, an X through the icon of a mapped network drive means the drive is unavailable or the drive has a new password. Windows will notify you of the problem the next time you start Windows.

Will Windows remember a password I entered to create a mapped network drive?

✔ When you create a mapped network drive, you may be asked for a password. Windows will remember the password so you do not have to type the password each time you want to access the information.

What drive letter should I select for the mapped network drive?

✔ You should choose a drive letter between F and Z. You should reserve the letters A through E for your floppy drive, hard drive, CD-ROM drive and any removable drives you use on your computer.

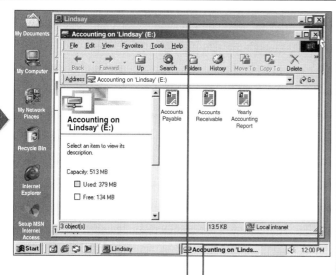

■ A window appears, displaying the contents of the drive or folder.

Note: The Enter Network Password dialog box appears if you need to type a password to access the drive or folder. Type the password and then press the Enter key.

7 When you finish viewing the contents of the drive or folder, click ☒ to close the window.

8 Click ☒ to close the My Network Places window.

VIEW MAPPED NETWORK DRIVES

1 Double-click My Computer.

■ The My Computer window appears.

■ The icon for the drive or folder on the network displays a disk attached to a cable. You can double-click the icon to access the contents of the drive or folder.

CHANGE COMPUTER AND WORKGROUP NAME

You can change the name of your computer and the workgroup your computer belongs to on a network. Windows uses this information to identify your computer to other people on the network. Before changing your computer or workgroup name, you should consult your network administrator.

Each computer on a network must have a unique name. A descriptive name such as "Johns_Computer"

makes a computer easier to identify than a name such as "Computer10." A computer name can contain up to 15 characters, including letters, numbers and underscore characters (_).

You can change the workgroup that your computer belongs to on the network. A workgroup name can contain up to 15 characters.

You can assign your computer a description. Assigning a description gives other people

on the network more detailed information about your computer, such as the computer's location.

You need to restart your computer before the changes will take effect. Make sure you close any open programs before restarting your computer.

After you change your computer or workgroup name, you should inform the people on the network who access resources on your computer.

CHANGE COMPUTER AND WORKGROUP NAME

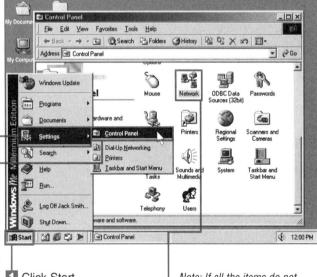

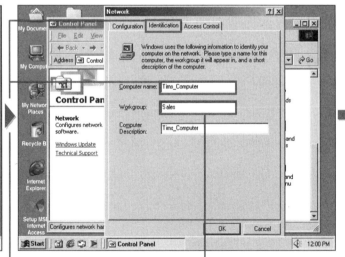

1 Click Start.

2 Click Settings.

3 Click Control Panel.

■ The Control Panel window appears.

Note: If all the items do not appear in the Control Panel window, click the view all Control Panel options link in the window to display all the items.

4 Double-click Network.

■ The Network dialog box appears.

5 Click the Identification tab.

6 This area displays the name of your computer. To change the name, type a new name.

7 This area displays the workgroup your computer belongs to. To change the workgroup, select the text and then type the name of another workgroup.

What is a workgroup?

✔ A workgroup is a group of computers that frequently share resources such as files and printers on a network. A workgroup often consists of computers located close to each other, such as computers in the accounting or sales department. If you do not know the name of your workgroup, ask your network administrator.

Can I create a new workgroup on the network?

✔ Yes. Display the Network dialog box and click the Identification tab. In the Workgroup area, type a workgroup name that does not currently exist. A new workgroup with the name you specified will be created on the network. You should consult your network administrator before creating a new workgroup.

My computer already displays a name and workgroup name. When was this information entered?

✔ The computer and workgroup names are often entered when Windows is installed on a computer.

How do I view descriptions for computers on the network?

✔ Double-click the My Network Places icon on the desktop and then locate the computers you want to view descriptions for. Select the View menu and then click Details. Descriptions are displayed in the Comment column.

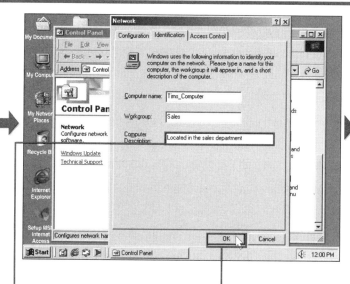

8 This area displays a description of your computer. To change the description, select the text and then type a new description.

9 Click OK to confirm your changes.

■ The System Settings Change dialog box appears, stating that Windows needs to restart your computer before the changes will take effect.

10 Click Yes to restart your computer.

EXCHANGE MESSAGES WITH WINPOPUP

Y ou can use WinPopup to exchange short messages with other people on your network. WinPopup is useful for asking questions, expressing ideas and making short announcements. For example, you can use WinPopup to let all the people on your network know when you are about to stop sharing information or a device such as a printer.

If you use WinPopup regularly, you can leave it open on the desktop or minimize it to a button on the taskbar. The WinPopup program must be running on your computer in order for you to receive messages. The WinPopup button on the taskbar displays the 🐾 symbol when you have messages. You can flip through all the messages you receive.

You can send a message to one person or to everyone in a workgroup. A workgroup is a group of computers on a network that frequently share resources.

EXCHANGE MESSAGES WITH WINPOPUP

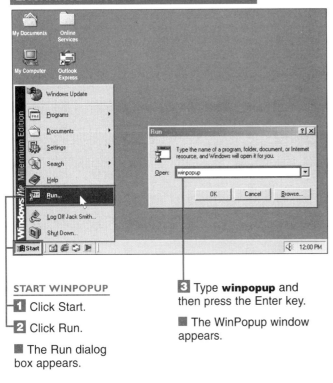

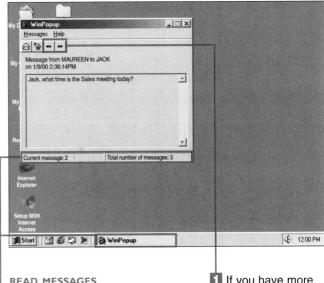

START WINPOPUP

■1 Click Start.

■2 Click Run.

■ The Run dialog box appears.

■3 Type **winpopup** and then press the Enter key.

■ The WinPopup window appears.

READ MESSAGES

■ The WinPopup button on the taskbar displays a symbol to indicate if you have (🐾) or do not have (🐾) messages.

■ This area shows the number of the currently displayed message and the total number of messages.

■1 If you have more than one message, click one of these buttons to display the previous (◄◄) or next (►►) message.

Can I save the WinPopup messages I receive?

✔ No. If you need to keep a WinPopup message, drag the mouse I over the text in the message to select the text. Right-click the selected text and then click Copy. You can then paste the text into a document in another program.

How do I delete a message?

✔ To delete the currently displayed message, click the Delete button (🖫). To delete all messages, choose the Messages menu and then select Clear All.

Can I make the WinPopup window appear automatically each time I receive a message?

✔ Yes. In the WinPopup window, choose the Messages menu and then select Options. In the Options dialog box, click the Pop up dialog on message receipt option (☐ changes to ☑) and then click OK. You can then minimize the WinPopup window. The window will automatically pop up on your screen when you receive a message.

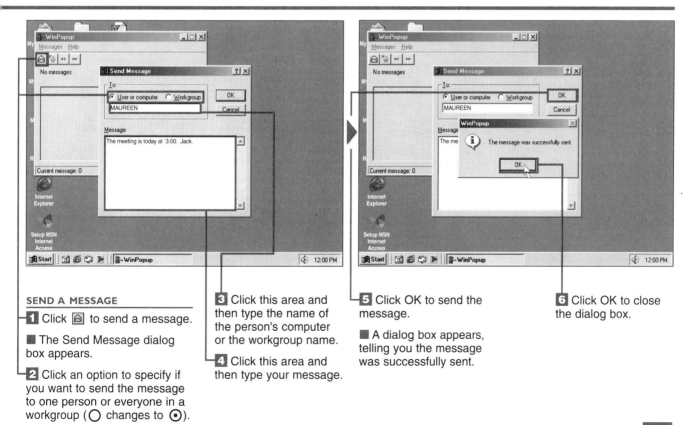

SEND A MESSAGE

■ 1 Click 📧 to send a message.

■ The Send Message dialog box appears.

■ 2 Click an option to specify if you want to send the message to one person or everyone in a workgroup (○ changes to ⊙).

■ 3 Click this area and then type the name of the person's computer or the workgroup name.

■ 4 Click this area and then type your message.

■ 5 Click OK to send the message.

■ A dialog box appears, telling you the message was successfully sent.

■ 6 Click OK to close the dialog box.

TURN ON SHARING

Before you can share information or a printer with other people on a network, you must set up your computer to share resources.

You may choose to share files stored on your computer with other people on the network. Sharing files is useful if you want your colleagues to be able to access information on your computer. You can share many types of files, such as programs, documents, videos, sounds and graphics.

You can also share a printer connected to your computer. After you share your printer, people on the network can use your printer to print documents.

Sharing a printer often helps companies reduce costs, since everyone on the network can share one central printer.

You will have to restart your computer before the new sharing settings will take effect. Make sure you close any open programs before restarting your computer.

TURN ON SHARING

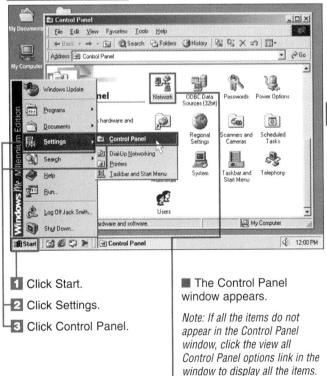

■ Click Start.

■ Click Settings.

■ Click Control Panel.

■ The Control Panel window appears.

Note: If all the items do not appear in the Control Panel window, click the view all Control Panel options link in the window to display all the items.

■ Double-click Network.

■ The Network dialog box appears.

■ Click File and Print Sharing.

■ The File and Print Sharing dialog box appears.

I turned on sharing, but my colleagues still cannot access my files and printer. What is wrong?

✔ Once you turn on sharing, you must specify exactly what you want to share on your computer. For information about sharing folders, see page 374. For information about sharing a printer, see page 378. You may also need to install the network protocol used by your network to exchange information. A network protocol is a set of rules that determines how computers on a network communicate. To install a network protocol, see page 390.

How do I turn off sharing on my computer?

✔ To turn off sharing on your computer, repeat steps 1 to 10 below (✔ changes to ☐ in steps 6 and 7). After your computer restarts, other people on the network will no longer be able to access your resources.

If I turn on sharing again, will Windows remember which resources I previously shared?

✔ Windows remembers which resources you were sharing. When you turn on sharing again, all the resources you previously shared are shared again.

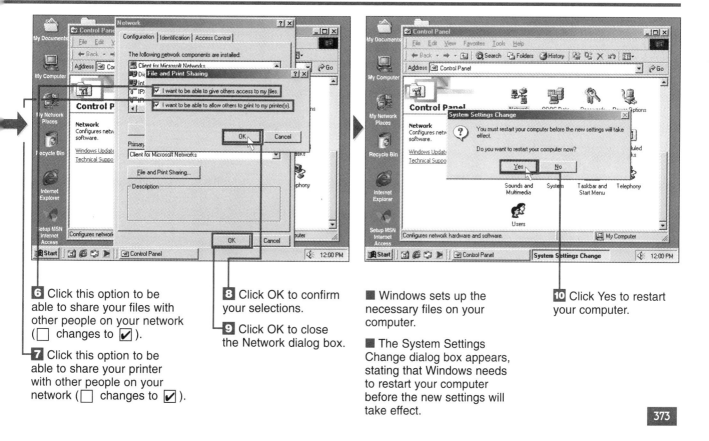

6 Click this option to be able to share your files with other people on your network (☐ changes to ✔).

7 Click this option to be able to share your printer with other people on your network (☐ changes to ✔).

8 Click OK to confirm your selections.

9 Click OK to close the Network dialog box.

■ Windows sets up the necessary files on your computer.

■ The System Settings Change dialog box appears, stating that Windows needs to restart your computer before the new settings will take effect.

10 Click Yes to restart your computer.

SHARE INFORMATION

Y ou can specify exactly what information on your computer you want to share with other people on a network. Sharing information is useful when people on a network are working together on a project and need to access the same files. Sharing information on a network is also very efficient. Computers can exchange information over a network in seconds.

When you share a folder on your computer, people on the network will have access to all the folders and files within the folder. They will be able to work with the files as if the files were stored on their own computers.

You can specify the name that the shared folder will display on the network. The name cannot contain more than 12 characters.

Specifying a name for a shared folder will not change the name of the folder on your computer. You can also add a comment to a shared folder to help people on the network identify the folder.

Before you can share information, you must set up your computer to share resources. To turn on file and printer sharing, see page 372.

SHARE INFORMATION

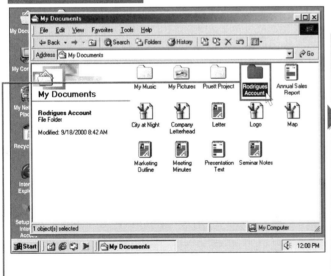

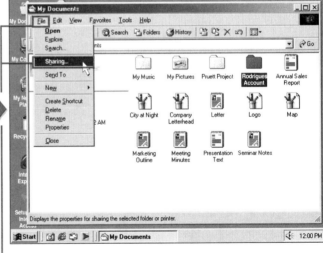

1 Click the folder you want to share with other people on your network.

2 Click File.

3 Click Sharing.

■ The Properties dialog box appears.

Can I share a drive on my computer?

✔ Yes. You can share your hard drive, floppy drive or CD-ROM drive the same way you would share a folder on your computer.

Can I hide a shared folder from other people on the network?

✔ In the Properties dialog box for the folder, type a dollar sign ($) at the end of the folder's name. This will ensure that other people on the network will not see your shared folder when they browse through the information on the network.

How can I view all the folders that are shared on the network?

✔ You can use My Network Places to see the folders shared by your computer and other computers on the network. To browse through shared folders on a network, see page 362.

How can I view the comments for shared folders on a network?

✔ When viewing shared folders on the network, you can display the comments entered for the folders. In the My Network Places window, click the View menu and then select Details to display the comment for each shared folder.

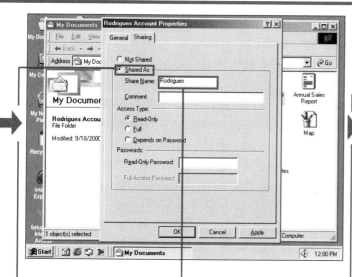

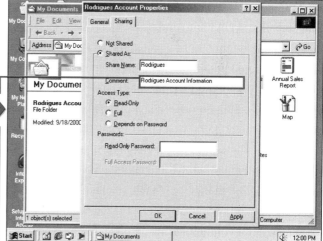

■4 Click Shared As to share the folder with other people on your network (○ changes to ⊙).

■ This area displays the name of the folder people will see on the network.

■5 To have the folder display a different name on the network, select the name and then type a new name.

■6 To enter a comment about the folder that people can see on the network, click this area and then type a comment.

CONTINUED

SHARE INFORMATION (CONTINUED)

You can give people on a network one of three types of access to a shared folder on your computer.

Read-Only access allows people on the network to read and copy files in a shared folder but not change, add or delete the files. Users must copy a shared file to their own computers before they can save changes to the file.

Full access allows people on the network to read, copy, change, add and delete shared files. You should not grant Full access to your main hard drive. If someone erases your computer's system files, you may not be able to use your computer.

Depends on Password access is a good way to share your folders. Windows allows you to set two passwords. One password assigns

Read-Only access to the folder. The other password gives people Full access to the folder.

Assigning a password to a shared folder on your computer prevents unauthorized people from accessing the folder. Assigning a password is optional when using the Read-Only and Full access types but is required when using the Depends on Password access type.

SHARE INFORMATION (CONTINUED)

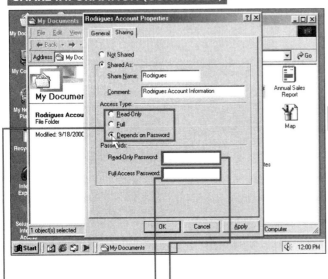

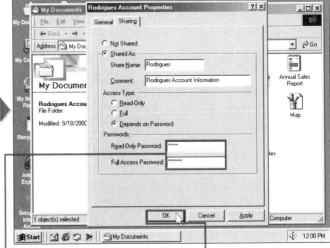

7 Click the type of access you want to assign to the folder (○ changes to ⊙).

8 If you selected Read-Only in step 7 and want to assign a password to the folder, click this area and type a password.

9 If you selected Full in step 7 and want to assign a password to the folder, click this area and type a password.

10 If you selected Depends on Password in step 7, perform steps 8 and 9 to enter both a Read-Only and Full access password.

Note: The passwords for Read-Only and Full access must be different.

11 Click OK to confirm your changes.

How do I stop sharing a folder?

✔ When you no longer want people on the network to have access to a folder, right-click the folder and then select Sharing. In the Properties dialog box that appears, click Not Shared.

What password should I use?

✔ The password you use should contain up to eight characters and consist of a mixture of letters and numbers. A password should not be a word in the dictionary and should not contain your name. When entering a password, a symbol (×) appears for each character you type to prevent others from seeing the password.

Can I find out if people are accessing my shared folder?

✔ Yes. Windows allows you to view information about a shared folder, such as who is accessing the folder and how many files they have open. For more information, see page 404.

How does sharing information affect the performance of my computer?

✔ When another computer accesses your shared information, the computer uses your computer to retrieve and then transfer the information through the network. Each time someone accesses your shared information, your computer may operate more slowly.

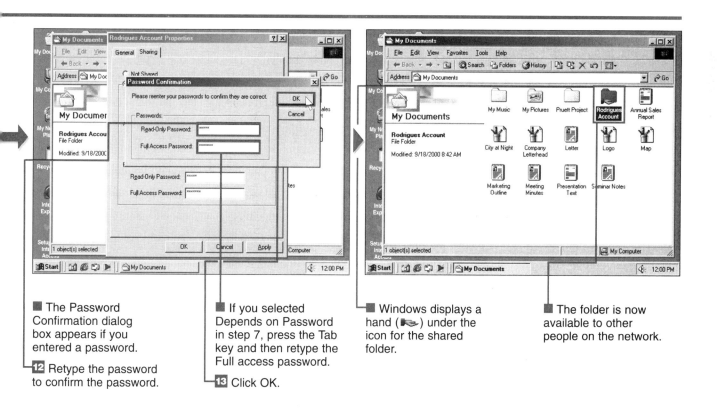

■ The Password Confirmation dialog box appears if you entered a password.

12 Retype the password to confirm the password.

■ If you selected Depends on Password in step 7, press the Tab key and then retype the Full access password.

13 Click OK.

■ Windows displays a hand (🖐) under the icon for the shared folder.

■ The folder is now available to other people on the network.

SHARE A PRINTER

You can share a printer connected to your computer with other people on a network. Sharing a printer allows others to use your printer to print documents.

When sharing a printer, you can assign a name and comment to the printer. Other people will be able to see the name and comment when they browse for shared printers on the network.

A descriptive name helps to identify your printer if there are several printers available on the network. You can use a comment to describe where your printer is located, such as "Dan's Office."

You can restrict access to a printer by assigning a password that people must enter to use your printer. Only people who know the password will be able to use your printer.

After you share your printer, you must make sure that both your computer and your printer are turned on and accessible when other people need the printer.

Before sharing your printer, your computer must be set up to share resources. To turn on file and printer sharing, see page 372.

Before sharing your printer, your computer must be set up to share resources. To turn on file and printer sharing, see page 372.

SHARE A PRINTER

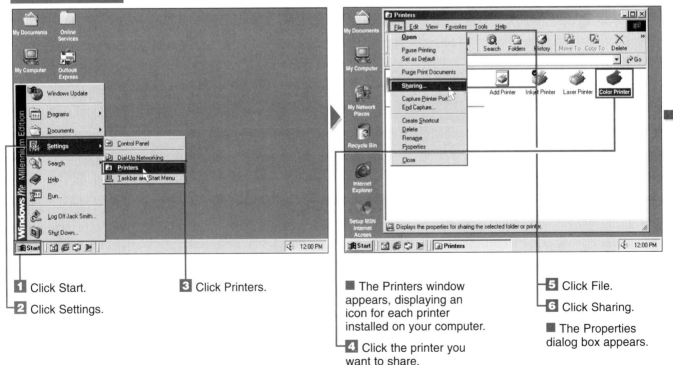

1 Click Start.

2 Click Settings.

3 Click Printers.

■ The Printers window appears, displaying an icon for each printer installed on your computer.

4 Click the printer you want to share.

5 Click File.

6 Click Sharing.

■ The Properties dialog box appears.

How do I stop sharing a printer?

✔ When you no longer want individuals on the network to use your printer, perform steps 1 to 6 on page 378 to display the Properties dialog box for the printer. Then click Not Shared and click OK.

Will sharing a printer affect my computer's performance?

✔ When people on the network send files to your printer, your computer temporarily stores the files before sending them to the printer. As a result, your computer may operate more slowly while other people are using your printer.

Can I hide my shared printer from other people on the network?

✔ In the Properties dialog box for the printer, type a dollar sign ($) at the end of the printer's name. This ensures that other people on the network will not see your printer when they browse for shared printers.

How do I connect to a shared printer on the network?

✔ If you want to use a shared printer on the network, you need to install the printer on your computer. See page 380 to install a printer located on the network.

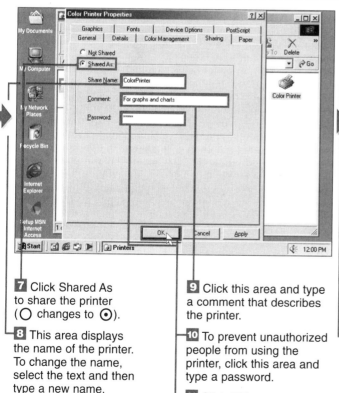

7 Click Shared As to share the printer (○ changes to ⊙).

8 This area displays the name of the printer. To change the name, select the text and then type a new name.

9 Click this area and type a comment that describes the printer.

10 To prevent unauthorized people from using the printer, click this area and type a password.

11 Click OK.

■ Your printer is now available to other computers on the network.

■ Windows displays a hand (👉) under the icon for the shared printer.

Note: If you entered a password in step 10, a dialog box appears, asking you to enter the password again to confirm the password. Type the password and then press the Enter key.

CONNECT TO A SHARED PRINTER

Before you can use a shared printer on your network, you need to set up a connection to the printer. You only need to set up a connection to a shared printer once.

Companies often connect printers to a network to help reduce printing costs. Everyone can then use the network printer instead of needing a printer connected to each computer.

Some printers on a network are connected to computers whose only function is to process print jobs for people on the network. This type of printer is known as a dedicated network printer. A dedicated network printer can be placed in a central part of an office to make the printer easy to access. Dedicated network printers often have additional capabilities that are not available on standard printers,

such as a job-sorting feature that organizes documents printed by many people.

When you set up a connection to a shared printer, you specify whether you will use the printer to print files from MS-DOS-based programs.

CONNECT TO A SHARED PRINTER

1 Click Start.

2 Click Settings.

3 Click Printers.

■ The Printers window appears, displaying an icon for each printer installed on your computer.

4 Double-click Add Printer to set up a connection to a shared printer on your network.

■ The Add Printer Wizard appears.

5 Click Next to continue.

Will the wizard require more information if I choose to print from MS-DOS-based programs?

✔ Yes. The wizard will ask you to specify which port you want the printer to use. Many MS-DOS-based programs must send information to a printer port, called an LPT port, to be able to print files.

Why does the printer take a long time to print my files?

✔ Most printers on a network are used by many people and may be used to print large files. These factors may slow down the printing of your files.

How do I delete a shared printer I no longer use on my computer?

✔ In the Printers window, click the printer you want to delete and then press the Delete key.

What is a print server?

✔ A print server is usually a computer that has a shared printer attached to it. A computer used for performing regular office tasks with a standard printer attached can be a print server. A print server can also be a computer that is used only for processing print jobs and is connected to several high-speed laser printers.

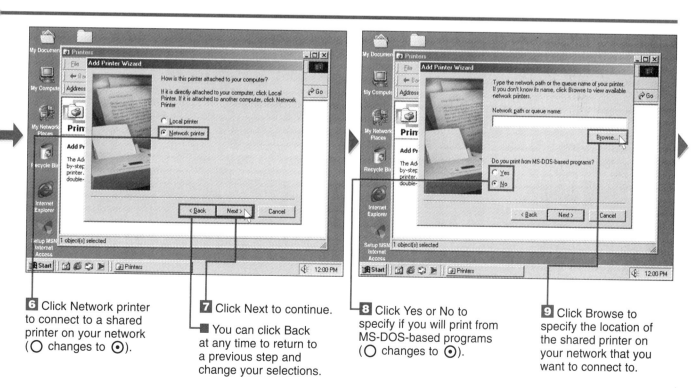

6 Click Network printer to connect to a shared printer on your network (○ changes to ⊙).

7 Click Next to continue.

■ You can click Back at any time to return to a previous step and change your selections.

8 Click Yes or No to specify if you will print from MS-DOS-based programs (○ changes to ⊙).

9 Click Browse to specify the location of the shared printer on your network that you want to connect to.

CONTINUED

CONNECT TO A SHARED PRINTER (CONTINUED)

The Add Printer Wizard allows you to locate the printer on your network that you want to connect to. Each item in the Browse for Printer dialog box displays a different icon to help you distinguish between the types of items on the network, such as workgroups (⚐), computers (🖳) and printers (🖨). You will need to locate first the workgroup and then the computer that shares the printer you want to connect to.

When connecting to a shared printer, you can specify a name for the printer. You may want to use a name that defines the location of the printer, such as "Dan's Office."

You can specify whether you want the shared printer to be your default printer. Files you print automatically print to the default printer. If you do not have other printers installed on your computer, the shared printer will automatically be set as the default printer.

Windows allows you to print a test page to confirm that the printer is working properly.

After you connect to a shared printer, an icon for the printer appears in the Printers window.

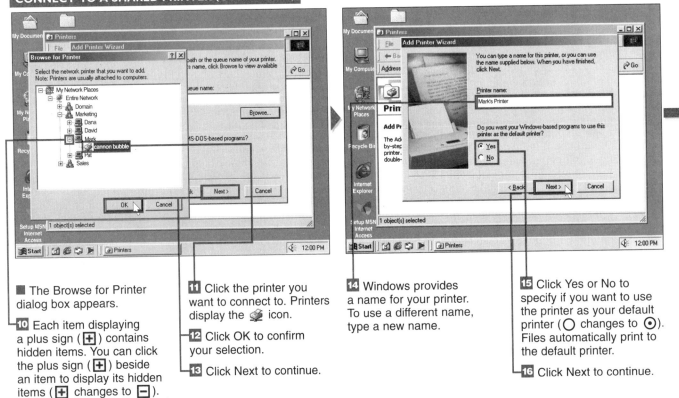

■ The Browse for Printer dialog box appears.

🔟 Each item displaying a plus sign (➕) contains hidden items. You can click the plus sign (➕) beside an item to display its hidden items (➕ changes to ➖).

11 Click the printer you want to connect to. Printers display the 🖨 icon.

12 Click OK to confirm your selection.

13 Click Next to continue.

14 Windows provides a name for your printer. To use a different name, type a new name.

15 Click Yes or No to specify if you want to use the printer as your default printer (○ changes to ⊙). Files automatically print to the default printer.

16 Click Next to continue.

Why am I unable to find the printer I want to connect to?

✔ If you want to connect to a printer that connects directly to the network, you may need to install a network service or protocol before you can access the printer. You should check with your network administrator to determine which network service or protocol you need to install. To install a network service, see page 394. To install a network protocol, see page 390.

Why does the wizard indicate that there is a print driver already installed for the printer?

✔ A print driver is software that enables Windows to communicate with your printer. When you set up a printer, Windows helps you select the correct print driver for your printer. If you previously set up a similar type of printer, the print driver needed for the printer you are currently setting up may already be installed. You can choose to keep the existing driver or install a new one for the current printer.

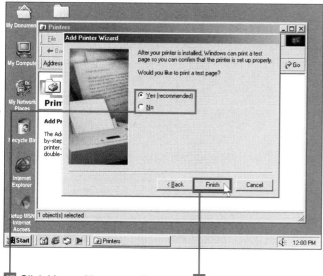

17 Click Yes or No to specify if you want to print a test page (○ changes to ⊙). A test page will confirm that the printer is set up properly.

18 Click Finish to complete the connection to the shared printer.

■ An icon for the printer appears in the Printers window.

■ The printer displays a check mark (✔) if you made the printer your default printer.

19 If you chose to print a test page, a dialog box appears, asking you to confirm the test page printed correctly. Click Yes if the page printed correctly.

20 Click ✕ to close the Printers window.

TURN ON USER-LEVEL ACCESS CONTROL

You can specify which people on your Microsoft network can have access to your shared resources. Resources you share can include information such as files and folders or devices such as a printer.

There are two ways you can control access to your shared resources–share-level access and user-level access. When you set up Windows to share resources, Windows uses share-level access control by default.

Share-level access control allows you to assign a password to each resource and give the password to specific people. Using share-level access control is suitable for small networks but can be unmanageable when there are many people who want to access your shared resources.

User-level access control is suitable for large networks and offers enhanced security. A computer, or server, on the network stores

a list of people on the network. You can use the list to determine who you want to be able to access your resources. You can grant access to specific individuals or entire groups. The people you select do not need to use a password to access your shared resources.

Contact your network administrator to find out if your network offers user-level access control.

TURN ON USER-LEVEL ACCESS CONTROL

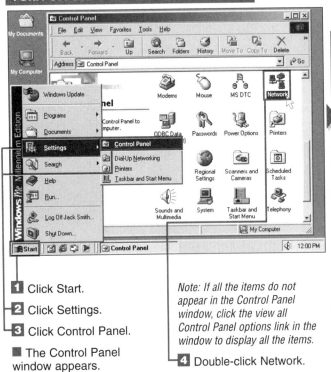

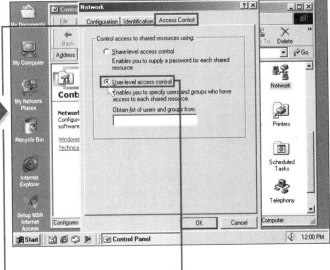

■ Click Start.

■ Click Settings.

■ Click Control Panel.

■ The Control Panel window appears.

Note: If all the items do not appear in the Control Panel window, click the view all Control Panel options link in the window to display all the items.

■ Double-click Network.

■ The Network dialog box appears.

■ Click the Access Control tab.

■ Click User-level access control to be able to select from a list of people to whom you want to grant access to your shared information (○ changes to ⊙).

Where is the list of users and groups stored?

✔ Your network administrator will set up the list of users and groups on a computer on your network. Once the list is set up, everyone connected to the network can access the list. Ask your network administrator for the name of the computer that stores the list of users.

After I turn on user-level access control, how do I share information on my computer?

✔ You will use the list of names on the network to specify who you want to have access to each folder and device you want to share on your computer. See page 388 to select the people you want to have access to your shared resources.

What will happen to the resources I previously shared after I turn on user-level access control?

✔ When you turn on user-level access control, all the resources you previously shared will no longer be shared. To once again share these resources, you will have to specify which users you want to access the resources.

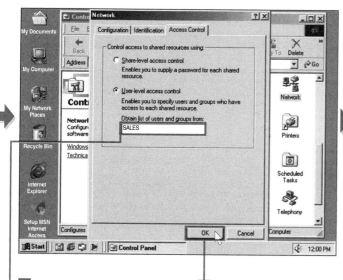

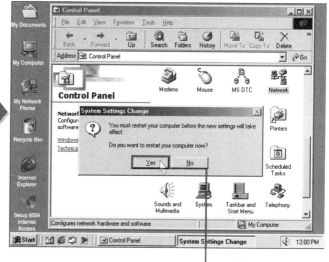

7 Click this area and then type the name of the computer or network domain that stores the list of people you want to use.

8 Click OK.

■ A dialog box may appear, stating that any folders you previously shared will no longer be shared. Click Yes to continue.

■ The System Settings Change dialog box appears, stating that Windows needs to restart your computer before the new settings will take effect.

9 Click Yes to restart your computer.

GRANT ACCESS TO SHARED INFORMATION

Y ou can share information on your computer with other people on your network.

If you set up your computer to use user-level access control, you can use a list of names on the network to determine who can access your shared information. You can grant access to specific individuals or entire groups. To

turn on user-level access control, see page 384.

You can choose the specific folders on your computer that you want to share. People you specify on the network will have access to all the folders and files within the shared folder and will be able to work with the files as if the files were stored on their own computers.

You can specify the name that the shared folder will display on the network. The name cannot contain more than 12 characters. Specifying a name for a shared folder will not change the name of the folder on your computer. You can also add a comment to a shared folder to help people on the network identify the folder.

GRANT ACCESS TO SHARED INFORMATION

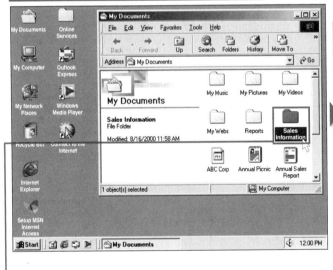

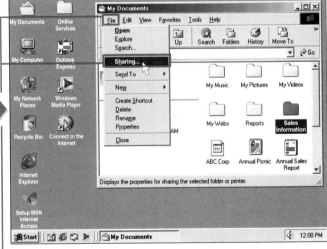

1 Click the folder you want to share with other people on your network.

2 Click File.

3 Click Sharing.

■ The Properties dialog box appears.

Can I grant access to a drive on my computer?

✔ Yes. You can grant access to your hard drive, floppy drive or CD-ROM drive as you would to a folder on your computer.

Can I grant access to my printer?

✔ Yes. You can grant access to your printer as you would to a folder on your computer. You can only grant access to a printer that is directly connected to your computer. To find the printer you want to share, click Start, select Settings and then click Printers. You can grant only full access to a shared printer.

How can I view the comments for shared folders on a network?

✔ When viewing shared folders on the network, you can display the comments entered for the folders. In the My Network Places window, click the View menu and then select Details to display the comment for each shared folder. For more information about My Network Places, see page 362.

How do I stop sharing a folder?

✔ When you no longer want people on the network to have access to a folder, right-click the folder and then select Sharing. In the Properties dialog box that appears, click Not Shared.

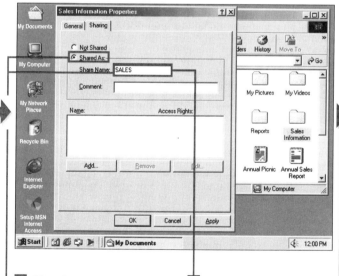

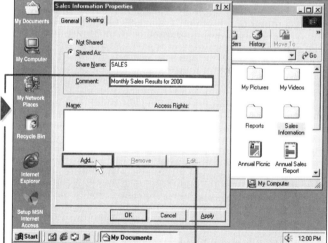

■4 Click Shared As to share the folder with other people on your network (○ changes to ⊙).

■ This area displays the name of the folder people will see on the network.

■5 To have the folder display a different name on the network, select the name and then type a new name.

■6 To enter a comment about the folder that people can see on the network, click this area and then type a comment.

■7 Click Add to specify which people on the network you want to grant access to the folder.

CONTINUED ▶

GRANT ACCESS TO SHARED INFORMATION (CONTINUED)

Y ou can specify every person and group on the network that you want to be able to access a shared folder. You can select a person, a group or several people and groups all at once.

There are three types of access you can grant. Read-Only access allows a person or group to read and copy shared files but not change, add or delete files.

Full access allows a person or group to read, copy, change, add and delete shared files. You should not grant Full access to your main hard drive. If someone erases your computer's system files, you may not be able to use your computer.

Custom access allows you to choose exactly what type of access you want to grant to people and groups. Granting custom access

gives you more control over the type of access people have to your folder. You should be very careful in selecting the types of access you grant. For example, if you grant Write to Files access to a person, you should also grant List Files access so the person can view the contents of the shared folder and Read Files access so the person can open files for editing.

GRANT ACCESS TO SHARED INFORMATION (CONTINUED)

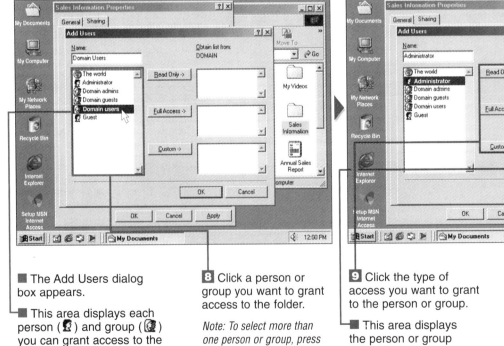

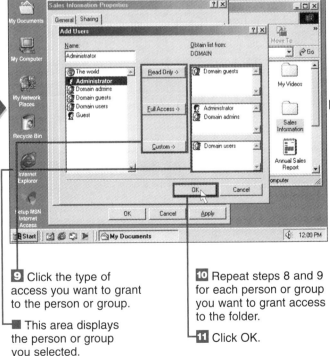

■ The Add Users dialog box appears.

■ This area displays each person (👤) and group (👥) you can grant access to the folder.

8 Click a person or group you want to grant access to the folder.

Note: To select more than one person or group, press and hold down the Ctrl key as you click each name.

9 Click the type of access you want to grant to the person or group.

■ This area displays the person or group you selected.

10 Repeat steps 8 and 9 for each person or group you want to grant access to the folder.

11 Click OK.

MASTER IT

What types of custom access rights can I grant?

✔ Read Files access allows people to read the files in the shared folder.

Write to Files access allows people to make changes to the files in the shared folder.

Create Files and Folders access allows people to create new files and folders in the shared folder.

Delete Files access allows people to delete files from the shared folder. This is a powerful type of access and should only be given to people you trust.

Change File Attributes access allows people to change the properties of files in the shared folder, such as making a file read-only.

List Files access allows people to view the contents of the shared folder.

Change Access Control access allows people to change the type of access granted to the shared folder.

How do I change the type of access I granted to a folder?

✔ Right-click the shared folder and then click Sharing. Select the person or group whose type of access you want to change. To grant a different type of access, click the Edit button and then select the type of access you want to grant. If you no longer want the person or group to have access to the folder, click the Remove button. A red X appears over the icon for the person or group.

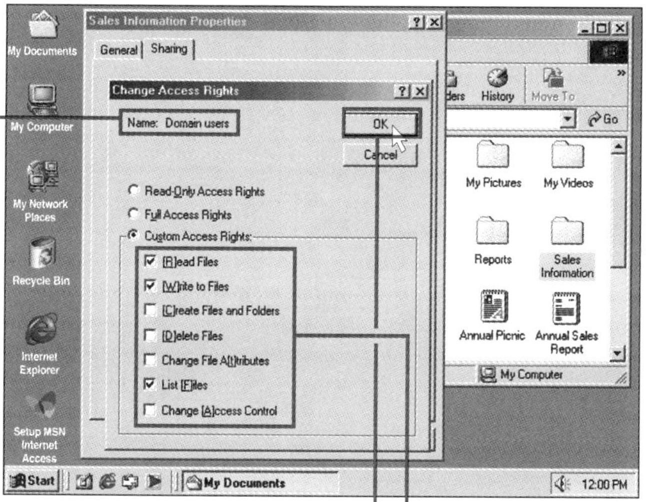

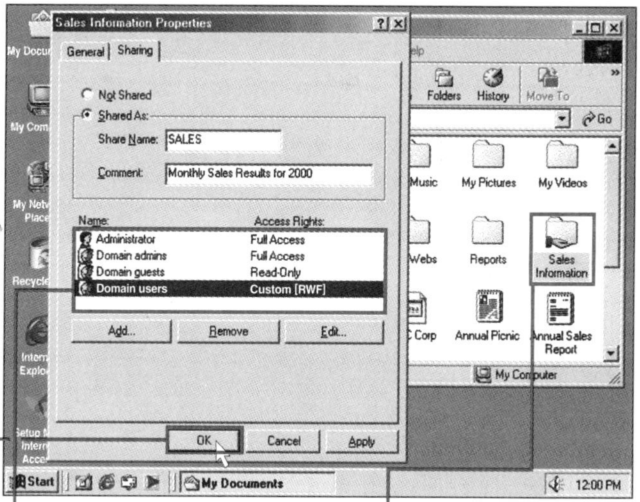

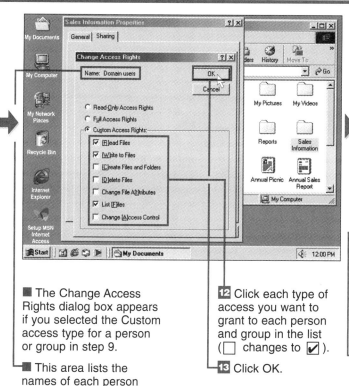

■ The Change Access Rights dialog box appears if you selected the Custom access type for a person or group in step 9.

■ This area lists the names of each person and group you granted custom access to.

12 Click each type of access you want to grant to each person and group in the list (☐ changes to ☑).

13 Click OK.

■ This area displays the name of each person and group you granted access to the folder.

14 Click OK to close the Properties dialog box.

■ Windows displays a hand ( ) under the icon for the shared folder.

■ The folder is now available to the people you specified on the network.

INSTALL A NETWORK PROTOCOL

Y ou may need to install a
network protocol to allow
your computer to exchange
information with other computers
and devices on a network. A
network protocol is a language,
or a set of rules, which determines
how computers on a network
communicate. A network protocol
determines how information
transfers from one computer
to another on a network.

All computers and devices on
a network must use the same
network protocol to communicate
with each other. For example, a
computer and a network printer
must use the same protocol before
the computer can successfully
send print jobs to the printer.

Many network protocols are
designed specifically for use with
one type of network. The type of
protocol you need to install is

determined by the type of network
you want to connect to. For
example, the protocol you need
to connect to a Novell network is
different than the protocol you
need to connect to a Windows
network.

When you install Windows, some
network protocols, such as TCP/IP,
are automatically installed on your
computer.

INSTALL A NETWORK PROTOCOL

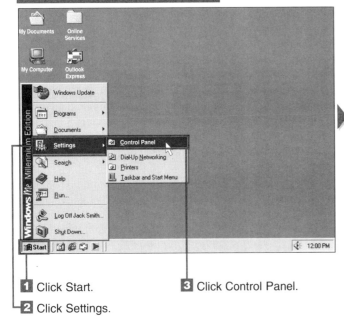

1 Click Start.

2 Click Settings.

3 Click Control Panel.

■ The Control Panel
window appears.

*Note: If all the items do not
appear in the Control Panel
window, click the view all
Control Panel options link
in the window to display all
the items.*

4 Double-click Network
to change the network
settings for your computer.

What are the most important features of a network protocol?

✔ A network protocol can check for errors when a computer transfers information over a network. Most network protocols can also correct errors by having a computer resend information.

The addressing feature lets a network protocol determine where to send information. The addressing feature also makes sure that information arrives at its intended destination.

Flow control helps regulate the flow of information so slower devices can process information they receive from faster devices on the network.

Can I remove a network protocol?

✔ Yes. You can remove a network protocol you no longer need. Removing unnecessary network protocols can improve the performance of your computer on the network. In the Network dialog box, click the network protocol you want to remove and then select the Remove button.

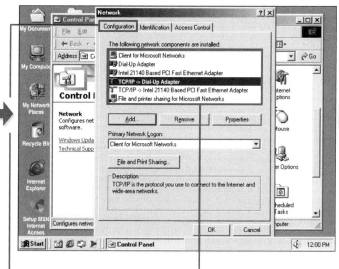

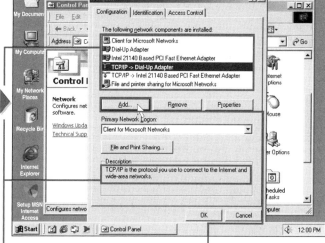

■ The Network dialog box appears.

5 Click the Configuration tab.

■ This area lists the network components installed on your computer. Network protocols display a cable symbol (🖧).

6 To display a description of a network protocol, click the name of the network protocol.

■ This area displays a description of the network protocol you selected.

7 Click Add to install a new network protocol.

CONTINUED ▶

INSTALL A NETWORK PROTOCOL
(CONTINUED)

When installing a network protocol, you must tell Windows which protocol you want to install. You may need to install a network protocol to exchange information with other computers on a network. You may also need to install a network protocol when the type of network you connect to changes.

There are many different types of network protocols you can add to a computer. A network can use several different types of network protocols at the same time. Any device that does not understand a protocol used by a computer on the network will simply ignore the information sent using that protocol.

Network protocols may be used for specific tasks on a network.

For example, the NetBEUI protocol may be used to control all the information transferred between computers on the network. The IPX/SPX protocol may be used to send documents to a network printer.

Windows includes support for the most popular types of network protocols, including IPX/SPX, NetBEUI and TCP/IP.

INSTALL A NETWORK PROTOCOL (CONTINUED)

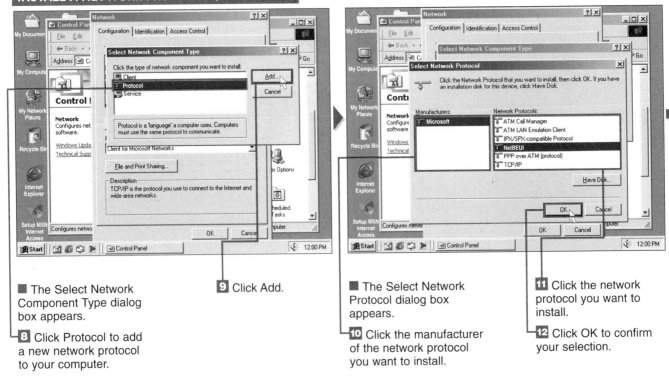

■ The Select Network Component Type dialog box appears.

8 Click Protocol to add a new network protocol to your computer.

9 Click Add.

■ The Select Network Protocol dialog box appears.

10 Click the manufacturer of the network protocol you want to install.

11 Click the network protocol you want to install.

12 Click OK to confirm your selection.

Which network protocols should I install?

✔ Internetwork Packet Exchange/Sequenced Packet Exchange (IPX/SPX) is a popular network protocol that allows computers on a Novell network to communicate. Many network devices, such as printers, also use the IPX/SPX network protocol.

NetBIOS Extended User Interface (NetBEUI) is a network protocol developed by IBM that allows computers on a Windows network to communicate. This network protocol is normally used on small networks.

Transmission Control Protocol/Internet Protocol (TCP/IP) is the network protocol that allows computers to connect to the Internet. Many network devices, such as printers, also use the TCP/IP network protocol.

What should I do if the network protocol I want to install does not appear in the list of protocols?

✔ If Windows does not provide the network protocol you want to install, you need to obtain the appropriate software from the manufacturer of the network operating system. In the Select Network Protocol dialog box, click the Have Disk button to use the disk provided by the manufacturer.

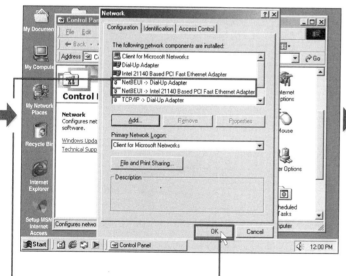

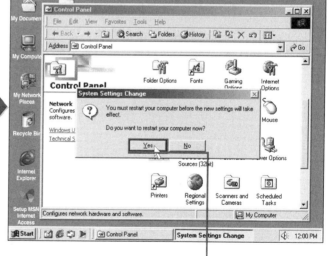

■ Windows adds the network protocol to the list of network components.

Note: If the protocol appears more than once in the list, Windows has set up the protocol to work with several devices, such as a modem and network interface card.

13 Click OK to install the network protocol.

■ The System Settings Change dialog box appears, stating that Windows needs to restart your computer before the new settings will take effect.

14 Click Yes to restart your computer.

INSTALL A NETWORK CLIENT

You can install a network client to control the flow of information between your computer and other computers on a network. A network client is software that lets your computer communicate with other computers on a network.

A network client determines whether information stays on your computer or is sent to another computer or device on the network. For example, when you send a document to a printer, the network client determines if the document will print on a printer attached to your computer or if it should be sent to a printer on the network.

A network client is sometimes referred to as a redirector because the client determines where information is sent.

A network client also allows a computer to communicate with a server on a network. A server is a computer that supplies information, such as files, to other computers on a network.

INSTALL A NETWORK CLIENT

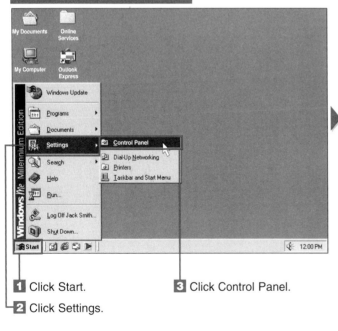

1 Click Start.

2 Click Settings.

3 Click Control Panel.

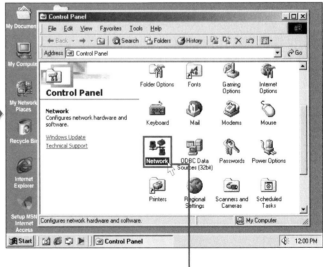

■ The Control Panel window appears.

Note: If all the items do not appear in the Control Panel window, click the view all Control Panel options link in the window to display all the items.

4 Double-click Network to change the network settings for your computer.

Why is there a network client already installed on my computer?

✔ When you installed Windows on your computer, the Client for Microsoft Networks was installed automatically. This client lets you connect to other Microsoft Windows computers and servers.

Can I install more than one network client?

✔ Yes. Installing more than one network client allows you to connect to more than one type of network. For example, you could connect to a Microsoft network to access a database and a Novell NetWare network to access files and printers.

Can I remove a network client I no longer need?

✔ Yes. Removing unnecessary network clients can improve the performance of your computer on the network. In the Network dialog box, click the network client you want to remove and then select the Remove button.

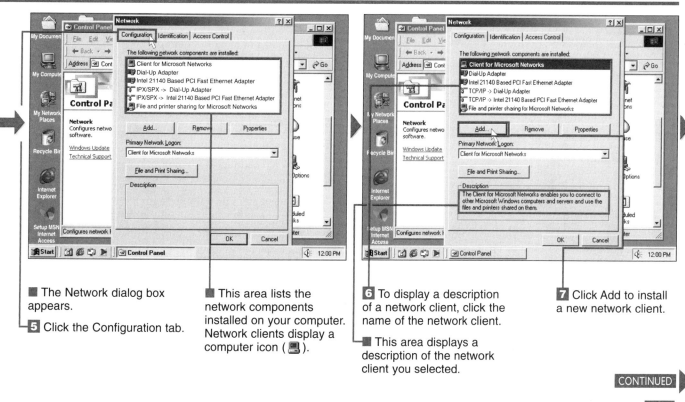

■ The Network dialog box appears.

■5 Click the Configuration tab.

■ This area lists the network components installed on your computer. Network clients display a computer icon (🖳).

■6 To display a description of a network client, click the name of the network client.

■ This area displays a description of the network client you selected.

■7 Click Add to install a new network client.

CONTINUED ▶

INSTALL A NETWORK CLIENT
(CONTINUED)

When installing a network client, you must tell Windows the manufacturer of the network client and the type of client you want to install. Windows includes client software for the most popular types of networks, including Microsoft and Novell NetWare networks.

The type of network you want to connect to determines the network client you need to install. You should check with your network administrator to confirm that any new client software you want to install will work with your network.

When installing a network client, you will need to restart your

computer before the new settings will take effect. Make sure you close any open programs before restarting your computer to avoid losing any work.

After you have installed the network client for each type of network you want to connect to, you can access information and devices on each network.

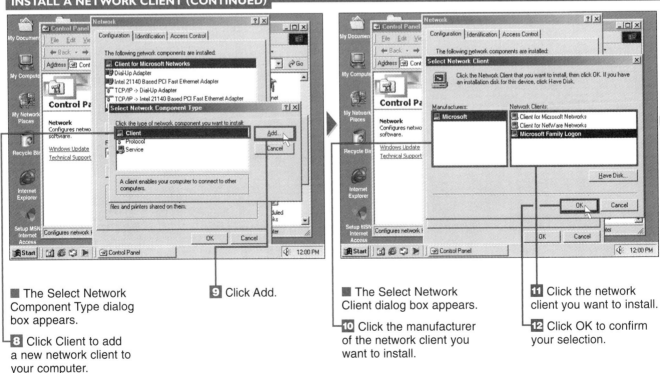

INSTALL A NETWORK CLIENT (CONTINUED)

■ The Select Network Component Type dialog box appears.

■8 Click Client to add a new network client to your computer.

■9 Click Add.

■ The Select Network Client dialog box appears.

■10 Click the manufacturer of the network client you want to install.

■11 Click the network client you want to install.

■12 Click OK to confirm your selection.

How do I add names to the list of people who have access to the computer for the Microsoft Family Logon client?

✔ You must first change the primary network client to the Microsoft Family Logon client. To change the primary network client, see page 398. To add a name to the list that appears each time Windows starts, create a new user on your computer. See page 218.

What should I do if the network client I want to install does not appear in the list of clients?

✔ If Windows does not provide the network client you want to install, you need to obtain the appropriate software from the manufacturer of the network operating system. In the Select Network Client dialog box, click the Have Disk button to use the disk provided by the manufacturer.

Which network client should I install?

✔ The Client for Microsoft Networks allows you to connect to other Windows computers and servers. The Client for NetWare Networks allows you to connect to Novell NetWare servers.

The Microsoft Family Logon client displays a list of people who have access to the computer each time Windows starts. This is useful if you share your computer with several people.

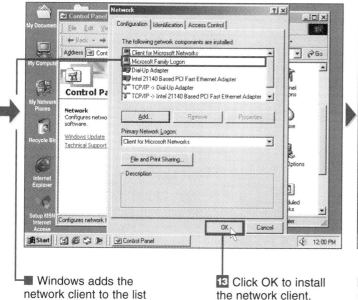

■ Windows adds the network client to the list of network components.

13 Click OK to install the network client.

■ The System Settings Change dialog box appears, stating that Windows needs to restart your computer before the new settings will take effect.

14 Click Yes to restart your computer.

SELECT A PRIMARY NETWORK CLIENT

Windows allows you to choose which network client you want to use as the primary, or main, network client. A network client is software that allows your computer to communicate with a specific network operating system.

When you start Windows, you need to enter logon information, such as a password. The primary network client determines which network

will check your logon information. When entered correctly, this information allows you to use the network.

The network clients installed on your computer depend on the type of networks you want to connect to, such as a Microsoft or Novell NetWare network. You must have a network client installed on your computer for each type of network you want to connect to.

When selecting the primary network client, you should choose the client for the network you use most often. For example, if you frequently use a Novell NetWare network to access files and printers and you occasionally use a Microsoft network to access a database, you should set the Novell NetWare client as your primary client.

SELECT A PRIMARY NETWORK CLIENT

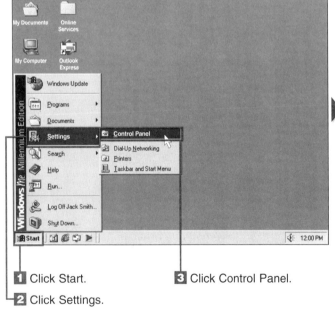

1 Click Start.

2 Click Settings.

3 Click Control Panel.

■ The Control Panel window appears.

Note: If all the items do not appear in the Control Panel window, click the view all Control Panel options link in the window to display all the items.

4 Double-click Network.

Why would I select the Windows Logon option when selecting a primary network client?

✔ The Windows Logon option allows you to log on to Windows. This option will not log you on to any networks. You may find the Windows Logon option useful when you are using a computer that is not connected to a network, such as when using a portable computer away from the office.

When would I need to change my primary network client?

✔ Once you select your primary network client, you will rarely need to change the client. If the network you usually connect to changes or you will be using another network for more than a few days, you may want to change your primary network client.

Why can't I find the client I want to use as the primary network client?

✔ If the client you want to use as the primary network client is not displayed in the Network dialog box, you must install the network client on your computer. To install a network client, see page 394.

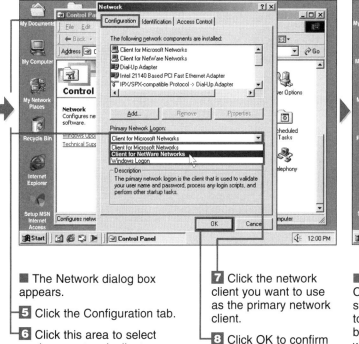

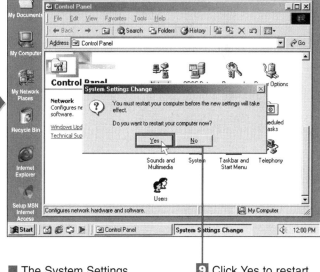

■ The Network dialog box appears.

5 Click the Configuration tab.

6 Click this area to select a primary network client.

7 Click the network client you want to use as the primary network client.

8 Click OK to confirm your change.

■ The System Settings Change dialog box appears, stating that Windows needs to restart your computer before the new settings will take effect.

9 Click Yes to restart your computer.

CHANGE SETTINGS FOR THE MICROSOFT NETWORKS CLIENT

Y ou can change the settings for the Microsoft Networks client to customize the way your computer connects to a network.

You can have Windows automatically connect to your Windows network each time you log on to Windows. You need to tell Windows the name of the domain or individual server you want to connect to. When you

log on to a network, the domain or server verifies your logon information before granting you access to the network. If you do not know the name of the domain or server, ask your network administrator.

Windows allows you to choose between a quick and a regular logon option to connect to your network. Most computers that connect to a network use the

regular logon option. If you plan to only use a few resources on the network, you may want to use the quick logon option.

If the Microsoft Networks client is not installed on your computer, you can install the client. See page 398 for information about installing a network client.

CHANGE SETTINGS FOR THE MICROSOFT NETWORKS CLIENT

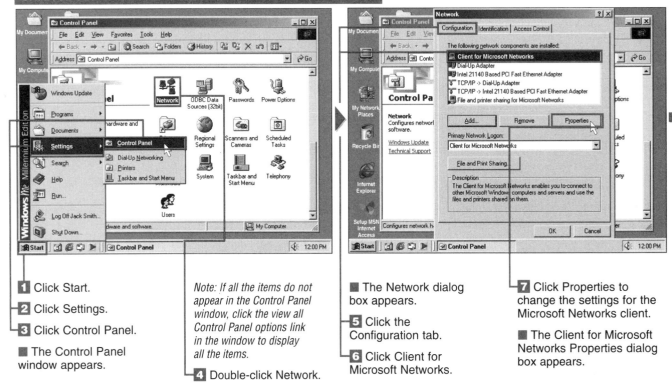

1 Click Start.

2 Click Settings.

3 Click Control Panel.

■ The Control Panel window appears.

Note: If all the items do not appear in the Control Panel window, click the view all Control Panel options link in the window to display all the items.

4 Double-click Network.

■ The Network dialog box appears.

5 Click the Configuration tab.

6 Click Client for Microsoft Networks.

7 Click Properties to change the settings for the Microsoft Networks client.

■ The Client for Microsoft Networks Properties dialog box appears.

What is the difference between a quick and a regular logon?

✔ If you choose a quick logon, Windows logs you onto the network but will only connect you to resources on the network when you access them. The quick logon option is useful if you plan to only use a few resources on the network every time you connect to the network. A regular logon connects you to each resource on the network every time you start Windows. You will immediately know if each resource is available, but this option increases the time it takes to log on to the network.

What is a domain?

✔ A domain is a name given to a collection of computers on a network. For example, a domain can consist of all computers in a particular department of a company. If a large network consists of many smaller networks connected together, each of the smaller networks is usually a different domain.

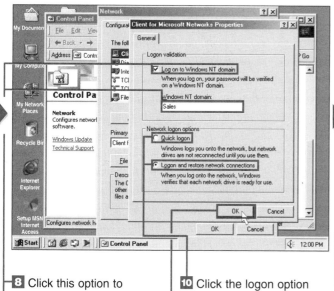

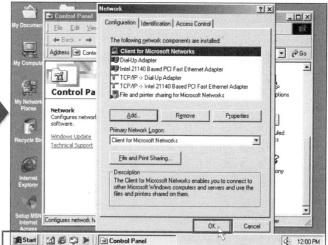

■8 Click this option to connect to a Windows network when you log on to Windows (☐ changes to ☑).

■9 Click this area and then type the name of the domain or server you want to connect to.

■10 Click the logon option you want to use each time you connect to the network (○ changes to ◉).

■11 Click OK to confirm your changes.

■12 Click OK to close the Network dialog box.

■ A dialog box appears, stating that Windows needs to restart your computer before the new settings will take effect. Click Yes to restart your computer.

CHANGE SETTINGS FOR THE NETWARE NETWORKS CLIENT

You may need to adjust the settings for your NetWare Networks client to customize the way your computer connects to a Novell network. Before you can adjust the settings, the NetWare Networks client must be installed on your computer. To install a network client, see page 394.

A Novell NetWare network can consist of many NetWare servers, which store information that people on the network can access. When changing the settings for the

NetWare Networks client, you need to enter the name of the server you want to connect to each time you log on to the network. This server will give you access to the network. If you do not know the name of the server, ask your network administrator.

You can choose the drive letter Windows will use for your first mapped network drive. This is useful if you use a removable drive that uses a certain letter.

You can also have Windows automatically run logon scripts when you connect to the network. A logon script is a series of instructions that Windows performs when you successfully connect to a NetWare server. For example, logon scripts can run a virus program to check your computer for viruses.

CHANGE SETTINGS FOR THE NETWARE NETWORKS CLIENT

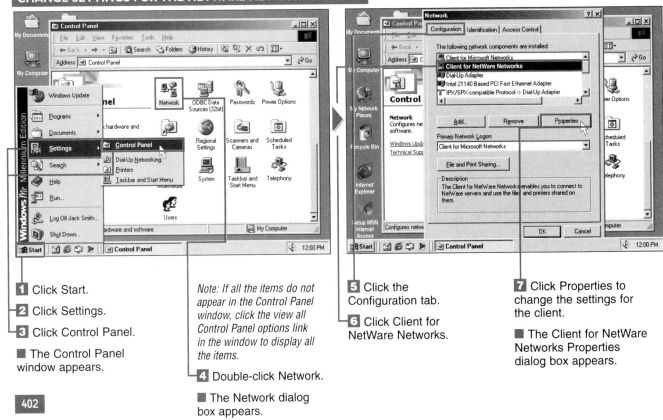

1 Click Start.

2 Click Settings.

3 Click Control Panel.

■ The Control Panel window appears.

Note: If all the items do not appear in the Control Panel window, click the view all Control Panel options link in the window to display all the items.

4 Double-click Network.

■ The Network dialog box appears.

5 Click the Configuration tab.

6 Click Client for NetWare Networks.

7 Click Properties to change the settings for the client.

■ The Client for NetWare Networks Properties dialog box appears.

What is a preferred server?

✔ A preferred server is the Novell NetWare server you connect to each time you log on to the network. The preferred server will check your user name and password before granting you access to the network.

Can I change the logon scripts?

✔ Only the network administrator can change the logon scripts. Novell NetWare logon scripts are text files that are stored on the network. Logon scripts are usually written and installed by the network administrator.

What is a mapped network drive?

✔ A mapped network drive provides a quick way to access information stored on a network. Mapping a network drive assigns a drive letter to a resource on the network and places an icon for the resource in the My Computer window. You can work with the information in the resource as if the information were stored on your own computer. See page 366 to create a mapped network drive.

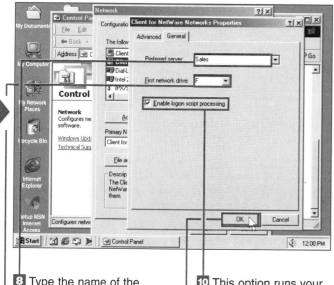

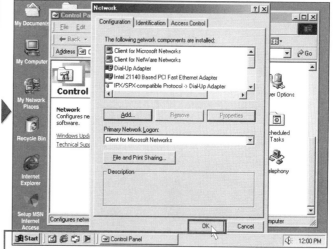

8 Type the name of the server you want to connect to each time you log on to the network.

9 This area displays the drive letter Windows uses for your first mapped network drive. You can click this area to select another letter.

10 This option runs your logon script when you connect to the network. You can click the option to turn the option on (✔) or off (☐).

11 Click OK.

12 Click OK to close the Network dialog box.

■ A dialog box will appear, stating that Windows needs to restart your computer before the new settings will take effect. Click Yes to restart your computer.

MONITOR SHARED RESOURCES USING NET WATCHER

You can use Net Watcher to monitor the shared resources on your computer.

Net Watcher can display information about the people currently accessing your computer, such as the name of each person, the number of files each person has open and the amount of time each person has been connected. You can determine which folders and files on your computer each

person is accessing. If you do not want certain people accessing files on your computer, you can restrict access to your shared information by using passwords.

Net Watcher can display a list of all the folders and printers you have shared on your computer. You can view details about the shared resources, such as the type of access assigned to each resource. Net Watcher can also

display a list of shared files on your computer that are currently being accessed by other people.

Monitoring how many people access your shared resources helps you determine how sharing affects the performance of your computer. If too many people access the information on your computer, your computer may operate slower.

MONITOR SHARED RESOURCES USING NET WATCHER

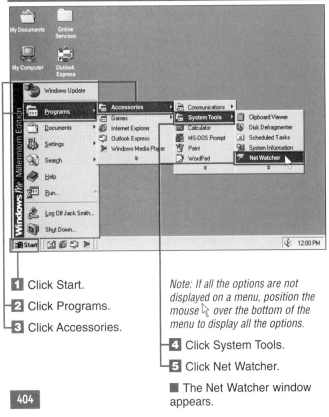

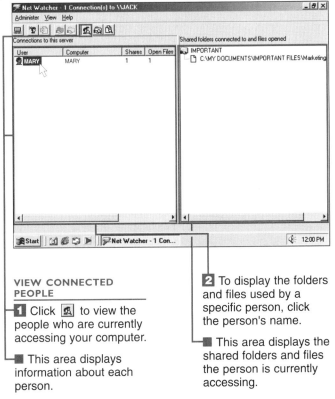

■1 Click Start.

■2 Click Programs.

■3 Click Accessories.

Note: If all the options are not displayed on a menu, position the mouse ℜ over the bottom of the menu to display all the options.

■4 Click System Tools.

■5 Click Net Watcher.

■ The Net Watcher window appears.

VIEW CONNECTED PEOPLE

■1 Click 🔲 to view the people who are currently accessing your computer.

■ This area displays information about each person.

■2 To display the folders and files used by a specific person, click the person's name.

■ This area displays the shared folders and files the person is currently accessing.

Why isn't Net Watcher on my Start menu?

✔ You may need to install the Net Watcher component on your computer. Net Watcher is located in the System Tools category. To add Windows components, see page 538.

Can I close a file currently being accessed on my computer?

✔ Yes. If you want to work with a file that another person has open, you can close the file. Click 🔲 in the Net Watcher window to display the files being accessed. Select the file you want to close and then click 🔲. The person using the file may lose data.

Can I disconnect a person who is accessing my computer?

✔ Yes. If you need to use a program that requires a lot of resources, you can disconnect a person to free up your computer's resources. Click 🔲 in the Net Watcher window to display the people accessing your computer. Select the name of the person you want to disconnect and then click 🔲.

Before you disconnect a person, you should give the person time to close any open files to prevent them from losing data.

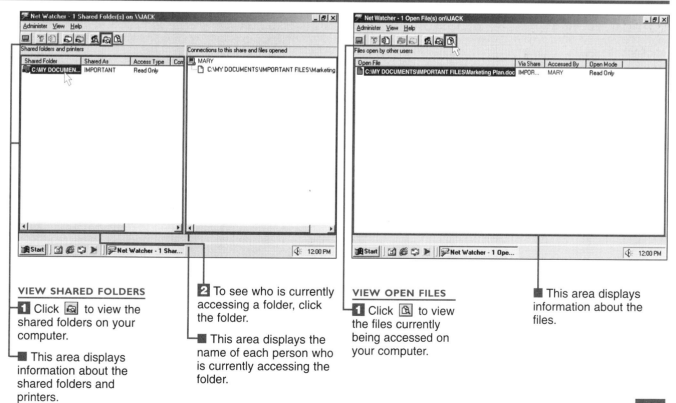

VIEW SHARED FOLDERS

■1 Click 🔲 to view the shared folders on your computer.

■ This area displays information about the shared folders and printers.

■2 To see who is currently accessing a folder, click the folder.

■ This area displays the name of each person who is currently accessing the folder.

VIEW OPEN FILES

■1 Click 🔲 to view the files currently being accessed on your computer.

■ This area displays information about the files.

SET UP A HOME NETWORK

If you have more than one computer at home, you can set up a network to share information and resources among the computers.

Before setting up a home network, you must install a Network Interface Card (NIC) in each computer you want to connect to the network. NICs control the flow of information between the network and the computers. Cables are required to physically connect each computer to the network. Your network may also require a hub, which provides a central location where the cables on the network meet. If you want computers on the network to be able to connect to the Internet, one computer will also need a device, such as a modem, to connect to the Internet.

One computer on the network must have Windows Me installed. The other computers on the network can use Windows 95, Windows 98 or Windows Me.

The Home Networking Wizard helps you set up a computer on your home network. You must run the wizard on each computer you want to set up on the network.

You can set up a computer on your home network to share its connection to the Internet with other computers. This is called Internet Connection Sharing (ICS).

SET UP A HOME NETWORK

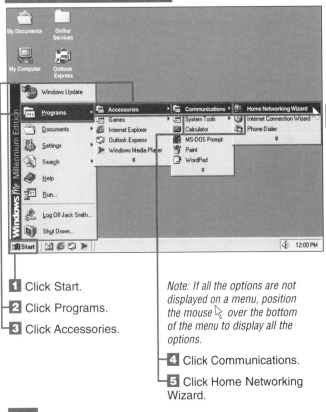

1 Click Start.

2 Click Programs.

3 Click Accessories.

Note: If all the options are not displayed on a menu, position the mouse ⌖ over the bottom of the menu to display all the options.

4 Click Communications.

5 Click Home Networking Wizard.

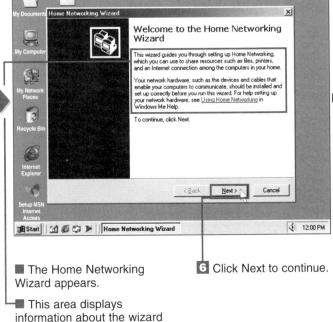

■ The Home Networking Wizard appears.

■ This area displays information about the wizard as well as a reminder that your network hardware should be installed and set up correctly before you use the wizard.

6 Click Next to continue.

What should I consider when sharing an Internet connection on my network?

✔ Your Internet Service Provider (ISP) may not allow more than one computer on your network to connect to the Internet through a single Internet connection. You can contact your ISP for more information.

Why does the Home Networking Wizard display a Setup options screen?

✔ You have already used the Home Networking Wizard to set up this computer on the network. The Setup options screen allows you to change the settings for this computer or create a floppy disk to set up other computers on the network. Click the option you want to use (○ changes to ⊙) and then click the Next button.

I need help setting up my home network. What can I do?

✔ Windows provides a step-by-step process that you can use if you need help setting up a home network. Click the Start button and select Help. In the Help and Support window, click the Home Networking link. In the Help & Information area, click the Using Home Networking link and then follow the instructions in the right side of the window.

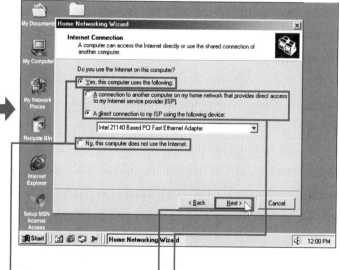

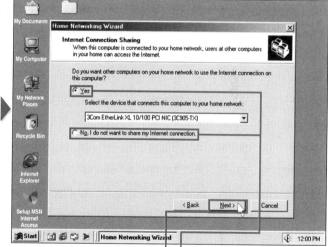

7 Click Yes or No to specify if you want to connect to the Internet from this computer (○ changes to ⊙).

8 If you selected Yes in step 7, click an option to specify how you want to connect to the Internet (○ changes to ⊙). You can connect to the Internet through a shared connection on another computer or directly through this computer.

9 Click Next to continue.

■ This screen appears if you chose to connect to the Internet directly through this computer.

Note: If this screen does not appear, skip to step 12 on page 408.

10 Click Yes or No to specify if you want to share your connection to the Internet with other computers on your network (○ changes to ⊙).

11 Click Next to continue.

CONTINUED

SET UP A HOME NETWORK
(CONTINUED)

When setting up a computer on your home network, you must specify a computer name and workgroup name for the computer.

A computer name identifies a computer on your network and can be a location, such as "den," or a person's name, such as "Pat." Each computer on a network must have a different name. A workgroup name identifies the group of

computers on your network. Windows recommends you use the default name MSHOME, but you can specify your own workgroup name. Each computer on a home network must have the same workgroup name.

The Home Networking Wizard allows you to share the My Documents folder on your computer with other people on your network. The My Documents folder is located on your desktop

and provides a convenient place to store your files. Many programs automatically store files you save in the My Documents folder. You can assign a password to the folder. Assigning a password to the My Documents folder will prevent unauthorized people from accessing the folder.

If you have a printer connected to your computer, you can also share the printer with other people on the network.

SET UP A HOME NETWORK (CONTINUED)

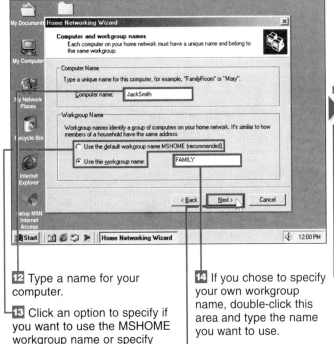

■12 Type a name for your computer.

■13 Click an option to specify if you want to use the MSHOME workgroup name or specify your own workgroup name (○ changes to ⊙).

■14 If you chose to specify your own workgroup name, double-click this area and type the name you want to use.

■15 Click Next to continue.

■16 This option allows you to share the My Documents folder on your computer with other people on your network. Click this option if you want to share the folder (☐ changes to ☑).

■17 If you chose to share the My Documents folder, click Password to assign a password to the folder that will prevent unauthorized people from accessing the folder.

Why does the wizard ask if I want my computer to connect to the Internet when another computer on the network needs access?

✔ If you chose to share your Internet connection and you have not saved the password you use to connect to the Internet, a screen appears allowing your computer to connect to the Internet automatically when another computer on the network needs access. To automatically connect to the Internet, click the Yes, connect to the Internet automatically option (○ changes to ⦿). Select the No option if you want to enter your password and connect your computer to the Internet before another computer can access the Internet.

Can I share other folders on my computer?

✔ Yes. After you complete the Home Networking Wizard, you can share other folders on your computer. To share other folders on your computer, see page 374.

I no longer want to share my printer on my home network. What can I do?

✔ If you no longer want people on the network to access your printer, you can stop sharing the printer. Click the Start button, choose Settings and then click Printers. In the Printers window, select the printer you want to stop sharing. Choose the File menu and then click Sharing. In the Properties dialog box, click Not Shared.

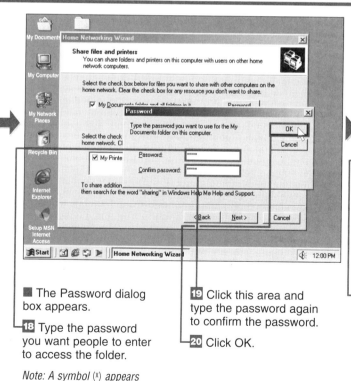

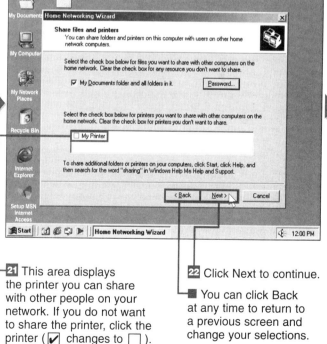

■ The Password dialog box appears.

18 Type the password you want people to enter to access the folder.

Note: A symbol (x) appears for each character that you type to prevent other people from seeing the password.

19 Click this area and type the password again to confirm the password.

20 Click OK.

21 This area displays the printer you can share with other people on your network. If you do not want to share the printer, click the printer (☑ changes to ☐).

22 Click Next to continue.

■ You can click Back at any time to return to a previous screen and change your selections.

CONTINUED ▶

SET UP A HOME NETWORK
(CONTINUED)

You can create a Home Networking Setup disk that will allow you to set up other computers that use Windows 95 or Windows 98 on your home network.

After you have completed the Home Networking Wizard, Windows may ask you to restart your computer. You must restart your computer to ensure that the changes you specified in the wizard take effect.

You must run the wizard on each computer you want to set up on your home network. If you do not run the wizard on every computer, the network may not work properly.

If you are using Internet Connection Sharing (ICS), you may have to adjust settings in programs such as Internet Explorer and Outlook Express to ensure the programs will connect to the Internet using the network.

Once you have set up a home network, you can access shared resources on the network. You can use My Network Places to see the resources shared by your computer and other computers on the network. To browse through shared resources on a network, see page 362.

SET UP A HOME NETWORK (CONTINUED)

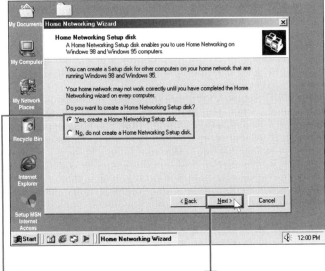

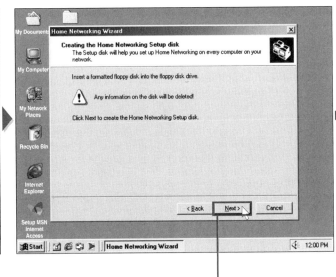

23 Click Yes or No to specify if you want to create a Home Networking Setup disk (○ changes to ⊙). You can use the disk to set up other computers that use Windows 95 or Windows 98 on your home network.

24 Click Next to continue.

Note: If you chose No in step 23, skip to step 28.

25 Insert a formatted floppy disk into your floppy drive. Windows will delete any information on the floppy disk.

26 Click Next to create the Home Networking Setup disk.

How do I set up a Windows 95 or Windows 98 computer on my home network?

✔ After you create a Home Networking Setup disk on a Windows Me computer, insert the disk into a Windows 95 or Windows 98 computer. Display the contents of the floppy disk and then double-click the Setup file to start the Home Networking Wizard. You can then follow the instructions on your screen to set up the computer on your home network.

What can I do if the home network I set up does not work properly?

✔ You can use the Home Networking Troubleshooter to solve problems you may be experiencing with your network. Click the Start button and select Help. In the top right corner of the Help and Support window, click the area below Search and type **home networking troubleshooter**. Then press the Enter key. A link appears for the Home Networking Troubleshooter. Click the link and then follow the instructions that appear in the right side of the window.

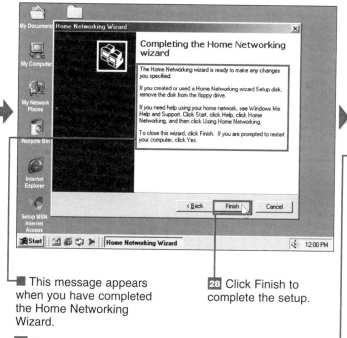

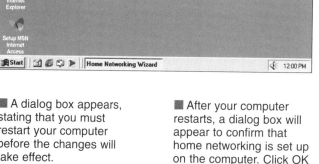

■ This message appears when you have completed the Home Networking Wizard.

27 If you created a Home Networking Setup disk, remove the floppy disk from your floppy drive.

28 Click Finish to complete the setup.

■ A dialog box appears, stating that you must restart your computer before the changes will take effect.

29 Click Yes to restart your computer.

■ After your computer restarts, a dialog box will appear to confirm that home networking is set up on the computer. Click OK to close the dialog box.

START MSN MESSENGER SERVICE

You can use MSN Messenger Service to see when your friends are online, send instant messages, call a computer and more.

The first time you start MSN Messenger Service, a wizard appears to help you set up the service.

You must have a Microsoft Passport to use MSN Messenger

Service. A Microsoft Passport is made up of a sign-in name and password. If you have a Hotmail account, you already have a Passport. If you do not have a Passport, you can obtain one free of charge when you set up MSN Messenger Service.

You use your sign-in name and password to sign in to MSN Messenger Service. You can have

Windows remember your sign-in name and password so you do not have to enter the information each time you sign in.

When a newer version of MSN Messenger Service is available, you will be notified. You can install the newer version on your computer to ensure you have access to the most up-to-date features the service has to offer.

START MSN MESSENGER SERVICE

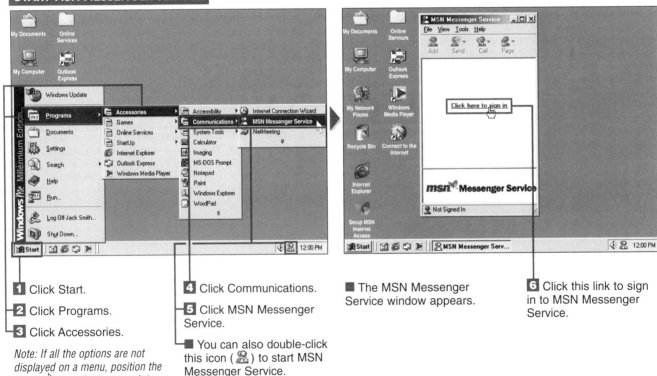

1 Click Start.

2 Click Programs.

3 Click Accessories.

Note: If all the options are not displayed on a menu, position the mouse ⬚ over the bottom of the menu to display all the options.

4 Click Communications.

5 Click MSN Messenger Service.

■ You can also double-click this icon (🧍) to start MSN Messenger Service.

■ The MSN Messenger Service window appears.

6 Click this link to sign in to MSN Messenger Service.

Why can't I find the MSN Messenger Service command on the Start menu?

✓ If you have installed a newer version of the service, the MSN Messenger Service command may have moved to another location on the Start menu. Choose the Start button, select Programs and then click MSN Messenger Service.

I cannot sign in because I forget my password. What can I do?

✓ If you forget your password, you can specify a new password. In the Sign in to Passport dialog box, click the Forgot your password? button and then follow the instructions on your screen.

Can I remove the MSN Messenger Service window from my screen?

✓ Yes. To remove the MSN Messenger Service window from your screen, but remain signed in to the service, click ⊠. A dialog box appears stating that the service will continue to run.

I am finished using MSN Messenger Service. How do I sign out?

✓ If you no longer want to use the service, you can sign out of the service without logging off the Internet. In the MSN Messenger Service window, choose the File menu and select Sign out.

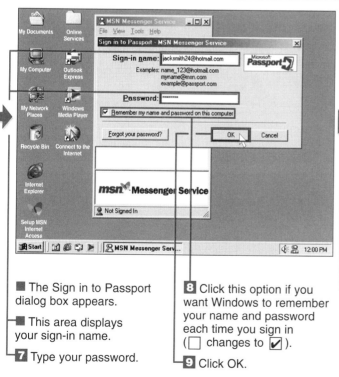

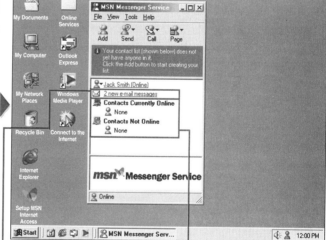

■ The Sign in to Passport dialog box appears.

■ This area displays your sign-in name.

7 Type your password.

8 Click this option if you want Windows to remember your name and password each time you sign in (☐ changes to ☑).

9 Click OK.

Note: If you are currently not connected to the Internet, a dialog box appears that allows you to connect.

■ This area displays the number of new e-mail messages you have received.

■ After you add contacts to your list, this area displays the contacts that are currently online and the contacts that are currently not online.

Note: To add contacts to your list, see page 414.

ADD A CONTACT TO YOUR LIST

You can add people to your contact list to see when they are online and quickly send them messages. MSN Messenger Service allows you to add up to 75 people to your contact list.

You need to specify the e-mail address of the person you want to add to your contact list. MSN Messenger Service uses the

e-mail address to determine if the person has a Microsoft Passport. If the person does not have a Passport, MSN Messenger Service allows you to send the person an e-mail message inviting them to obtain a Passport and install MSN Messenger Service. You cannot add the person to your contact list until they have obtained a Passport.

After you add a person to your contact list, MSN Messenger Service notifies the person and allows the person to choose whether they want you to see when they are online and be able to contact them.

ADD A CONTACT TO YOUR LIST

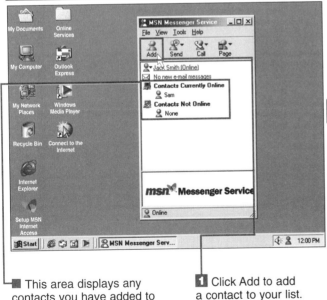

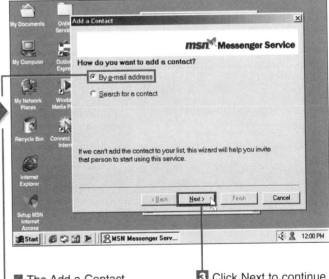

■ This area displays any contacts you have added to your list. You can see the contacts that are currently online and the contacts that are currently not online.

1 Click Add to add a contact to your list.

■ The Add a Contact wizard appears.

2 Click this option to add a contact by specifying the person's e-mail address (○ changes to ⊙).

3 Click Next to continue.

What can I do if I don't know the e-mail address of the person I want to add to my contact list?

✔ You can have MSN Messenger Service search for the person. When you start the Add a Contact wizard, click the Search for a contact option and click Next. Enter the information for the person you want to find and click Next. Select the name of the person you want to add to your contact list and click Next. For privacy reasons, MSN Messenger Service cannot add a person it finds in the Hotmail Member Directory to your contact list. You can send an e-mail message to the person asking them to contact you.

How do I remove a person from my contact list?

✔ Click the name of the person you want to remove from your contact list and then press the Delete key. People you remove from your list will still be able to contact you.

How can I let others know that I am not available?

✔ In the MSN Messenger Service window, click your name and then choose the option that best describes your status.

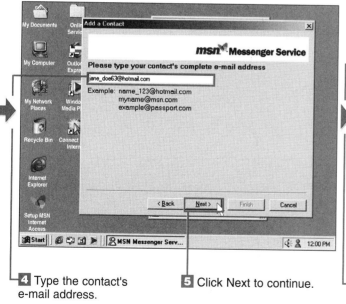

4 Type the contact's e-mail address.

5 Click Next to continue.

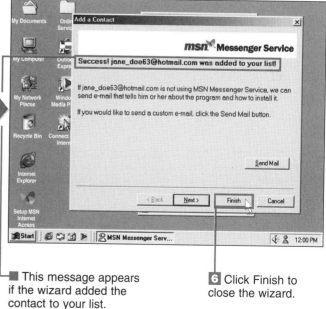

■ This message appears if the wizard added the contact to your list.

6 Click Finish to close the wizard.

SEND AN INSTANT MESSAGE

You can send an instant message to another person who is signed in to MSN Messenger Service. Instant messages you send can be up to 400 characters long.

You can start a conversation with one person and then invite other people to join the conversation. MSN Messenger Service allows you to exchange instant messages with up to four other people at once.

You can use emoticons in your instant messages. Emoticons are characters you type to represent facial expressions such as a smile or a frown. When you send an instant message, any emoticons in the message are automatically converted to graphic images.

The status bar at the bottom of the Instant Message window displays the date and time of the last message you received

or indicates when another person is typing a message.

When you receive an instant message that is not part of a conversation, your computer makes a sound and displays a box containing the first few lines of the message. You can click the box to see the entire message.

SEND AN INSTANT MESSAGE

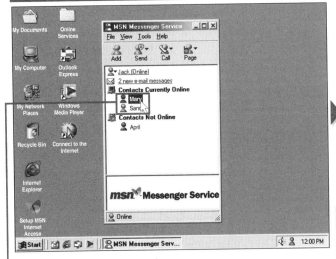

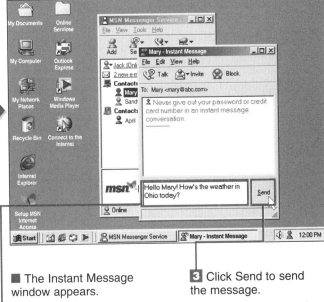

■1 Double-click the name of the person you want to send an instant message to.

■ The Instant Message window appears.

■2 Click this area and type your message.

■3 Click Send to send the message.

How do I send an instant message to someone who is not in my contact list?

✔ In the MSN Messenger Service window, click the Send button and then select Other. In the Send An Instant Message dialog box, type the person's e-mail address. The person must be signed in to MSN Messenger Service to receive the message.

How can I prevent a contact from sending me instant messages?

✔ Choose the Tools menu and select Options. On the Privacy tab, select the name of the person you do not want to receive instant messages from and then click the Block button.

Can I send an instant message to a cell phone or pager?

✔ To send an instant message to a person who has set up their mobile device to receive instant messages, you must add the person to your contact list and specify the address of their mobile device. To add a contact, see page 414. In the MSN Messenger Service window, click the Page button and select the mobile device you want to send a message. Type your message and then click Send. To set up a mobile device to receive instant messages, click the Page button, select Set up my pager address and then follow the instructions on your screen.

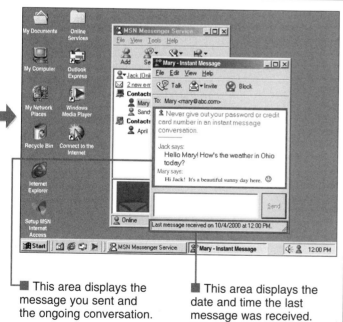

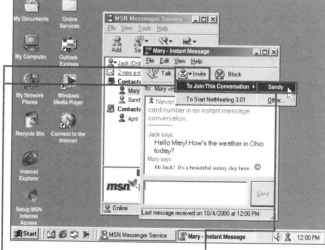

■ This area displays the message you sent and the ongoing conversation.

■ This area displays the date and time the last message was received. If the other person is typing a message, this area indicates that the person is typing.

EXCHANGE MESSAGES WITH SEVERAL PEOPLE

1 Click Invite to add a person to the conversation.

2 Click To Join This Conversation.

3 Click the name of the person you want to join the conversation.

CALL A COMPUTER

MSN Messenger Service allows you to call a computer to have a voice conversation with another person. Your computer and the computer you call must both have MSN Messenger Service installed. Both computers must also have a sound card, microphone and speakers.

The first time you call a computer, the Audio Tuning Wizard appears on your screen to help you adjust the volume of your speakers and microphone.

Before you can use your microphone to talk to another person, the person must accept your call.

You can send instant messages during a call. For information about sending instant messages, see page 416. You can also control the sound level of a call by adjusting the speaker volume or turning off your microphone so you cannot be heard.

MASTER IT

Can I call a phone number using MSN Messenger Service?

✔ You can place a free call to a phone number anywhere in Canada or the United States. In the MSN Messenger Service window, click the Call button and select Dial a Phone Number. Enter the phone number you want to call, including the country code and area code, and then click the Dial button.

CALL A COMPUTER

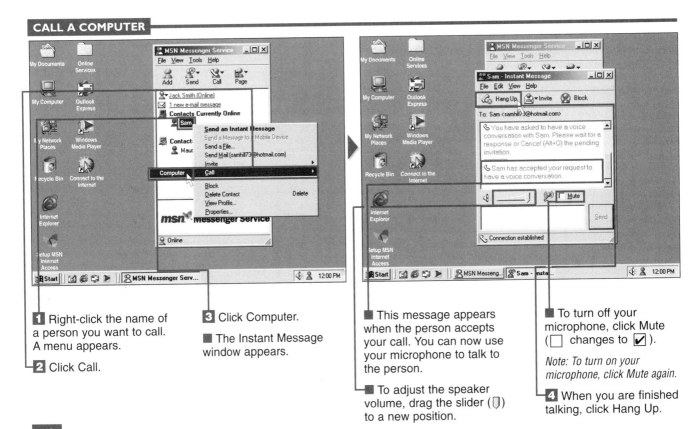

◀ **1** Right-click the name of a person you want to call. A menu appears.

2 Click Call.

3 Click Computer.

■ The Instant Message window appears.

■ This message appears when the person accepts your call. You can now use your microphone to talk to the person.

■ To adjust the speaker volume, drag the slider (⬚) to a new position.

■ To turn off your microphone, click Mute (☐ changes to ☑).

Note: To turn on your microphone, click Mute again.

4 When you are finished talking, click Hang Up.

READ E-MAIL MESSAGES

Y ou can use MSN Messenger Service to read your e-mail messages.

If the sign-in name you use to sign in to MSN Messenger Service is a Hotmail e-mail address, the MSN Messenger Service window will contain a link that displays the number of new e-mail messages you have received. You can select the link to open your Hotmail Inbox and access your messages. MSN Messenger Service will

also notify you when you receive new messages.

If you sign in to MSN Messenger Service using an e-mail address other than a Hotmail address, MSN Messenger Service will display a link to your e-mail program, but will not notify you when you receive new e-mail messages. You can select the link to open your default e-mail program and access your messages.

How do I send an e-mail message to a person in my contact list?

✔ In the MSN Messenger Service window, right-click the name of the person you want to send an e-mail message to and then select Send Mail. Your e-mail program opens and displays a message addressed to the person you specified.

READ E-MAIL MESSAGES

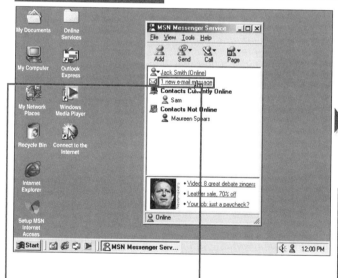

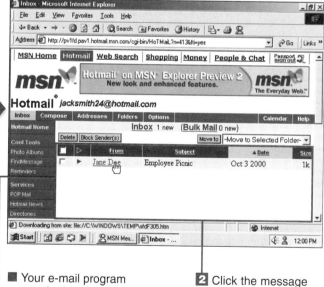

■ This link indicates how many new e-mail messages you have received.

1 Click the link to read your e-mail messages.

Note: Security Alert dialog boxes may appear. Click OK or Yes in the dialog boxes to continue.

■ Your e-mail program opens. In this example, a Web page displaying your Hotmail Inbox appears.

■ This area displays information about your e-mail messages.

2 Click the message you want to read.

■ The contents of the message appear.

SEND A FILE

You can send a file to another MSN Messenger Service user. You can send any type of file, including a document, image, sound, video or program.

Before a file you want to send is transferred, the other person must accept the file. If you accidentally send a file, you can cancel the transfer before the other person accepts the file.

When someone sends you a file, the sender's name appears in the Instant Message window, along with the name and size of the file. You can accept or decline the file.

Files you accept are automatically saved in the My Documents folder, in a subfolder called Messenger Service Received Files. After you have successfully received a file, the location and name of the file

appear as a link in the Instant Message window. You can click the link to open the file.

You should be very cautious of files you receive from people you do not know. When you receive a file, you should use an anti-virus program to check the file for viruses before opening the file.

SEND A FILE

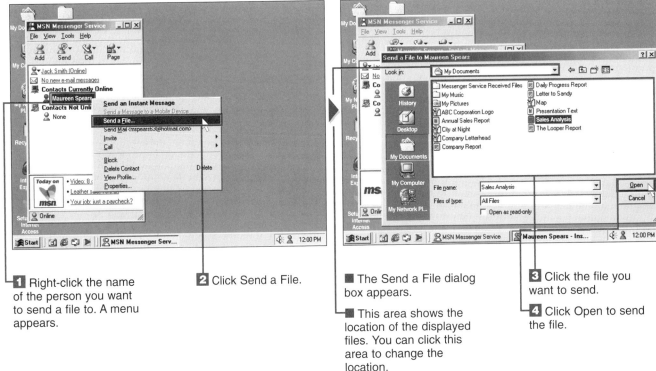

1 Right-click the name of the person you want to send a file to. A menu appears.

2 Click Send a File.

■ The Send a File dialog box appears.

■ This area shows the location of the displayed files. You can click this area to change the location.

3 Click the file you want to send.

4 Click Open to send the file.

MASTER IT

Can I change where MSN Messenger Service stores files I receive?

✔ Yes. In the MSN Messenger Service window, choose the Tools menu and click Options. In the Options dialog box, select the Preferences tab and then click the Browse button. In the Browse for Folder dialog box, select the folder where you want MSN Messenger Service to store files you receive.

How do I later open a file I received?

✔ In the MSN Messenger Service window, choose the File menu and select Open Received Files. Then double-click the file you want to open.

Can I send a file to someone who is not in my contact list?

✔ You can send a file to anyone who uses MSN Messenger Service. In the MSN Messenger Service window, choose the File menu, select Send a File To and then click Other. In the Send a File dialog box, enter the e-mail address of the person you want to send a file to and click then OK.

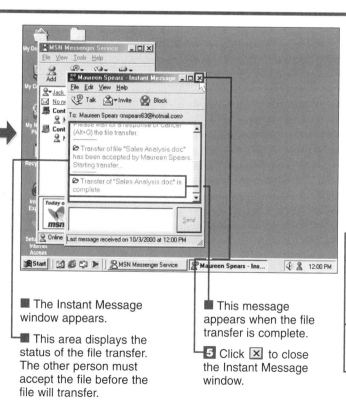

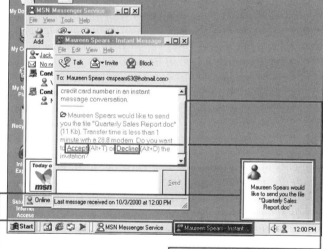

■ The Instant Message window appears.

■ This area displays the status of the file transfer. The other person must accept the file before the file will transfer.

■ This message appears when the file transfer is complete.

5 Click ☒ to close the Instant Message window.

RECEIVE A FILE

■ This message briefly appears when someone sends you a file.

1 Click the flashing button on the taskbar to display the Instant Message window.

■ This area displays information about the file.

2 Click Accept or Decline to accept or decline the file.

Note: If you select Accept, a dialog box will appear, warning that some files may contain viruses. Click OK to receive the file.

PLACE A CALL

NetMeeting allows you to communicate with other people on the Internet or on a network. A NetMeeting session can consist of two people or can be a conference with many participants working together at the same time.

You can use a computer name or computer IP address to place a call. An IP address identifies a computer on the Internet or on a network. You can only place

a call to contact a person who has NetMeeting open on their computer.

When you place a call, NetMeeting sends a message to the person you are calling, asking if they want to accept your call. The person can choose to accept or ignore the call.

Once the other person accepts your call, you can chat, exchange files, work together on files and more. If you have a microphone, you can

speak to the person. The person must have a sound card and speakers to hear sound. If you have a video camera, you can send video images to the person. You can only use voice and video communication with one person during a NetMeeting conference.

While you have NetMeeting open on your computer, other NetMeeting users can call you. You can accept or ignore a call.

PLACE A CALL

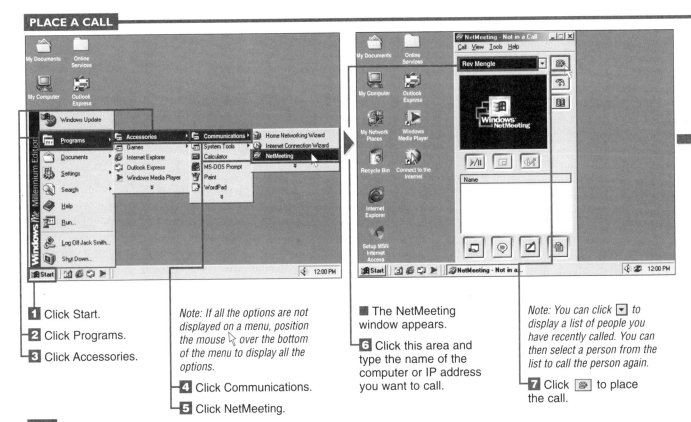

◼ Click Start.

◻ Click Programs.

◻ Click Accessories.

Note: If all the options are not displayed on a menu, position the mouse over the bottom of the menu to display all the options.

◻ Click Communications.

◻ Click NetMeeting.

◼ The NetMeeting window appears.

◻ Click this area and type the name of the computer or IP address you want to call.

Note: You can click ▾ to display a list of people you have recently called. You can then select a person from the list to call the person again.

◻ Click 🕿 to place the call.

How do I set up NetMeeting?

✔ The first time you start NetMeeting, you will be asked to provide information such as your name and e-mail address. You will also have the opportunity to tune your audio settings.

The other person cannot see my video image. What can I do?

✔ To start sending your video image to the other person, choose the Tools menu, select Video and then click Send.

Can I use a directory to place a call?

✔ You can visit the www.netmeet.net/ bestservers.asp Web site to find a list of directory servers you can use to place a call. After you find the server you want to use, choose the Tools menu in the NetMeeting window and select Options. On the General tab, select the text in the Directory area and enter the name of the directory server you want to use. Then click OK. In the NetMeeting window, click [image] to display the Find Someone dialog box. In the Select a directory area, click the name of the server you want to use. A list of people you can call appears. You can double-click the name of the person you want to call.

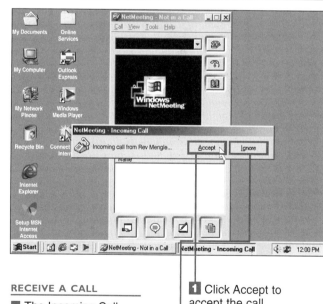

■ NetMeeting asks the other person if they will accept your call.

■ Once the person accepts your call, this area lists each person in the conference. You can immediately use your microphone to talk to the person.

■ If the other person has a video camera, this area may display a video.

8 When you want to end the call, click [image] to end the call.

RECEIVE A CALL

■ The Incoming Call dialog box appears when someone calls you.

1 Click Accept to accept the call.

■ If you do not want to accept the call, click Ignore.

USING CHAT

You can use Chat to send typed messages to the participants in a NetMeeting conference.

When one participant starts Chat, the Chat window appears on each participant's screen. You can choose to send a message to everyone in the conference. You can also send a private message to a specific person.

The text you type will not appear on the screens of the other participants until you press the Enter key. This lets you prepare your comments or questions before sending them to people in the conference. Each line in the Chat window is preceded by the name of the participant who entered the comment. In a large conference, you may want to use a moderator

or one participant who controls the flow of the chat.

When you close the Chat window, NetMeeting asks if you want to save the chat conversation as a file. Saving a chat conversation is useful when you want to keep a record of the chat session so you can review the conference again later or share the conference with other people.

USING CHAT

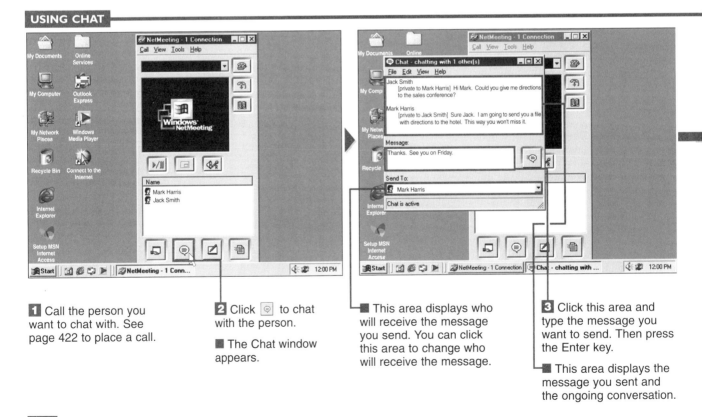

1 Call the person you want to chat with. See page 422 to place a call.

2 Click 🗨 to chat with the person.

■ The Chat window appears.

■ This area displays who will receive the message you send. You can click this area to change who will receive the message.

3 Click this area and type the message you want to send. Then press the Enter key.

■ This area displays the message you sent and the ongoing conversation.

Instead of Chat, can I use my microphone to communicate with other people in a conference?

✔ When you use a microphone, you can only communicate with one person at a time in a conference. The Chat feature allows you to communicate with many people at once, which is useful when you are in a conference with many participants. Chat also allows you to communicate with people who do not have a microphone or speakers.

Can I change the font of text in the Chat window?

✔ Yes. In the Chat window, choose the View menu and then select Options. In the Fonts area, click the button for the type of messages you want to display in a different font. In the dialog box that appears, select the font options you want to use.

Can I specify how information appears in the Chat window?

✔ Yes. In the Chat window, choose the View menu and select Options. In the Information display area, click each item you want to display in the Chat window. A check mark (✔) appears beside each item that will be displayed. In the Message format area, select the way you want to wrap text in the window (○ changes to ◉).

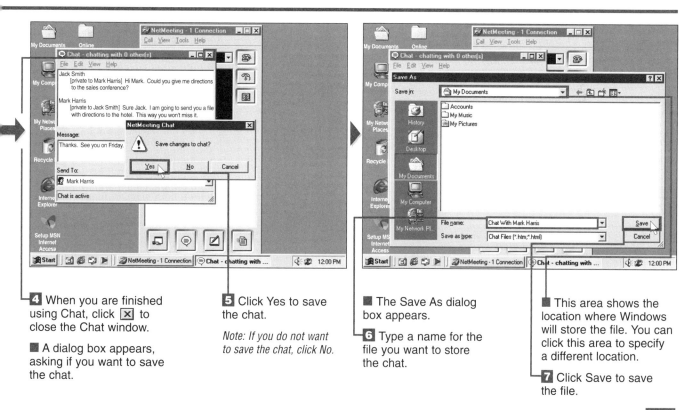

4 When you are finished using Chat, click ✕ to close the Chat window.

■ A dialog box appears, asking if you want to save the chat.

5 Click Yes to save the chat.

Note: If you do not want to save the chat, click No.

■ The Save As dialog box appears.

6 Type a name for the file you want to store the chat.

■ This area shows the location where Windows will store the file. You can click this area to specify a different location.

7 Click Save to save the file.

USING THE WHITEBOARD

The NetMeeting Whiteboard gives all conference participants the opportunity to share and comment on the information on a page.

All the participants in a conference can see the comments and drawings made on the Whiteboard page. The Whiteboard is useful for helping participants describe, create and edit a common project. The Whiteboard is especially useful for displaying and discussing images and designs.

The Whiteboard tools are similar to the tools found in Microsoft Paint. Participants can use the Whiteboard tools to create lines and other basic shapes, such as rectangles and ellipses. Each participant can also use the tools to type text on the page and highlight or underline text.

The Whiteboard provides a pointer tool that can be used to point out objects on the page. This allows a participant to easily draw attention to an object or area of the page.

You cannot tell who is making changes to the Whiteboard page when there are several participants in a NetMeeting conference.

When a participant closes the Whiteboard, they can save the current contents of the Whiteboard.

USING THE WHITEBOARD

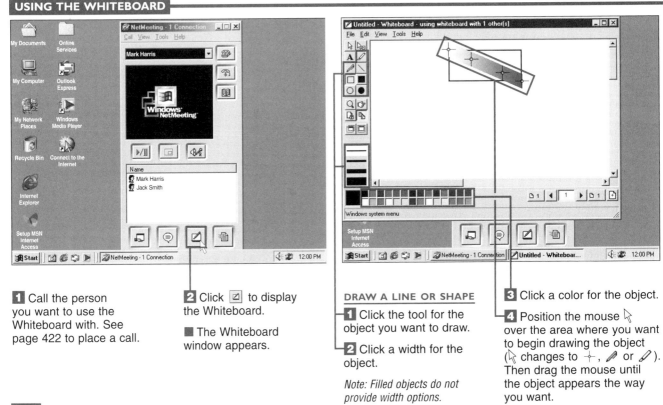

1 Call the person you want to use the Whiteboard with. See page 422 to place a call.

2 Click 🖉 to display the Whiteboard.

■ The Whiteboard window appears.

DRAW A LINE OR SHAPE

1 Click the tool for the object you want to draw.

2 Click a width for the object.

Note: Filled objects do not provide width options.

3 Click a color for the object.

4 Position the mouse ⬧ over the area where you want to begin drawing the object (⬧ changes to +, ✎ or ✐). Then drag the mouse until the object appears the way you want.

Can I add a new page to the Whiteboard?

✔ You can click 🗅 at the bottom of the Whiteboard window to insert a new page. You can then click the arrows (◀ or ▶) to move through the pages. When one participant moves to another page, all participants will also see the new page.

Can I rearrange the objects on the Whiteboard?

✔ Yes. Click the Selector tool (🔲) and then drag the object you want to move to the new location. You must position the mouse over an edge of an unfilled object you want to drag.

How do I delete an object on the Whiteboard?

✔ Click the Eraser tool (🔲) and then click the object or text you want to delete.

Can I place a document on the Whiteboard so all conference participants can see the document and make suggestions?

✔ Yes. Open the document you want to place on the Whiteboard. Switch back to the Whiteboard window and then click the Select Window tool (🔲). In the dialog box that appears, click OK. Then click anywhere in the document you want to display on the Whiteboard.

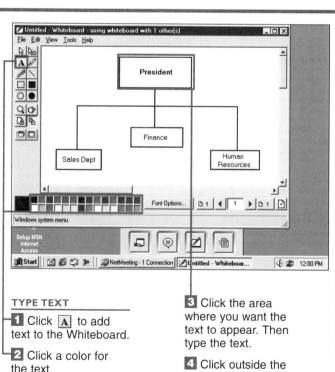

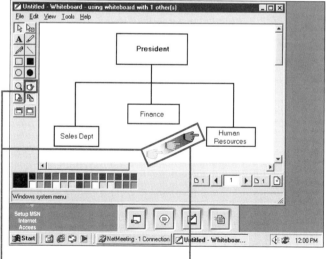

TYPE TEXT

1 Click A to add text to the Whiteboard.

2 Click a color for the text.

3 Click the area where you want the text to appear. Then type the text.

4 Click outside the text area when you finish typing the text.

POINT TO AN OBJECT

1 Click 🖑 to point to an object on the Whiteboard.

■ A hand (☞) appears on the Whiteboard.

2 Position the mouse ⇗ over the hand and then drag the hand to the object you want to point out.

Note: You can repeat step 1 to hide the hand.

SEND A FILE

You can send a file to the participants in a NetMeeting conference. You can send a file to all the participants or only one person in the conference.

NetMeeting can be used to send any type of file, including a document, spreadsheet, sound, video or program.

When you send a file, the file transfers in the background while you continue to work or chat. Each person you send a file to will see a window indicating the file is being transferred. Each participant can decide whether to keep the file or delete the file.

Files that participants receive are automatically saved in the NetMeeting folder, in a

subfolder called Received Files. You can find the NetMeeting folder in the Program Files folder on your hard drive.

You should be very cautious of files you receive from NetMeeting participants you do not know. When you receive a file, you should use an anti-virus program to check the file for viruses before opening the file.

SEND A FILE

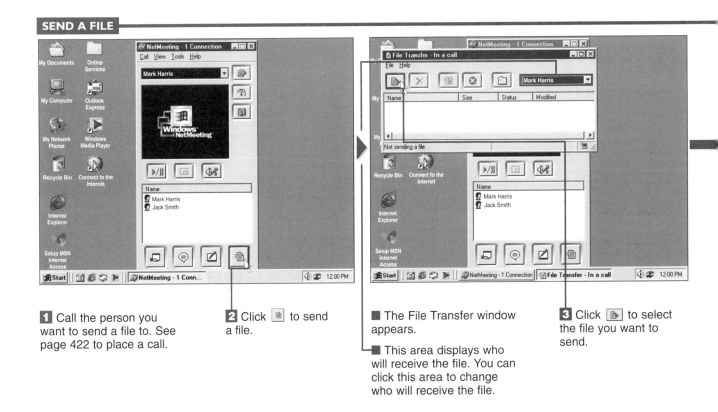

1 Call the person you want to send a file to. See page 422 to place a call.

2 Click to send a file.

■ The File Transfer window appears.

■ This area displays who will receive the file. You can click this area to change who will receive the file.

3 Click to select the file you want to send.

How do I remove a file I no longer want to send?

✔ To remove a file from the File Transfer window, click the file and then click ⊠.

I accidentally sent a file. Can I stop the transfer of the file?

✔ Yes. To cancel a file transfer before it is complete, click ⊘.

Can I change where NetMeeting stores files I receive?

✔ Yes. In the File Transfer window, choose the File menu and then click Change Folder. In the dialog box that appears, select the folder where you want NetMeeting to store files you receive.

How can I work with a file someone sends me?

✔ When someone sends you a file, a window appears, displaying information about the file. To open the file now, click Open. To delete the file, click Delete. To open the file later, click Close. When you want to open the file, click 🗀 in the File Transfer window to display a list of the files you have received. Then double-click the file you want to open.

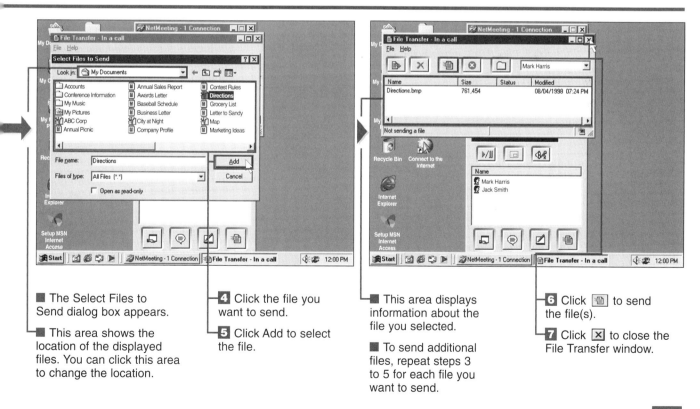

■ The Select Files to Send dialog box appears.

■ This area shows the location of the displayed files. You can click this area to change the location.

4 Click the file you want to send.

5 Click Add to select the file.

■ This area displays information about the file you selected.

■ To send additional files, repeat steps 3 to 5 for each file you want to send.

6 Click 🖼 to send the file(s).

7 Click ⊠ to close the File Transfer window.

SHARE A PROGRAM

You can share a program to work interactively with other participants in a NetMeeting conference.

Sharing a program lets you present a demonstration while other conference participants watch you work. Every participant will be able to see the program, even if they do not have the program installed on their computer.

You can give participants control of a shared program so they can

work with the program. To control a shared program, a participant must have NetMeeting 3.0 or later. Only one person at a time can control a shared program.

You can also use NetMeeting to share items such as your desktop or an open folder on your computer. If you share the desktop, your entire computer will be shared. If you share a folder, My Computer window or Windows Explorer window, NetMeeting will automatically

share all open folders and every program you open during the conference.

When you share a program, other participants cannot save or print information from the shared program on their own computer. If you want other participants to have a copy of the information, you must send them the file. To send a file using NetMeeting, see page 428.

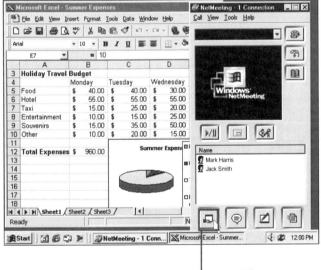

1 Call the person you want to share a program with. See page 422 to place a call.

2 Start the program you want to share.

3 Click 🖾 to share the program.

■ The Sharing window appears.

4 Click the name of the program you want to share.

Note: You can select Desktop to share your entire computer.

5 Click Share to share the program.

MASTER IT

How do I work with a program that someone else shared?

✔ In the shared program window, choose the Control menu and then click Request Control to ask permission to use the program. The person who shared the program must accept your request before you can work with the program. The Request Control option is only available if the person sharing the program has chosen to allow others to control the program.

The shared program is covered with a pattern of colored squares. What is wrong?

✔ The person who shared the program is currently using another program. You will only be able to properly view the shared program when the person makes the program the active window.

Can I have NetMeeting automatically give participants control of a program I shared?

✔ Yes. You can automatically grant control of a shared program if you do not want a dialog box to appear each time a participant requests control. In the Sharing window, click the Automatically accept requests for control option (☐ changes to ✔).

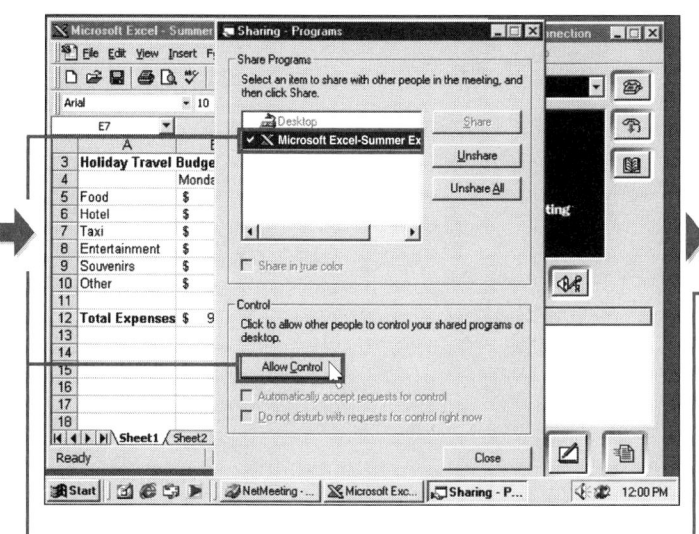

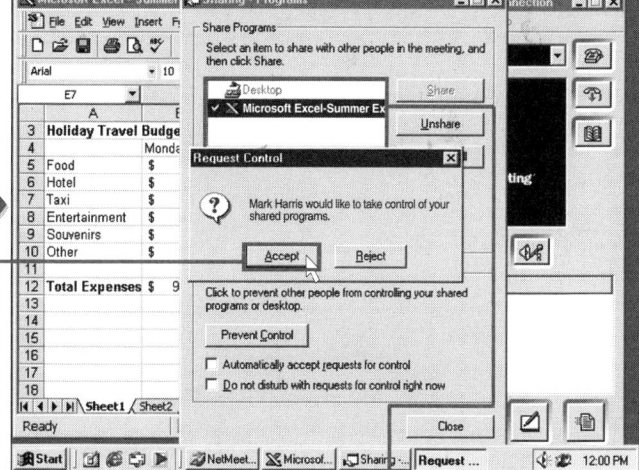

■ A check mark (✔) appears beside the name of the program you selected to share.

6 Click Allow Control if you want other people to be able to work with the program.

Note: When you click Allow Control, the button changes to Prevent Control. You can click Prevent Control at any time to stop allowing others to work with the program.

■ A dialog box appears when another person wants to control the program.

7 Click Accept to allow the person to take control of the program and make changes.

Note: To regain control of the program at any time, click your mouse.

■ To stop sharing a program, double-click the name of the program in the Sharing window. The check mark (✔) beside the program's name disappears.

SET UP AN INTERNET CONNECTION

You can use the Internet Connection Wizard to set up a connection to the Internet. You only need to set up a connection to the Internet once.

If you have an account with an Internet Service Provider (ISP), you can use the wizard to connect to the ISP using your phone line and modem. An ISP is a company that provides access to the Internet. You must have a modem

installed on your computer to connect to the Internet through a phone line. See page 324 to install a modem.

If your computer is connected to a Local Area Network (LAN), you can gain access to the Internet through the network.

When setting up a connection to an Internet service provider, you must enter the phone number

of your ISP. You must also specify the location of the ISP.

Once you are connected to the Internet, you can access the resources available on the Internet. You will be able to browse through information on the Web, exchange e-mail messages and read messages in newsgroups.

SET UP AN INTERNET CONNECTION

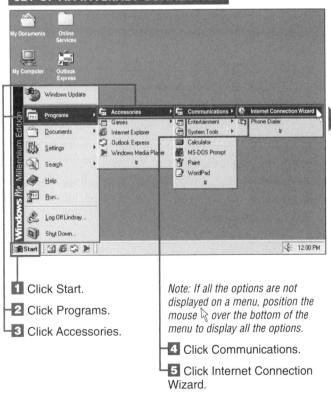

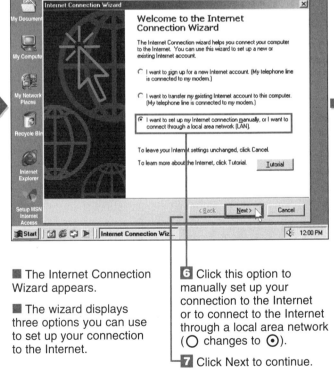

1 Click Start.

2 Click Programs.

3 Click Accessories.

Note: If all the options are not displayed on a menu, position the mouse ⇲ over the bottom of the menu to display all the options.

4 Click Communications.

5 Click Internet Connection Wizard.

■ The Internet Connection Wizard appears.

■ The wizard displays three options you can use to set up your connection to the Internet.

6 Click this option to manually set up your connection to the Internet or to connect to the Internet through a local area network (○ changes to ◉).

7 Click Next to continue.

Can I set up a connection to the Internet if I do not already have an account with an ISP?

✔ The Internet Connection Wizard can help you find an ISP in your area. Click the "I want to sign up for a new Internet account" option. The wizard displays a list of service providers in your area. Select the ISP you want to use and click Next. Then follow the instructions on your screen.

I have an existing account with an ISP but I am not connected to the Internet. What should I do?

✔ In the Internet Connection Wizard, click the "I want to transfer my existing Internet account to this computer" option. Then click Next and follow the instructions on your screen.

When setting up a connection to the Internet through a network, the wizard asks how I want to configure my proxy settings. What does this mean?

✔ If your network has a proxy server, Windows can use the proxy server to access the Internet. A proxy server is a computer that handles Internet requests for other computers on a network. To have Windows automatically find and set up the proxy server for you, make sure the "Automatic discovery of proxy server [recommended]" option is turned on (☑).

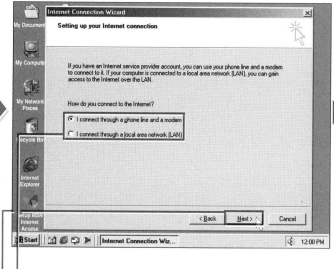

8 Click the way you want to connect to the Internet (○ changes to ⊙).

9 Click Next to continue.

Note: If you are connecting to the Internet through a network, a screen will appear that allows you to specify settings for your network. After you finish entering the information, click Next and then skip to step 19.

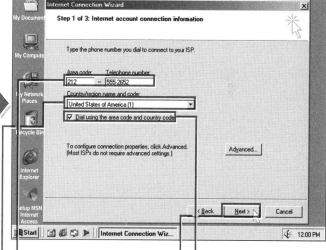

10 Double-click these areas and type the area code and phone number for your Internet service provider.

11 This area displays the location of your Internet service provider. You can click this area to change the location.

12 This option dials the area code and country code for your Internet service provider. You can click this option to turn the option on (☑) or off (☐).

13 Click Next to continue.

CONTINUED

SET UP AN INTERNET CONNECTION (CONTINUED)

To set up a connection to an Internet service provider, you must specify the user name and password you use to log on to your ISP in the Internet Connection Wizard. If you do not know this information, contact your ISP.

You can assign a name to the Internet connection. An icon displaying the name for the connection will appear in the Dial-Up Networking window.

The wizard allows you to set up an Internet mail account. An Internet mail account allows you to send and receive e-mail messages. If you have an e-mail account set up with your Internet service provider, the ISP will have provided you with the connection information. If you are missing any information the wizard requires, contact your ISP.

You can specify the name you want to appear on the messages you send. When you send an e-mail message, the name you specify will appear in the From field of the message.

SET UP AN INTERNET CONNECTION (CONTINUED)

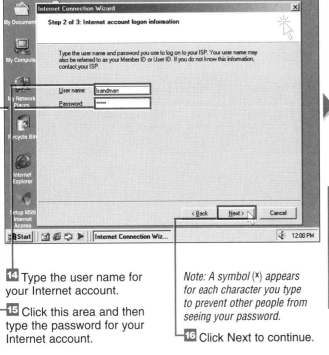

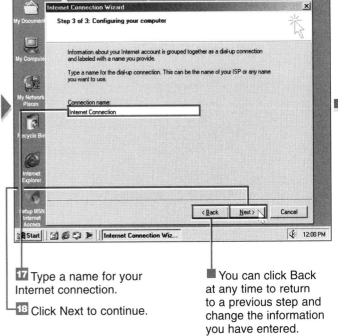

■14 Type the user name for your Internet account.

■15 Click this area and then type the password for your Internet account.

Note: A symbol (x) appears for each character you type to prevent other people from seeing your password.

■16 Click Next to continue.

■17 Type a name for your Internet connection.

■18 Click Next to continue.

■ You can click Back at any time to return to a previous step and change the information you have entered.

Can I set up an Internet mail account at a later time?

✔ Yes. If you selected No in step 19 below, you can set up an Internet mail account at a later time. Click 🖼 to open Outlook Express. The Internet Connection Wizard appears. You can then follow the instructions in the wizard to set up an Internet mail account.

I already have an e-mail account set up on my computer. Do I still need to create an account using the wizard?

✔ If you already have an e-mail account and you selected Yes in step 19 below, the wizard gives you the option of setting up a new e-mail account or using your existing account. Click the "Use an existing Internet mail account" option to use your existing account.

Can I change the settings for my Internet mail account later?

✔ Yes. Click 🖼 to open Outlook Express, select the Tools menu and then click Accounts. In the Internet Accounts dialog box, choose the Mail tab, select the Internet mail account you want to change the settings for and then click Properties. The Properties dialog box appears. You can then change the information for the mail account.

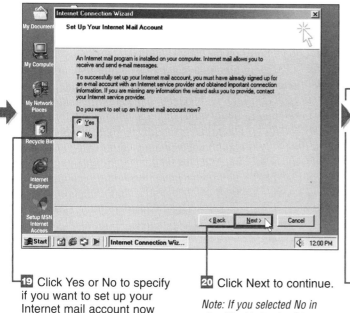

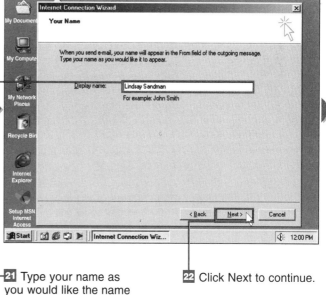

19 Click Yes or No to specify if you want to set up your Internet mail account now (○ changes to ⊙).

20 Click Next to continue.

Note: If you selected No in step 19, skip to step 34.

21 Type your name as you would like the name to appear when you send e-mail messages.

22 Click Next to continue.

CONTINUED ▶

SET UP AN INTERNET
CONNECTION (CONTINUED)

W hen setting up an Internet mail account, you must provide the Internet Connection Wizard with your e-mail address.

You must specify the type of mail server your Internet service provider uses to receive e-mail messages. The most common type of mail server is a POP3 server. You must also enter the addresses of the servers that send and receive your e-mail messages.

The wizard asks you to specify the account name and password provided by your ISP to log on to the Internet mail server. This information is usually the same as the name and password you use to connect to the Internet service provider.

You can also specify if your ISP requires you to use secure password authentication (SPA) to access your mail account. Most ISPs do not use SPA.

You can choose to automatically connect to the Internet when you close the wizard.

Once your computer is set up to connect to your Internet service provider, you can connect to the Internet at any time. To connect to your Internet service provider to access the Internet, click 🦋 on the taskbar. To exchange e-mail, click 📧.

SET UP AN INTERNET CONNECTION (CONTINUED)

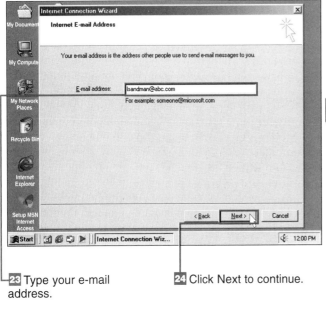

-23 Type your e-mail address.

24 Click Next to continue.

■ This area indicates the type of mail server your Internet service provider uses to receive e-mail messages. You can click this area to change the type of server.

25 Click this area and type the address of the mail server that receives e-mail messages.

26 Click this area and type the address of the mail server that sends e-mail messages.

27 Click Next to continue.

Can I change the way my computer dials in to my Internet service provider?

✔ Yes. You may want to change the phone number your computer dials or you may want Windows to display the progress of the connection. You can change the settings for an Internet connection as you would for any dial-up connection. For more information, see page 340.

Do I have to use the Internet Connection Wizard to change the settings of my Internet connection?

✔ You can use the Internet Options folder to change some of the settings. In the Control Panel window, double-click Internet Options and select the Connections tab. Select the connection you want to change the settings for and click Settings.

What can I do if the Internet connection I set up does not work?

✔ You can use the Internet Connections (ISPs) Troubleshooter to help you solve problems you may have when trying to connect to the Internet. Click the Start button and select Help. In the Search text box, type **internet connections troubleshooter** and press the Enter key. A link appears for the Internet Connections (ISPs) Troubleshooter. Click the link and then follow the instructions that appear in the right pane.

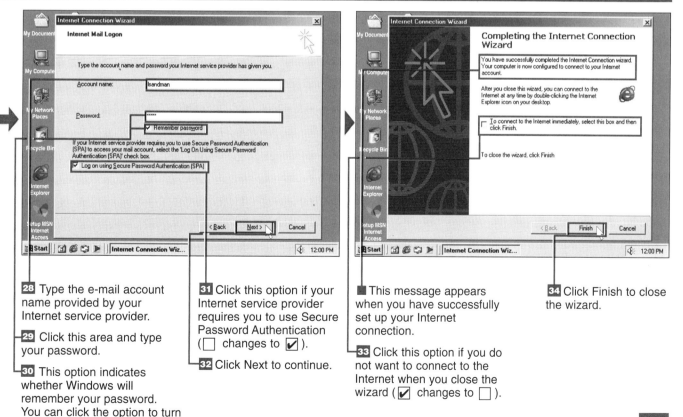

28 Type the e-mail account name provided by your Internet service provider.

29 Click this area and type your password.

30 This option indicates whether Windows will remember your password. You can click the option to turn the option on (☑) or off (☐).

31 Click this option if your Internet service provider requires you to use Secure Password Authentication (☐ changes to ☑).

32 Click Next to continue.

■ This message appears when you have successfully set up your Internet connection.

33 Click this option if you do not want to connect to the Internet when you close the wizard (☑ changes to ☐).

34 Click Finish to close the wizard.

DIAL IN TO AN INTERNET SERVICE PROVIDER

After you set up a connection to your Internet Service Provider (ISP), you can dial in to the ISP. Dialing in to an Internet service provider allows you to access the wide range of resources available on the Internet. You can browse through Web pages on various subjects, exchange electronic mail with friends and colleagues and read messages in newsgroups.

Windows displays an icon for each dial-up connection you have set up in the Dial-Up Networking window. To set up a connection to an Internet service provider, see page 432.

Windows needs to know your user name and password to dial in to your ISP. Your service provider should have provided you with this information when you set up your account.

You may not always have to perform the steps below to dial in to your Internet service provider. Most programs that access information on the Internet, such as Internet Explorer and Outlook Express, will automatically dial in to your Internet service provider when you start the program.

DIAL IN TO AN INTERNET SERVICE PROVIDER

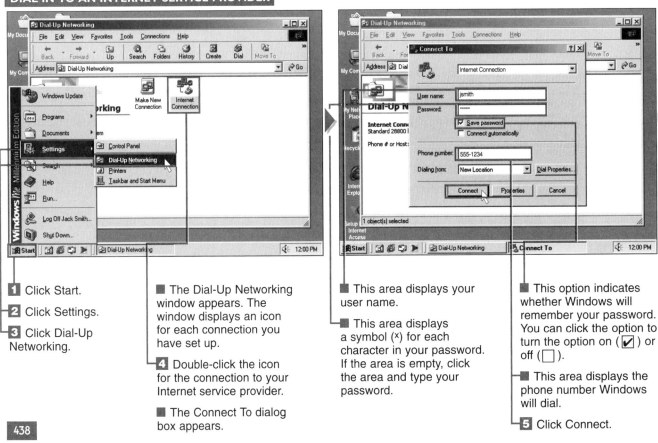

1 Click Start.

2 Click Settings.

3 Click Dial-Up Networking.

■ The Dial-Up Networking window appears. The window displays an icon for each connection you have set up.

4 Double-click the icon for the connection to your Internet service provider.

■ The Connect To dialog box appears.

■ This area displays your user name.

■ This area displays a symbol (×) for each character in your password. If the area is empty, click the area and type your password.

■ This option indicates whether Windows will remember your password. You can click the option to turn the option on (☑) or off (☐).

■ This area displays the phone number Windows will dial.

5 Click Connect.

Why can't I connect to my Internet service provider?

✔ You may have entered incorrect information when you set up the connection to your Internet service provider. You can display a terminal window after dialing in to your ISP to help you determine the problem. In the Dial-Up Networking window, right-click the icon for the connection to your ISP and then click Properties. Click the Configure button and then choose the Options tab. Select the Bring up terminal window after dialing option (☐ changes to ✔).

How can I test my connection to the Internet?

✔ Windows includes a program called PING that can use computer IP numbers to test a connection with another computer on the Internet. Your ISP can provide you with the IP number of a computer you can use to test the connection. Open the MS-DOS Prompt window and type **ping** followed by the IP number of the computer you want to communicate with. Then press the Enter key. PING will report how long it takes to send and receive a signal between your computer and the other computer. If PING displays a message stating that the request timed out, the connection is not working. See page 124 to open the MS-DOS Prompt window.

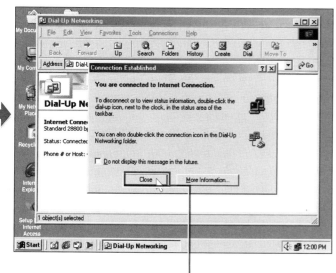

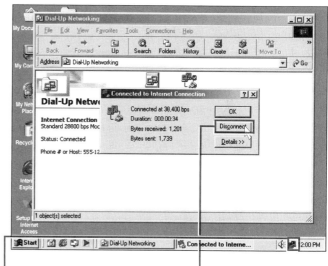

■ The Connection Established dialog box appears when you are successfully connected to your Internet service provider.

6 Click Close to close the dialog box.

■ You can now access information on the Internet.

END THE CONNECTION

■ An icon (💻) appears in this area when you are connected to your Internet service provider.

1 When you want to end the connection, double-click the icon (💻).

■ The Connected to dialog box appears.

2 Click Disconnect to end the connection.

START INTERNET EXPLORER AND DISPLAY WEB PAGES

You can use Internet Explorer to browse through information on the World Wide Web. The Web is part of the Internet and consists of a huge collection of documents, called Web pages, stored on computers around the world.

Web pages contain links, which are highlighted text or images on a Web page that connect to other pages on the Web. Links allow you to easily navigate through a vast amount of information by jumping from one Web page to another.

You can display a specific Web page that you have heard or read about if you know the address of the page. Each Web page has a unique address, called a Uniform Resource Locator (URL).

Internet Explorer remembers the addresses of Web pages you recently visited. You can select one of these addresses to quickly redisplay a Web page.

When you display a Web page, the text on the page transfers to your computer quickly so you can start reading the text right away. Images transfer more slowly, so you may have to wait a moment to clearly view the images.

START INTERNET EXPLORER AND DISPLAY WEB PAGES

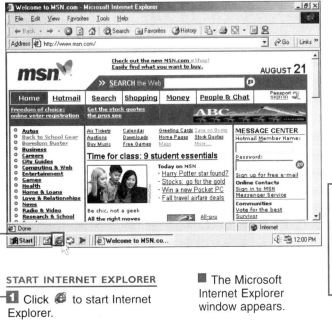

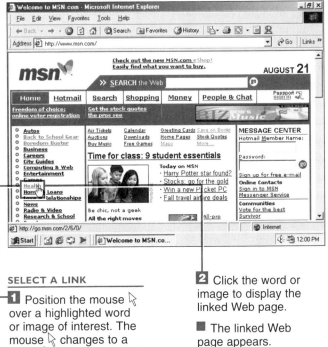

START INTERNET EXPLORER

1 Click 🅔 to start Internet Explorer.

Note: If you are not connected to the Internet, a dialog box appears that allows you to connect.

■ The Microsoft Internet Explorer window appears.

SELECT A LINK

1 Position the mouse ⌖ over a highlighted word or image of interest. The mouse ⌖ changes to a hand ⌙ when over a link.

2 Click the word or image to display the linked Web page.

■ The linked Web page appears.

Why does the Internet Connection Wizard appear when I start Internet Explorer?

✔ The Internet Connection Wizard appears the first time you start Internet Explorer to help you get connected to the Internet. See page 432 for more information.

Can I have more than one Internet Explorer window open at a time?

✔ If a Web page is taking a long time to transfer, you can open another Internet Explorer window to view other Web pages while you wait. From the File menu, select New and then choose Window.

Can I change the size of text displayed on Web pages?

✔ Yes. From the View menu, select Text Size and then choose the size you want to use. The current text size displays a dot (•).

How do I use Internet Explorer to disconnect from the Internet?

✔ Click ☒ to close the Internet Explorer window. A dialog box may appear, asking if you want to disconnect from the Internet. Click Disconnect Now to disconnect. The icon (🖳) that appears on the taskbar when you are connected to the Internet disappears.

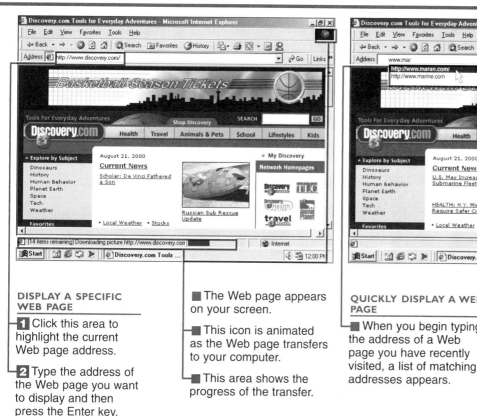

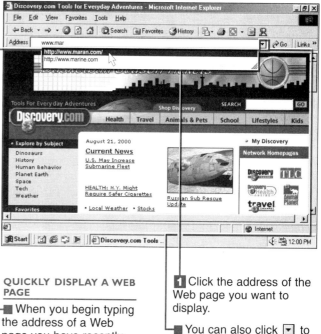

DISPLAY A SPECIFIC WEB PAGE

1 Click this area to highlight the current Web page address.

2 Type the address of the Web page you want to display and then press the Enter key.

■ The Web page appears on your screen.

■ This icon is animated as the Web page transfers to your computer.

■ This area shows the progress of the transfer.

QUICKLY DISPLAY A WEB PAGE

■ When you begin typing the address of a Web page you have recently visited, a list of matching addresses appears.

1 Click the address of the Web page you want to display.

■ You can also click ▾ to display the list of Web page addresses at any time.

WORK WITH WEB PAGES

Internet Explorer provides several toolbar buttons that help you work with Web pages.

If a Web page is taking a long time to appear on your screen or contains information that does not interest you, you can stop the transfer of the page.

You can move back or forward through the Web pages you have viewed since you last started Internet Explorer.

Refreshing a Web page allows you to transfer a fresh copy of the page to your computer. This is useful for updating Web pages that contain constantly changing information such as news, stock market data or images from a live camera.

Internet Explorer lets you produce a paper copy of a Web page. The page number and total number of pages that will print appear at the top of each printed page. The Web

page address and current date set in your computer appear at the bottom of each printed page.

You can display your home page at any time. The home page appears each time you start Internet Explorer.

WORK WITH WEB PAGES

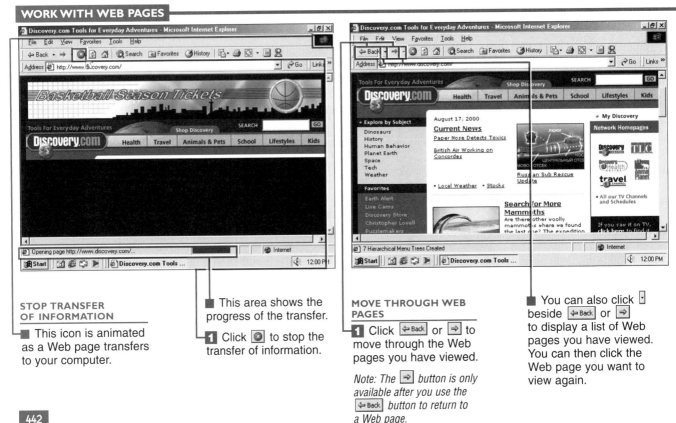

STOP TRANSFER OF INFORMATION

■ This icon is animated as a Web page transfers to your computer.

■ This area shows the progress of the transfer.

1 Click to stop the transfer of information.

MOVE THROUGH WEB PAGES

1 Click Back or to move through the Web pages you have viewed.

Note: The button is only available after you use the Back button to return to a Web page.

■ You can also click beside Back or to display a list of Web pages you have viewed. You can then click the Web page you want to view again.

Can I save a Web page?

✔ From the File menu, click Save As to name and save the Web page. Windows will create a folder in the location you specify to store the images for the page.

Can I save an image on a Web page?

✔ To save an image, right-click the image and then select Save Picture As. Type a name for the image and then click Save.

How do I open a Web page or image I saved?

✔ Locate the Web page or image on your computer and then double-click the page or image. Web pages you open appear in your Web browser. Images you open appear in the Image Preview window.

Can I find a word on a Web page?

✔ From the Edit menu, select Find (on This Page). Type the word you want to find and then click Find Next.

Can I find out how a Web page was created?

✔ Viewing the HTML code used to create a Web page is useful if you want to find out how the effects on a Web page were created. From the View menu, select Source.

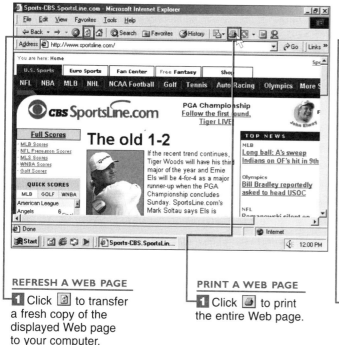

REFRESH A WEB PAGE

1 Click 🔄 to transfer a fresh copy of the displayed Web page to your computer.

PRINT A WEB PAGE

1 Click 🖨 to print the entire Web page.

DISPLAY YOUR HOME PAGE

1 Click 🏠 to display your home page.

■ Your home page appears.

Note: Your home page may be different than the home page shown above. To change your home page, see page 452.

SEARCH THE WEB

You can search for Web pages that discuss topics of interest to you. You can enter a word or phrase to display a list of Web pages that match the word or phrase you specified.

MSN Web Search is a search tool you can use to search for Web pages. Search tools often use software programs, called robots, to search the Web and catalog new Web pages. Many search tools also

have people who review cataloged Web pages and place them in appropriate categories. When you search for Web pages about a specific topic, a search tool searches its catalog for matching or related pages.

There are many other search tools available on the Web that you can use to search for Web pages. Some popular search tools include AltaVista (www.altavista.com) and

Yahoo! (www.yahoo.com). These search tools may allow you to perform more advanced searches.

Searching for information on the Web will give you a good starting point but will not find every page on the Web that discusses the topic. It is almost impossible to catalog every Web page because Web pages change frequently and new pages are created every day.

SEARCH THE WEB

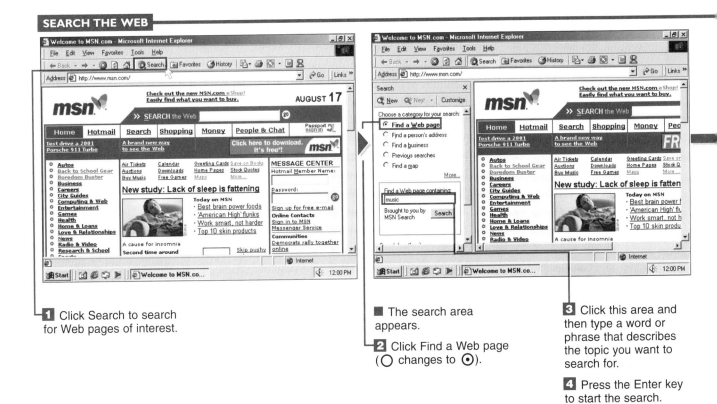

■ Click Search to search for Web pages of interest.

■ The search area appears.

■ Click Find a Web page (○ changes to ⊙).

■ Click this area and then type a word or phrase that describes the topic you want to search for.

■ Press the Enter key to start the search.

Is there a quicker way to search for Web pages?

✔ In the Address bar of the Microsoft Internet Explorer window, type a question mark (?) followed by a space and the word or phrase you want to search for. Then press the Enter key. Internet Explorer will locate Web pages that match the word or phrase you specified.

MSN Web Search did not provide the results I expected. What can I do?

✔ You can use another search tool provided with Internet Explorer to search for the word or phrase you specified. At the top of the search area, click ▼ beside the Next button and then select a search tool from the list.

Can I use the search area to find other types of information?

✔ Yes. You can search for information such as a person's e-mail address or a map. In the search area, select the type of information you want to search for (O changes to ⊙). Then enter the information you want to search for. To display more types of searches you can perform, click the More link.

How do I quickly clear the search area to start a new search?

✔ Click the New button at the top of the search area.

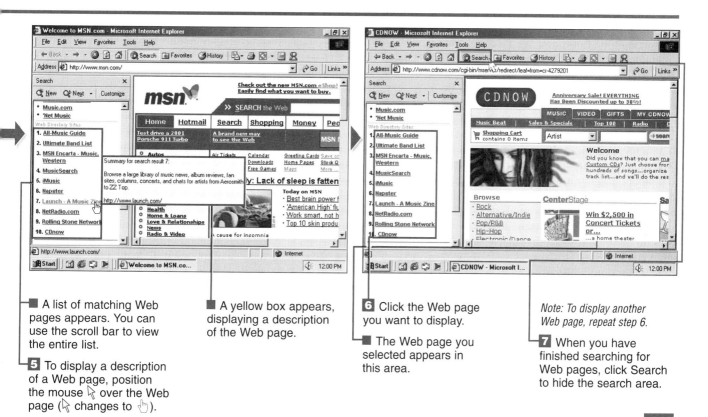

■ A list of matching Web pages appears. You can use the scroll bar to view the entire list.

5 To display a description of a Web page, position the mouse ⤢ over the Web page (⤢ changes to 👆).

■ A yellow box appears, displaying a description of the Web page.

6 Click the Web page you want to display.

■ The Web page you selected appears in this area.

Note: To display another Web page, repeat step 6.

7 When you have finished searching for Web pages, click Search to hide the search area.

ADD A WEB PAGE TO FAVORITES

The Favorites feature allows you to store the addresses of Web pages you frequently visit. When you know that you will be returning to a Web page, you can add the page to the Favorites list. You may return to the same Web page several times to investigate the page further or to check for new or updated information.

When you add a Web page to the Favorites list, you should give the page a meaningful name that clearly indicates its contents.

You can quickly access a Web page in the Favorites list. Selecting Web pages from the Favorites list saves you from having to remember and constantly retype the same addresses over and over again. Using the Favorites list also

eliminates the possibility that you will not be able to access a Web page because you have made a typing mistake in the address.

By default, the Favorites list includes the Links and Media folders, which contain Web pages you may find useful and interesting. The list also includes the MSN.com and Radio Station Guide Web pages.

ADD A WEB PAGE TO FAVORITES

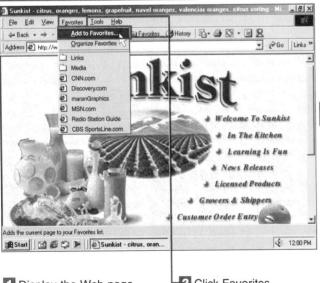
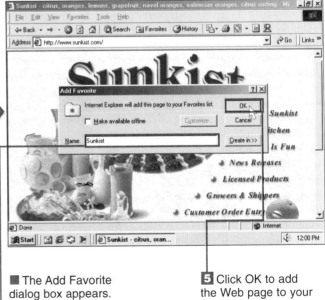

1 Display the Web page you want to add to your list of favorite Web pages.

2 Click Favorites.

3 Click Add to Favorites.

■ The Add Favorite dialog box appears.

4 This area displays the name of the Web page. To change the name, select the text and then type a new name.

5 Click OK to add the Web page to your list of favorites.

How can I make a favorite Web page available offline?

✔ Making a Web page available offline allows you to view the page even when you are not connected to the Internet. In the Add Favorite dialog box, click the Make available offline option (☐ changes to ✔) and then select the Customize button to display the Offline Favorite Wizard. You can use the wizard to specify the content you want to make available offline and to set up a schedule to automatically synchronize the Web page. Synchronizing ensures you have the most recent version of the Web page on your computer.

How do I add the currently displayed Web page to the Links folder?

✔ Drag the icon that appears beside the address of the page in the Address bar to the Links folder. Web pages you add to the Links folder are automatically added to the Links toolbar. To view the pages on the Links toolbar, click » on the Links toolbar button.

Is there another way to access the Favorites list?

✔ You can select the Favorites menu to display the list of your favorite Web pages. To display the Web pages stored in a folder, click the folder.

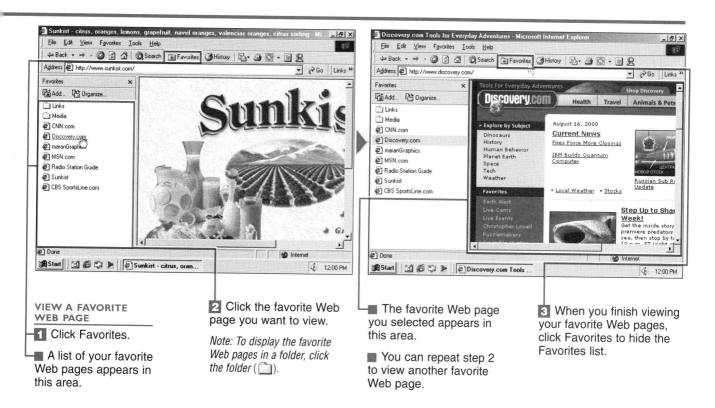

VIEW A FAVORITE WEB PAGE

◤1 Click Favorites.

■ A list of your favorite Web pages appears in this area.

◤2 Click the favorite Web page you want to view.

Note: To display the favorite Web pages in a folder, click the folder (☐).

■ The favorite Web page you selected appears in this area.

■ You can repeat step 2 to view another favorite Web page.

◤3 When you finish viewing your favorite Web pages, click Favorites to hide the Favorites list.

ORGANIZE FAVORITE WEB PAGES

Y ou can organize the Web pages in the Favorites list to help make the list easier to use.

Over time, your list of favorite Web pages may become large and unmanageable. To keep your Favorites list organized, you should delete the Web pages that you no longer visit or that no longer exist.

You can create new folders to organize your favorite Web pages. For example, you can create a folder called Hobbies to keep all your favorite hobby-related Web pages together. Web pages organized into folders are easier to find. To further organize your favorite Web pages, you can move a new folder you create into an existing folder. A folder

within another folder is called a sub-folder.

You can move your favorite Web pages to a new location in the Favorites list. This is useful if you want to organize your favorite Web pages by topic. For example, you can move Web pages that cover topics such as cooking and cycling to the Hobbies folder you created.

ORGANIZE FAVORITE WEB PAGES

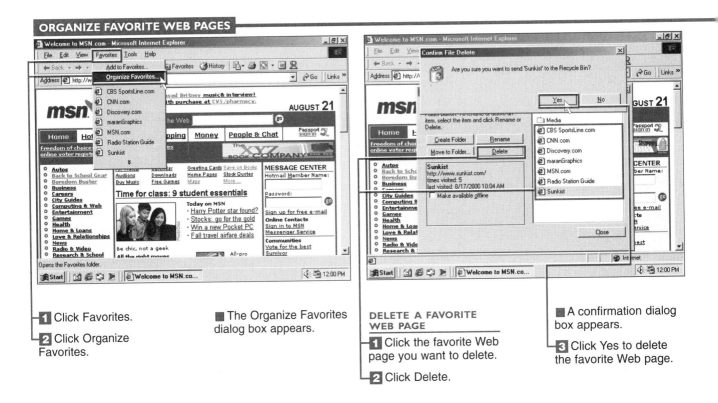

■1 Click Favorites.

■2 Click Organize Favorites.

■ The Organize Favorites dialog box appears.

DELETE A FAVORITE WEB PAGE

■1 Click the favorite Web page you want to delete.

■2 Click Delete.

■ A confirmation dialog box appears.

■3 Click Yes to delete the favorite Web page.

How do I delete a folder I created in the Favorites list?

✔ In the Organize Favorites dialog box, click the folder you want to delete and then select the Delete button. Any Web pages stored in the folder will also be deleted.

I have trouble dragging favorite Web pages to folders. Is there another way to move a favorite Web page?

✔ In the Organize Favorites dialog box, select the favorite Web page you want to move and then click the Move to Folder button. Select the folder you want to move the Web page to and then click OK.

Can I change the name of a favorite Web page?

✔ In the Organize Favorites dialog box, click the favorite Web page you want to rename and then select the Rename button. Type a new name for the page and press the Enter key.

Is there another way to organize the Favorites list?

✔ Click the Favorites button on the Standard Buttons toolbar to display the Favorites list. Then drag and drop Web pages to new locations in the list.

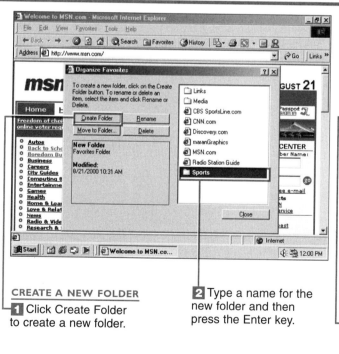

CREATE A NEW FOLDER

◼1 Click Create Folder to create a new folder.

◼2 Type a name for the new folder and then press the Enter key.

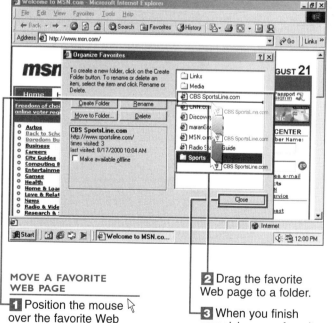

MOVE A FAVORITE WEB PAGE

◼1 Position the mouse over the favorite Web page you want to move.

Note: To display the favorite Web pages in a folder, click the folder (🗀).

◼2 Drag the favorite Web page to a folder.

◼3 When you finish organizing your favorite Web pages, click Close.

DISPLAY HISTORY OF VIEWED WEB PAGES

The History list keeps track of the Web pages you have recently viewed. You can select a Web page from the History list to return to the page. The History list keeps track of recently viewed Web pages even when you close Internet Explorer.

The list is organized into weeks and days so you can quickly find a Web page you viewed on a specific day. Each week and day contains an alphabetical listing of the Web sites you visited that week or day. When you select a Web site, a list of all the Web pages you visited at that site appears.

Your History list can grow quite large and may contain hundreds of Web pages. When the History list contains a large number of Web pages, Internet Explorer allows you to scroll through the list.

The History list also keeps track of any files you have recently worked with on your computer and the network.

DISPLAY HISTORY OF VIEWED WEB PAGES

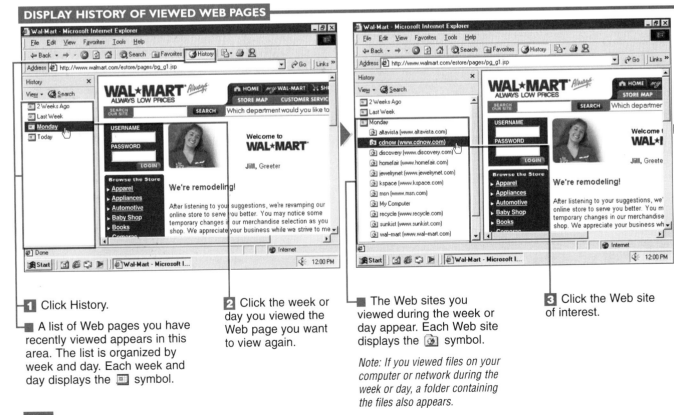

■1 Click History.

■ A list of Web pages you have recently viewed appears in this area. The list is organized by week and day. Each week and day displays the 📅 symbol.

■2 Click the week or day you viewed the Web page you want to view again.

■ The Web sites you viewed during the week or day appear. Each Web site displays the 🌐 symbol.

Note: If you viewed files on your computer or network during the week or day, a folder containing the files also appears.

■3 Click the Web site of interest.

How long does the History list keep track of recently viewed Web pages and files?

✔ The History list keeps track of the Web pages and files you have viewed over the last 20 days. You can change the number of days by choosing the Tools menu and then selecting Internet Options. In the History area, double-click the box beside Days to keep pages in history and then type a new number.

How do I clear the History list?

✔ Select the Tools menu and then click Internet Options. In the History area, click the Clear History button. Clearing the History list frees up space on your computer.

How can I sort the items displayed in the History list?

✔ At the top of the History list, click the View button and then click the way you want to sort the items.

Can I search for a specific Web page in the History list?

✔ Yes. At the top of the History list, click the Search button. Type a word that describes the Web page you want to find and then click the Search Now button.

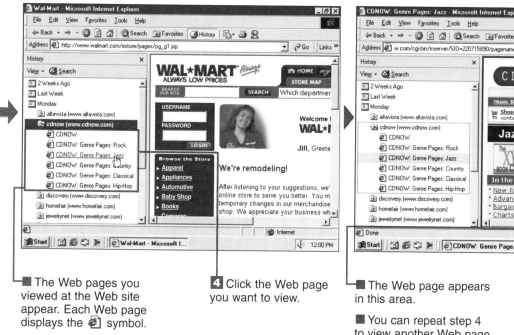

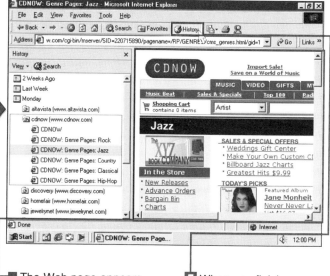

■ The Web pages you viewed at the Web site appear. Each Web page displays the 🗐 symbol.

4 Click the Web page you want to view.

■ The Web page appears in this area.

■ You can repeat step 4 to view another Web page at the Web site.

5 When you finish displaying recently viewed Web pages, click History to hide the History list.

CHANGE YOUR HOME PAGE

You can specify which Web page you want to appear each time you start Internet Explorer. This Web page is called your home page. While browsing the Web, you can use the Home button (🏠) to display your home page at any time.

You can use any page on the Web as your home page. You can choose a Web page that contains

news and information related to your personal interests or your work. You may want to use a Web page that provides a good starting point for exploring the Web, such as www.yahoo.com or www.altavista.com.

If you have a Web page creation program such as FrontPage, you can design and create your own home page. You can find Web

page creation programs on the Web or at computer stores.

You can also display a blank page when you start Internet Explorer. Displaying a blank page lets you start browsing the Web without having to wait for a home page to appear on your screen.

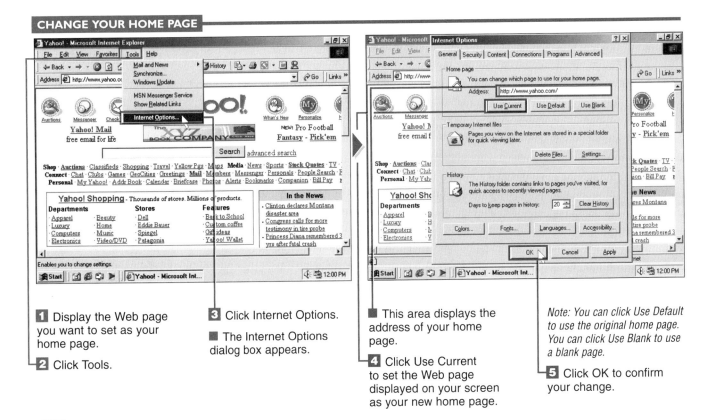

CHANGE YOUR HOME PAGE

1 Display the Web page you want to set as your home page.

2 Click Tools.

3 Click Internet Options.

■ The Internet Options dialog box appears.

■ This area displays the address of your home page.

4 Click Use Current to set the Web page displayed on your screen as your new home page.

Note: You can click Use Default to use the original home page. You can click Use Blank to use a blank page.

5 Click OK to confirm your change.

DELETE TEMPORARY INTERNET FILES

Y ou can delete temporary Internet files from your hard drive. Temporary Internet files are Web pages Internet Explorer stores on your hard drive while you are browsing the Web.

Before transferring a Web page to your computer, Internet Explorer checks to see if the page is stored in the temporary Internet files. If the Web page is stored in the temporary Internet files and you have already viewed the Web page

during the current Web browsing session, Internet Explorer displays the stored page rather than transferring the page to your computer from the Internet. This saves Internet Explorer from having to transfer the same pages to your computer over and over.

Temporary Internet files can take up valuable space on your hard drive. You can delete these files to free up space on your computer.

You can also delete Web pages stored on your computer for viewing when you are not connected to the Internet. Once you have deleted these Web pages, you will not be able to display the pages offline until Internet Explorer transfers the pages to your computer again. For information about making a Web page available offline, see the top of page 447.

DELETE TEMPORARY INTERNET FILES

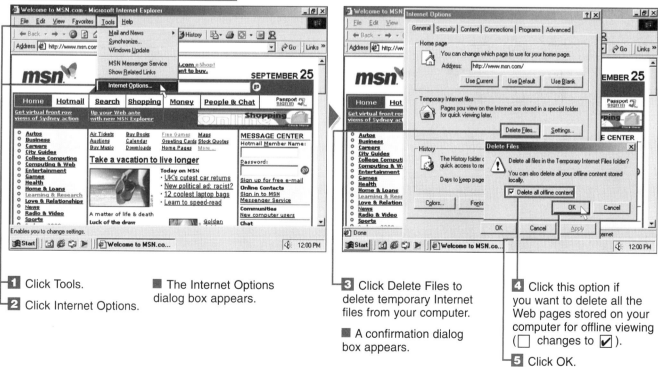

-1 Click Tools.

-2 Click Internet Options.

■ The Internet Options dialog box appears.

-3 Click Delete Files to delete temporary Internet files from your computer.

■ A confirmation dialog box appears.

-4 Click this option if you want to delete all the Web pages stored on your computer for offline viewing (☐ changes to ☑).

-5 Click OK.

VIEW SECURITY LEVELS FOR ZONES

You can assign Web sites available on the Internet and on an intranet to different zones.

The security level of the zone a Web site is assigned to determines the type of content that can be downloaded from the Web site. Some Web sites contain programs that may cause Internet Explorer to malfunction and may damage the information on your computer.

The Internet zone consists of Web sites not assigned to other zones

and has a medium security level. Internet Explorer will warn you before downloading potentially dangerous content from Web sites with the medium security level.

The Local intranet zone contains Web sites on your intranet and has a medium-low security level. Internet Explorer may warn you before downloading content from sites with the medium-low security level.

The Trusted sites zone contains Web sites you do not believe will

damage the information on your computer and has a low security level. Internet Explorer may not warn you before downloading content from sites with the low security level.

The Restricted sites zone contains Web sites that may include items that could damage the information on your computer. This zone is set to a high security level. Internet Explorer will not download any content that may pose a security problem from Web sites with the high security level.

VIEW SECURITY LEVELS FOR ZONES

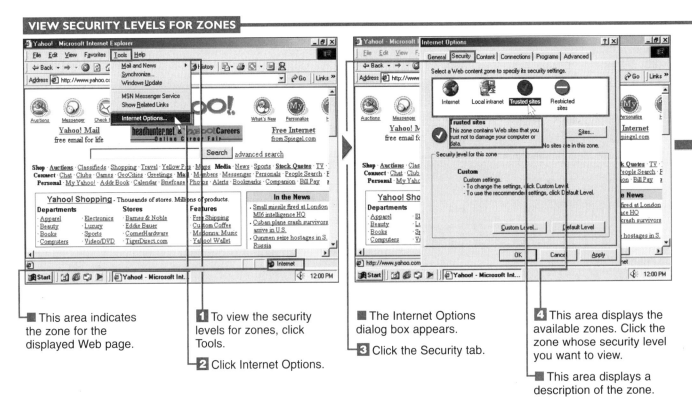

■ This area indicates the zone for the displayed Web page.

1 To view the security levels for zones, click Tools.

2 Click Internet Options.

■ The Internet Options dialog box appears.

3 Click the Security tab.

4 This area displays the available zones. Click the zone whose security level you want to view.

■ This area displays a description of the zone.

How do I assign a Web site to a zone?

✔ You can assign a Web site to the Local intranet, Trusted sites or Restricted sites zones. Select the zone you want to assign a Web site to and then click the Sites button. To assign a site to the Local intranet zone, you must then click the Advanced button. Type the full address of the Web site you want to assign to the zone and then click the Add button. When you assign a Web site to the Trusted sites zone, click the Require server verification (https:) for all sites in this zone option (☐ changes to ✔).

Can I specify custom security settings for a zone?

✔ Yes. Select the zone you want to specify custom security settings for and then click the Custom Level button. The Security Settings dialog box appears, displaying the settings you can change. You can choose to disable, enable or have Windows display a prompt for most settings.

Can I restore the original security level and settings for a zone?

✔ Yes. If you changed the security level or security settings for a zone, you can restore the original settings. In the Internet Options dialog box, click the Default Level button and then click OK.

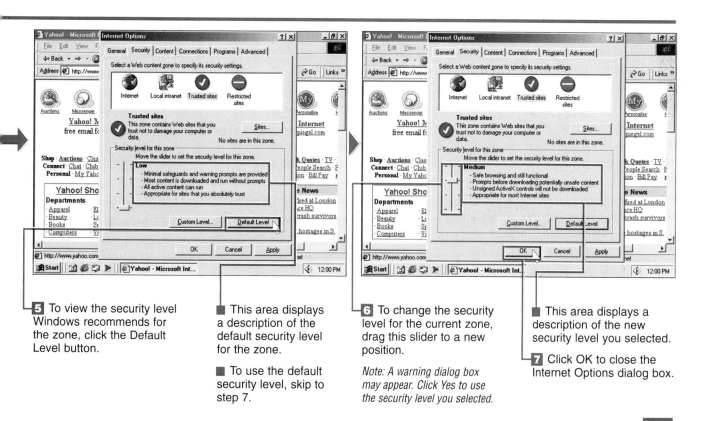

5 To view the security level Windows recommends for the zone, click the Default Level button.

■ This area displays a description of the default security level for the zone.

■ To use the default security level, skip to step 7.

6 To change the security level for the current zone, drag this slider to a new position.

Note: A warning dialog box may appear. Click Yes to use the security level you selected.

■ This area displays a description of the new security level you selected.

7 Click OK to close the Internet Options dialog box.

WORK WITH SECURE WEB CONTENT

Internet Explorer offers many features that can make exchanging information and browsing the World Wide Web more secure. Some people feel it is unsafe to send personal information, such as credit card numbers, over the Internet. However, the security features offered by Internet Explorer make it almost impossible for unauthorized people to access your personal information.

Internet Explorer allows you to connect to secure Web sites to create an almost unbreakable security system. When you connect to a secure Web site, other people on the Internet cannot view the information you transfer.

Addresses of secure Web sites start with "https" instead of "http." Internet Explorer may display a message when you

are about to access or leave a secure Web site. Internet Explorer also displays a lock icon (🔒) on the status bar when you are connected to a secure Web site.

Internet Explorer also includes features such as the Content Advisor, Certificates, AutoComplete and the Microsoft Profile Assistant to help meet your specific security needs.

WORK WITH SECURE WEB CONTENT

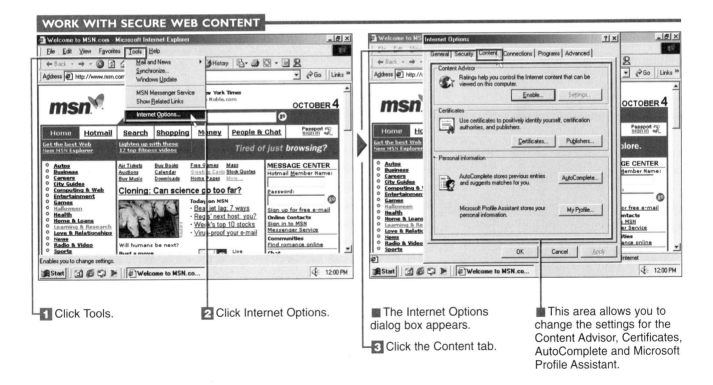

■1 Click Tools.

■2 Click Internet Options.

■ The Internet Options dialog box appears.

■3 Click the Content tab.

■ This area allows you to change the settings for the Content Advisor, Certificates, AutoComplete and Microsoft Profile Assistant.

Content Advisor

The Content Advisor allows you to restrict access to Web sites depending on the content of the sites. This is useful if you want to allow children to browse the World Wide Web while restricting their access to offensive material.

The Content Advisor lets you rate Web site content according to four categories: language, nudity, sex and violence. You can set a supervisor password to help prevent other people from changing the Content Advisor settings.

Although this rating system is gaining in popularity, many Web sites do not yet use the rating system. You can specify whether you want to be able to access Web sites that are not rated.

Certificates

A certificate is similar to an identification card. Personal certificates guarantee the identity of a person and can be obtained only from specific companies. Web site certificates ensure that Web sites are genuine. Web site certificates are often used to verify a program manufacturer's identity before you download a program from the Web site.

AutoComplete

The AutoComplete feature stores information you enter while browsing the Web, such as the addresses of Web pages. AutoComplete can also save user names and information you enter into forms. When you start typing text you have previously entered, Internet Explorer offers a list of suggestions for you to choose from. This saves you from having to type the same information over and over.

To protect your privacy, Internet Explorer does not allow a Web page to access all the information in AutoComplete. The Web page can access only the item you select from the AutoComplete list or the information you type.

Microsoft Profile Assistant

The Profile Assistant lets you use an electronic business card, or profile, to share personal information on the Internet. Profiles can contain information such as your e-mail address, phone number, where you work and if you can be contacted using Microsoft NetMeeting. Sending your profile to other people or to a Web site saves you from typing the same information over and over. Some Web sites use profiles to track visits from users.

CHAPTER 25

START OUTLOOK EXPRESS AND READ MESSAGES

Y ou can use Outlook Express to exchange e-mail messages with people around the world.

When you start Outlook Express, the window displays the folders that contain your messages, a list of the people in your address book and links that allow you to quickly perform common tasks.

Outlook Express has five folders to store your messages. The Inbox folder contains messages you

receive. Messages waiting to be sent are held in the Outbox folder. Copies of messages you have sent are stored in the Sent Items folder. The Deleted Items folder contains any messages you have deleted. Messages you have not yet completed are stored in the Drafts folder.

If a folder contains unread messages, the name of the folder appears in bold type. A number in parentheses beside a folder

indicates how many unread messages the folder contains. Each unread message in a folder displays a closed envelope and appears in bold type. After you read a message, the message displays an open envelope and appears in regular type.

Outlook Express automatically checks for new messages every 30 minutes, but you can check for new messages at any time.

START OUTLOOK EXPRESS

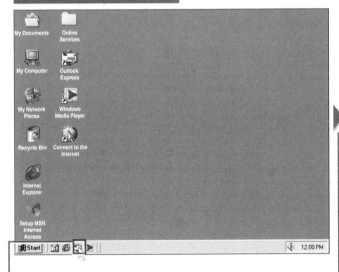

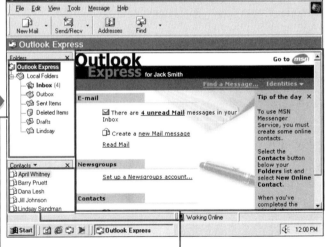

■1 Click 🖳 to start Outlook Express.

Note: If you are not currently connected to the Internet, a dialog box appears that allows you to connect.

■ The Outlook Express window appears.

■ This area displays the folders that contain your messages.

Note: A number in brackets beside a folder indicates how many unread messages the folder contains. The number disappears when you have read all the messages in the folder.

■ This area displays the Contacts list, which lists each person in your address book.

■ This area displays links that allow you to perform common tasks in Outlook Express.

How can I view the contents of a message in a larger area?

✔ You can double-click a message to view its contents in a separate window.

Can I make a message appear as if I have not read it?

✔ Yes. This is useful if you want to remind yourself to review the message at a later time. Click the message you want to appear as unread. From the Edit menu, select Mark as Unread.

How can I make an important message stand out?

✔ You can flag an important message to make the message stand out. Click the message you want to flag. From the Message menu, select Flag Message.

Can I change how often Outlook Express checks for new messages?

✔ Yes. Choose the Tools menu and then select Options. On the General tab, make sure the Check for new messages every option displays a check mark (✔). Then double-click the area beside the option and type the number of minutes Outlook Express should wait before checking for new messages.

How do I use Outlook Express to disconnect from the Internet?

✔ Click ✖ to close the Outlook Express window. A dialog box may appear, asking if you want to disconnect from the Internet. Click Disconnect Now to disconnect. The icon (🖳) that appears on the taskbar when you are connected to the Internet disappears.

READ MESSAGES

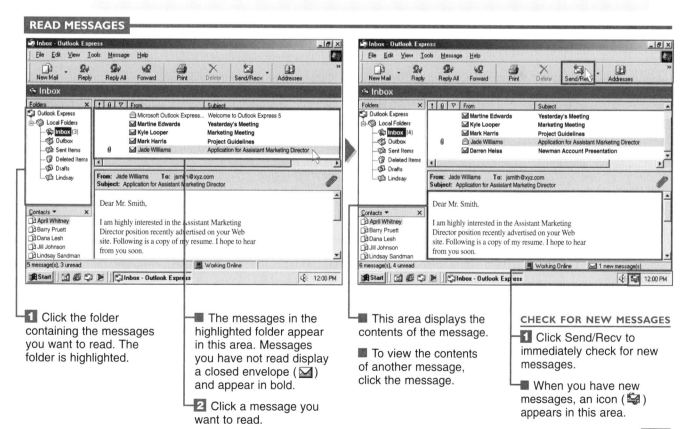

■1 Click the folder containing the messages you want to read. The folder is highlighted.

■ The messages in the highlighted folder appear in this area. Messages you have not read display a closed envelope (✉) and appear in bold.

■2 Click a message you want to read.

■ This area displays the contents of the message.

■ To view the contents of another message, click the message.

CHECK FOR NEW MESSAGES

■1 Click Send/Recv to immediately check for new messages.

■ When you have new messages, an icon (🖼) appears in this area.

REPLY TO OR FORWARD A MESSAGE

Y ou can reply to a message to answer a question, express an opinion or supply additional information.

You can send your reply to just the sender of the original message or to the sender and everyone who received the original message. When you reply to a message, a new window appears. The window displays the name of the recipients

and the subject of the message you are replying to.

The reply includes the contents of the original message. This is called quoting. Including the contents of the original message helps the reader identify which message you are replying to. You can save the reader time by deleting all parts of the original message that do not directly relate to your reply.

You can also forward a message to another person. When you forward a message, you can add your own comments to the original message. Forwarding a message is useful if you know that another person would be interested in the contents of the message.

REPLY TO A MESSAGE

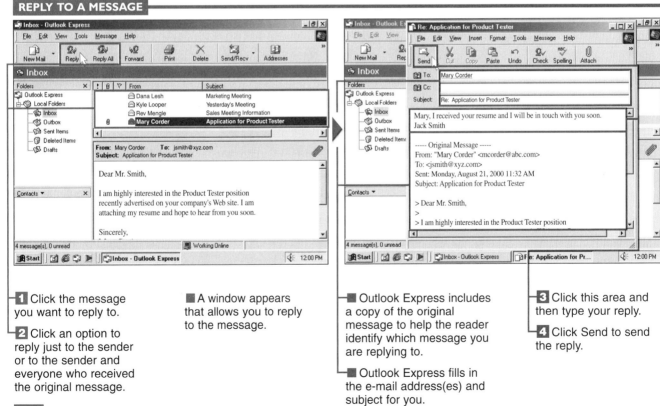

-1 Click the message you want to reply to.

-2 Click an option to reply just to the sender or to the sender and everyone who received the original message.

■ A window appears that allows you to reply to the message.

■ Outlook Express includes a copy of the original message to help the reader identify which message you are replying to.

■ Outlook Express fills in the e-mail address(es) and subject for you.

-3 Click this area and then type your reply.

-4 Click Send to send the reply.

How can I prevent Outlook Express from including the original message in my replies?

✓ If you do not want to include the original message in your replies, choose the Tools menu and then select Options. Select the Send tab and click the Include message in reply option (☑ changes to ☐).

Can I forward a message as an attached file?

✓ You can forward a message as an attached file instead of displaying the contents of the message. Click the message you want to forward as an attached file. From the Message menu, select Forward As Attachment.

How do I forward a message to more than one person?

✓ To forward a message to more than one person, perform steps 1 to 3 on this page. In step 3, separate each e-mail address with a semicolon (;) or a comma (,). You can also forward a message to more than one person by selecting names from the address book. To select names from the address book, see page 468.

FORWARD A MESSAGE

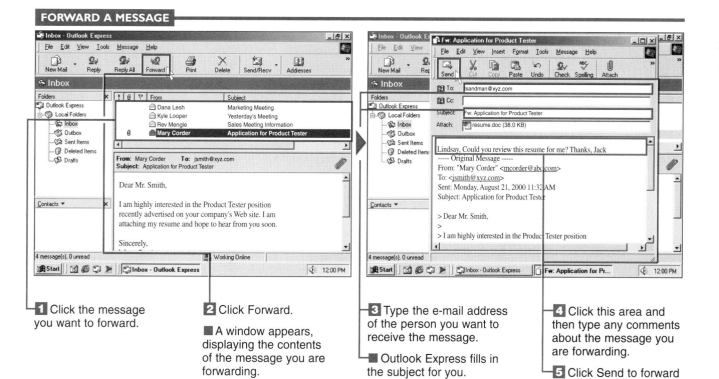

■1 Click the message you want to forward.

■2 Click Forward.

■ A window appears, displaying the contents of the message you are forwarding.

■3 Type the e-mail address of the person you want to receive the message.

■ Outlook Express fills in the subject for you.

■4 Click this area and then type any comments about the message you are forwarding.

■5 Click Send to forward the message.

SEND A MESSAGE

Y ou can send an e-mail message to express an idea or request information. To practice sending a message, you can send a message to yourself.

You can address a message to more than one person. You can enter the address of each person you want to receive the message in the To: area. You can use the Cc: area if you want to send a

copy of the message to a person who would be interested in the message, but is not directly involved.

You should include a subject in each message you send. A descriptive subject will help the reader quickly identify the contents of your message.

When composing the content of a message, you should use

both upper and lower case letters. A message written entirely in capital letters is difficult to read.

Outlook Express allows you to use the Contacts list to quickly address a message. The Contacts list displays the name of each person in your address book. For information about adding names to the address book, see page 464.

SEND A MESSAGE

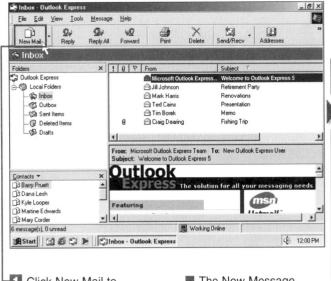

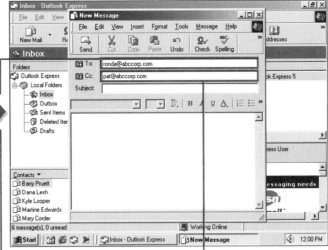

1 Click New Mail to send a new message.

■ The New Message window appears.

2 Type the e-mail address of the person you want to receive the message.

Note: To send the message to more than one person, separate each e-mail address with a semicolon (;) or a comma (,).

3 To send a copy of the message to another person, click this area and then type the e-mail address.

Note: To select a name from the address book, see page 468.

Is there another way to send a copy of a message?

✔ In the New Message window, choose the View menu and then click All Headers. The Bcc: area appears in the window. You can type an e-mail address in this area to send someone a copy of the message without anyone else knowing that the person received the message.

Can I spell check my messages?

✔ Outlook Express uses the spell checker provided with Microsoft Office programs, such as Word and Excel. If you do not have one of these programs installed, you cannot spell check messages. To spell check a message, click the Spelling button in the New Message window.

How can I indicate the importance of a message?

✔ In the New Message window, display the Message menu and then select Set Priority. You can choose a high, normal or low priority for the message. The recipient sees an exclamation mark (!) beside high priority messages and an arrow (↓) beside low priority messages.

Can I prevent Outlook Express from storing copies of messages I send in the Sent Items folder?

✔ In the Outlook Express window, choose the Tools menu, click Options and then select the Send tab. Click the Save copy of sent messages in the 'Sent Items' folder option (☑ changes to ☐).

QUICKLY ADDRESS A MESSAGE

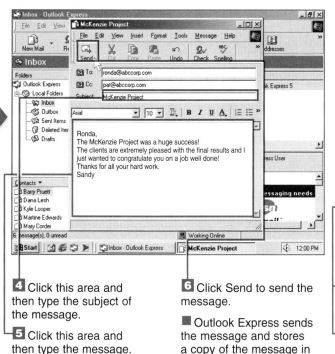

4 Click this area and then type the subject of the message.

5 Click this area and then type the message.

6 Click Send to send the message.

■ Outlook Express sends the message and stores a copy of the message in the Sent Items folder.

■ The Contacts list displays the name of each person in your address book.

1 To quickly send a message to a person in the Contacts list, double-click the name of the person.

■ The New Message window appears.

■ Outlook Express addresses the message for you.

2 To complete the message, perform steps 4 to 6.

ADD A NAME TO THE ADDRESS BOOK

You can use the address book to store the names and e-mail addresses of people you frequently send messages to.

When you add a new name to the address book, you can enter the person's first, middle and last name. Outlook Express also gives you the option of entering a nickname for the person. A nickname is a name or word that

describes the person. You can also enter the person's e-mail address.

When you send a message, you can select a name from the address book. You can also quickly address the message by typing the first few letters of the person's name, nickname or e-mail address. Outlook Express will automatically complete the name or e-mail address for you.

Using the address book to select names saves you from having to type the same e-mail addresses over and over. Using the address book also helps prevent typing mistakes in an address. Typing mistakes can result in a message being delivered to the wrong person or being returned to you.

Names you add to the address book also appear in the Contacts list.

ADD A NAME TO THE ADDRESS BOOK

1 Click Addresses to display the address book.

■ The Address Book window appears.

■ This area displays the name and e-mail address of each person in your address book.

2 Click New to add a name to the address book.

3 Click New Contact.

■ The Properties dialog box appears.

When I receive a message, can I add the sender to the address book?

✔ When you receive a message, you can quickly add the sender's name and e-mail address to the address book. Double-click the message and then choose the Tools menu. Select Add to Address Book and then click Sender.

Does Outlook Express automatically add names to the address book?

✔ Yes. Each time you reply to a message, the recipient's name and e-mail address are automatically added to the address book.

How do I change the information for a person in the address book?

✔ To change the information for a person in the address book, double-click the person's name in the Address Book window to display the information for the person. Click the Name tab and then make the changes.

How do I delete a person from the address book?

✔ To delete a person from the address book, click the person's name in the Address Book window and then press the Delete key.

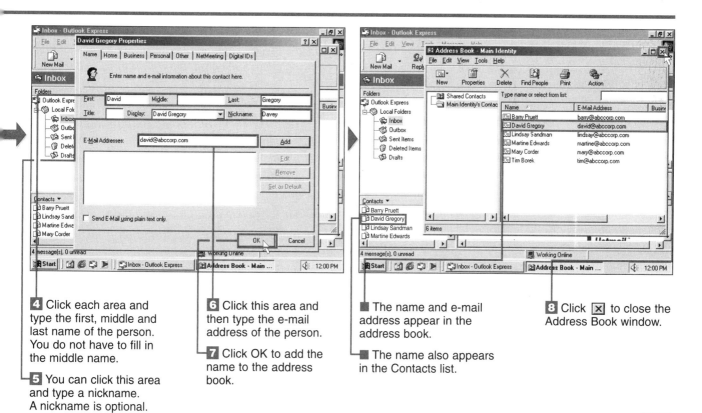

■ **4** Click each area and type the first, middle and last name of the person. You do not have to fill in the middle name.

■ **5** You can click this area and type a nickname. A nickname is optional.

■ **6** Click this area and then type the e-mail address of the person.

■ **7** Click OK to add the name to the address book.

■ The name and e-mail address appear in the address book.

■ The name also appears in the Contacts list.

■ **8** Click ✗ to close the Address Book window.

ADD A GROUP TO THE ADDRESS BOOK

You can add a group to the address book so you can quickly send the same message to every person in the group. Creating a group saves you the time of having to enter each person's e-mail address into a message. For example, if you are planning to send a message to your customers advising them of your monthly specials, you can create a group so you can

send the same message to all your customers at once.

You can use the addresses in your address book to create the new group. Each group appears as a name in the address book. You can create as many groups as you need.

When composing a message you want to send to a group, you can select the name of the group

from the address book. You can also type the name of the group in the New Message window. Outlook Express will send the message to everyone in the group.

Groups you add to the address book also appear in the Contacts list. This list allows you to quickly address a message.

ADD A GROUP TO THE ADDRESS BOOK

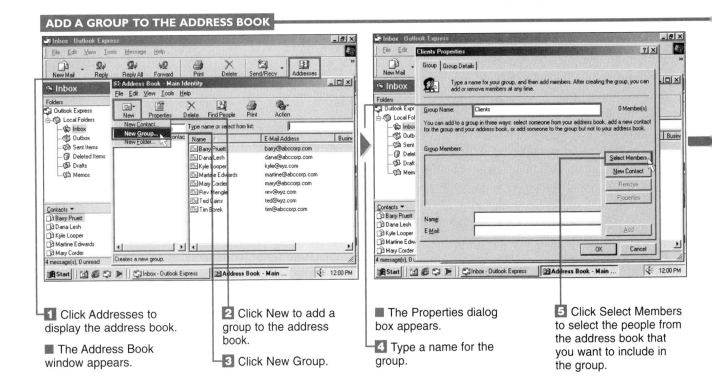

1 Click Addresses to display the address book.

■ The Address Book window appears.

2 Click New to add a group to the address book.

3 Click New Group.

■ The Properties dialog box appears.

4 Type a name for the group.

5 Click Select Members to select the people from the address book that you want to include in the group.

How can I add a name that is not in the address book to a group?

✔ In the Address Book window, double-click the group. At the bottom of the Properties dialog box, enter the person's name and e-mail address. Click the Add button and then click OK.

Can I add a name to a group and to the address book at the same time?

✔ Yes. In the Address Book window, double-click the group. In the Properties dialog box, click the New Contact button. Then perform steps 4 to 7 on page 465.

How do I remove a name from a group?

✔ In the Address Book window, double-click the group to display the list of names in the group. Select the name you want to remove from the group and then press the Delete key.

How do I remove an entire group from the address book?

✔ In the Address Book window, click the name of the group you want to remove and then press the Delete key.

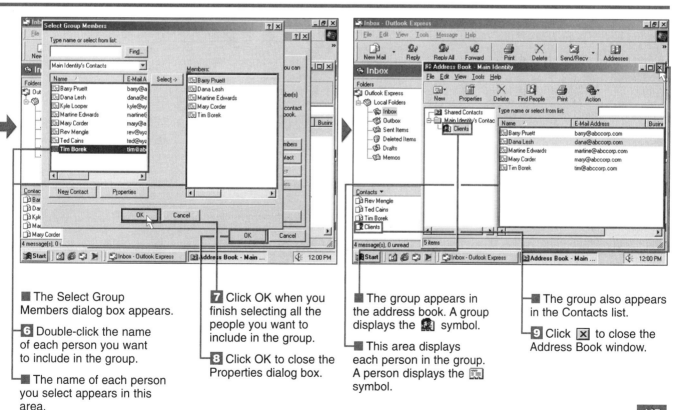

■ The Select Group Members dialog box appears.

6 Double-click the name of each person you want to include in the group.

■ The name of each person you select appears in this area.

7 Click OK when you finish selecting all the people you want to include in the group.

8 Click OK to close the Properties dialog box.

■ The group appears in the address book. A group displays the 🖳 symbol.

■ This area displays each person in the group. A person displays the 📧 symbol.

■ The group also appears in the Contacts list.

9 Click ☒ to close the Address Book window.

SELECT A NAME FROM THE ADDRESS BOOK

When sending a message, you can select the name of the person you want to receive the message from the address book. Selecting names from the address book saves you from having to type e-mail addresses you often use.

The address book makes it easy to send a message when you do not remember the recipient's e-mail

address. The address book also reduces the possibility that the message will be undeliverable because of a typing mistake in the address.

The address book allows you to send a message to several recipients. You can also send a copy of the message, called a carbon copy (Cc), to another person. This is useful if you

want to send a copy of the message to someone who is not directly involved, but would be interested in the message. The address book also lets you send a blind carbon copy (Bcc) of the message. A blind carbon copy is useful if you want to send a copy of the message to a person without anyone else knowing that the person received the message.

SELECT A NAME FROM THE ADDRESS BOOK

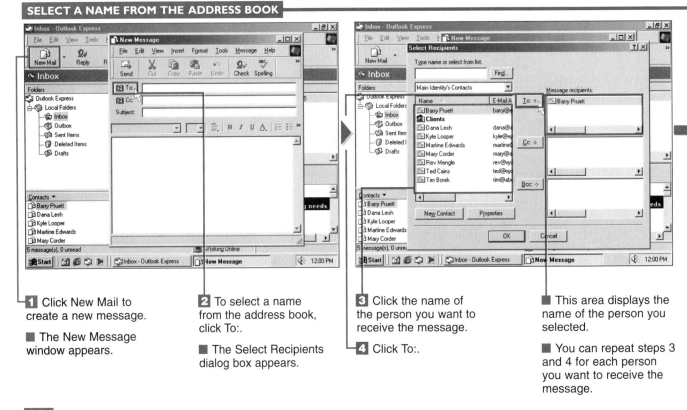

■1 Click New Mail to create a new message.

■ The New Message window appears.

■2 To select a name from the address book, click To:.

■ The Select Recipients dialog box appears.

■3 Click the name of the person you want to receive the message.

■4 Click To:.

■ This area displays the name of the person you selected.

■ You can repeat steps 3 and 4 for each person you want to receive the message.

How do I remove a name from the To:, Cc: or Bcc: area in the Select Recipients dialog box?

✔ To remove a name, click the name and then press the Delete key.

Is there a faster way to select a name from the address book?

✔ You can quickly enter a name from the address book by typing the first few letters of a person's name, nickname or e-mail address in the To: or Cc: areas of the New Message window. Outlook Express will automatically complete the name or e-mail address for you.

Can I mix names from the address book with addresses I type?

✔ Yes. After you select a name from the address book, you can type an e-mail address. Each name and address must be separated with a comma (,) or a semicolon (;).

How do I use the Contacts list to select a name from the address book?

✔ The Contacts list appears in the bottom left corner of the Outlook Express window and displays the name of each person in your address book. To quickly send a message to a person in the Contacts list, double-click their name. The New Message window appears with the To: area addressed to the person you selected.

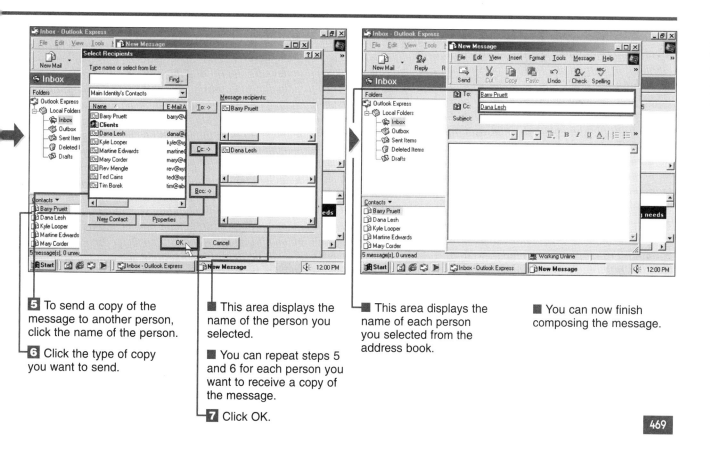

■ **5** To send a copy of the message to another person, click the name of the person.

■ **6** Click the type of copy you want to send.

■ This area displays the name of the person you selected.

■ You can repeat steps 5 and 6 for each person you want to receive a copy of the message.

■ **7** Click OK.

■ This area displays the name of each person you selected from the address book.

■ You can now finish composing the message.

ATTACH A FILE TO A MESSAGE

You can attach a file to a message you are sending. Attaching a file is useful when you want to include additional information with a message.

You can attach many different types of files to your messages, including document, image, program, sound and video files. The computer receiving the message must have the necessary

hardware and software to display or play the file you attach.

When you receive a message with an attached file, you can open and view the file. Some files, such as program files, can contain viruses. If you open a file that contains a virus, the information on your computer could be damaged. You should make sure the files you open are from reliable sources.

When you select a file you want to open, Outlook Express may ask if you want to open or save the file. Before you open the file, you should save the file on your computer and run an anti-virus program on the file.

Some pictures, such as those in the Bitmap, GIF and JPEG formats, are displayed in the body of a message, as well as in the list of attached files.

ATTACH A FILE TO A MESSAGE

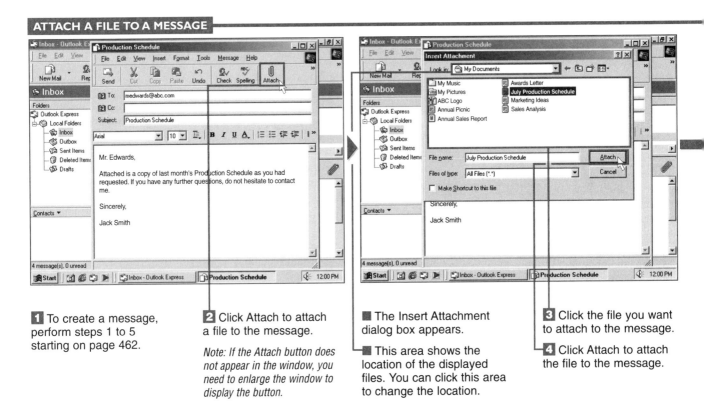

1 To create a message, perform steps 1 to 5 starting on page 462.

2 Click Attach to attach a file to the message.

Note: If the Attach button does not appear in the window, you need to enlarge the window to display the button.

■ The Insert Attachment dialog box appears.

■ This area shows the location of the displayed files. You can click this area to change the location.

3 Click the file you want to attach to the message.

4 Click Attach to attach the file to the message.

Can I drag and drop a file into a message?

✔ You can drag and drop a file from the desktop or any open window into a message. This is a quick way to attach several files to a message at once.

Instead of attaching a picture, can I send the picture as the background of a message?

✔ Yes. In the New Message window, choose the Format menu, select Background and then click Picture. In the Background Picture dialog box, click the Browse button to locate the file you want to use as a background picture.

Can I send a large message with many attachments?

✔ Many mail servers cannot send and receive messages larger than 1 MB. To send a large message, you can have Outlook Express break the message into several small messages. When an e-mail program receives the group of small messages, the program will combine the messages into one large message. In the Outlook Express window, select the Tools menu and then click Accounts. Choose the Mail tab, select the Properties button and then click the Advanced tab. Select the Break apart messages larger than option and then specify the maximum file size you can send.

OPEN AN ATTACHED FILE

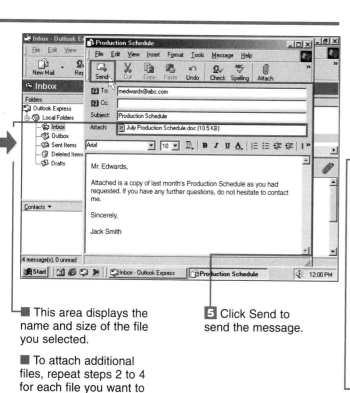

■ This area displays the name and size of the file you selected.

■ To attach additional files, repeat steps 2 to 4 for each file you want to attach to the message.

5 Click Send to send the message.

1 Click the message with an attached file. A message with an attached file displays a paper clip icon (📎).

2 Click the paper clip icon (📎) in this area to open the attached file.

3 Click the file you want to open.

■ A dialog box may appear, asking if you want to open or save the file.

FORMAT MESSAGES

Y ou can format the text in a message you are composing. The formatting features found in Outlook Express are similar to those found in most word processing programs.

You can change the design and size of the text in a message. Changing the design and size of text allows you to make your messages more interesting and can help make long messages

easier to read. You can use the bold, italic and underline styles to emphasize information. Changing the color of text helps to draw attention to important information and can make a message more attractive.

Outlook Express uses HyperText Markup Language (HTML) to format messages. HTML is the language used to create Web

pages. Most e-mail programs use HTML to format messages.

If the recipient of the message uses an e-mail program that cannot display HTML formatted text, the message will appear as plain text with no formatting. The message will include an attached file that the recipient can open in a Web browser to view the HTML formatted text.

FORMAT MESSAGES

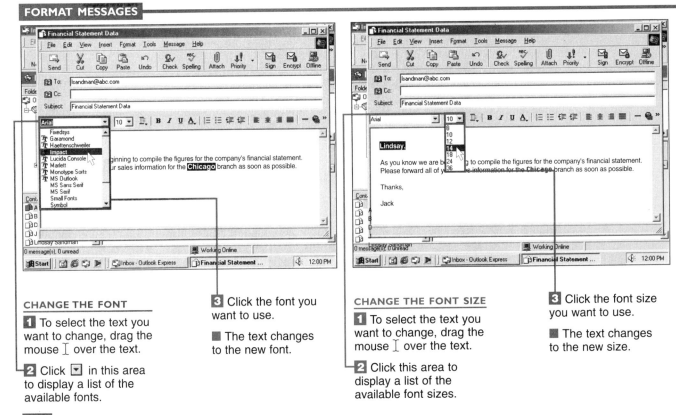

CHANGE THE FONT

1 To select the text you want to change, drag the mouse I over the text.

2 Click ▼ in this area to display a list of the available fonts.

3 Click the font you want to use.

■ The text changes to the new font.

CHANGE THE FONT SIZE

1 To select the text you want to change, drag the mouse I over the text.

2 Click this area to display a list of the available font sizes.

3 Click the font size you want to use.

■ The text changes to the new size.

Why can't I format a message?

✔ HTML formatting may be disabled. To enable HTML formatting, select the Format menu and then click Rich Text (HTML).

How can I change the background color of a message?

✔ Choose the Format menu and then select Background. Click Color and then select the background color you want to use. Make sure you use text and background colors that work well together. For example, red text on a blue background can be difficult to read.

Can I add a background design to a message?

✔ Yes. In the Outlook Express window, click ▪ beside the New Mail button and then click the design you want to use. The New Message window appears, displaying the background design.

Why does Outlook Express underline the e-mail and Web page addresses I type in a message?

✔ Outlook Express automatically converts any e-mail or Web page address you type into a link. The person who receives your message will be able to select the link to send a message or display the Web page.

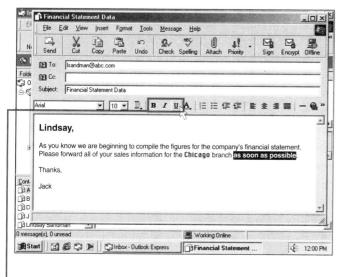

BOLD, ITALICIZE OR UNDERLINE TEXT

■ 1 To select the text you want to change, drag the mouse I over the text.

■ 2 Click bold (**B**), italic (*I*) or underline (U̲).

■ The text appears in the new style.

Note: To remove a bold, italic or underline style, repeat steps 1 and 2.

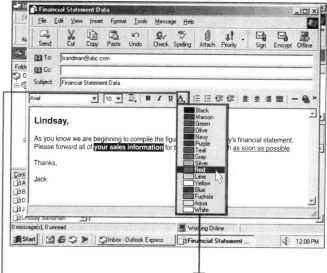

ADD COLOR

■ 1 To select the text you want to change, drag the mouse I over the text.

■ 2 Click ▲ to display a list of the available colors.

■ 3 Click the color you want to use.

■ The text appears in the color you selected.

ADD A SIGNATURE TO MESSAGES

You can have Outlook Express add information about yourself to the end of every message you send. This information is called a signature. A signature saves you from having to type the same information every time you send a message.

A signature can include information such as your name, e-mail address, occupation or Web page address. You can also use plain characters to display simple pictures in your signature. Many people use a signature to display their favorite humorous or inspirational quotation.

You should leave a blank line at the beginning of your signature to separate the signature from the body of your message. As a courtesy to the people who will be reading your messages, you should limit your signature to four or five lines.

You can have Outlook Express add your signature to all the messages you send, reply to and forward.

ADD A SIGNATURE TO MESSAGES

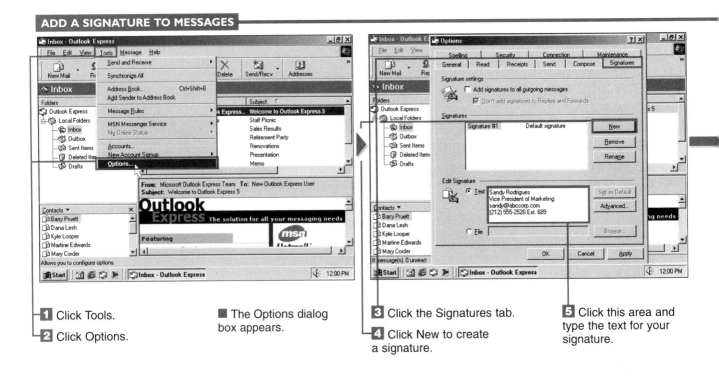

1 Click Tools.

2 Click Options.

■ The Options dialog box appears.

3 Click the Signatures tab.

4 Click New to create a signature.

5 Click this area and type the text for your signature.

How can I create multiple signatures?

✔ After creating your first signature, repeat steps 4 and 5 below for each additional signature you want to create. Turn off the Add signatures to all outgoing messages option (☑ changes to ☐) and click OK. To add a signature to a message you are composing, choose the Insert menu, select Signature and click the signature you want to include.

Can I use a text file on my computer as my signature?

✔ Yes. Perform steps 1 to 4 below and then select the File option (○ changes to ⦿). Click the Browse button to locate the text file and then perform steps 6 to 8.

Can I attach additional information to my messages?

✔ You can use a business card to send contact information to the recipients of your messages. To create a business card, perform steps 1 to 7 on page 464. You can use the tabs in the Properties dialog box to specify additional information. To add your business card to outgoing messages, choose the Tools menu in the Outlook Express window, select Options and click the Compose tab. In the Business Cards area, click the Mail option (☐ changes to ☑) and select your business card. A recipient can click the (⊞) symbol in your message to read your contact information.

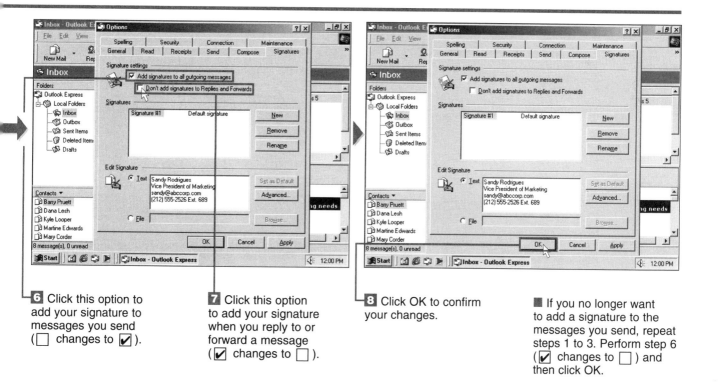

6 Click this option to add your signature to messages you send (☐ changes to ☑).

7 Click this option to add your signature when you reply to or forward a message (☑ changes to ☐).

8 Click OK to confirm your changes.

■ If you no longer want to add a signature to the messages you send, repeat steps 1 to 3. Perform step 6 (☑ changes to ☐) and then click OK.

SAVE A DRAFT

You can save a draft of a message you are unable to finish composing. Saving a draft allows you to complete the message at a later time. This is useful when you want to review the message again later before sending it. When you save a draft, Outlook Express stores the message in the Drafts folder until you are ready to complete and send the message.

When you want to complete a message you have saved as a draft, display the contents of the Drafts folder and double-click the message you want to complete. When you send the message, Outlook Express removes the message from the Drafts folder and places it in the Sent Items folder.

If you no longer want to complete and send a message you have saved, you can delete the message from the Drafts folder as you would delete any message. To delete a message, see page 478.

SAVE A DRAFT

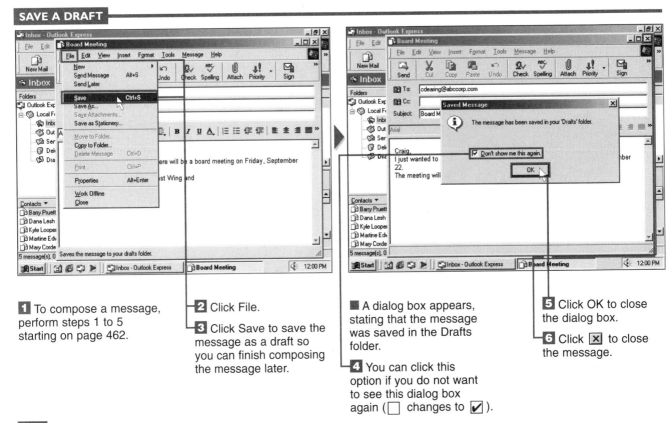

1 To compose a message, perform steps 1 to 5 starting on page 462.

2 Click File.

3 Click Save to save the message as a draft so you can finish composing the message later.

■ A dialog box appears, stating that the message was saved in the Drafts folder.

4 You can click this option if you do not want to see this dialog box again (☐ changes to ✔).

5 Click OK to close the dialog box.

6 Click ✕ to close the message.

CHECK FOR NEW MESSAGES AUTOMATICALLY

You can change how often Outlook Express checks for new messages. When Outlook Express checks for new messages, the new messages are transferred from the mail server at your Internet service provider to your computer.

If you have a constant connection to the Internet, such as at work, you may want to have Outlook Express check for new messages as often as every few minutes.

If you connect to the Internet using a modem, such as at home, you may want to have Outlook Express check for new messages less frequently. Checking for messages frequently can slow down other tasks you are performing, such as Web browsing.

If you are not connected to the Internet when it is time for Outlook Express to check for new messages, Outlook Express will not connect by default. You can specify if you

want to have Outlook Express always connect to the Internet automatically or connect only when you are not working offline.

You can click the Send and Receive button to check for new messages at any time. Clicking the Send and Receive button also immediately sends any messages stored in the Outbox folder.

CHECK FOR NEW MESSAGES AUTOMATICALLY

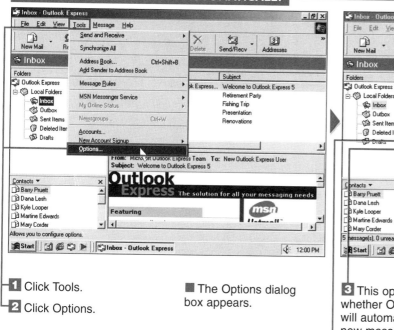

■ Click Tools.

■ Click Options.

■ The Options dialog box appears.

3 This option indicates whether Outlook Express will automatically check for new messages. Click this option to turn the option on (✔) or off (☐).

4 Double-click this area and type how often you want Outlook Express to check for new messages.

■ You can click ▼ in this area to specify what Outlook Express should do if you are not connected to the Internet.

5 Click OK.

WORK WITH E-MAIL MESSAGES

Outlook Express allows you to organize and manage your e-mail messages.

You can sort messages in Outlook Express so they are easier to find. You can sort by the name of the person who sent or received the message, the subject of the message or the date the message was sent or

received. Messages can be sorted in ascending or descending order. Messages are usually sorted by the date they were sent or received, in ascending order.

You can delete a message you no longer need. Deleting messages prevents your folders from becoming cluttered with messages. When you delete a message, Outlook Express

places the deleted message in the Deleted Items folder.

You can produce a paper copy of a message. A printed message is useful when you need a reference copy of the message. Outlook Express prints the page number and total number of pages at the top of each page. The current date prints at the bottom of each page.

WORK WITH E-MAIL MESSAGES

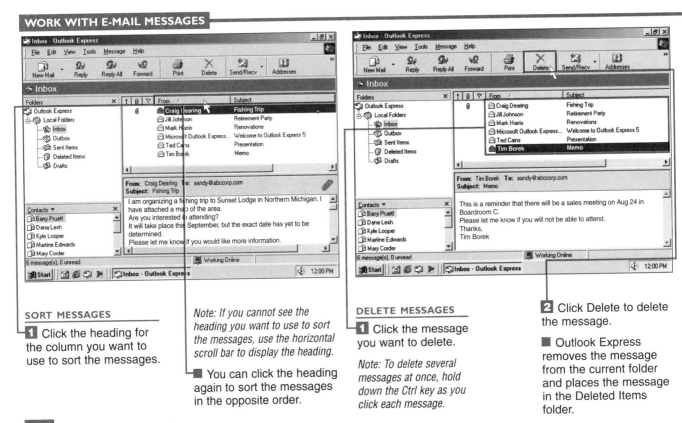

SORT MESSAGES

1 Click the heading for the column you want to use to sort the messages.

Note: If you cannot see the heading you want to use to sort the messages, use the horizontal scroll bar to display the heading.

■ You can click the heading again to sort the messages in the opposite order.

DELETE MESSAGES

1 Click the message you want to delete.

Note: To delete several messages at once, hold down the Ctrl key as you click each message.

2 Click Delete to delete the message.

■ Outlook Express removes the message from the current folder and places the message in the Deleted Items folder.

How do I change the width of a column?

✔ Position the mouse pointer on the right edge of the heading for the column you want to change. The mouse pointer changes to a double-headed arrow (✛). Drag the edge of the column until it displays the size you want.

Can Outlook Express automatically empty the Deleted Items folder?

✔ If you want the Deleted Items folder to automatically empty each time you close Outlook Express, choose the Tools menu and then click the Options command. Select the Maintenance tab and click the Empty messages from the 'Deleted Items' folder on exit option (☐ changes to ☑).

Can I empty the Deleted Items folder?

✔ You can empty the Deleted Items folder to permanently remove deleted messages from your computer. Right-click the Deleted Items folder and then select the Empty 'Deleted Items' Folder option.

Can I work with a message in another program?

✔ You can save a message as a text file so you can work with the message in another program. Click the message you want to save as a text file. Choose the File menu and then select Save As. In the Save Message As dialog box, change the Save as type option to Text Files.

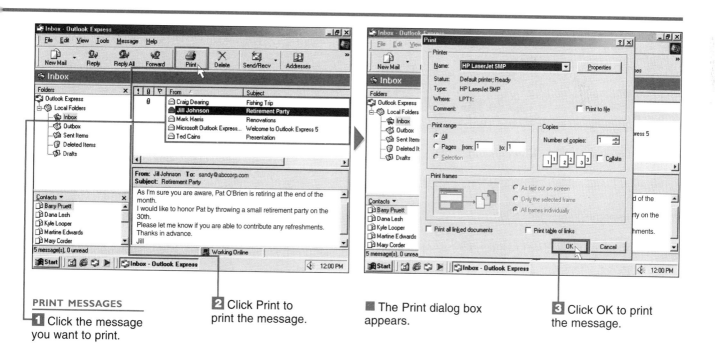

PRINT MESSAGES

■1 Click the message you want to print.

■2 Click Print to print the message.

■ The Print dialog box appears.

■3 Click OK to print the message.

CREATE A NEW FOLDER

You can create folders in Outlook Express to keep related messages together. Creating folders can help make your messages easier to find. For example, if you have many messages related to a specific project or client, you can create a folder to store all the messages in one location.

You can create a main folder that will appear with the Inbox, Outbox,

Sent Items, Deleted Items and Drafts folder. You can also create a folder that will appear within an existing folder. For example, you can create a folder within the Inbox folder.

You can use descriptive names to label the folders you create, but you should try to keep the names short. Long names may not be fully displayed in the Outlook Express

window. When you can see the full name of a folder in the Outlook Express window, you are able to work with the folder more easily.

After you create a folder, you can easily move messages into the folder.

CREATE A NEW FOLDER

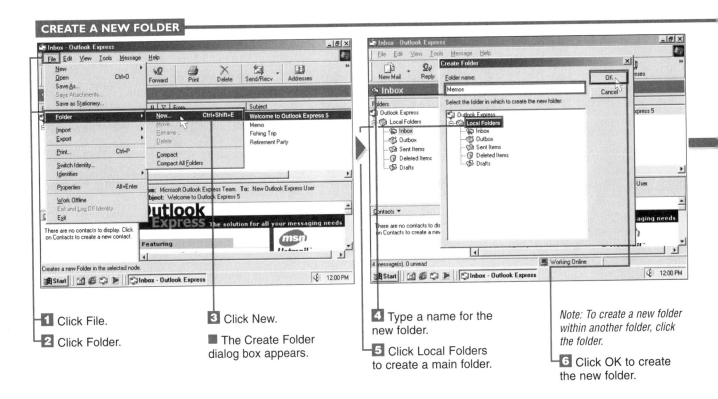

1 Click File.

2 Click Folder.

3 Click New.

■ The Create Folder dialog box appears.

4 Type a name for the new folder.

5 Click Local Folders to create a main folder.

Note: To create a new folder within another folder, click the folder.

6 Click OK to create the new folder.

Why can't I see the new folder I created?

✔ If you create a folder within another folder, the folder you created may be hidden. Click the plus sign (⊞) beside the folder that contains the folder you created (⊞ changes to ⊟).

How do I rename a folder?

✔ Right-click the folder you want to rename and then select Rename from the menu that appears. Type the new name and then press the Enter key. You can only rename folders that you have created.

How do I delete a folder I no longer need?

✔ Click the folder you want to delete and then press the Delete key. You can only delete folders that you have created. If you delete a folder that contains messages, the messages will also be deleted. Outlook Express places deleted folders in the Deleted Items folder. To permanently remove a folder from your computer, you must delete the folder from the Deleted Items folder.

Can I rearrange folders I have created?

✔ Yes. Position the mouse pointer over the folder you want to move and then drag the folder to a new location.

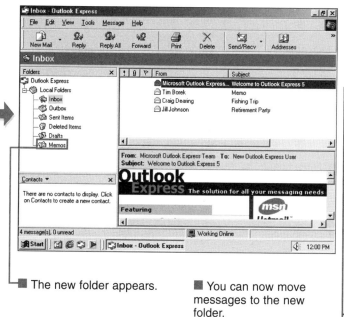

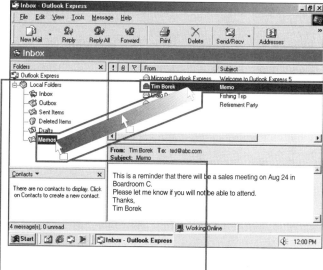

■ The new folder appears.

■ You can now move messages to the new folder.

MOVE MESSAGES TO ANOTHER FOLDER

1 Click the message you want to move to another folder.

2 Position the mouse ▷ over the message.

3 Drag the message to the folder you want to store the message.

■ Outlook Express moves the message to the folder.

FIND MESSAGES

If you cannot find a message you want to review, you can have Outlook Express search for the message. You should provide Outlook Express with as much information about the message as possible to help narrow your search.

If you know which folder contains the message, you can search a specific folder. You can also search all the folders for the message.

Outlook Express can search for a message you have received from a specific person. Outlook Express can also find a message you have sent to a certain person.

If you can only remember a word from the subject of the message you want to find, you can have Outlook Express search the subject area of your messages. You can also search for messages that contain specific text.

You may also want to search for messages received before or after a certain date, messages with attached files or messages you have flagged.

When the search is complete, Outlook Express displays a list of messages that match all of the information you specified. You can open and read the messages.

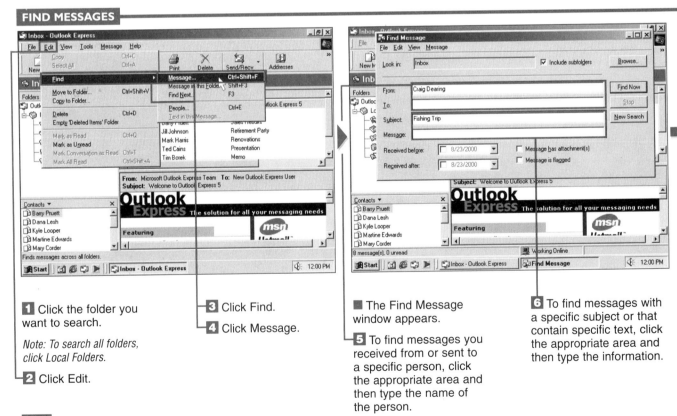

FIND MESSAGES

1 Click the folder you want to search.

Note: To search all folders, click Local Folders.

2 Click Edit.

3 Click Find.

4 Click Message.

■ The Find Message window appears.

5 To find messages you received from or sent to a specific person, click the appropriate area and then type the name of the person.

6 To find messages with a specific subject or that contain specific text, click the appropriate area and then type the information.

While specifying search options, can I change the folder Outlook Express will search?

✔ In the Find Message window, click the Browse button to select a different folder. Outlook Express will automatically search all the subfolders within the folder you select. If you do not want to search the subfolders, click the Include subfolders option to turn the option off (☑ changes to ☐).

Outlook Express didn't find the message I was looking for. What can I do?

✔ If the search did not provide the results you were expecting, you may have specified incorrect information. In the Find Message window, click the New Search button to clear the contents of the window and start a new search.

Can I search one message for specific text?

✔ If you are reviewing a message that contains a lot of text, you can use the Find feature to quickly locate a word in the message. Click anywhere in the message you want to search. From the Edit menu, select Find and then click Text in this message. Type the text you want to find and then click Find Next.

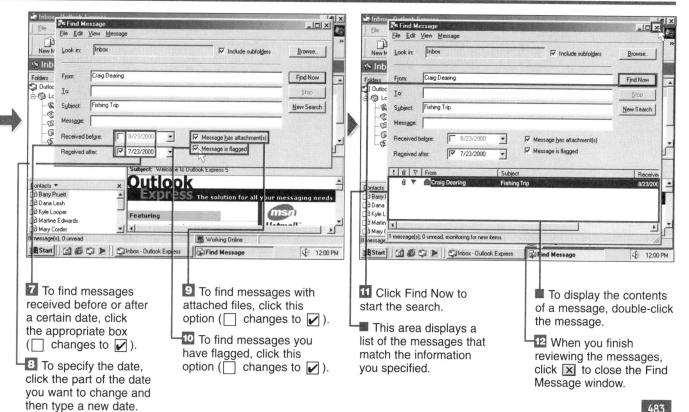

7 To find messages received before or after a certain date, click the appropriate box (☐ changes to ☑).

8 To specify the date, click the part of the date you want to change and then type a new date.

9 To find messages with attached files, click this option (☐ changes to ☑).

10 To find messages you have flagged, click this option (☐ changes to ☑).

11 Click Find Now to start the search.

■ This area displays a list of the messages that match the information you specified.

■ To display the contents of a message, double-click the message.

12 When you finish reviewing the messages, click ✕ to close the Find Message window.

SORT INCOMING MESSAGES

Y ou can have Outlook
Express sort the messages
you receive. This is useful
if you want to organize incoming
messages before you read them.

You can set up a rule to tell
Outlook Express how you want
to sort the messages you receive.
You need to select a condition
to specify which incoming
messages you want Outlook

Express to sort. For example,
you can sort incoming messages
that were sent by a specific
person. You could also sort
incoming messages that contain
specific words in the subject
or body of the message.

When setting up a rule, you will
also need to specify an action
you want Outlook Express to
perform on messages you

receive. Outlook Express can
automatically move or copy
messages to a specific folder,
delete messages you do not want
to read or forward messages to
another address. You can even
instruct Outlook Express to
automatically reply to messages.
Many people use automatic
replies to inform people that
they are on vacation.

SORT INCOMING MESSAGES

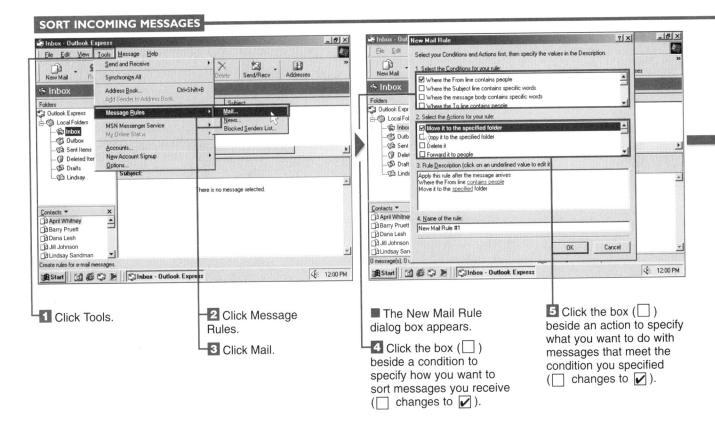

1 Click Tools.

2 Click Message Rules.

3 Click Mail.

■ The New Mail Rule dialog box appears.

4 Click the box (☐) beside a condition to specify how you want to sort messages you receive (☐ changes to ✔).

5 Click the box (☐) beside an action to specify what you want to do with messages that meet the condition you specified (☐ changes to ✔).

Why does the Message Rules dialog box appear instead of the New Mail Rule dialog box?

✔ If you have already created a rule, the New Mail Rule dialog box does not appear automatically. In the Message Rules dialog box, click the New button to display the New Mail Rule dialog box.

How do I quickly create a rule to sort messages from a specific person?

✔ Select a message from the person, choose the Message menu and then click Create Rule From Message. Outlook Express automatically fills in the condition for you using the e-mail address of the person. You must specify an action for the rule.

Can I select multiple conditions and actions for a rule?

✔ Yes. Click the check box beside each condition and action you want to use (☐ changes to ☑). If you select more than one condition, Outlook Express will only sort incoming messages that meet all the conditions. To sort incoming messages that meet any of the conditions, click 'and' in the Rule Description area and then select the Messages match any one of the criteria option in the dialog box that appears.

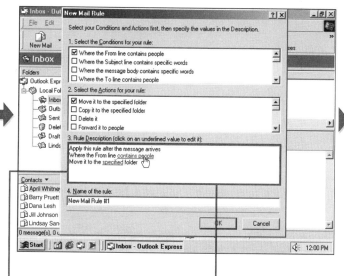

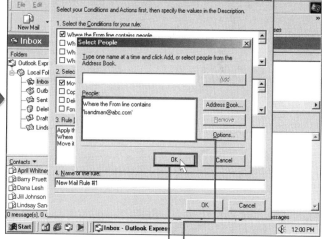

■ This area displays the condition and action you selected. You need to specify additional information for text that appears underlined and in blue.

Note: In this example, Outlook Express will move messages you receive from certain people to a specific folder.

6 Click the first instance of text that appears underlined and in blue to specify the required information.

Note: In this example, we click "contains people."

■ The Select People dialog box appears.

Note: The dialog box that appears depends on the text you selected in step 6.

7 Type an e-mail address you want to apply the rule to and then press the Enter key.

■ The e-mail address appears in this area.

8 To specify additional e-mail addresses, repeat step 7 for each address.

9 Click OK.

CONTINUED ▶

SORT INCOMING MESSAGES
(CONTINUED)

Outlook Express allows you to easily enter the information for a rule you are creating.

Once you have specified a condition and action for a rule, Outlook Express helps you complete the rule by displaying blue, underlined text to indicate where you must enter additional information. For example, when

you create a rule to move messages from certain people to a specific folder, Outlook Express indicates that you must enter the e-mail addresses of people whose messages you want to move and the folder to which you want to move the messages.

You can name a rule you create. A descriptive name can help you identify the rule later, which is

particularly useful if you create many rules for your e-mail messages.

Outlook Express displays rules you create in the Message Rules dialog box. You can perform steps 1 to 3 on page 484 to redisplay the dialog box at any time to review the rules for your e-mail messages.

SORT INCOMING MESSAGES (CONTINUED)

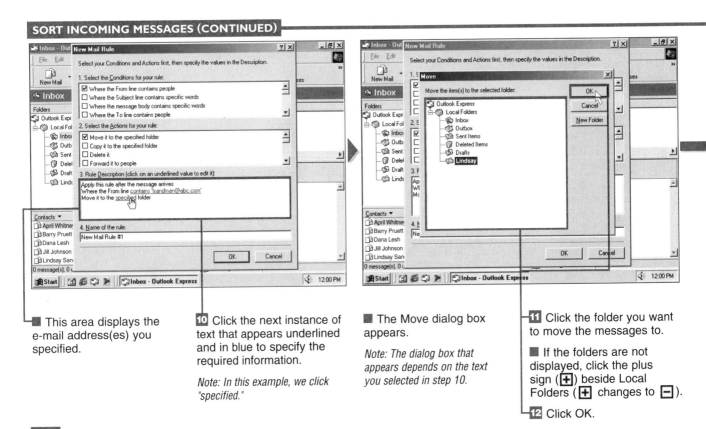

■ This area displays the e-mail address(es) you specified.

10 Click the next instance of text that appears underlined and in blue to specify the required information.

Note: In this example, we click "specified."

■ The Move dialog box appears.

Note: The dialog box that appears depends on the text you selected in step 10.

11 Click the folder you want to move the messages to.

■ If the folders are not displayed, click the plus sign (⊞) beside Local Folders (⊞ changes to ⊟).

12 Click OK.

Why are my messages not being sorted properly?

✔ If you are using more than one rule to sort your messages, the rules may not be affecting your messages in the proper order. The rule at the top of the Message Rules dialog box affects your messages first. To move a rule, select the rule and then click the Move Up or Move Down button.

Will a rule I create affect messages I have already received?

✔ No. A rule you create will only affect new messages you receive. To apply the rule to all your messages, click the Apply Now button in the Message Rules dialog box. In the dialog box that appears, click the rule and then click Apply Now.

How can I make changes to a rule I created?

✔ In the Message Rules dialog box, select the rule you want to change and then click the Modify button.

How do I remove a rule I no longer need?

✔ In the Message Rules dialog box, select the rule you no longer want to use and then click the Remove button.

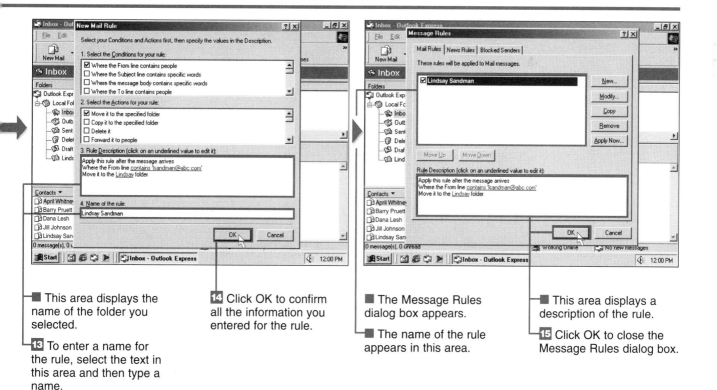

■ This area displays the name of the folder you selected.

13 To enter a name for the rule, select the text in this area and then type a name.

14 Click OK to confirm all the information you entered for the rule.

■ The Message Rules dialog box appears.

■ The name of the rule appears in this area.

■ This area displays a description of the rule.

15 Click OK to close the Message Rules dialog box.

SET UP A NEWS ACCOUNT

Before you can use Outlook Express to read or post newsgroup messages, you must set up a news account. Newsgroups allow people with common interests to communicate with each other.

The Internet Connection Wizard helps you set up a news account. You must provide the wizard with information, such as your name and e-mail address. If you have

already set up your e-mail account, the wizard may display your name and e-mail address.

When you post a message to a newsgroup, the name you specify in the wizard will appear in the From field of the message. If a reader wants to comment on a message you post, they can send you a reply. The reply will be sent to the e-mail address you specify in the wizard.

You do not have to use your real name and e-mail address. Specifying a false e-mail address prevents junk mailers from sending you automatic messages. Remember to include your real e-mail address in the body of your message if you want other readers to be able to contact you.

SET UP A NEWS ACCOUNT

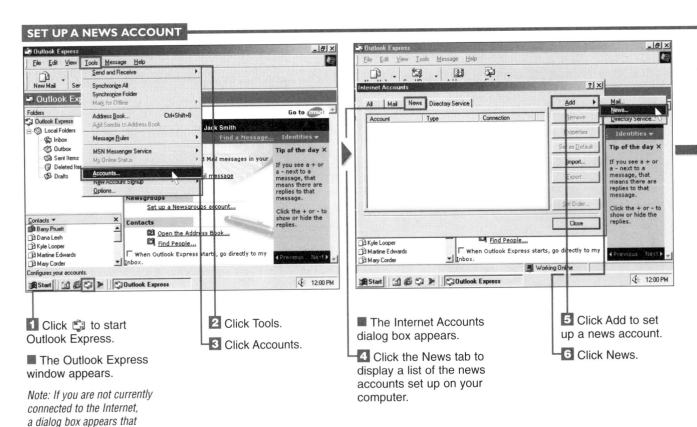

■ 1 Click 🛱 to start Outlook Express.

■ The Outlook Express window appears.

Note: If you are not currently connected to the Internet, a dialog box appears that allows you to connect.

■ 2 Click Tools.

■ 3 Click Accounts.

■ The Internet Accounts dialog box appears.

■ 4 Click the News tab to display a list of the news accounts set up on your computer.

■ 5 Click Add to set up a news account.

■ 6 Click News.

Is there another way to start the Internet Connection Wizard for the first time?

✔ Yes. In the Outlook Express window, select Outlook Express in the folders list. Then click the Set up Newsgroups link to display the Internet Connection Wizard.

How do I delete a news account I no longer use?

✔ In the Internet Accounts dialog box, select the news account you want to delete and then click the Remove button.

Can I set up more than one news account?

✔ You can set up multiple news accounts in Outlook Express. Setting up multiple news accounts allows you to access information from different news servers. For example, you could set up one news account to access newsgroups on your Internet service provider's news server and another account to access a news server set up by a company to provide product support.

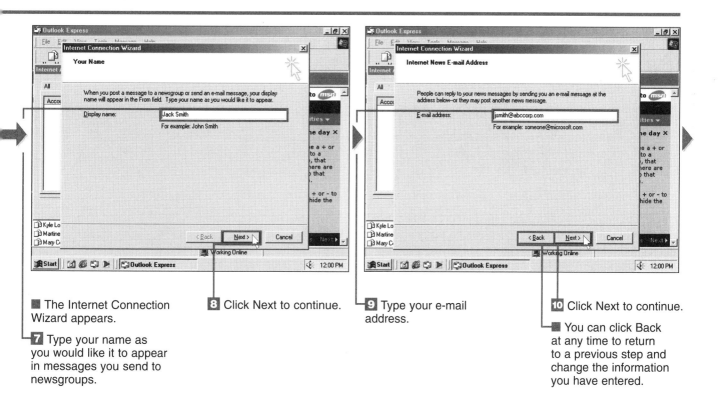

■ The Internet Connection Wizard appears.

7 Type your name as you would like it to appear in messages you send to newsgroups.

8 Click Next to continue.

9 Type your e-mail address.

10 Click Next to continue.

■ You can click Back at any time to return to a previous step and change the information you have entered.

SET UP A NEWS ACCOUNT
(CONTINUED)

Newsgroups are stored on computers called news servers, which are usually run and maintained by Internet service providers. When using the Internet Connection Wizard to set up a news account, you must specify the name of the news server you want to connect to. If you do not know the name of your news server, you can contact your Internet service provider.

Once you have set up your news account, you can have Outlook Express download a list of newsgroups from the news server. The available newsgroups depend on your news server. It may take Outlook Express a few minutes to download the entire list of newsgroups. You only need to download the entire list once.

After you download the list of newsgroups to your computer,

you can subscribe to a newsgroup you want to read on a regular basis. For information about subscribing to a newsgroup, see page 492.

The name of the news server you connect to appears in the folders list in the Outlook Express window.

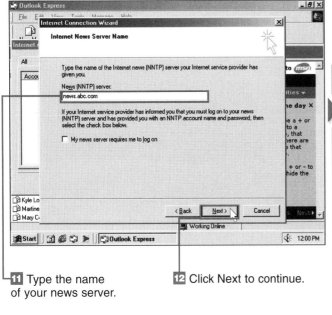

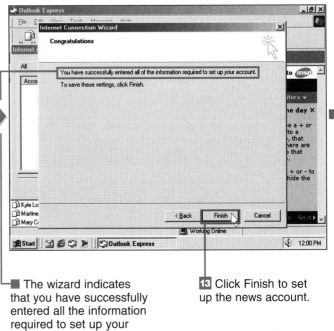

11 Type the name of your news server.

12 Click Next to continue.

■ The wizard indicates that you have successfully entered all the information required to set up your news account.

13 Click Finish to set up the news account.

My Internet service provider gave me an account name and password to log on to the news server. Where do I enter this information?

✔ After entering the name of your news server in the Internet Connection Wizard, click the My news server requires me to log on option and then click Next. Enter your account name and password and then click Next.

How do I change the settings for my news account?

✔ In the Internet Accounts dialog box, choose the News tab and then double-click the account you want to change. You can change information such as your name, e-mail address and the name of your news server.

Can I download the list of newsgroups from my news server at a later time?

✔ If you selected No in step 15, you can download the newsgroups at a later time. When you want to download the list of newsgroups, click the name of your news server in the folders list in the Outlook Express Window. In the dialog box that appears, click Yes.

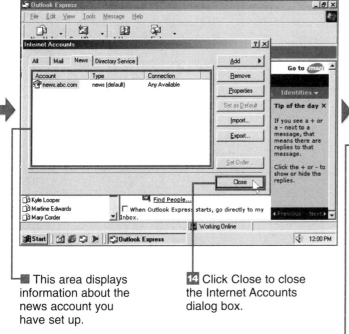

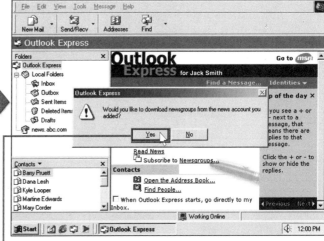

■ This area displays information about the news account you have set up.

14 Click Close to close the Internet Accounts dialog box.

■ A dialog box appears, asking if you want to download a list of newsgroups for the news account you have set up.

15 Click Yes to download the list of newsgroups to your computer.

■ A dialog box will appear, indicating the progress of the download.

Note: To subscribe to newsgroups you want to read on a regular basis, see page 492.

SUBSCRIBE TO NEWSGROUPS

Y ou can use Outlook Express to subscribe to newsgroups. Newsgroups allow people with common interests to communicate with each other. Subscribing gives you quick access to newsgroups you want to read on a regular basis.

Newsgroups are stored on computers called news servers, which are usually run and maintained by Internet service providers. The newsgroups

available to you depend on your news server. You can have Outlook Express display a list of all the newsgroups available to you.

There are thousands of newsgroups on every subject imaginable. The name of a newsgroup describes the type of information discussed in the newsgroup. A newsgroup name consists of two or more words, separated by dots (.). The first word describes the main topic

of the newsgroup. Each of the following words narrows the topic. For example, the rec.music.folk newsgroup contains messages from folk music enthusiasts.

The main newsgroup categories include alt (alternative), biz (business), comp (computers), k12 (kindergarten to grade 12 or education related), misc (miscellaneous), news, rec (recreation), sci (science), soc (social) and talk.

SUBSCRIBE TO NEWSGROUPS

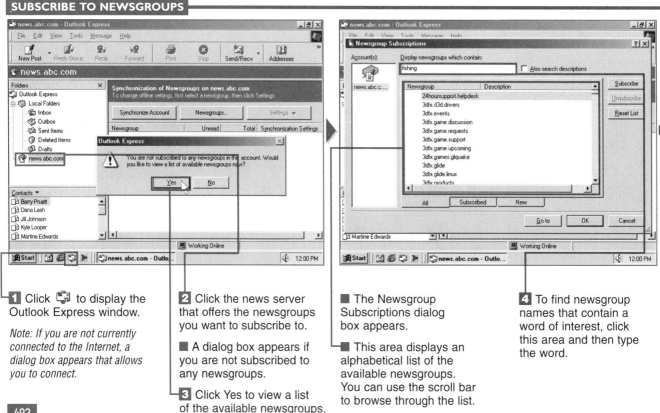

1 Click 🗔 to display the Outlook Express window.

Note: If you are not currently connected to the Internet, a dialog box appears that allows you to connect.

2 Click the news server that offers the newsgroups you want to subscribe to.

■ A dialog box appears if you are not subscribed to any newsgroups.

3 Click Yes to view a list of the available newsgroups.

■ The Newsgroup Subscriptions dialog box appears.

■ This area displays an alphabetical list of the available newsgroups. You can use the scroll bar to browse through the list.

4 To find newsgroup names that contain a word of interest, click this area and then type the word.

Are there any newsgroups designed for beginners?

✔ Yes. For example, the news.newusers.questions newsgroup provides useful information and lets you ask questions about newsgroups.

Can I view the messages in a newsgroup without subscribing to the newsgroup?

✔ Yes. In the Newsgroup Subscriptions dialog box, click the newsgroup that contains the messages you want to read and then click Go to.

Can I display descriptions for the newsgroups?

✔ You can display descriptions for some newsgroups. In the Newsgroup Subscriptions dialog box, click the Also search descriptions option. In the dialog box that appears, click Yes to download descriptions of the newsgroups.

How do I quickly display a list of newsgroups?

✔ The Newsgroup Subscriptions dialog box has three tabs. You can click the All tab to view all the available newsgroups. You can click the Subscribed tab to view newsgroups you are subscribed to. Click the New tab to display new newsgroups that have been added since you last connected to the news server.

How do I unsubscribe from a newsgroup?

✔ In the Outlook Express window, right-click the newsgroup you want to unsubscribe from and then click Unsubscribe.

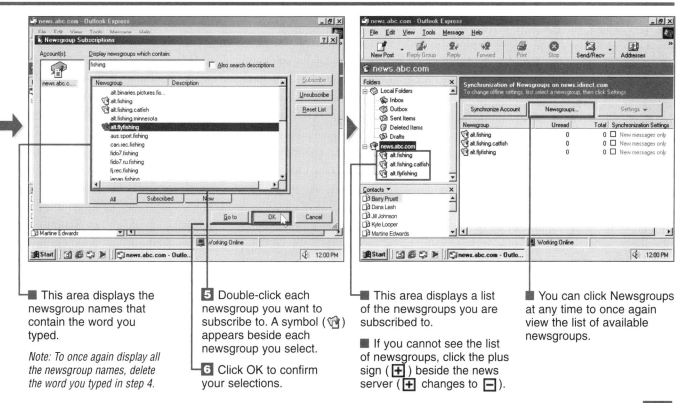

◼ This area displays the newsgroup names that contain the word you typed.

Note: To once again display all the newsgroup names, delete the word you typed in step 4.

5 Double-click each newsgroup you want to subscribe to. A symbol (🐷) appears beside each newsgroup you select.

6 Click OK to confirm your selections.

◼ This area displays a list of the newsgroups you are subscribed to.

◼ If you cannot see the list of newsgroups, click the plus sign (➕) beside the news server (➕ changes to ➖).

◼ You can click Newsgroups at any time to once again view the list of available newsgroups.

READ NEWSGROUP MESSAGES

You can read the messages in a newsgroup to learn the opinions and ideas of thousands of people around the world.

Newsgroup messages that people have replied to display a plus sign (⊞) and are called conversations. Outlook Express groups the original message and replies into a conversation to help you easily keep track of

related messages. For example, a message with the title "Tips for Windows Me" would be grouped with replies titled "Re: Tips for Windows Me". You can choose to view only the original message or the message and all of its replies.

Many newsgroups include a message called a FAQ (Frequently Asked Questions). A FAQ normally contains a list of questions and answers

that regularly appear in a newsgroup. A FAQ helps prevent new readers from posting questions to newsgroups that have already been answered. The news.answers newsgroup provides FAQs for a wide variety of newsgroups.

READ NEWSGROUP MESSAGES

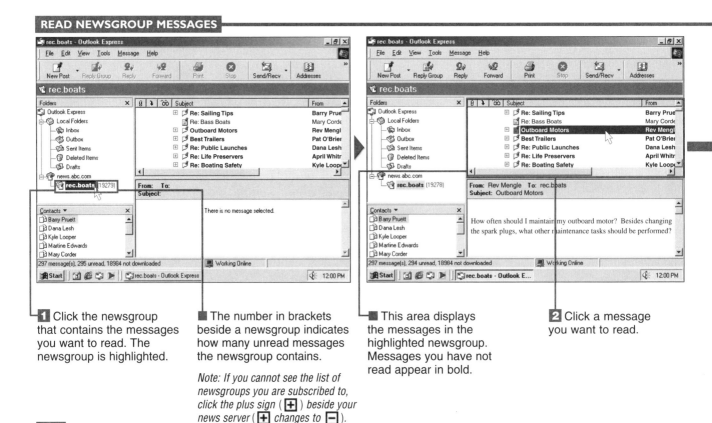

■1 Click the newsgroup that contains the messages you want to read. The newsgroup is highlighted.

■ The number in brackets beside a newsgroup indicates how many unread messages the newsgroup contains.

Note: If you cannot see the list of newsgroups you are subscribed to, click the plus sign (⊞) beside your news server (⊞ changes to ⊟).

■ This area displays the messages in the highlighted newsgroup. Messages you have not read appear in bold.

■2 Click a message you want to read.

Why didn't Outlook Express download all the messages in a newsgroup?

✔ Outlook Express automatically downloads only the first 300 messages in a newsgroup. To always download all messages, choose the Tools menu and then select Options. Click the Read tab and then select the box (✔) beside the Get 300 headers at a time option (✔ changes to ☐).

Can I expand all the conversations in a newsgroup at once?

✔ You can have Outlook Express automatically expand all the conversations every time you read newsgroup messages. From the Tools menu, select Options. On the Read tab, click the Automatically expand grouped messages option (☐ changes to ✔).

How can I view the contents of a message in a larger area?

✔ You can double-click a message to view the contents of the message in a separate window.

Can I forward an interesting message?

✔ Yes. Select the message you want to forward and then click the Forward button. Type the e-mail address of the person you want to receive the message and then click the Send button.

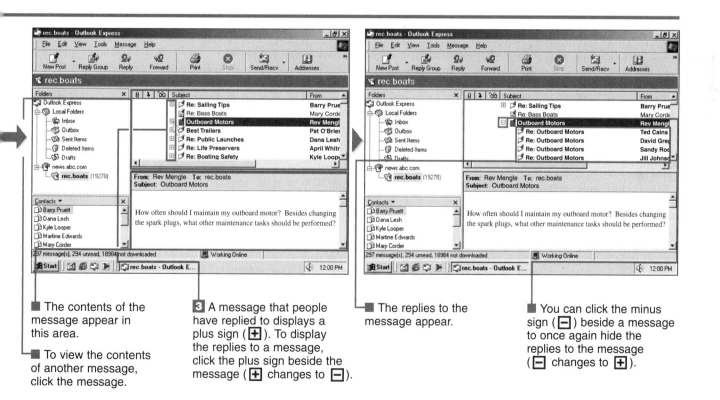

■ The contents of the message appear in this area.

■ To view the contents of another message, click the message.

3 A message that people have replied to displays a plus sign (⊞). To display the replies to a message, click the plus sign beside the message (⊞ changes to ⊟).

■ The replies to the message appear.

■ You can click the minus sign (⊟) beside a message to once again hide the replies to the message (⊟ changes to ⊞).

WORK WITH NEWSGROUP MESSAGES

You can copy a newsgroup message to a folder or change the display of messages to focus on messages of interest.

Messages posted to newsgroups are stored on the news server for only a limited amount of time. If you want to read a message later or keep a message for future reference, you can copy a message to a folder in Outlook Express. If the message has an attachment, such as an

image file, the attachment will also be copied to the folder.

You can choose to display all the messages in a newsgroup or hide the messages you have read. Hiding messages you have read allows you to quickly locate new messages.

Once you have viewed a message in a newsgroup, the message will be marked as read. You can mark messages as read without viewing

them. Marking messages as read takes the focus away from messages with subjects of no interest to you. You can mark a single message, an entire conversation or all the messages in a newsgroup as read. You can also select the Catch Up option to mark all the messages in a newsgroup as read, including messages you have not yet downloaded.

WORK WITH NEWSGROUP MESSAGES

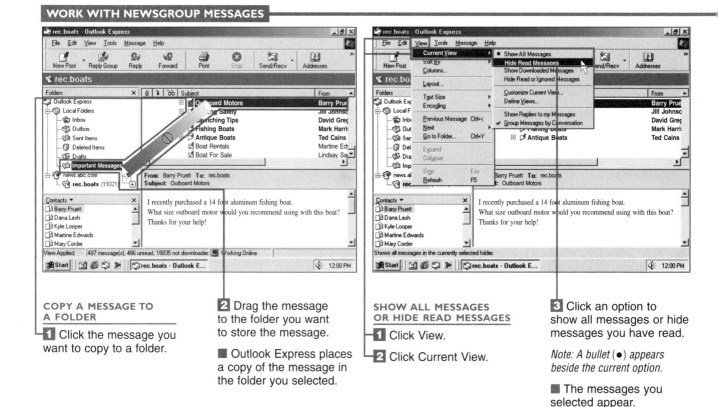

COPY A MESSAGE TO A FOLDER

1 Click the message you want to copy to a folder.

2 Drag the message to the folder you want to store the message.

■ Outlook Express places a copy of the message in the folder you selected.

SHOW ALL MESSAGES OR HIDE READ MESSAGES

1 Click View.

2 Click Current View.

3 Click an option to show all messages or hide messages you have read.

Note: A bullet (●) appears beside the current option.

■ The messages you selected appear.

Can Outlook Express automatically mark all messages as read when I leave a newsgroup?

✔ Yes. Select the Tools menu and then click Options. On the Read tab, select the Mark all messages as read when exiting a newsgroup option (☐ changes to ✔).

Can I sort newsgroup messages?

✔ Sorting messages can help you find messages on a certain subject or written by a particular person. To sort messages, click the heading for the column you want to use to sort the messages. To reverse the sort order, click the column heading again.

How can I print newsgroup messages?

✔ Click the message you want to print and then select the Print button.

How do I read the messages in a newsgroup when I am not connected to the Internet?

✔ Click the newsgroup that contains the messages you want to be able to read offline. From the Tools menu, choose Synchronize Newsgroup. Select the Get the following items option (☐ changes to ✔) and then click which messages you want to be able to read when you are offline (○ changes to ⊙). Outlook Express copies the messages to your computer.

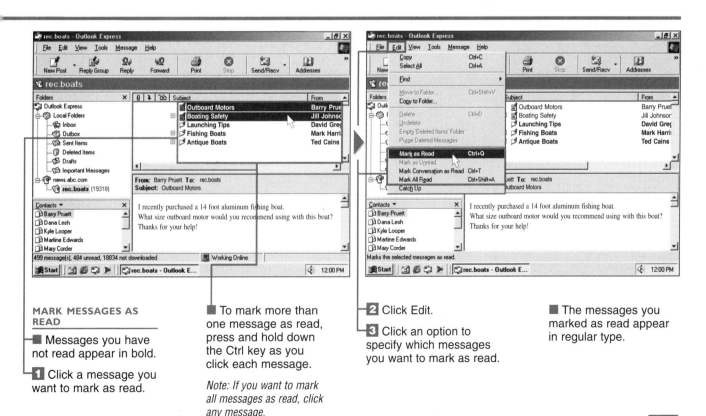

MARK MESSAGES AS READ

■ Messages you have not read appear in bold.

1 Click a message you want to mark as read.

■ To mark more than one message as read, press and hold down the Ctrl key as you click each message.

Note: If you want to mark all messages as read, click any message.

2 Click Edit.

3 Click an option to specify which messages you want to mark as read.

■ The messages you marked as read appear in regular type.

SEND A MESSAGE

You can send, or post, a new message to a newsgroup if you want to ask a question or express an opinion. Thousands of people around the world may read a message you post.

Before sending a message to a newsgroup, read the messages in the newsgroup for at least a week to learn how people in the newsgroup communicate.

Make sure you include a descriptive subject for a message you post. For

example, a subject that says "Read this now" is not very informative. Also, make sure the message is clear, concise and contains no spelling or grammar errors.

To practice sending a message, post a message to the misc.test newsgroup. If you send a test message to other newsgroups, you may receive unwanted replies or flames.

You can reply to a newsgroup message to answer a question or

supply information. You can send a reply to the entire newsgroup or only the author of the message.

When you reply to a message, Outlook Express includes a copy of the original message to help the reader identify which message you are replying to. This is called quoting.

POST A NEW MESSAGE

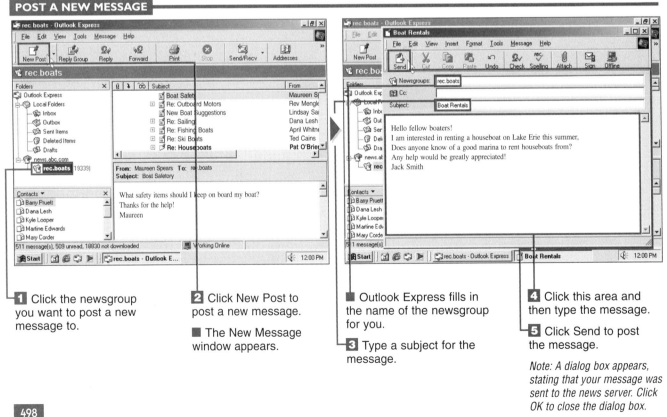

1 Click the newsgroup you want to post a new message to.

2 Click New Post to post a new message.

■ The New Message window appears.

■ Outlook Express fills in the name of the newsgroup for you.

3 Type a subject for the message.

4 Click this area and then type the message.

5 Click Send to post the message.

Note: A dialog box appears, stating that your message was sent to the news server. Click OK to close the dialog box.

Can I cancel a message I sent to a newsgroup?

✔ Yes. Select the newsgroup you sent the message to and then click the message you want to cancel. Choose the Message menu and then click Cancel Message. If someone downloaded the message before you canceled it, the message will not be removed from the person's computer.

What is a flame?

✔ When other readers do not like your message, they may reply to your message in a negative or hostile manner. These rude messages are called flames. You should ignore flames.

Do I have to use my real name in my messages?

✔ No. Choose the Tools menu and then click Accounts. Select the News tab and then click the Properties button to change the name and e-mail address that appear in your messages. Changing your e-mail address prevents junk mailers from sending you automatic messages. Remember to include your real e-mail address in the body of your message if you want other readers to be able to contact you.

REPLY TO A MESSAGE

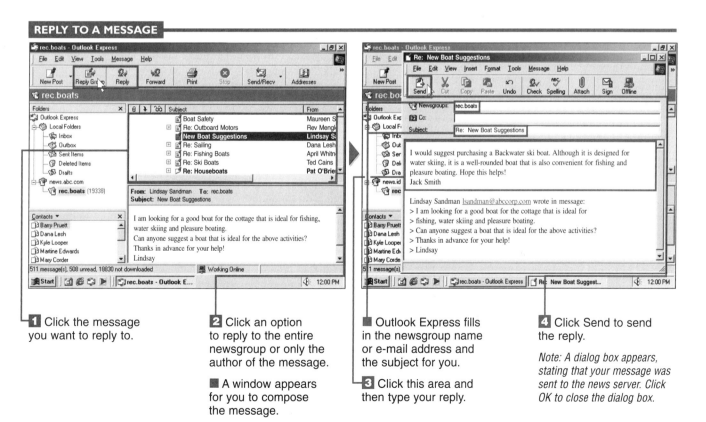

1 Click the message you want to reply to.

2 Click an option to reply to the entire newsgroup or only the author of the message.

■ A window appears for you to compose the message.

■ Outlook Express fills in the newsgroup name or e-mail address and the subject for you.

3 Click this area and then type your reply.

4 Click Send to send the reply.

Note: A dialog box appears, stating that your message was sent to the news server. Click OK to close the dialog box.

FORMAT FLOPPY DISKS

A floppy disk must be formatted before you can use it to store information. Floppy disks you buy at computer stores are usually formatted, but you may want to format a previously used floppy disk to prepare it for storing new information. Formatting removes all the information on the disk, so make sure the disk does not contain information you want to keep.

Floppy disks are available in two capacities. A double-density floppy disk can store 720 KB of information. A high-density floppy disk can store 1.44 MB of information, which is twice as much as a double-density disk.

The Quick (erase) format type removes all files from the disk but does not check the disk for damaged areas. You can only use this format type on a disk that was previously formatted. You should also be sure the disk does not have damaged areas.

The Full format type removes all files and checks the floppy disk for damaged areas. If Windows finds bad areas, the areas are marked so they will not be used.

Windows allows you to name the floppy disk so you can easily identify it later.

FORMAT FLOPPY DISKS

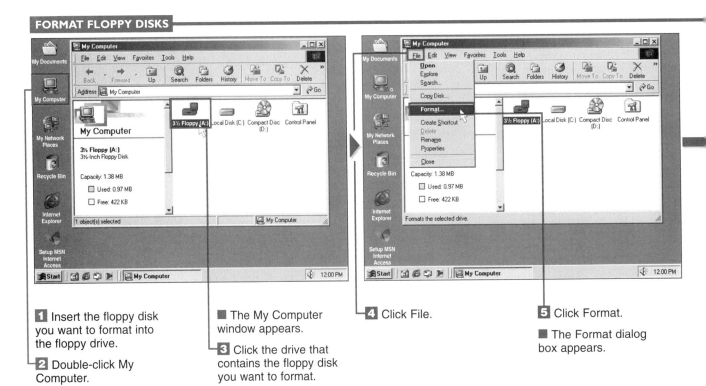

■ **1** Insert the floppy disk you want to format into the floppy drive.

■ **2** Double-click My Computer.

■ The My Computer window appears.

■ **3** Click the drive that contains the floppy disk you want to format.

■ **4** Click File.

■ **5** Click Format.

■ The Format dialog box appears.

How can I tell if a floppy disk is formatted?

✔ Windows displays an error message when you try to view the contents of a floppy disk that is not formatted. You cannot tell if a floppy disk is formatted just by looking at the disk.

A colleague gave me a floppy disk with documents on it, but Windows tells me the disk is not formatted. What is wrong with the disk?

✔ Your colleague may have formatted and used the floppy disk on a computer that uses a different filing system, such as a Macintosh computer. The floppy disk may also be damaged.

How can I protect my floppy disks from damage?

✔ You can help protect your floppy disks by keeping them away from moisture, heat and magnets.

Can I later rename a floppy disk I have formatted?

✔ Yes. Insert the disk into the floppy drive. In the My Computer window, right-click the drive containing the floppy disk and then select Properties from the menu that appears. In the Label area, type the new name and then press the Enter key.

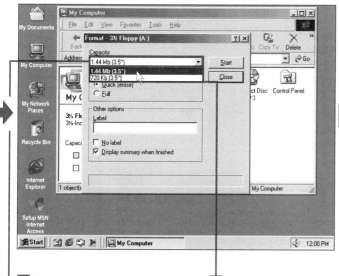

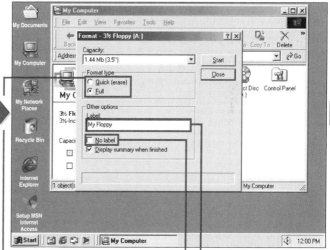

6 Click this area to specify how much information the floppy disk can store.

7 Click the storage capacity of the floppy disk.

8 Click the type of format you want to perform (○ changes to ⊙).

Note: If the floppy disk has never been formatted, select the Full option.

9 To name the floppy disk, click this area and type a name for the disk.

■ You can click this option if you do not want to name the floppy disk (☐ changes to ☑).

CONTINUED

FORMAT FLOPPY DISKS (CONTINUED)

You can have Windows display summary information about a floppy disk when the format is complete. The summary information includes information such as the total amount of disk space, the amount of space in bad sectors and the total available space on the disk.

The summary information also includes the number of allocation units available on the disk and the size of each unit. Each file is assigned to one or more allocation units on a disk. Each allocation unit can hold only one file. For example, on a disk with allocation units of 512 bytes, a file that is 200 bytes long still requires 512 bytes of disk space, or one allocation unit.

Windows shows the progress of the format as the floppy disk is formatted. Performing a full format on a floppy disk takes about two minutes.

When you finish formatting a floppy disk, you can format additional floppy disks. You may want to format several floppy disks at one time so you always have formatted disks available when you need them.

FORMAT FLOPPY DISKS (CONTINUED)

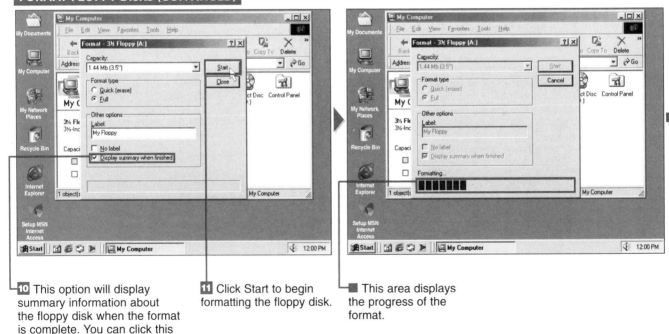

■10 This option will display summary information about the floppy disk when the format is complete. You can click this option if you do not want to display the summary information (☑ changes to ☐).

■11 Click Start to begin formatting the floppy disk.

■ This area displays the progress of the format.

I get an error message when I try to format my floppy disk. What is wrong?

✔ If you get an error message when you try to format a floppy disk, you should check the storage capacity you selected for the disk. An error message also appears if the disk is damaged or if files on the disk are open.

Can I format floppy disks from a Windows Explorer window?

✔ You can format a floppy disk from a Windows Explorer window by right-clicking the drive containing the disk and then selecting Format from the menu that appears.

What should I do if a floppy disk has bad sectors?

✔ Floppy disks can develop bad sectors for many reasons, such as exposure to magnets, dust accumulation on the disk surface, or general wear and tear. If an old floppy disk has damaged sectors, you should throw out the disk. If a new floppy disk has damaged sectors, you should return the disk to the manufacturer for a replacement.

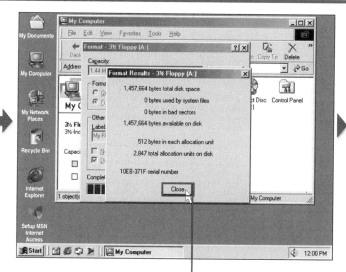

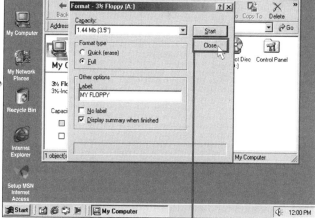

■ The Format Results dialog box appears when the format is complete, displaying information about the formatted disk.

Note: The dialog box does not appear if you turned off the Display summary when finished option in step 10.

12 When you finish reviewing the information, click Close to close the dialog box.

■ To format another floppy disk, insert the disk into the floppy drive and then repeat steps 6 to 12 starting on page 501.

13 Click Close to close the Format dialog box.

COPY FLOPPY DISKS

Y ou can easily make copies of your floppy disks. Copying a floppy disk is useful when you want to give a copy of a disk to a friend or colleague. You may also want to copy a floppy disk to make a backup copy of important information.

You can copy floppy disks even if your computer has only one floppy drive. Windows makes a

temporary copy of the information from the original floppy disk. When you insert the second disk, Windows copies the information to the disk.

Make sure the floppy disk receiving the copy does not contain information you want to keep. Copying removes all the existing information from the disk.

The original floppy disk and the disk that receives the copy must be able to store the same amount of information. A double-density floppy disk has one hole and can store 720 KB of information. A high-density floppy disk has two holes and can store 1.44 MB of information.

COPY FLOPPY DISKS

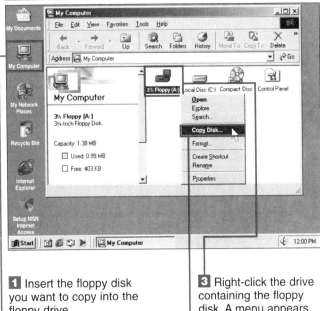

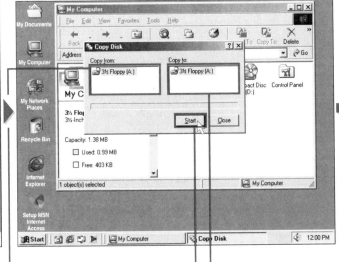

1 Insert the floppy disk you want to copy into the floppy drive.

2 Double-click My Computer to display the contents of your computer.

3 Right-click the drive containing the floppy disk. A menu appears.

4 Click Copy Disk.

■ The Copy Disk dialog box appears.

5 This area displays the drive that contains the disk you want to copy. If more than one drive is listed, click the drive that contains the disk.

6 This area displays the drive that will contain the disk you want to receive the copy. If more than one drive is listed, click the drive that will contain the disk.

7 Click Start to begin copying the disk.

Do I need to format the floppy disk I want to receive the copy?

✔ If the floppy disk is unformatted, Windows formats the disk before copying information to the disk.

How can I make several copies of a floppy disk without having to reinsert the disk each time?

✔ You may find it faster to first copy the contents of the floppy disk to a folder on your desktop. You can then copy the information onto the floppy disks from the desktop using the Send To menu. To copy files, see page 68.

Windows displayed a message saying the floppy disk receiving the copy could not be formatted. What is wrong?

✔ If this error message appears, make sure you properly inserted the floppy disk and the write-protect tab on the disk is closed. An error message also appears if the disk is damaged or if you are trying to copy the contents of a high-density disk onto a double-density disk.

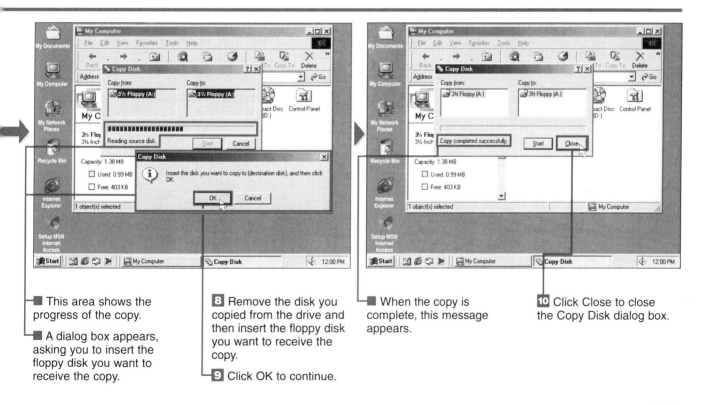

■ This area shows the progress of the copy.

■ A dialog box appears, asking you to insert the floppy disk you want to receive the copy.

8 Remove the disk you copied from the drive and then insert the floppy disk you want to receive the copy.

9 Click OK to continue.

■ When the copy is complete, this message appears.

10 Click Close to close the Copy Disk dialog box.

RENAME A DISK

You can rename your hard disk, removable disk and floppy disks. Renaming a disk allows you to more easily identify the disk. You cannot rename a CD-ROM disc.

You can use up to 11 letters or numbers to rename a disk. A name can contain spaces but cannot contain the \ / : * ? " < > or | characters.

When you change the name of your hard disk, the new name appears below the hard drive icon (⬚) in the My Computer window.

When you rename a removable disk or floppy disk, you change only the name of the disk currently in the drive. When you later insert the disk you renamed into a drive, you can

display the Properties dialog box to see the name.

The name that appears below the removable drive icon (⬚) or floppy drive icon (⬚) in the My Computer window will not change when you rename a disk. To rename a removable or floppy drive icon, right-click the icon and select Rename. Type a new name and then press the Enter key.

RENAME A DISK

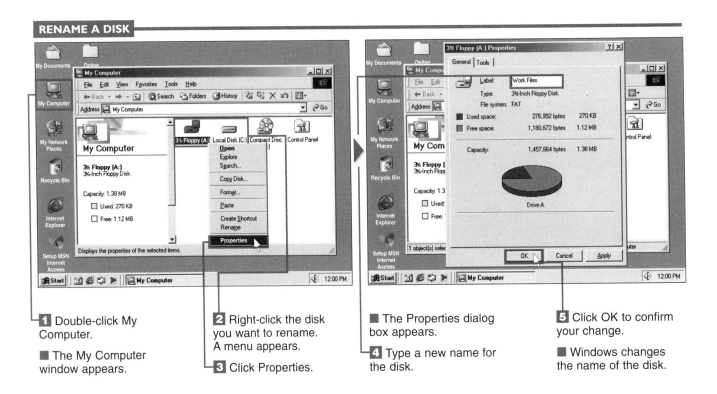

■1 Double-click My Computer.

■ The My Computer window appears.

■2 Right-click the disk you want to rename. A menu appears.

■3 Click Properties.

■ The Properties dialog box appears.

■4 Type a new name for the disk.

■5 Click OK to confirm your change.

■ Windows changes the name of the disk.

VIEW AMOUNT OF DISK SPACE

You can view the amount of used and free space on any disk, including hard disks, floppy disks, removable media and CD-ROM discs.

The amount of space on a disk is measured in bytes, megabytes (MB) and gigabytes (GB). One byte equals one character. One MB equals approximately one million characters. One GB equals approximately one billion characters.

You should check the amount of available disk space on your computer at least once a month. You should also check the amount of available disk space before you install a new program.

You should have at least 20% of your hard disk free. For example, if you have a 4 GB hard disk, make sure you have at least 0.8 GB free. This will help improve virtual memory performance as well as decrease fragmentation of files.

If you want to increase the amount of free space on your hard disk, you should delete files and programs you no longer use from your computer. You can also use the Disk Cleanup feature to remove unnecessary files. To use Disk Cleanup, see page 510.

VIEW AMOUNT OF DISK SPACE

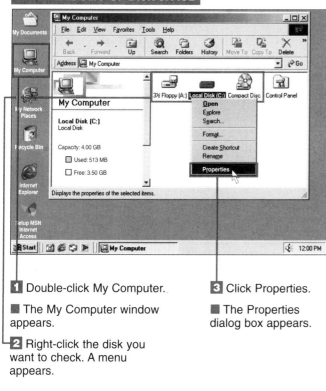

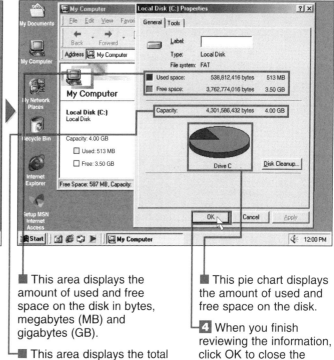

1 Double-click My Computer.

■ The My Computer window appears.

2 Right-click the disk you want to check. A menu appears.

3 Click Properties.

■ The Properties dialog box appears.

■ This area displays the amount of used and free space on the disk in bytes, megabytes (MB) and gigabytes (GB).

■ This area displays the total disk storage space, in both bytes and gigabytes (GB).

■ This pie chart displays the amount of used and free space on the disk.

4 When you finish reviewing the information, click OK to close the Properties dialog box.

DISPLAY VERSION AND REGISTRATION NUMBER

Y ou can find information about Windows and your computer by displaying the System Properties dialog box.

The System Properties dialog box displays a number that indicates the version of Windows you are using. Over time, Microsoft will make changes and additions to Windows Me. The version number may change to reflect these changes.

You can also find registration information, such as the user name that was entered when Windows Me was installed on your computer. The last line of the registration area displays the registration number for your copy of Windows. You should record the registration number for future reference in case you must re-install Windows on your computer. You will not

be able to re-install Windows without this number.

The System Properties dialog box also displays information about your computer's processor and the amount of memory (RAM) installed in your computer.

DISPLAY VERSION AND REGISTRATION NUMBER

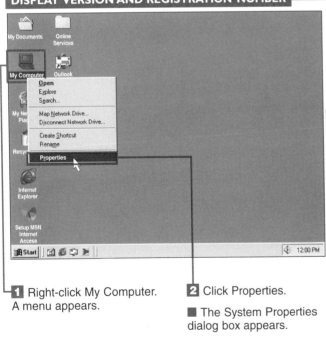

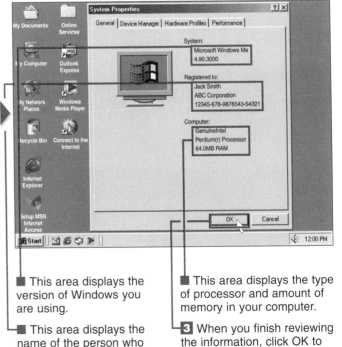

■1 Right-click My Computer. A menu appears.

■2 Click Properties.

■ The System Properties dialog box appears.

■ This area displays the version of Windows you are using.

■ This area displays the name of the person who is registered to use this copy of Windows and the registration number.

■ This area displays the type of processor and amount of memory in your computer.

■3 When you finish reviewing the information, click OK to close the System Properties dialog box.

CHECK PERFORMANCE STATUS

You can check the performance of your computer by viewing the items displayed on the Performance tab in the System Properties dialog box.

The first item, Memory, displays the amount of memory (RAM) in your computer. This amount will not change unless you add or remove memory in your computer. More memory means better performance.

The second item, System Resources, displays a percentage that will

change while you are working. When there is less than 30% free, you should close some programs or restart Windows to avoid potential problems.

The third and fourth items, File System and Virtual Memory, should both be set at 32-bit for the best performance.

The fifth item, Disk Compression, indicates if you have any disk compression software installed on your computer. This software

can affect your computer's performance, depending on the processor speed, the hard disk speed and the amount of memory installed.

PC Cards is the last item and applies to portable computers. This item indicates whether you have a PC Card installed on your computer and the type of PC Card installed.

CHECK PERFORMANCE STATUS

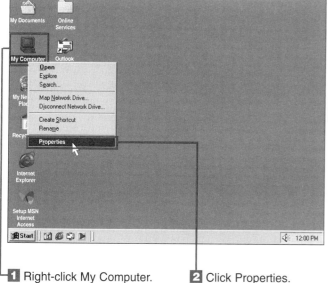

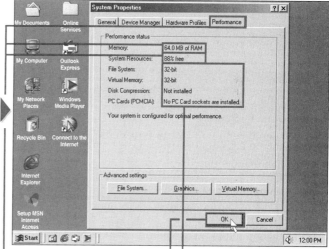

1 Right-click My Computer. A menu appears.

2 Click Properties.

■ The System Properties dialog box appears.

3 Click the Performance tab.

■ This area displays the amount of memory (RAM) in your computer.

■ This area displays the percentage of free system resources.

■ This area displays information about your computer's file system, virtual memory, disk compression software and PC Cards.

4 When you finish reviewing the information, click OK to close the System Properties dialog box.

USE DISK CLEANUP TO REMOVE UNNEEDED FILES

You can use Disk Cleanup to remove unnecessary files from your computer to free up disk space. Disk Cleanup can remove several types of files from your hard drive. You can select which types of files you want to remove.

Temporary Internet files are Web pages that Windows stores on your hard disk while you are browsing the Web. Using temporary Internet files saves Windows from having to transfer the same Web pages to

your computer each time you view them.

Downloaded program files are small program files that transfer automatically from the Internet when you view certain Web pages. Some Web pages require these files in order to display properly.

The Recycle Bin contains files you have deleted. These files are permanently removed from your computer when you empty the Recycle Bin.

While working, some programs store temporary files on your hard disk. If these files are not removed when the program has finished using them, they can take up valuable storage space.

Temporary PC Health files are files that the PC Health program uses to ensure your computer operates smoothly.

USE DISK CLEANUP TO REMOVE UNNEEDED FILES

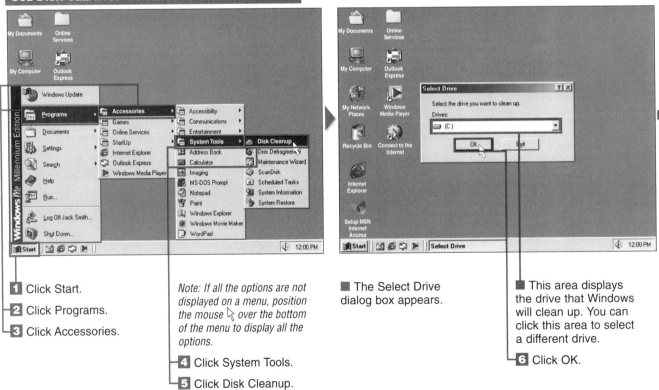

1 Click Start.

2 Click Programs.

3 Click Accessories.

Note: If all the options are not displayed on a menu, position the mouse ⬚ over the bottom of the menu to display all the options.

4 Click System Tools.

5 Click Disk Cleanup.

■ The Select Drive dialog box appears.

■ This area displays the drive that Windows will clean up. You can click this area to select a different drive.

6 Click OK.

How can I see which files will be removed?

✔ In the Disk Cleanup dialog box, select a file type and then click the View Files button. A window displays the files that will be removed. Depending on the file type you select, the View Files button may display a different name or may not be available.

Can Disk Cleanup help me free up even more disk space?

✔ Yes. In the Disk Cleanup dialog box, click the More Options tab. This tab can help you remove Windows components and programs you do not use or free up disk space by reducing the amount of storage space used by System Restore.

Can I change how much disk space is used by temporary Internet files or the Recycle Bin?

✔ To adjust the amount of disk space used by temporary Internet files, right-click the Internet Explorer icon on your desktop and select Properties. On the General tab, click the Settings button. You can drag the slider (⬚) to change the amount of disk space used to store temporary Internet files. To change the amount of disk space used by the Recycle Bin, see page 76.

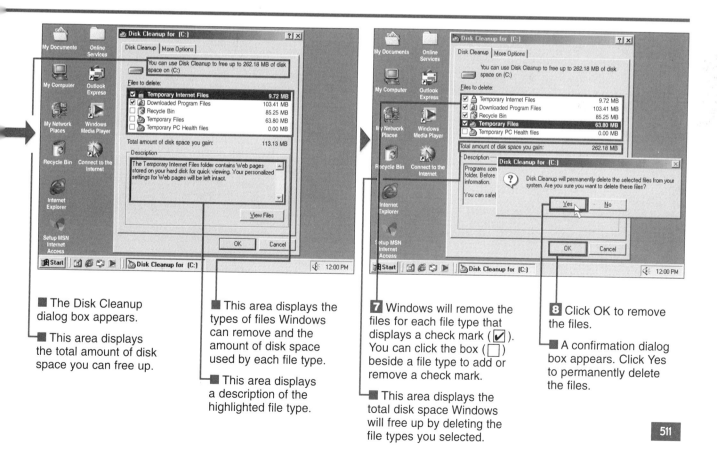

■ The Disk Cleanup dialog box appears.

■ This area displays the total amount of disk space you can free up.

■ This area displays the types of files Windows can remove and the amount of disk space used by each file type.

■ This area displays a description of the highlighted file type.

7 Windows will remove the files for each file type that displays a check mark (✔). You can click the box (☐) beside a file type to add or remove a check mark.

■ This area displays the total disk space Windows will free up by deleting the file types you selected.

8 Click OK to remove the files.

■ A confirmation dialog box appears. Click Yes to permanently delete the files.

CHECK FOR DISK ERRORS USING SCANDISK

You can use ScanDisk to detect and repair disk errors on hard disks, floppy disks and removable disks. ScanDisk cannot check for disk errors on CD-ROM discs or network drives.

The standard test checks for errors in files and folders. The thorough test performs the same check as the standard test and also checks the disk surface for physically damaged areas that can no longer be used to store information.

You can have ScanDisk automatically fix errors it finds.

When ScanDisk is finished checking a disk, a summary appears, displaying information about the disk. You can have ScanDisk display the summary only when errors are found.

You can save the results of each check in a file to keep track of the errors that occur over time. The file is named Scandisk.log and is stored on your hard drive.

ScanDisk checks for cross-linked files. Cross-linked files are two or more files stored in the same area of a disk. The data in crossed-linked files is often correct for only one of the files. The Make copies setting provides the best chance of recovering information from crossed-linked files.

CHECK FOR DISK ERRORS USING SCANDISK

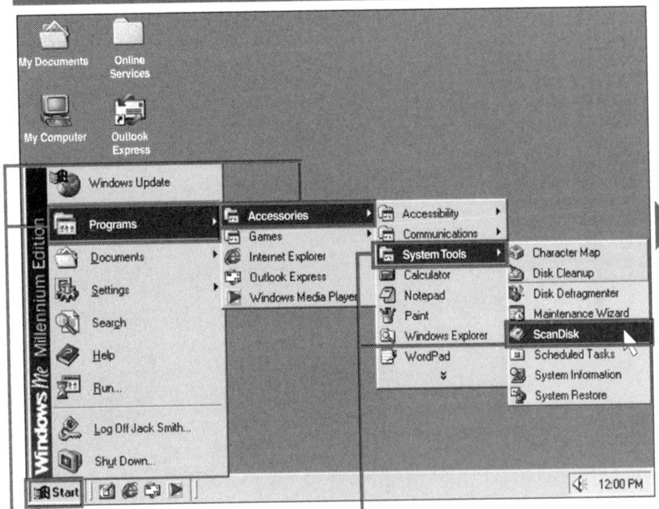

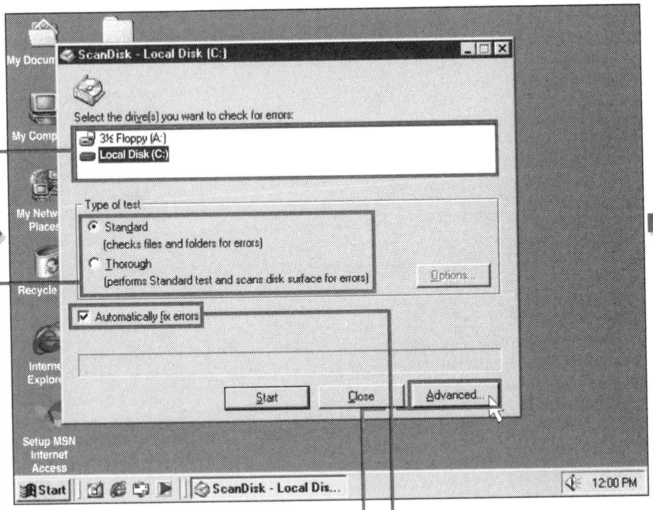

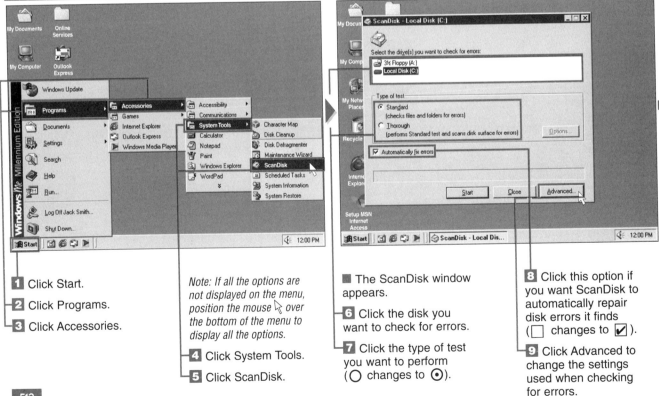

1 Click Start.

2 Click Programs.

3 Click Accessories.

Note: If all the options are not displayed on the menu, position the mouse over the bottom of the menu to display all the options.

4 Click System Tools.

5 Click ScanDisk.

■ The ScanDisk window appears.

6 Click the disk you want to check for errors.

7 Click the type of test you want to perform (○ changes to ⊙).

8 Click this option if you want ScanDisk to automatically repair disk errors it finds (☐ changes to ☑).

9 Click Advanced to change the settings used when checking for errors.

Can I change the settings ScanDisk uses when performing a thorough test?

✔ Yes. Select the Options button in the ScanDisk window and then click the settings you want to use (○ changes to ⊙). You can specify which areas of the disk you want to check, if you want ScanDisk to perform write-testing and which files you want ScanDisk to repair.

How often should I use ScanDisk to check for disk errors?

✔ You should perform the thorough test once a month. If you experience problems opening or saving files, you should check the disk immediately. You can perform the standard test as often as you like.

Can I find out when a disk was last checked for errors?

✔ Yes. Double-click My Computer on the desktop. Right-click the disk you want to check and select Properties from the menu that appears. In the Properties dialog box, click the Tools tab to view the error-checking status of the disk.

How long does the thorough test take?

✔ The thorough test can be time-consuming, especially on large disks. While the standard test takes a few minutes, the thorough test can take several hours.

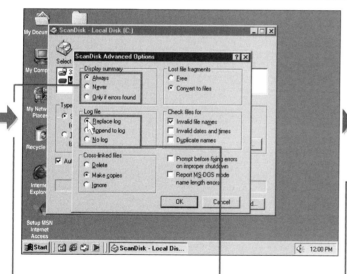

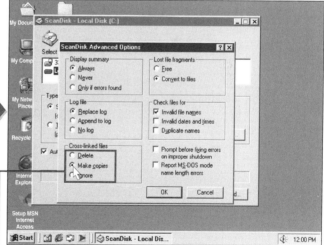

■ The ScanDisk Advanced Options dialog box appears.

10 Click an option to specify if you want to display a summary when ScanDisk finishes checking a disk (○ changes to ⊙).

11 Click an option to specify how you want to save the results of the ScanDisk check (○ changes to ⊙).

12 Click an option to specify what you want to do with files that use the same area of the disk (○ changes to ⊙).

CONTINUED ▶

CHECK FOR DISK ERRORS USING SCANDISK (CONTINUED)

Y ou can change the settings that ScanDisk uses when checking your files and folders for errors. ScanDisk checks for lost file fragments. Lost file fragments are pieces of data that are no longer associated with a file. The Convert to files setting saves file fragments so you can view their contents before you delete them.

You can check for files with invalid names. You may be unable to open files with invalid names. You can

also check files for invalid dates and times. Files with invalid dates and times may not sort correctly.

When file names become corrupted, two files in the same folder may have the same name. You can have ScanDisk locate and fix duplicate file names.

If you did not properly shut down Windows the last time you used the program, ScanDisk will automatically check for disk errors

the next time you turn on your computer.

You can have ScanDisk display a confirmation dialog box before repairing any errors it finds.

You can also check for folders with paths that exceed the MS-DOS limit of 66 characters. ScanDisk will move these folders to the top level, or root, folder. In most cases, you should not use this option.

CHECK FOR DISK ERRORS USING SCANDISK (CONTINUED)

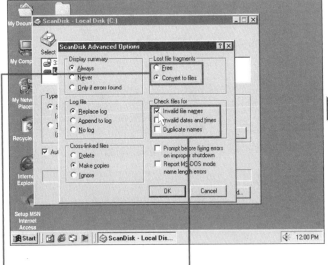

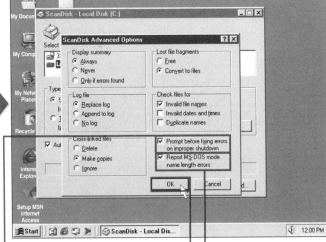

13 Click an option to specify what you want to do with lost fragments of files (○ changes to ⊙).

14 These options check files for invalid file names, invalid dates and times and identical names in the same folder. You can click an option to turn the option on (✔) or off (☐).

15 Click this option to display a confirmation dialog box before ScanDisk repairs errors when ScanDisk runs automatically after an improper Windows shut down (☐ changes to ✔).

16 Click this option to move folders with paths that exceed the MS-DOS limit of 66 characters to the top level folder (☐ changes to ✔).

17 Click OK to confirm your changes.

Can I use my computer while ScanDisk is running?

✔ You can use your computer while ScanDisk is running, but the check may take longer. ScanDisk will restart if Windows accesses the disk being checked. The use of a screen saver may also affect how long ScanDisk takes to check your disk for errors. You should run ScanDisk when you do not need to use your computer.

Can I schedule ScanDisk to run at a specified time?

✔ You can use the Task Scheduler to start ScanDisk automatically at dates and times you specify. You can choose times when you will not be using your computer, such as at lunchtime or at night. To use Task Scheduler, see page 520.

How can I view the file fragments that ScanDisk saves?

✔ When you use the Convert to files setting in ScanDisk, the file fragments are saved on your hard drive with names such as File0000. You may be able to open the file fragments using a simple text editor, such as Notepad or a specialized program for recovering data.

Can I stop ScanDisk before it is finished?

✔ Yes. Click the Cancel button to stop ScanDisk at any time.

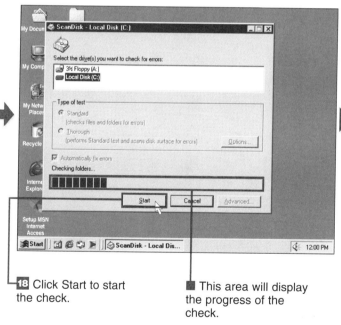

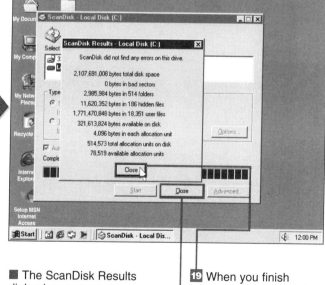

■18 Click Start to start the check.

■ This area will display the progress of the check.

■ The ScanDisk Results dialog box may appear when the check is complete. The dialog box displays information about the disk.

■19 When you finish reviewing the information, click Close to close the dialog box.

■20 Click Close to close the ScanDisk window.

DEFRAGMENT YOUR HARD DRIVE

You can improve the performance of your computer by defragmenting your hard drive.

A fragmented hard drive stores parts of a file in many different locations on the drive. Your computer must search many areas on the drive to retrieve a file. Disk Defragmenter reorganizes the information on the drive and places all the parts of a file in one location. This reduces the time your computer will spend locating files.

You can choose which drive you want to defragment. If you have more than one hard drive, you can choose to defragment all of your hard drives at once.

You can specify the settings you want to use when defragmenting a drive. You can have Disk Defragmenter rearrange your most frequently used program files so the programs will start faster. You can also check a drive for errors before defragmenting the drive. A drive that contains errors cannot be defragmented.

You can have Disk Defragmenter save the settings you selected for the defragmentation. This saves you from having to select the same settings the next time you defragment your hard drive.

DEFRAGMENT YOUR HARD DRIVE

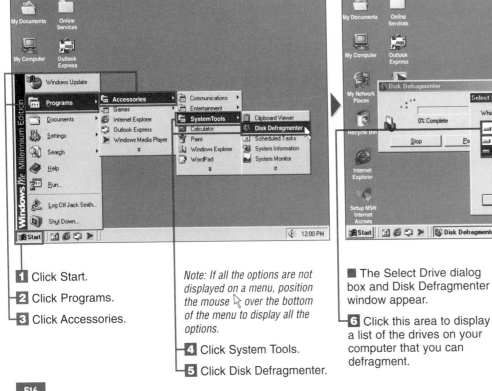

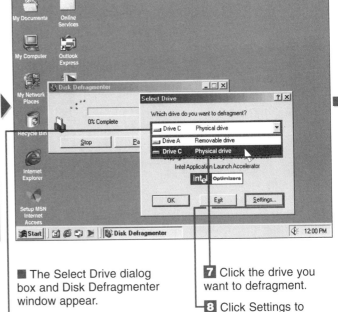

1 Click Start.

2 Click Programs.

3 Click Accessories.

Note: If all the options are not displayed on a menu, position the mouse ⫯ over the bottom of the menu to display all the options.

4 Click System Tools.

5 Click Disk Defragmenter.

■ The Select Drive dialog box and Disk Defragmenter window appear.

6 Click this area to display a list of the drives on your computer that you can defragment.

7 Click the drive you want to defragment.

8 Click Settings to change the settings Disk Defragmenter will use when defragmenting your drive.

How long will the defragmentation process take?

✔ The amount of time Disk Defragmenter takes to defragment a hard drive depends on several factors, including the amount of information on the drive, how fragmented the files are and whether you are working with files on your computer during the defragmentation process. An average hard drive can usually be defragmented within two hours.

What drives cannot be defragmented?

✔ Disk Defragmenter cannot defragment a CD-ROM drive or a network drive. Disk Defragmenter also cannot defragment a drive that has been compressed using a compression program that Windows does not support.

How can I find out when a drive was last defragmented?

✔ Double-click the My Computer icon on your desktop to display the My Computer window. Right-click the drive you want to check and then select Properties. In the Properties dialog box, click the Tools tab. The Defragmentation status area displays when the drive was last defragmented.

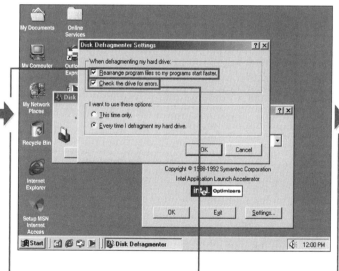

■ The Disk Defragmenter Settings dialog box appears.

9 This option rearranges your most frequently used program files to make your programs start faster. Click the option to turn the option on (☑) or off (☐).

10 This option checks the files and folders on your drive for errors before defragmenting the drive. Click the option to turn the option on (☑) or off (☐).

11 Click an option to specify if you want to use the settings you selected this time only or every time you defragment the drive (○ changes to ⊙).

12 Click OK to confirm your changes.

CONTINUED ▶

DEFRAGMENT YOUR HARD DRIVE (CONTINUED)

When defragmenting a hard drive, Disk Defragmenter displays the progress of the defragmentation. You can also have Disk Defragmenter graphically display the details of the defragmentation process.

You can use your computer to perform tasks while Disk Defragmenter is running, but your computer will operate more

slowly and the defragmentation process will take longer to finish.

Disk Defragmenter must restart each time another program accesses the drive. If Disk Defragmenter restarts too often, you may want to close other programs before defragmenting your drive.

You can schedule Disk Defragmenter to start automatically at a time when you will not be

using your computer, such as after work. To schedule tasks using Task Scheduler, see page 520.

For the best performance of your computer, you should defragment your hard drive at least once a month. Defragmenting a hard drive will not create more free space on the drive. Defragmenting only reorganizes the files on the drive to allow a computer to find and access the files faster.

DEFRAGMENT YOUR HARD DRIVE (CONTINUED)

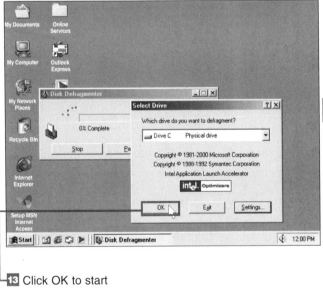

13 Click OK to start the defragmentation.

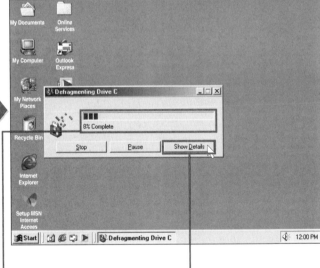

■ The Defragmenting Drive window appears.

■ This area shows the progress of the defragmentation.

14 Click Show Details to graphically display the defragmentation process.

Can I pause the defragmentation process?

✔ Pausing the defragmentation process allows you to run other programs faster and is useful if you need to finish another task immediately. To pause the defragmentation, click the Pause button. When you want to continue defragmenting your drive, click the Resume button. The defragmentation process will start over if your computer accesses the drive while Disk Defragmenter is paused.

Can I stop the defragmentation process?

✔ You can click the Stop button to stop defragmenting your drive. In the dialog box that appears, click the Exit button. The defragmentation process will not be completed.

When viewing the details of the defragmentation process, how can I find out what the colored blocks represent?

✔ After clicking the Show Details button to graphically display the defragmentation process, you can click the Legend button to display a description of what each colored block in the window represents.

Is there another way to run Disk Defragmenter?

✔ When you use the Maintenance Wizard to perform maintenance tasks on your computer, the wizard will run Disk Defragmenter. For information about the Maintenance Wizard, see page 528.

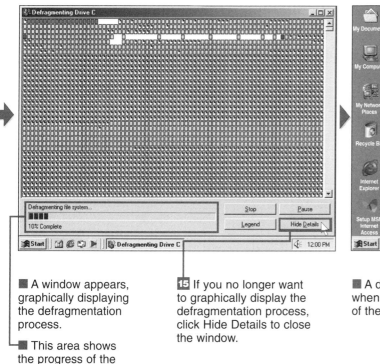

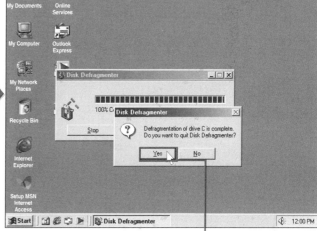

■ A window appears, graphically displaying the defragmentation process.

■ This area shows the progress of the defragmentation.

15 If you no longer want to graphically display the defragmentation process, click Hide Details to close the window.

■ A dialog box appears when the defragmentation of the hard drive is complete.

16 Click Yes to close Disk Defragmenter.

SCHEDULE A NEW TASK

You can use Task Scheduler to have Windows automatically run specific programs on a regular basis. You can schedule the programs to run at times that are convenient for you.

The Scheduled Task Wizard takes you step by step through the process of scheduling a new task. You can add any program on your computer to the list of programs that Task Scheduler will automatically start. Scheduling a task is ideal for running computer maintenance programs such as Disk Defragmenter, ScanDisk and Disk Cleanup on a regular basis.

Task Scheduler starts each time you start Windows and operates in the background.

Task Scheduler uses the date and time set in your computer to determine when to start scheduled tasks. You should make sure the date and time set in your computer is correct before scheduling tasks. To set the date and time, see page 164.

SCHEDULE A NEW TASK

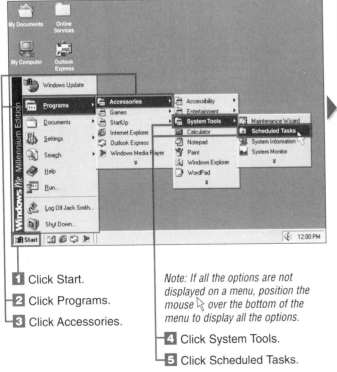

1 Click Start.

2 Click Programs.

3 Click Accessories.

Note: If all the options are not displayed on a menu, position the mouse ⟍ over the bottom of the menu to display all the options.

4 Click System Tools.

5 Click Scheduled Tasks.

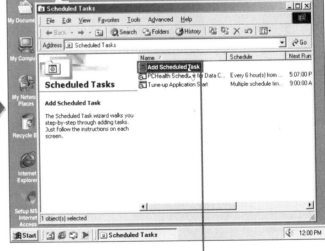

■ The Scheduled Tasks window appears.

6 Double-click Add Scheduled Task to schedule a new task.

MASTER IT

The program I want to schedule does not appear in the Scheduled Task Wizard. What should I do?

✔ You can click the Browse button in the wizard to search for the program on your computer.

How do I turn off Task Scheduler?

✔ In the Scheduled Tasks window, select the Advanced menu and then click Stop Using Task Scheduler. Your scheduled tasks will not run and Task Scheduler will not start the next time you start Windows. To once again turn on Task Scheduler, select the Advanced menu and then click Start Using Task Scheduler.

How do I remove a task from Task Scheduler?

✔ In the Scheduled Tasks window, click the task you want to remove and then press the Delete key. Removing a task from Task Scheduler stops the program from starting automatically but does not remove the program from your computer.

Is there another way to add tasks to Task Scheduler?

✔ You can use the Maintenance Wizard to add Disk Defragmenter, ScanDisk and Disk Cleanup to Task Scheduler. To use the Maintenance Wizard, see page 528.

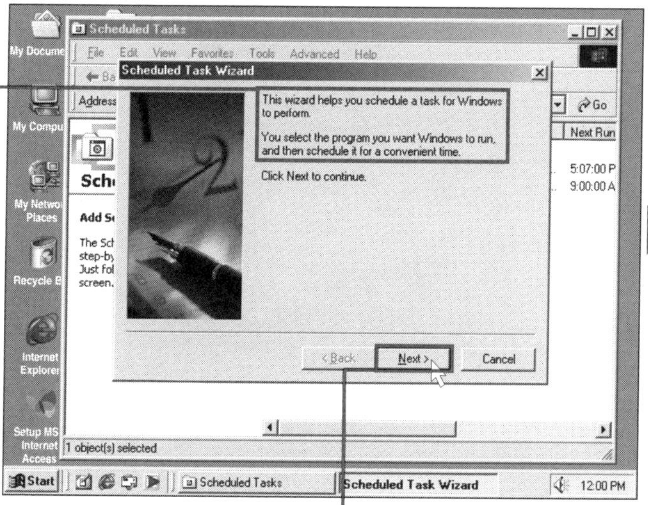

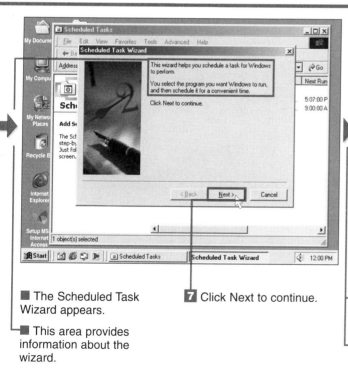

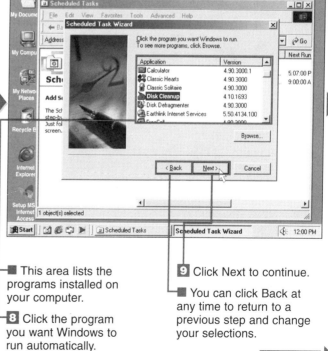

■ The Scheduled Task Wizard appears.

■ This area provides information about the wizard.

7 Click Next to continue.

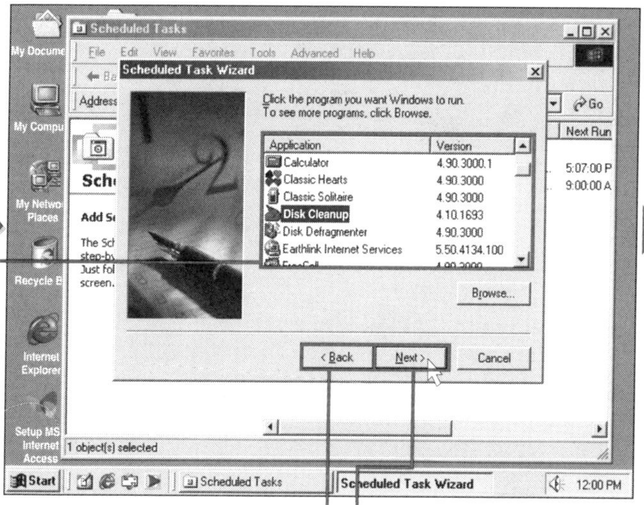

■ This area lists the programs installed on your computer.

8 Click the program you want Windows to run automatically.

9 Click Next to continue.

■ You can click Back at any time to return to a previous step and change your selections.

CONTINUED

SCHEDULE A NEW TASK (CONTINUED)

The Scheduled Task Wizard provides a name for the program you want to start automatically. You can change the name to a more descriptive name, which can help you more easily identify your scheduled tasks.

You can specify when you want a program to start. You can select a daily, weekly or monthly schedule. You can also schedule a program to start only once, start each time you turn on the computer or start each time you log on to the network.

Make sure you schedule a program for a time when your computer will be turned on.

Depending on the schedule you choose, additional options may be available. For example, if you select a weekly schedule, you can select which days of the week you want to run the program and at what time.

After you schedule a task, the task appears in the Scheduled Tasks window. The Scheduled Tasks window provides information about each task, such as when the task will run next and when the task was last run.

SCHEDULE A NEW TASK (CONTINUED)

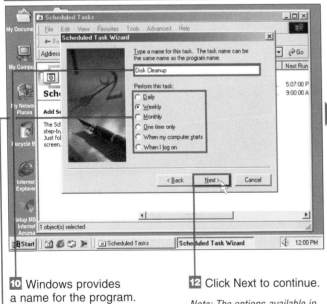

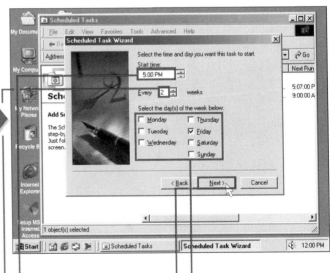

10 Windows provides a name for the program. To use a different name, type a new name.

11 Click an option to specify when you want the program to run (○ changes to ⊙).

12 Click Next to continue.

Note: The options available in the next screen depend on the option you selected in step 11.

13 To specify when you want the program to run, click the part of the time you want to change and then type a new time.

14 Windows will run the program every week. To run the program every few weeks, double-click this area and type a new number of weeks.

15 Click each day of the week you want the program to run (☐ changes to ☑).

16 Click Next to continue.

Can I stop a task while it is running?

✔ If a scheduled task begins to run at an inconvenient time, you can stop the task. Display the Scheduled Tasks window, right-click the task you want to stop and then select End Task.

Can I temporarily stop Task Scheduler from running all tasks?

✔ If you do not want to be interrupted while performing another task, you can temporarily stop Task Scheduler from running all tasks. In the Scheduled Tasks window, click the Advanced menu and then select Pause Task Scheduler. To once again run all scheduled tasks, click the Advanced menu and then select Continue Task Scheduler.

Why did a scheduled task not run?

✔ You can view the Task Scheduler log files to find out why a scheduled task did not run. In the Scheduled Tasks window, click the Advanced menu and select View Log.

How can I immediately run a task that I scheduled for a later time?

✔ Display the Scheduled Tasks window and right-click the task you want to run immediately. Then click Run on the menu that appears.

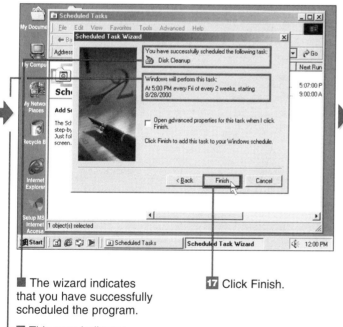

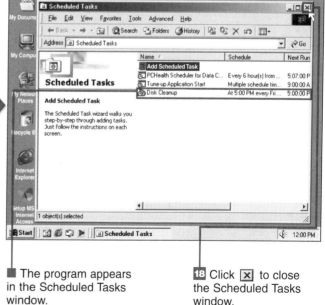

■ The wizard indicates that you have successfully scheduled the program.

■ This area indicates when Windows will run the program.

17 Click Finish.

■ The program appears in the Scheduled Tasks window.

18 Click ☒ to close the Scheduled Tasks window.

CHANGE A SCHEDULED TASK

I f you find that a scheduled task does not work the way you expected, you can change the properties of the task. For example, the program you scheduled may open, but the program may not perform the action you require. Changing the properties of the task allows you to control how and when Task Scheduler performs the task.

Some programs may require certain settings, or parameters, to perform the task you want. For example,

you may need to use parameters to specify exactly which backup job you want to perform for a backup program.

The program may need to access additional files stored on your computer to perform the task. If necessary, you can specify the location of the folder that contains the files.

Task Scheduler allows you to enter comments about a task

you have scheduled. Adding comments to your tasks will help you later identify each task.

You should make sure a task is turned on to ensure that the task will run when expected. If you do not want a scheduled task to interrupt your work, you can temporarily turn off the task.

CHANGE A SCHEDULED TASK

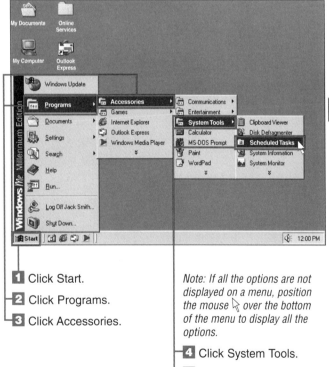

1 Click Start.

2 Click Programs.

3 Click Accessories.

Note: If all the options are not displayed on a menu, position the mouse ⌖ over the bottom of the menu to display all the options.

4 Click System Tools.

5 Click Scheduled Tasks.

■ The Scheduled Tasks window appears.

6 Double-click the task you want to change.

■ A dialog box appears, displaying properties that you can change for the task.

How can I find out which parameters a program needs to run correctly?

✔ You may find information about the parameters a program needs to run correctly in the documentation included with the program. You may also be able to find the parameters for a program using the MS-DOS Prompt. Click the Start button and select Programs. Choose Accessories and then click MS-DOS Prompt to display the MS-DOS Prompt window. At the command prompt, type the program's name followed by a space and /?. For example, type chkdsk /? to find the parameters you can use for the CheckDisk program.

Can I change the program that will run for a task?

✔ Yes. When viewing the properties of a task, select the Task tab. Click the Browse button to search your computer for the program you want to run. You can also type the location and name of the program in the Run area. If the location of the program includes spaces, place quotation marks ("") around the entire location.

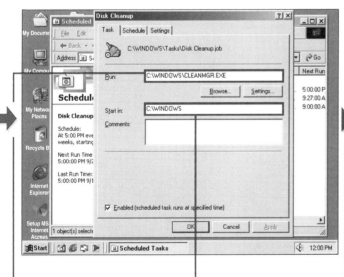

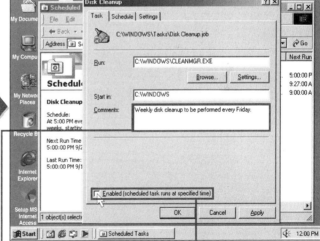

7 This area displays the location and name of the program that will run. If the program requires parameters, type the parameters at the end of the program name.

8 This area displays the location and name of the folder that contains the program or related files needed to run the program. To change the folder, select the text and then type a new folder location and name.

9 You can click this area and type comments about the task.

10 The task will run when a check mark (✔) appears in this area. You can click this option to temporarily turn off the task (✔ changes to ☐).

CONTINUED ▶

CHANGE A SCHEDULED TASK
(CONTINUED)

Task Scheduler allows you to change when a task will run. This is useful if a task runs at an inconvenient time or if you want to change how often the task runs.

You can have Task Scheduler delete a task when the task is not scheduled to run again. This is useful for tasks scheduled to run only once.

Task Scheduler lets you stop a task after the task has run for a certain length of time.

To prevent Task Scheduler from interrupting your work, you can have a task run only if you do not use your computer for a certain period of time. Task Scheduler can monitor your computer for a period of inactivity, during which it will run the task. If a task starts to run while you are using your computer, you can have Task Scheduler stop running the task.

You can prevent a task from starting while your computer

is running on batteries or stop performing a task if your computer switches to battery power. These options help conserve your batteries.

If your computer uses a sleep mode to conserve power, you can have Task Scheduler wake your computer to perform a task.

CHANGE A SCHEDULED TASK (CONTINUED)

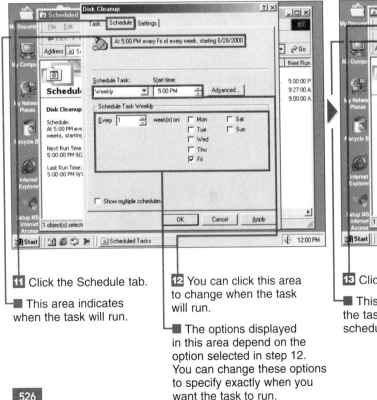

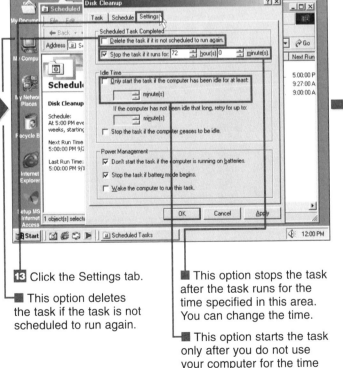

■11 Click the Schedule tab.

■ This area indicates when the task will run.

■12 You can click this area to change when the task will run.

■ The options displayed in this area depend on the option selected in step 12. You can change these options to specify exactly when you want the task to run.

■13 Click the Settings tab.

■ This option deletes the task if the task is not scheduled to run again.

■ This option stops the task after the task runs for the time specified in this area. You can change the time.

■ This option starts the task only after you do not use your computer for the time specified in this area. You can change the time

Can I have a task run only between certain dates?

✔ Yes. You may want to run a task only between certain dates, such as over a long weekend or while you are on vacation. When viewing the properties for a task, click the Schedule tab and then click the Advanced button. You can then select a start date and an end date for the task.

Why would I want to place a time limit on a task?

✔ You may want to stop running a task, such as disk defragmenting, if it takes a long time and interferes with your work. You may also want to use a time limit to close a program that does not close automatically when the program has finished running.

Can I have a task repeat each time it is scheduled to run?

✔ Yes. When viewing the properties for a task, select the Schedule tab and click the Advanced button. In the dialog box that appears, select the Repeat task option (☐ changes to ☑). You can then specify how often you want the task to repeat each time it runs.

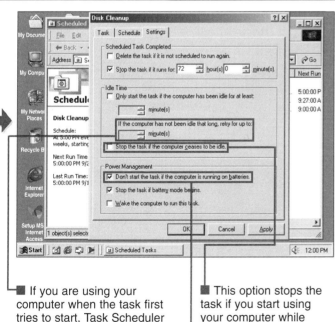

■ If you are using your computer when the task first tries to start, Task Scheduler will continue to check if you are using the computer for the time specified in this area. You can change the time.

■ This option stops the task if you start using your computer while the task is running.

■ This option prevents the task from starting if your computer is running on batteries.

■ This option stops performing the task if your computer starts running on batteries.

■ If your computer has entered a sleep mode, this option wakes the computer to run the task.

14 Task Scheduler will use each option that displays a check mark (✔). You can click an option to turn the option on (☑) or off (☐).

15 Click OK to confirm all your changes.

USING THE MAINTENANCE WIZARD

Y ou can use the Maintenance Wizard to schedule regular maintenance tasks to optimize the performance of your computer. The wizard can help make your programs run faster, free up space on your hard disk and check your hard disk for errors.

Windows allows you to select the maintenance settings you want to

use. The Express option uses the most common maintenance settings. The Custom option allows you to choose your own settings.

You can also specify when you want Windows to run the maintenance tasks on your computer. You may prefer to schedule maintenance tasks at night so they do not interfere with your work during the day.

You must ensure that your computer is turned on at the time the maintenance tasks are scheduled to occur.

Your computer may be set up to automatically open certain programs each time you start Windows. You can start Windows more quickly by preventing unnecessary programs from opening automatically.

USING THE MAINTENANCE WIZARD

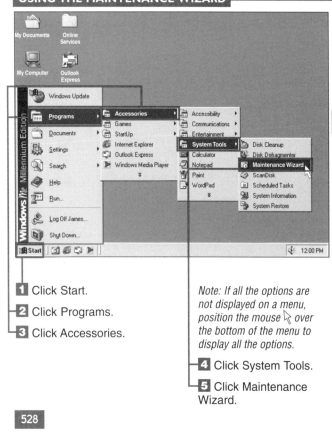

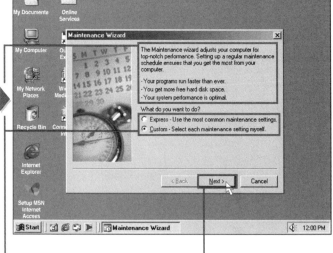

1 Click Start.

2 Click Programs.

3 Click Accessories.

Note: If all the options are not displayed on a menu, position the mouse ℝ over the bottom of the menu to display all the options.

4 Click System Tools.

5 Click Maintenance Wizard.

■ The Maintenance Wizard appears.

■ This area describes the Maintenance Wizard.

6 Click an option to use the most common maintenance settings or select your own settings (○ changes to ⦿).

7 Click Next to continue.

Note: The following steps depend on the option you selected in step 6.

Why does a different dialog box appear the next time I start the Maintenance Wizard?

✔ After you use the Maintenance Wizard to schedule maintenance tasks, a different dialog box will appear the next time you start the wizard. To run all the maintenance tasks, select the Perform maintenance now option. To review or change your maintenance settings, select the Change my maintenance settings or schedule option.

Should I prevent all of my programs from opening automatically?

✔ Opening too many programs automatically will make Windows start more slowly. You should only automatically open the programs you frequently use. For information about setting up programs to open automatically, see page 238.

How does Windows know when to start scheduled maintenance tasks?

✔ Windows uses the date and time set in your computer to determine when to start scheduled maintenance tasks. You should make sure the date and time set in your computer is correct before you schedule maintenance tasks. To change the date and time set in your computer, see page 164.

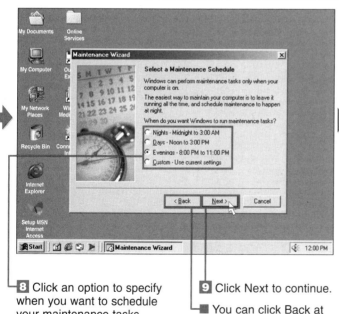

■8 Click an option to specify when you want to schedule your maintenance tasks (○ changes to ◉).

■9 Click Next to continue.

■ You can click Back at any time to return to a previous step and change your selections.

■ This area lists the programs that open automatically each time you start Windows.

Note: This screen does not appear if you have not set up any programs to open automatically. To continue, skip to step 12 on page 530.

■10 To start Windows more quickly, click the box beside each program you do not want to open automatically (☑ changes to ☐).

■11 Click Next to continue.

CONTINUED ▶

USING THE MAINTENANCE WIZARD (CONTINUED)

The Maintenance Wizard can run Disk Defragmenter to help make your programs operate faster. Over time, the files on a hard disk become more and more fragmented. To access a file, your computer must use many different areas on the hard disk. Disk Defragmenter reorganizes your files to reduce fragmentation so the programs operate more quickly.

You can also have the Maintenance Wizard run ScanDisk during the maintenance operation. ScanDisk is a program that detects and repairs errors on your hard disk.

The Maintenance Wizard can run Disk Cleanup to find and remove unneeded files on your hard disk as part of your maintenance. This can help increase the amount of available space on your hard disk. Disk Cleanup will find and remove several types of files, such as temporary Internet files and temporary files that your programs no longer need.

You can have Windows perform the maintenance tasks you have selected as soon as you finish using the wizard.

Disk Defragmenter, ScanDisk and Disk Cleanup also appear on the Start menu and you can run them at any time. For information on Disk Defragmenter, see page 516. For information on ScanDisk, see page 512. For information on Disk Cleanup, see page 510.

USING THE MAINTENANCE WIZARD (CONTINUED)

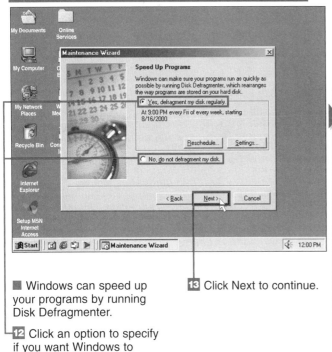

■ Windows can speed up your programs by running Disk Defragmenter.

12 Click an option to specify if you want Windows to defragment your hard disk regularly (○ changes to ◉).

13 Click Next to continue.

■ Windows can check your hard disk for errors by running ScanDisk.

14 Click an option to specify if you want Windows to check your hard disk for errors regularly (○ changes to ◉).

15 Click Next to continue.

Can I change the maintenance schedule and settings for Disk Defragmenter, ScanDisk and Disk Cleanup?

✔ The Reschedule button allows you to change the date and time when the Maintenance Wizard will run Disk Defragmenter, ScanDisk and Disk Cleanup. When setting up Disk Defragmenter or ScanDisk, the Settings button allows you to change the drive you want to defragment or check for errors. When setting up Disk Cleanup, the Settings button allows you to specify the types of files you want to delete.

How do I stop Windows from running a scheduled maintenance task?

✔ The Maintenance Wizard adds each maintenance task to the Scheduled Tasks window. To stop Windows from running a scheduled maintenance task, you must remove the task from the Scheduled Tasks window. Click Start, choose Programs and then select Accessories. Click System Tools and then select Scheduled Tasks. In the Scheduled Tasks window, click the task and then press the Delete key. For more information on the Scheduled Tasks window, see page 524.

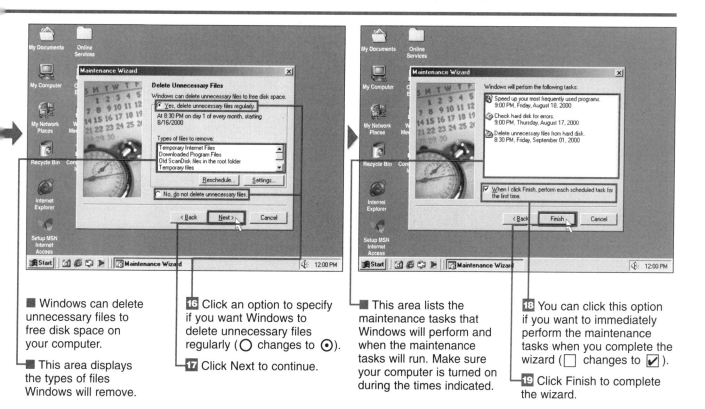

■ Windows can delete unnecessary files to free disk space on your computer.

■ This area displays the types of files Windows will remove.

16 Click an option to specify if you want Windows to delete unnecessary files regularly (○ changes to ⊙).

17 Click Next to continue.

■ This area lists the maintenance tasks that Windows will perform and when the maintenance tasks will run. Make sure your computer is turned on during the times indicated.

18 You can click this option if you want to immediately perform the maintenance tasks when you complete the wizard (☐ changes to ☑).

19 Click Finish to complete the wizard.

CHANGE POWER OPTIONS

Y ou can change the power options on your computer to reduce the amount of power the computer uses. This is useful if you want to reduce the energy consumption of your desktop computer or increase the battery life of your portable computer.

You can choose the power scheme that best describes the way you use your computer. A power scheme is a collection of settings that manage the power your computer uses.

Windows can conserve power by turning off your monitor and hard disks when your computer has been idle for a certain period of time. You can change the amount of time that passes before Windows turns off these items.

Windows can also place your computer on standby, which turns off items that use power, when you do not use the computer for a period of time you specify. Some computers also support the hibernate option, which saves everything on your computer and then turns off the computer after a period of inactivity you specify. When you restart your computer after hibernation, any open programs and documents will appear as you left them on your computer.

CHANGE POWER OPTIONS

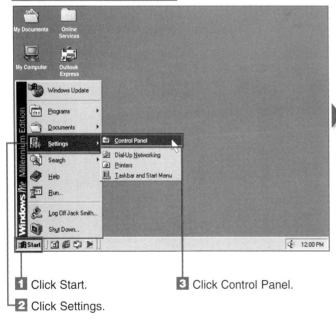

1 Click Start.

2 Click Settings.

3 Click Control Panel.

■ The Control Panel window appears.

Note: If all the items do not appear in the Control Panel window, click the view all Control Panel options link in the window to display all the items.

4 Double-click Power Options.

Why aren't all the power options available on my computer?

✔ The available power options depend on which options the hardware installed on your computer supports. If the option to change the amount of time that passes before your computer hibernates does not appear on the Power Schemes tab, either your hardware does not support hibernation or the hibernate feature is not enabled on your computer.

How can I create a new power scheme?

✔ In the Power Options Properties dialog box, click the Power Schemes tab and then select the options you want to use for the new power scheme. To save the new power scheme, click the Save As button.

How do I resume using my computer when it is in a low power mode?

✔ If your hard disk or monitor turns off or if your computer is on standby, you can move the mouse or press any key to resume working where you left off. To bring your computer out of hibernation, you must press the power button on your computer. Windows takes longer to bring your computer out of hibernation than out of standby.

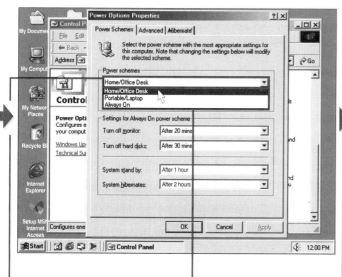

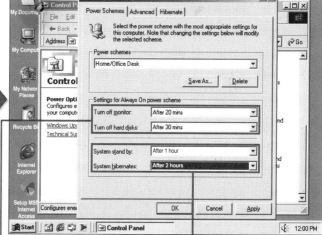

■ The Power Options Properties dialog box appears.

5 Click this area to display a list of the available power schemes.

6 Click the appropriate power scheme for the way you use your computer.

7 These areas display the amount of time your computer must be inactive before your monitor and hard disks automatically turn off. You can click an area to change the amount of time.

8 These areas display the amount of time your computer must be inactive before the computer goes on standby or hibernates. You can click an area to change the amount of time.

CONTINUED ▶

CHANGE POWER OPTIONS
(CONTINUED)

You can have Windows display a power icon on the right side of the taskbar. When you double-click the icon on a desktop computer, Windows displays the Power Options Properties dialog box so you can adjust your power options. If you are using a portable computer, double-clicking the icon displays the amount of power remaining on the battery.

You can also have Windows request a password when the

computer comes out of standby or hibernation. A password prevents unauthorized people from using your computer when it goes on standby or hibernates while you are away from your desk. The password you enter to bring the computer out of standby or hibernation is the same password you enter when you start Windows.

You can specify if you want the computer to go on standby,

hibernate or turn off when you press the power button on your computer.

If a computer supports hibernation, you can turn on the option that enables hibernation. You can also view the amount of free disk space on your computer and the amount of free disk space required to place your computer in hibernation.

CHANGE POWER OPTIONS (CONTINUED)

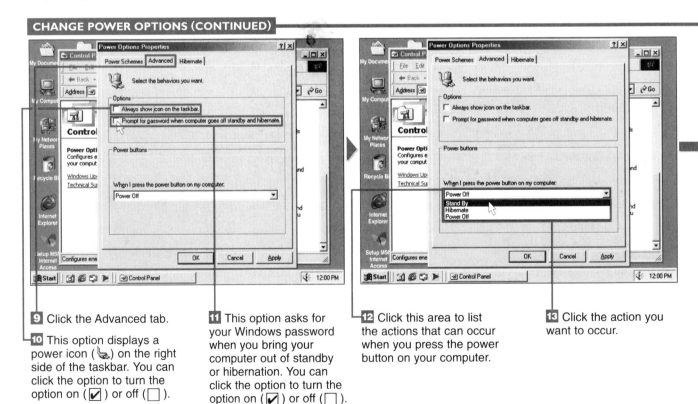

■9 Click the Advanced tab.

■10 This option displays a power icon (🔋) on the right side of the taskbar. You can click the option to turn the option on (✔) or off (☐).

■11 This option asks for your Windows password when you bring your computer out of standby or hibernation. You can click the option to turn the option on (✔) or off (☐).

■12 Click this area to list the actions that can occur when you press the power button on your computer.

■13 Click the action you want to occur.

How do I change the password required to bring my computer out of standby?

✔ You must change your Windows password. Click the Start button, select Settings and choose Control Panel. Double-click Passwords. In the Password Properties dialog box, click the Change Windows Password button. If a dialog box appears that lets you make your Windows password the same as other passwords, click OK to close the dialog box. To change your Windows password, type your old password and press the Tab key. Type your new Windows password and press the Tab key. Type the new password again and press the Enter key.

Will my portable computer warn me when battery power is low?

✔ If the Power Options Properties dialog box displays the Alarms tab, you can select sound or visual alarms that will warn you when battery power is low. You can also choose whether the computer goes into standby, hibernates or shuts down when the power is low.

How can I immediately put my computer on standby or hibernation?

✔ Click the Start button and then select Shut Down. In the Shut Down Windows dialog box, click ▾, select Stand by or Hibernate and then click OK.

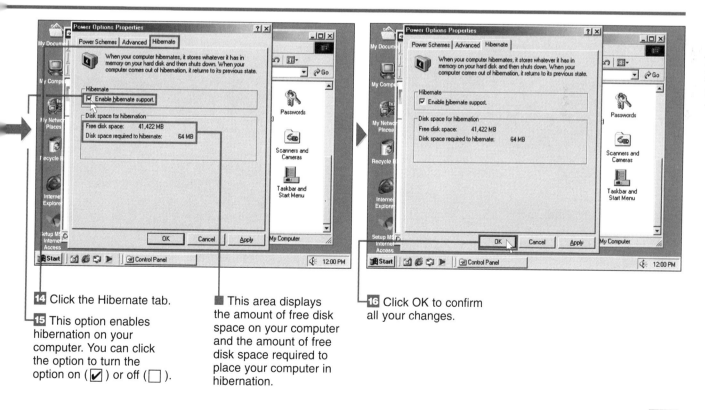

14 Click the Hibernate tab.

15 This option enables hibernation on your computer. You can click the option to turn the option on (✔) or off (☐).

■ This area displays the amount of free disk space on your computer and the amount of free disk space required to place your computer in hibernation.

16 Click OK to confirm all your changes.

CHANGE VIRTUAL MEMORY SETTINGS

Virtual memory is hard disk space Windows uses to store data that does not fit in Random Access Memory (RAM).

Your computer uses RAM to temporarily store information. The amount of RAM a computer has determines the number of programs the computer can run at once and how fast programs will operate.

Windows is constantly managing your computer's memory. When you choose a different font, open a new window or begin a task like printing, RAM is required. When your computer runs out of RAM, Windows places information in virtual memory on the hard disk and then retrieves the information when it is required. The hard disk space that Windows uses as virtual memory is also called a swap file.

Windows can manage the virtual memory settings on your computer or you can specify your own settings. You can specify the minimum and maximum amount of hard disk space you want to use as virtual memory. For example, you may want to increase the minimum amount of disk space if you frequently use programs that require large amounts of memory, such as multimedia programs.

CHANGE VIRTUAL MEMORY SETTINGS

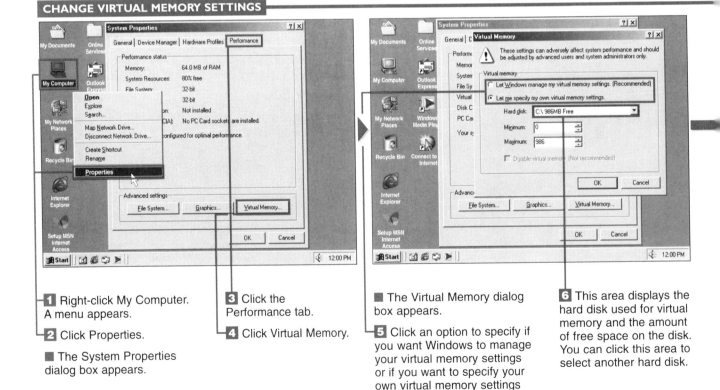

■1 Right-click My Computer. A menu appears.

■2 Click Properties.

■ The System Properties dialog box appears.

■3 Click the Performance tab.

■4 Click Virtual Memory.

■ The Virtual Memory dialog box appears.

■5 Click an option to specify if you want Windows to manage your virtual memory settings or if you want to specify your own virtual memory settings (○ changes to ⊙).

■6 This area displays the hard disk used for virtual memory and the amount of free space on the disk. You can click this area to select another hard disk.

Should I change the virtual memory settings?

✔ In general, you should not change the virtual memory settings. You should allow Windows to manage the virtual memory settings for you. If you change the virtual memory settings, you may not be able to restart your computer or your computer may not perform optimally. You should only change virtual memory settings if you are an advanced user or system administrator.

How can I optimize the virtual memory?

✔ If you have more than one hard drive, you could move the virtual memory from a slow drive to a faster drive or to a drive with more free space.

Some programs require more RAM than my computer has. Can I use virtual memory to make up the difference?

✔ No. Virtual memory cannot replace RAM. For example, if a program you want to run requires 64 MB of RAM and your computer has only 32 MB of RAM, virtual memory cannot be used to make up the additional RAM required to run the program.

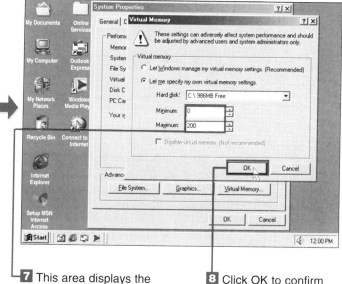

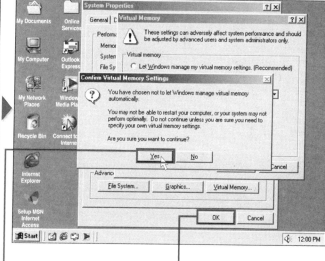

7 This area displays the minimum and maximum amount of hard disk space your computer can use as virtual memory. To change an amount, double-click an area and then type a new amount.

8 Click OK to confirm your changes.

■ The Confirm Virtual Memory Settings dialog box appears.

9 Click Yes to continue.

10 Click OK to close the System Properties dialog box.

■ Windows may ask you to restart your computer. Click Yes to restart your computer.

ADD WINDOWS COMPONENTS

You can add components to your computer that will add new programs and capabilities to Windows.

When Windows is installed on a computer, all of the components that come with Windows may not be installed. This helps prevent unneeded components from taking up valuable storage space on your computer. Components that are not required to perform essential

tasks or are of interest only to certain people, such as the Multilanguage Support component, are not typically installed.

Windows organizes components into various categories, such as Accessories, Communications and Multimedia. Each category contains similar types of components that you can install. You can view a description of

each category to help you determine which categories contain the components you want to add to your computer.

Windows indicates which categories contain components that are not yet installed on your computer. Windows uses check boxes to indicate whether all (☑), none (☐) or some (☑) of the components in a category are installed.

ADD WINDOWS COMPONENTS

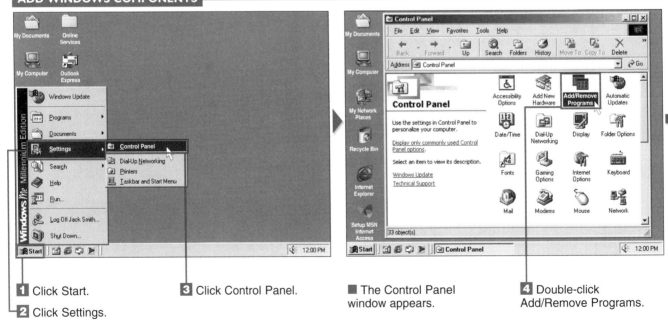

■ Click Start.

2 Click Settings.

3 Click Control Panel.

■ The Control Panel window appears.

4 Double-click Add/Remove Programs.

When would I use the Have Disk button?

✔ In the Add/Remove Programs Properties dialog box, you use the Have Disk button to install a Windows component that is not listed on the Windows Setup tab. For example, on some networks, the files necessary to install Windows components are not copied to each user's hard drive. You would use the Have Disk button to tell Windows where to find the necessary files on the network.

How do I remove a component I no longer need?

✔ You can remove components you no longer need to free up storage space on your computer. To remove a component you do not use, perform steps 1 to 10 starting on page 538. When you select a component you want to remove in step 8, ✔ changes to ☐. Some components, such as Briefcase, are no longer available after you install them, so you cannot remove these components.

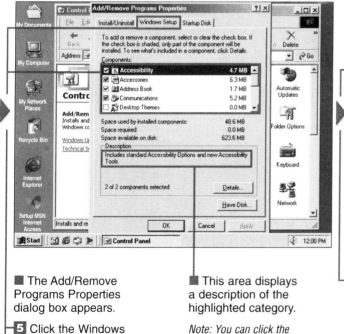

■ The Add/Remove Programs Properties dialog box appears.

5 Click the Windows Setup tab.

■ This area displays the categories of components you can add to your computer.

■ This area displays a description of the highlighted category.

Note: You can click the name of another category to display its description.

■ The box beside each category indicates if all (✔), some (✔) or none (☐) of the components in the category are installed on your computer.

CONTINUED

ADD WINDOWS COMPONENTS (CONTINUED)

There are many useful Windows components that you can add to your computer at any time.

The Accessories category has several useful components. Briefcase makes it easy to work with files away from the office. You can use Briefcase to make copies of your files and keep all copies up-to-date. You will also find additional desktop wallpaper and screen savers in the Accessories category.

The Communications category contains Direct Cable Connection, which allows you to create a simple network by attaching two computers with a cable. You will also find Internet Connection Sharing, which allows multiple computers to share a single connection to the Internet.

The System Tools category contains tools that allow you to optimize the performance of your computer. Character Map is invaluable when

you need to find a special character that is not available on the keyboard. Disk compression tools are helpful when you need to increase the amount of free space on your hard drive.

You can view all the components in a category and select the components you want to add to your computer.

ADD WINDOWS COMPONENTS (CONTINUED)

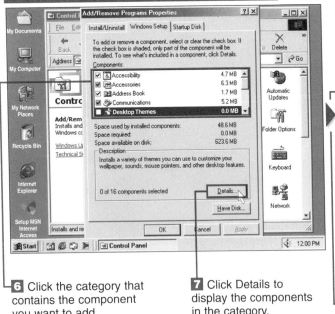

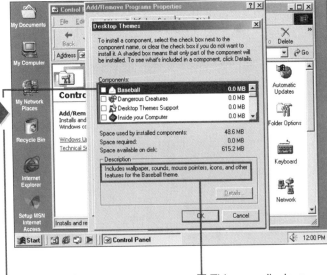

■6 Click the category that contains the component you want to add.

■7 Click Details to display the components in the category.

Note: If the Details button is dimmed, the category does not contain any components.

■ A dialog box appears.

■ This area displays the components in the category you selected.

■ This area displays a description of the highlighted component.

Note: You can click the name of another component to display its description.

What does the Multilanguage Support component do?

✔ Multilanguage Support installs the files needed to work with and create documents in several non-Western languages, including Greek and Turkish. There are five language groups you can choose from. To change your keyboard layout to work in one of these languages, see the top of page 166.

When I select a component to install, why does Windows ask if I want to install other components?

✔ Some components require other components to work properly. For example, to install a desktop theme, the Desktop Themes Support component must also be installed on your computer. When you select a component, Windows asks if you want to install all the components that are needed. To install the selected component and all the necessary components, click Yes in the dialog box that appears.

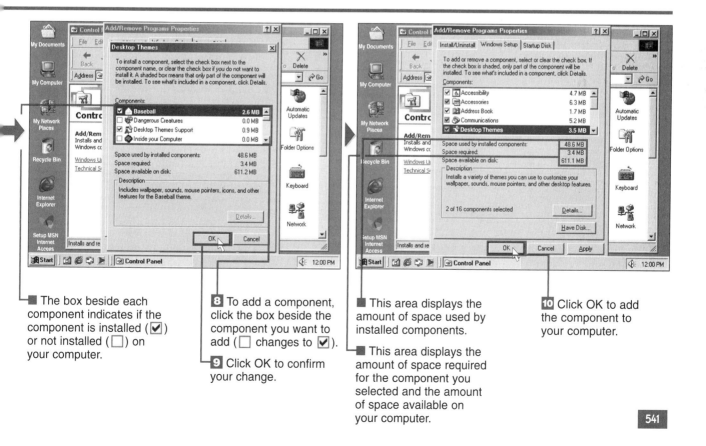

■ The box beside each component indicates if the component is installed (☑) or not installed (☐) on your computer.

8 To add a component, click the box beside the component you want to add (☐ changes to ☑).

9 Click OK to confirm your change.

■ This area displays the amount of space used by installed components.

■ This area displays the amount of space required for the component you selected and the amount of space available on your computer.

10 Click OK to add the component to your computer.

INSTALL A PROGRAM

You can install a new program on your computer. Programs are available on CD-ROM discs and floppy disks.

Most Windows programs available on a CD-ROM disc will automatically start an installation program when you insert the disc into a drive on your computer. If the installation program does not start automatically, you can have Windows start the installation process.

The installation program may ask you questions about your computer and how you would like to install the program. There are three common types of installations. A typical installation sets up a program with the most common components. A custom installation allows you to customize the program to suit your specific needs. A minimum installation sets up a program with a minimum number

of components. A minimum installation is ideal for computers with limited disk space.

After you install a new program, make sure you keep the program's CD-ROM disc or floppy disks in a safe place. If your computer fails or you accidentally erase the program files, you may need to install the program again.

INSTALL A PROGRAM

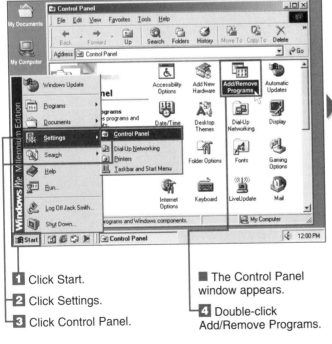

1 Click Start.

2 Click Settings.

3 Click Control Panel.

■ The Control Panel window appears.

4 Double-click Add/Remove Programs.

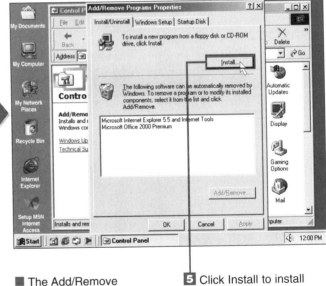

■ The Add/Remove Programs Properties dialog box appears.

5 Click Install to install a new program.

Windows did not find an installation program. What can I do?

✔ If Windows did not find an installation program, you can search for the program using the Browse button in the Run Installation Program dialog box. Display the contents of the drive containing the program's installation disk and look for a file named "setup" or "install."

How can I install a program if it does not have an installation program?

✔ If you are installing a program that does not have an installation program, create a new folder on your computer. Then copy all the files from the installation disk to the new folder. You can start the program from the folder.

Do I need to re-install all the programs on my computer after I upgrade to Windows Me?

✔ If you upgraded to Windows Me from a previous version of Windows, you do not have to re-install the existing programs on your computer.

What is a readme file?

✔ A readme file is a file usually found on a program's installation floppy disk or CD-ROM disc. This file may contain the latest information about the program or information that can help you install the program.

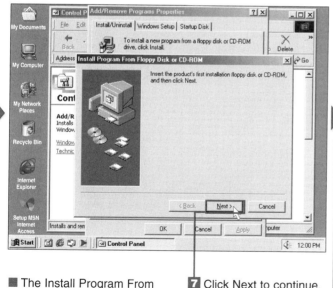

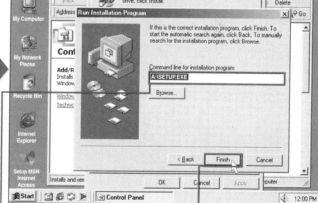

■ The Install Program From Floppy Disk or CD-ROM dialog box appears.

6 Insert the program's first installation floppy disk or CD-ROM disc into the appropriate drive on your computer.

7 Click Next to continue.

■ The Run Installation Program dialog box appears.

■ Windows locates the file needed to install the program.

8 Click Finish to install the program.

9 Follow the instructions on your screen. Every program will ask you a different set of questions.

REMOVE A PROGRAM

You can remove a program that you no longer use on your computer. Removing a program will free up space on your hard disk and allow you to install newer and more useful programs.

Windows keeps track of the programs you have installed on your computer. You can select the program you want to remove

from a list and have Windows automatically remove the program from your computer.

When you remove a program from your computer, Windows deletes the program's files and may reverse the computer settings that were changed when the program was installed. To avoid affecting other programs, Windows may leave some of the

files that other programs on your computer need to operate.

When you finish removing a program, you should restart your computer. This will ensure that any settings that were changed when the program was installed are reversed.

REMOVE A PROGRAM

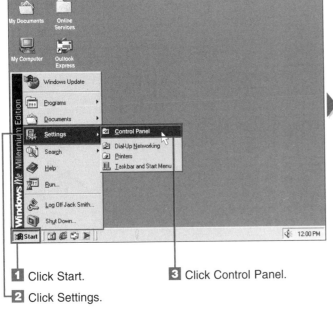

1 Click Start.

2 Click Settings.

3 Click Control Panel.

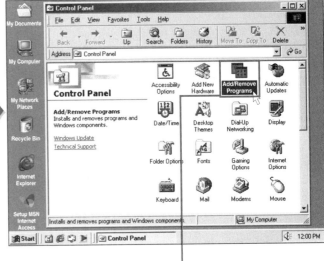

■ The Control Panel window appears.

4 Double-click Add/Remove Programs to remove a program from your computer.

How can I remove a program that Windows cannot automatically remove?

✔ Only programs designed for Windows will appear in the Add/Remove Programs Properties dialog box. For all other programs, check the documentation supplied with the program to determine which files you need to remove. Make sure you delete only the files for the program you want to remove. There are also many commercial uninstall programs you can purchase that can help you delete a program's files.

I removed a program from my computer, but the Start menu still displays the program. How do I remove a program from the Start menu?

✔ On the Start menu, right-click the program you want to remove and then select Delete from the menu that appears.

How do I delete a program's shortcut from my desktop?

✔ After deleting a program, you can drag any shortcuts you no longer need to the Recycle Bin.

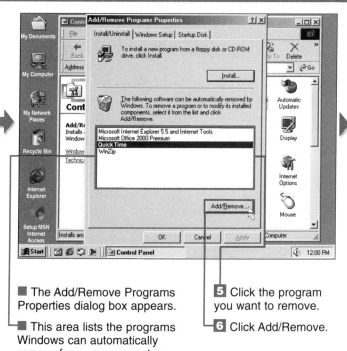

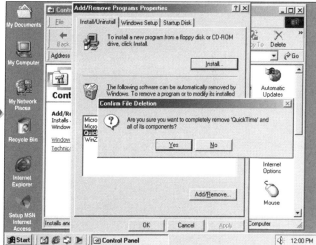

■ The Add/Remove Programs Properties dialog box appears.

■ This area lists the programs Windows can automatically remove from your computer.

5 Click the program you want to remove.

6 Click Add/Remove.

■ Windows begins the process of removing the program from your computer.

7 Follow the instructions on your screen. Every program will take you through different steps to remove the program.

INSTALL NEW HARDWARE

You can install new hardware on your computer, such as a network interface card, modem or printer. The Add New Hardware Wizard guides you step by step through the installation of new hardware.

Before installing new hardware, you should read any documentation that was included with the device and connect the device to your computer. You should also close all open programs on your computer.

Windows first searches your computer for Plug and Play hardware. Plug and Play hardware uses technology that allows Windows to automatically detect the device and set up the device to work properly with your computer. This makes Plug and Play devices easy to install.

If a new Plug and Play device is attached to your computer but is not detected by Windows, the device may not be working properly. You should check to make sure the device is properly connected to your computer.

INSTALL NEW HARDWARE

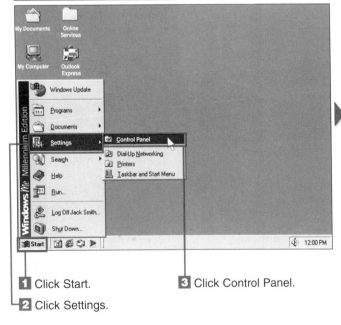

■ Click Start.

■ Click Settings.

■ Click Control Panel.

■ The Control Panel window appears.

Note: If all the items do not appear in the Control Panel window, click the view all Control Panel options link in the window to display all the items.

■ Double-click Add New Hardware.

Is there a faster way to install a new Plug and Play device?

✔ After you physically connect a Plug and Play device to your computer and turn the computer on, Windows automatically detects the device and installs the necessary software. If Windows requires information to install the device, Windows will ask you for the information.

What happens if the wizard finds a Plug and Play device?

✔ When the wizard finds a Plug and Play device, the wizard displays the name of the device it found. Click the device you want to install, click Next and then follow the instructions on your screen. If the device you want to install is not listed, select the No, the device isn't in the list option (○ changes to ⦿) and then click Next.

Do I need to use the Add New Hardware Wizard to install all devices?

✔ No. To install a printer using the Add Printer Wizard, see page 114. To install a modem using the Install New Modem wizard, see page 324. To install a game controller using the Gaming Options dialog box, see page 266.

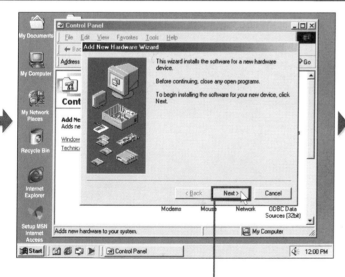

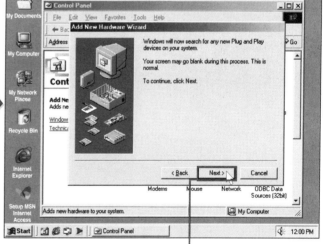

■ The Add New Hardware Wizard appears.

■ The wizard will install the software for your new hardware. Make sure you close any open programs before you continue.

5 Click Next to begin installing the new hardware.

■ Windows will now search for new Plug and Play devices on your computer. Your screen may go blank during the search.

6 Click Next to search for Plug and Play devices on your computer.

CONTINUED ▶

INSTALL NEW HARDWARE (CONTINUED)

Y ou can have Windows search your computer for new hardware that is not Plug and Play compatible. Windows may take several minutes to search your computer. If the search stops for a long time, you should restart your computer and try installing the new hardware again.

If the Add New Hardware Wizard does not find any new hardware

on your computer, the wizard allows you to select the type of hardware you want to install from a list.

When you install a device, you must ensure that the settings Windows uses for the device match the settings on the device. You may have to adjust the device settings to match the settings used by Windows. You can adjust the settings by

using the software that came with the device or by manually adjusting the jumpers or switches on the device. Consult the documentation that came with the device before making any adjustments. You can use Device Manager to view the settings Windows uses for the device. For information about Device Manager, see page 570.

INSTALL NEW HARDWARE (CONTINUED)

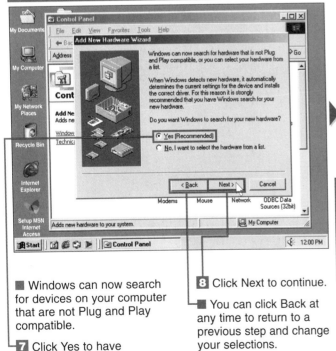

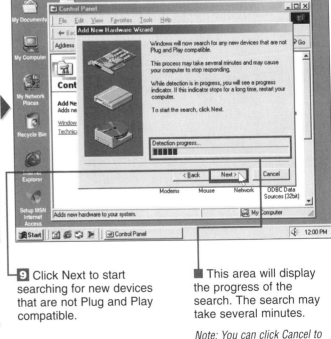

■ Windows can now search for devices on your computer that are not Plug and Play compatible.

7 Click Yes to have Windows search for new devices (○ changes to ⊙).

8 Click Next to continue.

■ You can click Back at any time to return to a previous step and change your selections.

9 Click Next to start searching for new devices that are not Plug and Play compatible.

■ This area will display the progress of the search. The search may take several minutes.

Note: You can click Cancel to stop the search at any time.

Why would I choose to select my hardware from a list instead of having Windows search for it?

✔ When Windows searches for and finds your new hardware, Windows determines the device's current settings and automatically installs a driver for the device. If you have a driver for the device that is more current than the one included with Windows, you can choose the "No, I want to select the hardware from the list" option to manually select the hardware and then install the new driver.

The type of device I want to install does not appear in the list. What should I do?

✔ You can select Other devices from the list and then click Next to display a list of computer product manufacturers that might provide the device. If you still cannot find the device, you can install the device using the installation disk for the device. Insert the installation disk into the drive. Click the Have Disk button in the Add New Hardware Wizard and then press the Enter key. If you do not have a disk for the device, try selecting a device that closely resembles the one you want to install.

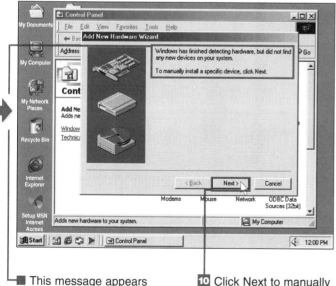

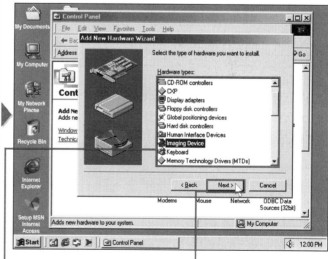

■ This message appears when Windows has finished searching for new devices. In this example, Windows did not find any new devices on the computer.

10 Click Next to manually install a device.

11 Click the type of hardware you want to install.

12 Click Next to continue.

Note: The following screens depend on the type of hardware you selected in step 11.

CONTINUED ▶

INSTALL NEW HARDWARE
(CONTINUED)

The type of hardware you choose to install will determine what steps you need to perform to finish installing the device.

If Windows did not automatically detect your new hardware, you must specify the manufacturer and model of the device. This allows Windows to select the correct driver for the device. A driver is software that enables Windows to communicate with the device.

When installing hardware, you may need to specify which port the device is connected to. A port is a connector that allows instructions and data to flow between the computer and a device. If Windows detected your device, you do not need to specify a port.

Windows may provide a name for the device you are installing. If you do not want to use the name Windows provides, you can change the name.

You may need to restart your computer to complete the installation of some devices.

INSTALL NEW HARDWARE (CONTINUED)

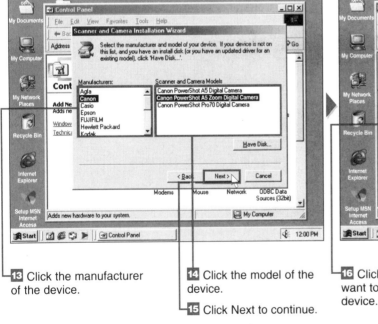

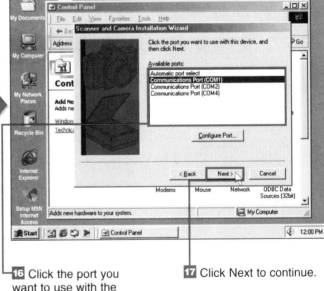

13 Click the manufacturer of the device.

14 Click the model of the device.

15 Click Next to continue.

16 Click the port you want to use with the device.

17 Click Next to continue.

What can I do if the device does not work after it is installed?

✔ You can use the Hardware Troubleshooter help topic to help you solve a problem you are having with your device. Click the Start button and then click Help. In the Help and Support window, click the Search area, type **hardware troubleshooter** and then press the Enter key. A link appears for the Hardware Troubleshooter. Click the link and then follow the instructions that appear in the right frame.

Why didn't my hardware device install properly?

✔ The device you installed may not be compatible with Windows Me. To ensure your new hardware device will work with Windows Me, check the documentation that came with the device or check Microsoft's hardware compatibility list at the www.microsoft.com/hcl Web site.

How do I uninstall hardware I no longer need?

✔ You can use the Device Manager to uninstall hardware. For information about using the Device Manager, see page 570.

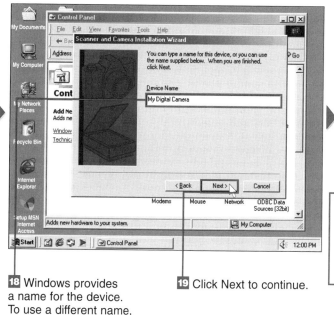

18 Windows provides a name for the device. To use a different name, type a new name.

19 Click Next to continue.

20 Click Finish to complete the installation of the device.

UPDATE DEVICE DRIVERS

Your hardware devices may work better if you are using the latest version of the software they need to operate. Hardware devices ranging from your mouse to your modem are all controlled by software, called drivers. A driver allows the computer to communicate with and control a device.

When you install a device, Windows checks for the hardware

and then installs the appropriate driver. Windows does not include all possible device drivers. If the correct driver is not installed, the device may not work properly. Updating the driver for the device may fix the problem.

When you purchase a device, the manufacturer may include drivers on a floppy disk or CD-ROM disc. To use the drivers, you should insert the floppy disk or CD-ROM

disc before performing the steps below.

You can also obtain new drivers directly from the manufacturer. Most manufacturers provide the latest drivers in the support area of their Web site. The latest driver for a device may improve the performance of the device and offer more features.

UPDATE DEVICE DRIVERS

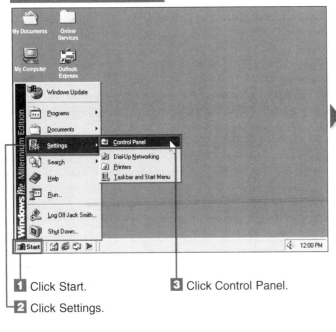

1 Click Start.

2 Click Settings.

3 Click Control Panel.

■ The Control Panel window appears.

Note: If all the items do not appear in the Control Panel window, click the view all Control Panel options link in the window to display all the items.

4 Double-click System.

What can I do if the device does not have a Driver tab?

✔ You may be able to change the settings for the device in the Control Panel. For example, to change the driver for a monitor, open the Control Panel window, double-click Display, choose the Settings tab and then select the Advanced button. In the dialog box that appears, click the Adapter tab.

How do I view a list of driver files a device is using?

✔ A device may use several driver files to operate. You can view the name and location of each file by clicking the Driver File Details button on the Driver tab. You should never delete a driver file that is being used by a device.

My printer is not listed in the Device Manager. How do I update my printer driver?

✔ Click the Start button, choose Settings and then click Printers. In the Printers window, right-click the printer you want to update and select Properties. In the dialog box that appears, choose the Details tab and click New Driver. In the Select Device dialog box, select the manufacturer and model of your printer.

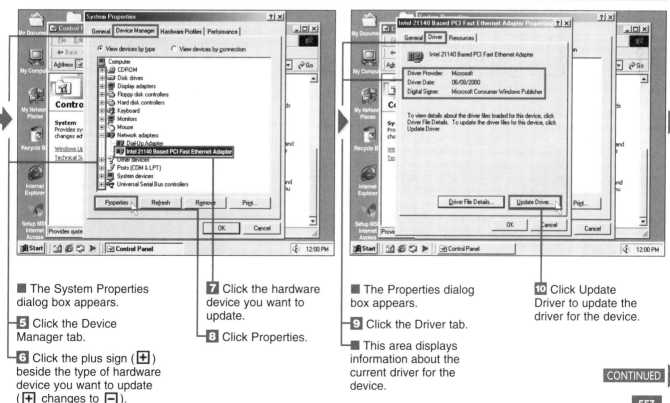

■ The System Properties dialog box appears.

5 Click the Device Manager tab.

6 Click the plus sign (⊞) beside the type of hardware device you want to update (⊞ changes to ⊟).

7 Click the hardware device you want to update.

8 Click Properties.

■ The Properties dialog box appears.

9 Click the Driver tab.

■ This area displays information about the current driver for the device.

10 Click Update Driver to update the driver for the device.

CONTINUED ▶

UPDATE DEVICE DRIVERS
(CONTINUED)

Whenever updating the driver for a device, you can have the Update Device Driver Wizard automatically search for a better driver.

The wizard will search the Windows drivers folder on your computer. This folder is a database on your hard drive that contains drivers. If you inserted a floppy disk or CD-ROM disc into a drive

before starting the wizard, Windows will search the contents of the drive for an updated driver.

When searching for updated drivers, the wizard always looks for a file with the .inf extension. The INF file contains information that tells the wizard how to install the driver. After the wizard reads the INF file, it will copy the files Windows needs and adjust any

settings that are required by the device. In addition to the INF file, the wizard may need files from the Windows CD-ROM disc.

If the new driver does not work properly, you may need to re-install the previous driver you were using. In some cases, you may need to remove the hardware and re-install it.

UPDATE DEVICE DRIVERS (CONTINUED)

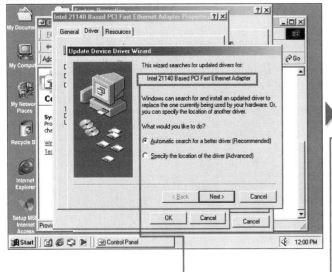

■ The Update Device Driver Wizard appears.

■ The wizard will search for updated drivers for the device shown in this area.

11 Click this option to have Windows automatically search for a better driver (○ changes to ⊙).

12 Click Next to continue.

■ Windows will search your floppy drive, CD-ROM drive and the Windows drivers folder for updated drivers.

The wizard did not find an updated driver, but says there are other drivers that may work with my device. What should I do?

✔ If you are satisfied with the driver currently installed on your computer, click Cancel. If the device is not working properly, you can try installing a different driver. Click the Install one of the other drivers option to view the drivers Windows found.

Can I manually search for a driver on my computer?

✔ If you know the location of the driver you want to update, you can select the Specify the location of the driver (Advanced) option in the wizard. Click Next and then select the "Display a list of all the drivers in a specific location, so you can select the driver you want" option. Then click Next and follow the instructions on your screen.

Is there another way I can search for new drivers?

✔ You can use the Windows Update feature to find new drivers on the Internet. Click the Start button and select Windows Update. For more information about Windows Update, see page 562.

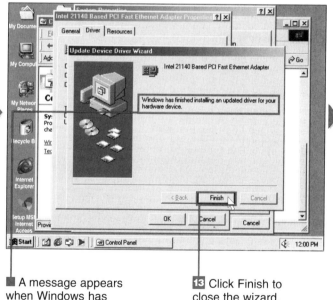

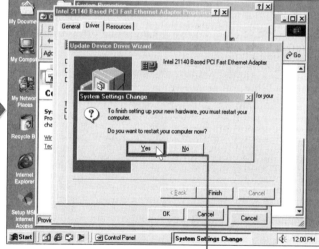

■ A message appears when Windows has finished updating the driver for the device.

Note: If Windows did not find a better driver for the device, a message appears, stating that the best driver for the device is already installed.

13 Click Finish to close the wizard.

■ A message may appear, stating that you must restart your computer to finish setting up the device.

14 Click Yes to restart the computer.

INSTALL WINDOWS ME

Y ou can install Windows Me to upgrade your computer's operating system from Windows 95, Windows 98 or Windows 98 Second Edition. When you upgrade to Windows Me, you replace the operating system currently installed on your computer, but you retain your settings and any programs you previously installed.

Before you upgrade to Windows Me, you should back up the files stored on your computer and ensure your computer meets the minimum hardware requirements for Windows Me.

The Windows Millennium Edition Setup Wizard guides you step by step through the installation process. The setup wizard displays the Microsoft

License Agreement. To continue with the installation, you must accept the terms of the license agreement.

You must enter the 25-character Product Key for your copy of Windows Me. You can find the Product Key on the CD-ROM's packaging or the documentation that came with the CD-ROM.

INSTALL WINDOWS ME

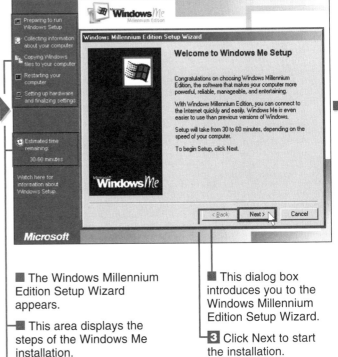

■1 Insert the Windows Me installation CD-ROM into a drive.

■ A dialog box appears, stating that the CD-ROM contains a newer version of Windows than you are currently using.

■2 Click Yes to upgrade your computer to Windows Me.

■ The Windows Millennium Edition Setup Wizard appears.

■ This area displays the steps of the Windows Me installation.

■ This area displays the estimated time remaining.

■ This dialog box introduces you to the Windows Millennium Edition Setup Wizard.

■3 Click Next to start the installation.

What are the minimum hardware requirements for Windows Me?

✔ To run Windows Me, your computer should at least have a 150 MHz Pentium processor, 32 MB of RAM and 320 MB of free hard disk space. Some features that come with Windows have higher hardware requirements. For example, to use Windows Movie Maker, you will need at least a 300 MHz processor, 64 MB of RAM and a video capture device.

The dialog box stating the CD-ROM contains a newer version of Windows than I am currently using did not appear. What should I do?

✔ Display the My Computer window and double-click the drive containing the CD-ROM. When the CD-ROM contents are displayed, double-click setup and then follow the steps below.

How do I install Windows Me on a computer that does not have an operating system currently installed?

✔ You can install Windows Me on a blank hard drive with a formatted partition. You can use the startup disk that comes with the full version of Windows Me to install Windows. Insert the startup disk, turn on your computer and then insert the Windows Me installation CD-ROM. Then follow the instructions on your screen to start the setup program.

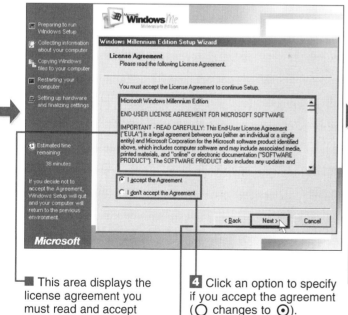

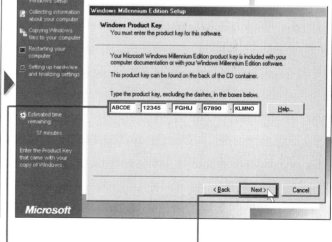

■ This area displays the license agreement you must read and accept before continuing.

Note: You can use the scroll bar to browse through the agreement.

4 Click an option to specify if you accept the agreement (○ changes to ⊙).

5 Click Next to continue.

6 Enter the 25-character Product Key for your copy of Windows Me.

7 Click Next to continue.

CONTINUED

INSTALL WINDOWS ME (CONTINUED)

During the installation, you can choose to save your existing operating system files. This will enable you to later uninstall Windows Me and return to your old operating system if you wish.

The Windows Millennium Edition Setup Wizard also creates a startup disk during the installation process. This disk will help you later start Windows Me if the operating system will not start normally. The floppy disk you use to create the startup disk must be able to store at least 1.2 MB of information. If your computer has more than one floppy disk drive, you should insert the disk into the A: drive. The A: drive is used to start the computer when the hard drive cannot.

Once the setup wizard has finished creating the startup disk, the wizard is ready to begin copying Windows Me files from the CD-ROM to your computer. It will take approximately 30 minutes to copy all the files to your computer.

INSTALL WINDOWS ME (CONTINUED)

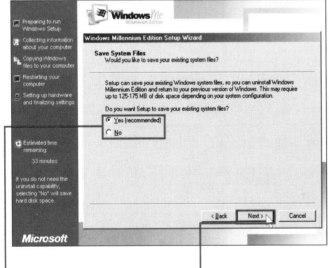

8 Click an option to specify if you want to save your existing operating system files (○ changes to ⊙).

9 Click Next to continue.

■ The setup wizard will now create a startup disk. You can use the disk if you have trouble starting Windows Me.

10 Label a floppy disk "Windows Millennium Edition Startup Disk."

11 Insert the floppy disk into drive A.

12 Click OK to continue.

What is on the startup disk?

✔ The startup disk contains basic operating system files that will allow you to start Windows Me if Windows will not start normally. The startup disk also contains generic CD-ROM drivers that let you access your CD-ROM drive. Several utility programs are also found on the startup disk. ScanDisk checks and repairs hard drive errors. FDISK allows you to partition your hard drive. Format allows you to format your hard drive.

Can I create a startup disk later?

✔ Yes. You can create a startup disk at any time after Windows Me is installed. For more information about creating a startup disk, see page 586.

Why did the wizard ask me to select a setup option?

✔ If you are installing Windows Me on a computer that does not currently have an operating system installed, you must select the type of setup you want to use. The setup you select will determine which components are installed with Windows Me. You can later add or remove components. See page 538 for information about Windows components.

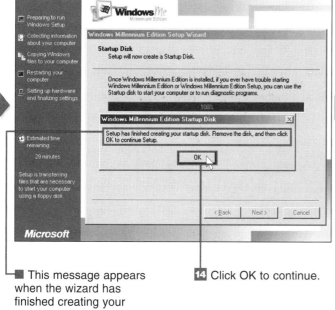

■ This message appears when the wizard has finished creating your startup disk.

13 Remove the floppy disk from the drive.

14 Click OK to continue.

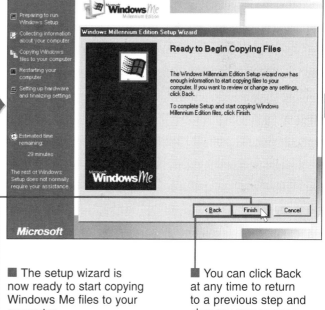

■ The setup wizard is now ready to start copying Windows Me files to your computer.

15 Click Finish to continue.

■ You can click Back at any time to return to a previous step and change your answers.

CONTINUED ▶

INSTALL WINDOWS ME (CONTINUED)

While the setup wizard copies Windows operating system files to your computer, the wizard takes the opportunity to tell you about the features and benefits of Windows Me.

When all the files have been transferred to your computer, the wizard restarts your computer to begin the final part of the installation process.

The wizard sets up any hardware devices and Plug and Play devices it finds on your computer. If you have new devices or devices that were not properly installed before, the wizard may install or correct the software for the devices. When the wizard has finished setting up hardware devices, it may restart your computer.

After setting up hardware, the wizard sets up components such as the Control Panel and

Windows Help. This may take several minutes. The wizard will automatically restart your computer once it has finished the installation.

When the installation process is complete, Windows Me plays a video highlighting the operating system's new features and enhancements. After you watch the video, you can access more information about the Windows Me features.

INSTALL WINDOWS ME (CONTINUED)

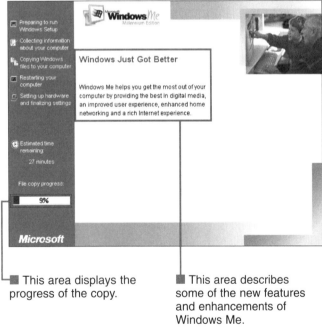

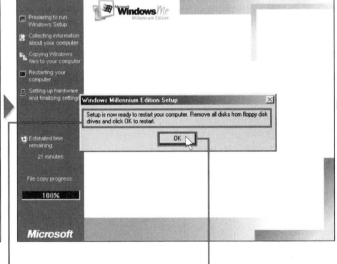

■ This area displays the progress of the copy.

■ This area describes some of the new features and enhancements of Windows Me.

■ This message appears when the setup wizard has finished copying files to your computer.

16 Click OK to restart your computer.

Note: Your computer restarts and the setup wizard finishes setting up Windows Me. When the wizard is finished, it restarts your computer again automatically.

Can I uninstall Windows Me after upgrading from a previous version?

✔ If you have not changed the file system or structure of your hard drive, such as converting to the FAT32 file system or partitioning your hard drive, you can uninstall the operating system. Display the Control Panel window and double-click the Add/Remove Programs icon. Click the Install/Uninstall tab, select Uninstall Windows Millennium and then click the Add/Remove button.

Can I remove the files for my old operating system?

✔ If you are sure you will not want to later uninstall Windows Me, display the Control Panel window and double-click the Add/Remove Programs icon. Click the Install/Uninstall tab, select Delete Windows Millennium uninstall information and then click the Add/Remove button.

Will Windows Me remember my passwords?

✔ Yes. If you used passwords with your previous version of Windows, you can continue to use the passwords with Windows Me. If your computer is connected to a network, installing Windows Me will not affect your network password. You should consult your system administrator before upgrading the computer to Windows Me.

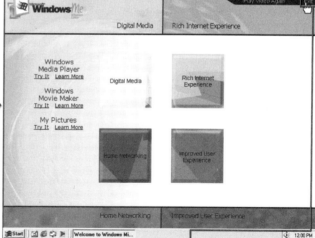

■ Windows Me starts.

■ A welcome video appears, introducing you to Windows Me.

■ This screen appears when the welcome video is finished playing.

■ You can move the mouse 🖑 over the screen to display links that you can click to use or learn more about some of the Windows Me features.

17 Click Exit to exit the welcome screen and begin using Windows Me.

UPDATE WINDOWS ME

You can set up Windows to automatically keep your computer up-to-date with the latest Windows components and information available on the Internet.

Instead of spending time to manually search for the latest updates for your computer, you can have Windows automatically search for important updates and information on the Internet.

Windows will search for updates only when you are connected to the Internet.

Windows can add new features to your computer and fix software problems to improve the performance of your computer. Windows will also use the latest information available on the Internet to check for outdated software on your computer.

No updates are installed at the time you set up automatic updating. After you set up Windows to automatically update your computer, Windows will check for updates when you are connected to the Internet and will download the updates so you can install them on your computer later.

SET UP WINDOWS TO UPDATE AUTOMATICALLY

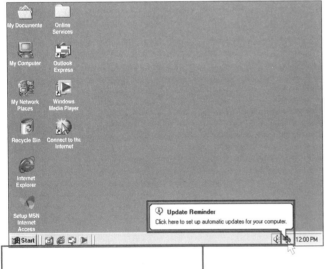

■ When you are connected to the Internet, this icon (🖳) and message appear when you can set up Windows to update your computer automatically.

1 Click the icon (🖳) to set up Windows to update your computer automatically.

■ The Updates wizard appears, stating that you can update your computer automatically by allowing Windows to search for important updates and information on the Internet.

2 Click Next to continue.

MASTER IT

Can I have Windows notify me before downloading updates?

✔ Yes. Click the Start button, choose Settings and then select Control Panel. In the Control Panel window, double-click Automatic Updates and then select the "Notify me before downloading any updates and notify me again when they are ready to be installed" option (○ changes to ⊙).

Can I update my computer manually?

✔ Yes. If you do not want Windows to automatically update your computer, click the Start button, choose Settings and then select Control Panel. Double-click Automatic Updates and then select the "Turn off automatic updating. I will update my computer manually" option (○ changes to ⊙).

Is there another way to update Windows?

✔ You can update Windows by using the Windows Update feature. This feature takes you to a Web site that can optimize the performance of your computer. The Web site scans your computer to determine additional components you can install to update Windows. To use the Windows Update feature, click the Start button and select Windows Update. Then follow the instructions on your screen.

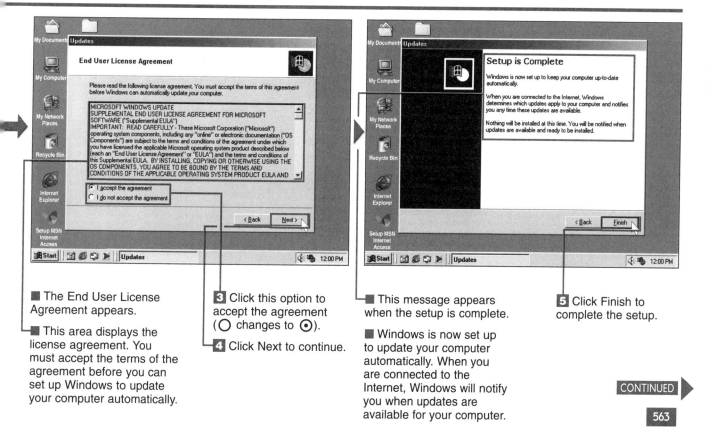

■ The End User License Agreement appears.

■ This area displays the license agreement. You must accept the terms of the agreement before you can set up Windows to update your computer automatically.

3 Click this option to accept the agreement (○ changes to ⊙).

4 Click Next to continue.

■ This message appears when the setup is complete.

■ Windows is now set up to update your computer automatically. When you are connected to the Internet, Windows will notify you when updates are available for your computer.

5 Click Finish to complete the setup.

CONTINUED

UPDATE WINDOWS ME (CONTINUED)

When you are connected to the Internet, Windows will automatically check for updates on the Internet that apply to your computer.

When Windows finds updates on the Internet that apply to your computer, it downloads the updates to your computer without interrupting your work.

After the download is complete, Windows displays an icon on the taskbar and a message stating that the updates are ready to be installed. When you click the icon, the Updates wizard appears, allowing you to install the updates on your computer.

You can view a list of the recommended updates before installing the updates. You

can also select which updates you want to install from the list.

Windows may ask you to restart your computer after you install certain updates. If you do not restart your computer, your computer may not function properly.

INSTALL UPDATES

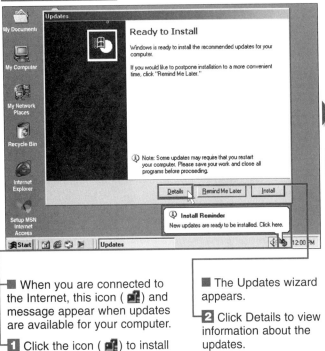

■ When you are connected to the Internet, this icon (🖳) and message appear when updates are available for your computer.

1 Click the icon (🖳) to install the recommended updates.

■ The Updates wizard appears.

2 Click Details to view information about the updates.

■ This area describes the updates that are recommended for your computer.

3 Windows will install each update that displays a check mark (✔). If you do not want to install an update, click the check mark beside the update (✔ changes to ☐).

4 Click Install to install the updates.

Can I postpone installing updates until a more convenient time?

✔ If you do not want to install updates when Windows displays the Update Reminder, you can have Windows remind you at a later time. Click the Update Reminder icon ( ) on your taskbar to display the Updates wizard and select the Remind Me Later button. A dialog box appears, allowing you to specify how long Windows should wait before reminding you again.

How can I find more information about a recommended update?

✔ When viewing the details for a recommended update, you can click the Read This First link to display additional information about an update.

If I choose not to install an update, can I install it later?

✔ Windows deletes updates if you choose not to install them. You can restore an update if you later change your mind. To restore an update, click the Start button, select Settings and choose Control Panel. In the Control Panel window, double-click Automatic Updates and then click the Restore Hidden Items button. Updates you have declined that still apply to your computer will appear the next time Windows notifies you of available updates.

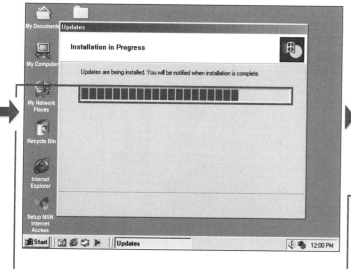

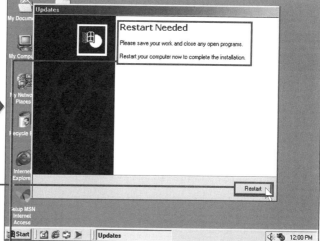

■ This area shows the progress of the installation.

■ This message appears if you need to restart your computer to complete the installation. Before restarting your computer, make sure you save your work and close any open programs.

5 Click Restart to restart your computer.

Note: If the "Installation Complete" message appears instead of the "Restart Needed" message, you do not need to restart your computer. Click OK to complete the installation.

CREATE A HARDWARE PROFILE

Y ou can create a new hardware profile for your computer. A hardware profile tells Windows which hardware devices to use when you start your computer.

Windows automatically creates profiles called Original Configuration and Undocked for a portable computer. For a desktop computer, Windows automatically creates the Original Configuration profile. To create a new hardware

profile, you copy an existing profile and then make changes to the copy.

A portable computer can be used in several different situations. For example, you may use the portable computer at an office where you connect to a docking station to access a network. At home, you may use the portable computer with a printer, monitor, keyboard and mouse. When traveling, you may use the

portable computer without any additional hardware. Each situation requires a different hardware setup.

To avoid having to install hardware devices on your computer each time you need to use a different hardware setup, you can save the hardware settings for each situation in a profile.

CREATE A HARDWARE PROFILE

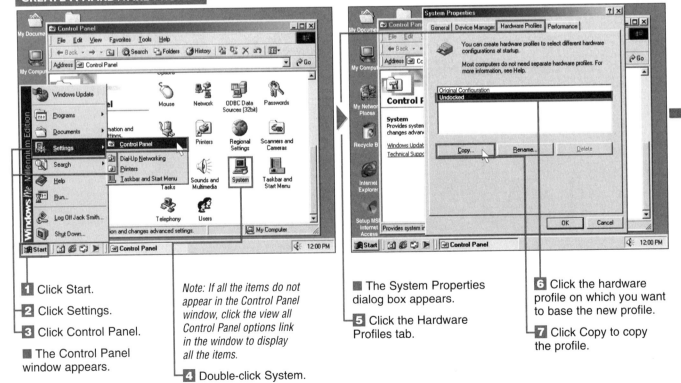

■ Click Start.

■ Click Settings.

■ Click Control Panel.

■ The Control Panel window appears.

Note: If all the items do not appear in the Control Panel window, click the view all Control Panel options link in the window to display all the items.

■ Double-click System.

■ The System Properties dialog box appears.

■ Click the Hardware Profiles tab.

■ Click the hardware profile on which you want to base the new profile.

■ Click Copy to copy the profile.

Which hardware profile should I copy as the basis for my new profile?

✔ You should choose a profile that has a large number of devices already installed, since it is easier to disable a device than it is to install one. For portable computers, this is probably the profile you use when docked and attached to a network.

How can I rename a profile I created?

✔ Display the System Properties dialog box and select the Hardware Profiles tab. Select the profile you want to rename and click the Rename button. Then type a new name for the profile.

When would I create a new hardware profile for my desktop computer?

✔ You may want to create a new profile for your desktop computer if you frequently add and remove a hardware device, such as a ZIP drive. Creating a profile that includes the ZIP drive saves you from having to install the drive each time you want to use it.

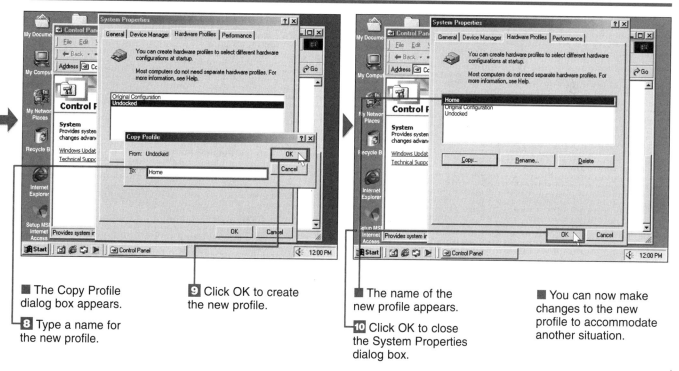

■ The Copy Profile dialog box appears.

8 Type a name for the new profile.

9 Click OK to create the new profile.

■ The name of the new profile appears.

10 Click OK to close the System Properties dialog box.

■ You can now make changes to the new profile to accommodate another situation.

CONTINUED

CREATE A HARDWARE PROFILE
(CONTINUED)

You create a new hardware profile by copying an existing profile and then changing the copied profile to suit your needs. Changing a copied profile does not affect any of the other profiles on your computer.

When you start your computer, Windows automatically uses the correct profile for the hardware it detects. If Windows does not

know which profile to use, you will be asked to choose a profile from a list that appears.

You can only make changes to the profile you used to start the computer.

To customize a hardware profile, you disable or enable devices in the profile to suit your needs. Disabling a device in a profile

stops Windows from loading the device's driver when you start your computer using the profile. A driver is the software Windows uses to communicate with a device. Windows displays a red X through the icon for each device you disable. There are some devices, such as CD-ROM and disk drives, which you cannot disable.

CREATE A HARDWARE PROFILE (CONTINUED)

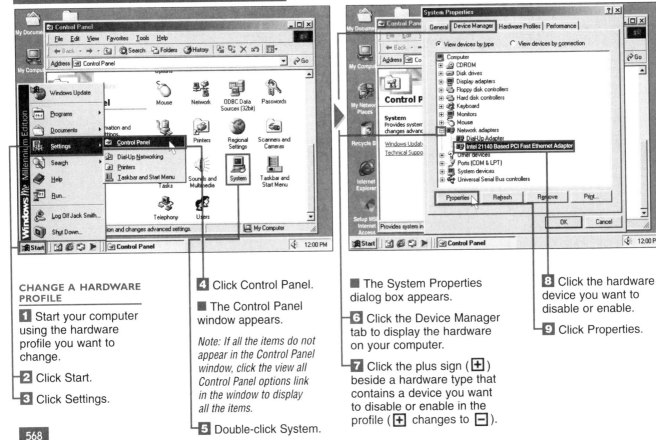

CHANGE A HARDWARE PROFILE

1 Start your computer using the hardware profile you want to change.

2 Click Start.

3 Click Settings.

4 Click Control Panel.

■ The Control Panel window appears.

Note: If all the items do not appear in the Control Panel window, click the view all Control Panel options link in the window to display all the items.

5 Double-click System.

■ The System Properties dialog box appears.

6 Click the Device Manager tab to display the hardware on your computer.

7 Click the plus sign (⊞) beside a hardware type that contains a device you want to disable or enable in the profile (⊞ changes to ⊟).

8 Click the hardware device you want to disable or enable.

9 Click Properties.

Do I need to disable the printer?

✔ It is not necessary to disable the printer. If you send documents to a printer that is not currently connected to your computer, Windows will store the print job until you reconnect to the printer. If you will not be using the printer in any of your profiles, you can remove the printer. For information about removing a printer, see page 113.

Can each hardware profile have its own screen resolution?

✔ Yes. When you change the screen resolution, it is automatically saved as part of the profile you are currently using. For information about changing the screen resolution, see page 172.

How do I delete a profile I no longer need?

✔ Display the System Properties dialog box and select the Hardware Profiles tab. Click the profile you want to remove and then click the Delete button.

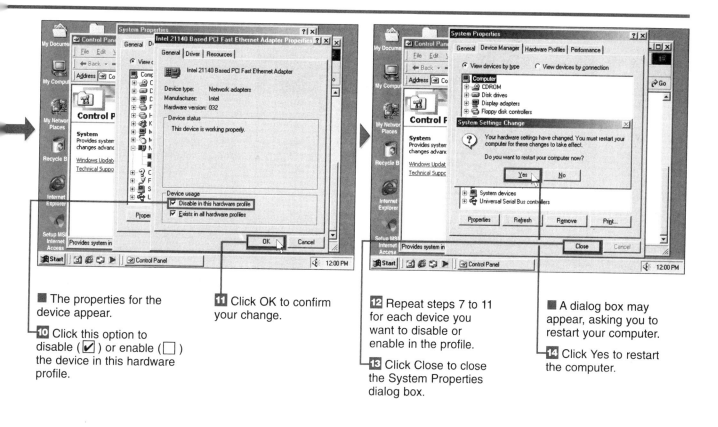

■ The properties for the device appear.

10 Click this option to disable (☑) or enable (☐) the device in this hardware profile.

11 Click OK to confirm your change.

12 Repeat steps 7 to 11 for each device you want to disable or enable in the profile.

13 Click Close to close the System Properties dialog box.

■ A dialog box may appear, asking you to restart your computer.

14 Click Yes to restart the computer.

USING DEVICE MANAGER

If you are having trouble with your computer, the Device Manager can often help you identify the problem and find a solution.

The Device Manager organizes hardware devices into categories, such as disk drives and monitors. Each category lists the specific hardware devices installed on your computer.

If there is a problem with a hardware device, the Device

Manager displays a yellow exclamation mark (!) over the icon for the device. For example, a hardware device that was not properly installed may display an exclamation mark. A hardware device with a red X through its icon indicates the device has been disabled. These symbols can simplify the task of identifying and solving problems with your hardware.

The Device Manager information can be helpful when adding a new

hardware device to your computer. You can quickly view which hardware devices are already installed on your computer.

If Windows does not start properly, you can start Windows in safe mode and use the Device Manager to determine whether a malfunctioning hardware device is causing the problem. For information about safe mode, see page 588.

VIEW HARDWARE INFORMATION

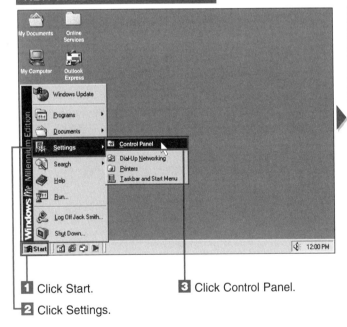

1 Click Start.

2 Click Settings.

3 Click Control Panel.

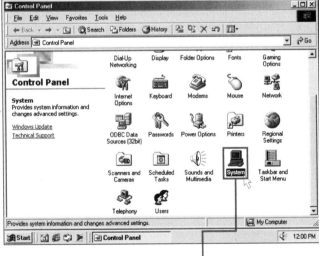

■ The Control Panel window appears.

Note: If all the items do not appear in the Control Panel window, click the view all Control Panel options link in the window to display all the items.

4 Double-click System.

How do I change the way devices are listed on the Device Manager tab?

✔ You can have the Device Manager list the hardware devices by type or by connection. To list the devices by type, display the Device Manager tab and select the View devices by type option. Listing by type lets you see the devices grouped under categories, such as CDROM and Display adapters. To list the devices by connection, select the View devices by connection option. If you list the devices by connection, the Device Manager organizes the devices under the hardware the devices are connected to, such as Plug and Play BIOS.

I just connected a device to my computer. Why doesn't the device appear in Device Manager?

✔ Many devices, such as PC cards for portable computers and devices that connect to a Universal Serial Bus (USB) port, can be attached to or disconnected from a computer while the computer is running. You do not need to restart your computer for these devices to work. After connecting or disconnecting a device, you can use the Refresh button on the Device Manager tab to update the list of devices.

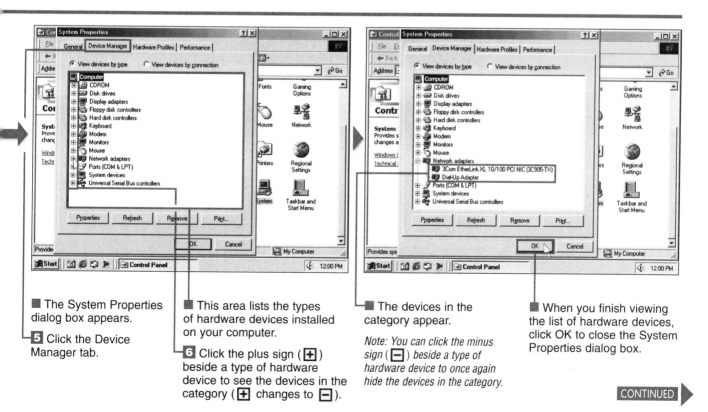

■ The System Properties dialog box appears.

5 Click the Device Manager tab.

■ This area lists the types of hardware devices installed on your computer.

6 Click the plus sign (⊞) beside a type of hardware device to see the devices in the category (⊞ changes to ⊟).

■ The devices in the category appear.

Note: You can click the minus sign (⊟) beside a type of hardware device to once again hide the devices in the category.

■ When you finish viewing the list of hardware devices, click OK to close the System Properties dialog box.

CONTINUED ▶

USING DEVICE MANAGER (CONTINUED)

You can use the Device Manager to display information about a hardware device, such as the manufacturer of the device and whether the device is working properly.

You can also use the Device Manager to display information about the driver for a hardware device. A driver is software that allows the computer to communicate with a hardware device. For more information about drivers, see page 552.

The Device Manager can identify which resources on your computer a hardware device uses. There are four main types of resources that control the communication between the computer and a hardware device. An Interrupt Request tells the computer that a device needs attention. A Direct Memory Access channel lets a device communicate directly with your computer's memory to speed up the processing of information. An Input/Output Range specifies which area of memory a device

uses to communicate with the computer. A Memory Range indicates which area of memory a device uses to perform functions.

You can use the Device Manager to find out if any conflicts exist that could cause problems with the operation of a hardware device. If the resource settings for a device conflict with the settings for another device, the devices may not work properly.

DISPLAY INFORMATION FOR A DEVICE

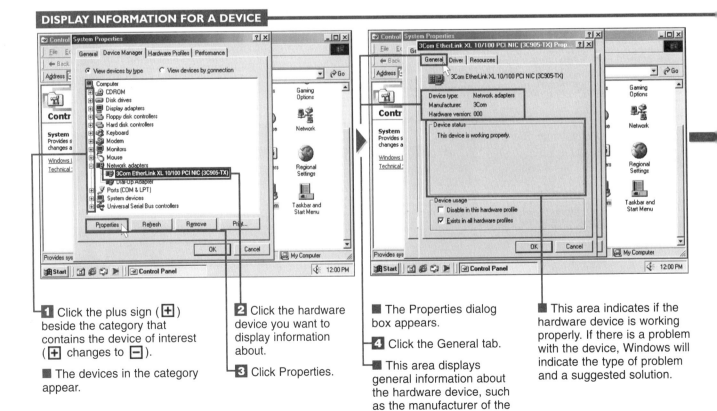

1 Click the plus sign (⊞) beside the category that contains the device of interest (⊞ changes to ⊟).

■ The devices in the category appear.

2 Click the hardware device you want to display information about.

3 Click Properties.

■ The Properties dialog box appears.

4 Click the General tab.

■ This area displays general information about the hardware device, such as the manufacturer of the device.

■ This area indicates if the hardware device is working properly. If there is a problem with the device, Windows will indicate the type of problem and a suggested solution.

Why don't all devices have a Resources tab?

✔ If a device does not have a Resources tab, the device does not use any resources directly. For example, the resources for a CD-ROM drive are usually set by the disk controller.

Why does a device display different tabs than shown below?

✔ The tabs that appear in the Properties dialog box depend on the device you selected. Additional tabs will appear if additional settings are available for the device. For example, you can use the Settings tab to display and change the settings for a CD-ROM drive.

How can I change a resource setting for a hardware device?

✔ If you have conflicts between your hardware devices, you may be able to change some of the resource settings the hardware devices use. Display the properties for the hardware device and select the Resources tab. Click the Use automatic settings option (☑ changes to ☐). Then select the resource you want to change from the resource list and click Change Setting. Change the value and make sure the Conflict information area displays "No devices are conflicting."

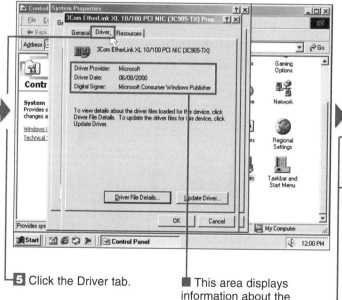

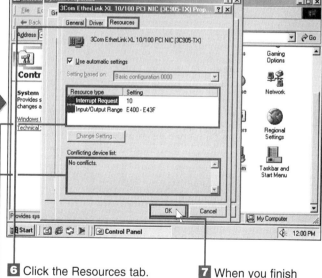

5 Click the Driver tab.

■ This area displays information about the driver the computer uses to communicate with the hardware device.

6 Click the Resources tab.

■ This area displays the resources used by the hardware device.

■ This area indicates if any conflicts exist that could cause problems with the operation of the hardware device.

7 When you finish reviewing information about the hardware device, click OK to close the Properties dialog box.

CONTINUED

USING DEVICE MANAGER (CONTINUED)

You can use the Device Manager to identify which resources on your computer are currently in use. This helps you determine which resources are available for new hardware.

The four main types of resources on your computer are Interrupt Requests (IRQ), Direct Memory Access (DMA) channels, Input/Output (I/O) addresses and Memory addresses. Hardware devices require several resources to run properly.

You can use the Device Manager to uninstall a device on your computer. You may want to uninstall a device when you are removing an old device and installing an updated version of the device. To uninstall a device, you remove the device from the Device Manager and then physically remove the device from your computer. Physically removing an uninstalled hardware device frees up the resources used by the device and ensures that

Windows will not automatically re-install a Plug and Play device.

After you uninstall a device, you should restart your computer. Restarting your computer resets the devices and software on your computer and makes sure the software for the uninstalled device is removed from memory.

DISPLAY RESOURCES USED BY ALL DEVICES

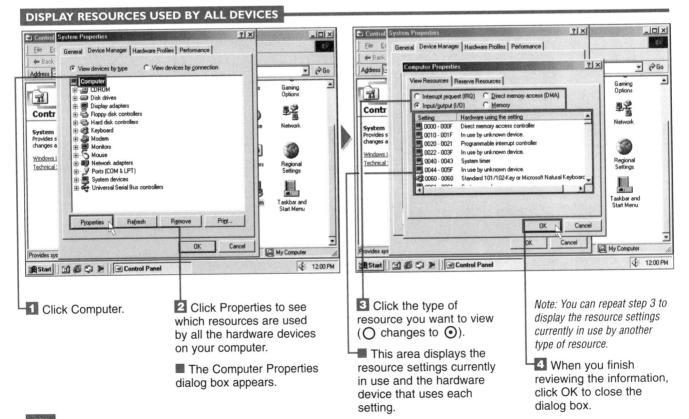

1 Click Computer.

2 Click Properties to see which resources are used by all the hardware devices on your computer.

■ The Computer Properties dialog box appears.

3 Click the type of resource you want to view (○ changes to ⊙).

■ This area displays the resource settings currently in use and the hardware device that uses each setting.

Note: You can repeat step 3 to display the resource settings currently in use by another type of resource.

4 When you finish reviewing the information, click OK to close the dialog box.

Can I print information about my hardware devices from the System Properties dialog box?

✔ Yes. To print information about a specific device or category, display the Device Manager tab, select the device or category and then click the Print button. In the Print dialog box, you can select an option for the information you want to print. The System summary option prints a report listing the system resources and the devices using each resource. The Selected class or device option prints a report listing the resources and drivers used by the selected category or device. The All devices and system summary option prints a resource listing for every device installed on your computer and a system summary report.

How do I re-install a hardware device on my computer?

✔ To re-install a hardware device, click the Start button, choose Settings and select Control Panel. In the Control Panel window, click Add New Hardware and follow the instructions on your screen. For more information, see page 546.

UNINSTALL A DEVICE

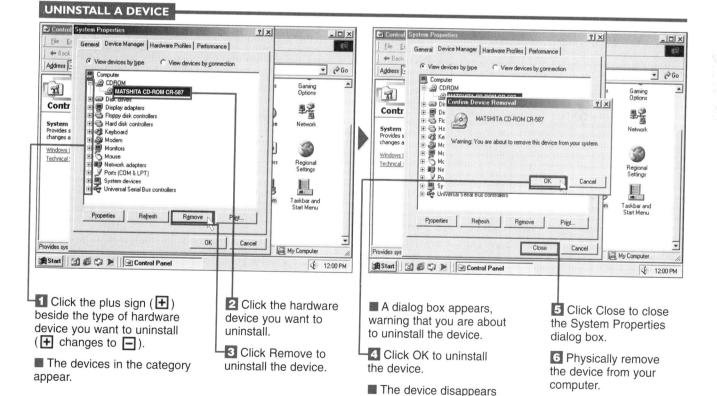

■1 Click the plus sign (⊞) beside the type of hardware device you want to uninstall (⊞ changes to ⊟).

■ The devices in the category appear.

■2 Click the hardware device you want to uninstall.

■3 Click Remove to uninstall the device.

■ A dialog box appears, warning that you are about to uninstall the device.

■4 Click OK to uninstall the device.

■ The device disappears from the Device Manager.

■5 Click Close to close the System Properties dialog box.

■6 Physically remove the device from your computer.

USING SYSTEM INFORMATION

You can use System Information to display detailed information about the hardware and software on your computer. You can use this information to learn more about your computer or troubleshoot a problem you are experiencing. The information provided may also help a support technician identify the cause of a problem and suggest a solution.

System Information is organized into categories. The System Summary category allows you to display general information about your computer and your operating system.

The Hardware Resources category displays information about the resources on your computer and how the hardware devices installed on your computer use the resources.

The Components category contains information about your Windows setup and the hardware devices on your computer. This category

is useful for determining the driver for a specific device.

The Software Environment category contains information about the software that is installed on your computer and the software currently running.

System Information may also display categories for some programs installed on your computer, such as Internet Explorer. These categories will display information specific to the program.

USING SYSTEM INFORMATION

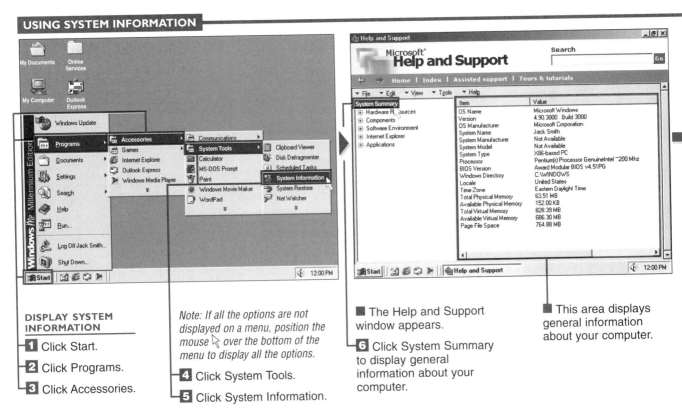

DISPLAY SYSTEM INFORMATION

1 Click Start.

2 Click Programs.

3 Click Accessories.

Note: If all the options are not displayed on a menu, position the mouse ⍾ over the bottom of the menu to display all the options.

4 Click System Tools.

5 Click System Information.

■ The Help and Support window appears.

6 Click System Summary to display general information about your computer.

■ This area displays general information about your computer.

How do I print the displayed system information?

✔ Select the File menu and then click Print.

Can I save the displayed system information?

✔ Yes. Select the File menu and then click Save. To later view the saved information, you must open System Information, select the File menu and then click Open.

How do I save the displayed system information so I can open the data with a text editor?

✔ Select the File menu and then click Export. Saving the information as a text file allows you to easily review the information and send the information to other people by e-mail or fax.

Can I search for specific system information?

✔ Yes. Select the Edit menu and click Find. In the Find what area at the bottom of the screen, type the information you want to find and then click Find to start the search. Click Find Next until the information of interest appears.

Can I display more advanced system information?

✔ Yes. Select the View menu and then click Advanced. The Advanced view is useful if you need to provide a support technician with more in-depth information.

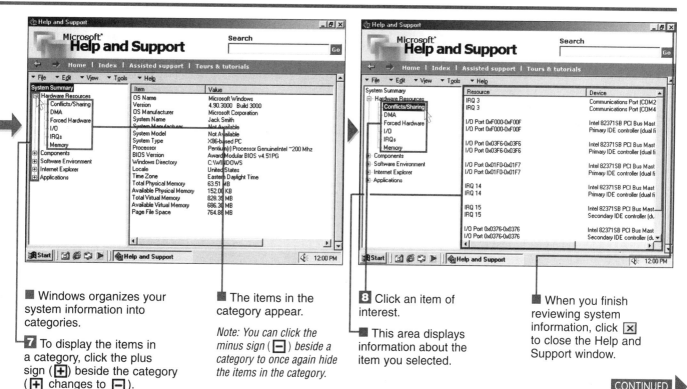

■ Windows organizes your system information into categories.

7 To display the items in a category, click the plus sign (⊞) beside the category (⊞ changes to ⊟).

■ The items in the category appear.

Note: You can click the minus sign (⊟) beside a category to once again hide the items in the category.

8 Click an item of interest.

■ This area displays information about the item you selected.

■ When you finish reviewing system information, click ☒ to close the Help and Support window.

CONTINUED

USING SYSTEM INFORMATION
(CONTINUED)

System Information contains several tools you can use to help identify and solve your computer problems. System Information includes tools such as Update Wizard Uninstall, Signature Verification Tool, Registry Checker, Automatic Skip Driver Agent, Dr. Watson and ScanDisk. Support technicians may ask you to run one or more of these tools when they are trying

to find the cause of a specific problem you are experiencing with your computer.

Although these tools were originally designed to be used when you are working with a support technician, you may want to run some of these tools on your own. These tools may help you troubleshoot and resolve a problem before asking

for assistance from a support technician.

Advanced users may want to use these tools even when they are not experiencing problems with their computer. The tools can help you learn more about the technical aspects of your computer, such as its capabilities and setup.

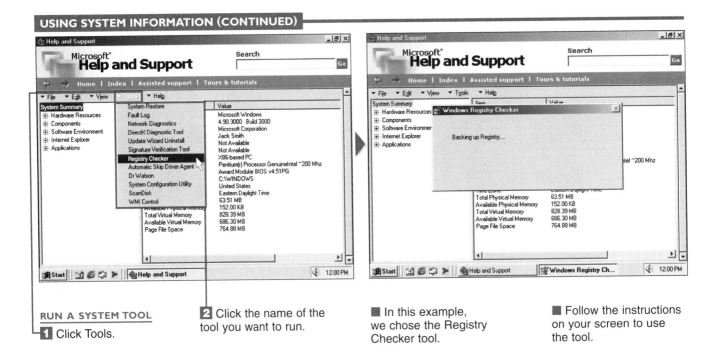

USING SYSTEM INFORMATION (CONTINUED)

RUN A SYSTEM TOOL

1 Click Tools.

2 Click the name of the tool you want to run.

■ In this example, we chose the Registry Checker tool.

■ Follow the instructions on your screen to use the tool.

System Information Tools

System Restore

If you are experiencing problems with your computer, this tool allows you to return your computer to a time before problems occurred. For more information about System Restore, see page 582.

Fault Log

This tool displays errors that have occurred on your computer in a text document. Viewing this information may help you troubleshoot a problem on your computer. This tool is only available if your computer has previously experienced an error.

Network Diagnostics

This tool gathers information about your network connection. You may find this information helpful when you are having problems connecting to a network.

DirectX Diagnostic Tool

DirectX is a set of components and drivers that are used by Windows programs to control graphics and sound. This tool can help you find out if DirectX is working properly.

Update Wizard Uninstall

This tool lets you remove some or all of the updates you installed from the Windows Update Web site or the updates Windows automatically installed. For information about automatically updating Windows, see page 562.

Signature Verification Tool

You can use the Signature Verification Tool to search for system files that are digitally signed. This helps you verify that a system file on your computer is an authentic file provided by the file's developer.

Registry Checker

Registry Checker scans the contents of your registry for problems and errors. Registry Checker runs each time you start Windows and creates a backup copy of the registry. If Registry Checker finds a problem, it may suggest that you restore the registry from the backup.

Automatic Skip Driver Agent

This tool checks for devices that do not respond properly when you start Windows. If a device does not respond properly, this tool prevents Windows from loading the driver for the device.

Dr. Watson

When your computer crashes, Dr. Watson records what your computer was doing at the time of the crash. This tool may be able to identify the cause of a problem and offer suggestions to help you fix the problem.

System Configuration Utility

This tool allows you to create and test different system configuration settings to help you determine the cause of a problem. Advanced users may also want to use this tool to change their system files.

ScanDisk

ScanDisk checks for and repairs errors on your hard disk. For more information about ScanDisk, see page 512.

WMI Control

The WMI (Windows Management Instrumentation) Control allows you to adjust WMI settings on your computer or on another computer on the network. This tool is usually used by network administrators for tasks such as setting up error logging.

MONITOR COMPUTER PERFORMANCE USING SYSTEM MONITOR

You can use System Monitor to monitor the performance of your computer.

System Monitor is often used to monitor the speed at which parts of a computer process information. If your computer is not working properly, this information can help you determine the cause of a problem. System Monitor can also help you decide whether you need to upgrade your computer hardware.

You may want to observe and keep records of how your computer performs when there are no problems. You can use this information in a comparison later if your computer's performance starts to deteriorate. You should monitor your computer's performance over an extended period of time to get a better estimate of what normal performance is. A good way to determine if your computer is running properly is to compare it with another computer that is set up in a similar way.

You can tell System Monitor which items you want to monitor. System Monitor will display graphs that show the performance of each item you selected.

Before you can use System Monitor, you may need to install the System Monitor component on your computer. System Monitor is located in the System Tools category. To add Windows components, see page 538.

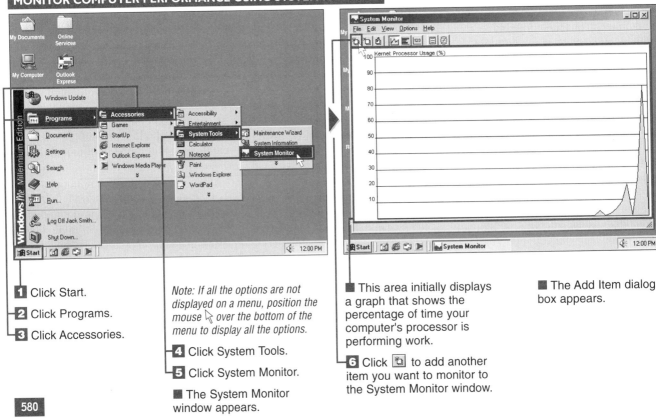

MONITOR COMPUTER PERFORMANCE USING SYSTEM MONITOR

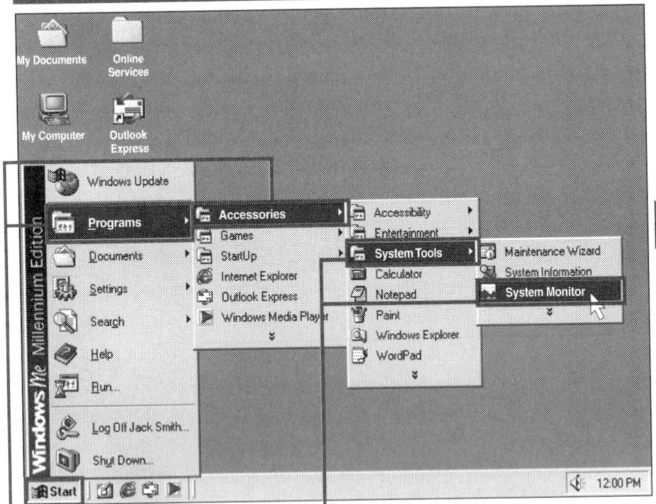

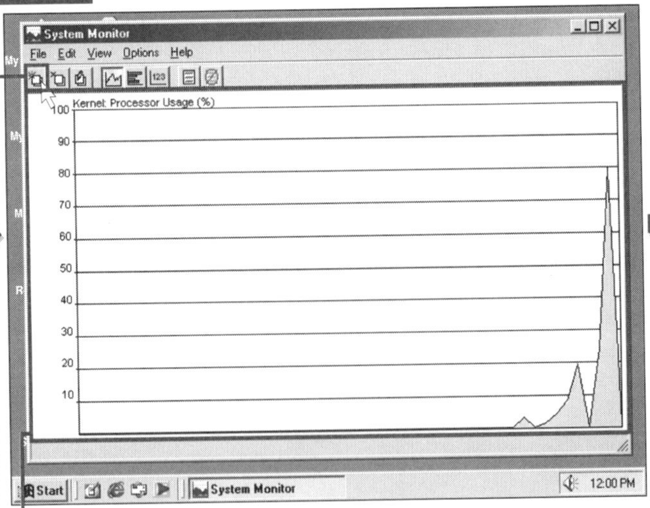

1 Click Start.

2 Click Programs.

3 Click Accessories.

Note: If all the options are not displayed on a menu, position the mouse over the bottom of the menu to display all the options.

4 Click System Tools.

5 Click System Monitor.

■ The System Monitor window appears.

■ This area initially displays a graph that shows the percentage of time your computer's processor is performing work.

6 Click to add another item you want to monitor to the System Monitor window.

■ The Add Item dialog box appears.

How do I remove an item from the System Monitor window?

✔ Click 🔲 to display a list of items currently shown in the System Monitor window. Select the item you want to remove and then click OK.

Can I save the information displayed by System Monitor in a text file?

✔ Yes. Click 🗏 to start saving information, type a name for the text file and then click Save. The value of each item is recorded in the file every five seconds. To stop saving information, click 🚫. You can open and print the text file from any word processing program.

Is there another way to view information about my computer's performance?

✔ You can use Resource Meter to monitor how your computer's resources are being used. You may need to install the Resource Meter component on your computer. Resource Meter is located in the System Tools category. To add Windows components, see page 538.

To start Resource Meter, perform steps 1 to 4 below and then select Resource Meter. When Resource Meter is running, an icon (🗏) appears on your taskbar. You can double-click the icon to display the Resource Meter window and view the information.

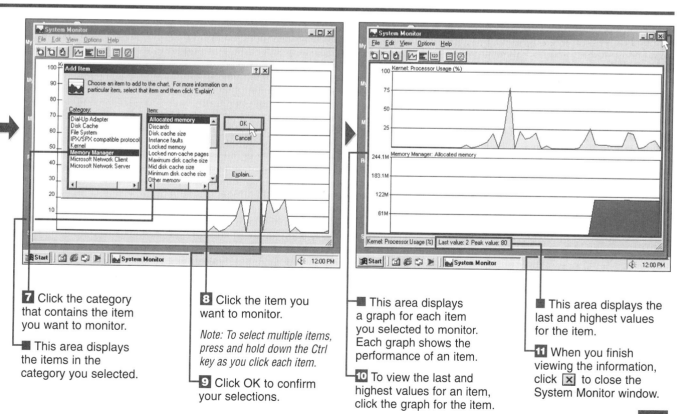

7 Click the category that contains the item you want to monitor.

■ This area displays the items in the category you selected.

8 Click the item you want to monitor.

Note: To select multiple items, press and hold down the Ctrl key as you click each item.

9 Click OK to confirm your selections.

■ This area displays a graph for each item you selected to monitor. Each graph shows the performance of an item.

10 To view the last and highest values for an item, click the graph for the item.

■ This area displays the last and highest values for the item.

11 When you finish viewing the information, click ☒ to close the System Monitor window.

RESTORE YOUR COMPUTER

I f you are experiencing problems with your computer, you can use the System Restore feature to return your computer to a time before the problems occurred. For example, if you accidentally delete program files, you can restore your computer to a time before you deleted the files. Problems may also occur when you install new hardware or software or make changes to your system settings.

When you restore your computer, you return your computer to an earlier, more stable time, called a restore point. Windows can store one to three weeks of restore points. The number of available restore points primarily depends on how frequently you use your computer.

Windows creates different types of restore points. An initial System CheckPoint is created when you first start Windows

after upgrading or installing Windows on a computer. Windows then regularly creates new System CheckPoint restore points. A Windows Automatic Update Install restore point is created when you install updates using the Windows Auto Update feature. For information about updating Windows, see page 562. Windows also creates restore points when you install certain programs.

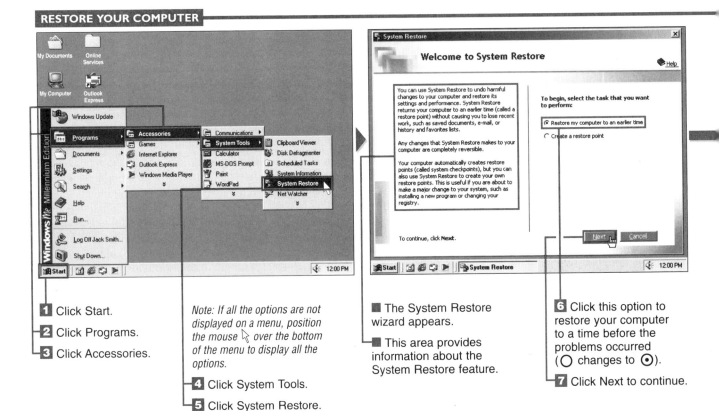

RESTORE YOUR COMPUTER

1 Click Start.

2 Click Programs.

3 Click Accessories.

Note: If all the options are not displayed on a menu, position the mouse ⬚ over the bottom of the menu to display all the options.

4 Click System Tools.

5 Click System Restore.

■ The System Restore wizard appears.

■ This area provides information about the System Restore feature.

6 Click this option to restore your computer to a time before the problems occurred (○ changes to ⊙).

7 Click Next to continue.

MASTER IT

When I try to start System Restore, why do I get a dialog box telling me System Restore is currently inactive?

✔ If you had 200 MB or less of free space on your hard drive when Windows was installed, System Restore is automatically turned off. To turn on System Restore, you must first delete unnecessary files and programs to free up over 200 MB of hard drive space. Then right-click My Computer on the desktop and select Properties to display the System Properties dialog box. On the Performance tab, click the File System button. In the File System Properties dialog box, click the Troubleshooting tab and then select the Disable System Restore option.

Can I create my own restore point?

✔ Yes. This is useful if you plan to make changes that could make your computer unstable. Perform steps 1 to 5 below to start System Restore. Select the Create a restore point option and click Next. Type a name for the restore point and click Next. Click OK to complete the wizard. The restore point will appear for the current day in the System Restore wizard.

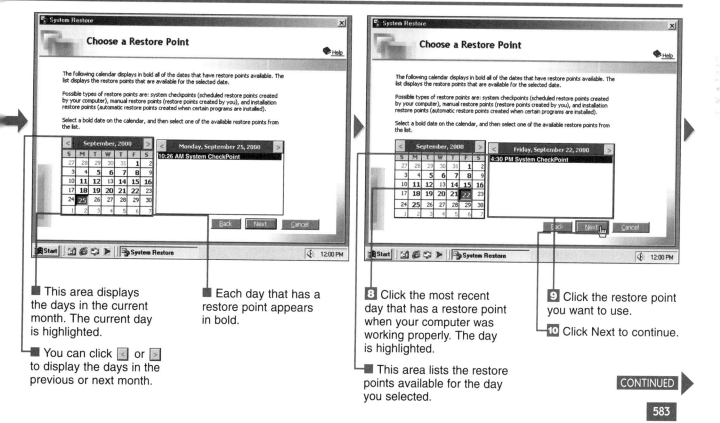

■ This area displays the days in the current month. The current day is highlighted.

■ You can click ◄ or ► to display the days in the previous or next month.

■ Each day that has a restore point appears in bold.

8 Click the most recent day that has a restore point when your computer was working properly. The day is highlighted.

■ This area lists the restore points available for the day you selected.

9 Click the restore point you want to use.

10 Click Next to continue.

CONTINUED ▶

RESTORE YOUR COMPUTER
(CONTINUED)

Restoring your computer will not cause you to lose any common types of files, such as word processing documents or spreadsheet files. If you want to ensure a specific file is not affected by the restoration, store the file in the My Documents folder. Any documents in the My Documents folder will not be affected. System Restore will also not affect your e-mail messages or the items on your Favorites list in Internet Explorer.

When you restore your computer to an earlier time, any programs you installed after that date will be uninstalled. Files you created using the program will not be deleted, but you will need to reinstall the program to work with the files again.

Before restoring your computer to an earlier time, you should close all open files and programs. When the restoration is in progress, you should not work with any files or programs.

Your computer will automatically restart when the restoration is complete. If there are any problems after a restoration, restarting your computer again may solve the problems.

RESTORE YOUR COMPUTER (CONTINUED)

■ A dialog box appears, asking you to close all open files and programs before restoring your computer.

11 Click OK to continue.

■ This area displays information about the restore point you selected.

12 Click Next to continue.

■ You can click Back at any time to return to a previous screen and change your selections.

Can I reverse the changes made when I restored my computer?

✔ Yes. Any changes that System Restore makes to your computer are completely reversible. To undo the last restoration, start System Restore by performing steps 1 to 5 on page 582. In the System Restore wizard, select the Undo my last restoration option (○ changes to ⊙). Then follow the instructions on your screen.

My computer started in safe mode. Can I run System Restore in safe mode?

✔ Windows may automatically start in safe mode if your computer cannot start properly. You can run System Restore in safe mode to return to a time when the computer did start properly. For more information about working in safe mode, see page 588.

When System Restore uninstalls a program, are all the program's files removed from my computer?

✔ Some of the program's files may remain on your computer. To completely remove all the program files, use the program's uninstall feature. For information on removing a program from your computer, see page 544.

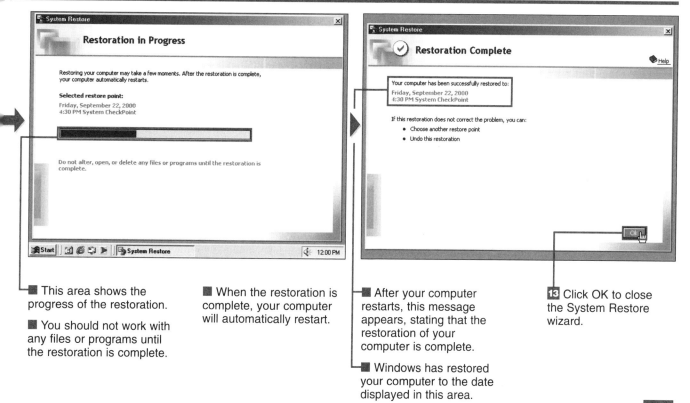

■ This area shows the progress of the restoration.

■ You should not work with any files or programs until the restoration is complete.

■ When the restoration is complete, your computer will automatically restart.

■ After your computer restarts, this message appears, stating that the restoration of your computer is complete.

■ Windows has restored your computer to the date displayed in this area.

13 Click OK to close the System Restore wizard.

CREATE A STARTUP DISK

You should create a startup disk and keep the disk on hand in case you have trouble starting Windows. When you cannot start Windows normally, you can insert the startup disk into your floppy drive to start your computer.

When you use a startup disk to start your computer, a command prompt similar to the MS-DOS command prompt appears on your screen. You can access several utility programs to try to solve the problem that prevents Windows from starting properly. You will not be able to log on to the network.

The floppy disk you use to create the startup disk must be able to store at least 1.2 MB of information. All files currently stored on the floppy disk will be erased when you create a startup disk.

After you create a startup disk, open the write-protect tab on the disk so you do not accidentally delete any files stored on the disk. Make sure you label your startup disk and keep the disk with your Windows installation CD-ROM disc.

CREATE A STARTUP DISK

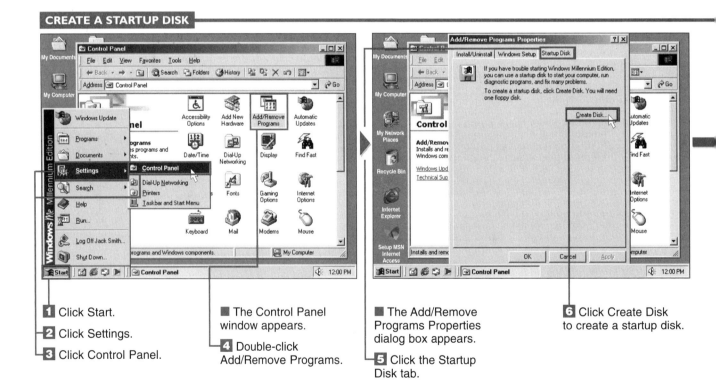

■ Click Start.

■ Click Settings.

■ Click Control Panel.

■ The Control Panel window appears.

■ Double-click Add/Remove Programs.

■ The Add/Remove Programs Properties dialog box appears.

■ Click the Startup Disk tab.

■ Click Create Disk to create a startup disk.

How can I create a startup disk if I am having trouble starting Windows?

✓ If you have trouble starting Windows and have not created a startup disk, you can create a startup disk using another Windows Me computer.

I inserted the startup disk, but my computer is still trying to start from the hard drive. What can I do?

✓ If your computer does not read the contents of the startup disk when you start your computer, you need to adjust the BIOS settings to have your computer start from the floppy drive. Consult your computer documentation or contact the manufacturer of your computer to find out how to adjust the BIOS settings.

What is on the startup disk?

✓ In addition to the system files needed to start a command prompt, the startup disk contains several utility programs. ScanDisk checks and repairs hard drive errors. FDISK allows you to partition your hard drive. Format allows you to format your hard drive. Edit is a text editor that lets you make changes to configuration files.

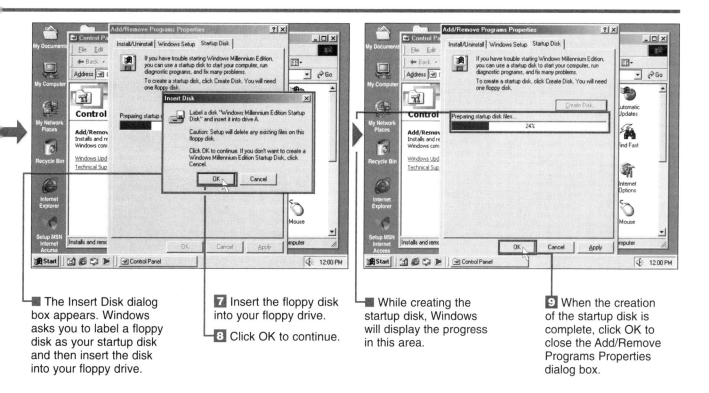

■ The Insert Disk dialog box appears. Windows asks you to label a floppy disk as your startup disk and then insert the disk into your floppy drive.

7 Insert the floppy disk into your floppy drive.

8 Click OK to continue.

■ While creating the startup disk, Windows will display the progress in this area.

9 When the creation of the startup disk is complete, click OK to close the Add/Remove Programs Properties dialog box.

START WINDOWS IN SAFE MODE

I f Windows does not start properly, you can start Windows in safe mode. In safe mode, you may be able to correct the problem that prevents Windows from starting normally.

Windows may not start properly for several reasons, such as if you accidentally deleted important files, changed certain Windows settings or added a new device that conflicts with an existing device.

Safe mode uses the minimum capabilities required to run Windows. In safe mode, you will not be able to access your CD-ROM drive, printer and other devices such as your sound card and modem. You will also not be able to connect to your network.

When using safe mode, your screen may use a lower resolution and fewer colors, which will change the overall appearance of your screen.

Any items you have added to the StartUp folder will not start automatically when your computer starts in safe mode.

Windows may automatically start in safe mode if your computer cannot start properly.

START WINDOWS IN SAFE MODE

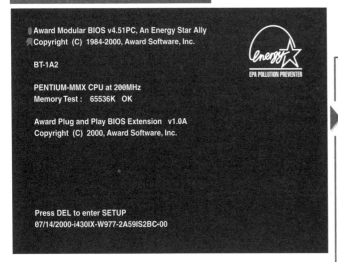

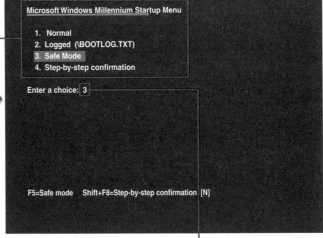

■1 Turn on your computer and monitor.

■2 Press and hold down the Ctrl key.

Note: You can press the F8 key instead of the Ctrl key on some computers.

■ The Microsoft Windows Millennium Startup Menu appears. The menu displays a list of options for starting Windows.

■3 Type the number **3** to start Windows in safe mode and then press the Enter key.

■ Windows starts in safe mode.

What are the other options for starting my computer?

✔ The Normal option starts Windows normally. The Logged option starts Windows normally and creates a hidden file named bootlog.txt on your hard drive that records actions performed during startup. You can use this file to help determine the cause of a startup problem. To display hidden files, see page 87. The Step-by-step confirmation option takes you through each activity that occurs during startup. You can choose which activities you want to occur so you can avoid activities that may be causing a problem.

How can I quickly fix the problem that prevents Windows from starting normally?

✔ You can use the System Restore feature to return your computer to a time before any problems occurred. For example, if you accidentally deleted important files, you can restore your computer to a time before you deleted the files. To use System Restore, see page 582.

How do I restart my computer after the problem is fixed?

✔ Click the Start button and then select Shut Down. In the Shut Down Windows dialog box, select Restart and then click OK.

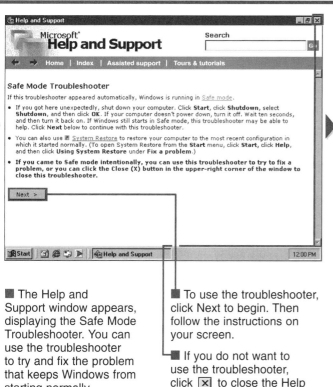

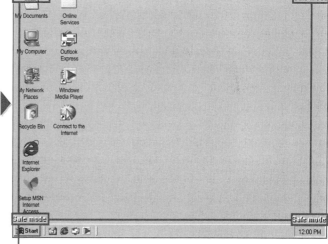

■ The Help and Support window appears, displaying the Safe Mode Troubleshooter. You can use the troubleshooter to try and fix the problem that keeps Windows from starting normally.

■ To use the troubleshooter, click Next to begin. Then follow the instructions on your screen.

■ If you do not want to use the troubleshooter, click ✕ to close the Help and Support window.

■ Windows displays the words "Safe mode" in each corner of your screen to indicate that you are in safe mode.

■ When you finish fixing the problem, you need to restart your computer. You should now be able to use your computer as usual.

WORK WITH THE REGISTRY

The Registry Editor is an advanced tool you can use to view and edit the registry. The registry contains information needed to run Windows with your hardware and software.

The contents of the registry are complex, so you should use the Registry Editor only when absolutely necessary. Before making any changes to the registry, you should create a backup copy of the registry and make sure you understand how to restore it.

The registry is made up of six main keys, also called branches. Each key can contain other keys, as well as pieces of information called values. Each value has a name and data.

The HKEY_CLASSES_ROOT key contains information about the associations between your programs and documents. HKEY_CURRENT_USER contains information specific to the current user and HKEY_LOCAL_MACHINE contains information about

your hardware and software. HKEY_USERS contains information about desktop settings and network connections. HKEY_CURRENT_CONFIG contains information about display and printer settings, while HKEY_DYN_DATA stores data from the computer's memory, including Plug and Play information.

START THE REGISTRY EDITOR

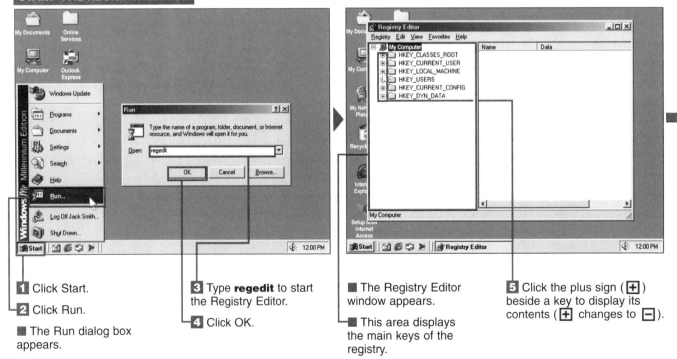

1 Click Start.

2 Click Run.

■ The Run dialog box appears.

3 Type **regedit** to start the Registry Editor.

4 Click OK.

■ The Registry Editor window appears.

■ This area displays the main keys of the registry.

5 Click the plus sign (⊞) beside a key to display its contents (⊞ changes to ⊟).

Can I check the registry for errors?

✔ You can use the Registry Checker system tool to scan the registry for errors. For information on running a system tool, see page 578.

How do I back up the registry?

✔ You can create a backup copy by exporting the registry to a text file as shown on page 596. You can also use a commercial backup program, such as VERITAS Backup Exec, to back up the registry. Using a backup program allows you to back up your registry onto floppy disks so you will be able to restore the registry if the files on your computer are damaged.

I forgot to back up the registry! Can I still restore the settings?

✔ If you made changes to the registry and Windows will not start properly, restart the computer and hold down the Ctrl key. When the Microsoft Windows Millennium Startup Menu appears, select the Safe mode option. After Windows starts in Safe mode, click Start and then click Run. In the Run dialog box, type **scanregw /restore** and press Enter. Then click Yes in the dialog box that appears. The Microsoft Registry Checker appears, displaying one or more previous settings. Select the setting for the last time Windows started successfully.

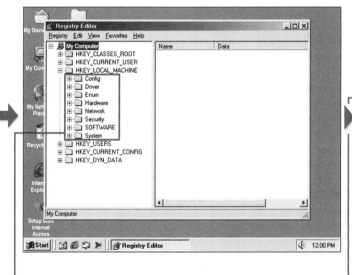

■ The contents of the key appear.

Note: You can click the minus sign (⊟) to once again hide the contents of the key.

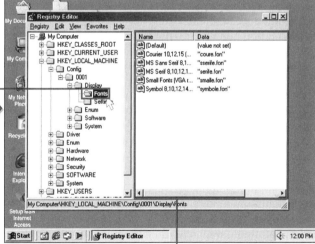

6 Repeat step 5 until the registry item you want to view appears.

7 Click the registry item to display its values.

■ This area displays the values for the registry item.

CONTINUED ▶

WORK WITH THE REGISTRY
(CONTINUED)

Looking for a specific key by browsing through the Registry Editor window can be time-consuming and difficult. The Find feature can help you quickly find a specific key in the registry.

The Registry Editor window has two panes. The left pane displays the list of keys contained in the registry. The right pane displays the values,

or information, stored in the current key. Each value has a name and data. By default, Windows will search all the keys, values and data in the registry for information. You can speed up the Find feature by choosing to search only keys, values or data.

You can also use the Match whole string only option to find only text that exactly matches

the text you specify. For example, "Directory" will not find "Download Directory."

When you use the Find feature to find a key, you must search for specific information. For example, if you want to find your screen appearance settings, search for the name of one of the appearance schemes, such as eggplant.

SEARCH THE REGISTRY

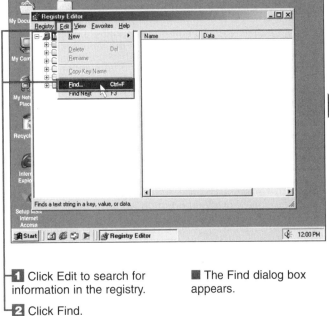

1 Click Edit to search for information in the registry.

2 Click Find.

■ The Find dialog box appears.

3 Type the text you want to find.

4 Windows will search for the text in each area that displays a check mark. You can click an option to add (✔) or remove (☐) a check mark.

5 This option finds only exactly matching text in the registry. You can turn this option on (✔) or off (☐).

6 Click Find Next.

What type of data can I search for?

✓ The Find feature can only search for string data. You will not be able to search for binary or DWORD data. String data appears in quotation marks. Binary data is typically presented as pairs of hexadecimal values. DWORD data displays 0x followed by 8 hexadecimal values and the decimal equivalent of the data in parentheses.

The Registry Editor's Find feature is slow. How can I perform faster searches?

✓ You can export the registry to a text file and then use a word processor, such as WordPad, to search the registry. To export the registry to a text file, see page 596.

I found the key I was searching for. How do I transfer the key's settings to another computer?

✓ Export the key to a text file and place the file on a floppy disk. To export part of the registry to a text file, see page 596. Insert the floppy disk into the other computer and then double-click the file you exported to merge the settings into the registry of the other computer.

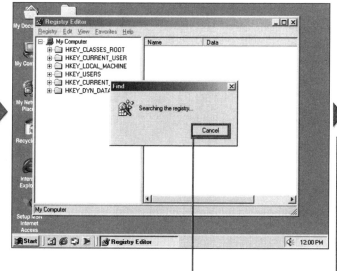

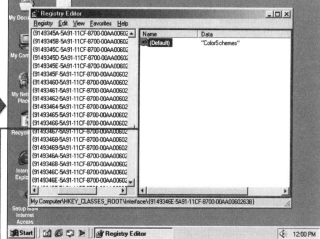

■ The Find dialog box appears while Windows searches the registry.

■ You can click Cancel to stop the search at any time.

■ This area displays the first item that matches the text you typed.

■ You can press the F3 key to find the next instance of the text in the registry.

CONTINUED ▶

WORK WITH THE REGISTRY
(CONTINUED)

You can use the Registry Editor to add or change information in the registry. The Registry Editor does not have an Undo feature and many changes to the registry are made immediately. If you make a mistake while editing the registry, Windows may not start. Before making any changes, you should create a backup copy of the registry. For more information, see page 596.

You can add information to the registry. For example, you can add a value to have a program start automatically without having to place the program in the StartUp folder. This is useful if you want to make sure a program runs every time you start your computer.

You can also change the information in the registry. You can change the data in an existing value or in a value you have added.

This is useful if you want to change the way Windows behaves. For example, you can prevent Windows from adding "Shortcut to" to shortcuts you create.

Any changes you make to the registry should be based on tested information from reliable sources. You can search the Web for sites that contain reliable information about changing the registry.

EDIT THE REGISTRY

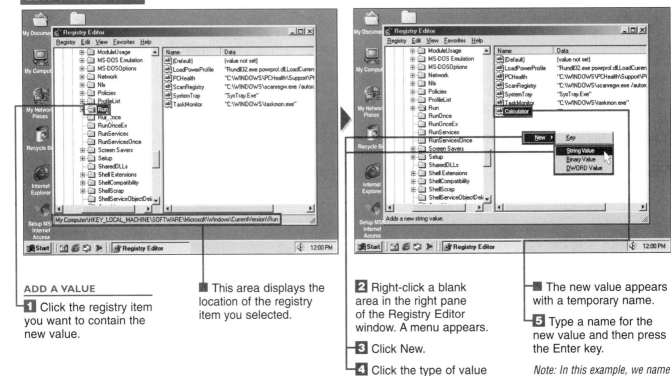

ADD A VALUE

1 Click the registry item you want to contain the new value.

■ This area displays the location of the registry item you selected.

2 Right-click a blank area in the right pane of the Registry Editor window. A menu appears.

3 Click New.

4 Click the type of value you want to add.

■ The new value appears with a temporary name.

5 Type a name for the new value and then press the Enter key.

Note: In this example, we name the new value Calculator.

Is there another way to make changes to the registry?

✔ Whenever possible, you should use the tools included with Windows, such as the tools in the Control Panel, to make changes to your computer. When you make changes using Window's tools, Windows makes the changes to the registry for you.

How do I delete a key or value?

✔ Click the key or value you want to remove and then press the Delete key. This is useful when you have removed a program from your computer but it is still listed in the Control Panel's Add/Remove Programs Properties dialog box. To remove the program from the dialog box, delete the program's key from HKEY_LOCAL_MACHINE\ Software\Microsoft\Windows\Current Version\Uninstall.

How else can I change a value?

✔ When the data for a value is "0" or "1" with no other letters or numbers, you can turn the value on or off by changing the data. In the data column, a "0" means the value is off and a "1" means the value is on.

How can I create shortcuts without the "Shortcut to" prefix?

✔ To prevent Windows from adding "Shortcut to" to your shortcuts, display the HKEY_CURRENT_USER\Software\ Microsoft\Windows\CurrentVersion\ Explorer key and change the value of link to 00 00 00 00.

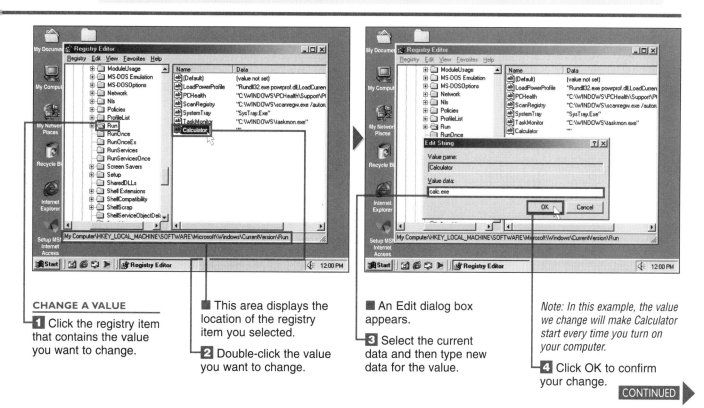

CHANGE A VALUE

◀1 Click the registry item that contains the value you want to change.

■ This area displays the location of the registry item you selected.

◀2 Double-click the value you want to change.

■ An Edit dialog box appears.

◀3 Select the current data and then type new data for the value.

Note: In this example, the value we change will make Calculator start every time you turn on your computer.

◀4 Click OK to confirm your change.

CONTINUED ▶

595

WORK WITH THE REGISTRY
(CONTINUED)

Y ou can copy, or export, your registry settings into a file that can be saved on your computer. When exporting the registry to a text file, you can choose to copy the entire registry or just one key.

Exporting your registry to a text file allows you to create a backup copy of your registry. If there is ever a problem with your settings,

you can use the backup to restore a working version of your registry. You should always back up your registry before making changes to the registry.

Exporting your registry to a text file also allows you to use a word processor to edit the registry. When you finish editing the registry, you can merge the exported file back into the

registry. Editing the registry with a word processor is convenient, since word processors have advanced features, such as Find and Replace. Keep in mind that the structure of the registry is complex and its rules for punctuation are complicated. It is easier to make an editing mistake when you use a word processor than when you use the Registry Editor.

EXPORT THE REGISTRY TO A TEXT FILE

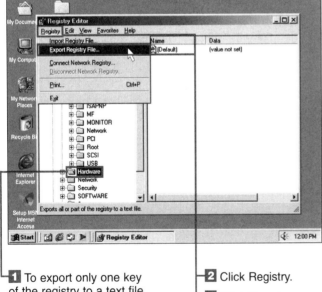

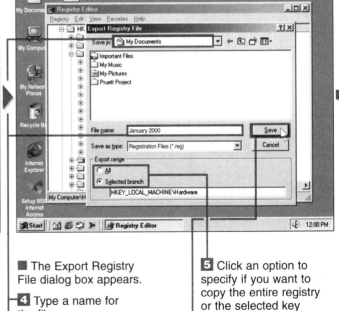

1 To export only one key of the registry to a text file, click the key you want to export.

Note: To export the entire registry, you do not need to click a key.

2 Click Registry.

3 Click Export Registry File.

■ The Export Registry File dialog box appears.

4 Type a name for the file.

■ This area shows the location where Windows will store the file. You can click this area to change the location.

5 Click an option to specify if you want to copy the entire registry or the selected key (○ changes to ⊙).

6 Click Save to create the registry file.

596

How do I merge the text file I created back into my registry?

✔ In the Registry Editor, choose the Registry menu and select the Import Registry File command. In the Import Registry File dialog box, click the file you want to import and click the Open button.

What happens to my current registry settings when I merge a text file into the registry?

✔ The contents of the file overwrite the current registry settings. If the settings in the file do not exist in the registry, they will be added. If settings exist in the registry and not in the file, the settings in the registry will not be affected.

Can I restore my computer to a prior state using the copy of my registry?

✔ Restoring your registry using a copy may not completely restore your computer to a prior state. To restore your entire computer, you may want to use System Restore. For more information about System Restore, see page 582.

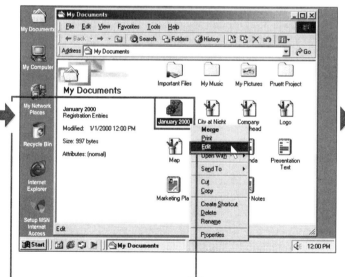

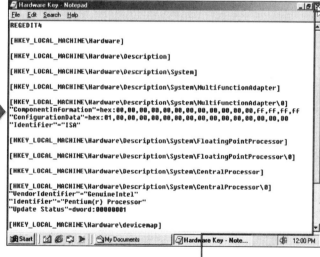

■ Windows creates the registry file.

7 To open the registry file in a word processor or text editor, right-click the registry file. A menu appears.

8 Click Edit.

Note: Do not double-click the file since this will merge the information back into the registry.

■ The registry file opens in WordPad or Notepad.

Note: The program the registry file opens in depends on the size of the registry file. A large registry file will open in WordPad.

9 Click ✕ to close WordPad or Notepad when you finish viewing the file.

APPENDIX

WHAT'S ON THE CD-ROM

The CD-ROM disc included in this book contains many useful files and programs that can be used when working with Windows Me Millennium Edition. You will find an e-version of this book, as well as several popular programs you can install and use on your computer. Before installing any of the programs on the disc, make sure a newer version of the program is not already installed on your computer. For information on installing different versions of the same program, contact the program's manufacturer.

SYSTEM REQUIREMENTS

While most programs on the CD-ROM disc have minimal system requirements, your computer should be equipped with the following hardware and software to use all the contents of the CD-ROM disc:

*   A Pentium or faster processor.
*   Microsoft Windows 95 or later.
*   At least 32MB of RAM.
*   180 MB of hard drive space.
*   A double-speed (2x) or faster CD-ROM drive.
*   A monitor capable of displaying at least 256 colors or grayscale.
*   A modem with a speed of at least 14,400 bps.
*   A sound card.

ACROBAT VERSION

The CD-ROM contains an e-version of this book that you can view and search using Adobe Acrobat Reader. You can also use the hyperlinks provided in the text to access all Web pages and Internet references in the book. You cannot print the pages or copy text from the Acrobat files. An evaluation version of Adobe Acrobat Reader is also included on the disc.

INSTALLING AND USING THE SOFTWARE

This CD-ROM disc contains several useful programs.

Before installing a program from this CD, you should exit all other programs. In order to use most of the programs, you must accept the license agreement provided with the program. Make sure you read any Readme files provided with each program.

Program Versions

Shareware programs are fully functional, free trial versions of copyrighted programs. If you like a particular program, you can register with its author for a nominal fee and receive licenses, enhanced versions and technical support.

Freeware programs are free, copyrighted games, applications and utilities. You can copy them to as many computers as you like, but they have no technical support.

GNU software is governed by its own license, which is included inside the folder of the GNU software. There are no restrictions on distribution of this software. See the GNU license for more details.

Trial, demo and evaluation versions are usually limited either by time or functionality. For example, you may not be able to save projects using these versions.

For your convenience, the software titles on the CD are listed alphabetically.

Acrobat Reader

For Microsoft Windows 95/98/NT/2000. Evaluation version.

This disc contains an evaluation version of Acrobat Reader from Adobe Systems, Inc. You will need this program to access the e-version of the book also included on this disc. For more information about using Acrobat Reader, see page 600.

Download Accelerator

For Microsoft Windows 95/98/NT/2000/Me. Beta version.

Download Accelerator is a download acceleration program that can improve download speeds by up to 300 percent. Download Accelerator works with Internet Explorer and Netscape Navigator Web browsers and offers features such as multi-server connections and automatic recovery from lost connections or other errors.

Download Accelerator is a free beta version from SpeedBit. You can obtain the latest version of Download Accelerator at www.speedbit.com.

MindSpring Internet Access

For Microsoft Windows 95/98. Commercial version.

You can use the CD-ROM disc to set up an account and start using the MindSpring Internet Service Provider (ISP) for a low monthly fee. If you are already on the Internet, you can find more information about MindSpring and the services they offer by visiting MindSpring's Web site at www.mindspring.com.

Note: If you already have an Internet service provider, installing MindSpring Internet Access may replace your current settings. You may no longer be able to access the Internet through your original ISP.

Netscape Communicator

For Microsoft Windows 95/98/NT. Commercial version.

Netscape Communicator is a suite of applications from Netscape Communications that includes the popular Web browser, Navigator. Netscape Communicator also includes other Internet related applications including the Winamp audio player, the Messenger e-mail program and the Netscape Instant Messenger communication program.

Netscape Communicator is a fully functional program. There is no charge for its use. The latest version of Netscape Communicator, as well as support files and additional components, are available at www.netscape.com.

Paint Shop Pro

For Microsoft Windows 95/98/NT. Evaluation version.

Paint Shop Pro is an image editing and creation program. Paint Shop Pro can be used to capture images from a computer screen or digital camera and then edit the images, adding special effects.

Paint Shop Pro is an evaluation version from Jasc Software, Inc. Paint Shop Pro is fully functional for 30 days, after which time you are required to register it with the author.

You can download additional components and access technical support for Paint Shop Pro at www.jasc.com.

RealPlayer

For Microsoft Windows 95/98/NT/2000. Plug-in.

RealPlayer lets you play audio and video files compatible with RealPlayer. RealPlayer also allows you to listen to or view streaming media from sources such as radio stations on the Internet.

RealPlayer is a free program from Real Networks.

You can download additional components and access technical support for RealPlayer at www.real.com.

Winamp

For Microsoft Windows 95/98/NT. Freeware version.

Winamp is a free audio player program that features built-in support for a variety of file formats, including MP3, MIDI and WAV. Winamp is customizable, allowing you to change the appearance of the player window and download plug-ins for additional file format support.

Winamp version 2.5 and higher is freeware from Nullsoft, Inc.

You can find the latest version of Winamp, additional components and technical support at www.winamp.com.

WinZip

For Microsoft Windows 95/98/NT/2000. Shareware version.

WinZip compresses files to make it easier and faster to transfer information from one computer to another. WinZip is commonly used to reduce the amount of disk space consumed by files and to reduce the size of files sent by e-mail. WinZip is a shareware version from Nico Mak Computing, Inc. You can use the program for free for 21 days. If you wish to continue using the program, you must pay a registration fee. For more information about WinZip, visit www.winzip.com.

TROUBLESHOOTING

We have tried our best to compile programs that work on most computers with the minimum system requirements. Your computer, however, may differ and some programs may not work properly for some reason.

The two most likely problems are that you do not have enough memory (RAM) for the programs you want to use or you have other programs running that are affecting the installation or running of a program. If you get error messages while trying to install or use the programs on the CD-ROM disc, try one or more of the following methods and then try installing or running the software again:

*   Close all running programs.
*   Restart your computer.
*   Turn off any anti-virus software.
*   Close the CD-ROM interface and run demos or installations directly from Windows Explorer.
*   Add more RAM to your computer.

If you still have trouble installing the programs from the CD-ROM disc, please call the IDG Books Worldwide Customer Service phone number: 800-762-2974.

APPENDIX

USING THE E-VERSION OF THE BOOK

You can view *Master Visually Windows Me Millennium Edition* on your screen using the CD-ROM disc included at the back of this book. The CD-ROM disc allows you to search the contents of each chapter of the book for a specific word or phrase. The CD-ROM disc also provides a convenient way of keeping the book handy while traveling.

You must install Adobe Acrobat Reader on your computer before you can view the book on the CD-ROM disc. This program is provided on the disc. Acrobat Reader allows you to view Portable Document Format (PDF) files, which can display books and magazines on your screen exactly as they appear in printed form.

To view the contents of the book using Acrobat Reader, display the contents of the disc. Double-click the Resources folder and then double-click the PDFs folder to display the contents of the folder. In the window that appears, double-click the icon for the section of the book you want to review.

USING THE E-VERSION OF THE BOOK

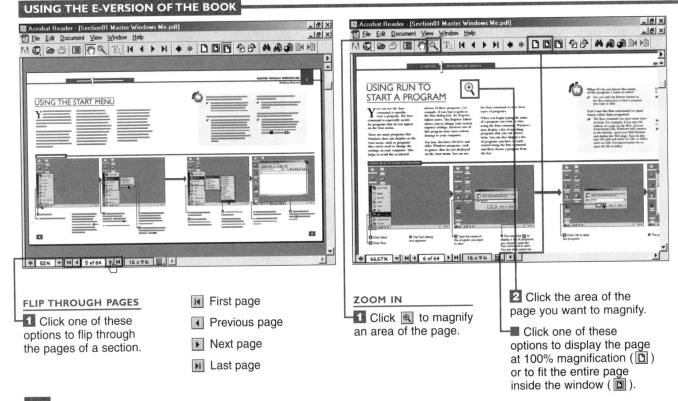

FLIP THROUGH PAGES

1 Click one of these options to flip through the pages of a section.

First page

Previous page

Next page

Last page

ZOOM IN

1 Click to magnify an area of the page.

2 Click the area of the page you want to magnify.

Click one of these options to display the page at 100% magnification () or to fit the entire page inside the window ().

How do I install Acrobat Reader?

✔ To install Acrobat Reader, insert the CD-ROM disc into a drive. In the screen that appears, click Software. Click Acrobat Reader and then click INSTALL at the bottom of the screen. Then follow the instructions on your screen to install the program.

How can I make searching the book more convenient?

✔ You can make searching the book more convenient by copying the .pdf files to your own computer. Display the contents of the CD-ROM disc and then copy the PDFs folder from the CD to your hard drive. This allows you to easily access the contents of the book at any time.

Can I use Acrobat Reader for anything else?

✔ Acrobat Reader is a popular and useful program. There are many files available on the Web that are designed to be viewed using Acrobat Reader. Look for files with the .pdf extension. For more information about Acrobat Reader, visit the Web site at www.adobe.com/products/acrobat/readermain.html.

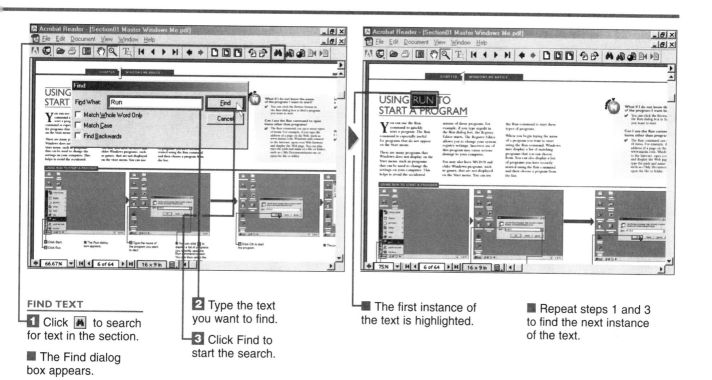

FIND TEXT

1 Click 🔍 to search for text in the section.

■ The Find dialog box appears.

2 Type the text you want to find.

3 Click Find to start the search.

■ The first instance of the text is highlighted.

■ Repeat steps 1 and 3 to find the next instance of the text.

APPENDIX

IDG BOOKS WORLDWIDE, INC.
END-USER LICENSE AGREEMENT

READ THIS. You should carefully read these terms and conditions before opening the software packet(s) included with this book ("Book"). This is a license agreement ("Agreement") between you and IDG Books Worldwide, Inc. ("IDGB"). By opening the accompanying software packet(s), you acknowledge that you have read and accept the following terms and conditions. If you do not agree and do not want to be bound by such terms and conditions, promptly return the Book and the unopened software packet(s) to the place you obtained them for a full refund.

1. License Grant. IDGB grants to you (either an individual or entity) a nonexclusive license to use one copy of the enclosed software program(s) (collectively, the "Software") solely for your own personal or business purposes on a single computer (whether a standard computer or a workstation component of a multi-user network). The Software is in use on a computer when it is loaded into temporary memory (i.e., RAM) or installed into permanent memory (e.g., hard disk, CD-ROM or other storage device). IDGB reserves all rights not expressly granted herein.

2. Ownership. IDGB is the owner of all right, title and interest, including copyright, in and to the compilation of the Software recorded on the CD-ROM. Copyright to the individual programs on the CD-ROM is owned by the author or other authorized copyright owner of each program. Ownership of the Software and all proprietary rights relating thereto remain with IDGB and its licensors.

3. Restrictions On Use and Transfer.

(a) You may only (i) make one copy of the Software for backup or archival purposes, or (ii) transfer the Software to a single hard disk, provided that you keep the original for backup or archival purposes. You may not (i) rent or lease the Software, (ii) copy or reproduce the Software through a LAN or other network system or through any computer subscriber system or bulletin-board system, or (iii) modify, adapt or create derivative works based on the Software.

(b) You may not reverse engineer, decompile, or disassemble the Software. You may transfer the Software and user documentation on a permanent basis, provided that the transferee agrees to accept the terms and conditions of this Agreement and you retain no copies. If the Software is an update or has been updated, any transfer must include the most recent update and all prior versions.

4. Restrictions on Use of Individual Programs. You must follow the individual requirements and restrictions detailed for each individual program in the "About the CD" section of this Book. These limitations are contained in the individual license agreements recorded on the CD-ROM. These restrictions may include a requirement that after using the program for the period of time specified in its text, the user must pay a registration fee or discontinue use. By opening the Software packet(s), you will be agreeing to abide by the licenses and restrictions for these individual programs. None of the material on this disc(s) or listed in this Book may ever be distributed, in original or modified form, for commercial purposes.

5. Limited Warranty.

(a) IDGB warrants that the Software and CD-ROM are free from defects in materials and workmanship under normal use for a period of sixty (60) days from the date of purchase of this Book. If IDGB receives notification within the warranty period of defects in materials or workmanship, IDGB will replace the defective CD-ROM.

(b) IDGB AND THE AUTHOR OF THE BOOK DISCLAIM ALL OTHER WARRANTIES, EXPRESS OR IMPLIED, INCLUDING WITHOUT LIMITATION IMPLIED WARRANTIES OF MERCHANTABILITY AND FITNESS FOR A PARTICULAR PURPOSE, WITH RESPECT TO THE SOFTWARE, THE PROGRAMS, THE SOURCE CODE CONTAINED THEREIN, AND/OR THE TECHNIQUES DESCRIBED IN THIS BOOK.

IDGB DOES NOT WARRANT THAT THE FUNCTIONS CONTAINED IN THE SOFTWARE WILL MEET YOUR REQUIREMENTS OR THAT THE OPERATION OF THE SOFTWARE WILL BE ERROR FREE.

(c) This limited warranty gives you specific legal rights, and you may have other rights which vary from jurisdiction to jurisdiction.

6. Remedies.

(a) IDGB's entire liability and your exclusive remedy for defects in materials and workmanship shall be limited to replacement of the Software, which may be returned to IDGB with a copy of your receipt at the following address: Disc Fulfillment Department, Attn: Master Visually Windows Me Millennium Edition, IDG Books Worldwide, Inc., 10475 Crosspoint Boulevard, Indianapolis, Indiana, 46256, or call 1-800-762-2974. Please allow 3-4 weeks for delivery. This Limited Warranty is void if failure of the Software has resulted from accident, abuse, or misapplication. Any replacement Software will be warranted for the remainder of the original warranty period or thirty (30) days, whichever is longer.

(b) In no event shall IDGB or the author be liable for any damages whatsoever (including without limitation damages for loss of business profits, business interruption, loss of business information, or any other pecuniary loss) arising out of the use of or inability to use the Book or the Software, even if IDGB has been advised of the possibility of such damages.

(c) Because some jurisdictions do not allow the exclusion or limitation of liability for consequential or incidental damages, the above limitation or exclusion may not apply to you.

7. U.S. Government Restricted Rights. Use, duplication, or disclosure of the Software by the U.S. Government is subject to restrictions stated in paragraph (c) (1) (ii) of the Rights in Technical Data and Computer Software clause of DFARS 252.227-7013, and in subparagraphs (a) through (d) of the Commercial Computer—Restricted Rights clause at FAR 52.227-19, and in similar clauses in the NASA FAR supplement, when applicable.

8. General. This Agreement constitutes the entire understanding of the parties, and revokes and supersedes all prior agreements, oral or written, between them and may not be modified or amended except in a writing signed by both parties hereto which specifically refers to this Agreement. This Agreement shall take precedence over any other documents that may be in conflict herewith. If any one or more provisions contained in this Agreement are held by any court or tribunal to be invalid, illegal or otherwise unenforceable, each and every other provision shall remain in full force and effect.

INDEX

INDEX

INDEX

Read Less, Learn More™

Visual

New Series!

The visual alternative to learning complex computer topics.

For experienced computer users, developers, network professionals who learn best visually.

Extra

Apply It

"Apply It" and "Extra" provide ready-to-run code and useful tips.

Title	ISBN	Price
Active Server™ Pages 3.0: Your visual blueprint for developing interactive Web sites	0-7645-3472-6	$24.99
HTML: Your visual blueprint for designing effective Web pages	0-7645-3471-8	$24.99
JavaScript™: Your visual blueprint for building dynamic Web pages	0-7645-4730-5	$24.99
Linux®: Your visual blueprint to the Linux platform	0-7645-3481-5	$24.99
Perl: Your visual blueprint for building Perl scripts	0-7645-3478-5	$24.99
Unix®: Your visual blueprint to the universe of Unix	0-7645-3480-7	$24.99
XML™: Your visual blueprint for building expert Web pages	0-7645-3477-7	$24.99

Over 10 million *Visual* books in print!

with these two-color Visual™ guides

The Complete Visual Reference

For visual learners who want an all-in-one reference/tutorial that delivers more in-depth information about a technology topic.

"Master It" tips provide additional topic coverage

Title	ISBN	Price
Master Active Directory™ VISUALLY™	0-7645-3425-4	$34.99
Master Microsoft® Access 2000 VISUALLY™	0-7645-6048-4	$39.99
Master Microsoft® Office 2000 VISUALLY™	0-7645-6050-6	$39.99
Master Microsoft® Word 2000 VISUALLY™	0-7645-6046-8	$39.99
Master Office 97 VISUALLY™	0-7645-6036-0	$39.99
Master Photoshop® 5.5 VISUALLY™	0-7645-6045-X	$39.99
Master Red Hat® Linux® VISUALLY™	0-7645-3436-X	$34.99
Master VISUALLY™ HTML 4 & XHTML 1	0-7645-3454-8	$34.99
Master VISUALLY™ Windows® 2000 Server	0-7645-3426-2	$34.99
Master VISUALLY™ Windows® Me Millennium Edition	0-7645-3496-3	$34.99
Master Windows® 95 VISUALLY™	0-7645-6024-7	$39.99
Master Windows® 98 VISUALLY™	0-7645-6034-4	$39.99
Master Windows® 2000 Professional VISUALLY™	0-7645-3421-1	$39.99

*The **Visual**™ series is available wherever books are sold, or call* **1-800-762-2974.**

Outside the US, call **317-572-3993**

ORDER FORM

IDG BOOKS®

TRADE & INDIVIDUAL ORDERS

Phone: **(800) 762-2974**
or **(317) 572-3993**
(8 a.m.–6 p.m., CST, weekdays)
FAX : **(800) 550-2747**
or **(317) 572-4002**

EDUCATIONAL ORDERS & DISCOUNTS

Phone: **(800) 434-2086**
(8:30 a.m.–5:00 p.m., CST, weekdays)
FAX : **(317) 572-4005**

CORPORATE ORDERS FOR 3-D VISUAL™ SERIES

Phone: **(800) 469-6616**
(8 a.m.–5 p.m., EST, weekdays)
FAX : **(905) 890-9434**

Qty	ISBN	Title	Price	Total

Shipping & Handling Charges

	Description	First book	Each add'l. book	Total
Domestic	Normal	$4.50	$1.50	$
	Two Day Air	$8.50	$2.50	$
	Overnight	$18.00	$3.00	$
International	Surface	$8.00	$8.00	$
	Airmail	$16.00	$16.00	$
	DHL Air	$17.00	$17.00	$

Subtotal _____

*CA residents add
applicable sales tax* _____

*IN, MA and MD
residents add
5% sales tax* _____

*IL residents add
6.25% sales tax* _____

*RI residents add
7% sales tax* _____

*TX residents add
8.25% sales tax* _____

Shipping _____

Total _____

Ship to:

Name_____

Address_____

Company _____

City/State/Zip _____

Daytime Phone_____

Payment: ☐ Check to IDG Books (US Funds Only)
☐ Visa   ☐ Mastercard   ☐ American Express

Card # _____ Exp. _____ Signature_____

maranGraphics™